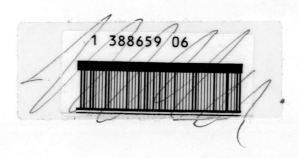

THE
NATURAL
HISTORY
OF
BRITAIN & EUROPE

General Editor
MICHAEL CHINERY

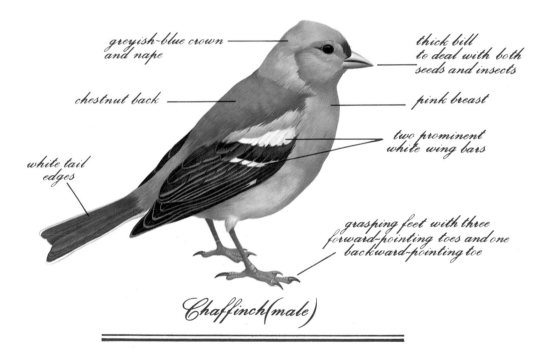

greyish-blue crown
and nape

thick bill
to deal with both
seeds and insects

chestnut back

pink breast

two prominent
white wing bars

white tail
edges

grasping feet with three
forward-pointing toes and one
backward-pointing toe

Chaffinch (male)

KINGFISHER BOOKS

GENERAL EDITOR
Michael Chinery

HOUSE EDITORS
Vanessa Clarke
Jane Olliver
Caroline Royds

PICTURE RESEARCH
Penny Warn

AUTHORS	PHOTOGRAPHERS
Neil Ardley	Heather Angel
Michael Chinery	Ardea
Marilyn Jones	A-Z Collection
Elizabeth Martin	Alan Beaumont
Derek Reid	Michael Chinery
Allan Watson	Bruce Coleman
Alwyne Wheeler	Sonia Halliday
	Brian Hawkes
ARTISTS	David Hosking
Norma Birgin	Ken Merrylees
Wendy Bramall	Pat Morris
Terry Callcut	Natural History
Martin Camm	Photographic Agency
Denys Ovenden	Nature Photographers
Gordon Riley	Maurice Nimmo
Bernard Robinson	Oleg Polunin
Rod Sutterby	Derek Reid
George Thompson	Seaphot
Norman Weaver	Zefa
David Wright	

Kingfisher Books, Grisewood & Dempsey Ltd,
Elsley House, 24–30 Great Titchfield Street,
London WIP 7AD

First published in 1982 by Kingfisher Books exclusively for WH Smith
Reprinted 1985, 1986
This edition published in 1988 by Kingfisher Books

BRITISH LIBRARY CATALOGUING IN PUBLICATION DATA
The Natural history of Britain and Europe.
1. Natural history – Europe
I. Chinery, Michael
591.941   QL253
ISBN 0 86272 382 5

Colour separations by Newsele Litho Ltd, Milan, Italy
Printed in Portugal

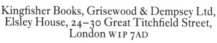

Contents

INTRODUCTION
Michael Chinery
PAGE 6

CHAPTER ONE
MAMMALS
Iain Bishop
PAGE 8

CHAPTER TWO
BIRDS
Neil Ardley
PAGE 38

CHAPTER THREE
REPTILES AND AMPHIBIANS
Michael Chinery
PAGE 106

CHAPTER FOUR
FISHES
Alwyne Wheeler
PAGE 118

CHAPTER FIVE
INVERTEBRATES
Michael Chinery
PAGE 130

CHAPTER SIX
WILD FLOWERS
Marilyn Jones
PAGE 210

CHAPTER SEVEN
TREES AND SHRUBS
Elizabeth Martin
PAGE 294

CHAPTER EIGHT
FERNS AND MOSSES
Michael Chinery
PAGE 354

CHAPTER NINE
FUNGI
Derek Reid
PAGE 362

CHAPTER TEN
SEAWEEDS AND OTHER ALGAE
Michael Chinery
PAGE 389

INDEX
PAGE 392

Introduction

The European continent is made up of four major life zones: the northern tundra, the coniferous forest belt, the deciduous forests of central regions, and the Mediterranean region with its largely evergreen vegetation. In addition there are the mountains, lakes, rivers and coastal waters, and vast areas of grassland created by human destruction of the original forests. The plant and animal life in these assorted habitats is not as rich and varied as that of the tropics, but there are still many thousands of species, each playing an important role in the ecology or natural history of its habitat. Wherever you go, whether it is simply into your garden or further afield to the forests or seashore, there will be plants and animals, and in this book you will find general and specific information about many of them. Clearly, not every species can be included, but those selected are among the most common and conspicuous ones – those that you are most likely to see. All the major habitats are covered except the little-visited tundra.

Distribution

The area covered by the book is essentially western Europe, although a few species from Greece and neighbouring areas are included. Unless otherwise stated, it may be assumed that a particular species occurs in suitable habitats throughout western Europe. For the purposes of this book, southern Europe includes everywhere south of the main alpine chain (south of 45°N). Central Europe stretches from the Alps to central Denmark (45° to 55°N) and includes Britain. Northern Europe is Scandinavia (north of 55°N).

Many animals, especially terrestrial invertebrates (animals without backbones), occur only at certain times of the year. The dates given in the descriptions are those at which adults are normally found, but it should be remembered that animals often have much longer seasons in southern Europe. If no dates are given, it may be assumed that the species can be found at all times of the year, although many animals may go into hibernation during the colder months.

Measurements

Unless otherwise stated, the sizes quoted for each species are the normal averages for mature specimens, but individuals vary a good deal and the measurements are no more than a guide. Most measurements are lengths or heights, but wingspans are quoted for many insects. The form of measurement employed is indicated in each chapter of the book. A range of sizes is given for species which are particularly variable or in which males and females have different sizes. Where males and females are significantly different in appearance, the illustrations are marked with the appropriate sex.

Classification

All the major groups of plants and animals are covered in this book, from mammals to jellyfishes and from the giant redwood trees to minute fungi and microscopic algae. The animals are arranged in their natural groupings, the largest of which are the phyla (singular: phylum). All the backboned animals (vertebrates) belong to the Phylum Chordata, and the mammals, birds, reptiles, amphibians and fishes fall into different classes of the phylum. Other phyla are similarly divided into classes. The classes are split into orders, and the orders into families. A family includes a number of species with many features in common and its name always ends in -idae. Plant classification follows similar lines, but the family names nearly all end in -aceae.

Apart from some of the flowerless plants, each species is assigned to its family when it is described, and where several members of one family appear there is usually a short paragraph giving the main characteristics of that family. If no family name appears under a species, it may be assumed that the species belongs to the same family as the preceding one.

English and Scientific Names

Most species in this book are given an English name and a scientific name, the latter consisting of two parts and conventionally printed in italics. The first part is the generic name (the name of the genus and possibly shared by several closely related species), while the second part is the specific name. Together, the two parts of the scientific name positively identify one particular kind, or species, of plant or animal. Scientific names are understood all over the world, but they are not entirely stable and you might find different names in different books. Such changes are confusing, but they are brought about when biologists make new discoveries about the relationships of different species. The Small White butterfly, for example, was for a long time known as *Pieris rapae* and was believed to be closely related to the Large White (*Pieris brassicae*), but recent research has revealed several anatomical differences between the two species. The Small White has therefore been placed in a different genus and is now called *Artogeia rapae*.

Many small invertebrates have no individual English names, and they are given just their scientific names in the text, as are many non-British creatures which have failed to acquire English names.

Conservation

Large areas of the countryside are disappearing every year as a result of house-building, road-building, and other human activity, and wildlife is declining as the available habitats shrink. A thoughtful approach to the plants and animals that you see can help to halt the decline. Small insects must be caught and examined closely if they are to be identified accurately, but they should be released afterwards. Try to identify wild flowers without picking them, and remember that many plants are now protected by law. A sensible attitude to the wildlife around us will ensure that it is still there for our descendants to enjoy.

Chapter One
Mammals

The mammals are backboned animals belonging to the class Mammalia. They are warm-blooded like the birds, but can be distinguished from all other vertebrates by the possession of hair (absent only from most of the whales) and by the fact that the females feed their young with milk. This is produced in the females' mammary glands, which give the class its name. There is an enormous range of size within the class—from the tiny Pygmy white-toothed shrew, a mere 40mm long, to the giant Blue whale, which can be 30m in length and weigh over 100 tonnes.

With the exception of the Australasian echidnas and the Duck-billed platypus, which lay eggs, all mammals bring forth live young. The majority, including the European mammals discussed in this book, belong to the group known as placentals. The young are retained in the mother's body for some time, nourished through a special organ called the placenta, and are born at various stages of development. Mice and rabbits, for example, are born blind and naked, usually in secure burrows, and require a good deal of care and protection during the first few days or weeks of their lives. Cats and other carnivores are also born with their eyes closed, although they usually have a good coating of fur. They can move around a little at birth, but need plenty of care and attention. Young carnivores tend to stay with their parents longer than many other mammals because they have to learn how to hunt. Hooved mammals, such as horses and antelopes, are born in a very advanced state and many can walk within an hour of birth. Within a day or two they can usually run with the herds—an absolute necessity if they are to escape from predators on the open plains. The other main group of mammals is the marsupials, or pouched mammals. These have no placenta and their young are born at a very early stage, but the babies are then nursed in their mother's pouch for quite a long time. Marsupials, represented by the kangaroos and wallabies, are found mainly in Australia.

The mammals eat a wide variety of plant and animal material, and their teeth are correspondingly varied. The basic complement is 44 teeth, with the upper and lower jaws each having 6 incisors, 2 canines or eyeteeth, 8 premolars and 6 molars. The moles, the Pyrenean desman and the Wild boar are the only European mammals to retain this full set of teeth. Some of the toothed whales have acquired even more teeth because of their fish-eating habits, but otherwise there has been a loss of teeth during evolution. Rodents, for example, have between 16 and 22 teeth, while cats have 30 and dogs 42. Meat-eaters usually have sharp, stabbing canines and sharp-edged cheek teeth (molars and premolars) for slicing meat. Grazing mammals have broad, flat surfaces to their cheek teeth, ideal for grinding plant matter. Canine teeth are normally absent in grazers and rodents. It is usually quite easy to identify mammals just from their jaws and teeth.

Mammals in all Habitats

Mammals are found all over the world. They colonize the polar regions and the high mountains: their fur coats and their ability to regulate their body temperatures enable them to live in some of the coldest places on earth. They are equally happy in deserts and tropical forests, as well as in all the other less extreme habitats.

Although they are essentially terrestrial animals walking on four legs, mammals exhibit many modifications of body and limbs associated with their many different modes of life. The whales and seals, for example, have streamlined bodies and paddle-like limbs for swimming; bats have evolved wings and have become the only truly aerial mammals; while many other species have become burrowers or climbers. The group as a whole is thus a very successful one.

Mammalian Orders

There are 16 orders of living mammals, of which just 9 are native to Europe—10 if we include our own species, which belongs to the order Primates. There are about 3,500 species in all, of which about 170 are native to Europe. A further 23 introduced species now run wild in Europe, and there are also a few feral species. These are domesticated species which have escaped and become established in the wild. Examples include the goat, the ferret and the domestic cat.

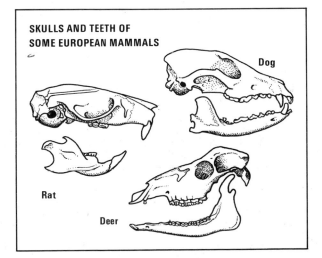

SKULLS AND TEETH OF SOME EUROPEAN MAMMALS

Dog

Rat

Deer

Left: The grey squirrel spends more time on the ground than the red squirrel and commonly uses tree stumps as dining tables. Acorns and other nuts are its main foods in autumn and winter and their remains are abundant at the feeding points.

Insectivores

This widely distributed and rather ancient group (Order Insectivora) includes some 300 species, most of which exhibit various primitive features. Many, for example, possess 44 teeth, which was the full complement for the earliest placental mammals. Most other mammals have lost some of their teeth during their evolution. There are 8 families of insectivores, of which just 3 occur in Europe—the hedgehogs (Erinaceidae), the moles and desmans (Talpidae), and the shrews (Soricidae). All are small, long-snouted, short-legged animals with sharp-cusped teeth and 5 clawed digits on each limb —another primitive feature. Although the name means 'insect-eaters', the insectivores actually eat a wide variety of small animals and some take vegetable food as well. They are extremely common animals and play an important role in the ecology of many habitats.

WESTERN HEDGEHOG
Erinaceus europaeus
Family Erinaceidae
Head and body 18–27cm: tail 2–3cm. Back and sides clothed with spines about 2cm long. Spines are modified hairs, dark brown or black with white tips. There is a narrow parting on the back of the head. Face, underside and limbs are clothed with soft hair.
Food and habits: eats slugs, worms, and a wide range of insects, together with fallen fruit and fungi. Almost entirely nocturnal, and very noisy when foraging. It can roll into a tight ball when disturbed. Sleeps by day among dead leaves and other rubbish in hedge bottoms and similar places. Hibernates October–April in a nest of dry leaves, but often active until well into winter. Swims and climbs well: can also burrow but rarely does so.

Habitat and range: common in most places apart from moors and marshes: abundant in parks, gardens and hedgerows. Western and northern Europe (see map). The Eastern hedgehog (*E. concolor*) of eastern Europe is very similar but has a white breast. The Algerian hedgehog (*E. algirus*) of the western Mediterranean region is paler all over, with a wide parting on the head.

NORTHERN MOLE
Talpa europaea Family Talpidae
Head and body 12–15cm: tail about 4cm. Front feet greatly enlarged and spade-like for digging. The animal lives almost entirely underground in an extensive tunnel system. Mole hills are the piles of soil excavated from the tunnels and periodically pushed up to the surface. The velvety black or dark grey fur can lie in any direction, allowing the animal to move backwards and forwards in its tunnels with equal ease. It feeds almost entirely on earthworms. The eyes are very small, although it is not completely blind. Active day and night, sometimes emerging to rummage in leaf litter.
Habitat and range: mostly in grassland and deciduous woodland, even where quite wet (the mole can swim well). Most of Europe apart from Ireland and the far north.

PYRENEAN DESMAN
Galemys pyrenaicus
Head and body 11–13·5cm, tail 13–15cm. Muzzle long, flat and broad; tail flattened from side to side and fringed with stiff hairs; hind feet large and webbed for swimming.
Range and habitat: mountain streams and canals in the Pyrenees and northern Spain and Portugal.
Food: small aquatic invertebrates.

SHREWS
Family Soricidae

This large family contains some 200 species. Shrews are small, short-legged animals with long pointed noses. Their fur is short and usually brown or grey, they have very small eyes and their senses of hearing and smell are well developed. Most species are terrestrial, active day and night and solitary. They are usually carnivorous or insectivorous, though a little plant food is eaten. Because the many species are difficult to identify, a detailed examination of teeth and skulls is often necessary. The 15 European species can be split into 2 main groups: the red-toothed shrews (*Sorex* and *Neomys*), in which the teeth have red tips, and the white-toothed shrews (*Suncus* and *Crocidura*).

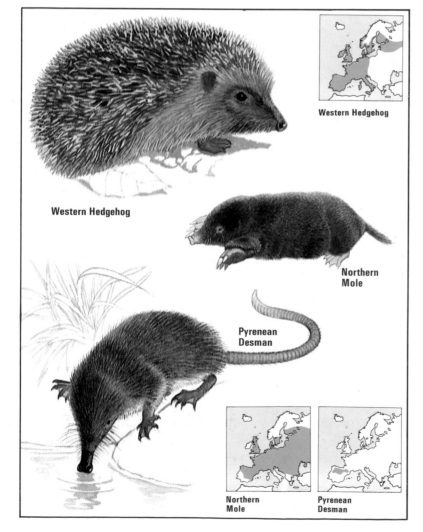

Western Hedgehog

Western Hedgehog

Northern Mole

Pyrenean Desman

Northern Mole

Pyrenean Desman

COMMON SHREW
Sorex araneus
Head and body 70–85mm, tail 45mm, hind foot 12–13mm. The teeth are red-tipped. The silky fur on the back is dark brown, the underside pale, and along the sides there is a distinct band of an intermediate colour.
Range and habitat: Britain, Scandinavia and eastern Europe, wherever the ground cover is sufficient. Abundant in grassland, woods and hedgerows. The very similar Millet's shrew (*S. coronatus*) inhabits most of western Europe.
Food and habits: eats mainly insects, worms and spiders; will also eat carrion.

PYGMY SHREW
Sorex minutus
Head and body 45–60mm, tail 40mm long. Distinctly smaller than the Common shrew and no band of intermediate colour is present on the flanks.
Range: widespread in Europe, but only at high altitude in the south.

GREATER WHITE-TOOTHED SHREW
Crocidura russula
Head and body 65–85mm, tail 35–50mm, hind foot 12–13mm. Has whiskers on the tail, and is greyish-brown above, fading to yellowish-grey below.
Range and habitat: dry grassland, woodland and hedges in southern and central Europe.

BICOLOURED WHITE-TOOTHED SHREW
Crocidura leucodon
Head and body 64–87mm, tail 28–39mm, hind foot 12–13mm. The dark grey upper side contrasts sharply with the yellowish-white below. Tail whiskered and clearly bicoloured.
Range and habitat: often found on the edges of woods in central Europe and on the steppes of eastern Europe.

PYGMY WHITE-TOOTHED SHREW or ETRUSCAN SHREW
Suncus etruscus
Head and body 36–50mm, tail 24–29mm, hind foot 7–8mm. The smallest mammal in the world. Usually weighing less than 2g. Long hairs form whiskers on the tail. Reddish-grey above, dull grey below.
Range and habitat: widespread in grassland and often found in arable farmland and gardens. Southern Europe.

WATER SHREW
Neomys fodiens
Head and body 70–90mm, hind foot 17–20mm. A large, dark shrew, nearly black above, with underside colour varying from silver-grey to black. Stiff hairs on the underside of the tail and on the hind feet assist swimming.
Range and habitat: found throughout Europe, except Ireland, in dense vegetation near fresh water.
Food and habits: insect larvae and other water invertebrates. Also uses its poisonous saliva to kill small fishes, frogs and even small mammals.

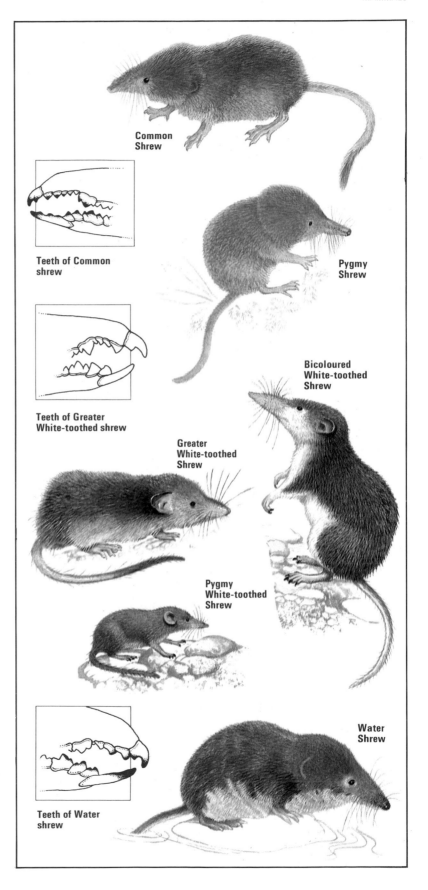

Common Shrew

Teeth of Common shrew

Pygmy Shrew

Teeth of Greater White-toothed shrew

Bicoloured White-toothed Shrew

Greater White-toothed Shrew

Pygmy White-toothed Shrew

Water Shrew

Teeth of Water shrew

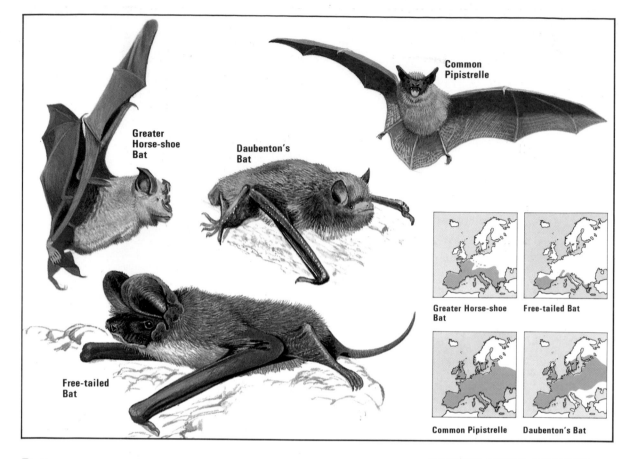

Greater Horse-shoe Bat

Daubenton's Bat

Common Pipistrelle

Free-tailed Bat

Greater Horse-shoe Bat

Free-tailed Bat

Common Pipistrelle

Daubenton's Bat

Bats

The bats, which belong to the order Chiroptera, are the only mammals that fly, though other kinds of mammals can glide from tree to tree. The bat's wings are skin membranes and they are supported by fingers, fore and hind limbs and tail. About 1,000 species are currently recognized. Bats are distributed throughout the world, with the exception of the polar regions, but most species are tropical or sub-tropical. Fruit bats (Sub-order Megachiroptera) are not found in Europe, but some 30 species of insectivorous bats (Sub-order Microchiroptera) have been recorded from the area. Bats usually fly at night using high-pitched sound pulses to navigate and find food. They spend the daylight hours in a torpid state in dark, sheltered cavities in trees, caves, attics or cellars. In temperate regions most bats hibernate in winter. Correct identification of some European bats is difficult and may depend upon minute details of structure of the skull or teeth, but many can be identified by looking at the face and ears and the membrane surrounding the tail, and also by measuring the length of the forearm (from elbow to thumb). Many bats have a prominent lobe of skin, called the tragus, standing up at the base of the ear, and the shape of this is a good guide to identification. All bats have a thin spur of cartilage, known as the calcar, attached to the ankle. It usually lies inconspicuously along the edge of the tail membrane, but in some bats the membrane extends as a small lobe beyond the calcar. Three families of bats occur in Europe. The Horse-shoe bats (Rhinolophidae) are represented by five species, all with horseshoe-shaped flaps of skin around the nose. Free-tailed bats (Molossidae), in which the tail extends well beyond the membrane, have a single representative in Europe. Most European bats belong to the Vespertilionidae, whose members can all be recognized by the possession of a tragus.

GREATER HORSE-SHOE BAT
Rhinolophus ferrumequinum
Family Rhinolophidae
The largest Horse-shoe bat in Europe. Head and body about 70mm, forearm 50–60mm. The thick fur is grey above, pale buff below. Ears large and broad with curved pointed tips. Flight is relatively slow, rather like that of a butterfly, and usually within a metre or so of the ground.
Range: south and central Europe; s.w. Britain only. Mainly wooded country.

FREE-TAILED BAT
Tadarida teniotis
Family Molossidae
Head and body up to 85mm, forearm 58–64mm; tail up to 55mm, of which about half is free of the membrane. The only bat in Europe with the tail extending more than 2 vertebrae beyond the membrane. It often lives in rocky areas and flies high and fast.
Range: Mediterranean area: often active throughout the year, with little or no hibernation.

VESPERTILIONID BATS
Family Vespertilionidae

This family of small bats includes about 280 species, of which 26 are European. The

DORMICE
Family Gliridae

A small family of about 10 species in Europe, Asia, and Africa. Five species live in Europe. Most dormice have bushy tails and resemble small squirrels. They also have large eyes, rounded ears, and short legs. They are climbing animals, living mainly in trees and bushes and feeding mainly on buds and fruit, including nuts. They are nocturnal and secretive and can be pests in orchards. They sleep through the winter in snug nests of leaves, usually on or under the ground or in hollow logs.

GARDEN DORMOUSE
Eliomys quercinus
Head and body 15cm, tail 9cm. The long slender tail has a flattened, black and white tuft at the tip. Body greyish-brown above, white below. Black mask on the face.
Range and habitat: Most of Europe, but not Britain or Scandinavia. Mainly in woodland, but also gardens, orchards and rocky areas.
Food and habits: spends much of its time on the ground. Eats a wide variety of food including insects, snails, birds' eggs and nestling small mammals and birds, as well as fruit and nuts. Becomes dormant in autumn after the summer fattening period. It is nocturnal, hiding in a hole during day.

FAT DORMOUSE
Glis glis
Head and body 14–19cm, tail 13cm. The largest dormouse. Grey-brown above, somewhat lighter below. Dark stripes on outside of legs, dark ring round eyes. Long bushy tail.
Range and habitat: Most of southern and central Europe: introduced to Britain in 1902 and now well established in Chiltern area. Mature woodlands and orchards.
Food and habits: eats nuts, seeds, fruit and insects. Can be pest of fruit and forestry crops. Becomes very fat in autumn and dormant October–April. Nocturnal. In Roman times fattened for the table and considered a delicacy.

COMMON DORMOUSE
Muscardinus avellanarius
Head and body 7cm, tail 7cm. A small dormouse, light tawny above, yellowish-white below. Throat and chest white. Tail thickly haired.
Range and habitat: deciduous forest with shrubs; copses and thick hedgerows. The summer nest is usually built in dense bushes. Most of Europe to southern Scandinavia.
Food and habits: eats nuts, seeds and some insects. Sleeps from October to April rolled in a ball.

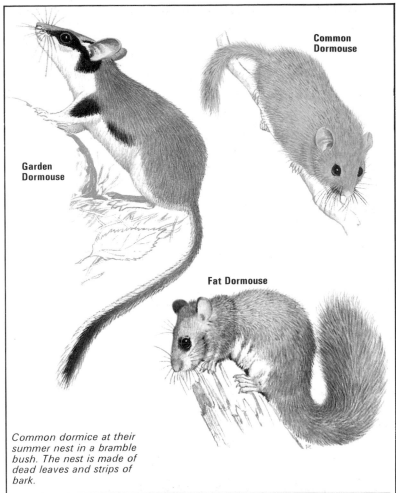

Garden Dormouse

Common Dormouse

Fat Dormouse

Common dormice at their summer nest in a bramble bush. The nest is made of dead leaves and strips of bark.

HAMSTERS, MOLES, RATS AND MICE
Family Muridae

This is the largest rodent family, containing over 1,000 species of rats, mice, voles, hamsters and their allies. Usually small, fast-breeding, short-lived animals, they are found in almost every corner of the world. All have 3 molar or cheek teeth in each jaw, but the shapes of these teeth vary a good deal. The family is divided into several distinct groups or sub-families. Many species are pests of agriculture and of stored products, and several carry diseases. Over 40 species are found in Europe, many of which are difficult to identify.

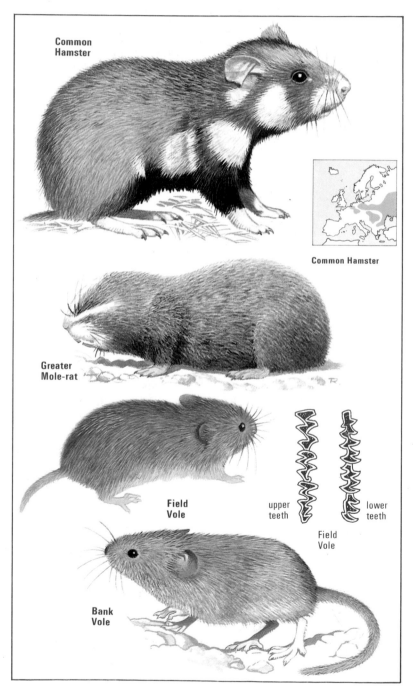

Common Hamster

Common Hamster

Greater Mole-rat

Field Vole

upper teeth

lower teeth

Field Vole

Bank Vole

HAMSTERS AND ALLIES
Sub-family Cricetinae

A widely distributed sub-family with 3 representatives in Europe. They are mostly small, terrestrial animals with simple grinding surfaces on the molars.

COMMON HAMSTER
Cricetus cricetus
Head and body 22–32cm, tail 3–6cm. Broad feet and large cheek pouches. **Habitat:** grassland, meadows and cultivated land usually near water. **Food and habits:** feeds mainly on seeds and grain, but also eats roots and insects. Makes extensive burrow systems with many chambers. Mainly nocturnal. Hibernates.

MOLE-RATS
Sub-family Spalacinae

A small group consisting of only 3 highly specialized rodents, 2 of which are found in Europe. They are adapted for burrowing and spend nearly all their life underground, although young animals may be found on the surface when dispersing to find new territories. They dig with their teeth, pushing loosened earth behind them with their feet. The jaw muscles are particularly strong, and the jaw is more mobile than in most rodent species.

GREATER MOLE-RAT
Spalax micropthalmus
Head and body 24–30cm. Soft velvety fur and clear white markings on head. **Range and habitat:** grassland and cultivated land of eastern Europe. **Food and habits:** feeds mainly on roots, bulbs and tubers and may pull whole plants down into burrow. Builds complex tunnel system with separate chambers for food, rest and latrine. The Lesser mole-rat (*S. leucodon*) of south-east Europe is smaller and darker.

LEMMINGS AND VOLES
Sub-family Microtinae

Some 25 species of this sub-family are found in Europe. They are characterized by their shortish tail, short legs and blunt muzzles, and by the complex patterns of enamel and dentine on the molar teeth. They are the predominant small grazing animals of European grasslands. Their numbers tend to fluctuate, periodically reaching plague levels.

FIELD VOLE
Microtus agrestis
Head and body 90–130mm, tail 30–45mm. Colour variable, yellow-brown to dark brown above, greyish-white below. Blunt head with short round hairy ears. Tail dark above, light below.
Range and habitat: an abundant and widespread species in grassland, meadows and marshland where ground cover is thick.
Food and habits: eats stems and leaves of grasses, reeds and sedges, and will take some animal food. May strip bark from trees in winter. Makes shallow burrows and a network of tunnels under vegetation on surface. Can cause extensive damage to crops and grassland pastures. Active day and night.
The voles are often confused with the mice (page 21), but the short ears and rounded snouts of the voles readily distinguish them.

BANK VOLE
Clethrionomys glareolus
Head and body 85–100mm, tail 40–65mm. Above, bright chestnut or reddish; below, yellowish, buff or grey-white. Patterns of enamel on cheek teeth are important for identification of this and allied forms.
Habitat: scrub, deciduous woodland and hedgerows.
Food and habits: eats a wide range of vegetable matter and some insects. Active day and night in short bursts, often climbing amongst bushes.

NORTHERN WATER VOLE
Arvicola terrestris
Head and body 16–19cm, tail 8–10cm. Like a large Field vole, but with a relatively long tail. Long, thick, glossy fur, blackish-grey or red-brown above, yellowish-grey below. Smaller and paler in southern part of range.
Habitat: edges of lakes and slow-moving rivers with good cover of vegetation on the banks, but can also be found in drier grassland. Most of Europe, but replaced by Southern Water Vole (*A. sapidus*) in south-west. Absent from Ireland.
Food and habits: eats mostly green vegetation, reeds, grass and some nuts and roots. Swims well, but is not pronouncedly adapted to aquatic habit. Burrows in river banks and makes a large grass-lined nest chamber. Some activity both day and night.

MUSKRAT
Ondatra zibethicus
Head and body 30–40cm, tail 19–27cm. A North American species introduced to Europe by escapes from fur farms. Much larger than all native voles and with a tail which is flattened from side to side. Dark brown above, dirty white below. Lives close to water and swims well, but feet not webbed.
Habitat: found mainly near slow-moving streams, canals and lakes.
Food and habits: eats river-side vegetation, but will take roots and crops when available. Nocturnal. Burrows in banks and may cause considerable damage to waterways.

NORWAY LEMMING
Lemmus lemmus
Head and body about 130mm, tail 20mm. The long fur is yellow-brown above, with a bold pattern of black streaks and patches; lighter below.
Range and habitat: tundra areas.
Food and habits: eats grass, roots, sedges, moss and lichens. Burrows just below surface in summer, below snow in winter.

WOOD LEMMING
Myopus schisticolor
Head and body 85–95mm, tail 16–18mm. Similar to a short-tailed vole. Grey with a reddish tinge above, grey below.
Habitat: northern coniferous forest.
Food: mainly mosses, liverworts and lichens.

Muskrat

Water Vole

Norway Lemming

Muskrat   Wood Lemming

Wood Lemming

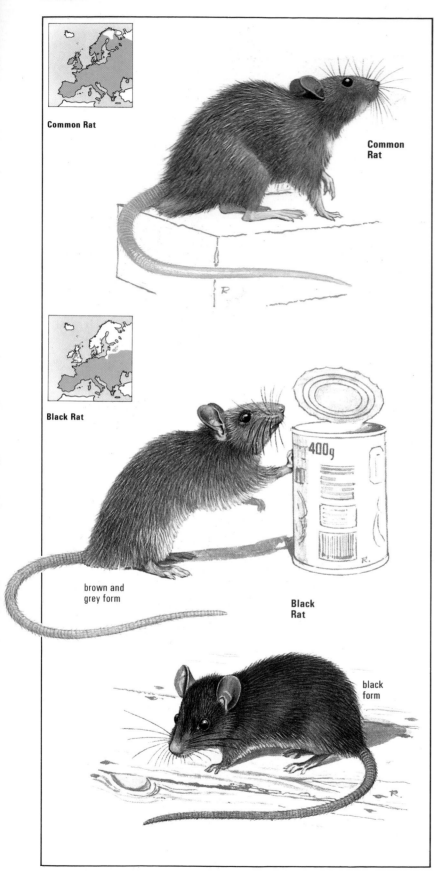

Common Rat

Common
Rat

Black Rat

brown and
grey form

Black
Rat

black
form

RATS AND MICE
Sub-family Murinae

The rats and mice form the large sub-family Murinae and can be distinguished from the voles by their long tails, large ears, and more pointed snouts. There are 3 molar teeth in each jaw, but they have rounded cusps quite unlike the flat grinding surfaces of the vole molars. Most of the rats and mice are of tropical origin, but 12 species occur in Europe. The animals are very adaptable, occupying a wide range of habitats including many man-made situations. The genera *Mus* and *Rattus* are almost world-wide as a result of their close association with man. Most of the species feed on seeds, but other plant materials are included in their varied diets, and some species, especially those associated with man, are distinctly omnivorous. Many species are pests of agriculture and stored products, and some are carriers of disease.

COMMON RAT or NORWAY RAT
Rattus norvegicus
Head and body 20–26cm, tail 17–23cm, hind foot 40–45mm. Usually brown, occasionally black above, grey below. Albino forms are used in research laboratories, and other colour forms have been bred for research and the pet trade.
Range and habitat: introduced to Europe from Asia in about AD 1500. Prefers habitats modified by man. Mainly terrestrial, but can swim well. Abundant in sewers, on rubbish dumps, and on farms: also on river banks and along estuaries.
Food and habits: eats grain and seeds when available, but will eat almost anything. A devastating pest of stored produce, often polluting far more than it eats and causing a vast amount of damage. Implicated in the spread of many diseases, including plague. Mostly nocturnal, spending the day in an extensive system of tunnels.

BLACK RAT or SHIP RAT
Rattus rattus
Head and body 16–23cm, tail 18–25cm, hind foot 30–40mm. Distinguished from Common rat by its relatively long tail and short hind foot, and also by its larger, rounded ears. Three colour forms are commonly found: dark grey or black all over, brown above with grey below, and brown above with white below.
Range and habitat: introduced from Asia at about the time of the Crusades, probably overland. More common in

southern Europe than the Common rat. Closely associated with man and is the familiar rat of ships and seaports.

Food and habits: omnivorous. Climbs more than the Common rat. A considerable pest of stored produce and a carrier of many diseases. Often nests in roofs and other places above ground.

WOOD MOUSE
Apodemus sylvaticus
Head and body 80–110mm, tail 70–110mm. Yellowish-brown above, silvery grey below. Usually has a small yellow patch on the chest which may extend to a streak. Eyes and ears large.
Habitat: very common in woodland, but frequently found in gardens and hedgerows, and often enters buildings.
Food and habits: eats mainly seeds, especially acorns, beech mast and hazel nuts, but also takes some insects and other invertebrate food. An agile climber. Nocturnal. A major source of food for owls and small mammals.

YELLOW-NECKED FIELD MOUSE
Apodemus flavicollis
Head and body 90–120mm, tail 90–135mm. Slightly larger and more brightly coloured than the Wood mouse. White below, and with the yellow chest spot large and usually extended sideways to form a collar.
Habitat: woodland, orchards and gardens, and often enters houses.
Habits: similar to the Wood mouse.

ROCK MOUSE
Apodemus mystacinus
Head and body 100–130mm, tail 105–140mm. Largest of the species of *Apodemus*. Sandy-grey above, white below. Lacks chest spot. Similar to a young rat, but more slender and with relatively small hind feet.
Range and habitat: Greece, Albania and the coastal mountains of Yugoslavia. Lives in open woodland and scrub, especially where rocks provide some shelter.
Habits: not well known but probably very similar to those of the Wood mouse.

STRIPED FIELD MOUSE
Apodemus agrarius
Head and body 90–115mm, tail 70–85mm. Very similar to the Wood mouse, but with a prominent dark stripe from nape of neck to base of tail. Reddish-brown above, white below.
Habitat: lives in scrub, grassland, hedgerows and woodland margins, but not found in dense woodland. More terrestrial than Wood mouse and less strictly nocturnal. Eastern Europe, as far west as Italy and Denmark. Could be confused with Birch mouse (page 22), but latter has a much longer tail.

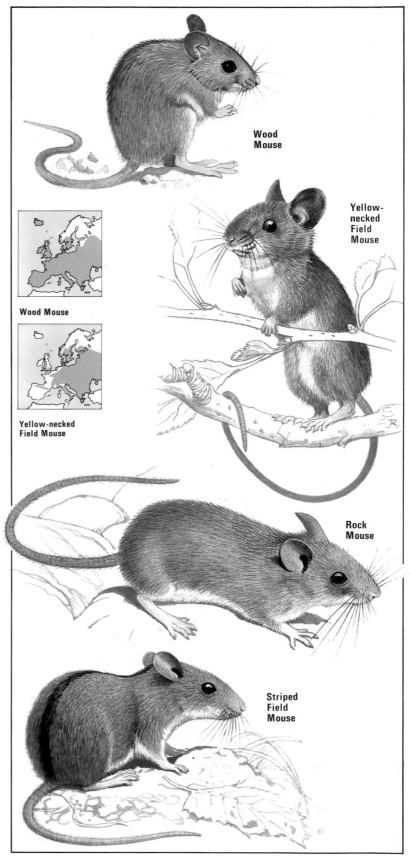

Wood Mouse

Yellow-necked Field Mouse

Wood Mouse

Yellow-necked Field Mouse

Rock Mouse

Striped Field Mouse

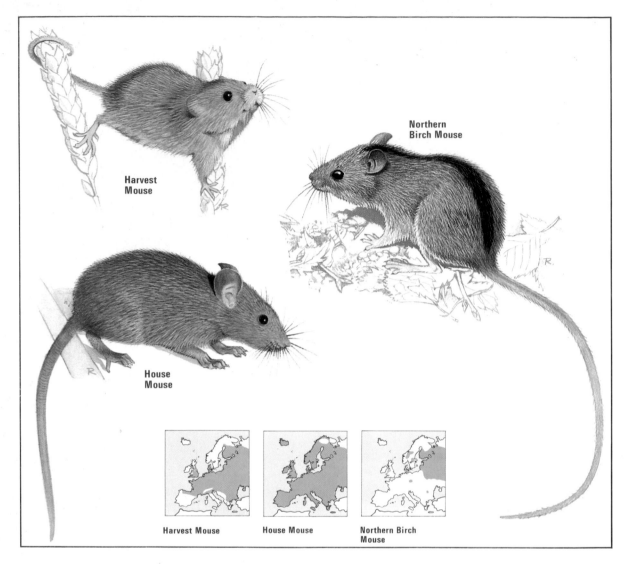

Harvest Mouse

Northern Birch Mouse

House Mouse

Harvest Mouse

House Mouse

Northern Birch Mouse

HARVEST MOUSE
Micromys minutus
Head and body 60–75mm, tail 50–70mm. A small rodent with thick, soft fur, brown above with a yellowish or russet tone; white below. Bicolored tail, partly prehensile, and used to assist climbing.
Habitat: hedgerows, tall grass and reed beds. The mice remain in thick cover and are difficult to observe. Modern farming methods may be causing some reduction in numbers through the removal of hedgerows, while combine harvesters now make life difficult in the grain fields, but the mice are still common in marshland.
Food and habits: eats mainly seeds, fruits, and bulbs, but takes some insect food, particularly in summer. Stores seed for winter below ground. Active day and night, and does not hibernate. but spends much more time under the ground in the winter. The summer nest is a spherical ball of woven grass attached to stems well above ground.

HOUSE MOUSE
Mus musculus
Head and body 70–95mm, tail 70–95mm. Size varies with habitat, and island forms often large. Soft brown-grey fur, slightly lighter below, but colour variable. Large eyes. Characteristic musty smell.
Range: origin probably central Asia, now worldwide associated with man.
Food and habits: eats almost anything, but prefers grain when available. A major pest of stored food and a carrier of several diseases. Mainly nocturnal.

BIRCH MICE
Family Zapodidae

A family of some 11 species, widely distributed in the northern hemisphere. Two species occur in Europe. Birch mice have exceptionally long prehensile tails and a dark stripe along the back. The upper jaw has an extra grinding tooth.

NORTHERN BIRCH MOUSE
Sicista betulina
Head and body 50–70mm, tail 75–100mm. Russet above, white below, but with a prominent dark stripe along the back from neck to base of tail.
Range and habitat: distributed patchily in Europe, but usually found in damp birch woodland with dense undergrowth.
Food and habits: feeds mainly on small invertebrates, but also eats seeds and bulbs. Nocturnal. Agile, and an especially good climber aided by the prehensile tail. Hibernates from October to April. The Southern Birch mouse (*S. subtilis*) of the steppes is very similar.

Right: Europe's smallest mouse: the harvest mouse does not even bend the cereal stalks as it climbs. Its prehensile tail acts like a safety belt in case the mouse should lose its footing.

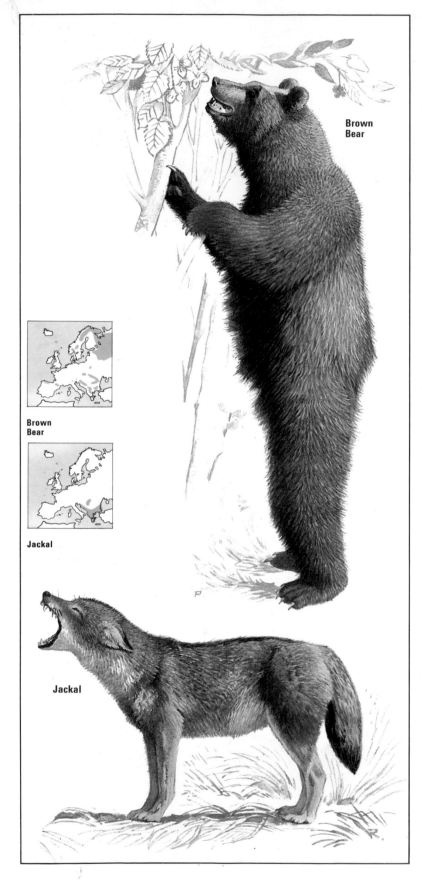

Brown Bear

Brown Bear

Jackal

Jackal

Carnivores

About 250 species of carnivores (Order Carnivora) are scattered around the world, although they were not present in Australia or New Zealand until introduced by man. About 25 species occur in Europe. The range of size in the group is enormous, from the tiny weasel to the polar bear. The name Carnivora means flesh-eater and, although the diets vary, most species are adapted for eating meat, with stabbing eye teeth and sharp-edged cheek teeth which shear cleanly through the flesh.

BEARS
Family Ursidae

There are about 10 species of bears distributed around the northern hemisphere and in northern South America. Bears are heavily-built animals with small ears and eyes. They have 5 digits in each foot and strong claws. They walk with the feet flat on the ground. The molars are not noticeably modified for shearing.

BROWN BEAR
Ursus arctos
Head and body up to 2m, tail vestigial. Colour of shaggy coat varying shades of brown. Weighs up to 250kg.
Range and habitat: wild, wooded country, often in mountains. Population in forests of western Europe heavily persecuted and the remaining specimens are smaller than their eastern and northern counterparts.
Food and habits: a very varied diet, mostly vegetarian with roots, bulbs, tubers, berries and grain. Also eats small mammals, eggs, and fish. Can open bees' nests for the honey. Solitary and mostly nocturnal.

DOGS AND ALLIES
Family Canidae

This family contains about 35 species, including the wolves and jackals. There are 5 species in Europe. Most members are long-legged, deep-chested animals with plenty of stamina for the chase. The claws are blunt and not retractable.

JACKAL
Canis aureus
Head and body up to 75cm, tail up to 36cm. Smaller and more lightly built than the wolf, the jackal can also be recognized by the reddish-brown

colouring on the side of the neck. Colour a dirty yellow mixed with black and brown hairs. Tail reddish with black tip.

Habitat: lives mainly in steppe and scrub vegetation.

Food and habits: feeds on small mammals, birds, eggs, fish and fruit. More nocturnal than the wolf.

WOLF
Canis lupus

Head and body up to 140cm, tail 40cm. The size is variable, with animals in the south being smaller. A dog-like animal with broad head and chest; long, bushy, drooping tail; and pointed ears. Colour variable, but usually a brownish- or yellowish-grey brindled with black.

Range and habitat: the original European population is now much reduced and the animals are found in the more remote forests, mountains and tundra.

Food and habits: feeds on deer, but will also take smaller prey. In summer lives in small family groups in specific territory, but in winter several groups may join together to form a large pack for hunting.

RED FOX
Vulpes vulpes

Head and body about 60 cm, tail about 40cm. Fur sandy to brownish-red above, greyish-white below. Has black markings on front of limbs and back of ears. Tail bushy, usually with a white tip.

Habitat: preferred habitat is woodland, but very adaptable and significant numbers are found in towns.

Food and habits: mainly small mammals, squirrels and rabbits, but also eats insects, small birds, eggs, grass, fruit and carrion. Mostly nocturnal.

RACCOON-DOG
Nyctereutes procyonoides

Head and body 50–55cm, tail 13–18cm. General colour yellowish-brown, with hairs on shoulder, back and tail tipped with black.

Range and habitat: a native of eastern Siberia and Asia, the Raccoon-dog has been brought to Europe for fur-farming and has now spread as far west as Germany. Lives mainly in river valleys, grassy plains and forests.

Food and habits: varied diet includes rodents, fish and fruit. Spends worst of winter in hibernation, the only member of the family to do so.

ARCTIC FOX
Alopex lagopus

Head and body up to 67cm, tail to 42cm. Colour variable, but summer coat usually greyish-brown, turning white in winter. A small percentage of animals are a smoky-grey colour throughout the year and are known as the Blue fox. Muzzle and ears are shorter than in Red fox.

Range and habitat: the Arctic tundra and the mountains of Scandinavia.

Food and habits: feeds mainly on voles and lemmings, birds, carrion and shellfish.

Wolf

Red Fox

Raccoon-dog

Wolf

Raccoon-dog

Arctic Fox

winter coat

summer coat

Arctic Fox

WEASELS AND ALLIES
Family Mustelidae

This family of carnivores is widely distributed around the world and includes about 70 species of short-legged, sinuous, long-bodied animals such as weasels, polecats, badgers, otters, mink and their allies. Most species produce a strong-smelling odour from anal glands. They are meat-eaters with prominent canines and well-developed shearing teeth. Many species are hunted for their fur; some have been persecuted because they are pests; others have been farmed and domesticated. They are mainly nocturnal.

WEASEL
Mustela nivalis
Head and body about 20cm, tail 6cm. Female smaller than male. The smallest European carnivore. Weasels of southern Europe are larger than those from the north. Smaller than the stoat, with relatively short tail with no black on tip. Reddish-brown above, white below, often with brownish markings. May turn white in north of range (Russia and Scandinavia). Musky smell from anal glands.
Habitat: found in nearly all habitats, even in towns. Active day and night, preying on mice and voles, other small rodents, birds and eggs. They are slender enough to chase small rodents in their burrows. As with stoat, numbers fluctuate according to population of prey, especially voles.

MARBLED POLECAT
Vormela peregusna
Head and body 30–38cm, tail 15–20cm. Similar to the other polecats in shape, but with distinctly mottled coat of dark brown and cream. Dark brown below.
Habitat: lives in open areas with scrub and trees, and is also found in farmland. South-east Europe.
Food: eats small mammals, birds, lizards and reptiles and some invertebrates.

WESTERN POLECAT
Mustela putorius
Head and body 30–44cm, tail 13–18cm. Coarse, dark brown hair above with yellowish underfur showing through. Black below. White on muzzle and between eyes and ears. The musky scent from the anal glands is particularly strong in this species, which is also known as the foulmart. Often killed as pest of game and poultry, and formerly for its fur. Once almost extinct in Britain, but recovering slowly.

Habitat: lives mainly in woodland and near water, although it rarely climbs or swims. Makes a den among rocks or tree roots, or sometimes in old rabbit holes.
The domestic ferret (*M. fero*), kept for hunting and controlling rabbits, is often thought to have originated from the Western polecat, although its skull shows some similarities with that of the Steppe polecat. It is the size of the Western polecat, but in captivity it is usually very pale and often albino. Feral populations, occurring in many areas, tend to resemble the polecat in colour and habits and interbreed with them when the opportunity arises.

STEPPE POLECAT
Mustela eversmanni
Head and body 30–44cm, tail 13–18cm. Very similar to the Western polecat, but paler in colour above.
Habitat: lives mainly in grassland, scrub and cultivated land.
Food and habits: grassland animals such as susliks and hamsters are prominent in diet. More active in daylight hours than western species. Habits otherwise similar, except that it usually lives in an underground burrow, often excavating for itself.

STOAT
Mustela erminea
Head and body 22–32cm, tail 8–12cm. Males considerably larger than females. Body long and slim with short legs. Reddish-brown above, white tinged with yellow below. Tip of tail black. In northern part of range winter coat is white, but tail tip remains black. Fur is known as *ermine*. This is harvested mainly in Russia, but supplies are declining. Musky odour produced by anal glands.
Habitat: lives mainly in woodland, but adaptable and found in hedgerows rough grassland and moorland.
Food and habits: diet almost entirely meat, especially rodents, rabbits, fish, birds and eggs. Mainly nocturnal, but may hunt by day. Numbers fluctuate with abundance of prey species. Regarded as pest of poultry and game birds, and much persecuted.

Left: The western polecat has an outer coat of glossy brown hairs, but these are often rather sparse and the yellow underfur shows through very clearly.

Western Polecat

Steppe Polecat

female

Weasel

male

Marbled Polecat

Steppe Polecat

Western Polecat

winter coat

Stoat

summer coat

Stoat

European Mink

European Mink

Pine Marten

Beech Marten

Beech Marten

Cretan form

Pine Marten

EUROPEAN MINK
Mustela lutreola

Head and body 35–40cm, tail 13–14cm. Male larger than female. A large weasel-like species. Dark brown all over, except for white markings above and below the mouth. No white around eye. Feet partially webbed; swims and dives well.

Habitat: lives in marsh lands and on the banks of lakes and rivers.

Food and habits: eats water voles, rodents, birds, frogs and fish. Nocturnal and solitary. Sleeps by day in a hole or burrow or in a hollow tree.

The American mink (*M. vison*), introduced to fur farms in Europe, has escaped and become established in Britain and elsewhere. It can be distinguished from the European mink because it has no white on upper jaw.

PINE MARTEN
Martes martes

Head and body 40–55cm, tail 22–27cm. Colour varies from brown to nearly black above and below. Conspicuous throat patch yellowish to orange, but never pure white. Sharp muzzle, prominent ears, long bushy tail.

Habitat: lives in woodlands, especially the pine woods of northern Europe; being a good climber, is often seen in trees. The Pine marten is trapped intensively for fur, and has become rare in many parts of range; also trapped to protect game birds.

Food and habits: feeds on small birds, squirrels and other small rodents, rabbits and eggs, but will also take honey and berries. Mainly nocturnal.

BEECH MARTEN
Martes foina

Head and body 40–48cm, tail 22–26cm. Similar to Pine marten, but with a pure-white throat patch, which is often divided by a dark streak. In Crete the throat patch is much reduced and may be absent.

Habitat: lives in deciduous woodland and rocky areas, and is often found near houses. Less often seen in trees than Pine marten. Absent from British Isles and Scandinavia.

Food and habits: preys on mice, shrews, birds, frogs and lizards; also eats some fruit and berries. Habits similar to those of Pine marten, but will make den in houses and barns and readily enters towns.

OTTER
Lutra lutra
Head and body 60–80cm, tail 35–45cm. Fur rich brown above, paler below, especially on throat. Thick underfur grey, mixed with long, glossy guard hairs. Long body with long tapering tail, short legs, webbed feet. Ears very small.
Habitat: lives by lakes and rivers and also inhabits coastal areas in wilder parts of its range. Widely distributed.
Food and habits: feeds mainly on fish of many kinds, although eels are often preferred. Also eats crayfish and other invertebrates, and water birds. On land will take voles, rabbits and other small mammals. Usually nocturnal. Spends much time in the water. Hunted for fur, sport and to protect fishing interests, the otter is becoming scarce in some parts of its range. Habitat destruction is also an important factor in its decrease, as is water pollution.

BADGER
Meles meles
Head and body 70–80cm, tail 12–19cm. Stout, squat body; head with long tapered snout. The rough coat is grey above, and black below and on limbs. Head white, with conspicuous black stripe on each side running through the eye to the small ears, which are tipped with white.
Habitat: lives mainly in woods and copses in extensive burrow systems called *sets*, which can be recognized by the great mounds of excavated earth surrounding the entrances. May also live in fields and hedgerows.
Food and habits: feeds on a wide range of animals and plants, including earthworms, small mammals, carrion, fruit, nuts and bulbs. Lives in family groups. Nocturnal.

WOLVERINE
Gulo gulo
Head and body 70–80cm, tail 16–25cm. Often known as the Glutton. Largest of the weasel family. Dense, shaggy coat of thick fur, dark brown above, with band of paler colour on side and dark below. Thick body with short, strong legs.
Range and habitat: lives in evergreen forests in colder parts of northern Europe and on the tundra. Persecuted by man for its fur and as a pest of domestic animals, but is still common in many parts of its range.
Food and habits: eats mostly rodents, birds, eggs, and invertebrates in summer, but mainly carrion in winter. Can attack sickly animals of larger size and may eat deer. Its particularly strong jaws are used to tear carrion. Hunts alone or in pairs. Nocturnal and relatively slow-moving.

Otter

Otter

Badger

Badger

Wolverine

Wolverine

MONGOOSES AND GENETS
Family Viverridae

A family of small- to medium-sized carnivores, including about 75 species of civets, genets, and mongooses widely distributed throughout both Asia and Africa. Ecologically, they are the tropical equivalents of the weasels and martens, which occur mainly in the cooler regions of the world. Three species occur in southern Europe. The family includes a number of species with striped and spotted coats, sinuous bodies and long bushy tails. Scent-gland secretions, known as *civet*, are taken from several species and used in the perfume and pharmaceutical industries. Unlike those of the mustelids, the secretions are not usually unpleasant and are not used for defence.

EGYPTIAN MONGOOSE
Herpestes ichneumon
Head and body 50–55cm, tail 35–45cm. Long sinuous body, grizzled grey all over. Tail tipped with black, tapering to a point.
Range and habitat: found in southern Spain and Portugal, probably as an introduction from Africa, where it is common from Egypt to the Cape. Lives in scrub and open woodland.
Food and habits: feeds on rodents, birds, eggs and reptiles. Known for ability to kill snakes by agility and speed of attack. Nocturnal, but sometimes active by day. Usually solitary, but sometimes found in small family groups.
The Indian Grey Mongoose (*H. edwardsi*) is slightly smaller and has a lighter tip to the tail, which is about the same length (45cm) as the head and body. It has been introduced to southern Italy from Asia.

GENET
Genetta genetta
Head and body 50–60cm, tail 40–50cm. Similar to a small, lightly built cat. Coat spotted dark brown on pale ground colour; tail banded light and dark. Short legs, large ears and pointed muzzle.
Range and habitat: range includes most of Africa and Arabia, together with Iberia and much of France. Lives in bush and scrub country.
Food and habits: eats mainly small mammals, birds and insects. Nocturnal, usually solitary.

RACCOONS
Family Procyonidae

A small family of about 18 species, including raccoons and kinkajous. Some scientists include the Lesser and Giant pandas of Asia in this family, but otherwise the family is confined to the Americas. Most species are small- to medium-sized carnivores with long tails, and generally rather flat, non-slicing cheek teeth. One species has been introduced to Europe.

RACCOON
Procyon lotor
Head and body 50–60cm, tail 30–40cm. About the size of a cat, but easily identified by its black mask contrasting with white face markings, and by its distinctly banded tail. General colour greyish-brown.
Range and habitat: widespread in the Americas, and now established in Germany, the Netherlands and Luxembourg. Lives mainly in woodland often close to water. Nocturnal
Food and habits: feeds mainly on aquatic animals, especially crayfish, fish and insects in the water, and rodents and a little plant food on land.

CATS
Family Felidae

A family of about 36 species of carnivores widely distributed around the world. Although differing greatly in size and coat pattern—many are beautifully striped or spotted—all are unmistakably cat-like in appearance, with supple, muscular bodies, rounded heads and short jaws, eyes with pupils that contract to vertical slits, and well-developed whiskers. They have fewer teeth than other carnivores, but the cheek teeth are superbly suited to shearing through flesh and the canines are large and dagger-like. The claws can be retracted as a rule, and the animals walk on their toes like dogs—not on the soles of their feet like bears. There are nocturnal and diurnal species, and some which hunt by night and day. Most species hunt by creeping stealthily towards their prey and then pouncing or rushing the last few metres. There are 2 native species in Europe.

WILD CAT
Felis sylvestris
Head and body 50–65cm, tail 30cm. About the size of a large domestic cat, but somewhat more robust. Can be distinguished from domestic cats by its short bushy tail, which is marked with clear, separate dark rings; the coat, which is usually clearly striped; and the pale paws.
Habitat: lives in dense woodland and on rocky hills. Southern Europe, Alps and Scotland.
Food and habits: eats mostly small mammals, hares and rabbits, but may also kill small deer and lambs, birds, fish and some insects. Nocturnal.

LYNX
Felis lynx
Head and body 80–130cm, tail 11–25cm. A medium-sized cat with long legs, markedly tufted ears and a ruff round the face. Tail short, black towards the tip. Coat reddish with dark spots which vary in number and are often indistinct, especially in the north of the range. Some scientists consider the Spanish lynx to be a separate species, as it is smaller and more heavily spotted.
Range and habitat: formerly widespread in Europe. Now very scarce in most of range and protected in many areas. Lives mainly in coniferous forest and mountainous country—mainly in Scandinavia and Spain.
Food and habits: feeds on hares, rodents and young deer. Nocturnal.

The wild cat hunts by night, but has a favourite resting place in its territory and can sometimes be seen sunning itself there by day.

Wild Cat

Lynx

Hooved Mammals

The hooved mammals, or ungulates, are mostly large grazing and browsing animals which walk on tip-toe and have tough hooves to protect their toes. Walking on tip-toe increases the effective length of the leg, and therefore the stride, and enables the animals to run faster—an important factor for animals living, as most ungulates do, on open grasslands. Batteries of grinding cheek teeth crush the the food, and most species employ armies of intestinal bacteria to digest the cellulose. There are two distinct orders which are not closely related. The Perissodactyla, represented by the horses and asses, the tapirs, and the rhinoceroses, are known as odd-toed ungulates because the feet normally have 1 or 3 toes. The weight is all borne on the central toe. The Artiodactyla contain the even-toed ungulates, or cloven-hooved mammals, which have 2 or 4 toes on each foot and support their weight on the two middle toes. They include pigs, sheep, deer, antelopes, cattle and camels—in fact, almost all the world's large herbivores. Many are ruminants—cud-chewing animals with complex stomachs.

HORSE
Equus caballus
Family Equidae
The many breeds of domestic horse are descendants of a wild horse known as the Tarpan (*E. ferus*), which roamed the steppes of Asia and eastern Europe until about 200 years ago. No truly wild horses are found in Europe today, although relatively unimproved breeds survive in several areas, some almost wild.
New Forest ponies and Exmoor ponies in Britain and the Camargue horses in France are examples. The Przewalski horse of China and Mongolia most closely resembles truly wild stock and many herds are kept in captivity.
Horses are distributed worldwide as a result of introduction by man. Colour and size vary enormously, but all have the characteristic long heads and long, maned necks.

WILD BOAR
Sus scrofa
Family Suidae
Head and body 1·8m, tail 30cm. Size very variable, larger in eastern part of range. Has a dense, bristly coat of grey to black colour and a long, mobile snout. Canine teeth well developed, giving tusks up to 30cm long in large males. Young has yellow stripes along the body. Ancestor of the domestic pig.
Habitat: lives mainly in deciduous woodland. Not in Britain (see map).
Food: diet mostly vegetable (roots, bulbs, acorns and beech mast), but also takes animal food. Can be pest by digging up root crops.

CATTLE, SHEEP, GOATS AND ALLIES
Family Bovidae

There are more than 100 species in this widely distributed family, ranging from graceful antelopes to huge bison and buffalo. All have complex stomachs and all chew the cud. Most species have unbranched horns with a bony core fixed permanently to the bones of the skull and covered with a sheath of horny material. Horns are found in both sexes in most species. Many species are gregarious and form large herds. Most live in open country and many are mountain animals.

MOUFLON
Ovis musimon
Head and body 120cm, tail 6cm, shoulder height 70cm. A truly wild sheep with a short rough coat, reddish-brown in colour, with dark markings, a white patch on each flank, and white legs and muzzle.
Range and habitat: lives in open woodland in mainland Europe, in open country on Mediterranean islands.
Food and habits: eats mainly grasses, herbs and sedges, and some shrubs.

DOMESTIC GOAT
Capra hircus
Size very variable: colour ranges from white to black, often piebald. Horns long and divergent in male, often turning up at the tips: shorter in female. Adult males are bearded.
Habitat: feral herds, usually with rather shaggy coats, live in many parts of Europe, roaming on rocky hillsides and scrub.
Food and habits: browses on shrubs and trees, often standing on hind legs to reach branches. Also grazes. Domestic goats are descended from the true Wild Goat (*C. aegagrus*), which is probably extinct, although feral herds on Crete are thought to resemble the original stock very closely. Their horns diverge little and sweep back in a smooth curve.

ALPINE IBEX
Capra ibex
Head and body 140cm, tail 15cm, shoulder height 75cm. Females distinctly smaller. A wild goat with a mostly grey coat with some darker colour and a black streak along lower flanks. White below. Horns heavy and curved with prominent ridges on the fronts. In females, horns sweep straight back and are smaller.
Range and habitat: lives in Alpine meadows and hillsides above treeline.
Food and habits: mainly shrubs, grasses and sedges; in winter may eat lichens.

CHAMOIS
Rupicapra rupicapra
Head and body 90–130cm, tail 3–4cm, shoulder height 75–80cm. Goat-like, with stiff coarse hair, which is tawny brown in summer, changing to a longer, nearly black coat in winter. Lighter in colour below, with white throat patch. Horns up to 20cm long, bent sharply back like a hook at tip.
Habitat: lives on wooded slopes and above the tree line in mountainous areas. Moves down to lower slopes in winter.
Food and habits: mainly herbs in summer, lichens and mosses in winter, but will eat young tree shoots. Gregarious, and forms large herds in winter.

Left: The sturdy Dartmoor pony is one of several breeds living semi-wild in various parts of Europe. They nearly all live in small groups.

Wild
Boar

Mouflon

Domestic
Goat

Alpine
Ibex

Chamois

Wild Boar

Mouflon

Alpine Ibex

Chamois

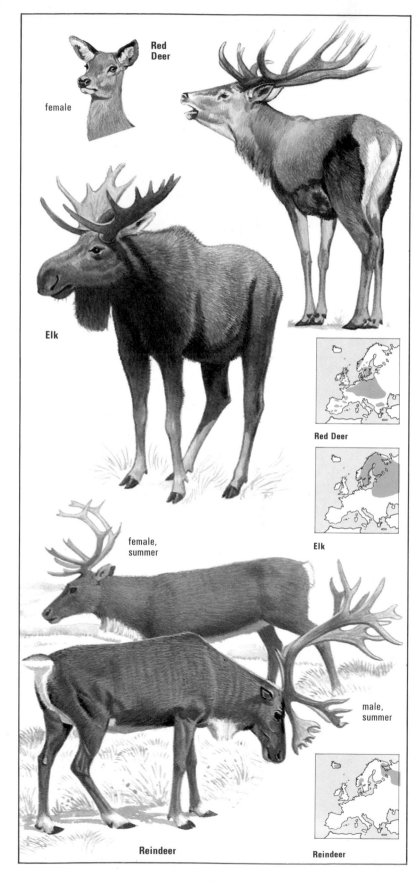

Red Deer

female

Elk

female, summer

male, summer

Reindeer

Red Deer

Elk

Reindeer

DEER
Family Cervidae

A family of about 53 species widely distributed in the Americas and Eurasia, including tropical areas. Ten species live in Europe, of which half are introduced. Nearly all species have antlers. These are solid bony appendages of the skull, developed each year and shed after the *rut*, or breeding season. Growing antlers are covered in blood-rich skin called velvet. With the exception of the reindeer, only males carry antlers. Like the cattle and antelopes, deer are cud-chewing animals. Males are usually larger than females.

RED DEER
Cervus elaphus
Shoulder height up to 140cm. A large species with a reddish-brown summer coat changing to a thicker brown-grey coat in winter. Whitish below; patch around tail buff-coloured.
Habitat: lives in dense deciduous forest, but in some areas has adapted to moorland and open woodland.
Food and habits: mainly browsing animals, eating young shoots and leaves of deciduous trees and shrubs, but will also eat nuts and fruits.

ELK
Alces alces
Shoulder height 1·8–2m. The largest deer. Colour grey-brown to black above, lighter on snout and legs. Broad muzzle. Males carry large palmate antlers with numerous branches.
Range and habitat: Scandinavia. Once close to extinction, but herds are now expanding in many areas. Lives in marshlands in summer, moving to drier land, often woodland, in winter.
Food and habits: eats leaves and young shoots, particularly birch and willow, and aquatic plants in summer. In winter subsists on bark and shoots. Spends much time in or near water, and can swim well.

REINDEER
Rangifer tarandus
Shoulder height 110–120cm. Coat thick, and variable in colour, but often a dark grey-brown in summer and paler in winter. Ears small, tail short. Hooves particularly broad and deeply cleft. Both sexes carry complex antlers.
Range and habitat: lives on the tundra and taiga of northern Europe. Domesticated in parts of northern Europe especially Lapland. Domestic animals small and very variable in colour.
Food and habits: grasses and sedges in summer; lichens and young shoots in winter. Wild herds are migratory, and strong swimmers.

MONK SEAL
Monachus monachus
Length 2·7m. Colour is a uniform brown on back, greyer below and usually with a white patch on belly. Pups black.
Range: Mediterranean and Black Sea, but now rare.

COMMON PORPOISE
Phocoena phocoena
Family Phocoenidae
Length up to 1·8m. The smallest cetacean. Stoutly built, without a beak and carrying a small, broad dorsal fin. Black above, white below. Flippers black. Colour can be variable, with some grey on the sides. Teeth 22–27 on each side of each jaw, but flattened, not conical as in dolphins.
Range and habitat: widely distributed in North Atlantic and from White Sea to Mediterranean and Black Seas. Prefers coastal waters, and may enter estuaries and larger rivers.
Food and habits: eats fish, cuttlefish and crustaceans. Found in small groups. Relatively slow swimmer.

COMMON DOLPHIN
Delphinus delphis
Family Delphinidae
Length up to 2·4m. Beak long (about 10–12cm), slender and separated by a distinct groove from forehead. Colour black above, white below, with a complex pattern of grey, yellow and white on sides. Two conspicuous waves of colour meet below dorsal fin. Dark circle around eye extending on to forehead. Teeth simple and about 3mm in diameter. There are 40–50 on each side of each jaw.
Range and habitat: worldwide in temperate and warm seas, but occasionally ventures into colder Arctic waters. Common in Black Sea, Mediterranean and northwards to southern Britain.
Food and habits: feeds mainly on fish, squid and cuttlefish. Gregarious in habits. A fast swimmer, reputed to reach 25 knots.

LONG-FINNED PILOT WHALE
Globicephala melaena
Length up to 8·5m. Bulbous forehead, with a very short beak. Black, except for white throat and chest. Dorsal fin large and recurved, about half-way down back. Long, slender, tapering flippers. Teeth 8–10 on each side of both jaws and arranged near front of jaw. Teeth are small, conical and about 10mm in diameter.
Range and habitat: the Atlantic and southern oceans. Frequently seen in coastal waters from Arctic to Mediterranean.
Food and habits: eats mainly cuttlefish and squid. Usually gathers in large schools of up to 100 animals. Migrates north in summer. Herded in Faroe Islands and driven ashore.

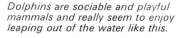

Dolphins are sociable and playful mammals and really seem to enjoy leaping out of the water like this.

Chapter Two

Birds

The birds make up the class Aves – one of the major divisions of the backboned or vertebrate animals. There are about 9,000 species, found in all kinds of habitats from the open oceans to the deserts and from the polar ice-caps to the equatorial forests. There is enormous variation in shape and size – from the ostrich, perhaps 2·7 metres high and weighing over 150 kg, to the little bee hummingbird of Cuba which has a body length of about 60 mm and weighs a mere 2 g. Behaviour is correspondingly varied, but no-one ever has any difficulty in recognizing a bird as such because of the characteristic coating of feathers. No other kind of animal possesses feathers. Other features which are characteristic of birds include the beak, or bill, and the modification of the front limbs to form wings, although not all birds can actually fly.

Feathers and Flight

The birds are undoubtedly descended from reptiles, and their feathers are modified scales. Their primary function was insulation, in association with the birds' warm-bloodedness, and the soft down feathers still play a major role in keeping the birds warm. At a later stage of evolution the feather-covered front limbs were used for gliding, and they eventually evolved into wings. The feathers on the wings became large and strong and they now provide both the lift and the propulsion during flight. Wing shapes vary a great deal according to the life style of the birds.

Streamlining is very important for flying birds, and the surface feathers, known as contour feathers, form a very smooth outline to both wings and body. The feathers do not last for ever, and the birds renew them at least once a year. This is called moulting and it usually takes place in late summer. Not all the feathers

are lost at one time, but the bird may take on quite a different appearance during the moult.

Beaks and Feet

The beaks and feet of birds can tell us a lot about their habits, and especially about their diets. The beaks normally have to catch or pick up the food, and then they have to crush or tear it, and so their shape is very much geared to the type of diet. Seed-eating birds have fairly short, but heavy beaks for crushing hard seeds; insect-eaters have either very slender beaks for picking up small creatures or wide-gaping beaks for scooping them up in mid-air; and the flesh-eaters have sharp, hooked beaks which tear up their food. There are several other specialized types of beak, and also a number of all-purpose beaks like those of the crows. The feet very often reveal a bird's habitat. Marsh-loving birds, for example, usually have long legs and long, spreading toes, while swimmers usually have webbed feet. The perching birds, which include all the common garden birds, have three forward-pointing toes and one backward-pointing toe on each foot.

Identifying Birds

Size and colour are clearly the main features to look for when trying to identify a bird, and in the following pages the description of each species begins with size, from the tip of the beak to the end of the tail, and the diagnostic points of that species. Habits and habitats can also help, and songs can be very useful. Songs are difficult to describe, however; and little attempt is made to describe them here. The best way to learn the songs is to listen to the good recordings that are now available or to go bird-watching with an expert and learn the songs as you watch.

Left: Most birds, like the pair of bullfinches seen here with their young, build nests for their eggs and youngsters.

Below: A male chaffinch in breeding plumage, showing the main areas used when describing a bird.

The maps on the following pages show in which parts of Europe a bird is likely to be found and at which times of the year. Many birds, such as swallows and most of the warblers, visit Europe only for the summer and have no blue on their maps because they spend the winter in Africa. A bird is unlikely to be found in a white area unless migrating to or from its breeding grounds.

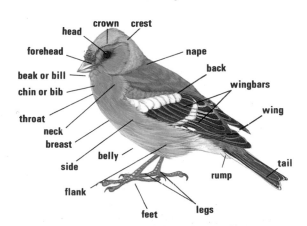

head, crown, crest, forehead, nape, beak or bill, back, chin or bib, wingbars, throat, wing, neck, breast, belly, tail, side, rump, flank, legs, feet

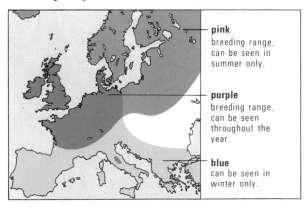

pink
breeding range, can be seen in summer only.

purple
breeding range, can be seen throughout the year.

blue
can be seen in winter only.

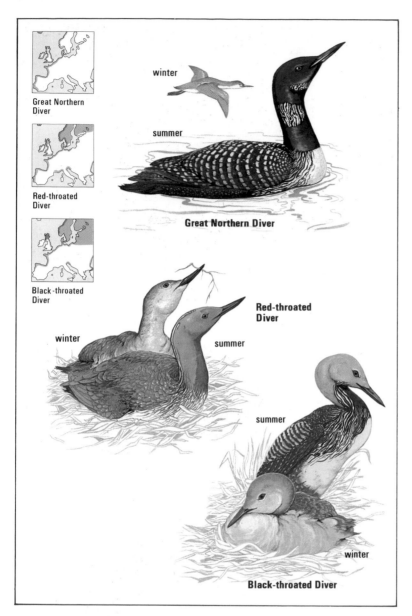

Great Northern Diver

Red-throated Diver

Black-throated Diver

winter

summer

Great Northern Diver

Red-throated Diver

winter

summer

summer

winter

Black-throated Diver

Divers

Divers are really at home underwater, where they catch fish and crustaceans. They either dive suddenly from the surface or sink slowly into the water. On land, divers walk clumsily and they normally come ashore only to breed. In winter, all divers become grey-brown above and white below. They can then only be told apart by their size, bill shape and the colours of their backs. Divers belong to the order Gaviiformes, of which there is just one family – the Gaviidae.

GREAT NORTHERN DIVER
Gavia immer
76 cm. Heavy bill. Summer: all-black head; chequered back. Winter: grey-brown back. Breeds on lakes in Iceland. Found at coast at other times.

RED-THROATED DIVER
Gavia stellata
56 cm. Thin, upturned bill. Summer: red throat patch; plain grey back. Winter: grey-brown back, speckled with white. Breeds by coast and on lakes, flying daily to the sea to feed. May be seen on reservoirs and lakes as well as at coast during autumn and winter.

BLACK-THROATED DIVER
Gavia arctica
63 cm. Intermediate bill. Summer: black throat patch; dark spotted back. Winter: blackish back. Breeds at remote lakes or lochs, usually on rocky islands. Seen at coasts in autumn and winter, often in small flocks.

Great Crested Grebe

summer

winter

Great Crested Grebe

Grebes

Grebes are elegant water birds with colourful breeding plumage in spring and summer. The boldly patterned heads and necks, with their ear tufts and frills, clearly mark them out from other birds. In winter, grebes lose their colour and adornments, becoming grey-brown above and white below. Then they look like divers, but are smaller and have wedge-shaped heads.

Grebes feed by diving for fish and other water animals. Although agile in the water, they are not good fliers and may escape danger by partly submerging themselves until only the head remains above water.

Grebes build nests of water plants among reeds at the edges of lakes and rivers, and lay about four eggs. The eggs may be covered with vegetation. Before building the nest, the birds perform extraordinary courtship dances in which they rush to and fro over the water and freeze in absurd postures. The chicks are often carried on the parents' backs, even during dives.

Grebes spread to the coast and open water in autumn and winter. They belong to the Podicipitidae, the only family in the order Podicipediformes.

GREAT CRESTED GREBE
Podiceps cristatus
46 cm. Long white neck and pink bill. Summer: large ear tufts and frill. Found on inland waters in summer and winter, also at coast in winter. Once hunted for its plumage, it came near to extinction in Britain in 1800s. Recovery mainly due to protection, though building of reservoirs has enabled it to expand.

RED-NECKED GREBE
Podiceps grisegena
43 cm. Medium-sized neck and black and yellow bill. Summer: red neck and pale grey cheeks but no frill. Found on inland waters in summer: usually at coast in winter.

SLAVONIAN GREBE or HORNED GREBE
Podiceps auritus
36 cm. Blue-grey bill. Summer: golden ear tufts and chestnut neck. Winter: white cheeks. Found on inland waters in summer and at estuaries in winter.

BLACK-NECKED GREBE
Podiceps nigricollis
30 cm. Slightly upturned bill. Summer: black neck and chestnut ear tufts. Winter: dusky neck and cheeks. Often seen in small flocks on inland waters in summer and on estuaries and inland in winter.

LITTLE GREBE or DABCHICK
Tachybaptus ruficollis
25 cm. Duck-like shape with almost no tail. Summer: rust-coloured neck. Found on inland waters in summer and winter, also at coast in winter.

A pair of red-necked grebes in summer plumage. The nest floats among reeds at the edge of a lake. A chick nestles between the wings of the parent bird on the nest.

Leach's Petrel

Great
Shearwater

Sooty
Shearwater

Cory's
Shearwater

Storm
Petrel

Manx
Shearwater

light phase

Fulmar

dark phase

Fulmar

Cory's
Shearwater

Great
Shearwater

Sooty
Shearwater

Storm Petrel

Leach's Petrel

Manx
Shearwater

Fulmars, Petrels and Shearwaters

The fulmar and shearwaters (family Procellariidae) and petrels (family Hydrobatidae) form the order Procellariiformes. They are ocean birds that normally come ashore only to breed. They may then be seen in colonies on coastal cliffs and islands. Some shearwaters are southern birds that visit European waters when migrating.

FULMAR
Fulmarus glacialis
46 cm. Thick neck; stubby bill; light grey with white head and underparts (light phase) or smoky grey all over (dark phase). Often follows ships, but may come ashore and occupy buildings. Nests in colonies on cliffs. Parents protect the young by ejecting a foul-smelling oily liquid at intruders.

CORY'S SHEARWATER
Calonectris diomedea
46 cm. Light brown head; yellow bill. Breeds on Mediterranean islands and ventures into Atlantic in autumn. Does not follow ships.

MANX SHEARWATER
Puffinus puffinus
36 cm. Dark upperparts and white underparts; small size. Breeds in colonies in burrows on islands and cliff-tops. Does not follow ships. Commonest European shearwater.

GREAT SHEARWATER
Puffinus gravis
46 cm. Black cap and white throat; white at base of tail. Breeds in south Atlantic in winter and visits open north Atlantic in summer and autumn. Sometimes seen offshore.

SOOTY SHEARWATER
Puffinus griseus
41 cm. Dark all over; narrow wings. Breeds in south Atlantic in winter and visits north Atlantic in summer and autumn. May be seen offshore.

STORM PETREL
Hydrobates pelagicus
15 cm. Square tail; flitting and pattering flight. Nests in crevices in rocks or stone walls on islands. Can be seen following ships, flitting over the waves summer and autumn. May be seen offshore.

LEACH'S PETREL
Oceanodroma leucorhoa
20 cm. Shallow fork in tail, erratic flight. Breeds in burrows on islands. Flight is more erratic than storm petrel, and does not follow ships or patter over waves.

Gannets, Pelicans and Cormorants

Gannets (family Sulidae), pelicans (family Pelecanidae) and cormorants (family Phalacrocoracidae) are the largest European sea birds. Although they all have webbed feet, they are not habitual swimmers. They all have different and interesting methods of fishing.
All belong to the order Pelecaniformes.

GANNET
Sula bassana
91 cm. White body with pointed tail; black wingtips; yellow head with blue eye-ring. Breeds in summer in vast colonies on cliffs, mainly on rocky islands. Winters at sea, but may be seen offshore. May follow ships. Makes spectacular dive into the water to catch fish.

CORMORANT
Phalacrocorax carbo
91 cm. Atlantic form: all black with white chin. Continental form: black with white head and neck in summer. Found at seashores and on inland waters. Flies low over water but settles on surface before diving for fish. Often perches with wings outspread, probably to dry them. Atlantic form is found in Britain, Norway and Iceland and breeds on rocky cliffs. Continental form is found in mainland Europe and nests in trees and bushes.

SHAG
Phalacrocorax aristotelis
76 cm. Green-black; yellow base of bill. Identical to cormorant in behaviour, but smaller in size and rarely seen inland at any season. Breeds on rocky cliffs at coast.

PYGMY CORMORANT
Phalacrocorax pygmaeus
48 cm. Breeding: dark spotted plumage; rust-coloured head. Non-breeding: unspotted plumage, white throat, rust-coloured breast. Usually found on inland waters. Nests in trees and bushes.

WHITE PELICAN
Pelecanus onocrotalus
168 cm. Underside of wings white at front, dark at rear; flesh-coloured feet. Breeds in swamps and marshes in eastern Mediterranean. May also be seen at coast in winter. Uses pouch beneath bill as net to catch fish. Rare.

DALMATIAN PELICAN
Pelecanus crispus
168 cm. Underside of wings all white except for dark wingtips; grey feet. Same habitat and behaviour as white pelican and inhabits same areas. Rare.

Gannet   Cormorant

Shag   Pygmy Cormorant

Continental form

Atlantic form

Cormorant

Gannet

Shag

Pygmy Cormorant

White Pelican   Dalmatian Pelican

White Pelican

Dalmatian Pelican

Grey Heron

Purple Heron

Little Egret

summer

winter

Great White Egret

Night Heron

Squacco Heron

Grey Heron	Purple Heron	Little Egret	Great White Egret	Squacco Heron	Night Heron

Herons and Allies

These birds are elegant long-legged waders belonging to the order Ciconiiformes. They feed in shallow water, lowering their long necks and bills to catch aquatic animals. Some herons spread their wings while fishing, perhaps to cut out the reflection of the sky. Herons and bitterns (family Ardeidae) and storks (family Ciconiidae) all have straight bills. They can easily be identified in flight because herons and bitterns draw back their heads whereas storks fly with necks outstretched.

GREY HERON
Ardea cinerea
91 cm. Pale grey and white with black crest; black wing edges. The most common and largest European heron. Found on inland water and at seashore, where it stands motionless in or near water then suddenly darts head down after prey. Also perches in trees, where it usually nests in colonies.

PURPLE HERON
Ardea purpurea
79 cm. Long S-shaped chestnut neck with black stripe; reddish underparts. Found in swamps and marshes, where it breeds in colonies.

LITTLE EGRET
Egretta garzetta
58 cm. Yellow feet. May be found at shallow water of any kind. Usually nests near water. In summer develops a long white crest of hanging plumes, for which it was once hunted.

GREAT WHITE EGRET
Egretta alba
89 cm. Black feet; no summer crest. Found by shallow water; nests in reed-beds. Resembles little egret but is much larger and less common.

SQUACCO HERON
Ardeola ralloides
46 cm. Thick neck and stocky shape; buff body with white wings, but looks white in flight. Found in marshes and swamps and at small stretches of water, where it nests among reeds or in bushes or trees. It is like a bittern in shape but is much less shy.

NIGHT HERON
Nycticorax nycticorax
61 cm. Stocky with rather short legs, black back, white breast; black cap. Usually seen feeding at dusk in pools and marshes, or roosting in bushes and trees during the day.

White Stork

Black Stork

Little Bittern

Bittern

Greater Flamingo

A pair of white storks. These birds often nest on buildings, and this pair have built their nest on a chimney cowling.

Black Stork

White Stork

Bittern

Little Bittern

Greater Flamingo

LITTLE BITTERN
Ixobrychus minutus
36 cm. Black wings with buff patch, black back (male) or brown back (female). Hides away and nests among dense reeds and thickets near water. May escape detection by freezing stock-still.

BITTERN
Botaurus stellaris
76 cm. Large stocky shape. Same habitat and behaviour as little bittern, but much larger size. Freezes with bill pointing upwards. Foghorn-like booming call may be heard at a great distance.

WHITE STORK
Ciconia ciconia
102 cm. White neck and upperparts; red bill and legs. Found in marshes, farmland and open country. Nests on buildings, often on special platforms, or in trees near farms and villages. Walks slowly over ground.

BLACK STORK
Ciconia nigra
96 cm. Black neck and upperparts. Frequents marshes and pools among forests, where it nests in trees. Uncommon.

GREATER FLAMINGO
Phoenicopterus ruber
125 cm. Large bent bill; very long neck and legs; pink and black wings (in flight). Found in flocks only in the nature reserves of the Camargue region in southern France, where it breeds, and of the Coto de Doñana in southern Spain, where breeding is rare. Single birds seen in the wild have probably escaped from collections. Wades in shallow water, dipping its bill to strain tiny creatures from the water, and nests on mudflats or on heaps of mud in water.

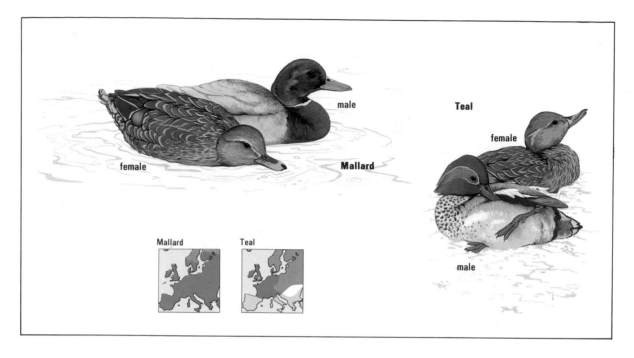

male

Teal

female

female

Mallard

male

Mallard

Teal

Waterfowl or Wildfowl

This group of birds consists of ducks, geese and swans. They are all water birds, and use their webbed feet to swim strongly. The young are born with feathers and can walk and swim soon after hatching. Many species can be seen on lakes in parks. All belong to the Anatidae, the only family in the order Anseriformes.

DUCKS
Family Anatidae

Ducks are usually smaller in size and have shorter necks than geese and swans. In addition, the two sexes have different plumage, although in late summer the drakes (males) moult and for a time resemble the ducks (females). Ducks nest on the ground or in holes. There are three main groups of ducks. *Surface-feeding* or *dabbling ducks* live in shallow water, where they feed on water plants by dabbling or up-ending. They leap into the air to get airborne, and have a brightly coloured patch of glossy wing feathers called a *speculum*. The colour of the speculum is important in identifying the

drably coloured females. *Diving ducks* dive from the surface for water plants and animals, and so prefer deeper water than do dabbling ducks. Their legs are set farther back so that they can swim underwater, and they run along the surface to take wing. The third group of ducks, the *sawbills*, are also divers.

MALLARD
Anas platyrhynchos
58 cm. Male: dark green head; chestnut breast. Female: blue-purple speculum. Dabbling duck, very common on all kinds of inland waters and at coasts and estuaries. Often seen in flocks. Most domestic ducks, though different in colour, are descended from wild mallards.

TEAL
Anas crecca
36 cm. Male: brown and green head. Female: small size, green speculum. Dabbling duck. Smallest European duck. Prefers secluded inland waters in summer, spreads to open waters and coasts in winter.

GADWALL
Anas strepera
51 cm. Male: grey body with black rear; brown wing panel; black and white speculum. Female: white belly, black and white speculum. Dabbling duck. Prefers inland waters.

GARGANEY
Anas querquedula
38 cm. Male: white stripe on head. Female: blue-grey forewing; indistinct

speculum. Dabbling duck. Prefers inland waters, seldom seen on coast.

WIGEON
Anas penelope
46 cm. Male: chestnut head with light crown; white forewing. Female: black and green speculum; white belly. Dabbling duck. Prefers inland waters in summer, spreads to coast in winter, when it may be seen in flocks. May graze on land.

PINTAIL
Anas acuta
63 cm. Large but slim build. Male: long pointed tail; white neck stripe. Female: Long neck, long tail. Dabbling duck. Prefers inland waters in summer, but coasts in winter. Breeds on moors, marshes.

SHOVELER
Anas clypeata
51 cm. Spoon-shaped bill. Male: green head, white breast and chestnut flanks. Female: blue forewing with dark green speculum. Dabbling duck. Usually found on ponds and in marshes. The odd-shaped bill, unlike that of all other ducks, is used to strain tiny plants and animals from the water.

MANDARIN DUCK
Aix galericulata
46 cm. Male: orange sidewhiskers, orange 'fins' on wings. Female: white eye-ring and stripe; white chin; spotted underparts. Dabbling duck. Introduced from China and seen mainly on park lakes, nests in tree holes. Escaped birds live in the wild, preferring ponds surrounded by trees.

female
male
Gadwall

female
Garganey
male

female
Wigeon
male

male
Pintail

female

female
male
Shoveler

female
male
Mandarin Duck

Gadwall Garganey

Wigeon Pintail Shoveler Mandarin Duck

Red-crested Pochard

Scaup

Tufted Duck

male female **Red-crested Pochard**

male female **Scaup**

male female **Eider**

male female **Tufted Duck**

female male **Ferruginous Duck**

female male **Pochard**

Pochard

Ferruginous Duck

Eider

RED-CRESTED POCHARD
Netta rufina
56 cm. Male: chestnut head with red bill; long white wingbar; white flanks. Female: brown plumage with light cheeks and long white wingbar. Diving duck. Prefers inland waters.

SCAUP
Aythya marila
46 cm. Male: as tufted duck, but no crest and with grey back. Female: as tufted duck, but no crest and with larger white face patch. Diving duck. Breeds inland, but otherwise seen at coast and on estuaries.

TUFTED DUCK
Aythya fuligula
43 cm. Male: drooping crest; dark head and neck, black back and tail with white belly. Female: small crest; small white patch at base of bill, white wingbar. Diving duck. Often seen on lakes and ponds; also at seashore and estuaries in winter.

POCHARD
Aythya ferina
46 cm. Male: dark chestnut head and neck with pale grey back; black breast. Female: brown head with light stripe through eye; blue band on bill; grey wing band. Diving duck. Breeds among reeds on inland waters, otherwise seen mainly on lakes and at estuaries.

FERRUGINOUS DUCK
Aythya nyroca
41 cm. Male: rich brown head, neck and breast; white eye; white patch under tail; bold white wingbar. Female: as male but dull brown and brown eye; white patch under tail and white wingbar. Diving duck. Breeds among reeds on inland waters; winters at open inland waters, rarely at coast.

EIDER
Somateria mollissima
61 cm. Male: white back and black belly. Female: brown plumage closely barred with black. Diving duck. Most marine of all ducks, seldom found inland. Breeds at seashore, lining nest with soft breast feathers known as eider down.

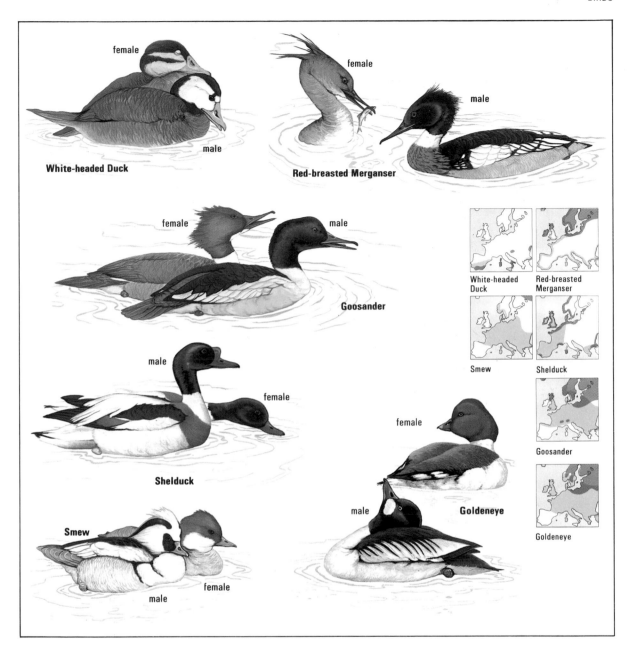

White-headed Duck

Red-breasted Merganser

female
male

female
male

Goosander

male
female

Shelduck

female

male

Goldeneye

Smew

male
female

White-headed
Duck

Red-breasted
Merganser

Smew

Shelduck

Goosander

Goldeneye

WHITE-HEADED DUCK
Oxyura leucocephala
46 cm. Male: white head; blue bill (in summer). Female: light cheek with dark line. Diving duck. Confined to inland waters. Often points tail upwards when swimming. Uncommon. Very similar Ruddy duck *Oxyura jamaicensis* has been introduced into Britain.

GOLDENEYE
Bucephala clangula
46 cm. Male: round white patch before eye. Female: brown head with white collar. Diving duck. Nests in tree holes and burrows near fresh water; winters on lakes, rivers and coastal waters. Drakes raise bill in courting display in early spring. Wings whistle in flight.

SHELDUCK
Tadorna tadorna
61 cm. Male: green-black head and white body with broad chestnut band; red knob over bill. Female: as male but no red knob. Large goose-like duck. Nests in hollow trees and burrows or among bushes. Winters mainly at coasts, often on mudflats.

RED-BREASTED MERGANSER
Mergus serrator
56 cm. Male: green-black head with double crest, white collar and chestnut breast band. Female: chestnut head with double crest. Sawbill. Breeds near fresh or salt water, hiding nest among rocks or vegetation. Mainly found at coasts in winter.

GOOSANDER
Mergus merganser
66 cm. Male: dark green head with long thin red bill, pinkish-white breast and flanks. Female: as female red-breasted merganser, but with single crest and striking white throat. Sawbill. Nests in tree cavities and burrows near fresh water. Usually remains inland in winter.

SMEW
Mergus albellus
41 cm. Male: white with black markings, especially patch around eye. Female: white head and throat with chestnut cap and nape. Sawbill (but duck-like appearance). Nests in holes in trees near inland waters. Also found at coast in winter.

Bean Goose

dark-bellied form

light-bellied form

Brent Goose

Pink-footed Goose

Greenland race

Greylag Goose

White-fronted Goose

Lesser White-fronted Goose

Main race

Pink-footed Goose

Lesser White-fronted Goose

Eastern race

Western race

White-fronted Goose

Brent Goose

Bean Goose

Greylag Goose

GEESE
Family Anatidae

Geese are between ducks and swans in size. They graze mainly on land, and the legs are set forward so that they can walk easily. The sexes are alike. There are two groups of geese. Geese of the genus *Anser* are grey-brown and those of the genus *Branta* are black and white.

GREYLAG GOOSE
Anser anser
84 cm. Pink feet and legs with head and neck no darker than body, orange bill (western race) or pink bill (eastern race). Very common. Breeds on moors, marshes, reedy lakes, and offshore islands. Winters in fields, inland and coastal marshes and at estuaries. There are two subspecies, or races. The

western race (*A.a. anser*) is found in Iceland, Britain and western Europe; the eastern race (*A.a. rubrirostris*) inhabits eastern Europe. All domestic geese are descended from the greylag.

WHITE-FRONTED GOOSE
Anser albifrons
71 cm. White patch at base of bill; irregular black bars on belly, pink bill (main race) or yellow or orange bill (Greenland race). Found in same habitat as greylag goose in winter, but breeds in far north. The Greenland race (*A.a. flavirostris*) migrates from Greenland to winter in Ireland and western Scotland. The main, or typical, race (*A.a. albifrons*) breeds in northern Russia and winters in the rest of mainland Europe and in Britain.

LESSER WHITE-FRONTED GOOSE
Anser erythropus
61 cm. As main race of white-fronted goose, but smaller size and with yellow eye-ring and larger white patch. Similar habitat to white-fronted goose.

BEAN GOOSE
Anser fabalis
76 cm. Orange-yellow feet and legs; dark head and neck; black and orange-yellow bill. Breeds in northern woods and tundra; winters inland in fields near water.

PINK-FOOTED GOOSE
Anser brachyrhynchus
68 cm. As bean goose, but pink feet and legs and pink and black bill. Breeds in Arctic; similar winter habitat to bean goose.

BRENT GOOSE
Branta bernicla
58 cm. Black head and neck with small white neck mark. Winter visitor to coasts and estuaries. Feeds mainly on eel grasses in water, and feeding times depend on tides. There are two subspecies. The light-bellied form (*B.b. hrota*) breeds in Greenland and Spitsbergen, and the dark-bellied form (*B.b. bernicla*) in northern Russia.

BARNACLE GOOSE
Branta leucopsis
63 cm. White face, black neck and breast. Winter visitor from Arctic to salt marshes and estuaries and surrounding fields. The odd name comes from a medieval belief that the birds hatch from goose barnacles instead of eggs.

CANADA GOOSE
Branta canadensis
97 cm. Long black neck, black head with white throat, light breast. Largest European goose. Introduced from North America to parks. Escaped birds now breed in Britain and Sweden, and may move further south for the winter. Wild birds nest on islands in lakes and graze in marshes and fields by lakes and rivers.

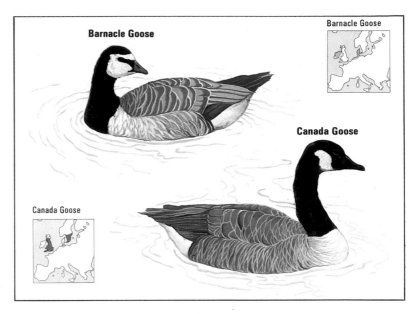

SWANS
Family Anatidae

Swans are the largest waterfowl and immediately recognised by their long elegant necks, which they lower into the water or to the ground to pull up plants. The sexes are alike. The black swan seen in parks has been introduced from Australia. The birds should be approached with caution, especially when breeding. Juveniles of all European species are brown, with indistinct bill patterns.

MUTE SWAN
Cygnus olor
152 cm. Orange bill with black knob, neck usually curved. Very common. Often found in tame state on park lakes and village ponds and along rivers. Usually nests at banks of rivers and lakes; winters on open waters and at coast.

WHOOPER SWAN
Cygnus cygnus
152 cm. Yellow bill with black tip; neck usually straight. Nests in swamps and by lakes in far north; winters further south along coasts and on lakes and rivers. Its name refers to whooping sound of call.

BEWICK'S SWAN
Cygnus columbianus
122 cm. Black bill with yellow base; neck usually straight. Winter visitors from Arctic. Similar habitat to whooper swan, though prefers larger areas of water in more open country.

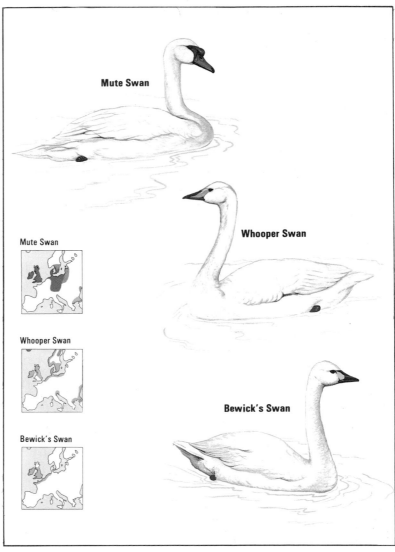

Birds of Prey

The birds of prey hunt other animals. They usually catch them alive – on the ground, in the air or in the water – but sometimes they eat dead animals. Some other birds, such as kingfishers and crows, may take similar prey, but the true birds of prey, often called raptors, have sharp talons with which they catch their victims. Their hooked beaks then tear the flesh. Eagles, falcons and vultures are all birds of prey and all are included in the order Falconiformes. The owls also have sharp talons and hooked beaks, but they hunt mainly by night and, although they are birds of prey, they are placed in a separate order (pages 73–74).

Black Vulture

Griffon Vulture

Lammergeyer

Egyptian Vulture

Egyptian Vulture

Griffon Vulture

Black Vulture

Lammergeyer

VULTURES, EAGLES, BUZZARDS, HAWKS, KITES AND HARRIERS
Family Accipitridae

Most of these birds of prey soar through the air, keeping a sharp lookout for prey below and then dropping on an unsuspecting victim. However, vultures land on the ground to feed on carrion (dead animals) and on refuse. Eagles mainly seek live prey as they soar. Buzzards and kites also soar and look rather like small eagles, though buzzards may also be seen perching and kites can be told by their long forked tails. Hawks and harriers fly near the ground, hawks dashing rapidly through the air and harriers gliding gently.

EGYPTIAN VULTURE
Neophron percnopterus
63 cm. Long thin bill with bare yellow skin on face; white plumage with black wingtips. Usually seen in mountains, but comes to rubbish dumps in villages. In Africa, it is well known for its habit of dropping stones on ostrich eggs to break them open.

GRIFFON VULTURE
Gyps fulvus
100 cm. White neck and head with white ruff. Usually found in mountains. Unlike eagles, has head and tail that appear very small in flight.

BLACK VULTURE
Aegypius monachus
102 cm. Dark patches on head and long bare neck with dark ruff. Usually found in mountains and plains, but rare. If all three vultures arrive at a carcass together, the black vulture feeds first, then the griffon vulture and finally the Egyptian vulture.

LAMMERGEYER or BEARDED VULTURE
Gypaetus barbatus
110 cm. Long narrow wings and long diamond-shaped tail; orange breast. Found in mountains; does not join other vultures to feed. Well known for unusual habit of dropping bones on to rocks to break them open.

Golden Eagle

Bonelli's Eagle

light form

Short-toed Eagle

dark form

Booted Eagle

dark form

light form

Imperial Eagle
Spanish form

Honey Buzzard

Golden Eagle

Bonelli's Eagle

Imperial Eagle

Booted Eagle

Short-toed Eagle

Honey Buzzard

GOLDEN EAGLE
Aquila chrysaetos
84 cm. Dark brown all over with golden feathers on head. Usually seen soaring above mountain slopes, though may hunt near the ground. May also be found at coasts and in woods and fields. Nests in trees or on rock ledges.

IMPERIAL EAGLE
Aquila heliaca
81 cm. White shoulders; white wing patches (Spanish form only). Found in low-lying forests, woods, plains and marshes. Nests in tall trees.

BONELLI'S EAGLE
Hieraaetus fasciatus
71 cm. White underparts; wings dark above or white with dark band beneath. Usually found in mountains, but may

also be seen in more open country in winter. Dashes rapidly through the air, hunting for small mammals and birds. Nests in trees and on rock ledges.

BOOTED EAGLE
Hieraaetus pennatus
51 cm. Small size like buzzard but long narrow tail. Plumage varies from light to dark, but light birds are more common than dark birds. Usually found in forests or woods, hunting in clearings. Nests in trees.

SHORT-TOED EAGLE
Circaetus gallicus
66 cm. White underparts with white underwings and often dark breast and head. Head plumage may be light or dark, dark being more common. Found in mountains and gorges, plains and

woods and at coasts. Often hovers, seeking snakes, lizards and frogs. Nests in trees.

HONEY BUZZARD
Pernis apivorus
53 cm. Like buzzards, but longer tail with black bands. Colour varies from cream to dark brown. Usually found in clearings and at edges of forests and woods. Gets its name from its habit of feeding at the nests of bees and wasps, though for grubs and not for honey. Nests in trees.

Buzzard

light form

dark form

Rough-legged Buzzard

Goshawk

Montagu's Harrier

female

male

female

male

Sparrowhawk

| Buzzard | Rough-legged Buzzard | Sparrowhawk | Goshawk | Montagu's Harrier |

A female Montagu's harrier arriving at her nest.

BUZZARD
Buteo buteo
53 cm. Like small golden eagle but broad rounded tail. Plumage varies from cream to dark brown. Found in woods, fields and plains, at coasts and on mountain slopes and hillsides. Often soars, but hunts near the ground. Nests in trees and on rock ledges.

ROUGH-LEGGED BUZZARD
Buteo lagopus
56 cm. Dark belly; white tail with black band at tip. Found in winter on moors and in marshes and fields, in summer among mountains. Nests on cliff ledges or on ground in Arctic. Often hovers before swooping on small mammals; also hunts birds.

SPARROWHAWK
Accipiter nisus
33 cm. Broad rounded wings with long tail; closely barred underparts. Usually seen in forests and woods, but also among scattered trees and bushes. Dashes through trees and hops over hedges, hunting small birds. Female is much larger than male. Nests in trees and bushes.

GOSHAWK
Accipiter gentilis
53 cm. Both sexes similar to sparrowhawk but larger size. Female is larger than male. Usually seen in woods and forests, dashing through trees in pursuit of birds. Nests mainly in fir trees.

MONTAGU'S HARRIER
Circus pygargus
43 cm. Male: as male hen harrier but black wingbar, grey rump and streaky underside. Female: very similar to female hen harrier. Found in same places and has similar flight and nesting habits to hen harrier.

RED KITE
Milvus milvus
63 cm. Like buzzard, but reddish colour and deeply forked tail. Usually found in woods, but also among scattered trees. Nests in trees.

BLACK KITE
Milvus migrans
53 cm. As red kite, but dark plumage and shallow forked tail. Usually seen near lakes and rivers surrounded by trees. In southern Europe, also found in more open country and searching for refuse in towns and villages. Nests in trees.

WHITE-TAILED EAGLE or SEA EAGLE
Haliaeetus albicilla
81 cm. White tail with brown body. Found at coasts and remote lakes. Takes fish from surface of water or plunges; also hunts mammals and birds. Nests in trees and on rock ledges.

MARSH HARRIER
Circus aeruginosus
51 cm. Male: grey wing patch and tail. Female: pale crown and throat. Usually seen flying low over swamps and marshes and nearby fields. Nests in reed-beds.

HEN HARRIER
Circus cyaneus
46 cm. Male: grey with white rump and underside. Female: streaky brown with white rump (very like Montagu's harrier). Hunts while flying low over moors, heaths, fields, marshes and swamps. Makes its nest on the ground.

OSPREY
Family Pandionidae

The osprey is placed in a family by itself because it differs in several ways from the other birds of prey. In particular, the osprey has a reversible outer toe, which is used in catching and holding slippery fishes, and it can also close its nostrils – a useful feature for a bird which plunges into the water.

OSPREY
Pandion haliaetus
56 cm. Dark above and white below, with white head crossed by dark line. Found on lakes and rivers and at coast, where it hunts fish by soaring or hovering high over the water and then plunging in feet-first. Carries fish back to perch near water.

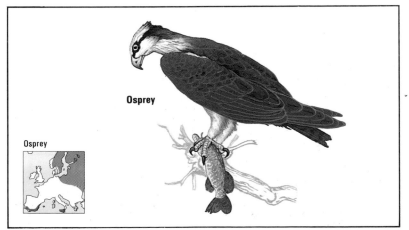

FALCONS
Family Falconidae

Falcons are generally smaller than other birds of prey, and have long, pointed wings and long tails. They are ferocious hunters, diving on or chasing their prey at great speed. Falconers train falcons to hunt and bring their prey back to them.

HOBBY
Falco subbuteo
33 cm. Streaky underside and chestnut 'trousers'. Lives in light woodland and among scattered trees, streaking through the air in pursuit of small birds such as larks, swallows and swifts, as well as flying insects. Nests in trees.

PEREGRINE FALCON
Falco peregrinus
43 cm. Light underside with bars and dark grey back; black moustache marking. Found among cliffs and crags, on which it nests, and also on flat coasts and marshes in winter; sometimes seen in forests and towns. Hunts by diving steeply at great speed, wings drawn back, mainly after birds, especially pigeons. Has become rare, suffering badly from effects of pesticides and raids by egg collectors.

GYRFALCON
Falco rusticolus
53 cm. Like large peregrine falcon, but grey (or rarely white) above and below; no moustache marking. Found in mountains and at coasts and forest edges. Nests on cliff ledges. Hunts like peregrine falcon but is not so fast in flight.

MERLIN
Falco columbarius
30 cm. Male: blue-grey back with red-brown streaky underside. Female: as male but brown back. Found in open country, on hills and moors in summer and also at coast in winter. Nests on ground or in trees. Darts through the air close to the ground, chasing small birds. May be seen hovering and perching.

KESTREL
Falco tinnunculus
33 cm. Male: grey-blue head and nape, reddish back and wings with dark spots, grey-blue tail with black band. Female: as male but brown head and nape, bars on back and wings, and brown tail with black bands. Very common bird of prey. Found in all kinds of places, including cities and towns; often spotted alongside motorways. Usually seen hovering 5-15 metres above the ground, flapping wings quickly, and then diving down in pursuit of rodents and insects.

LESSER KESTREL
Falco naumanni
30 cm. Male: like male kestrel, but unspotted back and wings. Female: very like female kestrel but seldom hovers. Found in open and rocky country and marshes, and often in fields around towns and villages. Nests on cliffs and buildings.

Right: The hobby is not much of a builder. It usually takes over the nest of another bird, or even a squirrel's drey, in which to lay its two or three eggs.

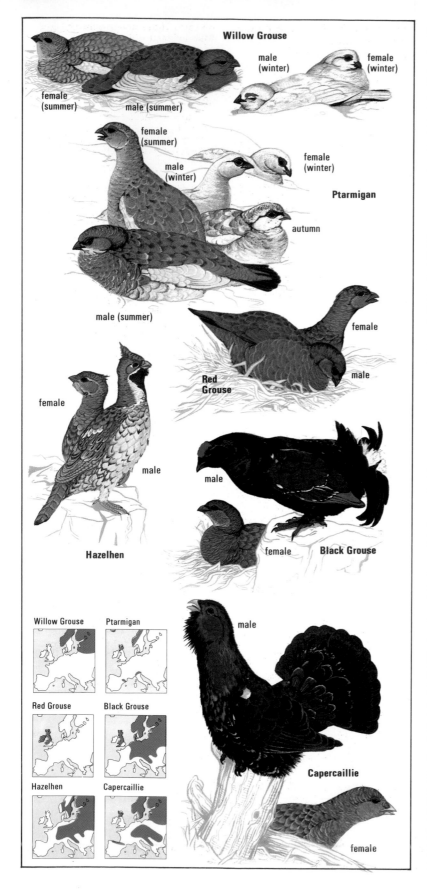

Willow Grouse

female (summer)

male (summer)

male (winter)

female (winter)

female (summer)

male (winter)

female (winter)

Ptarmigan

autumn

male (summer)

Red Grouse

female

male

female

male

Hazelhen

male

male

female

Black Grouse

Willow Grouse

Ptarmigan

Red Grouse

Black Grouse

Hazelhen

Capercaillie

male

Capercaillie

female

Game Birds

These birds are plump in shape, rather like chickens. They rarely fly very far or high and prefer to run or hide from danger, only taking to the air at the last moment. They spend most of their time on the ground rooting for seeds and insects, and they also nest on the ground.

The game birds all belong to the order Galliformes, of which two families occur in the wild in Europe.

GROUSE
Family Tetraonidae

These birds live in cold places, and their legs and sometimes their feet are covered with feathers for warmth.

WILLOW GROUSE
Lagopus lagopus
38 cm. Male: in summer, red-brown body with white wings and belly; in winter, pure white with black tail (but exactly like female ptarmigan). Female: in summer, as male, but body less red and more barred; in winter, as male. Found on moors, often living among heather and scattered bushes. Plumage changes from white in winter to brown and white in summer, helping to hide the bird among both winter snow and summer vegetation.

RED GROUSE
Lagopus lagopus scoticus
38 cm. Male: red-brown body with dark wings and tail edges. Female: as male, but body less red and more barred. A variety of willow grouse found only in the British Isles. No colour change takes place because snow does not always fall in winter. Lives among heather on moors, but also found in fields in winter.

PTARMIGAN
Lagopus mutus
36 cm. Male: as willow grouse, but greyer body in summer and autumn, and black face patch in winter. Female: very like female willow grouse. Found on high mountain slopes, usually above tree level. Plumage changes from brown and white in summer to grey and white in autumn and pure white in winter.

BLACK GROUSE
Lyrurus tetrix
53 cm. Male: glossy black with lyre-shaped tail. Female: grey-brown with slightly forked tail, 41 cm. Found on moors, in woods, among scattered trees and in fields. In spring, groups gather at courting grounds and the males display themselves before the females, spreading their wings and raising their tail feathers in a fan.

CAPERCAILLIE
Tetrao urogallus
Male: 86 cm. Dark grey with broad fan-shaped tail; brownish wings. Female: 61 cm. As female black grouse, but with fan-shaped tail and reddish breast patch. Lives among fir trees on hills and mountains. Male raises tail in a fan when courting female.

HAZELHEN or HAZEL GROUSE
Tetrastes bonasia
36 cm. Male: black throat and grey tail with black band. Female: as male but whitish throat. Lives in woods, usually hiding among bushes and thickets.

PARTRIDGES AND PHEASANTS
Family Phasianidae

Unlike grouse, these birds have bare legs and feet and are not found in cold places. Brightly coloured pheasants from other parts of the world are seen in parks. Some now live in the wild.

Pheasants make their nests on the ground and produce large numbers of young birds. Partridges too nest on the ground and are difficult to see. Quail are small shy birds prized as a delicacy.

PHEASANT
Phasianus colchicus
Male: 84 cm. Very long tail with green head and red eye patch. Female: 58 cm. Mottled brown body with long pointed tail. Often seen in fields, especially in winter, also in woods and marshes. Pattern of male varies; for example some have white neck-ring while others do not. Introduced from Asia, probably in ancient times. Most pheasants are semi-domesticated, being protected during the breeding season by gamekeepers to raise numbers for hunting later. Some are truly wild.

QUAIL
Coturnix coturnix
18 cm. Striped head; dark throat patch (male only). The smallest European game bird, and the only one that migrates. Hides among grass and crops. May be seen in bevies (small flocks) during migration, but is usually a solitary bird.

ROCK PARTRIDGE
Alectoris graeca
33 cm. Red legs; white throat patch surrounded by solid black band. Found on rocky ground and among trees, usually in hills. Looks very like red-legged partridge, but lives in different countries.

RED-LEGGED PARTRIDGE
Alectoris rufa
34 cm. Like rock partridge, but with black streaks below breast band. Found on moors and in fields and low treeless hills, often in dry and stony places.

PARTRIDGE
Perdix perdix
30 cm. Grey legs; orange-brown face and throat; dark belly patch (male only). Seen mainly in fields, but also on moors and heaths and in marshes, sand dunes and low treeless hills.

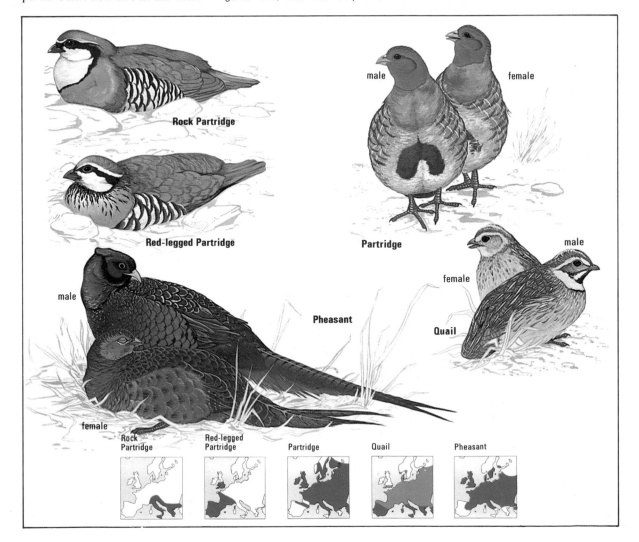

Rock Partridge

male

female

Red-legged Partridge

Partridge

male

female

Quail

male

Pheasant

female

| Rock Partridge | Red-legged Partridge | Partridge | Quail | Pheasant |

59

Crane Water Rail Spotted Crake

Baillon's Crake Little Crake Corncrake

Crane

Corncrake

Water Rail

Spotted Crake

Baillon's Crake

female

male

Little Crake

Cranes, Rails and Bustards

All these birds have long legs and many of them wade in shallow water. Cranes (family Gruidae) are tall, elegant birds living on dry land and in marshes, whereas rails, crakes, gallinules, moorhens and coots (family Rallidae) are mainly water birds, small to medium in size and chunky in shape. Bustards (family Otididae) are land birds, medium to large in size with long thick necks.
These birds all belong to the order Gruiformes.

CRANE
Grus grus
114 cm. Red crown and white cheek stripe; bushy drooping tail. Nests on the ground in swamps and among reeds; in winter moves to rivers, fields and plains. Told from storks and herons by bushy tail. Flies with neck out-stretched, migrating in long lines or V-formations. In spring, cranes perform crazy leaping dances before nesting.

CORNCRAKE or LAND RAIL
Crex crex
25 cm. Buff plumage with reddish wing patches. Hides away and nests among long grass and crops in mead-ows and fields. Mowing machines and other changes in agriculture have caused a drop in numbers.

WATER RAIL
Rallus aquaticus
28 cm. Long red beak. Usually hides among reeds in marshes and ponds, and nests on concealed platform of reeds built above water. Likely to come into the open during cold weather.

SPOTTED CRAKE
Porzana porzana
23 cm. Dark brown spotted and streaky plumage. Location and behaviour simi-lar to water rail, but even more shy.

BAILLON'S CRAKE
Porzana pusilla
18 cm. Grey underside with bars on flanks; flesh-coloured legs. Same loca-tion and behaviour as water rail, and similar appearance but much smaller. Very shy.

LITTLE CRAKE
Porzana parva
19 cm. Male: as Baillon's crake, but no bars on flanks and green legs. Female: as male, but buff underside. Same location and behaviour as water rail but much smaller. Very shy.

A moorhen on its nest in the reeds. The nest is a bulky platform of dead plant material, usually built close to the water's edge.

Moorhen

Coot

Little Bustard

Moorhen

Coot

Little Bustard

female   male

MOORHEN
Gallinula chloropus
33 cm. Black body with red bill and shield above bill and white feathers under the tail. Lives on ponds, lakes and streams, bobbing its head up and down and flicking its tail as it swims to and fro. Sometimes dives for food. Often seen in parks. Nests in reeds, bushes and trees, usually near the water. Often feeds on grassy banks and in nearby fields.

COOT
Fulica atra
38 cm. Black body with white bill and shield. Found on lakes, reservoirs and rivers, and in parks. Also on coasts and estuaries winter. Prefers larger stretches of water than moorhen, and dives more often. Usually seen in groups, with the birds always quarrelling.

LITTLE BUSTARD
Otis tetrax
43 cm. Male: black and white pattern on neck (summer only). Female and male in winter: streaky brown head and neck. Hides by crouching flat when danger approaches. Grassland.

Oystercatcher

Oystercatcher

Lapwing

Ringed
Plover

Little
Ringed
Plover

Kentish
Plover

Grey
Plover

winter   summer

Lapwing   Ringed Plover   Little Ringed
Plover   Kentish
Plover   Grey Plover

Waders, Gulls and Auks

This is a huge group of birds with widely differing appearances, although they all belong to the order Charadriiformes. There are many families. The birds are all closely associated with water for at least a part of their lives. Many live by the sea. The waders, which include the plovers and sandpipers and several other groups, are long-legged birds and, as the name suggests, they spend much of their time wading in shallow water where they find their food.

OYSTERCATCHERS
Family Haematopodidae

OYSTERCATCHER
Haematopus ostralegus
43 cm. Black and white plumage with long orange beak. The only European member of its family. Seen at seashore, prizing shellfish open with its chisel-like beak. Also probes for food in mud. May also be found inland on moors and by lakes and rivers.

PLOVERS
Family Charadriidae

Plovers can be told from almost all other waders by their short beaks. They probe for worms, grubs and shellfish.

LAPWING, PEEWIT or GREEN PLOVER
Vanellus vanellus
30 cm. Black and white plumage with crest; glossy dark-green back. Very common plover. Found in fields and marshes and on moors; also at coast in winter. Usually in large flocks.

RINGED PLOVER
Charadrius hiaticula
19 cm. Black breast band and orange-yellow legs; white wingbar in flight. Usually found on sandy and stony beaches, sometimes inland.

LITTLE RINGED PLOVER
Charadrius dubius
15 cm. As ringed plover but no wing-bar and legs often pink. Lives on sandy or stony shores of lakes and rivers, and in old gravel pits.

KENTISH PLOVER
Charadrius alexandrinus
15 cm. As ringed plover, but breast band incomplete and legs black. Found at seashore, on sandy or stony beaches.

GREY PLOVER
Pluvialis squatarola
28 cm. Summer: black below and silver-grey above. Winter: white below and grey above. Found on mudflats and sandy beaches.

GOLDEN PLOVER
Pluvialis apricaria
28 cm. Summer: black below and golden-brown above. Winter: white below and golden-brown above. Nests on moors in summer. In winter, also found in fields and at seashore, usually with lapwings.

DOTTEREL
Eudromias morinellus
23 cm. White eye-stripe and breast band; chestnut belly and dark underparts. Paler in winter. Nests on barren high ground. Found in fields and on the seashore in winter.

TURNSTONE
Arenaria interpres
23 cm. Summer: brown and black patterned wings. Winter: generally paler, but with dark breast band and orange legs. Found at coast, usually on rocky and stony shores. Gets its name from its habit of turning over stones, shells and seaweed when looking for food.

SANDPIPERS
Family Scolopacidae

These are wading birds with long bills. Most also have long legs. They may be found inland at damp places as well as at the seashore, and they usually nest on the ground. Flocks of several different kinds of sandpipers can often be seen feeding together at the shore, poking their bills into the water, mud or sand to find shellfish and worms. The different kinds of birds have bills of various lengths, so that they probe at different depths and live on different kinds of food.

SNIPE
Gallinago gallinago
27 cm. Long straight beak with dark stripes along head. Hides away in marshes, bogs and damp meadows. Flies away with zigzag flight when disturbed. Often dives from sky, making a drumming noise with its tail.

JACK SNIPE
Lymnocryptes minimus
19 cm. As snipe but shorter bill and pointed tail. Found in same places as snipe and behaves in same way, except that when disturbed it flies off with a more direct flight. Its call sounds rather like a distant galloping horse.

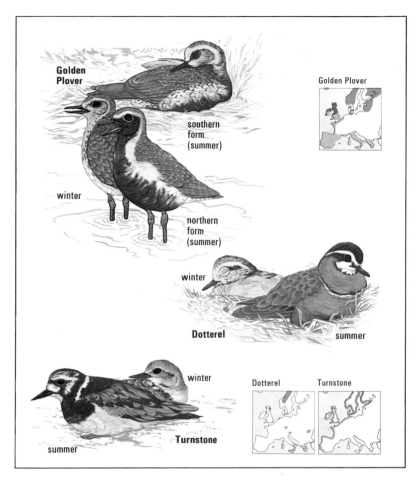

Woodcock

Curlew

Whimbrel

Black-tailed Godwit

Bar-tailed Godwit

Green Sandpiper

Woodcock

Curlew

Whimbrel

Green Sandpiper

summer · Bar-tailed Godwit

winter · winter

summer

Black-tailed Godwit

WOODCOCK
Scolopax rusticola
36 cm. Long beak with dark stripes across head. Stout shape. Hides away among damp woodland. Most likely to be seen at dawn or dusk flying through the trees or in circles above the trees.

CURLEW
Numenius arquata
56 cm. Very long down-curving bill and plain head. Nests on moors and in marshes, damp meadows and sand dunes. In winter, also seen on mudflats at seashore.

WHIMBREL
Numenius phaeopus
41 cm. As curlew, but shorter bill and striped head. Found in same places as curlew, and looks like a small curlew, but told apart by its head pattern.

BLACK-TAILED GODWIT
Limosa limosa
41 cm. Summer: long bill (very slightly upturned) with chestnut breast and white tail with black band at end. Winter: as summer but grey breast. Broad white wing bar clearly seen in flight. Nests in damp meadows and on boggy land. In winter, also seen on mudflats and in marshes.

BAR-TAILED GODWIT
Limosa lapponica
38 cm. As black-tailed godwit, but upturned bill and barred tail and no wing bar. Nests in marshes in Arctic, and migrates to spend winter at seashore.

GREEN SANDPIPER
Tringa ochropus
23 cm. White rump with dark legs, no wingbar. Not green. Nests in swamps in woodland. Winters in marshes and on lakes and rivers, seldom at coast.

WOOD SANDPIPER
Tringa glareola
20 cm. White rump with pale legs; no wingbar. Found in northern forests and in Arctic, where it nests on ground near water and in old nests in trees.

COMMON SANDPIPER
Tringa hypoleucos
20 cm. Dark rump, white wingbar seen in flight; bobs its tail and nods its head as it wades. Nests beside streams, rivers and lakes, usually in hills. In winter, also seen at seashore.

REDSHANK
Tringa totanus
28 cm. White rump with long red legs; white band at back of wing in flight. Nests among grass in meadows and inland and coastal marshes and on moors and heaths. In winter, usually found at seashore.

SPOTTED REDSHANK
Tringa erythropus
30 cm. Summer: black with red legs, no wingband. Winter: pale grey with red legs, no wingband. Nests in far north and migrates to spend winter at seashore and in marshes.

GREENSHANK
Tringa nebularia
30 cm. White rump with greenish legs; no wingband. Nests on ground on moors or in forests, usually near water.

KNOT
Calidris canuta
25 cm. Summer: reddish underparts. Winter: stout body, short neck, pale tail. A winter visitor from the Arctic. Seen at mudflats along seashores, often in flocks. Birds in summer plumage may be seen in spring and autumn.

DUNLIN
Calidris alpina
18 cm. Summer: black patch on underside. Winter: dark above and pale below with down-curving beak. Nests on moors and in marshes, spends winter in flocks on mudflats at or near coast and also inland. Flies in tight groups known as 'wader smoke' from the way the birds twist and turn through the air.

Sanderling

winter

summer

Male displaying
in summer

Ruff

male (winter)

female

Sanderling

Ruff

SANDERLING
Calidris alba
20 cm. Summer: reddish plumage with white belly. Winter: almost white with black spot at front of wing. Seen in winter at sandy beaches, racing about as if chasing the waves. Migrates to Arctic to breed.

RUFF
Philomachus pugnax
Male: 30 cm; easily identified by the ruff, or collar, in spring and summer; autumn plumage is brown, heavily mottled with black. Female: as autumn male, but smaller (23 cm). Nests on moors and in marshes and meadows; also found beside rivers and lakes in winter. In late spring and early summer, the males attract the females by raising a beautiful ruff of feathers around the neck. The colour of the ruff varies greatly. The female is also known as a reeve. Has recently recolonized Britain after earlier extinction as a breeding species.

AVOCETS AND STILTS
Family Recurvirostridae

These birds are the most elegant wading birds. They pick their way through the shallow water on stilt-like legs, snapping up insects from the air or lowering their long thin beaks into the water.

AVOCET
Recurvirostra avosetta
43 cm. Long up-turned bill; black and white back. Nests in marshes at or near coast; spends winter at estuaries. Best seen at bird reserves. Beak curves upwards so that the end skims surface of water when feeding.

BLACK-WINGED STILT
Himantopus himantopus
38 cm. Long straight bill; black back and white underside; long pink legs. Found in marshes and lagoons, often wading deeply in large stretches of water.

PHALAROPES
Family Phalaropodidae

RED-NECKED PHALAROPE
Phalaropus lobatus
18 cm. Female: orange-red neck and white throat in summer. Male: as female but less bright. Both sexes are grey and white in winter, when they can be recognized by the rather slender bill and the large dark eye-patch. Nests in marshes and beside lakes; spends winter out to sea. Often swims, unlike other waders, floating high in

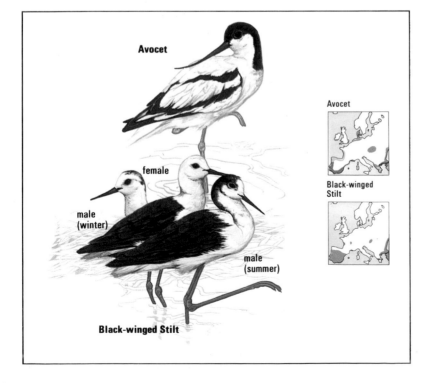

Avocet

female

male
(winter)

male
(summer)

Black-winged Stilt

Avocet

Black-winged
Stilt

the water and sometimes spinning in circles to stir up small animals from the bottom. Phalaropes are unusual birds. The females court the males, and the males build the nests, sit on the eggs and raise the young.

THICK-KNEES
Family Burhinidae

STONE CURLEW
Burhinus oedicnemus
41 cm. Large yellow eyes and white wingbar on ground; double white wingbar in flight. Gets its name because it is often found in stony and rocky places, and because its call (usually heard after dark) is like that of a curlew. It likes open treeless country. Runs with its head down when disturbed. Thick-knees got their strange name because their 'knees' (which in fact are their heels) appear to be swollen.

PRATINCOLES
Family Glareolidae

PRATINCOLE
Glareola pratincola
25 cm. Light throat patch; reddish-brown under wings. Found on dried mudflats and grassy plains, and at open spaces in marshes. Pratincoles fly and look like large swallows, but also run about on the ground. They often stand on tiptoe and stretch their necks, as if trying to see something.

SKUAS
Family Stercorariidae

Skuas are fast-flying sea birds with hooked beaks. They are sometimes called the pirates of the skies, for they often chase other sea birds and make them drop a fish they have just captured or even half eaten! The skua then swoops down to catch its stolen meal before it hits the water below.

GREAT SKUA
Stercorarius skua
58 cm. Fan-shaped tail without long protruding feathers. Nests among grass or heather on moors and spends winter out to sea. May be seen at coast on migration in spring and autumn.

ARCTIC SKUA
Stercorarius parasiticus
46 cm. Fan-shaped tail with long protruding central feathers. Lives in similar places to great skua. The neck, breast and underparts may be light, dark or any shade between.

male (summer)

Red-necked Phalarope

winter

female (summer)

Red-necked Phalarope

Stone Curlew

Pratincole

Stone Curlew

Pratincole

Great Skua diving

Great Skua

Great Skua

dark form

Arctic Skua

light form

Arctic Skua

A flock of gulls. These birds often follow ploughs to pick up worms and grubs as the soil is turned over. The gulls are helpful to farmers because they devour pests in this way.

Little Gull in winter

Little Gull summer

Glaucous Gull

Herring Gull

Common Gull

Herring Gull   Common Gull   Glaucous Gull   Little Gull

GULLS AND TERNS
Family Laridae

These two kinds of sea birds are easy to tell apart. Gulls have broad wings and fan-shaped tails, and their beaks are usually heavy with a hooked tip. They can be seen in flocks at the seashore and at harbours, constantly making mewing cries as they wheel to and fro in the air. To feed, they settle on the water and seize some floating waste or dip their heads under the water to catch a fish. They also follow ships, but not out of sight of land. Gulls also fly inland, especially in winter. They nest in colonies on the ground and on cliffs. Young gulls look brown and white until they are as much as four years old. Terns have slender wings and forked tails, and sharp beaks that often point downwards during flight.

HERRING GULL
Larus argentatus
56 cm. Pale grey back and wings, with black and white wingtips and red spot on yellow bill; legs usually pink. A very common gull, seen both at the coast and inland.

COMMON GULL
Larus canus
41 cm. As herring gull, but yellow-green legs and greenish bill without red spot. Found at coast and inland. In spite of its name, it is not the most numerous gull.

GLAUCOUS GULL
Larus hyperboreus
71 cm. Silver-grey back and wings; no dark patches at wingtips. Nests in Iceland and in Arctic; seen at coasts and harbours in winter, rarely inland. Preys on eggs and small birds.

LITTLE GULL
Larus minutus
28 cm. Like small black-headed gull but black head (not dark brown) in summer, no black on wingtips and dark beneath wings. Gets its name because it is noticeably smaller than other gulls. Nests in marshes and swamps, but seen at coast and inland at other times. Catches insects in flight.

BLACK-HEADED GULL
Larus ridibundus
38 cm. Dark-brown head in summer, becoming white with a dark spot behind the eye in winter; white patch on front of wings and black edge on back of wings; red legs. A very common gull, often seen inland. Nests in marshes, on moors, and by lakes and rivers. At other times found at coasts and harbours, and in fields and towns. Eats anything, including fish, worms, flying insects and even garbage.

KITTIWAKE
Rissa tridactyla
41 cm. Solid black wingtips and black legs. Nests in colonies on cliff ledges and also on buildings in coastal towns. Usually spends winter far out to sea.

GREAT BLACK-BACKED GULL
Larus marinus
68 cm. Black back and wings, pink legs. Usually seen at rocky coasts and offshore islands; may be seen inland, especially in winter. Often feeds on eggs and young of other sea birds.

LESSER BLACK-BACKED GULL
Larus fuscus
53 cm. Grey to dark grey back and wings (British form) or black back and wings (Scandinavian form); legs usually yellow or orange. The British form (*Larus fuscus graellsii*) has a lighter back than the Scandinavian form (*Larus fuscus fuscus*), which looks like a small great black-backed gull. Often seen at seashore and harbours and also inland.

Black-headed
Gull in winter

Great
Black-backed
Gull

Black-headed
Gull

summer

Kittiwake

Scandinavian
form

British
form

Lesser Black-backed Gull

*Kittiwakes nesting on
narrow cliff ledges in
the Farne Islands. The
nests are made of
grass and seaweed,
firmly cemented
together and fixed to
the rocks with mud.*

Black-headed
Gull

Kittiwake

Great Black-
backed Gull

Lesser Black-
backed Gull

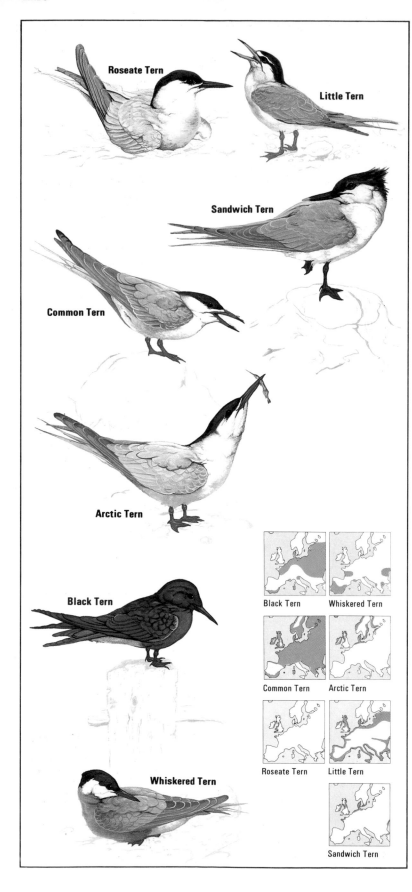

ROSEATE TERN
Sterna dougallii
38 cm. All-black bill, sometimes with red base; very long tail. Distinctive barking call note. Pink flush to breast in spring. Nests on rocky islands and beaches, sometimes with common terns and Arctic terns; seldom found inland.

LITTLE TERN
Sterna albifrons
24 cm. Yellow bill with black tip; white forehead. The smallest European tern. Nests mainly on sandy and stony beaches, but sometimes inland.

SANDWICH TERN
Sterna sandvicensis
41 cm. Black bill with yellow tip; slight crest. Nests in colonies on sandy and stony beaches and also on offshore islands. Rarely found inland. Named after Sandwich in Kent, where a famous colony once existed.

COMMON TERN
Sterna hirundo
36 cm. Orange bill, black tip. Nests on beaches, among sand dunes, in coastal swamps, on offshore islands and by lakes. Often seen flying along seashore and diving for fish.

ARCTIC TERN
Sterna paradisaea
36 cm. All-red bill, short legs; greyer breast than common tern. Found in same kinds of places as common tern, but less likely inland. May migrate as far south as the Antarctic to spend the winter.

BLACK TERN
Chlidonias niger
24 cm. Black head and body, grey wings and tail. Builds floating nest on lakes and marsh pools; may be seen at coast during migration in spring and autumn. Chases insects in air; rarely dives into water.

WHISKERED TERN
Chlidonias hybridus
24 cm. Grey belly, white cheeks. Found in same places as black tern, but often dives for food.

Black Tern   Whiskered Tern

Common Tern   Arctic Tern

Roseate Tern   Little Tern

Sandwich Tern

NOTE: the descriptions and illustrations on these pages are of birds in summer plumage. Terns may also be seen in winter plumage, when they all have white foreheads and dark bills, and are very difficult to tell apart. In addition, the black tern and whiskered tern become white beneath.

The beak of the puffin has saw-tooth edges so that it can hold several fish in its beak at once.

summer

winter

Puffin

Guillemot

summer

winter

Razorbill

summer

winter

summer

Black Guillemot

winter

winter

Little Auk

Black Guillemot

Razorbill   Little Auk   Puffin   Guillemot

AUKS
Family Alcidae

Auks look and behave very much like penguins. They dive for fish and chase them underwater, using their wings like oars and their feet like a rudder. On land, they sit up and waddle about. Also like penguins, they spend most of the year at sea and only come ashore to breed. However, unlike penguins, they can fly well – although the great auk, which is now extinct, could not. It was a very easy target for hunters, and the last pair of birds was killed in 1844. The great auk was a large bird as big as a goose.

RAZORBILL
Alca torda
41 cm. Broad dark bill with white marks. Breeds in colonies on cliff ledges at coast, often with guillemots. Spends winter out at sea, although storms may force it back to shore.

LITTLE AUK
Alle alle
20 cm. Small size and short bill distinguish this species. Nests in Arctic and spends winter in northern seas, but may be driven ashore by storms.

PUFFIN
Fratercula arctica
30 cm. Triangular beak (bright red and yellow in summer). Nests in colonies in burrows in steep slopes by sea. May run down slope to get into the air. Can hold several fish at once in its parrot-like beak. Spends winter far out to sea and is seldom blown ashore.

BLACK GUILLEMOT
Cepphus grylle
33 cm. Summer: black body with white wing patch. Winter: mottled grey back with white wing patch. Nests in holes and crevices on rocky shores and sea cliffs, but not in large colonies. Stays near shore in winter.

GUILLEMOT
Uria aalge
41 cm. Slender pointed bill. Breeds in large colonies on coastal cliffs and on offshore islands. The guillemot's egg is laid on bare rock and is pear-shaped, so that it rolls in a circle and not over the edge, if knocked. Spends winter out at sea, but may be driven ashore by gales.

71

Woodpigeon

The town pigeon, descended from the wild rock dove, grows fat on food dropped or purposely provided by people.

Collared Dove

Stock Dove

Rock Dove

Woodpigeon   Turtle Dove   Collared Dove

Stock Dove   Rock Dove

Turtle Dove

Pigeons and Doves

These birds have plump bodies, small heads and short legs. They can all fly very fast, and people raise pigeons for racing.
They belong to the family Columbidae in the order Columbiformes.

STOCK DOVE
Columba oenas
33 cm. Grey rump, no obvious neck mark or wing marks. Found in woods and on farmland; may also be seen in parks and on cliffs and sand dunes along coast. Often found in the company of woodpigeons.

ROCK DOVE
Columba livia
33 cm. White rump, no neck mark, two black wing stripes. Lives on rocky coasts and on mountains, and nests in caves and on cliff ledges. The pigeons that can be seen in city squares and parks, as well as the pigeons that people raise for racing, are all descended from the wild rock dove. Some of these pigeons still look like their wild ancestor, but many now have different plumage. The pigeons are interbreeding with rock doves, and the truly wild species is slowly disappearing. Because the wild birds are naturally at home on cliffs, pigeons can live and nest on the ledges of buildings. They have long been a companion of man, carrying messages for him as well as providing him with a source of food.

WOODPIGEON
Columba palumbus
41 cm. Grey rump, white neck mark, white wingbar. Found in woods and on farmland, and also in parks and gardens. Often seen in flocks containing stock doves and domestic pigeons.

TURTLE DOVE
Streptopelia turtur
28 cm. Black tail with white edges; white neck patch with black stripes. Found in spring and summer in light woods and among scattered trees and bushes; also on farmland and in parks and gardens.

COLLARED DOVE
Streptopelia decaocto
30 cm. Black stripe edged with white at back of neck. Usually found in towns or close to houses and farms. Nests on buildings or in trees nearby. It has spread rapidly through Europe from the Balkans during the last few decades. It first nested in Britain in 1955 and is now found throughout the British Isles.

Cuckoos

Cuckoos are famous for laying their eggs in the nests of other birds and leaving the other birds to bring up the young cuckoos. Both of the cuckoos found in Europe breed in this way. They belong to the family Cuculidae in the order Cuculiformes.

CUCKOO
Cuculus canorus
33 cm. Grey head and breast with bars on white underside; but female sometimes red-brown with bars all over body. Found in woodland, open ground with scattered trees and bushes, and on moors. Only the male makes 'cuckoo' call; female has babbling call. The female cuckoo lays several eggs, one each in the nests of other birds. Small birds are chosen, such as meadow pipits and robins, but each female cuckoo always uses nests of the same species. When it hatches, the young cuckoo pushes out any other eggs and nestlings, but its adopted parents continue to feed it, driven by instinct.

GREAT SPOTTED CUCKOO
Clamator glandarius
41 cm. White spots on wings, grey crest, long white-edged tail. Found in woods and among scattered trees. Does not call 'cuckoo'. Usually lays its eggs in the nests of crows, particularly magpies.

Owls

The owls are mainly nocturnal hunters, feeding mostly on small rodents. Some also eat other birds and insects. They are not closely related to the diurnal birds of prey (pages 52–57) and they are placed in the order Strigiformes. They have powerful talons and a large, hooked beak, although the beak is partly buried in the feathers and does not look very large. The eyes look forward and are extremely efficient. The ears are also very sensitive, allowing the owls to hear their prey on the ground. Feathery edges to the wings allow the owls to fly silently. The barn owl belongs to the family Tytonidae, while all the other owls belong to the Strigidae.

Cuckoo
red form (young)
grey form (adult)
Great Spotted Cuckoo
Cuckoo
Great Spotted Cuckoo

dark-breasted form
light-breasted form
Barn Owl
Scops Owl
Barn Owl
Scops Owl

Pygmy Owl

brown form

Tawny Owl

grey form

Short-eared Owl

Little Owl

Snowy Owl

Snowy Owl

Little Owl

Short-eared Owl

Pygmy Owl

Eagle Owl

Tawny Owl

Long-eared Owl

Long-eared Owl

Eagle Owl

BARN OWL
Tyto alba
36 cm. Heart-shaped face; brown back with white or buff unstreaked breast (may look all white at dusk). Found on farmland and in marshes but also occupies unused buildings, such as barns and church towers, and ruins. Most likely to be seen at dusk. Two forms occur, a white-breasted form (*Tyto alba alba*) in south and west Europe, and a buff-breasted form (*Tyto alba guttata*) in north and east Europe.

SCOPS OWL
Otus scops
19 cm. Small, with short ear tufts. Found among trees, often near buildings, as well as in ruins. Rarely seen in daytime. Like many other owls, has ear tufts that are not ears but merely tufts of head feathers.

PYGMY OWL
Glaucidium passerinum
18 cm. Very small, with round head, no ear tufts; flicks tail up and down when sitting on perch. Usually seen in fir forests. Active day and night, chasing small birds through air. Smallest European owl.

LITTLE OWL
Athene noctua
23 cm. Small, with flattened head, no ear tufts. Found among scattered trees in fields and on open ground, often near buildings. May be seen in daytime bobbing its head as it perches on a post or branch.

TAWNY OWL
Strix aluco
38 cm. Streaky plumage with black eyes; stocky shape and no ear tufts. A very common owl. Lives in woods and also in parks and gardens. Usually hunts by night, but may be seen sleeping in tree during daytime, when it is sometimes bothered by small birds. Colour varies from brown to grey.

EAGLE OWL
Bubo bubo
68 cm. Huge, with long ear tufts. Largest European owl. Lives in forests, among mountain crags and gorges, and on dry plains. Active at dawn and dusk, when it hunts animals as large as hares. Rare.

SNOWY OWL
Nyctea scandiaca
61 cm. White plumage, large yellow eyes. Lives and nests in Arctic, Norway and Iceland, and sometimes in the Shetland Isles. Many move further south for the winter. May then be seen on moors, in marshes, and at lake shores and coast. Hunts by day, but white plumage may conceal it against snow.

LONG-EARED OWL
Asio otus
36 cm. Slender shape and long ear tufts. Sleeps in woods, especially in fir trees, by day and comes out to hunt,

often over open ground, at dusk. May be seen sleeping in groups in winter.

SHORT-EARED OWL
Asio flammeus
38 cm. Similar to tawny owl but yellow eyes and lighter plumage. Seen hunting over moors, marshes and open ground during daytime and at dusk. Ear tufts are very short, often invisible.

Nightjars

The nightjars (family Caprimulgidae) are nocturnal birds with long wings and tail and a very agile, silent flight. The bill is short, but opens very widely to scoop up insects in flight. The name is derived from the penetrating churring song which can be heard at dusk. Two species breed in Europe. The birds belong to the order Caprimulgiformes.

NIGHTJAR
Caprimulgus europaeus
28 cm. Plumage pattern looks like dead leaves from above; fine bars below. Lives in woods, among bracken in clearings and on hillsides, on moors and sand dunes. Unless disturbed, it is very difficult to spot. Sleeps during the day and hunts for insects at night. Lays eggs on the ground.

Swifts

Swifts are masters of the air and are usually seen in flocks, wheeling high in the sky at great speed. They may spend weeks in the air without coming down, as they catch flying insects for food and can sleep in flight. Swifts have weak feet and if they land on the ground, they cannot walk and find it hard to get back into the air. Instead, they usually cling to vertical surfaces and simply fall off them to become airborne. The small feet are responsible for the family name of Apodidae, which actually means 'footless'. The birds belong to the order Apodiformes, which also includes the hummingbirds.

SWIFT
Apus apus
16 cm. Dark body; shallow forked tail. Nests in holes in trees, crevices in cliffs, and under the eaves of buildings. Often to be seen at dusk, dashing around rooftops in noisy flocks. May

Nightjar

male

female

Nightjar

A nightjar nesting.

Swift

Alpine Swift

Alpine Swift

Swift

Bee-eater

Roller

Kingfisher

crest up

Hoopoe

crest down

Bee-eater

Roller

Kingfisher

Hoopoe

be seen with swallows, but can easily be recognized by dark underparts and shallow forked tail.

ALPINE SWIFT
Apus melba
20 cm. White belly and throat with dark breast band; very long wings. Found in mountains, at cliffs and around buildings. Nests in crevices. Has very long wings, unlike similar sand martin.

Kingfishers and Related Birds

Any birds in this mixed group are worth a special effort to see, for they are the most colourful and spectacular birds to be seen in Europe. None is like any other and they all belong to different families. The kingfisher belongs to the family Alcedinidae, and the bee-eater to the family Meropidae. The roller is a member of the family Coraciidae, and the hoopoe of the family Upupidae. All belong to the order Coraciiformes.

KINGFISHER
Alcedo atthis
16 cm. Blue-green back and orange underparts. Seen by rivers and lakes, perching on a branch beside the water or darting down to plunge for a fish. May also be seen at coast in winter.

BEE-EATER
Merops apiaster
28 cm. Yellow throat and blue-green breast. Found in open country among scattered trees and bushes, often perching on bushes or telegraph wires. Nests in hole dug in bank of river or pit, or in burrow dug in the ground. Chases flying insects, especially bees and wasps.

ROLLER
Coracias garrulus
30 cm. Blue-green with chestnut back. Found in open country with scattered trees and in woods. Nests in hole in tree or bank. Often seen perching and then swooping down to catch insects and other small animals. Gets its name from the way it rolls over in flight to attract a mate during the spring courtship.

HOOPOE
Upupa epops
28 cm. Black-and-white striped wings; large black-tipped crest. Seen among scattered trees and in woods; sometimes in parks and gardens. Nests in hole in tree or wall. Often seen perching, usually with its crest down. Named after its call. Several recent nesting records from Britain (not mapped).

Woodpeckers

Woodpeckers are members of the family Picidae in the order Piciformes. They are often heard before being seen. Their sharp beaks make a loud rat-a-tat as they chisel into the bark of a tree in search of insects. They also dig out holes for nesting.

Woodpeckers grip the trunk or branch with sharp claws and thrust their tails stiffly against the bark to prop themselves up and give a powerful blow with the beak. In the spring, they make a drumming noise by clattering their beaks on a piece of wood; this is part of their courtship.

GREEN WOODPECKER
Picus viridis
30 cm. Greenish back and yellow rump; large red crown. Thick black (female) or red (male) moustache. Dull-green upperparts. Found in woods and forests, usually of broad-leaved trees, and in open country with scattered trees. Also seen on ground, feeding at anthills. Seldom drums.

GREY-HEADED WOODPECKER
Picus canus
25 cm. Grey head with thin moustache; only male has red forehead. Found in same places as green woodpecker. Often drums in spring, unlike green woodpecker.

THREE-TOED WOODPECKER
Picoides tridactylus
23 cm. White back, black cheeks and striped flanks. Yellow crown (male only). Lives in forests on mountains and in far north.

BLACK WOODPECKER
Dryocopus martius
46 cm. Black body, with red crown in male (slightly crested) and crimson patch on the back of the head in female. Lives in woods and forests, often in mountains. Largest European woodpecker.

Black Woodpecker

male

female

Grey-headed Woodpecker

male

female

Three-toed Woodpecker

female

male

foot

Green Woodpecker

male

female

Black Woodpecker

Grey headed Woodpecker

Three-toed Woodpecker

Green Woodpecker

female

male

Middle Spotted
Woodpecker

male

female

Great Spotted
Woodpecker

female

male

female

White-backed
Woodpecker

Lesser Spotted
Woodpecker

male

Wryneck

Lesser Spotted
Woodpecker

Middle Spotted
Woodpecker

White-backed
Woodpecker

Great Spotted
Woodpecker

Wryneck

LESSER SPOTTED WOODPECKER

Dendrocopos minor

15 cm. Black and white stripes on back with no red under tail. Crown red (male) or whitish (female). Lives in same places as middle spotted woodpecker, but may also be found in parks and orchards. Smallest European woodpecker.

WHITE-BACKED WOODPECKER

Dendrocopos leucotos

25 cm. As lesser spotted woodpecker, but larger and with white rump and red under tail. Found in woods and forests, though not often among fir trees.

MIDDLE SPOTTED WOODPECKER

Dendrocopos medius

20 cm. As great spotted woodpecker, but red crown in both sexes and less black on face. Lives in woods and forests, though seldom among fir trees. Usually stays high up in trees.

GREAT SPOTTED WOODPECKER

Dendrocopos major

23 cm. Large white wing patch and black crown (red in young); black stripe across neck; red patch at back of head (male only). Found in woods and forests of all kinds, and also in parks and gardens. Comes to bird tables,

being able to hang upside-down to feed as tits do. Also likes to wedge nuts into cracks in bark and hammer them open with bill. Known for its habit of drumming very rapidly on dead branches. The most common and widespread European woodpecker.

WRYNECK

Jynx torquilla

16 cm. Long banded tail; small beak. Lives in light woodland, and in open country with scattered trees, bushes and hedges, orchards, parks and gardens. Does not look like a woodpecker and does not chisel into bark. Often feeds on ground and nests in existing holes, including nest-boxes. Gets its name from the way it can turn its head round.

Perching Birds and Songbirds

These birds make up the biggest group of birds – the order Passeriformes, which contains more than half of all bird species. There are many families. They are found everywhere. None is very large, and most are fairly small. Their feet have three toes in front and a long one behind, which enables them to perch easily – although, of course, other birds can perch too. Many, but by no means all, can sing well and, in a few cases, the song must be heard to be sure of the bird's identity.

LARKS
Family Alaudidae

These birds are most often seen in the air, singing strongly. They make their nests on the ground where, being dull-coloured, they are difficult to spot. However, they may sometimes be seen running along the ground. Some larks look rather like buntings (page 104), but have thin beaks whereas buntings have stout beaks.

CRESTED LARK
Galerida cristata
16 cm. Large crest. In southern Spain, almost identical Thekla lark (*Galerida theklae*) may be seen. Found on stony and sandy ground and in fields; also seen on waste land in towns and villages and beside roads.

WOODLARK
Lullula arborea
15 cm. Black and white mark at front of wing; all-brown tail; slight crest. Found in fields and open country, often among scattered trees and bushes and at woodland edges. Often flies in circle while singing; also sings while perched.

SKYLARK
Alauda arvensis
18 cm. White edges to tail; slight crest. Found in all kinds of open country – moors, marshes, fields and sand dunes. Rises straight up into air and may hover while singing.

SHORE LARK
Eremophila alpestris
16 cm. Horns on head (male only); black and yellow face pattern. Nests on rocky ground in far north or high in mountains. Spends winter at beaches, and in marshes and fields along coast.

A skylark feeds its young at the nest. The youngsters gape as soon as they see the parent with food.

Woodlark

Crested Lark

Skylark

Shore Lark

Crested Lark   Woodlark   Skylark   Shore Lark

79

Sand Martin

Swallow

House Martin

Red-rumped
Swallow

Crag
Martin

Swallow

Red-rumped
Swallow

Crag Martin

House Martin

Sand Martin

SWALLOWS AND MARTINS
Family Hirundinidae

Swallows and martins fly very fast, often near the ground, twisting and turning in the air as they chase flying insects. Swifts (page 75) are similar, but have longer wings that they hold out stiffly as they fly. Unlike swifts, which cannot perch, flocks of swallows and martins often perch on telegraph wires, especially when they are about to migrate.

SAND MARTIN
Riparia riparia
13 cm. As crag martin but brown breast band. Lives in open country, especially near ponds, lakes and rivers. Nests in colonies in holes dug in banks of rivers, cuttings and pits, and also in cliffs.

HOUSE MARTIN
Delichon urbica
13 cm. Deep blue back with white rump, underside completely white. Often seen in towns and villages, but also lives in open country. Builds mud nest with tiny entrance hole beneath eaves of buildings, under bridges, and also on rock faces and cliffs.

SWALLOW
Hirundo rustica
19 cm. Deeply forked tail, red throat, deep blue back. Builds an open nest of mud and straw on beams and ledges in farm buildings and sheds. Hunts for insects in nearby fields, often swooping low in flight over water.

RED-RUMPED SWALLOW
Hirundo daurica
18 cm. As swallow but without red throat and with buff (not red) rump. Usually found in rocky country and at coast. Builds mud nest with long narrow entrance on walls of caves, cliffs or rocks, under bridges, or on buildings.

CRAG MARTIN
Hirundo rupestris
14 cm. Brown back and underside completely pale buff. Lives in mountains and on sea cliffs. Builds cup-shaped mud nest on rock face or cave wall, and sometimes on buildings.

ORIOLES
Family Oriolidae

Most orioles are brightly coloured birds of tropical forests. Only one species breeds in Europe

GOLDEN ORIOLE
Oriolus oriolus
24 cm. Male: bright yellow with black wings. Female: head and body green above and streaky white below. Found in woods and orchards, and among trees in parks. Usually hides among leaves in tops of trees. Has recently colonized small areas of England (not mapped).

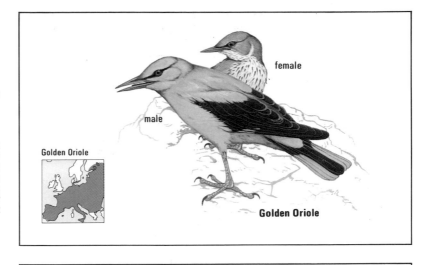

female

male

Golden Oriole

Golden Oriole

CROWS
Family Corvidae

Crows are the largest perching birds and they are among the cleverest of all birds. They search boldly for all kinds of food, and will avoid traps and ignore scarecrows that farmers put out to stop them robbing crops. They may also store food for the winter, and open snails by dropping them on to a stone.

RAVEN
Corvus corax
63 cm. Huge all-black body with massive black beak and wedge-shaped tail. Lives on sea cliffs and crags, in woods and open country, especially in hills and mountains and usually far from towns and villages. Builds huge nest on rock ledge or in tree. Often makes acrobatic display in the air, especially in spring. Hunts animals such as rabbits, hedgehogs and rats, but usually eats dead animals. The largest all-black bird in Europe.

CARRION CROW
Corvus corone corone
46 cm. Medium size; all-black body with heavy black beak. Found on moors, at coasts, and in fields, parks and gardens. Often seen alone or in pairs, and pairs nest alone in trees or on cliffs. Usually simply called crow rather than carrion crow.

HOODED CROW
Corvus corone cornix
46 cm. Like carrion crow but grey back and belly. Found in similar habitats and lives in same way as carrion crow. Belongs to same species as carrion crow, and interbreeds with it in places where their ranges overlap, producing birds intermediate in appearance between them.

Hooded Crow

Carrion Crow

Raven

Carrion Crow   Raven   Hooded Crow

A rookery. Rooks build their untidy nests high in the tree tops for safety. They build their nests in such large colonies because they are sociable birds. Jackdaws and owls may sometimes take over nests that have been abandoned by rooks.

Rook

Jackdaw

Jackdaw   Rook

ROOK
Corvus frugilegus
46 cm. Like carrion crow, but grey patch at base of beak (making beak look large). Found in fields surrounded by trees or small woods, in which it nests in colonies called rookeries. Also at seashore and open ground in winter. Usually seen in groups.

JACKDAW
Corvus monedula
33 cm. Black body but back of head and neck is grey. Found in fields and open country and at rocky coasts, nesting in holes in trees and rocks. Also seen on farms, and in towns and villages, where it nests in old buildings. Usually seen in flocks, walking jerkily or flying acrobatically.

MAGPIE
Pica pica
46 cm. Black and white body with very long tail. Found in fields and open country with scattered trees and bushes, in which it builds a large dome-shaped nest. Often seen in town parks and gardens. May steal bright objects, and store them in its nest. It has a characteristic pattern of flight, in which it intermittently glides and then rapidly flaps its wings.

NUTCRACKER
Nucifraga caryocatactes
33 cm. Brown body with white spots; white under tail. Lives in mountain forests, usually among conifer trees. Feeds mainly on conifer seeds but also very fond of hazel nuts, which it may store in the autumn and find months later, even under snow.

JAY
Garrulus glandarius
36 cm. Blue and white patch on wing; white rump. Found in woods and orchards and sometimes in town parks and gardens. Fond of acorns, which it stores for the winter by burying them in the ground. Can hold as many as six acorns in its mouth. It is a very lively and active bird and often flicks its tail.

CHOUGH
Pyrrhocorax pyrrhocorax
38 cm. Black body with red legs and red curved beak. Lives in mountains and on cliffs by sea; may also be found in quarries. Nests on ledges and in caves and crevices. Often performs acrobatics in flight.

ALPINE CHOUGH
Pyrrhocorax graculus
38 cm. As chough, but yellow beak. Lives on high mountains, right up to the snowy summits. Alpine choughs have even been seen near the top of Mount Everest, higher than any other bird. Comes down to mountain villages in winter to feed on any scraps it can find.

Jay

Nutcracker

Chough

Alpine Chough

Magpie

Nutcracker

Chough

Magpie

Jay

Alpine Chough

An Alpine chough. This bird follows mountaineers and may be seen at the top of the highest mountains, particularly in the Alps and Pyrenees and the mountains of the Balkans. The Alpine chough is a strong flier and can be seen soaring high in the sky in these areas.

Great Tit · Blue Tit · Coal Tit · Crested Tit · Marsh Tit · Willow Tit

Blue Tit

Great Tit

Willow Tit

Crested Tit

Marsh Tit

Coal Tit

The tits feed mainly on insects, especially in summer, and this marsh tit has found a nourishing meal for itself or its family.

TITS
Family Paridae

Tits are mainly woodland birds, but several kinds are frequent visitors to gardens. They can easily be told from other common woodland and garden birds as they have chunky rounded bodies. In woods, they flit through the branches and hang from twigs to get at insects, buds and seeds; they nest in holes in trees, laying at least four or five eggs and sometimes as many as twenty. Tits can easily be attracted to a garden; they are bold birds and show little fear of man. Their agility enables them to feed easily at bird tables and to take food hung from a branch or a gutter. Being hole nesters, they also come readily to nest boxes.

GREAT TIT
Parus major
14 cm. Yellow breast with black central stripe. Very often seen in woods, parks and gardens. Often pecks through milk bottle tops to reach the cream.

BLUE TIT
Parus caeruleus
11 cm. Blue cap, wings and tail. Very often seen in woods, parks and gardens. Like great tit, it often opens milk bottles. Blue tits also tear strips from wallpaper, books and newspapers, an activity thought to be an extension of their habit of tearing bark from trees to find insects.

COAL TIT
Parus ater
11 cm. White patch at back of head. Common in woods, especially pine woods. Less often seen in gardens than great tit or blue tit.

CRESTED TIT
Parus cristatus
11 cm. Speckled crest on head. Usually found in woods, especially among coniferous trees. Rarely seen in gardens.

MARSH TIT
Parus palustris
11 cm. Black crown without white nape of coal tit. Common in woods and often found in gardens. In spite of its name, it does not usually frequent marshes. Nests in natural holes in walls or trees.

WILLOW TIT
Parus montanus
11cm. As marsh tit, but with light wing markings and a less glossy crown. Common in woods, usually in damp places. Excavates nesting hole in rotten wood.

LONG-TAILED TITS
Family Aegithalidae

Several families of birds are called tits, which is simply an old word meaning little. If it were not for their tails, which take up more than half their length, long-tailed tits would be among the world's tiniest birds. Only one species is found in Europe.

LONG-TAILED TIT
Aegithalos caudatus
14 cm. Very small black and white body with very long tail. Found among bushes, thickets and hedges in woods, farmland and sometimes parks and gardens. Builds delicate globe-shaped nest with tiny entrance hole. The parent bird has to fold its long tail over its back when it is inside the nest.

NUTHATCHES AND WALLCREEPERS
Family Sittidae

Nuthatches are very agile tree birds and are to be seen clambering up or running headfirst down trunks and along branches, picking insects from the bark.
Wallcreepers climb over rock faces as well as walls, looking more like treecreepers than nuthatches. They also flutter through the air like butterflies.

NUTHATCH
Sitta europaea
14 cm. Blue-grey back, short tail. Lives in woods, parks and gardens; may visit bird tables. Nests in hole in tree, often plastering up entrance hole with mud. As well as eating insects, it wedges nuts into bark crevices and hammers them open with its beak. There are two distinct colour forms: birds with a white underside in northern Europe (*Sitta europaea europaea*), and birds with a buff underside elsewhere (*Sitta europaea caesia*). In Yugoslavia, Greece and Turkey the very similar rock nuthatch (*Sitta neumayer*) may be seen climbing rock faces.

WALLCREEPER
Tichodroma muraria
16 cm. Crimson wing patch. Lives on mountain slopes, among gorges and cliffs; descends to valleys and foothills in winter, when it may be seen on buildings. Nests in rock cavities.

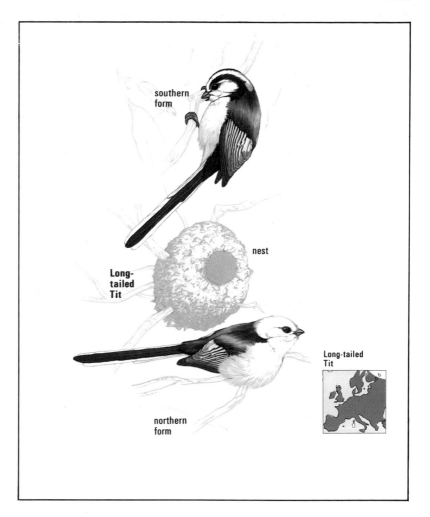

southern form

nest

Long-tailed Tit

Long-tailed Tit

northern form

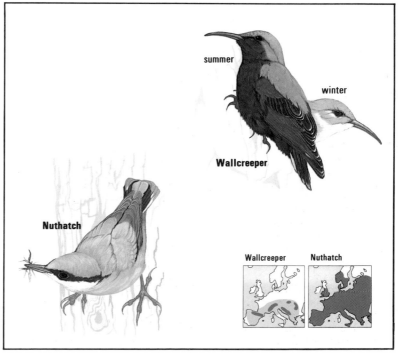

summer

winter

Wallcreeper

Nuthatch

Wallcreeper   Nuthatch

BABBLERS
Family Timaliidae

Babblers get their name from their constant chatter. Only one species is found in Europe.

BEARDED TIT or REEDLING
Panurus biarmicus
16 cm. Tawny body with very long tail; black moustache mark (male only). Lives among reeds, seen in flocks during winter. Gets its name from the large moustache marking of the male bird.

TREECREEPERS
Family Certhiidae

These birds are named after the way they creep up tree trunks, seeking insects in the bark. They nest in holes and crevices in trees and behind ivy.

TREECREEPER
Certhia familiaris
13 cm. Curved beak; streaky brown back and all-white underside. Found in woods, parks and gardens. Often seen with tits in winter.

SHORT-TOED TREECREEPER
Certhia brachydactyla
13 cm. Very similar to treecreeper, but may have buff flanks. Lives in same places as treecreeper. In central and southern Europe, this species is usually found at low altitude, whereas the treecreeper often prefers the mountains here.

WRENS
Family Troglodytidae

All but one of the members of the wren family live in America. They are all very small birds.

WREN
Troglodytes troglodytes
10 cm. Small size, upturned tail. Lives among low plants almost anywhere, from mountains, coasts and moors to woods, fields, parks and gardens. Often seen scurrying about in a flower bed or along the bottom of a hedge or wall, seeking insects among the litter on the ground. Nests in hedges and bushes and in holes in walls and trees.

DIPPERS
Family Cinclidae

Dippers are unusual perching birds because they are water birds. They can swim and dive, and may even walk along the bottom of a stream to look for small freshwater animals. They are called dippers not because they are continually taking a dip, but because they bob up and down as they perch on boulders in the stream. Only one species is found in Europe.

DIPPER
Cinclus cinclus
18 cm. Dark with white breast. Lives by streams in mountains; may also be found by water at lower levels and at seashore in winter. Builds nest in river banks, under bridges or behind waterfalls.

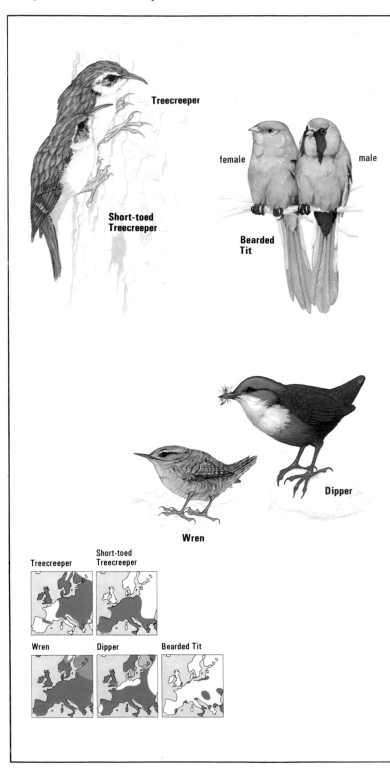

Treecreeper

Short-toed Treecreeper

female

male

Bearded Tit

Wren

Dipper

Treecreeper

Short-toed Treecreeper

Wren

Dipper

Bearded Tit

THRUSHES
Family Turdidae

This large family contains several birds that are well-known garden visitors. They feed mainly on berries and other fruits and insects, but are often to be seen looking for worms. Thrushes have beautiful songs, which they seem to perform just for the pleasure of singing.

MISTLE THRUSH
Turdus viscivorus
28 cm. Grey-brown back; heavily spotted breast, white underwing, white on outer tail feathers. Found in woods, farmland, parks and gardens; also on moors in winter. Nests in trees.

FIELDFARE
Turdus pilaris
25 cm. Grey head and rump, chestnut back. Breeds in northern Europe, forming colonies in birchwoods and also in parks and gardens, where it builds in trees or on buildings. In winter it moves south in flocks to fields and open country with hedges and scattered trees.

SONG THRUSH
Turdus philomelos
23 cm. Similar to mistle thrush, but smaller size, brown back, breast more lightly spotted, buff underwing and all-brown tail. Often seen in woods and orchards, among scattered bushes and hedges, and in parks and gardens. May be seen on lawns cocking its head to one side, as if listening but in fact looking for a worm. Hammers snails on to a stone (called an anvil) to break open their shells. Nests in trees, bushes and hedges, and also on buildings.

REDWING
Turdus iliacus
20 cm. Reddish flanks and underwing; light stripe over eye. Breeds in northern Europe in woods and in parks and gardens, nesting in trees or on the ground. Moves south for the winter to fields and open country.

ROCK THRUSH
Monticola saxatilis
19 cm. Male: blue head, orange breast and tail, white band across back. Female: mottled brown with chestnut tail. Lives and nests on rocky ground and among trees high in mountains in western Europe, but lower down in eastern Europe.

BLUE ROCK THRUSH
Monticola solitarius
20 cm. Male: blue body with dark wings and tail. Female: as female rock thrush but dark brown tail. Lives on rocky and stony ground from the sea-

Song Thrush   Redwing   Mistle Thrush   Fieldfare

Rock Thrush

Blue Rock Thrush

Fieldfare

Redwing

Rock Thrush

male

female

Song Thrush

Mistle Thrush

Blue Rock Thrush

male

female

Ring Ouzel

male

female

male

female

Blackbird

Black
Wheatear

male

female

male

female

Wheatear

female

black-throated
form

male

male

female

Black-eared Wheatear

Stonechat

male

female

female

male

Whinchat

| Blackbird | Ring Ouzel |

| Wheatear | Black-eared Wheatear | Black Wheatear | Stonechat | Whinchat |

shore up to mountain tops. May be seen in towns in southern Europe. Nests in holes in rocks or cliffs or on buildings.

RING OUZEL
Turdus torquatus
24 cm. Male: black with white breast band. Female: brown with just a dull white crescent on breast. Lives on moors and mountain slopes, often where there are scattered trees and bushes. Nests among low plants or on rock ledges or walls.

BLACKBIRD
Turdus merula
25 cm. Male: all black with bright yellow beak. Female: dark brown all over. Very often seen in woods, orchards, hedges, parks and gardens; also in fields in winter. Nests in trees, bushes or hedges, on the ground or on buildings. Some blackbirds are albino birds that have white patches or may even be entirely white.

WHEATEAR
Oenanthe oenanthe
15 cm. Male in summer: black patch over eye with grey crown, grey back and rump. Female and male in autumn: white stripe over eye and grey-brown back with white rump. Lives in open country, from high moors and grassy hillsides down to coasts. Nests in holes in ground or in walls and rocks.

BLACK-EARED WHEATEAR
Oenanthe hispanica
14 cm. Male: black patch over eye with white to chestnut crown, buff back and white rump; black patch may extend to throat. Female: as female wheatear but dark cheek patch and darker wings. Found in rocky and sandy places, often among scattered trees and bushes. Nests in holes in walls and rocks.

BLACK WHEATEAR
Oenanthe leucura
18 cm. Male: black body. Female: dark chocolate-brown body. Both have white rump. Lives in rocky mountains and at sea cliffs. Nests in holes in rocks, often hiding entrance with pile of stones.

STONECHAT
Saxicola torquata
13 cm. Male: black head (brownish in winter) with chestnut breast. Female: as male but much paler. Found on moors, on headlands at coast, and on rough ground with bushes, especially gorse. Often seen perching, flicking its tail up and down. The nest is hidden in a bush or among grass.

WHINCHAT
Saxicola rubetra
13 cm. Male: dark cheeks with white stripe over eye; white at base of tail. Female: as male but paler. Lives in similar places to stonechat, but also likes grassy areas and fields. Behaves in the same way as stonechat.

REDSTART
Phoenicurus phoenicurus
14 cm. Male: black throat with orange breast; reddish tail. Female: buff breast and reddish tail. Found in woods and among scattered trees; also in parks and gardens and rocky hillsides. Constantly flicks its tail up and down. Nests in holes in trees, walls and rocks.

BLACK REDSTART
Phoenicurus ochruros
14 cm. Male: black with reddish tail. Female: as female redstart but darker and greyer. Found on rocky ground and cliffs; also in towns, especially around factories. Constantly flicks its tail. Nests in holes in rocks and walls, and on buildings.

NIGHTINGALE
Luscinia megarhynchos
16 cm. Brown back and chestnut tail with plain breast. Hides away among undergrowth in woods, and in thickets and hedges, sometimes around gardens. Nest concealed near ground. Very difficult to spot, but beautiful, musical song can often be heard, especially at night (though other thrushes may also sing at night).

BLUETHROAT
Luscinia svecica
14 cm. Male: blue throat with red or white patch in centre. Female: dark breast band and orange patches on tail. Hides away among thickets and hedges, often close to water. Nest concealed near ground. There are two colour forms: the white-spotted bluethroat (*Luscinia svecica cyanecula*) of central and southern Europe, in which the blue throat patch of the male has a white centre; and the red-spotted bluethroat (*L. svecica svecica*) of northern Europe, in which it has a red centre. The blue is obscured during the winter.

ROBIN
Erithacus rubecula
14 cm. Orange-red face and breast. Very often seen in woods, hedges, parks and gardens, hopping over the ground. Nests in holes in trees and walls. In Britain, robins are bold birds and often come to bird tables, but elsewhere in Europe they are shy. Robins are usually seen alone, or at most in pairs during spring and summer. They are so aggressive towards each other that they will even mistake their own reflection for another bird and attack it.

Cetti's Warbler

Grasshopper Warbler

Savi's Warbler

Grasshopper Warbler

white form

Cetti's Warbler

Great Reed Warbler

Savi's Warbler

Moustached Warbler

Great Reed Warbler

Moustached Warbler

WARBLERS
Family Sylviidae

Warblers are small birds that flit about among trees, bushes and reeds, restlessly searching for insects to eat. They are named after their warbling songs, which vary widely from one species to another. The birds are often shy and difficult to spot. Most have dull colours with no very obvious marks to give away their identity. Recognizing the song of a warbler is therefore helpful in making sure of its identity.

CETTI'S WARBLER
Cettia cetti
14 cm. Unstreaked red-brown back. Song: repeated 'chewee' in bursts. Hides away and nests among dense thickets and reed-beds beside streams and swamps. Flicks tail.

GRASSHOPPER WARBLER
Locustella naevia
13 cm. Streaked back with faint eye-stripe. The underparts may be white or yellowish. Hides away and nests in dense undergrowth, long grass and reeds in marshes, and in more open country with scattered trees and bushes. Named after the grasshopper-like whirring sound of its song, which is held for a long time.

SAVI'S WARBLER
Locustella luscinioides
14 cm. Plumage like reed warbler but white chin. Song: like grasshopper warbler's, but lower and held for short time. Lives and nests among reeds and bushes in marshes and swamps. May be seen singing while perched on the tip of a reed or top of a bush.

MOUSTACHED WARBLER
Acrocephalus melanopogon
13 cm. Dark streaked back; dark cap with vivid eye-stripe. Song: sweet warble with 'tu-tu-tu' sounds. Lives and nests among reeds and small bushes in swamps and beside streams. Bobs its tail up and down, unlike similar sedge warbler and aquatic warbler.

GREAT REED WARBLER
Acrocephalus arundinaceus
19 cm. Large bird; unstreaked brown back with eye-stripe. Song: loud and strident with harsh sounds. Found among reeds beside lakes and rivers. Builds nest around reed stems. Sings from tops of reeds and may be seen on perch in the open. Largest European warbler.

Right: A pair of reed warblers at their nest, which is elaborately woven around the reed stems, usually over standing water.

Reed Warbler   Sedge Warbler   Marsh Warbler

Sedge Warbler

Marsh Warbler

Reed Warbler

REED WARBLER
Acrocephalus scirpaceus
13 cm. Like great reed warbler, but smaller and with faint eye-stripe. Song: monotonous mixture of sweet and harsh sounds. Lives and nests among reeds and low bushes beside water and sometimes in fields. Perches on reed to sing, and suspends nest among reeds.

MARSH WARBLER
Acrocephalus palustris
13 cm. Like reed warbler, but olive-brown back and pink legs. Song: varied and musical with trills. Lives and nests among low bushes in thickets and swamps and beside ditches and streams; also in cornfields. Sings from low visible perch.

SEDGE WARBLER
Acrocephalus schoenobaenus
13 cm. Like moustached warbler, but paler. Song: varied mixture of sweet and harsh sounds. Lives and nests among reeds, low bushes and hedges, usually near water; also among crops. Sings from perch at top of reed, and also during short flights.

MELODIOUS WARBLER
Hippolais polyglotta
13 cm. Green-grey with yellow under-side; brown legs. Song: rapid and varied, but musical. Lives in woods and among bushes along rivers, also in parks and gardens. Nests in bushes and hedges. Very similar to icterine warbler in plumage, but the two species are found together only in a narrow band across the centre of Europe.

ICTERINE WARBLER
Hippolais icterina
13 cm. Like melodious warbler, but blue-grey legs. Song: repeated notes, both sweet and harsh. Lives and nests in similar habitats to the melodious warbler, but less likely to be found near water.

OLIVACEOUS WARBLER
Hippolais pallida
13 cm. Grey-brown above and white below, with buffish eye-stripe. Song: like sedge warbler's. Lives and nests in trees, bushes and hedges in light woods, fields, orchards, parks and gardens. Similar to garden warbler, but the two species are usually found in different parts of Europe.

BARRED WARBLER
Sylvia nisoria
15 cm. Bars on underside. Song: musical, but in short bursts interrupted by chatter. Lives and nests in bushes and hedges in woods and fields. Usually shy, but may be seen and heard singing in flight.

ORPHEAN WARBLER
Sylvia hortensis
15 cm. Black cap extending below straw-coloured eye. Song: warble of repeated phrases. Lives and nests in bushes and trees in woods and orchards.

GARDEN WARBLER
Sylvia borin
14 cm. Light brown above and grey-white beneath, with no obvious mark-ings at all. The plainest of all European birds. Song: musical and liquid, soft but held for a long time. Hides away and nests in the undergrowth in woods and among thickets, hedges and bush-es, often in parks and gardens.

BLACKCAP
Sylvia atricapilla
14 cm. Male: black cap, a glossy black crown down to eye level. The sides of the head and the underparts are ash-grey. The female has a red-brown cap and browner underparts. Song: varied warble held for short time. Lives and nests among undergrowth, bushes and hedges in woods, parks and gardens. Usually shy, but may come to bird tables in winter. The blackcap can be distinguished from the orphean and Sardinian warblers by the sharply-defined cap and the lack of white in the tail.

Icterine Warbler

Melodious Warbler

Melodious Warbler

Icterine Warbler

Olivaceous Warbler

Olivaceous Warbler

Barred Warbler

Orphean Warbler

female   male

Blackcap

Garden Warbler

Barred Warbler   Orphean Warbler

Blackcap   Garden Warbler

WHITETHROAT
Sylvia communis
14 cm. White throat with plain grey (male) or brown (female) head; red-brown wings. Song: short bursts of chatter. Lives and nests among low bushes, hedges and brambles around woods and in fields, also in gardens. Very active, darting in and out of cover and making short flights, singing in air.

LESSER WHITETHROAT
Sylvia curruca
13 cm. Like whitethroat, but dark patch around eye and grey-brown wings. Song: fast rattle-like sound, often preceded by a short warble. Hides away and nests among bushes and trees in woods, parks and gardens.

DARTFORD WARBLER
Sylvia undata
13 cm. Red-brown breast, cocked tail. Song: short musical phrases with vary-ing pauses. Lives and nests among low bushes, especially gorse, and heather on dry open ground and hillsides. Very shy, but may sing in flight. Has generally spread its breeding range during the last few years, but could be vulnerable in Britain, partly due to cold winters and heath fires in hot summers.

WILLOW WARBLER
Phylloscopus trochilus
11 cm. Grey-green back. Yellowish underside, white eye-stripe, legs usu-ally pale. Song: liquid warble of de-scending notes. Found scurrying and flitting about in woods, among scat-tered trees and bushes, and in parks and gardens. Usually nests on the ground among bushes. Virtually iden-tical to chiffchaff, except for song.

CHIFFCHAFF
Phylloscopus collybita
11 cm. Like willow warbler, but legs usually dark. Song: repeated 'chiff-chaff' sounds. Found in same places and as restless as willow warbler, but prefers areas with trees. Nests above ground.

WOOD WARBLER
Phylloscopus sibilatrix
13 cm. Yellow throat and breast; yellow eye-stripe. Song: liquid trill followed by a few long notes. Lives and nests among woods and forests. Very active, singing as it moves through the leaves and flies from tree to tree.

BONELLI'S WARBLER
Phylloscopus bonelli
11 cm. Like willow warbler, but greyer above, whiter beneath and with yellow-ish rump. Song: short trills. Lives in woods and forests, usually on hills and mountainsides. Nests on the ground, among trees.

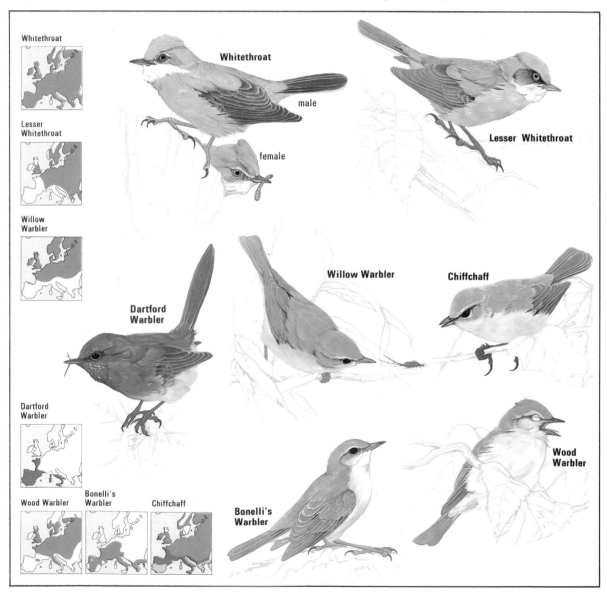

FLYCATCHERS
Family Muscicapidae

These birds are well named, for they are most likely to be seen sitting watchfully on a perch and then suddenly darting out to capture a fly or some other flying insect or swooping down to the ground to make a catch there. They often return to the same perch to wait for the next meal.

SPOTTED FLYCATCHER
Muscicapa striata
14 cm. Grey-brown with lightly streaked breast and head. Found at the edges of woods, among scattered trees, and in parks, orchards and gardens. Nests on buildings and tree trunks, often behind creepers. Flicks its tail as it perches. Only young birds are spotted; the adults are lightly streaked instead.

PIED FLYCATCHER
Ficedula hypoleuca
13 cm. Male in summer: black back and white underside with white wing patch. Male in autumn and female: brown back with white wing patch. Found in woods, parks and gardens. Nests in hole in tree or wall, also in nest boxes. Flicks tail, but does not often return to same perch after chasing insects.

COLLARED FLYCATCHER
Ficedula albicollis
13 cm. In spring and summer the male's plumage varies. In Italy and central Europe, the western form (*Ficedula albicollis albicollis*), which has a white collar, is found. The eastern form (*F. albicollis semi-torquata*), which is found in eastern Europe, lacks the white collar. Female and male in autumn: very like pied flycatcher. Lives in similar places and behaves in same way as pied flycatcher.

RED-BREASTED FLYCATCHER
Ficedula parva
11 cm. Orange (male) or buff (female) throat; white tail edges. The male looks rather like a small robin, except for the white on its tail. Found in woods and parks, usually feeding among leaves in trees but sometimes chasing insects. Nests in hole in tree or wall and also on tree trunk.

Spotted Flycatcher

Pied Flycatcher

female (and male in autumn)

male (summer)

female (and male in autumn)

Collared Flycatcher

male, western form (summer)

Red-breasted Flycatcher

male

female

Spotted Flycatcher

Pied Flycatcher

Collared Flycatcher

Red-breasted Flycatcher

GOLDCRESTS
Family Regulidae

Goldcrests are active little birds that flit through bushes and trees, hunting for insects. In the winter, they may join flocks of tits seeking food. Two species are found in Europe and they are the smallest European birds.

GOLDCREST
Regulus regulus
9 cm. Tiny; orange (male) or yellow (female) stripe on crown. Found in woods and forests, especially in conifer trees; also in hedges, low bushes and undergrowth in winter. Builds basket-like nest of moss, often hung in conifer tree or among ivy.

FIRECREST
Regulus ignicapillus
9 cm. Like goldcrest, but black and white stripe over eye. Found in same places as goldcrest, but has no preference for conifer trees. Nest may be hung in bushes or creepers as well as in trees.

ACCENTORS
Family Prunellidae

Accentors are small birds that root about on the ground or among low plants seeking insects and spiders to eat, and also seeds in winter. Two species are found in Europe.

DUNNOCK or HEDGE SPARROW
Prunella modularis
15 cm. Grey head and breast with brown back. Resembles female house sparrow but is recognized by its narrow bill and dark grey head and underside. Found in woods, bushy countryside, hedges, parks and gardens, where it shuffles through flower beds. Nests in hedges, bushes and low plants.

ALPINE ACCENTOR
Prunella collaris
18 cm. Spotted throat and streaky flanks. Lives on rocky mountain slopes, though may descend for the winter. Nests in holes in rocks.

A hard-working dunnock feeds a hungry young cuckoo hatched from an egg left in its nest.

Tawny Pipit   Meadow Pipit   Tree Pipit   Water Pipit   Rock Pipit

Tawny Pipit

Meadow Pipit

Tree Pipit

winter

summer

Rock Pipit

Water Pipit

PIPITS AND WAGTAILS
Family Motacillidae

Pipits and wagtails are small birds that spend most of their time on the ground in search of insects. Pipits look like several other streaky brown ground birds, such as buntings and larks, but they can be recognized by their narrow beaks and slender bodies. Wagtails have long tails, which they wag up and down all the time.

TAWNY PIPIT
Anthus campestris
16 cm. Sandy unstreaked breast and faintly streaked neck. Lives on dry, open, often sandy ground, also in fields. Nests in low plants on ground.

MEADOW PIPIT
Anthus pratensis
15 cm. Pale breast with dark streaks; brown legs. Found in all kinds of open country — moors, fields, dunes, grassy slopes — and in winter in marshes and along rivers, often at the coast. Makes its nest on the ground hidden among low plants. May be seen and heard singing as it makes short flights rising from and returning to the ground.

TREE PIPIT
Anthus trivialis
15 cm. Breast buff with dark streaks; pink legs. Lives in light woods and clearings and among scattered trees and bushes. Nests among low plants on ground. May be seen and heard singing in short spiral flight rising from a perch.

WATER PIPIT
Anthus spinoletta spinoletta
16 cm. Summer: unstreaked breast with grey back. Winter: like rock pipit, but white eye-stripe. Lives in mountains in spring and summer, nesting in holes in rock. Descends for winter, usually living near water.

ROCK PIPIT
Anthus spinoletta petrosus
16 cm. Dark and streaky all over; dark legs; grey edges to tail (white in other pipits). Belongs to same species as water pipit, but lives at coast, often among rocks. Nests in rock crevices.

97

White Wagtail

Pied Wagtail

White Wagtail

Pied Wagtail

Grey Wagtail

Yellow Wagtail

male
(summer)

female

male
(winter)

**Grey
Wagtail**

male

**Yellow
Wagtail**

female

WHITE WAGTAIL
Motacilla alba alba
18 cm. Black and white, with very long tail; grey back. Often found in open country, usually near water, and also on farms and in villages and towns. Nests in holes and on ledges among rocks and on buildings. In winter, large groups sleep on buildings and in trees in cities and towns.

PIED WAGTAIL
Motacilla alba yarrellii
18 cm. As white wagtail, but black back in spring and summer. Form of white wagtail found mainly in the British Isles. Lives and nests in similar places to the white wagtail.

GREY WAGTAIL
Motacilla cinerea
18 cm. Grey back with yellow underside; male has black throat in summer. In spring and summer, found by streams and rivers, mostly in hills and mountains, where it nests in holes in wall or rock beside water. In winter, moves to lowland rivers and lakes, sewage farms and coast.

YELLOW WAGTAIL
Motacilla flava
16 cm. Green-brown back and bright yellow underside (pale in female). Found in marshes and fields, usually near water. Nests on the ground, among grass or crops. Several forms with different head patterns and different names live in Europe. They all have their own regions, but where these meet, intermediate forms may be seen. In southern Scandinavia and central Europe, the blue-headed wagtail (*Motacilla flava flava*) – blue-grey crown, white stripe over eye, yellow throat – is found. Britain is the home of the yellow wagtail (*Motacilla flava flavissima*) – olive and yellow head. The Spanish wagtail (*Motacilla flava iberiae*) – grey crown, white stripe starting from eye, white throat – lives in Spain, Portugal and southern France. The ashy-headed wagtail (*Motacilla flava cinereocapilla*) – grey head, no stripe over eye, white throat – lives in Italy and Albania. The black-headed wagtail (*Motacilla flava feldegg*) – black head, no stripe over eye, yellow throat – is found in south-east Europe. Each kind may sometimes stray from its own region.

WAXWINGS
Family Bombycillidae

Waxwings are unusual birds because they do not have particular homes. Except when nesting, they continually wander in flocks from place to place, looking for fruits, berries and insects to eat. They may be seen in one place for a short time and then not again for years.

WAXWING
Bombycilla garrulus
18 cm. Large crest; yellow tip on tail and waxy red tips to secondary wing feathers. Found in woods, parks and gardens, busily eating berries and fruits. Nests in Arctic and spreads into Europe in winter in search of food.

SHRIKES
Family Laniidae

Shrikes are like small birds of prey. The shrike darts after its prey and snaps it up in its hooked beak. The victim is then usually taken to the shrike's 'larder', a sharp thorn or barbed wire fence where it is impaled so that the shrike can tear it apart – a habit that has earned the shrike its other name of butcherbird. Insects are the main prey, but the larger shrikes also catch lizards, small birds and rodents.

GREAT GREY SHRIKE
Lanius excubitor
24 cm. Black and white with grey back and crown. Found at edges of woods, among scattered trees and bushes and in hedges and orchards. Nests in trees and bushes.

LESSER GREY SHRIKE
Lanius minor
20 cm. As great grey shrike but black forehead. Found among scattered trees and bushes. Nests in trees.

WOODCHAT SHRIKE
Lanius senator
18 cm. Chestnut crown with white wing patch and rump (female paler than male). Found in scattered trees, bushy countryside, orchards and woods. Nests in trees.

RED-BACKED SHRIKE
Lanius collurio
18 cm. Male: grey crown with chestnut back and wings. Female: plain brown back with bars on breast. Found in bushy places and among brambles and thickets. Nests in bushes and small trees.

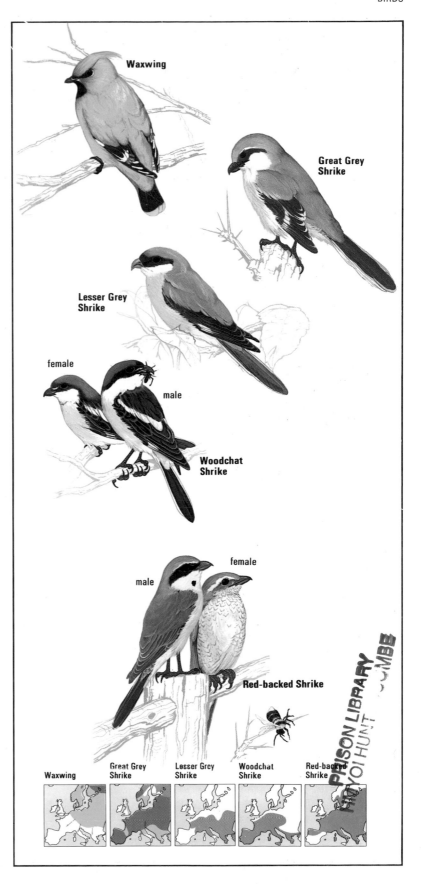

Waxwing

Great Grey Shrike

Lesser Grey Shrike

female   male

Woodchat Shrike

male   female

Red-backed Shrike

| Waxwing | Great Grey Shrike | Lesser Grey Shrike | Woodchat Shrike | Red-backed Shrike |

Starling

winter

Starling

summer

Starlings gather at the communal roost just before nightfall. They fly in from many miles around to sleep in large flocks.

STARLINGS
Family Sturnidae

Starlings like each other's company and live in flocks that in winter may contain thousands of birds. They wander over the ground, busily pecking here and there for food. They chatter constantly, often copying other sounds.

STARLING
Sturnus vulgaris
21 cm. Summer: slightly-speckled glossy black with green-purple sheen. Winter: black with white spots. Found throughout the countryside and also in towns, where flocks sleep on buildings and in trees. Nests in holes in trees or ground, on buildings and in nest boxes. As spring arrives, it loses the white spots of its winter plumage because the white tips of its feathers wear away. Also, the beak, which is dark in winter, turns yellow. Youngsters are dull brown, without spots, and may be confused with female blackbirds, but they have longer beaks than black-birds.

FINCHES
Family Fringillidae

Like tits, finches are generally among the most well-known and liked of birds, for they often come to gardens and parks, adding a touch of colour with their bright plumage. They are less likely to be seen in the summer when they are nesting. They are primarily seed-eaters and have stout beaks.

GREENFINCH
Carduelis chloris
15 cm. Green-brown with yellow edges to wings and tail (female paler than male). Often seen among scattered trees and bushes, in fields, parks and gardens. Clings to net bags or wire baskets of nuts to feed, like tits. Nests in trees and bushes.

HAWFINCH
Coccothraustes coccothraustes
18 cm. Huge beak above small black bib; wide white wingbar. Lives in woods, orchards, parks and gardens, but may hide away among leaves, especially in Britain. Nests in trees and bushes. Huge beak can crack open hard seeds.

GOLDFINCH
Carduelis carduelis
13 cm. Red patch on face; wide yellow

wingbar. Lives and nests in same places as greenfinch, but does not come to feed on nuts. Often seen climbing over thistles or on high perch.

SISKIN
Carduelis spinus
12 cm. Male: yellow-green with black crown and chin. Female: grey-green with streaky breast, yellow tail edges. Found in woods, usually nesting in conifer trees and, in winter, feeding in alder and birch trees. Also seen in parks and gardens.

LINNET
Acanthis cannabina
13 cm. Male: red forehead and breast (pale in winter), grey wing patch. Female: as twite but streaky throat and grey wing patch. Nests in low bushes, thickets and hedges, usually in open country but sometimes in parks and gardens. Roams over fields, rough pastures, and marshes in winter.

TWITE
Acanthis flavirostris
14 cm. Streaky brown back, head and breast, but unstreaked throat; yellow beak (winter only); pinkish rump (male). Lives on moors and hills in summer, nesting among heather and bushes and in stone walls and rabbit burrows. Descends for winter and roams over open fields, marshes and seashores, where it can often be seen in large flocks.

female

Chaffinch

male
(summer)

male
(winter)

male

female

Parrot Crossbill

male

Crossbill

female

female

male
(summer)

male
(winter)

Brambling

| Chaffinch | Brambling | Crossbill | Parrot Crossbill |

CROSSBILL
Loxia curvirostra
16 cm. Crossed bill (not always easy to see); orange-red (male) or green (female) with dark wings and tail. Lives and nests among conifer trees (especially spruce) in woods and forests. The tips of its bill are crossed so that it can lever open the cones to get at the seeds. When cones are scarce, it may spread in search of food, reaching the British Isles, France and Italy in great numbers.

PARROT CROSSBILL
Loxia pytyopsittacus
17 cm. As crossbill but heavier bill and larger head. Lives and nests mainly among pine trees, feeding in the same way as crossbill. Less likely to spread in search of food. Gets its name from the way it holds a cone while opening it, rather as a parrot holds a fruit while eating it (though crossbill performs same action).

CHAFFINCH
Fringilla coelebs
15 cm. Male: pink breast, grey-blue head (summer only) and green rump; two white wingbars and white edges to tail. Female: yellow-brown with two white wingbars and white tail edges.

Often found in woods, among scattered trees and bushes, and in fields, hedges, orchards, parks and gardens. Nests in trees and bushes; spreads to more open country in winter.

BRAMBLING
Fringilla montifringilla
15 cm. Male: orange breast and base of wing; white rump; black (summer) or brown (winter) head and back. Female: as winter male but paler. Nests in trees in woods, and spreads south to fields, parks and gardens in winter, often with chaffinches and other finches. Found especially in beech woods.

Corn Bunting

Yellowhammer

male / female

Cirl Bunting

male / female

male (summer) / male (winter)

female

Reed Bunting

female / male

Ortolan Bunting

Corn Bunting | Yellowhammer

Reed Bunting | Ortolan Bunting

Snow Bunting | Cirl Bunting

female / male (winter) / male (summer)

Snow Bunting

BUNTINGS
Family Emberizidae

Buntings are small seed-eating birds like finches, and have similar stout bills to crack open seeds. Buntings are most likely to be seen feeding on the ground in winter, often in groups, and also singing from a perch in spring and summer.

CORN BUNTING
Miliaria calandra
18 cm. Large, streaky brown. Found in open fields and on rough ground with scattered bushes. Hides its nest in grass or low bushes. May be seen perching on a post, wall or telegraph wires.

YELLOWHAMMER
Emberiza citrinella
16 cm. Male: yellow head and underparts, chestnut rump. Female: streaky pale yellow head and breast, chestnut rump. Found in clearings and at edges of woods, among scattered bushes, and in fields and hedges. Nests on the ground or in a low bush or hedge. Sings throughout spring and summer, repeating its famous phrase that seems to say 'little bit of bread and *no* cheese' – in fact, a group of short notes and a long one.

CIRL BUNTING
Emberiza cirlus
16 cm. Male: black throat. Female: as female yellowhammer but olive rump. Found among scattered trees and bushes and in hedges, where it nests near ground.

REED BUNTING
Emberiza schoeniclus
15 cm. Male: black (summer) or brown (winter) head and throat with white moustache and collar. Female: streaky brown with white moustache. Lives mainly in reed beds and swamps but also among bushes and hedges where it nests on or near the ground. Spreads to fields in winter, and may come to bird tables in gardens.

ORTOLAN BUNTING
Emberiza hortulana
16 cm. Male: green-grey head with yellow throat. Female: streaky brown with yellow throat. Found among scattered trees and bushes, often in hills; also in fields and gardens. Nests among low plants.

SNOW BUNTING
Plectrophenax nivalis
16 cm. Large white wing patch with white head (male in summer), sandy head (male in winter), or grey-brown head (female). Nests in crevices in rocks, usually high up in mountains. Spreads in winter to open coasts, hills and fields. Usually seen in winter in flocks, known as snowflakes from the way the little white birds dance through the air.

SPARROWS
Family Ploceidae

No bird is better known than the house sparrow, which lives with man almost everywhere. Sparrows are small streaky brown birds with stout bills, rather like several buntings but having special marks that are easy to recognize.

HOUSE SPARROW
Passer domesticus
15 cm. Male: grey crown and black bib. Female: streaky back with plain light breast; dull eye-stripe. Found in city centres and squares, parks and gardens, farms and fields, rarely far from human habitation. Nests under eaves, in holes in walls and rocks, and in nest boxes; also builds domed nest in creepers, bushes and trees. In Italy, Corsica and Crete, the Italian sparrow (*Passer domesticus italiae*) is found. It is a form of house sparrow with a chestnut crown and white cheeks.

SPANISH SPARROW
Passer hispaniolensis
15 cm. Male: as male Italian sparrow but with large black breast patch. Female: as female house sparrow but streaky flanks. Found in woods and among scattered trees and bushes. Nests in trees and bushes, often in old nests of other birds. Less common in towns than house sparrow and tree sparrow.

TREE SPARROW
Passer montanus
14 cm. Chestnut crown with black spot on cheek (both sexes). Found in woods and among scattered trees and bushes, and in fields and gardens. Nests in holes in trees. Also lives and nests in towns and villages like house sparrow, especially in southern and eastern Europe.

SNOW FINCH
Montifringilla nivalis
18 cm. White wings with black tips, grey head and dark chin (female duller than male). Lives on bare mountain slopes and summits, nesting in crevices. Spends winter lower down, often visiting huts and houses. Belongs to sparrow family, in spite of its name and bunting-like appearance.

ROCK SPARROW
Petronia petronia
14 cm. Pale with stripes on head, spots on tail, yellow spot on breast. Found in rocky and stony places, sometimes in gardens and among buildings. Nests in holes in rocks and trees.

female
House Sparrow
male
Italian Sparrow (male)

Tree Sparrow

male
female
Spanish Sparrow

Snow Finch

Rock Sparrow

House Sparrow

Spanish Sparrow

Tree Sparrow

Snow Finch

Rock Sparrow

Chapter Three

Reptiles and Amphibians

The reptiles and amphibians are backboned animals belonging to the classes Reptilia and Amphibia respectively. Both groups are cold-blooded, meaning that their body temperatures fluctuate with the surrounding air or water instead of remaining more or less constant as in birds and mammals. The animals are not necessarily cold, and in really hot weather they may actually be warmer than birds and mammals. They cannot stay active in very low temperatures, however, so, with the exception of a few Mediterranean species, European reptiles and amphibians go into hibernation for the colder months. In the far north, this can mean sleeping for as much as seven or eight months of the year.

Reptiles

The reptiles arose from some kind of amphibian ancestor about 280 million years ago, and many thousands of strange species have come and gone since then, including the famous dinosaurs. About 6,000 species of reptiles are alive today, of which the great majority are snakes and lizards (Order Squamata). Some 330 kinds of turtles and tortoises (Order Chelonia), 21 species of crocodiles and alligators (Order Crocodilia), and the solitary tuatara of New Zealand (Order Rhynchocephalia) make up the rest of the class.

Reptiles are all air-breathing animals and the great majority live on land. Most have tough, waterproof skins clothed with horny scales – a feature which readily distinguishes the lizards from the newts and salamanders. Basically, reptiles have four limbs, but these are reduced or absent in several groups of lizards and totally absent in all but a few snakes. With the exception of the tortoises and one or two other species, all European reptiles are carnivores, and most of them will take only living prey.

Some snakes and lizards give birth to active young, but most species lay eggs. Fertilization always takes place internally. The eggs, which are laid on land, have shells which are either leathery or hardened by impregnation with lime. Some reptiles guard their eggs, but most species abandon them. The youngsters are essentially similar to the adults and have no larval stage such as we find in most amphibians.

Left (above): A female sand lizard basking on a rock. Being cold-blooded, lizards commonly sunbathe to absorb sufficient warmth for their high-speed activity. Sunbathing is especially important for pregnant females, which need extra warmth for the development of their eggs or young. The scaly reptile skin is clearly seen in the picture.

Left (below): An edible frog leaping through the air, propelled by its powerful back legs. These limbs also provide the propulsive force for swimming.

Amphibians

The amphibians include the frogs and toads (Order Anura), the newts and salamanders (Order Caudata), and the worm-like caecilians (Order Apoda) which burrow in tropical soils. There are about 4,400 species, of which some 4,000 are anurans. Like the reptiles, the great majority live in the tropics.

Amphibians first appeared on the Earth about 350 million years ago, having evolved from some kind of fish that was able to struggle out of the water and breathe air. Although most of today's adult amphibians can survive well on land, they nearly all have to return to the water to breed, for the young stages are fish-like tadpoles which breathe with gills. As a result of this dependence on water, the amphibians never dominated the land in the way that the dinosaurs and other reptiles did, but the living amphibians are still a very successful group within the environments open to them. They do not occur in the sea, but most freshwater habitats support them and certain species have managed to adapt themselves to some surprisingly dry places. The amphibian skin is always very thin, though some of the toads have wart-like thickenings, and, except in some of the caecilians, it is totally devoid of scales. Mucus-secreting glands keep the skin moist, and some frogs and toads also have poison glands in the skin. A moist skin is essential because a good deal of respiration takes place through the body surface and oxygen cannot pass through the skin unless it is first dissolved in water. Most adult amphibians have lungs as well, but these are often poorly developed: some species which spend all their lives in water have no lungs at all.

Apart from the apodans, the amphibians typically have four legs. These are all more or less alike in the tailed amphibians (Caudata), but among the anurans the hind legs are much larger than the front ones. They provide the propulsive force for swimming and for leaping on land.

Courtship is often elaborate among the newts, with the males adopting splendid crests and colours and dancing in front of the females. There is no actual mating, however, for the males simply deposit packets of sperm which the females then pick up in their genital regions. Male frogs and toads attract their mates with loud calls. The vocal sacs in which the calls are amplified often swell enormously under the throat or from the sides of the neck. The males fertilize the eggs as the females lay them. The eggs, usually laid in water, have no tough coats, but a coating of jelly swells up around them as they make contact with the water. A number of amphibians give birth to active young, however, and some have managed to dispense with the water altogether by passing the entire larval stage inside the egg or even inside the mother's body.

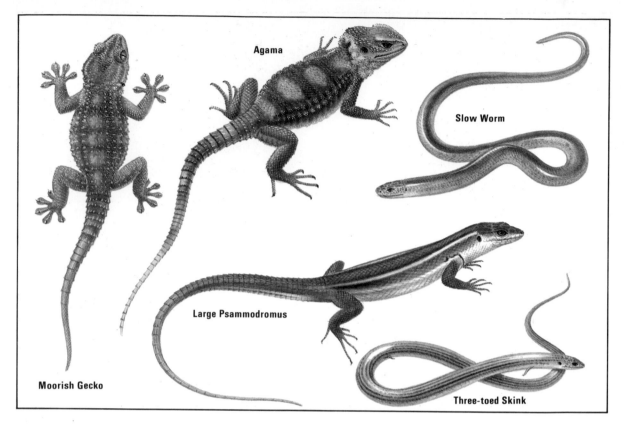

Agama

Slow Worm

Large Psammodromus

Moorish Gecko

Three-toed Skink

Lizards

There are about 3,000 species of lizards. Together with the snakes, they form the Order Squamata. They are mostly rather small and very active reptiles, typically with four legs, although these are reduced in the skinks and some other groups and absent altogether in the slow worms. Geckoes have adhesive pads on their toes, enabling them to climb smooth surfaces and even to run across ceilings. The tail is long in most lizards, but easily shed if the animal is caught by it. It can be re-grown, but rarely becomes as long as the original and often has a different scale pattern. Most lizards are active by day, usually only in sunny weather, and they feed mainly on small insects. The lengths given here are from the snout to the back legs.

MOORISH GECKO
Tarentola mauritanica
Family Gekkonidae
Up to 7 cm: tail about the same length. Pads extend all along the toes. A rather flat greyish-brown body with prominent tubercles.
Habitat: mainly nocturnal, but active by day in cooler months. On rocks and walls and in buildings: often lurks near lights to capture insects. Mediterranean: mainly near the coast.

AGAMA
Agama stellio
Family Agamidae
Up to 12 cm: tail up to 18 cm. Head sometimes yellowish, especially in males. Body flattened, with a well-defined neck which often raises the head' well above the body; head frequently bobs up and down.
Habitat: a sun-loving species found on rocks and tree trunks; often eats flowers and fallen fruit as well as insects. The only member of its family in Europe, it occurs in Greece: often called the Rhodes Dragon.

THREE-TOED SKINK
Chalcides chalcides
Family Scincidae
Up to 20 cm: tail about the same. A slender, cylindrical body clothed with large shiny scales. Tiny 3-toed legs. Sandy to brownish-green, with or without longitudinal stripes. Gives birth to active young – up to 23 at a time.
Habitat: damp meadows with dense herbage. Active by day, but secretive: very fast despite short legs. Eats a wide range of invertebrates. Southern Europe, from Italy westwards.

SLOW WORM
Anguis fragilis
Family Anguidae
Up to 50 cm in total, over half being tail in complete specimens but difficult to see where body ends and tail begins because there are no legs. Tail very fragile and easily broken and hardly grows again. Very smooth and shiny: grey to coppery colour. Female often has stripe along back: male may have blue spots. Easily distinguished from snakes by the presence of eye-lids. Gives birth to active young.
Habitat: damp places with lush vegetation. Spends much time under stones but ventures out at dusk and after rain; rather slow. Eats slugs. Absent from far north, Ireland, and southern Spain.

TYPICAL LIZARDS
Family Lacertidae

Very active diurnal lizards with slender bodies and well developed legs. Large scales clothe the head, which is larger in males than in females. Most numerous in southern Europe, where they revel in the hot, dry summers. Many of these southern species have very restricted distributions.

LARGE PSAMMODROMUS
Psammodromus algirus
Up to 8 cm: tail very long – up to 3 times body length. Scales large and pointed, with prominent keel. Stripes white or yellow. Males often have blue

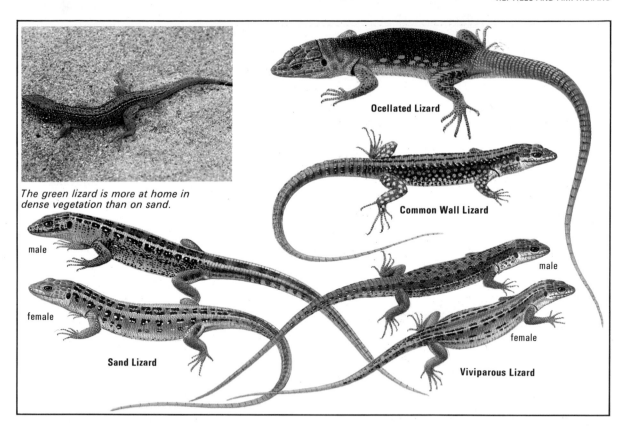

The green lizard is more at home in dense vegetation than on sand.

Ocellated Lizard

Common Wall Lizard

male

female

Sand Lizard

male

female

Viviparous Lizard

spots near the shoulder, and in the breeding season they have orange throat and cheeks.
Habitat: dense scrub: sometimes climbs the bushes but found mainly on the ground. Iberia (the commonest lizard in many places) and southern France.

GREEN LIZARD
Lacerta viridis
Up to 13 cm: tail up to twice body length. Male normally all green with black stippling: blue throat when mature. Female may be green or brown, often blotched and frequently with pale stripes. Scales are strongly keeled.
Habitat: dense vegetation, especially with bushes, which it often climbs. Eats some fruit and even birds' eggs as well as insects. Southern and central Europe: not in Britain or southern Spain. Present in Channel Islands.

OCELLATED LIZARD
Lacerta lepida
Up to 25 cm: tail up to 50 cm. This, the largest European lizard, is easily recognized just by its size when mature. The male has a very large head. Body is sometimes grey or brownish and the blue spots are not always present on the sides. The black stippling often forms distinct patterns on the back. The scales are not strongly keeled. Youngsters are dull green with white spots, often ringed with black.
Habitat: dry, scrubby places, including roadside banks, stone walls and vineyards. Food includes insects, fruit, birds' eggs and nestlings, and other

lizards. Iberia (where it largely replaces the green lizard) and southern France.

SAND LIZARD
Lacerta agilis
Up to 9 cm, but usually somewhat less: tail about 1½ times body length. A stocky species with relatively short legs and a very deep head, especially in the male. The body colour is extremely variable. The typical male has green sides (very bright in the breeding season) and a brown back with a darker central stripe. Both the back and the sides bear dark blotches, but a pale unmarked stripe runs along the upper part of each side. Some males are entirely green, especially in eastern Europe. Females are grey or brown and only rarely have green on the sides. The dark stripe in the middle of the back is usually fragmented. Both sexes may have a plain chestnut back (not in Britain).
Habitat: mainly dry areas, with shorter and less dense vegetation than required by the Green Lizard: rarely climbs. Roadsides, sand dunes, heathland and rough pasture: often high in mountains in the south. From southern Scandinavia to Alps and Pyrenees: local and rare in Britain: absent from Italy and most of Iberia and Greece.

COMMON WALL LIZARD
Podarcis muralis
Up to 8 cm, but usually less: tail up to 2¼ times body length. A rather flattened body and extremely variable in pattern, especially in southern Europe. In western and central Europe it is basically

brown or grey, usually with a thin dark stripe in the middle of the back and often with black and white patches on the sides of the tail. Males tend to be more strongly marked than females, and markings are also heavier in the south. The lizards are often heavily marked with green in Italy and parts of Spain.
Habitat: dry, rocky places, especially sunny banks. Runs on walls, rocks and tree trunks and is the most common lizard around houses. Prefers slightly damper places in the south, often high in the mountains. From southern Holland southwards, but absent from most of Iberia (where replaced by the very similar Iberian Wall Lizard): not in Britain.

VIVIPAROUS LIZARD
Lacerta vivipara
Up to 6·5 cm: tail up to twice body length and relatively stout. Body little flattened, with relatively small head and short legs. Grey, brown, or olive green with a variable pattern of streaks and spots. Underside white, yellow, or brick-red. Normally gives birth to active young, which are bronzy-black, but occasionally lays eggs in southern mountains.
Habitat: dense vegetation in fairly humid climates: grassland, heathland, sand dunes, bogs and moorland, and roadsides. Most of Europe, including the Arctic, but absent from most of Iberia and the Mediterranean region. The commonest lizard in most central and northern regions: also known as the Common Lizard in Britain.

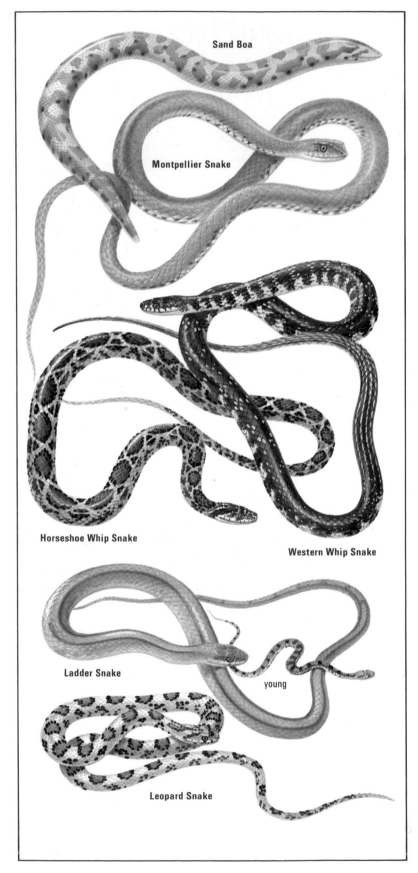

Sand Boa

Montpellier Snake

Horseshoe Whip Snake

Western Whip Snake

Ladder Snake

young

Leopard Snake

Snakes

Although they have no legs, the snakes flourish in many terrestrial and aquatic environments.

With a few exceptions, snakes catch live prey, which they find largely by smell. A snake is continually flicking out its tongue to pick up scent from the surroundings. Most snakes simply grab their prey in their jaws and swallow it. Constricting snakes wind their bodies around the prey and kill it by stopping it from breathing. The venomous snakes kill their prey with poison injected by special teeth (fangs). Prey is swallowed whole, and a snake can actually swallow prey of greater diameter than its own body.

Only 27 of the 2,700 known species of snake live in Europe. The measurements given on these pages are total lengths.

SAND BOA
Eryx jaculus Family Boidae
Up to 80 cm. Stout body and blunt tail. Grey to reddish-brown. The only European member of the family. Gives birth to active young.
Habitat: dry and mainly sandy places. Hunts at night, feeding mainly on small rodents which are caught in their burrows or on the surface and killed by constriction. South-eastern Europe.

COLUBRID SNAKES
Family Colubridae

A very large family containing most of the European snakes. There are large scales on the top of the head. Most species are non-poisonous and simply grab prey in their jaws. A few species are constrictors. Mainly diurnal.

MONTPELLIER SNAKE
Malpolon monspessulanus
Up to 200 cm. Readily identified by prominent ridges running over the large eyes and on to the snout. Grey, brown, olive, or black: often uniform but may have light or dark spots.
Habitat: dry, rocky and scrubby places mainly. Hunts mainly by sight, feeding mostly on lizards, small mammals, and other snakes. Venomous, but fangs are at the back of the mouth and not dangerous to man. Iberia and Mediterranean.

HORSESHOE WHIP SNAKE
Coluber hippocrepis
Up to 150 cm. Slender, with row of very small scales below eye. Ground colour yellow, greenish or reddish but largely obscured by black pattern.

Habitat: dry and rocky places: often around houses. Eats mammals, birds and lizards. Iberia and Sardinia only.

WESTERN WHIP SNAKE
Coluber viridiflavus
Up to 150 cm. Slender, with rather blunt snout. Yellowish-green with black markings: sometimes all black above.
Habitat: dry, rocky and scrubby places. Very fast, eating lizards and small mammals. Mainly France and Italy.

LADDER SNAKE
Elaphe scalaris
Up to 160 cm. Yellowish-grey to brown with 2 darker stripes on back. Named for ladder-like pattern of young.
Habitat: stony and bushy places; climbs well. Feeds mainly on small mammals and nestling birds. Iberia and Mediterranean coast of France.

LEOPARD SNAKE
Elaphe situla
Up to 100 cm. Yellowish or greyish-brown with variable, but very characteristic rust-coloured spots or stripes.
Habitat: mainly stony places, sometimes around buildings. Preys almost entirely on small mammals. South-eastern Europe.

GRASS SNAKE
Natrix natrix
Up to 120 cm (rarely 200 cm). Colour varies, but usually greyish-green, often with black spots, and with a yellowish, cream or orange collar.
Habitat: damp places, including river banks and ditches. Swims well. Feeds largely on frogs and toads. Most of Europe except far north: not Ireland.

VIPERINE SNAKE
Natrix maura
Up to 70 cm (rarely 100 cm). Brown or grey, usually with yellow or orange tinge and 2 rows of dark blotches on the back. May resemble adder, but easily distinguished by round pupil and large head scales.
Habitat: in or near water and in damp meadows. Eats fish and amphibians. South-western Europe.

SMOOTH SNAKE
Coronella austriaca
Up to 80 cm. Greyish to reddish-brown, usually with dark blotches on back: generally a dark stripe from neck, through eye, to nostril. Eye has round pupil. Brings forth active young.
Habitat: dry sunny places. Feeds mainly on lizards and snakes, often subduing them by constriction. Most Europe: southern Britain only.

CAT SNAKE
Telescopus fallax
Up to 80 cm (occasionally over 100 cm). Deep body and broad, flat head. Pupil vertical. Grey or brown, usually with dark collar and blotches on back.
Habitat: rough and stony places. Hunts mainly at dusk, feeding largely on lizards. Venomous fangs at back of mouth: not dangerous to man. South-eastern Europe.

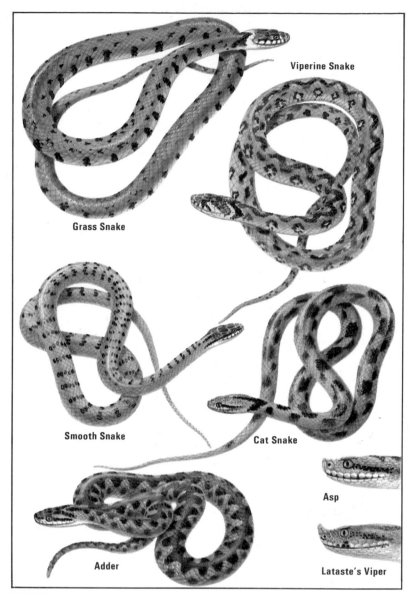

Viperine Snake

Grass Snake

Smooth Snake

Cat Snake

Adder

Asp

Lataste's Viper

VIPERS
Family Viperidae

Venomous snakes with large, erectile fangs at front of mouth. The only dangerous snakes in Europe. Heavy-bodied and relatively slow-moving. Pupil vertical. Head scales small. Most give birth to active young. There are seven European species.

ADDER
Vipera berus
Up to 70 cm (rarely 90 cm). Also known as the Common viper. Usually a clear dark zig-zag stripe along the back — especially prominent in males, which tend to have pale grey ground colour. Females often brownish and stripe less obvious. Some individuals are black. In Iberia, zig-zag may be replaced by a straight brown stripe with dark spots on each side.
Habitat: very varied, but generally heathland in north and on mountains further south. Mainly diurnal, feeding on small mammals and lizards. Most of Europe, including the Arctic, but not Ireland or Mediterranean.

ASP
Vipera aspis
Up to 75 cm (usually under 60 cm). Similar to Adder in appearance and habits, but distinguished by up-turned snout. More venomous than adder.
Habitat: very varied, from high mountains to coast. Pyrenees, Alps, Italy and most of France.

LATASTE'S VIPER
Vipera latasti
Up to 60 cm. Similar to last two species but with distinct nose horn.
Habitat: rocky hillsides and open woods. Iberia only.

Hermann's Tortoise

European Pond Terrapin

Stripe-necked Terrapin

Tortoises and Terrapins

The reptiles in this very ancient group (Order Chelonia), which has existed almost unchanged for over 200 million years, are easily recognized by the box-like shells in which they live. The shell is composed largely of bony plates, and there are two main parts – a domed carapace on the top and a flatter plastron underneath. The two parts are normally joined along the middle of each side, with gaps for the head, legs and tail. Head and limbs can be retracted when danger threatens. The carapace is decorated with a number of horny plates (tortoiseshell), whose pattern is characteristic for each species. The name tortoise is usually used for terrestrial forms, while freshwater species are often called terrapins and the marine species are usually called turtles. The tortoises are essentially vegetarians, while the terrapins and turtles are mainly carnivorous. None has any teeth, but a horny beak serves the same function. All species lay eggs. The sexes are much alike, but males have longer tails and slightly concave plastrons, allowing them to mount the females more easily.

HERMANN'S TORTOISE
Testudo hermanni
Family Testudinidae
Up to 20 cm long and strongly domed. It differs from the two other European tortoises in having a large scale on the tip of the tail and usually two shell plates immediately above the base of the tail: the others have no scale on the tail and just one plate above it.

Habitat: very varied: dry or moist with dense vegetation. Mediterranean.

EUROPEAN POND TERRAPIN
Emys orbicularis
Family Emydidae
Up to 30 cm long. Black or dark brown, usually with yellowish spots and streaks.

Habitat: still and slow-moving water with plenty of submerged and emergent vegetation. Basks at water's edge; dives when disturbed. Eats fishes, amphibians and various invertebrates. South and central Europe: not in Britain.

STRIPE-NECKED TERRAPIN
Mauremys caspica
Up to 20 cm long. Flattened and rather oval like the previous species but with a central keel — at least in hind region. Lighter than previous species, but fewer markings except that the neck bears prominent yellow stripes.
Habitat: like that of *Emys*, but often in larger bodies of water. Both species, which are the only European terrapins, will tolerate brackish waters. Iberia and south-east Europe.

Right: A common frog resting on a waterside rock. Only in the breeding season does the frog spend any length of time in the water. At other times it inhabits damp vegetation and rocky areas close to the water where it can find plenty of small invertebrates to eat.

Painted Frog

Yellow-bellied Toad

eggs

Common Spadefoot

Midwife Toad

Parsley Frog

eggs

Common Toad

Natterjack

Green Toad

Frogs and Toads

Frogs and toads (Order Anura) are tailless amphibians with squat bodies and long back legs. In common parlance, smooth-skinned species are usually called frogs, while rougher-skinned species are called toads, but many families contain both smooth and warty species and the common names do not necessarily signify any relationship. Tree frogs, for example, are more closely related to the common toad than to the common frog. Toads tend to live in drier places than frogs and they have better-developed lungs. All capture living prey, such as worms, slugs and insects; most catch it with a long, sticky tongue which is fired out at great speed. There are about 25 species in Europe, all with the typical life history involving free-swimming tadpoles. Females are usually larger than males.

MIDWIFE TOAD
Alytes obstetricus
Family Discoglossidae
Up to 5 cm. Plump; grey, green, or brown. Vertical pupil. Tongue is disc-shaped in this family and cannot be fired out. Male carries string of eggs wrapped round hind legs and enters water when they are ready to hatch.
Habitat: mainly on land, in varied places, including gardens. Mainly nocturnal. Western Europe from Germany southwards: introduced into Britain.

YELLOW-BELLIED TOAD
Bombina variegata
Up to 5 cm. Rather flattened, with orange or yellow underside which is displayed when alarmed. Pupil round, triangular or heart-shaped.
Habitat: stays mainly in shallow water. Mainly diurnal. South and central Europe: not Iberia or Britain.

PAINTED FROG
Discoglossus pictus
7 cm. Plump and shiny, rather like common frog but pupil is round or triangular. Colour varies from grey to brick red, usually with pale-edged dark spots.
Habitat: stays mainly in or close to water. Active day and night. Iberia, south-west France, Sicily, Malta.

COMMON SPADEFOOT
Pelobates fuscus
Family Pelobatidae
Up to 8 cm. Smooth-skinned with large eyes, vertical pupils and a swelling on top of head. A pale projection (the spade) on each hind leg is used for digging burrows. Colour and pattern very variable.

Habitat: sandy ground, including cultivated land. Strictly nocturnal outside breeding season. Central Europe: not in Britain. Western Spadefoot of south-west Europe is similar, but has black spade.

PARSLEY FROG
Pelodytes punctatus
Up to 5 cm. Long-legged and named for bright green decoration on warty grey back. Pupil vertical.
Habitat: shrubby vegetation: agile and climbs well. Nocturnal, resting under stones by day. South-west Europe, from Belgium southwards.

COMMON TOAD
Bufo bufo
Family Bufonidae
Up to 15 cm (usually less). Very warty, usually some shade of brown: pale below. Pupil horizontal.
Habitat: a wide variety of places, often quite dry. Mainly nocturnal. Walks rather than leaps, except when disturbed. As in all members of the family, eggs are laid in long strings. Most of Europe: not in Ireland.

NATTERJACK
Bufo calamita
8 cm. Brown, grey or greenish, usually with clear yellow stripe on back. Pupil horizontal.
Habitat: varied, but usually sandy places in north. Often in brackish pools by sea. Nocturnal. South-west and central Europe: rare in Britain.

GREEN TOAD
Bufo viridis
Up to 10 cm. Easily identified by colour pattern. Has shrill, warbling song.
Habitat: varied, often quite dry. Not uncommon around buildings. Mainly eastern Europe, including Italy and Denmark.

COMMON TREE FROG
Hyla arborea
Family Hylidae
Up to 5 cm. Usually bright green, but sometimes brownish and may be blotchy. A brown stripe on each side. Toes have suction pads, allowing them to cling to shiny leaves. Male has enormous vocal sac which swells like a balloon under chin when calling.
Habitat: bushes and other dense vegetation near water: very agile and climbs well. Mainly nocturnal. Southern and central Europe: introduced into Britain.

COMMON FROG
Rana temporaria
Family Ranidae
Up to 10 cm. Grey, brown, pink or yellow with darker blotches. Always a dark patch enclosing eye and eardrum, although this feature is shared with several similar species. Horizontal pupil and clear fold along each side of the back are typical of the family. Eggs laid in masses.
Habitat: damp vegetation: rarely in water outside breeding season. All Europe except Iberia and Mediterranean.

The stripeless tree frog (Hyla meridionalis) lives in southern Europe and lacks the brown stripe of the common tree frog.

eggs

tadpole

Edible Frog

Common Frog

Common Tree Frog

Marsh Frog

EDIBLE FROG
Rana esculenta
Up to 12 cm. Green or brown with dark spots, but no dark eye-patch. Vocal sacs bulge from each side of the throat: very noisy.
Habitat: largely aquatic, even out of breeding season. Active day and night. Southern and central Europe but not Iberia: southern Britain only.

MARSH FROG
Rana ridibunda
Up to 15 cm. Similar to the previous species but darker: often brown. Very noisy, with vocal sacs at side of throat.
Habitat: usually in or near water all year. Active day and night. Southern and central Europe: introduced in Britain.

Marbled Newt

Warty Newt

Palmate Newt

male

tadpole

Smooth Newt

egg

female

A male alpine newt, showing the unspotted belly typical of this species.

Newts and Salamanders

Newts and salamanders (Order Caudata) are tailed amphibians. Some salamanders breed in water, but the animals are largely terrestrial and some have dispensed with the free-living tadpole stage. They inhabit damp places and forage for small invertebrates at night. Outside the breeding season, the newts behave much like the salamanders, but they all return to the water to breed. Males become very colourful at this time and display themselves in front of the females, who lay their eggs singly on water plants and wrap the leaves around them. Unlike the anuran tadpoles, newt tadpoles keep their feathery gills until they leave the water and, because the adults have tails, there is a much less dramatic change between larval and adult state. Newt tadpoles are entirely carnivorous, whereas those of frogs and toads eat a good deal of vegetable matter.

There are 20 species in Europe, the 9 described here all belonging to the Family Salamandridae.

MARBLED NEWT
Triturus marmoratus
Up to 15 cm. Easily identified by its colour. Female lacks crest, as in all newts, and has a yellow stripe along the back. Male has no crest outside breeding season. Skin velvety on land.
Habitat: breeds in weedy pools but may wander far from water outside breeding season. Iberia and western France.

WARTY NEWT
Triturus cristatus
Up to 14 cm. Breeding male dark grey with black spots and a spiky crest. Female and non-breeding male appear jet black. Yellow or orange below. Coarse, warty skin.
Habitat: may stay in weedy pools all year, but often on land in summer. Most Europe, but not Iberia or Ireland.

PALMATE NEWT
Triturus helveticus
Up to 9 cm. Pale brown or sometimes greenish, with or without spots. Female and non-breeding male may be confused with smooth newt, but distinguished by unspotted throat. Breeding male has low, smooth crest on back and a higher one on the tail: latter ends abruptly in a small filament.
Habitat: breeds in still, clear water. Western Europe: not in Ireland.

SMOOTH NEWT
Triturus vulgaris
Up to 11 cm. Smooth-skinned, dry and velvety on land. Female and non-breeding male pale brown, often with 2 darker stripes on the back. Breeding male heavily spotted on the back and with a large, continuous, wavy crest on back and tail.
Habitat: breeds in still water with plenty of weeds, including garden ponds. Non-breeders roam far from water in a wide variety of habitats. Most Europe except south west and far north.

ALPINE NEWT
Triturus alpestris
Up to 12 cm. Similar to Smooth Newt, but orange or yellow underside is rarely spotted. Breeding male has a yellowish crest, much lower and smoother than in the previous species.
Habitat: aquatic for much of the year in cool, clear pools. Sometimes on land, but rarely far from water. Alps, Pyrenees and much of central Europe (often at low level): not in Britain.

FIRE SALAMANDER
Salamandra salamandra
Up to 20 cm (rarely 25 cm). A slow-moving species easily recognized by its colour, although spots may be quite small or even run together to form stripes. No other European species has similar coloration. Colours warn of unpleasant skin secretion. Pairs on land in summer, but eggs are kept in female's body until the spring: only then does she go to the water. The eggs have hatched by this time and she dips her hind end into the water to allow the young to swim away. In some areas female retains young in her body until they have turned into miniature adults: she never goes to the water.
Habitat: mainly damp upland woods. Southern and central Europe: not in Britain.

SPECTACLED SALAMANDER
Salamandrina terdigitata
Up to 11 cm. Dull black or brown above with red or yellow patch on head. Undersides of adult legs and tail bright red and exposed if alarmed. Four toes on hind foot (all other European species have five).
Habitat: dense vegetation on wooded mountain slopes, usually near streams. Breeds in water. Confined to Italy.

ALPINE SALAMANDER
Salamandra atra
Up to 16 cm. All black, often with a prominent ribbed appearance.
Habitat: forests and damp meadows, usually between 800 and 2000 metres up in the mountains. Mainly nocturnal, but often about after rain in the day-time. Gives birth to miniature adults and never needs to return to the water. Alps and northern Yugoslavia.

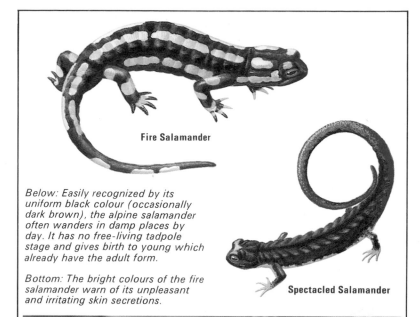

Fire Salamander

Spectacled Salamander

Below: Easily recognized by its uniform black colour (occasionally dark brown), the alpine salamander often wanders in damp places by day. It has no free-living tadpole stage and gives birth to young which already have the adult form.

Bottom: The bright colours of the fire salamander warn of its unpleasant and irritating skin secretions.

Chapter Four
Fishes

The general term fishes covers three very different groups of aquatic animals: the lampreys and hagfishes (Superclass Agnatha), the sharks and rays (Class Chondrichthyes) and the bony fishes (Class Osteichthyes). The last two classes belong to the Superclass Gnathostomata and so, while all three groups are very distinct, the sharks and rays and the bony fishes are more closely related to one another than either group is to the lampreys.

The lampreys have no jaws and they feed mostly as blood-suckers. They have no vertebrae, the backbone being a cartilaginous rod called a notochord. The rest of the skeleton is also made of cartilage.

The sharks and rays and the bony fishes have jaws and most feed by eating smaller animals, although some are specialized for other diets. Sharks and rays have no bone in their skeletons, which are made of cartilage although a chalky inclusion often makes it look like bone. They also have a series of separate gill slits, through which water passes out during breathing movements. Bony fishes have skeletons of real bone and their gills are concealed by a flap-like gill-cover with a single opening at the rear.

Fins
Among the most distinctive features of a fish are its fins, which are primarily designed to assist in swimming, although some fins serve other functions. Lampreys have only two simple fins – a flap of cartilage-supported tissue on the back (the dorsal fin), and another under the tail (the anal fin). The fins of sharks are more complicated; there are often two dorsal fins and usually an anal fin, together with two pairs of fins at the sides – one pair behind the head (pectoral fins) and another pair on the belly (pelvic fins) – and a well-developed tail fin with the tail running up the upper lobe. All the fins contain cartilaginous supports.

The fins of bony fishes are more complex still, although most of these fishes retain the dorsal, tail, anal, pectoral and pelvic fins seen in the sharks. Most species have strong spines in the fins – very well developed in the perch, for example – and all support the fins with bony rays, although the trout and some other fishes have an adipose fin on the back without any

skeleton. The fins are generally more mobile than among the sharks, but some bony fishes have lost certain fins during their evolution. Eels, for example, have no pelvic fins.

Scales
The scales are another obvious feature of fishes. They are best developed in the bony fishes, although some species, including the wels and the sea horse, have none. The scales form a protective covering, but as they are fixed only at the front end they do not prevent the fish from flexing its body as it swims. They are actually covered by a very thin skin which produces the slightly antiseptic slime so characteristic of fishes and provides a first defence against infection.

Senses
Many fishes have small holes in a series of scales down each side of the body – or pores in the skin if they are scaleless. These openings lead to special sense organs, unique to fishes and some amphibians, which can detect pressure changes in the surrounding water and alert the fish to approaching prey or predators, or to any obstruction in its path. Pores are also present on the head and the whole system is known as the lateral line.

The senses of smell, taste and touch are far more highly developed in fishes than in our own bodies. Hearing is also good in many species, although they are adapted to an underwater life, and many fishes can produce sounds – often quite loud – for communication. Vision is good in those fishes that live in shallow, well-lit habitats, and many species can see in colour.

In general, fishes are well organized for life in the sea and in fresh water and, with about 20,000 known species, they have proved to be the most successful group of vertebrate animals. Unless otherwise stated, the species described here occur in suitable habitats throughout the region. The sizes given are recorded maximum lengths.

Right: a typical bony fish showing the main external features.

Left: A perch putting all its fins into operation for a mid-water manoeuvre. The bony fin-rays are clearly seen, including the spines at the front of the dorsal fin, and the lateral line is very well marked.

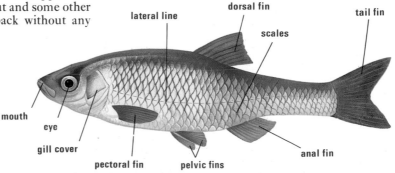

Freshwater Fishes

LAMPREY FAMILY
Petromyzonidae

One of the two living groups of jawless vertebrates, with about 30 species, mostly in fresh water. The mouth is a circular suction pad, with teeth in adults. Some species are blood-sucking parasites of other fishes. All feed on minute organisms in the mud when young.

LAMPERN
Lampetra fluviatilis
50 cm. Grey or greeny-brown on back, yellowish or white ventrally. Two dorsal fins.

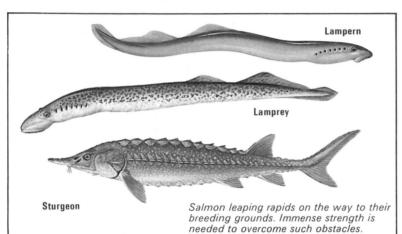

Lampern

Lamprey

Sturgeon

Salmon leaping rapids on the way to their breeding grounds. Immense strength is needed to overcome such obstacles.

Habitat: young spend 5 years in muddy river bed, then migrate to sea. Adults move up-river August-November, spawning on shingle beds in April. They attack estuarine and freshwater fishes.

LAMPREY
Petromyzon marinus
91 cm. Olive or yellow, heavily mottled with black on the back; pale underneath. Two dorsal fins.
Habitat: young are blind and spend 5 years in muddy river bed; then migrate to sea. Adults are parasitic on a wide range of sea and estuarine fishes. They spawn May-June on pebble beds in the rivers.

STURGEON FAMILY
Acipenseridae

STURGEON
Acipenser sturio
3·5 m for females; males smaller. 5 rows of bony plates on body; upper lobe of tail longer; mouth small and tubular, with 2 pairs of barbels.
Habitat: breeds in large rivers May-June. The young live in fresh water for 3 years and then go to sea. Adults return to the sea after spawning. Feeds on bottom-living animals. Rare in Europe, breeding in only a few southern rivers; more common in the Black Sea.

SALMON FAMILY
Salmonidae

Native to the northern hemisphere, these fishes live in the sea and in fresh water, but all breed in fresh water. They have a scaleless head and all have a fleshy adipose fin on the back between the dorsal and tail fins. None of the fin rays is spiny.

SALMON
Salmo salar
1·5 m. Very narrow just in front of tail fin: upper jaw reaches to rear edge of eye. Young fish (parr) have 8-11 dark smudges on each side.
Habitat: eggs are laid in river gravel in mid-winter. Parr live in river for 3 years, then migrate to sea as smolts. After 1-4 years in sea, feeding on fishes and crustaceans, then return to the rivers they were born in to spawn.

BROWN TROUT
Salmo trutta
1·4 m. Body deep just before tail fin: upper jaw reaches beyond eye.
Habitat: eggs are laid in river gravel in winter. Some brown trout live permanently in rivers but others move to lakes or the sea (sea trout).

RAINBOW TROUT
Salmo gairdneri
1 m. Heavily spotted with rainbow stripe along each side.
Habitat: a North American fish introduced to Europe in lakes and rivers.

ARCTIC CHARR
Salvelinus alpinus
1 m. Scales minute; pectoral, pelvic, and anal fins reddish with light margins.
Habitat: mostly mountainous lakes (where rarely over 25 cm long); in rivers and sea in Scandinavia.

The following four fishes were once included in the Salmon family, but they differ in small details and are now placed in three separate families.

POWAN
Coregonus lavaretus
Family Coregonidae
70 cm. Blunt-snouted, upper jaw longer than lower.
Habitat: mountain lakes in Britain and the Alps (where no more than 20 cm) and in the Baltic Sea.

VENDACE
Coregonus albula
35 cm. Lower jaw longer than upper.
Habitat: mountain lakes in Britain and Europe, and around the Baltic Sea.

SMELT
Osmerus eperlanus
Family Osmeridae
30 cm. With large fragile scales and large, strongly-toothed jaws. Smells strongly of cucumber.
Habitat: northern Europe only. Breeds in spring in rivers on sand or gravel within tidal influence and generally migrates to the sea and estuaries for the winter.

GRAYLING
Thymallus thymallus
Family Thymallidae
50 cm. Stout bodied with large scales and a large dorsal fin.
Habitat: cool, clean clear streams, often in fast-flowing water. Also in large mountain lakes. Spawns in spring in gravelly shallows; the colourful male displays to the female.

PIKE FAMILY
Esocidae

PIKE
Esox lucius
1·5 m. Powerful body with a large mouth and big teeth in the lower jaw only. Dorsal and anal fins near tail.
Habitat: lakes and rivers, usually close to weed beds from which it charges at passing fishes in daytime. Spawns in early spring at the water's edge.

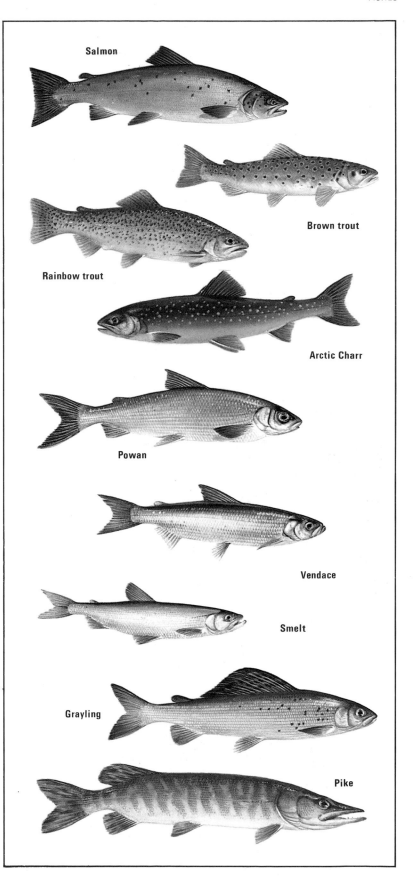

Salmon

Brown trout

Rainbow trout

Arctic Charr

Powan

Vendace

Smelt

Grayling

Pike

CARP FAMILY
Cyprinidae

One of the largest families of fishes, and the dominant freshwater family in most parts of the world. Mostly scaly fishes with no spines in their fins, scaleless heads, and toothless jaws.

ROACH
Rutilus rutilus
53 cm. Deep-bodied, with dorsal fin origin above the pelvic fin base. Eye and pelvic and anal fins reddish.
Habitat: abundant in lakes and in slow-moving rivers throughout Europe. Feeds on whatever insect larvae, crustaceans or snails are common locally. Spawns April-June; the yellow eggs are shed on plants in shallow water and hatch in 9-12 days.

MODERLIESCHEN
Leucaspius delineatus
12 cm. Slender-bodied, with a small head, large eyes, and a steeply-angled mouth. Scales thin and fragile. Lateral line is incomplete.
Habitat: a small schooling fish living in lakes, ponds and sometimes in slow-flowing rivers. Spawns in summer, the eggs being looped in strands round water plants. Not in Britain.

IDE
Leuciscus idus
1 m. Slender body, with humped back and broad head; scales small.
Habitat: not native to Britain, but widespread in Europe in lower reaches of rivers and large lowland lakes; eats aquatic invertebrates.

DACE
Leuciscus leuciscus
30 cm. Slender bodied with a narrow head; scales moderately large; anal fin concave.
Habitat: widespread in clean small rivers and brooks, in moderate current. Swims in schools, feeding on insect larvae and often taking adults at the surface. Spawns in early spring in gravel shallows.

ASP
Aspius aspius
70 cm. Compressed body with a sharp keel on belly; head pointed, with a prominent lower jaw.
Habitat: lowland rivers and lakes in central Europe, migrating into the Black and Caspian Seas. Eats small fishes and invertebrates.

CHUB
Leuciscus cephalus
61 cm. Slender body, but broad across the head and back; scales large; anal fin rounded.
Habitat: rivers, usually with moderate current; also in large lakes. Eats aquatic invertebrates and small fishes.

NASE
Chondrostoma nasus
50 cm. Slender-bodied, with a small head and protuberant snout; mouth small with hard horny lips.
Habitat: confined to mainland Europe and most abundant in swift-flowing rivers. Forms large schools and feeds on algae growing on rocks and other surfaces, including other plants.

RUDD
Scardinius erythrophthalmus
45 cm. Deep-bodied, with a small head and steeply-angled mouth. Dorsal fin placed behind level of pelvic fins; a sharp keel on the belly. Eye is golden; the pelvic and anal fins blood-red.
Habitat: lakes and backwaters of rivers, swimming in schools near the surface. Feeds on crustaceans and insects, often taking adults at the surface. Spawns April-June, the eggs sticking to plants.

MINNOW
Phoxinus phoxinus
12 cm. Round-bodied with a short, broad head; scales minute. Breeding males have red bellies and black throats.
Habitat: small clean rivers; rarely in large lakes. Forms large schools in shallow water, and spawns in spring over stones. Feeds on insect larvae and crustaceans. Lives in deeper water in winter.

TENCH
Tinca tinca
70 cm. Thickset fish with rounded fins and a deep tail. One pair of barbels at corners of mouth. Scales very small. Body with thick slime layer.
Habitat: slow-flowing rivers, canals and lakes, usually among water plants near the bottom. Buries in mud in winter; can survive high temperatures and low oxygen levels in summer. Feeds on molluscs and insect larvae.

GUDGEON
Gobio gobio
20 cm. Rather round-bodied with a large head; mouth ventral with a pair of barbels. Scales moderately large, 38-44 in lateral line.
Habitat: mainly a river fish of moderately fast currents, but also in slow-moving water and lakes. Lives on the bottom in small schools, and eats various invertebrates.

BITTERLING
Rhodeus sericeus
9 cm. Rather deep-bodied with large scales; the lateral line extends only to 5 or 6 scales. Pinkish on the sides, with a metallic blue streak; males are brighter.
Habitat: native only in mainland Europe, but introduced to England. Lives in still and slow-moving water, feeding mainly on planktonic crustaceans. Female uses her long egg-laying tube to deposit a few eggs inside the gill chamber of a freshwater mussel. The eggs develop inside the mussel.

BLEAK
Alburnus alburnus
20 cm. Slender and bright silvery, with compressed sides and a sharp keel on belly; anal fin long-based.
Habitat: very common in rivers, in large schools near the surface. Across Europe, but only in eastern England. Feeds on planktonic animals, especially crustaceans, and insects at the water's surface.

BARBEL
Barbus barbus
90 cm. Round in cross-section although belly is flattened. Mouth ventral, lips fleshy; 2 pairs of long barbels.
Habitat: lowland rivers with moderate currents and a sandy or gravelly bottom; particularly common in weir pools. Feeds on bottom-living invertebrates, particularly insect larvae, worms and molluscs. Breeds on river gravel in late spring.

CRUCIAN CARP
Carassius carassius
51 cm. Deep-bodied; long-based dorsal fin has a convex edge. Head small with no barbels.
Habitat: overgrown pools and lakes and river backwaters; very resistant to low oxygen levels and high and low temperatures. Feeds on plants, insect larvae and water snails. Spawns May-June; the golden eggs stick to water plants; the fry stay attached to the plants for the first few days.

CARP
Cyprinus carpio
1 m. Heavy-bodied; long-based dorsal fin with a concave edge. Head rather large; 4 barbels on the lips.
Habitat: lowland lakes and slow-moving rivers with much vegetation. Feeds mainly on bottom-living insect larvae and snails, also some plant material. Eggs are attached to water plants in spring. Native to eastern Europe; introduced to Britain and western Europe.

SILVER BREAM
Blicca bjoerkna
25 cm. Moderately deep-bodied with flattened sides. Anal fin long-based, with 22-24 rays. Eyes large. Pelvic fins reddish.
Habitat: slow-flowing lowland rivers, lakes and reservoirs, often among vegetation. Eats plants and bottom-living insect larvae, crustaceans and molluscs. The yellow eggs are attached to plants in summer.

COMMON BREAM
Abramis brama
80 cm. Deep-bodied with a high back, flat sides, and a sharp keel under the belly. Anal fin long-based with 25-31 rays. Eye moderately large.
Habitat: abundant in lakes and slow-flowing lowland rivers. Lives in schools and, in a head-down posture, uses its tubular mouth to pick insect larvae, worms and molluscs out of the mud.

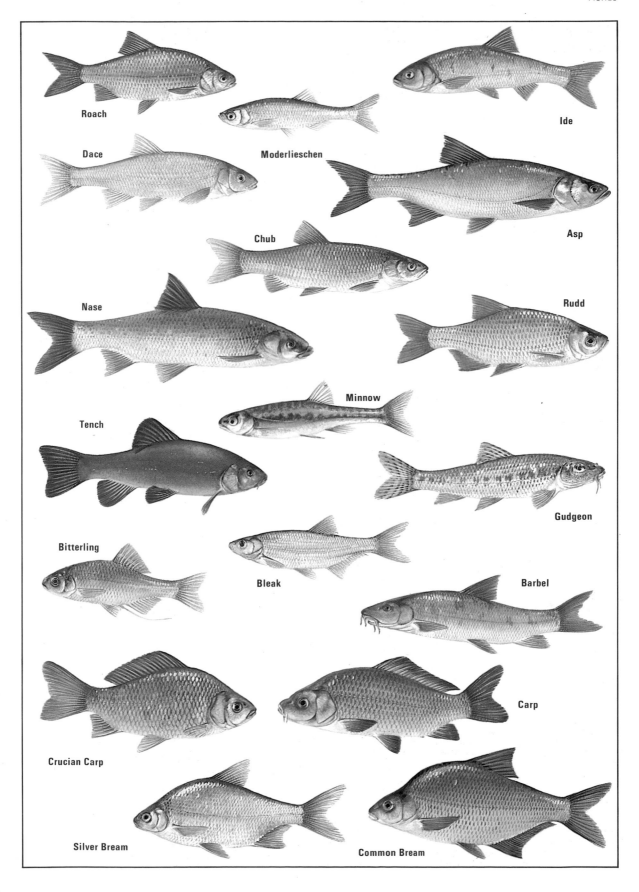

Roach

Ide

Dace

Moderlieschen

Asp

Chub

Nase

Rudd

Minnow

Tench

Gudgeon

Bitterling

Bleak

Barbel

Crucian Carp

Carp

Silver Bream

Common Bream

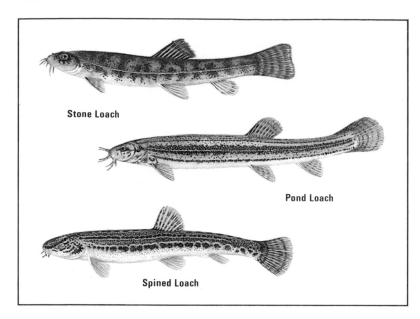

Stone Loach

Pond Loach

Spined Loach

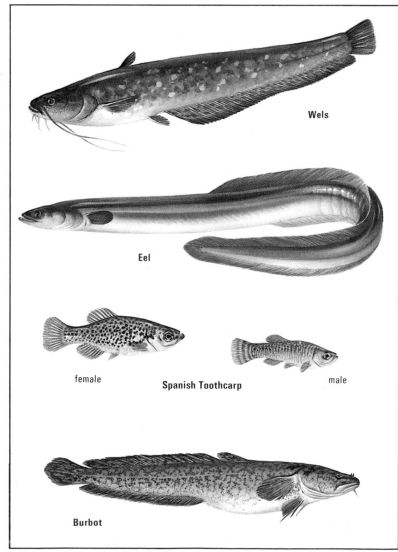

Wels

Eel

female

Spanish Toothcarp

male

Burbot

LOACH FAMILY
Cobitidae

A family of freshwater fishes, related to the carps. Slender and small, they burrow in the bottom; most have barbels round mouth.

STONE LOACH
Noemacheilus barbatulus
15 cm. 6 barbels; no spine under eye.
Habitat: streams and shallow rivers with stony bottoms and dense weed beds. Active at night and on dull days; feeds on bottom-living crustaceans and worms.

POND LOACH
Misgurnus fossilis
15 cm. 5 pairs of barbels.
Habitat: lowland ponds, marshes, and river backwaters with dense weed and mud; breathes air. Not in Britain.

SPINED LOACH
Cobitis taenia
11 cm. Very compressed sides; head small with very small barbels; sharp spine under each eye.
Habitat: slow-flowing rivers; buries in the mud and weed on the bottom. Active mostly at night.

CATFISH FAMILY
Siluridae

WELS
Silurus glanis
3 m. Head broad; 2 long barbels on upper lip, 2 pairs under chin.
Habitat: lowland rivers and lakes. Native to Europe; introduced to England. Mainly nocturnal; eats fishes, amphibians and water birds.

EEL FAMILY
Anguillidae

EEL
Anguilla anguilla
1 m. Female larger than male. Lower jaw projecting. Dorsal, tail and anal fins joined.
Habitat: rivers and lakes. Feeds on insect larvae, crustaceans and dead fish; mainly nocturnal. Can wriggle some distance over land.

TOOTHCARP FAMILY
Cyprinodontidae

SPANISH TOOTHCARP
Aphanius iberus
5 cm. Dorsal and anal fins opposite.
Habitat: coastal regions of Spain; in ditches and brackish lagoons. Feeds on small crustaceans.

CODFISH FAMILY
Gadidae

BURBOT
Lota lota
1 m. 2 dorsal fins, the second long.

Head broad with a chin barbel.
Habitat: lowland rivers and large lakes. Mainly nocturnal. Feeds on fishes, crustaceans and bottom-living insect larvae. Probably extinct in England.

PERCH FAMILY
Percidae

Freshwater fishes native to the northern hemisphere. All have 2 dorsal fins, the first with sharp spines, and an anal fin with 2 spines at the front.

PERCH
Perca fluviatilis
51 cm. Dark bars on sides; black spot at rear of first dorsal fin.
Habitat: lowland rivers, lakes, and ponds, usually in small schools close to tree roots or weed beds. Eats crustaceans and insect larvae when young; fishes when older.

ZANDER
Stizostedion lucioperca
1·3 m. Long-bodied; head pointed with several large fangs in jaws.
Habitat: lowland rivers. Native to eastern Europe, introduced to western Europe and England. Hunts in schools, feeding on smaller fishes.

RUFFE
Gymnocephalus cernuus
30 cm. Dorsal fins joined together; first 11-16 rays spiny.
Habitat: native to continental Europe and eastern England. Abundant in lowland lakes and slow-flowing rivers. Feeds close to the bottom, mainly on burrowing insect larvae and worms.

BULLHEAD FAMILY
Cottidae

BULLHEAD
Cottus gobio
17 cm. Broad flattened head with a short spine on gill cover.
Habitat: streams, small rivers, and lakes with stony beds; usually hides under stones or in dense weed beds. Lays eggs in cavities under stones.

STICKLEBACK FAMILY
Gasterosteidae

NINE-SPINED STICKLEBACK
Pungitius pungitius
7 cm. 8-10 short spines on back; tail long and narrow.
Habitat: ponds and rivers with dense vegetation and minimal flow. Nest built in plant stems in early summer.

THREE-SPINED STICKLEBACK
Gasterosteus aculeatus
10 cm. 2-3 long spines on back; tail deep and short.
Habitat: rivers, streams and ponds; the sea in the north. Nest built of plant fibres on the bottom.

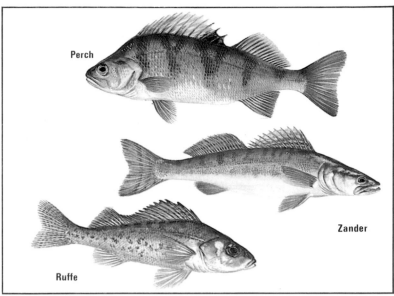

Three-spined sticklebacks, with male (bottom) in breeding dress. He displays his red belly to the female during his courtship dance. He also builds a nest for the eggs.

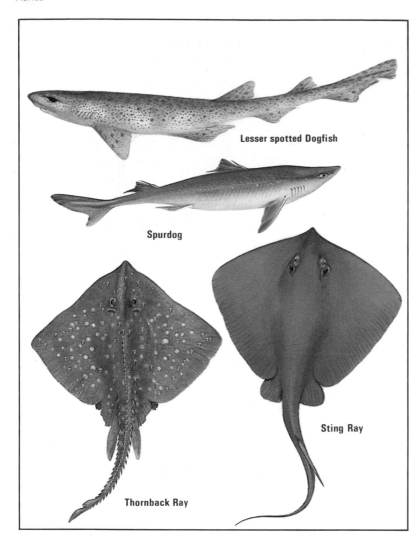

Lesser spotted Dogfish

Spurdog

Thornback Ray

Sting Ray

Coastal Fishes

CARTILAGINOUS FISHES

LESSER SPOTTED DOGFISH
Scyliorhinus canicula
Family Scyliorhinidae
1 m. Nostrils with large flaps with a small gap in between.
Habitat: sandy or gravel bottoms in shallow water. Lays eggs in long, leathery cases attached to seaweed.

SPURDOG
Squalus acanthias Family Squalidae
1·2 m. Long sharp spine before each dorsal fin; no anal fin.
Habitat: common mid-water shark in depths of 10-200 m. Feeds on small schooling fishes and hunts in packs. Gives birth to live young.

THORNBACK RAY
Raja clavata Family Rajidae
85 cm. Large thorns on tail and body.
Habitat: mostly on mud, sand and shingle in shallow water. Feeds on crabs and bottom-living fishes.

STING RAY
Dasyatis pastinaca Family Dasyatidae
1·4 m. No dorsal fin; serrated venomous spine at base of long tail.
Habitat: bottom-living, mainly on sand or mud. Feeds on crustaceans and molluscs.

BONY FISHES

ANCHOVY
Engraulis encrasicolus
Family Engraulidae
20 cm. Rounded snout; large jaws giving an enormous gape.
Habitat: in schools near the surface, feeding on planktonic animals. Migratory; a summer visitor in north.

HERRING
Clupea harengus Family Clupeidae
43 cm. Flat-sided with a rounded belly; dorsal fin origin above pelvics.
Habitat: in schools in the surface waters and migrating considerable distances. Feeds on plankton, chiefly crustaceans and fishes.

GARFISH
Belone belone Family Belonidae
93 cm. Long jaws with moderately large teeth.
Habitat: surface-living and migratory; inshore summer and autumn. Eats fishes, squid and crustaceans.

CONGER
Conger conger Family Congridae
2·7 m. Upper jaw longer; pectoral fins pointed.
Habitat: among rocks on shore and in wrecks and pier pilings; hidden in crevices and hunting mainly by night. Feeds on crabs and other crustaceans, octopus and fishes. Breeds in deep water in tropical Atlantic. Young are thin and transparent and drift at the surface.

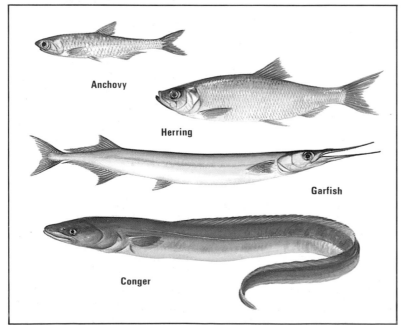

Anchovy

Herring

Garfish

Conger

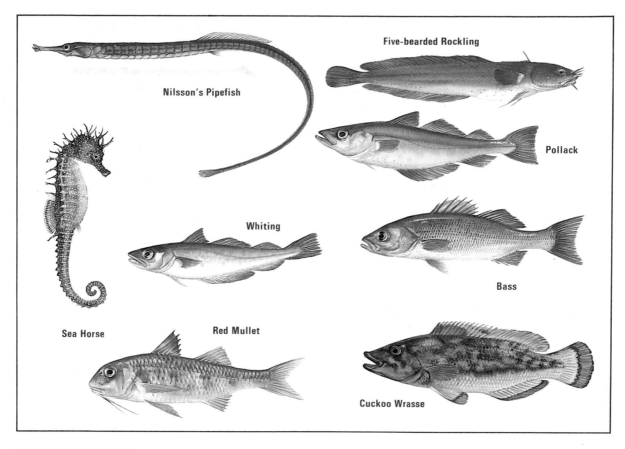

Nilsson's Pipefish

Five-bearded Rockling

Pollack

Sea Horse

Whiting

Bass

Red Mullet

Cuckoo Wrasse

NILSSON'S PIPEFISH
Syngnathus rostellatus
Family Syngnathidae
17 cm. Body rings distinct, 13-17 rings between pectoral and anal fins; tail fins present.
Habitat: common on sandy bottoms in shallow water in northern Europe; also among floating seaweed and eel grass, especially in estuaries. Breeds in spring; the male carries eggs in brood pouch under the tail. Young about 14 mm at birth. Feeds on small crustaceans and larval fish.

SEA HORSE
Hippocampus ramulosus
15 cm. Head set at angle to body; no tail fin. Snout long, more than a third of head length.
Habitat: lives among seaweed and eel grass in shallow water, but also in the open sea. Found mostly in the Bay of Biscay and the Mediterranean, but ocean currents occasionally carry it northwards to British and northern waters. Breeds in summer; males carry eggs and new-born young in brood pouch on tail. Feeds on small crustaceans.

FIVE-BEARDED ROCKLING
Ciliata mustela
Family Gadidae
25 cm. Fine fringe of rays form first dorsal fin; second dorsal and anal fins long. 4 barbels on snout, 1 on chin.
Habitat: common among rocks and under weed, on shore and in shallow

water down to 20 m on sand, mud and gravel bottoms. Feeds on small crustaceans and fishes. Breeds in winter in deep water; the young are silvery and surface-living and drift inshore with the tide.

POLLACK
Pollachius pollachius
1·3 m. 3 dorsal and 2 anal fins. Lateral line dark and sharply curved over the pectoral fin.
Habitat: in loose schools around rocks and wrecks down to 100 m; young in shallow water over sandy bottoms. Feeds on fishes and crustaceans. Spawns in early spring in deeper water; the eggs and larvae are pelagic but drift shorewards.

WHITING
Merlangius merlangus
70 cm. 3 dorsal and 2 anal fins, all close together. Chin barbel minute. Dusky spot at base of pectoral fin.
Habitat: very common in inshore shallow water between 10 and 100 m, usually over sandy or muddy bottoms. Young mostly in shallower depths. Very young shelter among tentacles of jelly fishes. Eats small fishes and crustaceans, and spawns in spring in shallow water.

BASS
Dicentrarchus labrax
Family Percichthyidae
1 m. 2 dorsal fins, the first spiny; forward pointing spines on the lower

edge of the gill cover.
Habitat: in schools over reefs, off rocky headlands, and in open bays, chiefly on ocean coasts. Young are common in estuaries and harbours and form large schools. An active predator, feeding mainly on fishes, squid and shrimps. Breeds in spring in inshore waters. Rare north of Britain.

RED MULLET
Mullus surmuletus
Family Mullidae
40 cm. Reddish, with 2 long barbels on chin: young are blue-backed with silvery sides.
Habitat: bottom-living, most common on sand and mud in shallow water of 3-90 m. Probes the seabed with its barbels in search of food, mainly worms, molluscs and crustaceans; sometimes burrows into sand to seize food. Young are pelagic. Rare north of British waters.

CUCKOO WRASSE
Labrus mixtus
Family Labridae
35 cm. Long dorsal fin with 16-18 spiny rays in front. Head pointed, with large mouth and strong teeth. Females and young males pinkish-orange with 3 brown blotches on back; adult males with blue heads and yellowish-orange sides.
Habitat: close to rocks in 10-100 m depth. Feeds on crabs, other crustaceans and molluscs. Spawns in spring in a seabed nest guarded by the male.

LESSER WEEVER
Echiichthys vipera
Family Trachinidae
14 cm. Short and deep-bodied; mouth strongly oblique; pectoral fin rounded. First dorsal fin jet black, with 4 venomous spines. Gill-cover spines also with venom glands.
Habitat: from low tide mark to 50 m, buried in clean sand. Forages up shore with return of tide, feeding on small crustaceans, fishes and worms. Venom spines give intensely painful sting which requires medical treatment.

DRAGONET
Callionymus lyra
Family Callionymidae
30 cm. Belly flattened; eyes on top of head; 3 upward-pointing spines and a forward-pointing one at side of gill-cover. Males brighter and with longer fins than females.
Habitat: common on mud and sandy bottoms at depths of 10-100 m. Burrows in seabed, but actively hunts for bottom-living worms, crustaceans and molluscs. Spawns in spring, male making an elaborate courtship display; both eggs and larvae are surface living.

THICK-LIPPED GREY MULLET
Chelon labrosus
Family Mugilidae
75 cm. Streamlined with a broad head; upper lip very thick and covered with coarse papillae.
Habitat: usually in schools near the surface of inshore waters, harbour mouths and estuaries. Feeds on rich organic mud, consuming soil and grit as well as the small animals and algae in it.

MACKEREL
Scomber scombrus
Family Scombridae
66 cm. First dorsal fin with 11-13 slender spines; 2 small keels at the base of the tail fin.
Habitat: a schooling fish living near the surface and in mid-water in huge numbers; close to the coast in summer, when it moves northwards. Spawns in summer; both eggs and young are pelagic. Feeds on surface-living crustaceans and fishes, but in winter retires to deep water and feeds much less.

GREATER SANDEEL
Hyperoplus lanceolatus
Family Amodytidae
32 cm. Long slender body with pointed lower jaw; a distinct black smudge on the sides of the snout.
Habitat: on clean sand from low tide mark to 150 m. Forms large schools. Often swims in oblique head-down posture. Dives into sand at great speed when alarmed. Eats fish eggs and young and crustaceans.

SAND-SMELT
Atherina presbyter
Family Atherinidae
21 cm. 2 dorsal fins, the first with slender spines. A bright silvery stripe along the sides: back clear green.
Habitat: a common inshore and estuarine fish, migrating northwards and closer inshore as the water warms in summer. Most abundant over sandy seabeds at 0-20 m depth. Eggs are attached to seaweed in mid-summer. Young are found in shore pools in late summer. Feeds on small crustaceans.

SHANNY
Lipophrys pholis
Family Blenniidae
16 cm. Pelvic fins with two rays only; no tentacles on head.
Habitat: an abundant shore-fish living in rock pools, under stones and seaweed, and even in sandy shore pools where there is seaweed shelter. Also to depths of 30 m. Feeds on algae and a wide range of crustaceans; young fishes nip off the arms of barnacles. Eggs are laid on the underside of large stones or in rock crevices. The male guards the eggs.

MONTAGU'S BLENNY
Coryphoblennius galerita
8·5 cm. Pelvic fins with 2 rays only; a triangular flap of skin between the eyes, followed by short tentacles. Males are strongly blue-spotted, with yellow edge to head crest and upper lip.
Habitat: lives up to mid-tide level in shore pools containing little seaweed except the reddish encrusting *Litho-thamnion* and shrubby *Corallina*. Feeds on barnacles, nipping off their limbs when they are extended; also eats other small crustaceans and algae. Eggs are laid in rock crevices in summer. Common only in southern Europe.

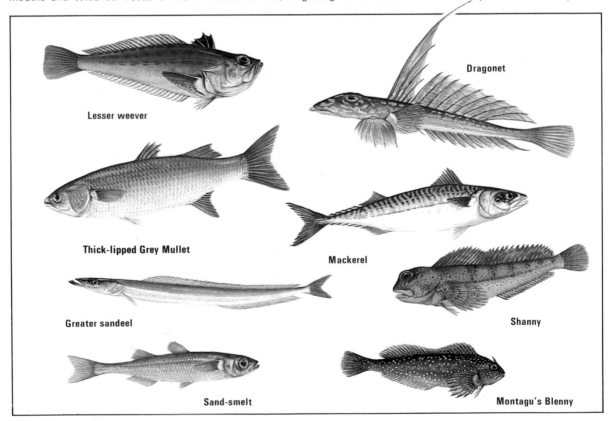

Lesser weever

Dragonet

Thick-lipped Grey Mullet

Mackerel

Greater sandeel

Shanny

Sand-smelt

Montagu's Blenny

BUTTERFISH
Pholis gunnellus
Family Pholidae
25 cm. Long, slender and compressed, with exceptionally slippery skin. Dorsal fin long, low and mostly spiny; pelvic fins minute spines.
Habitat: shallow seas close to the bottom and on the shore, mainly in rock pools, but also under damp rocks and seaweed. Depth range 0-100 m. Spawns January-February, the eggs laid in clumps in crevices or under shells and guarded by the adult. Eats worms, small crustaceans and molluscs. Rare south of Britain.

RED GURNARD
Aspitrigla cuculus
Family Triglidae
40 cm. Heavy-headed with stout spines on the gill-covers. Lateral line with broad, flat scales. Bright red; pectoral fins greyish-red.
Habitat: shallow inshore waters from 20-200 m, usually on sand, gravel or mud. Eats bottom-living invertebrates and fishes, the former detected by the long, lower pectoral rays which act as feelers as the fish creeps over the sea-bed. Grunts loudly in water and when caught.

SEA SCORPION
Taurulus bubalis
Family Cottidae
17 cm. A long, strong spine in front of gill-cover; a small flap of skin on the end of the upper jaw.
Habitat: common in pools and under seaweed on rocky shores, and also

below tide marks at depths of 0-60 m. Eggs are laid among seaweed in early spring. Feeds on crustaceans, worms and small fishes. Not found south of Biscay.

COMMON GOBY
Pomatoschistus microps
Family Gobiidae
6·4 cm. Rather stout, with a broad head and thick lips. Scales moderate in size. A dusky triangular patch at the base of pectoral fin, and a dusky blotch at the base of tail fin. Pelvic fins are united to form a disc.
Habitat: abundant in tide pools; on muddy and sandy shores; also in river mouths and drainage ditches close to the sea. Migrates into deeper water in winter. Eggs are laid underneath shells, and guarded by the male. Feeds mainly on small crustaceans.

BRILL
Scophthalmus rhombus
Family Scophthalmidae
75 cm. Broad-bodied flatfish, lying on right side with its eyes on left side of head. Mouth large; front rays of dorsal fin branched and free of membrane. Body scaly.
Habitat: common inshore on sandy bottoms and gravel, less so on mud, mostly at depths of 9-73 m. Feeds on bottom-living and mid-water fishes, squid and crustaceans. Eggs and larvae are pelagic and, like all flatfishes, the young have an eye each side of the head at first. As the fish grows, one eye moves over the top of the head, so that both are on the same side.

DAB
Limanda limanda
Family Pleuronectidae
42 cm. Lies on left, with eyes on right side of head. Lateral line strongly arched above pectoral fin; scales very rough on coloured side.
Habitat: a common flatfish of sandy or shell grounds at 2-40 m depth. Feeds mainly on worms and small crustaceans, occasionally molluscs. Spawns in spring and early summer; the eggs and larvae are pelagic.

FLOUNDER
Platichthys flesus
51 cm. Eyes usually on right side of head, often on left. Prickles at bases of dorsal and anal fins, and above pectoral fin.
Habitat: common at 0-55 m depth, mostly on mud and sand. Regularly comes into fresh water and extremely common in river mouths. Feeds on molluscs, worms and crustaceans, and is most active at night. Breeds offshore in spring; eggs and larvae pelagic.

PLAICE
Pleuronectes platessa
91 cm. Lies on left, with eyes on right side of head. Scales smooth; a series of rounded bumps running from between eyes back to level of pectoral fins. Bright orange spots on coloured side.
Habitat: abundant on sand and gravel, less often on mud, from 0-200 m. Feeds on bottom-living invertebrates. Spawns in early spring; eggs and larvae pelagic.

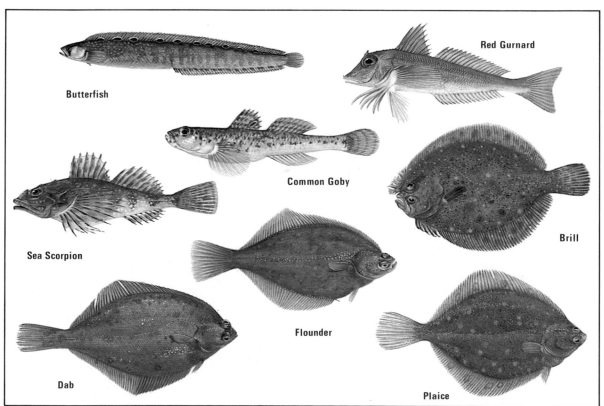

Butterfish

Red Gurnard

Common Goby

Sea Scorpion

Flounder

Brill

Dab

Plaice

Chapter Five
Invertebrates

The invertebrates are all those animals which have no backbones. They belong to some 29 different phyla and far outnumber the vertebrates, or back-boned animals, which belong to just one phylum – the Chordata. Invertebrates cannot compete in size with the largest vertebrates, but there is actually a tremendous range of sizes among them – from microscopic organisms (see below) to squids 15 m long (including their tentacles) and giant clams weighing 275 kg. These monstrous invertebrates are many thousands of times heavier than the smallest vertebrates.

Many invertebrates have no skeleton at all and rely entirely on the pressure of their body fluids to maintain their shape. Many others, however, have external skeletons or shells, technically known as exoskeletons, which give them their shape and also afford a good deal of protection. Crabs and snails are obvious examples.

One-Celled Animals
The simplest invertebrates are the protozoans (Phylum Protozoa), with bodies consisting of just one microscopic cell. And yet, within that one cell go on all the essential processes of life – breathing or respiration, the digestion of food and the elimination of waste, and reproduction. In addition, the cell is aware of its surroundings and can move or otherwise react to any changes. There are several distinct groups of protozoans, among which the amoebae are probably the best known. Occasionally reaching the size of a pin-head, but usually much smaller, these animals are sometimes described as shapeless blobs of jelly. In fact, each animal is continually changing its shape as it 'flows' along, putting out 'arms' here and there to engulf small food particles. Most amoebae live in water or in damp soil. Reproduction is most commonly effected simply by splitting into two: each half then continues to grow until it is ready to divide again.

The Major Groups of Invertebrates
The many-celled invertebrates are usually much larger than the protozoans and they belong to several phyla, although many of these groups are rather small. Some phyla contain just a few kinds of rarely-seen animals. Most of the invertebrates that you see belong to just five major phyla, and the following pages are devoted to these five groups.

Left: The sunstar (bottom left) exhibits the rough skin, water-filled tube feet and radial symmetry typical of the echinoderms. The top shell (top right) browses on seaweeds and is a typical gastropod mollusc, with a single, coiled shell. The orb-web spider (bottom right) is a typical arachnid, clearly displaying its four pairs of jointed legs. The wings of the small tortoiseshell butterfly (top left) clearly show that it is an insect – no other invertebrates have wings.

The largest of all the animal phyla is the Arthropoda. The name means 'jointed feet', and adult members of the group all have distinctly jointed limbs. Their bodies are also divided into a number of segments, although this division is sometimes obscured, and the animals are all enclosed in tough and sometimes very hard exoskeletons. The main classes within the Arthropoda are the crustaceans, the insects, the arachnids (spiders and scorpions), the centipedes and the millipedes. They total in the region of a million species.

The Phylum Mollusca, which includes the slugs and snails, the squids, and all the sea shells, comes second to the Arthropoda but, with only about 80,000 species, it is a long way behind. The animals are all soft-bodied creatures without any sign of segmentation. Most of them are protected by hard shells.

The Phylum Annelida includes a wide variety of aquatic and terrestrial worms – mostly slender creatures whose bodies are clearly divided into segments. This segmentation separates the annelids from the roundworms or nematodes, and other worm-like creatures.

Members of the Phylum Echinodermata are confined to the sea. They include the starfishes and sea urchins and their relatives. All have rough and often very spiny skins and they are all built on a radially symmetrical (circular) plan, meaning that cutting along any diameter will produce two more or less identical halves. Most other animals are bilaterally symmetrical, with only one possible way of cutting to produce two similar halves.

The fifth major phylum, the Coelenterata, is another radially symmetrical group. It includes the sea anemones and the jellyfishes.

Measurements and Dates
In the following pages the measurements given are the normal maximums for adults, although a range of sizes is given where the animals are particularly variable – where males and females are of different sizes, for example. Unless otherwise stated, the sizes given indicate body length (without legs), but where insects are normally shown with their wings outstretched (e.g. butterflies and dragonflies) the measurements indicate the wingspan.

Most aquatic invertebrates can be found at any time of the year. Many terrestrial species can also be found at all seasons, although some may go into hibernation in autumn. Many insects, however, are distinctly seasonal in their appearance and the times given are those at which the adults are most likely to be seen. In southern Europe they may appear earlier and continue later than indicated. Where no dates are given, it may be assumed that adults can be found at any time.

Echinoderms

The starfishes and sea urchins belong to the Phylum Echinodermata, whose members are built on a basically circular plan. Their skins are rough, often very spiny, and they all live in the sea. Many occur in coastal waters and can be found on the shore. Water-filled tubes run through the body, and slender branches, known as tube-feet, emerge from the surface. These are used for feeding and for locomotion and generally have disc-shaped suckers at their tips. Reproduction is extremely simple, most species merely releasing eggs and sperm into the water and leaving fertilization to chance. Most echinoderms have planktonic larvae which bear little resemblance to the adults.

There are five classes of echinoderms. The starfishes (Class Asteroidea) are flattened animals, usually with five arms. The arms are not clearly separated from the central disc. The mouth is on the underside and there are rows of tube-feet under the arms. Many simply sweep debris into the mouth, but some use the powerful suction of their tube-feet to open bivalve shells and then eat the animals inside. Brittle stars (Class Ophiuroidea) are similar to starfishes but their arms are more slender and are clearly separated from the central disc. Some feed on detritus, while others catch small prey with their arms. The sea urchins (Class Echinoidea) are rather more spiny than other echinoderms, and mostly globular. They have a chalky shell called a test just under the skin, and this is often washed up on the shore when the animal dies. Five bands of tube-feet run over the surface and the mouth is on the underside. The animals either sift food from the mud or scrape algae from the rocks. Sea cucumbers (Class Holothuroidea) are sausage-shaped creatures with the mouth at one end. Often living at great depths, the animals gather food from the mud. The Class Crinoidea (not illustrated) contains the sea lilies and feather stars, whose arms spread out like the petals of a flower and collect food particles from the water.

Sea Urchins

EDIBLE SEA URCHIN
Echinus esculentus
Up to 16 cm across, but usually less. Pink, red or purple and densely spined. Test deep pink with white spots: quite thick and often washed up on the shore intact. Long tube-feet, mostly with strong suckers, drag the animal along and also anchor it when necessary. Rocky and gravelly bottoms, usually just off-shore. It scrapes algae with strong teeth around the mouth. Edible parts are the bulky reproductive organs.

ROCK URCHIN
Paracentrotus lividus
Up to 6 cm across. Green, brown or violet with strong spines. Usually on soft limestone rocks in shallow water, often in rock pools. Often excavates a small cavity in the rock and may cover its upper surface with shell and sea-weed fragments, held on by the tube-feet. Feeds mainly on debris. Mediterranean and Atlantic.

VIOLET HEART URCHIN
Spatangus purpureus
Up to 12 cm long. Heart-shaped, having lost the radial symmetry. Spines are short and fur-like on top, but some on the underside are paddle-like and used for burrowing in sand and mud. Tube-feet lack suckers and mouth lacks teeth. It feeds on detritus. Test very thin.

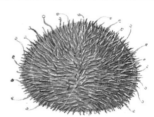

Edible Sea Urchin

**Test of
Violet Heart Urchin**

Above left: Rock urchins resting in hollows which they have worn in the soft limestone with their spines and teeth. Below left: Violet heart urchins showing their dense, fur-like spines. They live under the sand.

Sea Cucumbers

HOLOTHURIA FORSKALI
Up to 30 cm long. Dark brown to greenish-black with a leathery texture and only scattered chalky plates embedded in the skin. Suckered tube-feet on ·the lower surface move it about, while branched ones around the mouth scoop detritus from the seabed for food. Lives on mud and sand and in rocky crevices.

SEA GHERKIN
Cucumaria planci
Up to 15 cm long. Leathery, with five rows of suckered tube-feet which it uses for climbing over rocks. Prefers stony bottoms with a certain amount of mud. The branching tentacles filter food particles from the water and also sweep up detritus from the surrounding rocks. Mediterranean.

Starfishes

SUNSTAR
Solaster papposus
Up to 25 cm across. Purple or red with 8-15 arms (sometimes more in old specimens). Tube-feet with suckers. On sand and stones, feeding on other echinoderms. English Channel northwards.

CUSHION STAR
Asterina gibbosa
Up to 7 cm across. Yellow or green (sometimes brick-red). On rocks and under stones. Suckered tube-feet allow it to climb. Eats molluscs and other echinoderms. Lays eggs under stones. English Channel southwards.

ASTROPECTEN IRREGULARIS
Up to 12 cm across. Red to purplish-brown. Often called a comb star because of the spines on the edges of the arms. Burrows in sand and mud. Tube-feet without suckers. Eats worms, molluscs and other echinoderms.

COMMON STARFISH
Asterias rubens
Up to 30 cm across. Pale yellow, through red, to violet. Tube-feet with suckers. On stones and coarse sand, feeding mainly on bivalve molluscs: a pest on oyster farms.

Brittle Stars

OPHIOTHRIX FRAGILIS
Disc 2 cm across. Arms brittle and up to 7 cm long. Colour very variable. Tube-feet without suckers. Coils arms round stones to pull itself along and also uses them to filter food particles from the water. Common under stones and seaweeds near low-water mark.

SERPENT STAR
Ophiura texturata
Disc 3 cm across. Arms up to 15 cm long: grey to reddish-brown. On mud and sand, burrowing when tide is out but roaming the seabed at other times and capturing prey with the arms.

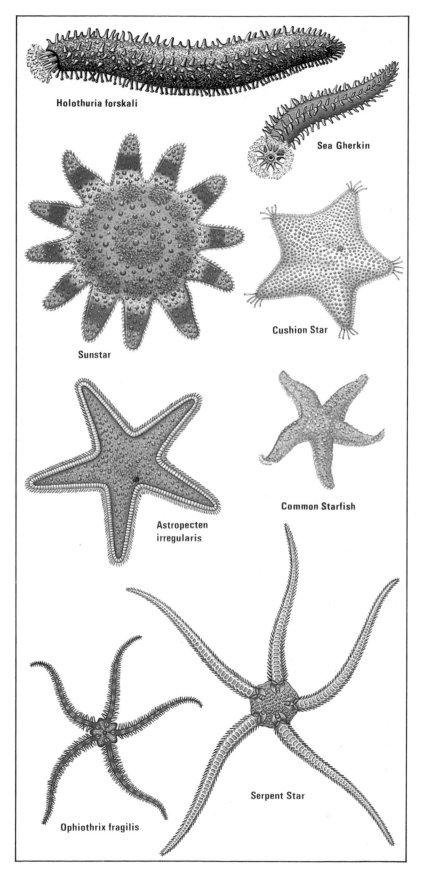

Holothuria forskali

Sea Gherkin

Sunstar

Cushion Star

Astropecten irregularis

Common Starfish

Ophiothrix fragilis

Serpent Star

Molluscs

The molluscs (Phylum Mollusca) are soft-bodied invertebrates, most of which are protected by a hard shell. There are about 80,000 known species, ranging from the highly mobile oceanic squids to the slow-moving slugs and snails of our gardens and the completely sedentary oysters. Because the animals are so varied, it is not possible to give a simple definition of the molluscs, but one feature which is present in all the major groups is the mantle. This is a thick cloak of skin which envelops at least a part of the body. The space between the mantle and the rest of the body is called the mantle cavity and it is connected to the outside world by one or more openings. In most aquatic molluscs the cavity contains gills: water is pumped in and out of the cavity and the gills absorb oxygen from it. The gills also play a part in food collection in many molluscs. In land molluscs and many freshwater snails the mantle cavity acts as a lung: if you watch pond snails for a while, you will see them come to the surface and expel a bubble of stale air from the lung before taking in a fresh supply.

The mantle is also responsible for producing the shell, which has three main layers. There is an outer horny layer, which gives the shell much of its colour, a middle layer composed of columnar crystals of calcium carbonate, and a smooth inner layer which is often pearly. The outer and middle layers are secreted by cells around the edge of the mantle, while the inner layer is secreted by the general mantle surface. If a shell is damaged, the inner layer can thus be repaired, but the mollusc cannot restore the other layers.

Slugs and Snails

These animals belong to the Class Gastropoda, which is by far the largest of the six classes into which the molluscs are divided. There are over 60,000 species, living on land, in the sea and in fresh water. Gastropoda means 'belly-footed' and refers to the large muscular organ, known as the foot, on which the animals glide along. The head, with its one or two pairs of retractile tentacles, is not clearly separated from the foot. Most of the snail's internal organs are contained in the visceral hump, which is coiled on top of the foot and enclosed in the mantle

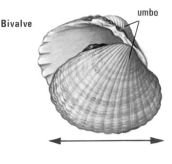

The tusk shells (Dentalium *species*) belong to the Class Scaphopoda. The tubular shell is open at both ends. The animal protrudes from the wide end and feeds in the mud. It lives in fairly deep water.

and shell. The snail can pull the foot into the shell as well, and many species can close the shell with a horny disc called the operculum. Most frequent in sea snails, the operculum can be seen at the tip of the foot when the animal is active. Slugs are simply snails which have lost their shells during evolution. Their internal organs have been packed into the foot and the mantle has been much reduced: in the sea slugs it has been completely lost.

All gastropods possess a rasp-like tongue called a radula. It is clothed with horny teeth and nibbles away at the animal's food rather like a cheese-grater. The teeth are quickly worn down, especially in those species which rasp algae from the rocks, but they are formed on a kind of conveyor belt and new teeth are continuously brought forward from the back.

Most gastropods have separate sexes. Many marine species merely scatter eggs and sperm into the water and leave fertilization to chance, but the more advanced species pair up and fertilization takes place internally. There is often a free-swimming larval stage which helps to scatter the species. Many land snails and slugs are hermaphrodite, with male and female organs in the same individual. They still pair up and mate, however, and often have very elaborate mating behaviour.

The Bivalves

The bivalves, in which the shell is composed of two halves or valves, belong to the Class Lamellibranchia. The valves may or may not be alike, but each valve is asymmetrical in itself and usually has a prominent point called the umbo. The valves are hinged around the umbo, usually with interlocking teeth and a

Bivalve molluscs (left) have two halves or valves to the shell, hinged at the top. They are usually measured by width. Univalves (right), which have a single, usually coiled valve, are measured by height. The opening of the univalve shell is nearly always on the right (dextral condition) as you look at the shell.

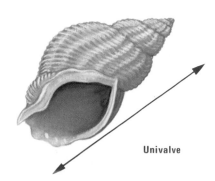

Bivalve

umbo

Univalve

tough, horny ligament. Strong muscles close the shell, but when they relax the hinge ligament causes it to gape. If you look at an empty shell you can see the scars where the closing muscles were attached.

All of the 7,500 species of bivalves live in water and all are filter-feeders. Their very large gills are used to strain food particles from the stream of water passing over them. The two flaps of the mantle may be free at the edges, but are often joined in places and frequently drawn out to form two siphons – one to carry water in to the gills, and one to carry it out again. Some bivalves have very long inlet siphons which they use to suck debris from the sea bed. Most have a muscular foot with which they can burrow in sand or mud, but no head; the foot is absent in the completely sedentary oyster. Most bivalves have separate sexes, although a few are hermaphrodite, and some actually start off as males and become females later in life. Eggs and sperm are usually simply scattered into the water, but some females retain their eggs in the mantle cavity, where they are fertilized by sperms drawn in with the water.

Squid, Cuttlefish and Octopus

These animals form the Class Cephalopoda, in which the foot is divided into a number of tentacles surrounding the mouth. There are about 600 species, all marine and all active predators with well developed eyes. There is no real shell, although the squid's body is supported by a horny plate embedded in the mantle and the cuttlefish is similarly supported by the familiar chalky 'cuttlebone'. The body behind the head and tentacles is enclosed in a very thick, muscular mantle which opens to the outside by way of a tubular funnel. Rapid contraction of the mantle cavity forces water out through the funnel or siphon, and sends the animal speeding along by jet-propulsion. It usually goes backwards, but can change direction by bending the siphon in different directions. The sexes are always separate and there are often complex courtship rituals.

Other Molluscs

The other three molluscan classes are all quite small and are confined to the sea. They are the Scaphopoda (see above left), the Amphineura, and the Monoplacophora. The Amphineura contains the chitons, or coat-of-mail shells, in which the flat, oval body is protected by eight shell plates (see page 139). The animals glide over rocks on a broad foot, and if detached can roll into a ball. The Monoplacophora is a very ancient class, represented today only by a deep-sea creature called *Neopilina*. This has a limpet-like shell and foot, but is otherwise unlike any other living mollusc.

*Above right: Two great grey slugs (*Limax maximus*) mating while hanging at the end of a string of mucus which they themselves produce after climbing a wall or tree trunk. The large white structures are the genital organs, which coil around each other to exchange sperm.*

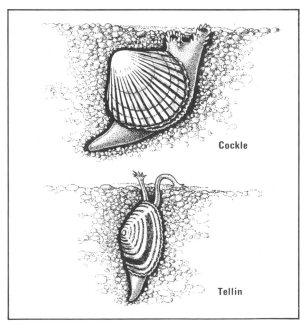

Cockle

Tellin

Right: The cockle (top) feeds by sucking water in through its siphon. The tellin (below) uses its long siphon like a vacuum cleaner to suck debris from the seabed.

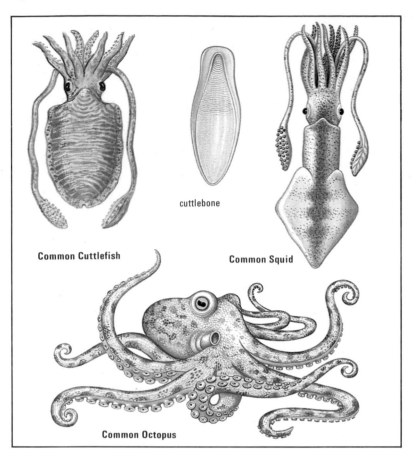

Common Cuttlefish

cuttlebone

Common Squid

Common Octopus

Cephalopods

These are very mobile, predatory, marine molluscs with a number of sucker-covered arms and extremely large and efficient eyes. There is a horny, parrot-like beak at the base of the arms and the salivary glands secrete a poison which quickly paralyzes prey. The group contains the largest of all invertebrates, but most members are quite small and, despite their sinister reputations, most are quite harmless to humans.

COMMON CUTTLEFISH
Sepia officinalis Family Sepiidae
Up to 30 cm long. Flattened and oval with 8 short arms and 2 longer ones which can be shot out to catch shrimps and similar prey. Keeps close to sea bed, usually over sand or eel-grass, and can change colour to match different backgrounds. Swims by jet-propulsion or slowly by waving fin surrounding the mantle. Chalky white cuttlebone often washed up on the beach. One of several similar species.

COMMON SQUID
Loligo vulgaris Family Loliginidae
Up to 50 cm long. Slender, cylindrical body with diamond-shaped stabilizing tail fin. Cream or pink with purplish-brown spots. 8 short arms and 2 longer ones which can be shot out to catch prey. Free-swimming, often in large shoals. Often at surface; never on sea bed. Feeds mainly on fishes. Mainly Dutch coast southwards. One of several similar species.

COMMON OCTOPUS
Octopus vulgaris Family Octopodidae
Up to 3 m across extended arms, but usually much less: arms often under 50 cm long. Bag-like body grey to brown, often mottled and changing colour to match various backgrounds. 8 arms, each with 2 rows of suckers. Lurks in rocky crevices on seabed and darts out to catch fishes and crustaceans. A shy animal, it will inflict a painful bite if handled. English Channel southwards: rare in Britain.

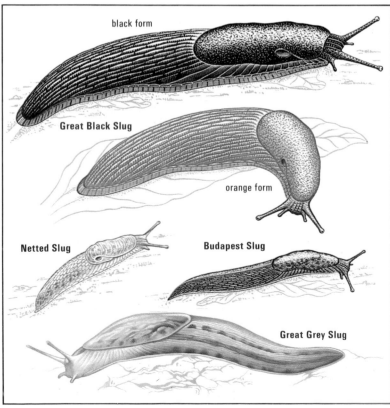

black form

Great Black Slug

orange form

Netted Slug

Budapest Slug

Great Grey Slug

Slugs and Snails

These are herbivorous or carnivorous gastropods, active mainly by night but also after daytime rain. They have two pairs of tentacles, usually with eyes at the tips of the longer ones. Slugs have a small saddle-like mantle, usually near the front. A coating of slime, especially thick and sticky in slugs, helps to prevent desiccation and also gives some protection from enemies.

Garden Snail

Roman Snail

Strawberry Snail

Kentish Snail

Brown-lipped Snail

Two-toothed Door Snail

Round-mouthed Snail

Garlic Glass Snail

Great Pond Snail

Great Ram's Horn

The animals may be active all year, but they hide away in very cold or dry weather. Snails often seal up their shells with slime which hardens into a parchment-like cap. Very few land snails have an operculum. All the species on these pages eat living or dead plant matter.

GREAT BLACK SLUG
Arion ater Family Arionidae
Up to 15 cm. May also be grey, brown, or orange, especially in south. A round-backed slug with no keel on back. Lung opening near front of mantle on right. Contracts to hemisphere and sways from side to side if disturbed. Eats rotting vegetation.

NETTED SLUG
Deroceras reticulatum Family Limacidae
Up to 5 cm. Cream to brown or grey, often speckled with black. Keel on hind end. Lung opening near back of mantle on right. Exudes milky slime when handled. A pest of vegetable crops.

GREAT GREY SLUG
Limax maximus
Up to 20 cm. Keel on hind end. Tentacles reddish-brown. Lung opening near back of mantle on right. Eats fungi and decaying matter. Aerial mating (see page 135).

BUDAPEST SLUG
Milax budapestensis Family Milacidae
Up to 6 cm. Pale to dark grey with yellow or orange keel along back. Lung opening near back of mantle on right. A serious crop pest, especially on roots. Mainly cultivated land.

GARDEN SNAIL
Helix aspersa Family Helicidae
Shell more or less globular, up to 3·5 cm high. Yellowish-brown with variable dark markings. A common garden pest, nibbling a wide range of plants. South and central Europe.

ROMAN SNAIL
Helix pomatia
Shell globular, up to 5 cm high. Creamy-white with pale brown bands. On lime-rich soils. South and central Europe: southern Britain only.

STRAWBERRY SNAIL
Trichia striolata
Shell flattened, up to 1·4 cm across. Sandy to purplish-brown, with a white rib just inside mouth when mature. Mainly damp places: a pest in gardens. Britain eastwards to Rhine Valley.

KENTISH SNAIL
Monacha cantiana
Shell slightly flattened, up to 2 cm across: creamy-white with reddish tinge near mouth. Often looks greyish with snail in it. Grassy places. South and central Europe.

BROWN-LIPPED SNAIL
Cepaea nemoralis
Shell rounded, up to 20 mm high. Ground colour yellow, pink, or brown, with up to 5 spiral brown bands: often yellow with no bands in grassland. Shell lip is dark brown. Woods, hedgerows, grassland and gardens. *C. hortensis* is very similar, but shell has a white lip.

GARLIC GLASS SNAIL
Oxychilus alliarius Family Zonitidae
Shell flattened, up to 7 mm across. Shining, translucent brown. Animal smells of garlic if touched. Damp places. Western Europe.

ROUND-MOUTHED SNAIL
Pomatias elegans Family Pomatiidae
Shell up to 1·3 cm high, with distinctly rounded whorls and a round opening. Thick: greyish to yellow. One of very few land snails with an operculum. Rough vegetation on lime-rich soils. Western Europe: not in north.

TWO-TOOTHED DOOR SNAIL
Clausilia bidentata
Family Clausiliidae
Shell spindle-shaped, up to 1·2 cm high. Reddish-brown and sinistral — with opening on the left as you look at it. Damp walls and rocks, eating moss and algae.

GREAT POND SNAIL
Limnaea stagnalis
Family Limnaeidae
Shell up to 6 cm long. Thin and pale brown. Tentacles flat, with eyes at base of hind pair. No operculum. Still and slow-moving water with plenty of lime and lots of weed. Eats plant and animal matter, living or dead. Air-breathing.

GREAT RAM'S HORN
Planorbis corneus
Family Planorbidae
Deep-brown shell coiled in a flat spiral up to 3 cm across. Animal deep brown or red. Tentacles long and slender. No operculum. Weedy ponds, eating plant matter. An air-breather, but comes to the surface much less than the previous species because body contains haemoglobin and can absorb oxygen from the water.

Sea Snails and Sea Slugs

These animals, like their terrestrial counterparts, belong to the Class Gastropoda. The head bears one or two pairs of sensory tentacles, usually with eyes at the base of one pair. The rasping radula (see page 134) is used to obtain either animal or vegetable food and can even be used to drill through the shells of other molluscs. Many sea snails have long inlet siphons through which water is drawn into the mantle cavity. The siphon is housed in a grooved extension of the lip of the shell, but can be extended way beyond the shell. Sea slugs have lost their shells and they have lost the mantle and mantle cavity as well. They breathe with the aid of false gills developed on the back. Sea snails and sea slugs live mainly on rocky seabeds and shores, sheltering under seaweeds when the tide goes out in the daytime but often moving about to feed in the damp air at night. Empty shells may be washed up on all kinds of beaches. Unless otherwise stated, the measurements given for snails are shell heights (see page 134).

COMMON ORMER
Haliotis tuberculata Family Haliotidae
Up to 8 cm long. Greenish-brown to brick-red, coiled only at apex and looking like half of a bivalve shell, but the row of small breathing holes identifies it. Very pearly inside. Among rocks and stones, eating algae. Channel Islands southwards.

COMMON LIMPET
Patella vulgaris Family Patellidae
Up to 6 cm in diameter. Shell conical and more or less circular at base. Those on highest parts of shore are taller than those further down. Greenish-grey or brown: pearly white inside. Foot more or less circular. Attaches itself very firmly to rocks of the upper and middle shore, where it wears a shallow groove into which it fits perfectly. Scrapes algae from rocks. Several similar species live on lower and middle shore. Western and northern shores.

BLUE-RAYED LIMPET
Patina pellucida
Up to 2 cm diameter. Shell conical with oval base. Translucent, yellowish with blue stripes. On oarweeds and related seaweeds. Western and northern shores.

PAINTED TOP SHELL
Calliostoma zizyphinum
Family Trochidae
Up to 4 cm. Orange, pink, or red with darker red spots. Outer layer often wears away to reveal thick pearly layer in places. On rocks on lower shore, browsing on seaweeds: usually below low-tide level in northern regions.

TOWER SHELL
Turritella communis Family Turritellidae
Up to 5 cm. Yellowish-brown to brick-red. Common in mud and sand just offshore, usually buried up to tip of spire. Feeds on algae and detritus.

NEEDLE SHELL
Bittium reticulatum Family Cerithiidae
Up to 1·5 cm. Tightly whorled, each whorl decorated with spiral rows of small bumps. Pale to dark brown, with short siphon canal at side of shell opening. Browses on seaweeds on mud and sand.

COMMON PERIWINKLE
Littorina littorea Family Littorinidae
Up to 3 cm. Dark greenish-grey or almost black, sometimes with paler bands. Shell thick. This is the familiar winkle of the fishmonger's slab. Browses on seaweeds on rocks and stones at around low-tide level.

FLAT PERIWINKLE
Littorina littoralis
Up to 1·5 cm. Yellow to orange or pale brown, with or without banding. Flatter than other winkles, often almost circular in outline. Browses on seaweeds on rocks of middle shore.

COMMON WENTLETRAP
Clathrus clathrus Family Epitoniidae
Up to 4·5 cm. White to rusty or purplish-red, with prominent ridges crossing the tightly-packed whorls. In sand and mud below low-tide level. Carnivorous.

SLIPPER LIMPET
Crepidula fornicata Calyptraeidae
Up to 6 cm long. Cream to brown, often spotted with red. Resembles half a bivalve shell, but with a thick white plate extending half way across the underside. Often found in 'chains', with three or more shells fixed to each other. A filter-feeder. Often causes damage to mussel and oyster beds by settling all over the shells and denying them food. Introduced from America.

PELICAN'S FOOT
Aporrhais pespelecani
Family Aporrhaidae
Up to 5 cm. Yellow to dark brown. Named for the way in which lip of adult shell is drawn out into the shape of a bird's foot. Opening is straight and narrow. Burrows in mud and sand: eats detritus.

EUROPEAN COWRIE
Trivia monacha Family Cypraeidae
Up to 1·2 cm long. Oval shells, flattened on one side and with a long, narrow opening. Strongly ribbed, pale pink to greyish-brown with 4-6 darker spots. Mantle is folded back over shell in life. Rocky shores, feeding on small sea-squirts. Several similar species.

MUREX BRANDARIS
Family Muricidae
Up to 9 cm, with long spines and a very long siphon canal. Pale grey or yellowish. On mud and stones, eating other molluscs and carrion. Contains a rich purple dye. Mediterranean.

COMMON DOG WHELK
Nucella lapillus
Up to 4·5 cm. Very thick shell, brown or yellow and often banded with white. A short siphon groove. Abundant on rocks on middle shore. Feeds on other molluscs and barnacles, using the radula, which is at the end of a slender proboscis, to drill through their shells. Western and northern coasts.

STING WINKLE
Ocinebra erinacea
Up to 6 cm. Thick, with prominent ribbing. White to sandy grey. On stones and firm mud, especially among eelgrasses. Drills holes in other mollusc shells with radula, aided by chemical secretions.

COMMON WHELK
Buccinum undatum Family Buccinidae
Up to 12 cm, with short, curved siphon canal. White to sandy-grey. On sand, mud and stones. Eats carrion and also preys on bivalves, wedging the shells open with the lip of its own shell and inserting the radula on its long proboscis. Northern and western shores.

SEA HARE
Aplysia depilans Family Aplysiidae
Up to 25 cm long. Olive-green or brown with pale spots. 4 stout tentacles. Thin shell completely covered by mantle folds. Browses on algae on mud and sand, usually below low-tide level. Mediterranean. Several similar species.

SEA SLUG
Dendronotus frondosus
Family Dendronotidae
Up to 6 cm long. Cream, yellow or pale pink, with branched white tentacles and numerous branched gills on the back. No shell. Browses on small coelenterates on rocky shores. Northern and western coasts.

GREY SEA SLUG
Aeolidia papillosa Family Aeolidiidae
Up to 9 cm. Grey to brown, with many white-spotted, unbranched gills on the back. No shell. On sand and rocks, feeding on sea anemones. Bay of Biscay northwards. Several similar species.

Coat-of-Mail Shells

GREY CHITON
Lepidochitona cinerea
Family Lepidochitonidae
Up to 3 cm long. One of the coat-of-mail shells (see page 135) with 8 protective plates. Colour ranges from grey to green or brick-red. Clings tightly to other shells and to rocks in coastal zone: browses on algae. Several similar species.

Common Ormer

Common Limpet

Blue-rayed Limpet

Painted Top Shell

Tower Shell

Needle Shell

Common Periwinkle

Flat Periwinkle

Common Wentletrap

Slipper Limpet

Pelican's Foot

European Cowrie

Murex brandaris

Common Dog Whelk

Sting Winkle

Common Whelk

Sea Hare

Sea Slug

Grey Sea Slug

Grey Chiton

Bivalve Sea Shells

Huge populations of bivalves, belonging to hundreds of species, live on the seabed, usually burrowing in sand or mud. When they die, their empty shells are often cast up on the shore, sometimes forming huge banks. The hinges usually break as the shells are thrown about by the waves, and most of the shells on the shore are just single valves. The arrangement of the hinge teeth and muscle scars on the inside of the shell often help in identification, especially if the colours have faded. The habitats given are those preferred by the living animals. Measurements are taken across the width of the shell (see page 134).

DOG COCKLE
Glycimeris glycimeris
Family Glycimeridae
Up to 10 cm. Almost circular. Straw-coloured to brick-red: many hinge teeth. Each valve with a broad, grooved inner rim. Sandy shores.

COMMON MUSSEL
Mytilus edulis Family Mytilidae
Up to 10 cm. Hinged on front (narrow) part of curved side; a few small teeth. Brown, blue or black. Attached to rocks and stones by tough, horny threads (the byssus): usually in exposed places where currents bring plenty of food.

QUEEN SCALLOP
Chlamys opercularis Family Pectinidae
Up to 9 cm. Almost circular with a straight, toothless hinge and slightly unequal 'ears'. One valve slightly more convex than the other. Yellow, through orange, to brown: 18-22 prominent ribs. Lies freely on coarse sand: swims by flapping valves.

OYSTER
Ostrea edulis Family Ostreidae
Up to 15 cm. Almost circular. Grey, with rough concentric growth lines. Left valve bowl-shaped and fixed to rocks and stones. Right valve flat and forms a lid. From low-tide level to depths of about 50 m.

PORTUGUESE OYSTER
Crassostrea angulata
Up to 10 cm. Similar to the oyster, but longer and narrower and left valve much deeper – usually with deeply-indented margins into which the lid fits very neatly. One purple muscle scar in each valve. Atlantic.

COMMON COCKLE
Cardium edule Family Cardiidae
Up to 5 cm. White to mid-brown with 22-26 coarse ribs. Two main teeth close to the umbo. Abundant in mud and sand from lower shore downwards, including estuaries.

PRICKLY COCKLE
Cardium echinatum
Up to 8 cm. Very thick shell with 20-30 ribs bearing short, blunt spines. White to mid-brown. In mud, usually below low-tide level.

BLUNT TELLIN
Tellina crassa Family Tellinidae
Up to 5 cm. Cream or grey, sometimes with faint pink stripes and red umbo: orange inside. Like all tellins, it has long siphons and sucks debris from seabed (see page 135). Sand: off-shore.

THIN TELLIN
Tellina tenuis
Up to 3 cm. Yellow, pink or red. Very thin, but hinge is tough and valves commonly remain joined after death. Sand near low-tide level.

BANDED WEDGE SHELL
Donax vittatus Family Donacidae
Up to 3 cm. Distinctly oblong with umbo very much off-centre. Shiny: yellow to brown outside, with or without darker bands, and purplish or yellowish inside. Sand near low-tide level. Siphons long, as in tellins.

RAYED ARTEMIS
Dosina exoleta Family Veneridae
Up to 5 cm. Thick shell with curved and pointed umbo. White or cream, usually with reddish-brown rays. 3 teeth under umbo. Sand.

BANDED CARPET SHELL
Venerupis rhomboides
Up to 5 cm. Sandy brown with 3 or 4 darker radiating stripes: often with zig-zag brown lines near the margin when mature. 3 converging teeth under umbo. Mud and sand.

LARGE RAZOR SHELL
Ensis siliqua Family Solenidae
Up to 20 cm. Open both ends. Hinged near one end, with 2 large teeth and dark external ligament. Lives vertically in sand and burrows very quickly. There are several similar, but smaller species, including *Ensis ensis* which is strongly curved.

RAYED TROUGH SHELL
Mactra corallina Family Mactridae
Up to 7 cm. Shell thin with a blunt umbo. Alternating yellowish and brown bands: numerous narrow white rays. Pink to violet inside. Sand.

COMMON OTTER SHELL
Lutraria lutraria Family Lutrariidae
Up to 14 cm. Distinctly elliptical. Dirty white to pinkish, with brown outer skin which flakes off in patches. Gapes slightly at each end. Burrows deeply in sand and mud: long siphons.

COMMON PIDDOCK
Pholas dactylus Family Pholadidae
Up to 12 cm. White and gaping at both ends. Valves thin, with no hinge ligament. A curved spine just under umbo in each valve. Front end of shell rasp-like and used to drill burrows in soft rocks.

SAND GAPER
Mya arenaria Family Myidae
Up to 15 cm. White to sandy, with darker concentric bands and peeling grey skin. Gapes at both ends. Left valve smaller and more domed than right and containing large, spoon-like tooth. Right valve has deep groove to hold tooth. Mud and sand.

Freshwater Bivalves

PAINTER'S MUSSEL
Unio pictorum Family Unionidae
Up to 14 cm. One of several rather similar bivalves living in still and slow-moving water with plenty of mud on the bottom. Yellowish-green to brown and tapering markedly towards the back. Named because artists once used the shells to hold their paints.

The painter's mussel, showing the frilly edges of the siphons through which water enters and leaves.

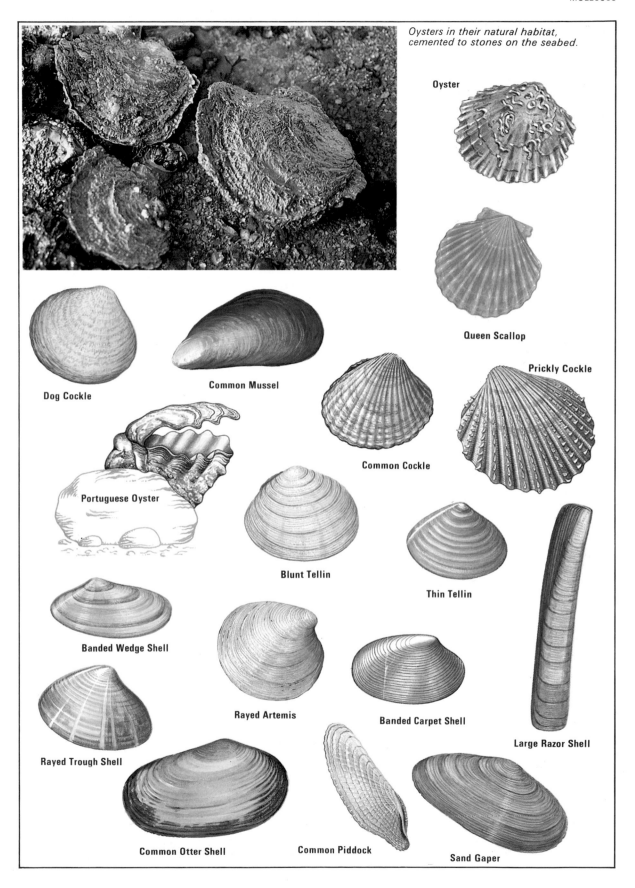

Oysters in their natural habitat, cemented to stones on the seabed.

Oyster

Queen Scallop

Dog Cockle

Common Mussel

Prickly Cockle

Common Cockle

Portuguese Oyster

Blunt Tellin

Thin Tellin

Banded Wedge Shell

Rayed Artemis

Banded Carpet Shell

Large Razor Shell

Rayed Trough Shell

Common Otter Shell

Common Piddock

Sand Gaper

Crustaceans

The crabs and their relatives form the Class Crustacea, one of the major divisions of the arthropods. They nearly all live in water and they are covered with a hard exoskeleton heavily impregnated with calcium carbonate. The head bears two pairs of antennae, but otherwise the animals are extremely varied and it is impossible to give a simple description of the group. They range from minute floating creatures, such as water fleas, to lobsters and crabs weighing several kilogrammes. There are several to many pairs of legs, and in some of the more primitive crustaceans, such as the Fairy shrimp, they are all alike and function simultaneously as food gatherers, paddles and gills. The more advanced crustaceans have specialized feeding limbs near the front and walking or swimming legs further back. The gills are outgrowths from some of the limbs. Most of the animals are scavengers and many have complex life histories with several kinds of larvae. Only a few of the more advanced species are shown here.

Woodlice

This is the only group of crustaceans that has really invaded the land, although several species still live in water and most are restricted to damp places. Most are flattened and all have seven pairs of similar legs. The woodlice belong to the order Isopoda.

ONISCUS ASELLUS
Family Oniscidae
12-16 mm. Glossy grey with a pale margin; sometimes all yellowish. Abundant under stones and in rotting wood. Feeds on decaying vegetable matter of all kinds.

SEA SLATER
Ligia oceanica
Family Ligiidae
20-25 mm. Greyish-green, often blackish when young. Scavenges on the shore at night, hiding in rock crevices by day – usually close to high tide level.

WATER LOUSE
Asellus aquaticus
Family Asellidae
18-25 mm. Male much larger than female and often carries her about clasped to his belly. Abundant in weedy ponds and streams, where it feeds on assorted debris and sometimes on filamentous algae.

Amphipoda

An order of marine or freshwater crustaceans which have laterally compressed bodies, usually with three pairs of swimming legs and three pairs of jumping legs on the abdomen. There are four pairs of walking and grasping legs at the front.

FRESHWATER SHRIMP
Gammarus pulex
Family Gammaridae
15-30 mm. Male larger than female and often carries her about in the breeding season. Grey to reddish-brown. Abundant in shallow streams, especially in lime-rich areas, usually hiding under stones and vegetation. Body curved at rest, but straightens when swimming – usually on one side. Feeds on detritus and also nibbles algae.

SAND HOPPER
Orchestia gammarella
10-20 mm. Greenish-brown to chestnut. Abundant on sea shore, under the piles of decaying seaweed and other rubbish on which it feeds. Leaps away vigorously when disturbed.

Decapoda

The creatures in this order are almost all marine, with five pairs of walking legs of which one or more pairs may bear pincers for catching food. Most are flesh-eaters, taking carrion as well as living food. The abdomen often bears five pairs of swimming legs (also used to carry eggs in female), but crabs have a very small abdomen tucked under thorax.

COMMON SHRIMP
Crangon crangon
4-7 cm. Grey or brown. Abundant in coastal waters, usually burrowing in sand or mud with just eyes showing.

COMMON PRAWN
Palaemon serratus
10 cm. Common in coastal waters over rocky bottoms, generally hiding by day and hunting by night. Easily distinguished from shrimp by the toothed rostrum on the head.

NORWAY LOBSTER
Nephrops norvegicus
10-20 cm. On sandy and muddy seabeds from 30-200 m deep. Marketed as scampi or Dublin Bay prawns.

SPINY LOBSTER
Palinurus vulgaris
20-40 cm. Also called crawfish. No pincers, but the thick, spiny antennae can inflict damage. Rocky seabeds below 10 m. Mainly southern; as far north as Holland. A favourite food.

LOBSTER
Homarus vulgaris
20-60 cm. The largest European crustacean and much in demand for food. Rocky coasts from low-tide level downwards, hiding in crevices by day and hunting at night. Becomes red when cooked.

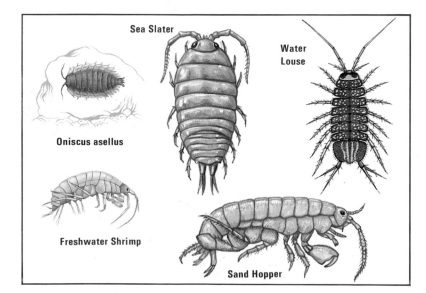

Sea Slater

Water Louse

Oniscus asellus

Freshwater Shrimp

Sand Hopper

CRAYFISH
Potamobius pallipes
10 cm. A freshwater species found in clean streams with sandy or gravelly beds, usually in chalk and limestone areas. It usually hides by day under stones or in holes in the bank and hunts by night. The slightly larger *P. fluviatilis*, recognized by the red underside of its claws, is reared for food on the continent.

EDIBLE CRAB
Cancer pagurus
7-20 cm. Lives on rocky coasts, from the shore to quite deep water. Much sought after for food.

SHORE CRAB
Carcinus maenas
4-6 cm. Common on sandy and rocky shores and, like most crabs, walks sideways. Often in estuaries.

VELVET CRAB
Portunus puber
6-7 cm. Named for its hairy coat, this is one of the swimming crabs. The hind legs are broad and flat and are used to row the crab through the water, although it can also crawl on the bottom. Rocky and sandy coasts.

HERMIT CRAB
Eupagurus bernhardus
10 cm. Unlike true crabs, the abdomen is quite long, but it is very soft and the hermit crab protects it by taking up residence in empty shells. As it grows, it moves to larger shells. The large right claw is used to close the opening when the crab retires into the shell.

Cirrepedia

ACORN BARNACLE
Balanus balanoides
5-15 mm diameter. Adults are cemented to inter-tidal rocks and surrounded by chalky plates. When submerged, feathery limbs emerge and comb food particles from the water. The plates close up when the tide recedes. Young stages are free-swimming.

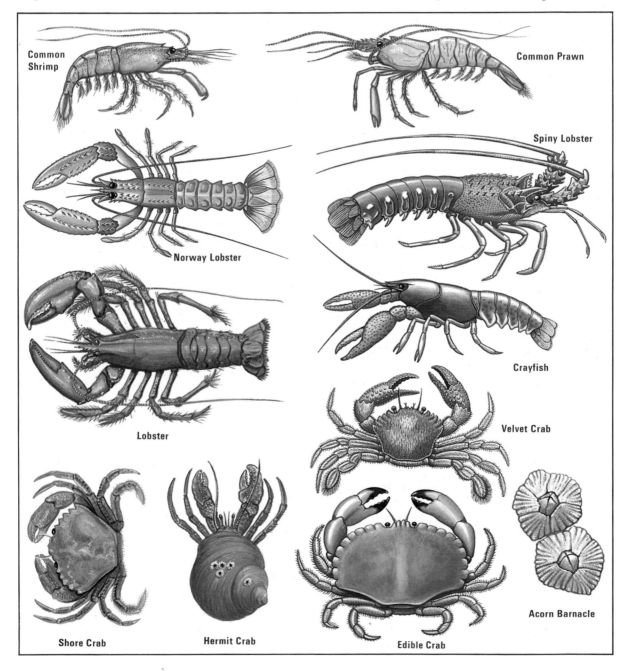

Common Shrimp

Common Prawn

Spiny Lobster

Norway Lobster

Crayfish

Lobster

Velvet Crab

Shore Crab

Hermit Crab

Edible Crab

Acorn Barnacle

Spiders and their Relatives

The spiders and their relatives, which include the scorpions and the mites and ticks, make up the Class Arachnida – another major division of the arthropods. They are easily distinguished from insects by the four pairs of legs and the lack of antennae, although a pair of palps just behind the mouth may look like either legs or antennae. There are no real jaws, but there is always a pair of claw-like limbs called chelicerae just in front of the mouth. Most arachnids are carnivorous, although many of the mites are plant-feeders.

Spiders (order Araneida) have two distinct body sections, the front one of which is covered by a fairly tough shield or carapace. The hind region is usually softer and rather bulbous. The front region carries all the legs, and there are usually six or eight eyes distributed over the front end. The palps are quite short and function like antennae, although they are swollen at the tips in males. The chelicerae are in the form of poison fangs. Some large spiders eat birds and lizards and even small mammals, but most spiders eat insects. Many spin elaborate webs to catch their prey, but others simply go hunting or lie in ambush for their prey. The venom from the fangs paralyzes the prey and the spider then sucks it dry.

Males are often much smaller than females and they usually put on some elaborate courtship displays to ensure that the females recognize them. Even so, many males are eaten by their mates. All spiders make silk, even if they do not make webs. It is used for many purposes, including wrapping up prey and protecting the eggs.

Spiders

AMAUROBIUS SIMILIS
Family Amaurobiidae
6 mm (male); 12 mm (female). Lives in crevices in bark and old walls and also around window frames, making a rather irregular lacy web around its retreat. Crawling insects are entangled in the web and quickly drawn into the spider's lair, usually being pulled in by one leg. All year. *A. fenestralis* is very similar, but less common on buildings.

DADDY-LONG-LEGS SPIDER
Pholcus phalangioides
Family Pholcidae
8-10 mm. Easily recognized by its slender body and extremely long legs, this spider is most likely to be found in caves and buildings. It makes an irregular web, like flimsy scaffolding, and when prey stumbles into it the spider actually throws more silk over it with its back legs. It regularly feeds on other spiders as well as insects. All year, but becomes quiescent in winter. Southern and central Europe: mainly southern Britain.

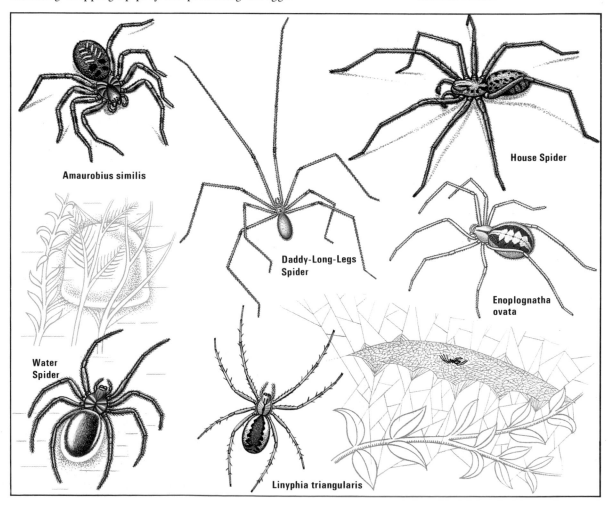

Amaurobius similis

Daddy-Long-Legs Spider

House Spider

Enoplognatha ovata

Water Spider

Linyphia triangularis

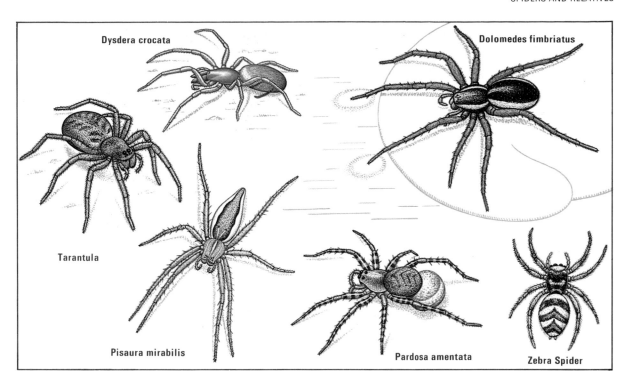

Dysdera crocata

Dolomedes fimbriatus

Tarantula

Pisaura mirabilis

Pardosa amentata

Zebra Spider

HOUSE SPIDER
Tegenaria gigantea
Family Agelenidae
11-15 mm. This is one of the spiders that commonly scuttle across the floor in the evening. It is especially common in outbuildings and also found out of doors. The web is a roughly triangular horizontal sheet (cobweb), spun in a corner with a tubular retreat in the angle. It is not sticky, but small insects get their feet entangled in the dense mat of threads and are easily caught by the spider. Adult in late summer and autumn. It is one of several similar species.

WATER SPIDER
Argyroneta aquatica
8-15 mm (sometimes much larger). Male often larger than female. It is the only spider living permanently under water. It builds a silken bell in ponds and other still waters and fills it with air brought from the surface among the body hairs. It sits in the bell by day, perhaps darting out after passing prey, and goes out to hunt at night. All year.

LINYPHIA TRIANGULARIS
Family Linyphiidae
5-6 mm. Abundant late summer and autumn, forming hammock webs on almost every bush and clump of grass. The spider hangs below the hammock, waiting for insects to collide with the scaffolding above and fall on to the sheet.

ENOPLOGNATHA OVATA
Family Theridiidae
3-6 mm.. Upper side of abdomen may be all cream, all red, or just with the 2 red lines. Abundant among brambles,

nettles and other dense vegetation, including garden plants. Female rolls up a leaf to form a shelter and rests there with her blue-green egg cocoon. The web is a loose 3-dimensional scaffold with sticky threads on the outside. More silk is thrown over trapped victims. Adult June-August.

DYSDERA CROCATA
Family Dysderidae
9-15 mm. A slow-moving hunter living under stones and logs, often in a silk-lined cell. It makes no web and hunts at night, specializing in woodlice, which it captures with its huge fangs: one pierces the underside of the wood-louse and the other goes in through the top. Early summer.

PISAURA MIRABILIS
Family Pisauridae
12-15 mm. Abundant in dense vegetation, this is one of the wolf spiders which roam around in search of prey and chase after it. It often rests with the two front pairs of legs held close together and pointing forward at an angle of about 30° to the body. Female carries her egg cocoon around in her fangs, attaching it to a plant when the eggs are about to hatch and then covering it with a silken tent. She stands guard over it until the young have dispersed. Adult May-July.

DOLOMEDES FIMBRIATUS
9-13 mm (male); 13-25 mm (female). Another wolf spider, inhabiting marshes and the edges of ponds and streams. It often sits on a floating leaf with the front legs resting on the water, and if it senses an insect on the water nearby it

skates after it. When alarmed, the spider may walk down plant stems into the water. May-July.

PARDOSA AMENTATA
Family Lycosidae
5-7 mm. A very common wolf spider which hunts on the ground and is regularly seen sunbathing on rockery stones and in other exposed places. The female carries her egg cocoon attached to the spinnerets at her hind end, and when the eggs hatch she carries the babies on her back for a few days. April-September. One of several very similar species.

TARANTULA
Lycosa narbonensis
25 mm. This is the famous tarantula of southern Europe – a wolf spider whose bite was supposed to be fatal unless the victim embarked on a long and furious dance which became known as the tarantella. In fact, although the bite may be troublesome, it is not really dangerous. The spider lives in a burrow and hunts on the ground. Like all wolf spiders, it has large eyes. All year.

ZEBRA SPIDER
Salticus scenicus
Family Salticidae
5-7 mm. Common on sunny rocks and walls, including house walls, this is one of the jumping spiders, with very large eyes. It hunts by sight like the wolf spiders, but when it spots prey it creeps slowly towards it and then, when within range, leaps on to it. The prey is held down by the sturdy front legs and then bitten by the fangs. The spider can leap many times its own length. April-September.

145

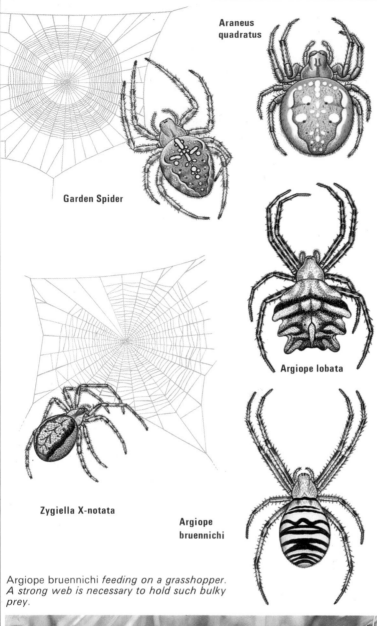

Araneus quadratus

Garden Spider

Argiope lobata

Zygiella X-notata

Argiope bruennichi

Argiope bruennichi *feeding on a grasshopper. A strong web is necessary to hold such bulky prey.*

ORB-WEB SPIDERS
Family Argiopidae

These spiders spin the circular webs which are so beautiful when covered with dew or frost in autumn. The spiders mature at this time and the webs are at their largest. The spider may rest at the centre of its web, but more often hides under a nearby leaf until an insect flies into the web. Eggs are laid in silken cocoons, often on walls and fences, and they hatch in spring.

GARDEN SPIDER
Araneus diadematus
4-8 mm (male); 10-12 mm (female). One of the commonest of the orb-web spiders, abundant on fences and hedges August-October. Pale brown to almost black, the white cross on abdomen rather variable.

ARANEUS QUADRATUS
6-8 mm (male); 9-15 mm (female). The very rounded abdomen, usually with 4 distinct white spots, distinguishes this species which varies from greenish-yellow to dark brown. August-October, especially on heathland.

ZYGIELLA X-NOTATA
3·5 mm (male); 6·5 mm (female). Colour varies, but usually a distinct leaf-like pattern on abdomen. Very common July-October, especially on and around buildings. Web has a missing segment (see illustration).

ARGIOPE LOBATA
7 mm (male); 20 mm (female). Makes a web similar to that of *A. bruennichi*. August-October. Mediterranean region.

ARGIOPE BRUENNICHI
4 mm (male): 11-14 mm (female). This striking spider makes a web with a zig-zag band of silk across the middle, usually from top to bottom, to strengthen it. August-October. Southern and central Europe: rare in southern Britain.

CRAB SPIDERS
Family Thomisidae

Mostly crab-like in appearance with front two pairs of legs usually larger than the rest and often walking sideways. They spin no webs and usually lie in ambush for their prey, although they may hunt.

XYSTICUS CRISTATUS
4-7 mm. Very common in low herbage in spring and summer. Male sticks female down with silk before mating.

MISUMENA VATIA

3-4 mm (male); 10-11 mm (female). Greenish, yellow or white according to background. Usually lurks in flowers and catches insects that come to feed. May-July. Not in north.

Harvestmen

These arachnids (Order Opiliones) are often confused with spiders, but the body is not clearly divided into two sections. There are no poison fangs and the animals produce no silk. There are two eyes, perched on a turret near the middle of the back. Most species mature in late summer – hence their common name. They are mostly nocturnal and eat a wide range of living and dead animal matter.

PHALANGIUM OPILIO

4-9 mm. Female larger than male. Underside of body pure white. Chelicerae of male bear large, forward-pointing brown horns. Very common in rough herbage.

LEIOBUNUM ROTUNDUM

3·5-6 mm. Female longer than round-bodied male and heavily mottled. Abundant in rough herbage in all kinds of habitats, often resting on walls and tree trunks by day.

False Scorpions

These very small arachnids (Order Pseudoscorpiones) resemble scorpions in having relatively large claws but lack their tails. Many species, rarely more than 3 mm long, live in leaf litter and other debris, feeding on various small animals. *Lamprochernes nodosus* is a common example.

Scorpions

EUSCORPIUS FLAVICAUDUS
Family Chactidae

35 mm. One of the smallest scorpions, but endowed with the typical claws (modified palps) and long tail of the group. The sting is rarely, if ever, used and the animal is not dangerous. It hides in crevices, especially in old walls, with the claws protruding at night to capture small animals. Mainly southern Europe, but established elsewhere, including some port areas of Britain. All year.

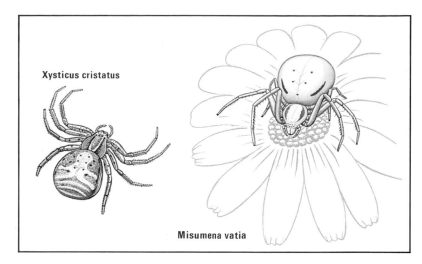

Xysticus cristatus

Misumena vatia

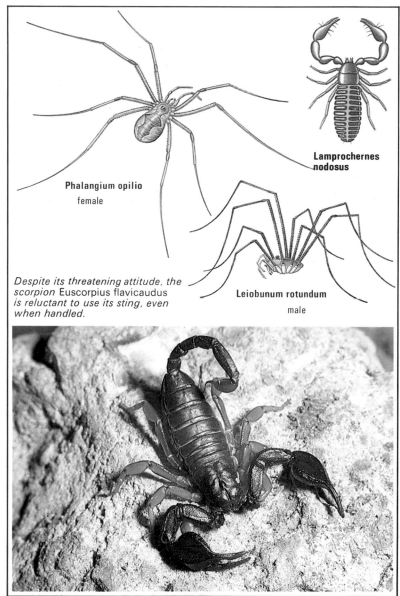

Phalangium opilio
female

Lamprochernes
nodosus

Leiobunum rotundum
male

Despite its threatening attitude, the scorpion Euscorpius flavicaudus *is reluctant to use its sting, even when handled.*

Insects

The insects (Class Insecta) form the largest class of the arthropods and are, in fact, the largest of all animal groups, with something like a million known species and certainly many more to be discovered. Their extraordinary success is due in part to their small size – the *average* size is rather less than a grain of rice – which enables them to occupy habitats denied to larger animals and to exist in immense numbers in small areas.

Adult insects can almost all be recognized by their three pairs of legs, one pair of antennae, and a body clearly divided into three sections – head, thorax and abdomen. Most adult insects also have two pairs of wings, but there are many wingless species and some have only one pair of wings. There is great variation in the form of the wings.

Very few insects live in the sea, but they can be found in almost every terrestrial and freshwater habitat, feeding on just about everything from nectar to wood and from blood to dried dung. To deal with such varied diets, they have an extraordinary range of mouthparts – from slender tubes for drinking nectar, to the powerful jaws needed to chew solid wood.

Insect Life Cycles

The insects exhibit two main types of life history. In the first, exemplified by the grasshoppers, the youngster looks much like the adult except that it lacks functional wings. Such a youngster is called a nymph and it usually eats the same kind of food as the adult. It moults its skin periodically and the wing buds on its back get larger at each moult. At the final moult, the adult insect, complete with fully developed wings, crawls out of the old nymphal skin. This type of life history, in which the young gradually assume the adult form, is called a partial metamorphosis. Dragonflies, bugs and earwigs all have this kind of life history.

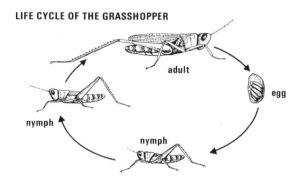

LIFE CYCLE OF THE GRASSHOPPER

adult

egg

nymph

nymph

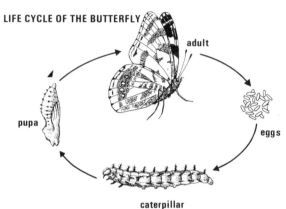

LIFE CYCLE OF THE BUTTERFLY

adult

eggs

pupa

caterpillar

Top: The partial metamorphosis of the grasshopper, with a gradual change from young to adult form. Above: The complete metamorphosis of the butterfly, involving a sudden change in the pupal stage.

Opposite page: A honey bee (top left), a stick insect (bottom left), a longhorn beetle (top right) and an emperor dragonfly show something of the wide variety of insect life. The few European stick insects (Order Phasmida) are all wingless, although many tropical ones have wings.

The second type of life history, typified by the butterflies and moths, involves a youngster which is very different from the adult. It is called a caterpillar or larva and it often exists on quite different food from the adult. The butterfly caterpillar, for example, is a leaf-feeder, while the adult sips nectar from flowers. The larva moults periodically, but does not gradually assume the adult form and shows no sign of wings. When fully grown, it turns into a pupa or chrysalis, and it is in this stage that the larval body is converted into that of the adult. This type of life history, shown by flies, bees and beetles, as well as butterflies and moths, is known as a complete metamorphosis.

The Orders of Insects

The insects are arranged in about 30 orders, most of which are named according to the structure of the wings. Butterflies and moths, for example, belong to the Lepidoptera, which means 'scale-winged' and refers to the coating of scales on the wings. Beetles, with their tough horny front wings, belong to the Coleoptera or 'sheath-winged' insects.

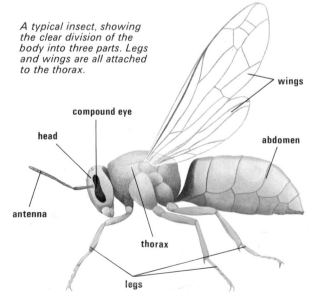

A typical insect, showing the clear division of the body into three parts. Legs and wings are all attached to the thorax.

wings

compound eye

head

abdomen

antenna

thorax

legs

Dragonflies

Dragonflies (Order Odonata) are long-bodied insects with 2 pairs of gauzy wings and very short bristle-like antennae. The eyes are very large. Dragonflies eat other insects which they scoop up in mid-air with their spiky legs. There are two main groups: The Anisoptera or true dragonflies, and the Zygoptera or damselflies. The true dragonflies are again divided into hawkers and darters. Hawkers spend most of their time on the wing, hawking to and fro in search of prey, while darters spend much time resting on the vegetation and simply dart out when prey approaches. Damselflies are much daintier than the hawkers and darters and generally fly rather slowly. They feed largely by plucking small insects from the vegetation. True dragonflies rest with wings outstretched, but damselflies normally fold their wings together over the body.

All dragonflies spend their early life in water. The nymphs are fiercely carnivorous, shooting out their spiky jaws to impale other small animals. The nymphs usually climb reeds when it is time for the adults to emerge. There is no chrysalis stage. Adult colours may take several days to develop fully. The larger dragon-flies are strong fliers and often roam far from water, but the insects are most commonly seen close to ponds and streams. Sizes given are wingspans.

EMPEROR DRAGONFLY
Anax imperator
Family Aeshnidae
105 mm. Male has bright blue abdomen; female normally green with a brown tip, although some old females are blue. Both sexes with green thorax. A hawker, found mainly near still water such as canals and large ponds, May-August. Southern and central Europe.

BROWN AESHNA
Aeshna grandis
100 mm. Only male has blue spots at front of abdomen. Hawks to and fro along a definite beat, usually over or along the edge of water, June-October. Prefers still or slow-moving water. Most of Europe, including the Arctic, but not Scotland.

DOWNY EMERALD
Cordulia linaenea
Family Corduliidae
60-70 mm. A fast-flying hawker, easily recognized by the green eyes, metallic green thorax, and bronzy abdomen. The thorax is also very hairy. May-August over ponds and canals. Widespread, but local.

GOLD-RINGED DRAGONFLY
Cordulegaster boltonii
Family Cordulegasteridae
100 mm. Hawks low over small streams May-September. Female uses her long ovipositor to dig her eggs into the silt at the bottom of the stream. The insect prefers upland areas and is common on heaths and moors in most parts of Europe. *C. bidentatus* of southern and central Europe is very similar but lacks the small yellow spots at hind edge of each segment.

LIBELLULA DEPRESSA
Family Libellulidae
75 mm. A fast-flying darter. Female is brown with yellow spots along sides of abdomen: male is also like this when young, but develops blue colour as he matures. Dark patch at base of each wing distinguishes this species from several similar ones. Flies May-August and perches more or less horizontally on bushes and other vegetation, often selecting a dead twig. Prefers still and slow-moving water and will breed in brackish pools by the sea.

FOUR-SPOTTED LIBELLULA
Libellula quadrimaculata
75 mm. Easily recognized by the 4 spots – one near the middle of the front edge of each wing. Both sexes are brown, but may be distinguished by the larger claspers of the male. Flies May-August, often rests on ground. Prefers boggy pools and wet heaths.

RUDDY SYMPETRUM
Sympetrum sanguineum
55 mm. One of several similarly coloured darters, but male is distinguished by the strongly constricted abdomen. Female is orange-brown. Legs are black without a yellow stripe in both sexes. Flies June-September, breeding in ponds and ditches where reedmace and horsetails grow. Settles on bare ground, rocks and twigs, often with wings drooping.

BANDED AGRION
Agrion splendens
Family Agriidae
60-65 mm. One of the largest of the damselflies. Female has a greener metallic body and uniform yellowish-green wings. Flies May-October, preferring quiet streams with muddy bottoms and plenty of weeds. Weak-flying female spends most of the time on the vegetation; males 'dance' quite rapidly over the waterside plants, often in large numbers. Most of Europe, but not Scotland.

LARGE RED DAMSELFLY
Pyrrhosoma nymphula
Family Coenagriidae
40-50 mm. Female has more black on the abdomen, including a black line down the centre. Legs black in both sexes (the Small Red Damselfly has red legs). It is one of the commonest damselflies and one of the first to appear in spring. It flies April-September, inhabiting still and slow-moving water, including peat bogs.

COMMON BLUE DAMSELFLY
Enallagma cyathigerum
35-40 mm. Male usually easily distinguished from similar blue and black damselflies by the stalked black spot at front of abdomen. Female is green and black and may be recognized by a small spine under 8th segment of abdomen. Flies May-September at edges of still and slow-moving water with plenty of vegetation.

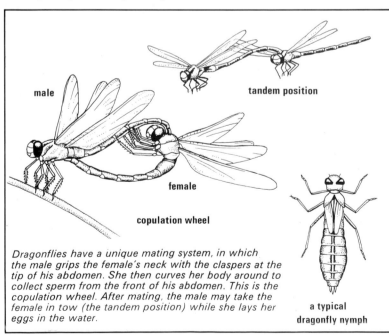

male

tandem position

female

copulation wheel

a typical dragonfly nymph

Dragonflies have a unique mating system, in which the male grips the female's neck with the claspers at the tip of his abdomen. She then curves her body around to collect sperm from the front of his abdomen. This is the copulation wheel. After mating, the male may take the female in tow (the tandem position) while she lays her eggs in the water.

Emperor Dragonfly
male

Gold-ringed Dragonfly
male

Brown Aeshna
male

Downy Emerald
male

Ruddy Sympetrum
male

Libellula depressa
male

Four-spotted Libellula
male

Banded Agrion
male

Large Red Damselfly
male

Common Blue Damselfly
male

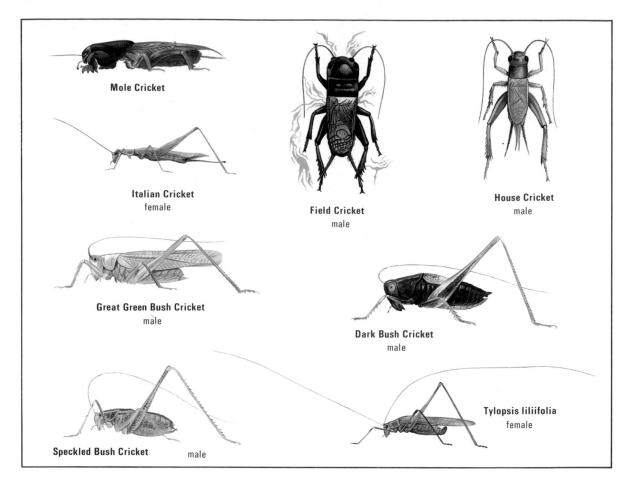

Mole Cricket

Italian Cricket
female

Field Cricket
male

House Cricket
male

Great Green Bush Cricket
male

Dark Bush Cricket
male

Tylopsis liliifolia
female

Speckled Bush Cricket   male

Grasshoppers and Crickets

These insects (Order Orthoptera) generally have tough front wings and membranous hind wings, although many species are wingless. The hind legs are long and used for jumping. The males of most species 'sing' by rubbing one part of the body against another. There is no chrysalis stage and young resemble adults.

MOLE CRICKET
Gryllotalpa gryllotalpa
Family Gryllotalpidae
35-45 mm. Front legs modified for digging; front wings short. Spends much time underground, feeding on roots and insect grubs, but can fly. Damp meadows in late summer and again in spring after hibernation. Very rare in Britain.

TRUE CRICKETS
Family Gryllidae

The front wings, when present, form a box-like cover for the body, distinctly flattened on top. Males sing by rubbing the two front wings together. Females have a slender, spear-like ovipositor (egg-layer).

FIELD CRICKET
Gryllus campestris
20 mm. A warmth-loving insect of dry grassland. It is flightless and lives in burrows. Female is browner. Male has a shrill song. Spring and early summer, mainly diurnal. Southern and central Europe: now rare in Britain.

HOUSE CRICKET
Acheta domesticus
15 mm. Mainly nocturnal. Hind wings project like tails from end of body when folded. Both sexes fly well. Male has shrill song. Mostly in buildings. All year.

ITALIAN CRICKET
Oecanthus pellucens
9-15 mm. A delicate insect of shrubs and other tall vegetation. Female wings are much narrower on top than male's. Male has a beautiful soft warbling song at nightfall. July-October. Southern Europe.

BUSH CRICKETS
Family Tettigoniidae

These insects differ from true crickets in having no large flat area on top. They are like grasshoppers in shape but have longer antennae. Males sing by rubbing the front wings together. Females have a broad, sabre-like ovipositor – long and straight or short and strongly curved. Most eat both plant and animal matter – usually insects – and are active mainly towards evening. They usually inhabit scrubby places and mature in late summer. The group is now usually split into several families.

GREAT GREEN BUSH CRICKET
Tettigonia viridissima
40-50 mm. Bright green with brown on top of head and at base of male front wing. Song loud, in long bursts. Not in northern Britain.

SPECKLED BUSH CRICKET
Leptophyes punctatissima
9-17 mm. Bright green with dark spots. Wings minute; front ones forming a

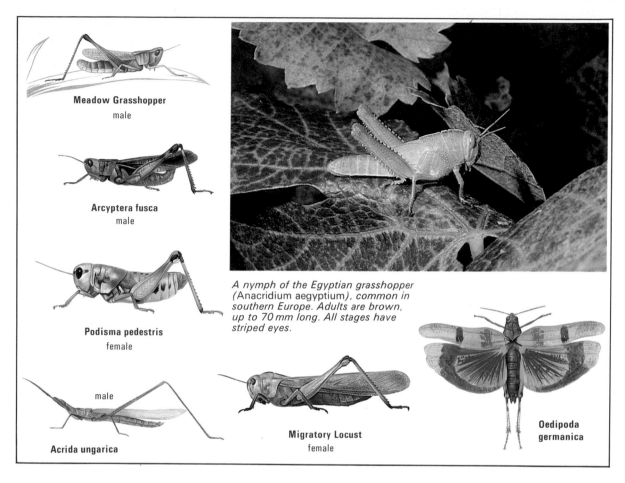

Meadow Grasshopper
male

Arcyptera fusca
male

Podisma pedestris
female

male

Acrida ungarica

A nymph of the Egyptian grasshopper (Anacridium aegyptium), *common in southern Europe. Adults are brown, up to 70 mm long. All stages have striped eyes.*

Migratory Locust
female

Oedipoda germanica

little saddle in male. Song almost inaudible. Ovipositor short and curved.

DARK BUSH CRICKET
Pholidoptera griseoaptera
13-20 mm. Yellowish-brown to black. Front wings are small flaps in male; female wingless. Ovipositor long. Song is a series of short chirps.

TYLOPSIS LILIIFOLIA
13-23 mm. Brown or green, with very long antennae. Both sexes fly well. Ovipositor short and curved. Song very faint. Southern Europe.

GRASSHOPPERS
Family Acrididae

These are mostly sturdily-built, bullet-shaped insects with short antennae and narrow front wings, although many are wingless, especially montane species. Females are usually larger than males. Males sing by rubbing their back legs against veins on front wings, but many species are silent. They are usually active only in sunshine. All are vegetarian. The group is now usually split into several families.

MEADOW GRASSHOPPER
Chorthippus parallelus
10-24 mm (female much larger than male). Colour may be any combination of green, brown, pink and red. Female front wings much shorter than male: hind wings absent in both sexes, therefore flightless. Song is a buzzing sound lasting for up to 3 seconds and getting louder. Most kinds of grassland July-November.

ARCYPTERA FUSCA
22-40 mm. Female longer and fatter than male but with shorter wings (flightless). Song very loud: starts with a few short notes, turns into a warble, and then dies away with a few more short notes. Grassy places in mountains July-September. Not Britain.

MIGRATORY LOCUST
Locusta migratoria
30-50 mm. Male much smaller than female shown here. Colour varies, but males often brownish and females largely green. It forms huge swarms in some areas – especially in Africa – and is then greyish-brown or yellow. Most European specimens are of the solitary phase, always found alone and distinguished by the prominently domed thorax. They occur in all kinds of habitats July-November and may hibernate as adults to reappear in spring. Mainly in southern Europe, but it is strong-flying and occasionally migrates to Britain and other northern regions.

ACRIDA UNGARICA
30-75 mm. Female much larger than male. Green or brown, sometimes with light and dark patterns, and very hard to see when it is sitting upright among the grasses. July-October, mainly in the damper grasslands. Mediterranean.

PODISMA PEDESTRIS
15-30 mm. Female larger than male. Flightless, with wings reduced to tiny flaps in both sexes. A montane species, rarely found below 1,000 metres. Stony ground in August and September. Not in Britain. (The closely related *P. alpina* has yellow hind tibiae.)

OEDIPODA GERMANICA
15-30 mm. Female somewhat larger than male. At rest on the ground, the insect is well camouflaged, but if disturbed it flies away and flashes its red hind wings. It quickly drops to the ground again and this is believed to confuse the enemy, which continues to search for something red. The song is very quiet and produced only in the presence of a female. June-November in dry fields and hillsides, especially in stony areas. Southern and central Europe: not in Britain. (The closely related *O. coerulescens* has bright blue hind wings.)

153

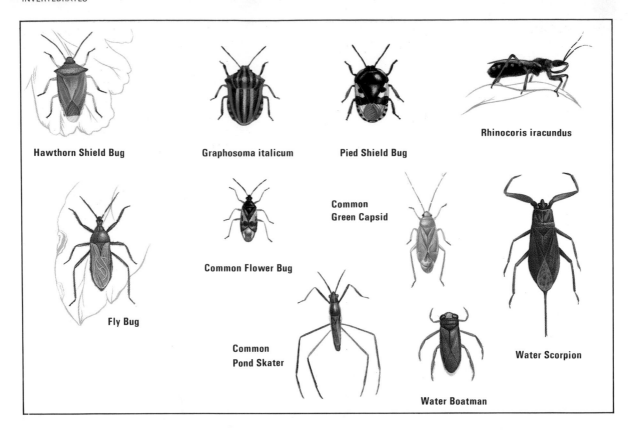

Hawthorn Shield Bug

Graphosoma italicum

Pied Shield Bug

Rhinocoris iracundus

Fly Bug

Common Flower Bug

Common Green Capsid

Common Pond Skater

Water Boatman

Water Scorpion

Bugs

This order (Hemiptera) is extremely varied, but all members possess a needle-like beak for piercing and sucking up fluids. Most have 4 wings, but many are wingless. There are two major divisions – the Heteroptera and the Homoptera. The front wings of the Heteroptera, when present, have a horny basal area and a membranous tip. The front wings of the Homoptera, when present, are of uniform texture throughout – either horny or membranous. There are also some differences in the beaks of the two groups. The Heteroptera include both plant and animal feeders and all the water bugs. The Homoptera are all terrestrial plant-feeders. Each group has many families. The young resemble the adults and there is no chrysalis stage.

HETEROPTERA

HAWTHORN SHIELD BUG
Acanthosoma haemorrhoidale
Family Acanthosomatidae
14 mm. One of many shield bugs, so called for their shape. It feeds on haw-

thorn leaves and berries in autumn and again after hibernation.

GRAPHOSOMA ITALICUM
Family Pentatomidae
10 mm. The bright colours of this shield bug warn of a most unpleasant taste. It feeds on a variety of umbelliferous plants August-October. Southern and central Europe: not in Britain.

PIED SHIELD BUG
Sehirus bicolor
Family Cydnidae
5-7 mm. Feeds mainly on the sap of white deadnettle, on which it can be found at most times of the year. Adults hibernate under the ground.

RHINOCORIS IRACUNDUS
Family Reduviidae
12 mm. One of the assassin bugs – predatory species with strong, curved beaks. It feeds on a variety of insects, plunging its beak into them to drain out the fluids. Summer and autumn. Southern and central Europe: not Britain.

FLY BUG
Reduvius personatus
17 mm. Another of the assassin bugs, usually found in houses and stables. It feeds on silverfish, flies and various other insects including bedbugs. Rarely bites man. All summer. Southern and central Europe: southern Britain only.

COMMON FLOWER BUG
Anthocoris nemorum
Family Cimicidae
3-4 mm. A very common predatory bug

found on leaves and flowers. It feeds on aphids and other small creatures, including the red spider mite which infests fruit trees. Spring to autumn: adults, especially females, hibernate under bark and in rubbish.

COMMON GREEN CAPSID
Lygocoris pabulinus
Family Miridae
5-6 mm. Abundant on trees and shrubs in spring and on a wide range of herbaceous plants in summer. Often a pest of soft fruit, which it punctures with its beak.

COMMON POND SKATER
Gerris lacustris
Family Gerridae
12 mm. Lives on the surface of still water, skating around on long 2nd pair of legs. Hind legs used as a rudder, and front legs for catching other small insects. April-November.

WATER BOATMAN
Corixa punctata
Family Corixidae
12-13 mm. Antennae hidden, as in most aquatic bugs. Swims with hairy back legs and feeds on algae. All year.

WATER SCORPION
Nepa cinerea
Family Nepidae
20 mm. Creeps slowly around in ponds, mainly on the bottom, and catches other animals with its powerful front legs. It draws air from the surface through the tube at the back. All year.

HOMOPTERA

CICADETTA MONTANA
Family Cicadidae
15-25 mm. Female larger than male. The only cicada found in Britain (New Forest only), but widely distributed in Europe. Rests on tree trunks and branches and sucks sap with stout beak. Male makes a rather bubbling whistle. Nymphs feed underground on the roots of trees and shrubs. May-July. (Several larger cicadas with much louder calls live in southern Europe.)

COMMON FROGHOPPER
Philaenus spumarius
Family Cercopidae
6 mm. Pattern varies. Abundant on trees and shrubs, leaping strongly when disturbed. Nymph lives in 'cuckoo spit', which protects it while it feeds on sap. June-September.

CERCOPIS VULNERATA
10 mm. This brightly coloured froghopper lives on various plants, mainly in wooded regions. The nymph lives on roots in a mass of solidified froth. April-August. Not in the north.

IASSUS LANIO
Family Cicadellidae
7-8 mm. One of a large group of leaping bugs known as leafhoppers. Usually on oaks July-October. Most leafhoppers are green or brown. They are distinguished from froghoppers by having lots of small spines on hind legs. The nymphs do not live in froth.

BUFFALO HOPPER
Stictocephala bisonia
Family Membracidae
10 mm. The pronotal shield just behind the head is extended back to the tip of the body. A native of North America, it is now well established in southern Europe. July-October.

BLACKFLY
Aphis fabae Family Aphididae
2-3 mm. Also called the black bean aphid, this pest lives in large numbers on beans, spinach, sugar-beet and many other plants. In spring and summer all the aphids are females, giving birth to many young without mating. They may be winged or wingless. April-October.

ROSE APHID
Macrosiphum rosae
2-3 mm. One of several very similar aphids collectively known as greenfly. Green or pink, with long black tubular outgrowths (siphunculi) at the hind end. Winged or wingless, it lives on roses in spring and early summer and then moves to teasels and scabious. Males occur only in late summer.

CABBAGE WHITEFLY
Aleyrodes proletella
Family Aleyrodidae
1-4 mm. Moth-like with tiny wings clothed with waxy powder. Feeds on the undersides of cabbage leaves in summer.

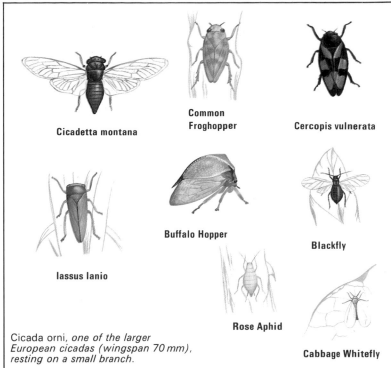

Cicadetta montana

Common Froghopper

Cercopis vulnerata

Iassus lanio

Buffalo Hopper

Blackfly

Rose Aphid

Cabbage Whitefly

Cicada orni, *one of the larger European cicadas (wingspan 70 mm), resting on a small branch.*

Butterflies

Butterflies, like moths, belong to the order Lepidoptera. Their wings are clothed with minute scales. All have clubbed antennae. European butterflies fly by day and rest with the wings held vertically over the body. The front legs are reduced in some families. Where only one insect is shown, the sexes are similar. Sizes given are wingspans.

SWALLOWTAILS AND APOLLOS
Family Papilionidae

A group with over 500 mostly large and colourful butterflies, mainly tropical. Most have tailed hind wings and all have 3 pairs of functional legs. The caterpillar has a retractable fleshy process behind the head. The pupa is usually attached to the foodplant in an upright position by tail hooks and a girdle of silk.

SWALLOWTAIL
Papilio machaon
60-98 mm. Flies between April and August in meadows and on flowery hillslopes in the lowlands and mountains up to about 2,000 metres. Occurs in North Africa, through most of Europe and across Asia as far as Japan. It is common in parts of continental Europe, but rare in Britain and found only in the marshy fens of East Anglia. There is usually one generation in the north but up to three in warmer parts of Europe.
The caterpillar feeds exclusively on the leaves of umbellifers, chiefly those of the Milk Parsley (*Peucedanum palustre*) in England, but on other species elsewhere. The caterpillar is at first black and white and looks like a bird-dropping, but later becomes green, ringed with black and orange, and has an orange retractable process behind the head.
Identification The Corsican Swallowtail (*P. hospiton*) resembles the Swallowtail, but it has a much more wavy edge to the dark band near the outer edge of the forewing, especially on the underside.

SCARCE SWALLOWTAIL
Iphiclides podalirius
65-84 mm. Now a protected species in parts of Europe, but widespread and quite common in places in North Africa and other parts of Europe northwards to the Baltic and across Asia to China. Specimens rarely reach England and Scandinavia, and never overwinter successfully. There are usually two generations each year flying in May and June and July and August. It is attracted to flowers and tree blossom in meadows, orchards and gardens, on grassy slopes, and along margins of woods; in places up to 1,800 metres.
The caterpillar is green, lined with yellow. It feeds on leaves of oak (*Quercus*), Blackthorn (*Prunus spinosa*) and other wild trees, as well as on cultivated cherries and other *Prunus* species.

APOLLO
Parnassius apollo
50-100 mm. Fairly common in the mountains of Europe (but not Britain) up to about 3,000 metres, and also at low elevations in Scandinavia and Finland. The single generation flies between May and September, usually in sunny places where the butterflies are attracted to flowers. The species is protected by law in many parts of Europe.
The caterpillar is black with grey-blue processes along the body, and orange spots along each side; it also has a Y-shaped retractable process behind the head. Stonecrops (*Sedum*) and, less often, saxifrages (*Saxifraga*) are the caterpillar's foodplants. The Apollo overwinters as a young caterpillar inside the unbroken egg-shell. It often starts to feed in the spring before the snow has all melted, but only does so in full sunshine.

caterpillar

Swallowtail

Scarce Swallowtail

Apollo

WHITES AND YELLOWS
Family Pieridae

A worldwide group of about 2,000 medium-sized species, with about 40 species in Europe.
Males usually differ slightly from females in colour-pattern. All six legs are functional. The caterpillars lack spines and are usually green in colour. Most feed on legumes (Pea family) or crucifers (Cabbage family) and some are agricultural pests.
The chrysalis is attached head-up to the foodplant, or elsewhere, by tail hooks and a girdle of silk.

LARGE WHITE
Pieris brassicae
56-67 mm. A common butterfly in gardens, agricultural land and hill slopes up to 2,000 metres. There are two or three generations each year, on the wing from April to August. Found in North Africa, in most of Europe and across Asia to the Himalayas. Often migrates in large numbers.
The caterpillar feeds in groups on cabbage (*Brassica*) and other crucifers, but also on garden Nasturtium (*Tropaeolum*). It is green striped with yellow, and mottled with black.

SMALL WHITE
Artogeia rapae
46-54 mm. A common species in most of Europe, North Africa, northern Asia and North America. In gardens, meadows and agricultural land during most of the summer, with usually two generations in northern and up to four in southern Europe. Sometimes migrates in large numbers. Cabbage (*Brassica*) is a common foodplant, but wild crucifers like Hedge Mustard (*Sisymbrium officinale*) are also eaten.
The caterpillar is green lined with yellow, and often chooses sheltered places on fences in which to pupate.
Identification Two southern European whites resemble the Small White: the Mountain Small White (*A. ergane*), which lacks black spots on the underside of the wings, and the Southern Small White (*A. mannii*), which has a larger black marking at the outer edge of the forewing.

GREEN-VEINED WHITE
Artogeia napi
39-51 mm. A migratory butterfly (less so than the Small White), but usually not a pest. Prefers meadows and hedgerows and often visits flowers. Except at high altitudes, there are usually two generations flying in May and June and in July and August. Found in North Africa, most of Europe, temperate Asia and North America.
The caterpillar is pale green lined with dark green and yellow. It feeds mainly on Charlock (*Sinapis arvensis*) and other wild crucifers.

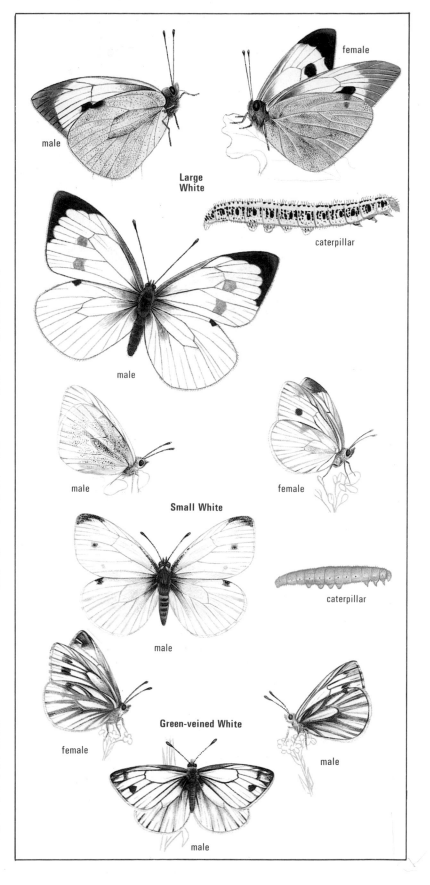

Large White

male

female

caterpillar

male

Small White

male

female

caterpillar

male

Green-veined White

female

male

male

157

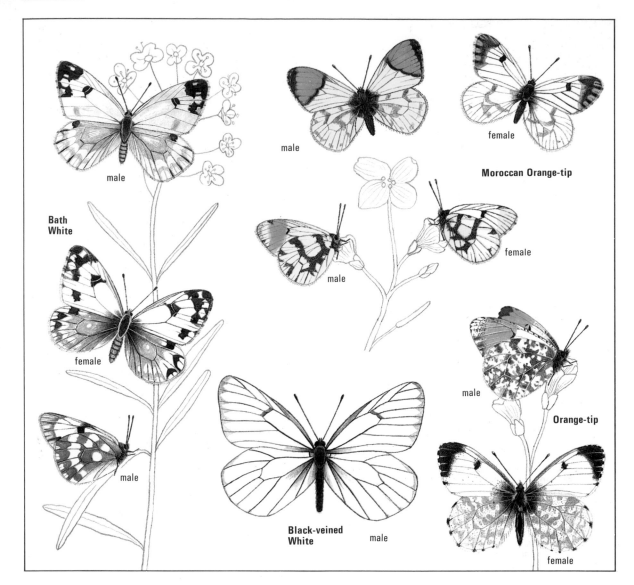

male

male

female

Moroccan Orange-tip

**Bath
White**

female

male

female

female

male

male

Orange-tip

**Black-veined
White** male

female

BLACK-VEINED WHITE
Aporia crataegi
57-67 mm. This butterfly is common along hedgerows, in fields of Lucerne (*Medicago sativa*) and open country in some parts of Europe, North Africa and temperate Asia, and can be a pest in orchards. In Britain it is now extinct. The single generation flies in May, June and July. The female forewing is almost transparent.
The caterpillar feeds in groups on the foliage of hawthorn (*Crataegus*), Blackthorn (*Prunus spinosa*) and apple (*Malus*), and rests in a large silken nest. It is black, lined with orange, above, and grey, spotted with white, below. The partly grown caterpillars overwinter inside the nest.

BATH WHITE
Pontia daplidice
40-51 mm. A Continental European butterfly commonest in southern Europe, but migrating specimens occasionally reach England. Bath Whites fly during much of the summer in two or more generations on grass-covered hills and in meadows up to about 2,000 metres. Found in North Africa, Europe and temperate Asia as far as Japan.
The caterpillar is violet-grey, lined with pale yellow. It feeds on Mountain Alison (*Alyssum montanum*) and many other crucifers.
Identification Separable from the similarly coloured female Orange-tip (*Anthocharis cardamines*) by the more strongly marked upper side of the forewing.

ORANGE-TIP
Anthocharis cardamines
33-48 mm. The butterflies of the single yearly generation usually emerge between March and July. They fly along hedgerows and in meadows, often near woods, and are frequently attracted to flowers. Found in most of Europe as far north as the Arctic Circle and across Asia to Japan.
The caterpillar is green with black spots and white lines. It feeds on Cuckoo Flower (*Cardamine pratensis*) and other crucifers and eventually changes into a chrysalis on or near the foodplant.

MOROCCAN ORANGE-TIP
Anthocharis belia
32-39 mm. This butterfly often visits flowers in open, uncultivated land and in woodland glades. The single generation flies between May and July in Europe, but often earlier in North Africa. Found only in southern Europe and North Africa, usually in mountainous country up to 1,800 metres.
The caterpillar is green, with white lines on the sides and black and yellow on the back. It feeds on *Biscutella* and other crucifers.

MOUNTAIN CLOUDED YELLOW
Colias phicomone

39-47 mm. An alpine butterfly found in meadows and on grass slopes up to 2,400 metres. Restricted to the Alps and Pyrenees. There is usually one generation, flying in July and August, but sometimes two, with a second flight in late August and September.

The caterpillar is green mottled with black, and has a white stripe on the sides. It feeds on various kinds of vetches, including *Vicia* and *Coronilla*, lucerne (*Medicago sativa*) and other legumes. Overwintering caterpillars start to feed again early in the spring.

Identification This is the only western European Clouded Yellow living in mountainous regions that has greyish-yellow wings, but the Pale Arctic Clouded Yellow (*C. nastes*) of the far north is quite similar.

CLOUDED YELLOW
Colias crocea

47-61 mm. Migrates northwards during the summer, but a year-long resident in southern Europe, south-western Asia and North Africa. Flies from early spring until October in a succession of generations. Found in meadows up to about 1,500 metres, and often common in fields of lucerne and clover.

The caterpillar is green, with a line of yellow and red, and a row of black spots on the side. It feeds on clovers and lucerne and other legumes and changes into a chrysalis on the food-plant. The last generation of the year overwinters in the caterpillar stage.

Identification The normal female is slightly paler than the male and has yellow spots in the black borders. There is, however, a very pale variety of the female with dusky hind wings. Known as *helice*, it makes up about 10 per cent of the female population. It is easily confused with the female Pale Clouded Yellow, but the black margins are much less extensive in this latter species and the underside of the hind wing is a much brighter yellow, without any grey clouding.

PALE CLOUDED YELLOW
Colias hyale

44-54 mm. Less of a southern species than the Clouded Yellow. Resident in southern and central Europe, migrating in warm years to Britain and Scandinavia. Occurs also in temperate western and central Asia. There are two generations each year, the first flying in May and June, the second in August and September. Often visits fields of lucerne (*Medicago sativa*) and clover (*Trifolium*), but also found in grassy country up to about 2,000 metres.

The caterpillar feeds on vetches (*Hippocrepis* and *Coronilla*), lucerne, clovers and other legumes. It is green, striped with white, orange and yellow. Caterpillars of the second generation overwinter.

male

female

Mountain Clouded Yellow

male

female (form *helice*)

female (typical form)

caterpillar

Clouded Yellow

male

male

female

male

Pale Clouded Yellow

caterpillar

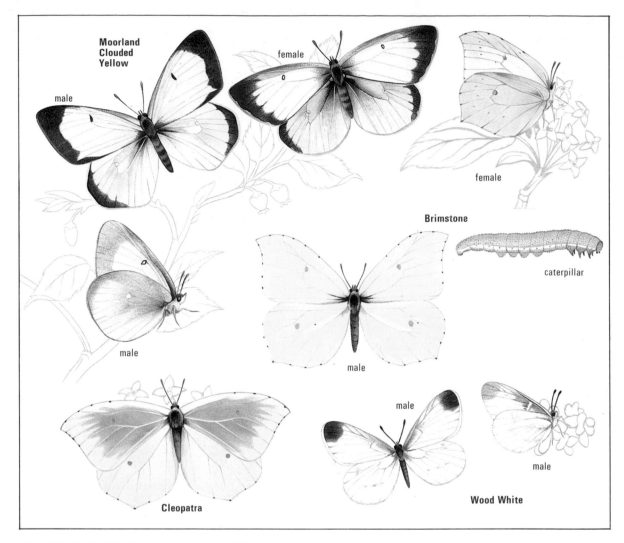

Moorland Clouded Yellow

male

female

female

Brimstone

caterpillar

male

male

male

male

Cleopatra

Wood White

MOORLAND CLOUDED YELLOW
Colias palaeno

38-42 mm. A locally common butterfly, but decreasing in numbers following drainage of marshes and wet moors and meadows where the caterpillar's foodplant grows. Flies in June, July and August in a single generation, often near woods from sea-level to 2,500 metres. Found in France and northern Europe (but not Britain) across Asia to Japan, and also in North America.

The caterpillar is green, striped with yellow and black, and feeds on Northern Bilberry (*Vaccinium uliginosum*) and other species of *Vaccinium*. It overwinters.

CLEOPATRA
Gonepteryx cleopatra

50-60 mm. Flies from May onwards in open woods or scrubland, often on mountain slopes up to 2,000 metres. Found only in southern Europe and western Asia. There is usually one generation in Europe but more than one in Asia.

The caterpillar feeds mainly on species of *Rhamnus*. It is similar to the caterpillar of the Brimstone but is more bluish in colour.

Identification The males differ from the Brimstone (*G.rhamni*) chiefly in the much more orange colour of the upper side of the forewing; the female differs most noticeably on the underside of the forewing, where there is a faint orange area near the base.

BRIMSTONE
Gonepteryx rhamni

50-62 mm. Overwinters as an adult, and one of the first butterflies to appear in the spring. Flies on heaths, and along hedges and the edges of woods during June and July, before hibernating and reappearing in February or March. Often in gardens.

The caterpillar feeds on Buckthorn (*Rhamnus catharticus*) and, less often, on Alder Buckthorn (*Frangula alnus*). It is green, spotted with black and striped with darker green and white.

Identification The males are easily distinguished from male Cleopatra butterflies (*G.cleopatra*) by the yellow forewings; the greenish-white females are identified mainly by the absence of an orange area on the underside of the forewing.

WOOD WHITE
Leptidea sinapis

35-46 mm. A mainly woodland species found in clearings and along the edges of woods up to about 1,900 metres. Occurs in most of Europe, except for Scotland and the Arctic, and in temperate Asia as far east as Japan. It is on the wing with a characteristic weak flight in a single generation in May and June in the north, and with a second flight later in the year in warmer parts.

The caterpillar feeds on vetches (*Vicia*), trefoils (*Lotus*) and other legumes. It is green, striped with dark green and yellow.

Identification Separable from the Eastern Wood White (*L.duponcheli*) by the white patch under the club of the antenna. The dark apical mark on the forewing is less well marked in the female, especially in second brood insects where it may be absent altogether.

SNOUT BUTTERFLIES
Family Libytheidae

There is just one European species in this mainly tropical family. Female forelegs well-developed; males have reduced forelegs, as in the closely related Family Nymphalidae. Both sexes have a toothed margin to the forewing and most have long, beak-like palps. The chrysalis is suspended from hooks at the tail end.

NETTLE-TREE BUTTERFLY
Libythea celtis
36-42 mm. Found only where there are Nettle-trees (*Celtis australis*) and restricted to North Africa, southern Europe up to about 800 metres, and across Asia to Japan. Flies in June, July and August in a single generation, but also in early spring when overwintering butterflies reappear.
The caterpillar is brown or green, striped with white and black. It feeds on Nettle-tree foliage.

ADMIRALS, EMPERORS, VANESSIDS AND FRITILLARIES
Family Nymphalidae

A worldwide group of several thousand medium-sized species, with about 70 representatives in Europe. All the species have reduced forelegs and most are colourful, strongly flying butterflies. The upper-side colour-pattern usually differs from that of the underside, but males and females resemble each other fairly closely. The caterpillars are generally covered with spines. The chrysalids are often ornamented with shiny gold or silver markings, and are suspended from hooks at the tail end.

PURPLE EMPEROR
Apatura iris
64-80 mm. Males usually fly around the upper branches of oak trees (*Quercus*), but may be attracted to rotting animal material and damp patches on the ground. Fairly common in July and August up to about 1,500 metres in much of Europe, including Britain, but not in Sweden or Norway.
The caterpillar, which overwinters, is green, marked with yellow and white, and has two long horns on the head. It feeds mostly on sallows (*Salix*), resting along the middle of a leaf on a layer of silk.

Nettle-tree Butterfly

male

Purple Emperor

male

female

A purple emperor caterpillar feeding on sallow leaves. The diagonal stripes make it look just like a rolled leaf.

male

**Lesser
Purple
Emperor**

male

male

**Poplar
Admiral**

Southern White Admiral

White Admiral

caterpillar

LESSER PURPLE EMPEROR
Apatura ilia
64-70 mm. A rather scarce butterfly of open woodlands, up to about 1,500 metres. On the wing between April and June and again in August and September, but with only one generation in the north and the Alps. Found in southern and central Europe (not Britain or Scandinavia) and in temperate Asia as far east as Japan.
The caterpillar is green, spotted and striped with yellow, and has two processes on the head. It feeds mainly on Black Poplar (*Populus nigra*) and other poplars, but probably also on willow (*Salix*) and other trees. The caterpillar overwinters.
Identification Separated from the Purple Emperor (*A. iris*) by the orange margin around the dark spot near the edge of the upper side of the forewing.

POPLAR ADMIRAL
Limenitis populi
70-80 mm. Common in woodland clearings up to about 1,500 metres in some areas but rare and local in others. The male usually flies high up in the trees, but may descend to feed on rotting animal matter and fruit. Appears in June and July in a single flight. Found in central and northern Europe, but not in Britain.
The caterpillar is mostly green, with two rows of fleshy processes along the back, and four shiny patches on the middle of the back. It feeds on Aspen (*Populus tremula*) and other poplars and overwinters in a rolled dead leaf.

SOUTHERN WHITE ADMIRAL
Limenitis reducta
42-48 mm. Widespread and locally common near woods and in woodland glades up to about 1,000 metres. Flies throughout the summer in one to three broods. Found in southern and central Europe and western Asia.
The caterpillar is green, striped with white, and has two rows of red spines along the body. It feeds on Honeysuckle (*Lonicera*), spinning a web under a leaf. Caterpillars of the autumn generation overwinter.
Identification Unlike the White Admiral, this species has only one row of black spots on the underside along the margin of the hind wing. The white spot near the centre of the front wing also identifies it.

WHITE ADMIRAL
Limenitis camilla
52-60 mm. A woodland species often attracted to Bramble (*Rubus*) flowers and decaying animal matter. Fairly common in a single flight during June and July up to 1,500 metres in most of Europe, except for the extreme south and north, and also found in temperate Asia as far east as Japan.
The caterpillar is green, striped with purple and white, and when young, attaches droppings to its body as camouflage. It feeds on Honeysuckle and overwinters on the foodplant.

CAMBERWELL BEAUTY
Nymphalis antiopa
60-73 mm. An elegant, strongly flying, migratory butterfly of open woodlands, particularly in hilly areas up to about 1,500 metres. Fond of feeding on rotting fruit and animal matter. The single yearly flight appears in June and July and continues until the autumn, when the survivors hibernate until early the following year. Found in North America and temperate Asia and in most of Europe, but in Britain only as a rare migrant.
The caterpillar is black with red markings and numerous hairy spines. It feeds on sallows (*Salix*) and other trees.

LARGE TORTOISESHELL
Nymphalis polychloros
54-66 mm. Usually found near woods, along old hedgerows, or in orchards where rotting fruit proves attractive. The butterflies emerge in July and August, then hibernate and fly again in the spring. Found in eastern England, most of continental Europe from sea-level to 1,300 metres, North Africa and western Asia.
The caterpillar is black, striped with brownish-orange, and has numerous yellow spines. It feeds in a group on elm, sallow and other trees.
Identification Separated from the Small Tortoiseshell by its size and the colour-pattern of the hind wing.

SMALL TORTOISESHELL
Aglais urticae
44-52 mm. One of the most abundant European butterflies wherever there are flowers, and a common visitor to Ice-plant (*Sedum*) and *Buddleia* flowers. This species does migrate, but not in great numbers. It overwinters as an adult butterfly and can be seen as early as March, flying until September or October in two or more generations. Found throughout Europe and temperate Asia to Japan from sea-level to 3,500 metres.
The caterpillar lives with others in a large web on nettles (*Urtica*). It is usually black above and greenish below, with several rows of spines.
Identification Best separated from the Large Tortoiseshell by the uniformly black base to the hind wing.

PEACOCK
Inachis io
56-68 mm. Regularly visits *Buddleia* in gardens and attracted to knapweeds (*Centaurea*) and other flowers. The main flight is from June onwards, the survivors overwintering until the following spring to produce the next year's generation. Generally common in Europe up to about 1,500 metres, except in Arctic Scandinavia, and across Asia to Japan. The unusual colour-pattern of the upper side possibly scares away small birds when the butterfly suddenly opens its wings.
The caterpillar feeds in a group on the young leaves of nettles (*Urtica*). It is black, spotted with white, and has numerous branched, black spines.

Camberwell Beauty

Large Tortoiseshell

Small Tortoiseshell

caterpillar

Peacock

caterpillar

Red
Admiral

Painted
Lady

Comma

male
(first
generation)

male
(first
generation)

male
(second
generation)

Map Butterfly

RED ADMIRAL
Vanessa atalanta
56-68 mm. A generally common species of meadows, hedgerows, orchards and gardens, and attracted to flowers and rotten fruit. Possibly overwinters as an adult in Britain, but usually first appears in May as a migrant from the south and produces a main flight in late summer together with further migrants. Found in much of Europe and across Asia to India, in North Africa, and in North and Central America.
The caterpillar is mainly black, with brown and yellow spines. It feeds alone, in a web, usually on nettles

PAINTED LADY
Cynthia cardui
54-65 mm. Sometimes common in northern Europe and even in Iceland as a migrant, but overwinters probably only in warmer regions. Flies in gardens, often visiting *Buddleia* flowers, and up to 3,000 metres in open country and woodland clearings. Occurs throughout the year in the tropics but has only two generations in the north. Almost worldwide in distribution but not known in South America.
The caterpillar feeds alone in a web under leaves of thistles (*Carduus* and *Cirsium*), nettles (*Urtica*) and other plants. It is mainly black, and is covered with yellow or yellow and black spines.

COMMA
Polygonia c-album
44-54 mm. First-brood insects fly June to August, and a 2nd brood, much darker than 1st, flies August to October. The 2nd-brood insects then hibernate and reappear in March and April. Found in orchards and gardens and along hedgerows and woodland margins in most of Europe. Often attracted to *Buddleia* and ice plant (*Sedum*) flowers.
The caterpillar lives alone in a small web under a leaf, usually on nettles (*Urtica*). It is black, marked with yellow and white, and is covered with white or yellow spines.
Identification Differs from the Southern Comma (*P.egea*) in the distinctly comma-like white marking under the hind wing (Y-shaped in *egea*).

MAP BUTTERFLY
Araschnia levana
32-40 mm. First brood insects (April to early July) are orange and black, those of the second generation (July and August) black and white. Generally a lowland species, but sometimes occurs up to about 1,000 metres. Found fairly commonly in France and Germany, but not in Britain nor in most of southern Europe or Scandinavia. Also occurs in Japan and much of temperate Asia.
The caterpillar feeds on nettles (*Urtica*), at first in a group but later alone. It is black or brown, with many long yellow and black spines.

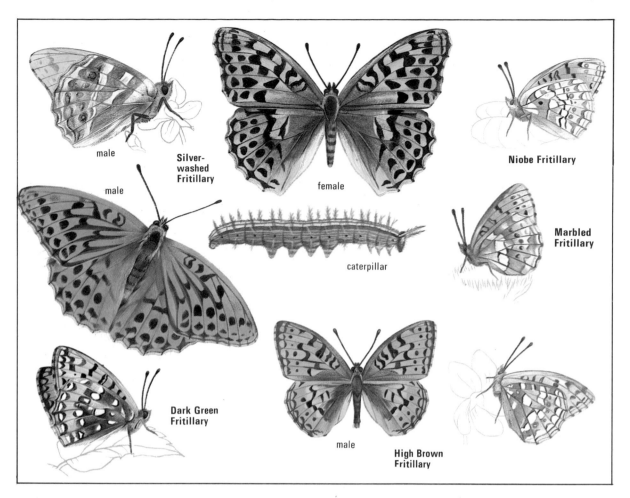

male

Silver-washed Fritillary

male

female

Niobe Fritillary

caterpillar

Marbled Fritillary

Dark Green Fritillary

male

High Brown Fritillary

SILVER-WASHED FRITILLARY
Argynnis paphia
56-74 mm. Flies in or near woods between June and September in a single yearly generation, and can be quite common up to about 1,000 metres. Often visits Bramble (*Rubus*) flowers. Found in most of Europe, including Britain, but not in Arctic Scandinavia.
The caterpillar feeds chiefly on Dog Violet (*Viola riviniana*), but in the first few months of its life it overwinters in the crevices of the bark of oaks (*Quercus*) and pines (*Pinus*).

DARK GREEN FRITILLARY
Mesoacidalia aglaja
48-65 mm. Inhabits wooded areas, but also heaths and hillsides with shrubs. Flies from June to August in a single generation, usually at low elevations in the north, but generally at high elevations in the south and up to 2,000 metres in North Africa. Widely distributed in Europe, except in the Arctic, and in temperate Asia eastwards to Japan.
The caterpillar feeds usually on Violets (*Viola*). It hibernates on the foodplant soon after hatching. When full-grown it is black and red, spotted with white and orange, and has numerous black spines along the body.
Identification Like the High Brown

Fritillary, but lacks a row of round spots near the outer edge of the hind wing on the underside.

NIOBE FRITILLARY
Fabriciana niobe
46-60 mm. Not known in Britain or northern Scandinavia, but otherwise widely distributed in Europe and western Asia. Locally common in a single flight during June, July and August in grassy and shrubby country up to 2,000 metres. Overwinters as an unhatched caterpillar inside the egg-shell.
The caterpillar usually feeds on Violets (*Viola*), and when full-grown is brown, striped with black and white, and is covered with pink spines.
Identification Differs from the High Brown Fritillary mainly on the underside of the hind wing, where there is usually a black-centred yellow spot in the cell.

HIGH BROWN FRITILLARY
Fabriciana adippe
50-64 mm. The single flight of this species extends from June to August. The butterflies are equally at home in woodland clearings and in more open country, from sea-level to about 2,000 metres. Fairly local in Britain, but quite common in parts of continental

Europe, except for northern Scandinavia. Found also in North Africa and temperate Asia, including Japan.
The caterpillar can be seen inside its egg-shell in the autumn, but does not hatch out until the spring. It feeds on Violets (*Viola*), and when full-grown is brown, with red or pink spines.
Identification Separable from the Dark Green Fritillary by the row of round spots on the underside near the margin of the hind wing.

MARBLED FRITILLARY
Brenthis daphne
42-54 mm. Flies during June and July in dry woodland meadows up to 1,500 metres, often visiting Bramble (*Rubus*) flowers. Common in some Swiss localities but generally uncommon in Europe. The range includes southern Europe and much of temperate Asia, including Japan.
The caterpillar, which overwinters, is brown, striped with white and yellow, and has numerous yellow spines along the body. It feeds on Violets (*Viola*), Raspberry and Bramble.
Identification Upper side similar to Small Pearl-bordered Fritillary (page 166), but the purplish-brown band on underside of hind wing readily distinguishes the Marbled Fritillary.

The small pearl-bordered fritillary feeds from various kinds of flower.

QUEEN OF SPAIN FRITILLARY
Issoria lathonia
36-48 mm. A rare migrant in Britain and northern Scandinavia, but often common in continental Europe, North Africa and temperate Asia in rough grassy country, regularly visiting scabious, thistles and other flowers. The single northern generation flies in May and June, but there are up to three generations in the south between February and October. Migrants to the north may breed and produce another generation, but the offspring never overwinter successfully.
The caterpillar is black, marked with white, and has many black and brown spines. It feeds on Violets (*Viola*). Autumn caterpillars overwinter.
Identification The large silver spots on the underside readily identify this species.

CRANBERRY FRITILLARY
Boloria aquilonaris
32-40 mm. A butterfly of wet moors and bogs, where it flies in June and early July. Found up to 1,500 metres in northern Europe (including the Arctic but not Britain), in parts of central Europe as far south as the Alps, and probably in Asia. Locally quite common.
The caterpillar feeds on Cranberry (*Vaccinium oxycoccus*), and overwinters amongst moss at the foot of the foodplant.

SMALL PEARL-BORDERED FRITILLARY
Clossiana selene
36-44 mm. A fairly common butterfly of woodland margins, but occurs also in more open situations, such as meadows and moorland. There is usually a single flight during June and July at high elevations and in the north, but two generations elsewhere, flying in April and May and in July and August. Found throughout Europe (except for Ireland and the extreme south), in temperate Asia across to the Pacific, and in much of North America. Rarely present above 1,500 metres.
The caterpillar is brown, spotted with white, and has short yellow-brown spines. It feeds on violets (*Viola*), and overwinters in a curled leaf bound with silk.

PEARL-BORDERED FRITILLARY
Clossiana euphrosyne
38-46 mm. Locally common in woodland clearings, and attracted to flowers and rotting animal matter. There is a single generation in the north flying during May and June, but two in the south between April and August. Found in most of Europe, including the Arctic and across Asia to the eastern Soviet Union. Occurs up to 1,800 metres in the Alps.
The caterpillar is black, spotted with white, and has numerous yellow and black spines. It feeds on violets (*Viola*) and overwinters.
Identification The single large silver spot in middle of underside of hind wing distinguishes this species from the Small Pearl-bordered Fritillary.

VIOLET FRITILLARY
Clossiana dia
30-34 mm. Can be common on sunny, grassy slopes and in woodland clearings up to about 1,500 metres. There is a single flight at higher elevations and in the north, but up to three generations in warmer areas between April and October. Found in the mountains of southern Europe, northwards to the Baltic (but not Britain or Scandinavia), and across Asia to western China.
The caterpillar is black or grey, striped with yellow, black and red, and with rows of yellow and white spines. It feeds on violets (*Viola*), knotgrasses (*Polygonum*) and other plants. Autumn caterpillars overwinter when partly grown.

ARCTIC FRITILLARY
Clossiana chariclea
32-34 mm. Probably the most northern of all butterflies and a generally rare species found only in Arctic Europe, northern North America, Greenland, and probably Arctic Asia. On the wing during the short Arctic summer in July and August. Often rests on stones in the sunshine.

KNAPWEED FRITILLARY
Melitaea phoebe
40-48 mm. Found mainly in grassy hilly country, up to 2,000 metres, and can be locally common. At high altitudes flies only in July, but at lower elevations has two or three generations flying between April and August. A resident of North Africa, central and southern Europe, and Asia as far as China.
The caterpillar is spiny and grey, striped with black and white, and feeds on knapweeds (*Centaurea*), plantains (*Plantago*) and other plants.

GLANVILLE FRITILLARY
Melitaea cinxia
32-45 mm. Widely distributed in continental Europe, North Africa and temperate Asia but in Britain confined to the Isle of Wight. Flies between May and September in one or two generations, in meadows and grassy hillslopes up to 2,500 metres.
The caterpillar is black, with rows of spiny processes along the body. It feeds in groups on plantains (*Plantago*) and other plants, and lives in a silk nest when resting or overwintering.

SPOTTED FRITILLARY
Melitaea didyma
36-42 mm. Flies in grassy or stony areas in usually two or three generations, and often common up to 1,800 metres. Found in the southern half of Europe, North Africa and central Asia.
The caterpillar feeds on speedwells (*Veronica*), plantains (*Plantago*) and several other plants. It is grey, ringed with black, and has rows of light-coloured spines along the body. Caterpillars of the last generation of the year overwinter.
Identification A very variable insect, although orange bands on underside of hind wing are fairly constant. In southern areas upper side may have just a few small spots, especially in late broods. In the mountains, front wings of female may be greyish-yellow.

HEATH FRITILLARY
Mellicta athalia
36-42 mm. One of the most common Fritillaries in Europe on heaths, in grassland and in woodland clearings up to 1,800 metres. There is a single midsummer flight in the north, but two generations are on the wing in the south between May and September. Rare in southern England.
The caterpillar is black, spotted with white, and covered with short, hairy spines. It feeds with others in a web on plantains (*Plantago*), Cow-wheat (*Melampyrum pratense*) and on other plants. Autumn-generation caterpillars overwinter.

MARSH FRITILLARY
Eurodryas aurinia
34-46 mm. Flies between April and July in a single flight, and can be common locally in marshy land and wet moors up to about 2,000 metres. Found in much of Europe (including Britain, but excluding northern Scandinavia), in North Africa and in temperate Asia eastwards to Korea.
The caterpillar, which overwinters, spins a web and lives in a large group on plantains (*Plantago*), gentians (*Gentiana*) and other plants. It is mostly black, marked with white, and has several short, black spines along the body.
Identification Separable from other similarly patterned Fritillaries by the combination of a strongly marked upper side and a usually pale underside to the forewing.

Queen of Spain Fritillary

Glanville
Fritillary

Cranberry
Fritillary

Knapweed
Fritillary

male

Small
Pearl-bordered
Fritillary

female   Spotted
Fritillary

Pearl-
bordered
Fritillary

Heath Fritillary

Violet Fritillary

Arctic Fritillary

Marsh
Fritillary

Marbled White

caterpillar

Western
Marbled White

male

Woodland
Grayling

male

female

BROWNS
Family Satyridae

This large family, with over 3,000 species, is most abundant in temperate regions. Over 100 species live in Europe, many of them in the mountains. Most have eye-spots on the wings, and the males of many species have a dark patch near the centre of the front wing. This patch, known as a scent brand, consists of scent-emitting scales used during courtship. The caterpillars are usually green or brown, finely hairy, and tapered at both ends. There is a short forked 'tail'. They feed almost entirely on grasses. The chrysalids either hang from tail hooks or lie in a loose cocoon on the ground.

MARBLED WHITE
Melanargia galathea
45-56 mm. A common butterfly of open, flowery grassland up to 1,800 metres. Flies in June and July in a single generation and has a characteristic, slow flight. Found in southern and central Europe, including southern England, and in North Africa.
The caterpillar is green or brown; it hibernates soon after hatching, and starts to feed early the next year on fescues (*Festuca*) and other grasses.

WESTERN MARBLED WHITE
Melanargia occitanica
50-56 mm. A locally common butterfly of rocky mountain slopes up to 1,800 metres, where it flies between April and June in a single generation. Found in south-western and central southern Europe and in North Africa.
The caterpillar feeds on False Brome (*Brachypodium*) and other grasses. It is brownish-grey, striped on the sides with yellow, and has a green head. It is the overwintering stage.
Identification Usually less heavily marked than Marbled White, from which it is also distinguished by the narrow black line crossing the cell. Brown veins on the underside of hind wing distinguish it from Esper's Marbled White (*M. russiae*), which has black veins.

WOODLAND GRAYLING
Hipparchia fagi
65-76 mm. A locally common butterfly of open woodlands and scrubland, usually below 1,000 metres. Often rests on tree-trunks, where it is well camouflaged. Usually emerges in July and August in a single flight. Found in central and southern Europe. Not found in Britain.
The caterpillar is brown, striped with dark brown and yellow, and feeds at night on Creeping Soft Grass (*Holcus mollis*) and other grasses.

female

Tree Grayling

female

Grayling

male

male

male

The Hermit

male

male

Striped Grayling

GRAYLING
Hipparchia semele
48-60 mm. Widespread and common in open, grassy places and on heaths up to 1,500 metres in a single flight between May and September. Often visits thyme (*Thymus*) flowers, but usually rests on the ground with the closed wings inclined towards the sun so that little shadow is cast, making the butterfly difficult to detect. Found in most of Europe.
The caterpillar is yellow, striped along the body with brown and dull yellow. It feeds on various kinds of Grass and overwinters when half grown.

TREE GRAYLING
Neohipparchia statilinus
46-53 mm. Locally common, but becoming more rare in some areas. On the wing between July and October, in a single flight, the males always emerging several days before the females. Found on heaths and in rocky places on mountain slopes in southern and central Europe (not Britain or Scandinavia) and in western Asia.
The caterpillar is yellow, striped with brown and feeds on fescues (*Festuca*), meadow grass (*Poa*) and other grasses. It overwinters, partly grown, at the base of the grass.

STRIPED GRAYLING
Pseudotergumia fidia
48-52 mm. Prefers dry, stony slopes with a few trees, up to 1,500 metres. Flies in July and August in one generation and can be common locally in North Africa, Spain and Portugal, southern France and the western Alps of Italy.
The caterpillar is yellow or brown, striped along the body with black or yellow. It feeds on grasses and probably overwinters.

THE HERMIT
Chazara briseis
40-52 mm. The single yearly generation flies between May and September, chiefly in dry, grassy places in chalk or limestone regions, up to 1,800 metres. Found in central and southern Europe, North America and western Asia, but not in Britain.
The caterpillar is greyish-yellow, striped with grey. It feeds on fescues and other grasses, and overwinters at the base of the foodplant.

Baltic
Grayling

Black
Satyr

female

male

Dryad

male

male

female

Great Banded Grayling

BALTIC GRAYLING
Oeneis jutta
43-50 mm. Prefers boggy places near coniferous forests at low elevations. Emerges during June and July in a single flight. Males in particular often rest on tree-trunks. Found throughout the Arctic and the northern part of the Northern Hemisphere from Scandinavia across northern Asia to Alaska and northern Canada. Flies every year, but the caterpillar overwinters twice, and odd-year butterflies are slightly different in colour-pattern from even-year butterflies.
The caterpillar is brown, striped with darker brown, and feeds on grasses.

BLACK SATYR
Satyrus actaea
48-58 mm. Common in parts of southern France, but usually locally distributed, on dry mountain slopes up to 1,800 metres and seldom below 1,000 metres. On the wing in a single flight during June, July and August. Found in southern Europe, from Spain to north-western Italy, and in western Asia as far east as Iran.
The caterpillar is brown, striped with darker brown and white, and feeds and brome (*Bromus*) and other grasses.
Identification The Great Sooty Satyr (*S. ferula*) is similar, but the male has 2 or more eye-spots on the front wing and no scent brand. Female *ferula* is brighter, with an orange patch enclosing the eye-spots.

DRYAD
Minois dryas
54-63 mm. A butterfly of damp moors and meadows, often near woods, usually below 1,000 metres. Usually emerges in July and August in a single generation, flying quite slowly and close to the ground. Occurs in colonies in central Europe (not Britain or Scandinavia), and in temperate Asia, including Japan.
The caterpillar is yellow-grey, striped with dark grey and brown. It feeds on Purple Moor Grass (*Molinia caerulea*) and other grasses, and overwinters partly grown.
Identification The blue-centred eye-spots readily distinguish this species from the very similar Great Sooty Satyr (*Satyrus ferula*), which has white-centred eye-spots. It also has white bands on the underside of hind wing.

GREAT BANDED GRAYLING
Brintesia circe
65-73 mm. Common at times in open Oak woods at low elevations during June, July and August in a single flight. Often rests on tree-trunks or branches, and if disturbed flies long distances before resettling. Resident in southern and central Europe (as far north as central France and Germany) and in south-western Asia.
The caterpillar is brown, striped with black and darker brown, and feeds on Rye-grass (*Lolium*) and other Grasses. It overwinters partly grown.

Mountain Ringlet

Scotch Argus

Almond-eyed Ringlet

caterpillar

Ringlet

female

male

Meadow Brown

Dewy Ringlet

caterpillar

MOUNTAIN RINGLET
Erebia epiphron
35-40 mm. Appears during June and July in a single flight in northern Britain (not Ireland), but is more widespread in the mountains of southern Europe from the Pyrenees to the Carpathians. Flies in wet, grassy forest clearings and on moors up to 3,000 metres, usually close to the ground.
The caterpillar is green, striped with yellow and white, and feeds on Hairgrass (*Deschampsia*) and other grasses. It overwinters partly grown.
Identification Upper and lower sides are quite similar. This is one of several rather similar European species, many of them with restricted distributions in the mountains. Some are restricted to just a few neighbouring peaks.

SCOTCH ARGUS
Erebia aethiops
40-53 mm. The single flight of this species takes place between July and early September, the butterflies seldom taking to the wing unless the weather is sunny. Found in Scotland and northern England, central and south-eastern Europe and in western Asia. Restricted to grassy areas, usually near forests in hills and mountains up to 2,000 metres, but also occurs near the coast in Belgium.
The caterpillar is usually yellow-brown, striped with darker and lighter brown. It feeds on Couch Grass (*Agropyron*) and other grasses, and overwinters when partly grown.

ALMOND-EYED RINGLET
Erebia alberganus
38-43 mm. Forms isolated colonies in mountain meadows, usually in or near woods, from about 1,000 to 2,000 metres. Emerges in a single flight between late June and August in the Alps, the mountains of Italy and in Bulgaria.
The caterpillar is green, striped with white and brown, and feeds on fescues (*Festuca*) and other grasses. It probably overwinters.

RINGLET
Aphantopus hyperantus
40-50 mm. Generally common near and in woods and along old hedgerows up to about 1,500 metres in a single flight during June and July. Often visits flowers. Found in most of Britain and continental Europe (except for southern Spain and Italy and Arctic Scandinavia), and also in northern Asia as far east as Siberia.
The caterpillar, which overwinters, is yellow-brown with darker stripes, and feeds on meadow grasses (*Poa*) and other grasses, and rarely on sedges (*Carex*).

DEWY RINGLET
Erebia pandrose
36-46 mm. A butterfly of stony fields and mountain slopes, and locally common in some years. Emerges in a single flight between the end of June and the beginning of August in Scandinavia and Finland at moderate altitudes, and between 1,500 and 3,000 metres in the mountains of southern Europe. Occurs also in western and central Asia.
The caterpillar is green, striped with black. It feeds on grasses, and overwinters.

MEADOW BROWN
Maniola jurtina
44-50 mm. Often very common on grass and heathland up to about 1,500 metres in much of Europe, including Britain but excluding northern Scandinavia. Found also in Asia as far east as the Ural mountains of central Russia and in North Africa and the Canaries. There is probably only one generation each year, which is on the wing from June to September. Upper side of male darker than female, with very little orange.
The caterpillar is green, spotted with black, and striped with white and dark green. It feeds on grasses, often meadow grasses (*Poa*), and overwinters partly grown.

Eye-spots are typical not only of this large heath butterfly but of browns (Satyridae) in general.

GATEKEEPER
Pyronia tithonus
36-42 mm. Common in places, especially near woods and along hedgerows, and often attracted to the flowers of Wood Sage (*Teucrium scorodonia*). Appears in July and August in a single flight, usually at low elevations but up to 1,000 metres in southern Europe. Found in most of Europe but not in Scandinavia or northern Britain.
The caterpillar is either green or brown, striped along the body with black, brown and white. It feeds on Cocksfoot (*Dactylis glomerata*) and other grasses, and overwinters partly grown.
Identification Separable from the Southern Gatekeeper (*P.cecilia*) by the presence of eye-spots on the underside of the hind wing.

LARGE HEATH
Coenonympha tullia
35-40 mm. A butterfly of wet meadows, moors and bogs, on the wing in a single flight during June and July, at low elevations in the north but up to 2,000 metres in the mountains of southern Europe. Much less common in Britain now than in the past, probably as a result of improved land drainage. Found in isolated colonies in most of Europe, including Britain but excluding Arctic Scandinavia and south-western and south-eastern Europe. Occurs also in northern Asia and North America.
The caterpillar is green, spotted with white, and striped with dark green and white. It feeds on Beak-sedge (*Rhynchospora*) and various grasses, and overwinters at the base of the foodplant.
Identification Resembles the Small Heath (*C.pamphilus*), but on the upper outer edge of the wings. A rather variable species.

SMALL HEATH
Coenonympha pamphilus
27-34 mm. On the wing, usually in two or more generations, from April onwards, often settling on flowers or on the ground. A common species of grassy places from sea-level to 2,000 metres in western Asia and most of Europe, including Britain but not the extreme north of Scandinavia.
The caterpillar is green, spotted with white, and striped with darker green, and feeds on various species of grass. In northern Europe some caterpillars from each generation overwinter.

DUSKY HEATH
Coenonympha dorus
32-34 mm. Locally common in dry, rocky places up to about 2,000 metres in Spain, Italy and southern France, but found only between 1,500 and 1,800 metres in North Africa. The single yearly flight usually emerges in June or July.
The caterpillar feeds on fescues (*Festuca*), bents (*Agrostis*) and other grasses. It overwinters.

PEARLY HEATH
Coenonympha arcania
35-40 mm. A generally common butterfly of meadows, in or near woodlands. On the wing during June, July and August in a single flight. Found from sea level to 2,000 metres in much of Europe, but not Britain, the Low Countries or Norway. Occurs also in temperate Asia as far east as the Ural mountains.
The caterpillar is green, striped along the body with dark green, white and yellow. It overwinters, partly grown, on the foodplant, melic (*Melica*) and other grasses.

SPECKLED WOOD
Pararge aegeria
35-45 mm. A butterfly of woodlands and old hedgerows, where its colour-pattern makes it difficult to see in broken sunlight. Flies in a series of

generations from March onwards, but with only one flight in parts of Scandinavia. Found in North Africa, Madeira, the Canaries, most of Europe (except for northern Scotland and northern Scandinavia), and across Asia to the Ural mountains.
The caterpillar is green, striped with dark green and yellow, and feeds on Couch Grass (*Agropyron*) and other grasses. Some of the Autumn generation overwinter as caterpillars, others in the chrysalis stage.
Identification Occurs in 2 distinct forms: in south-west Europe (Italy, southern France, and Iberia) the pale spots are orange, while elsewhere they are creamy white.

WOODLAND BROWN
Lopinga achine
48-54 mm. Occurs in widely separated colonies up to 1,000 metres in woodland meadows and along edges of woods in central and northern Europe (excluding Britain and north-western Germany), and across temperate Asia to Japan. Appears in a single flight between June and August, the males emerging before the females.
The caterpillar is green, striped with dark green and white, and feeds on Rye-grass (*Lolium*), various other grasses and sedges (*Carex*). It overwinters.

WALL BROWN
Lasiommata megera
35-40 mm. Prefers sunny, dry places and often basks in the sunshine on a wall, rock or pathway. Attracted to *Buddleia* and other garden flowers. Often common up to about 1,200 metres from March onwards, usually in two or more generations. Found in Europe (including Britain, but excluding northern Scandinavia), North Africa, Madeira, the Canaries and western Asia.
The caterpillar is blue-green, striped along the body with dark green and white, and feeds on Cocksfoot (*Dactylis glomerata*) and other grasses. Autumn caterpillars overwinter, some feeding throughout the winter.
Identification Separable from the Large Wall Brown (*L.maera*) chiefly by the presence of two dark-brown bars across the cell on the upper side of the forewing.

LARGE WALL BROWN
Lasiommata maera
44-54 mm. Common in rocky, grassy places in or near woodlands, up to about 2,000 metres in the Alps. The single northern and high-elevation flight is in June and July, but there are two generations on the wing elsewhere between May and September. Resident in North Africa, much of Europe (but not Britain), and in western Asia as far east as the Himalayas.
The caterpillar is green, striped with white and dark green, and feeds on various species of grasses. Autumn generation caterpillars overwinter.

male

female

Gatekeeper

male

Large Heath

Dusky Heath

male

Small Heath

Pearly Heath

Speckled Wood

Wall Brown

Large Wall Brown

male

female

Large Wall Brown

male

Woodland Brown

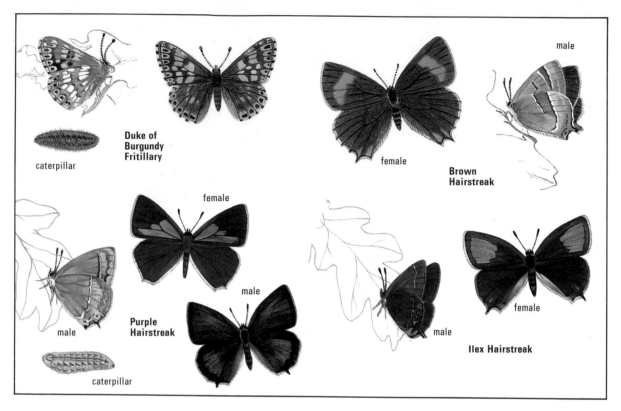

Duke of Burgundy Fritillary

caterpillar

Brown Hairstreak

male

female

Purple Hairstreak

female

male

caterpillar

male

Ilex Hairstreak

female

male

METALMARKS AND OTHERS
Family Riodinidae

Mainly a Central and South American group, with just a single Fritillary-like species in Europe. The front leg is much reduced, as in the Nymphalidae, but the family is probably more closely related to the Lycaenidae. Many species are very colourful or have shiny metallic markings on the wings. The caterpillars are slug-like in shape and rather hairy.

DUKE OF BURGUNDY FRITILLARY
Hamearis lucina
27-34 mm. Flies in woodland clearings and along the edges of woods, during May and June in a single northern generation, or from May to August in the south where there are two flights. Usually rests on a leaf, but is sometimes attracted to Bugle (*Ajuga reptans*) flowers. Found in Spain, Sweden, much of central Europe (not the Low Countries), and in western Asia. Prefers limestone regions in Britain and is absent from Ireland and northern Scotland.
The caterpillar is brown and feeds on Primrose (*Primula vulgaris*) and other species of *Primula*.

HAIRSTREAKS, COPPERS AND BLUES
Family Lycaenidae

A worldwide group of several thousand, mainly small species, best represented in the tropics of the Old World but with about 100 species in Europe. The wings are mostly blue, green, brown, orange or red above, but usually very differently coloured on the underside. Most Hairstreaks have one or more short tails to the hind wing. All three pairs of legs are fully developed. Females usually differ from the males in colour-pattern.

The chrysalis is short and stout. It may hang from its tail end, be fixed in an upright position by a girdle of silk, or lie on the ground.

BROWN HAIRSTREAK
Thecla betulae
34-36 mm. This butterfly normally flies high up amongst the branches of Oak trees, but is sometimes attracted to flowers at ground level. Appears in August and September in a single flight, and is fairly common locally up to 1,500 metres in central and northern Europe (including Ireland and southern England). Overwinters in the egg stage.

The caterpillar is green, striped with yellow, and feeds chiefly on Blackthorn (*Prunus spinosa*).

PURPLE HAIRSTREAK
Quercusia quercus
24-29 mm. Emerges in a single flight between June and August, and often common in oak forests, flying high up in the trees but occasionally attracted to flowers near the ground. Found in North Africa, western Asia and much of Europe, including Britain but excluding Arctic Scandinavia. Overwinters in the egg stage.
The caterpillar is brown, marked with black and white, and looks rather like the oak buds on which it feeds.

ILEX HAIRSTREAK
Nordmannia ilicis
32-37 mm. Locally common on hills with oak scrub, up to 1,500 metres. Emerges in a single flight during June and July. Found in southern and central Europe: not Britain.
The caterpillar, which overwinters under a leaf, is green, striped with dark green and yellow. It feeds on oaks (*Quercus*) and other trees, and is often attended by ants.

WHITE-LETTER HAIRSTREAK
Strymonidia w-album
24-38 mm. Sometimes common where there are elm and lime trees, and feeding on bramble blossom in June. July and August in a single yearly emergence. Found in Europe (not Ireland, Scotland or Portugal), seldom

White-letter Hairstreak

Blue-spot Hairstreak

Green Hairstreak

male

Small Copper

Scarce Copper

male

female

Purple-shot Copper

male

female

male

caterpillar

female

above 1,000 metres, and across temperate Asia to Japan. Overwinters in the egg stage.

The caterpillar is greenish-yellow and green, and feeds on the buds, flowers and leaves of elms and limes.

Identification The upper side is entirely sooty brown in both sexes. The Black Hairstreak (*S. pruni*) is similar but lacks the clear W-shaped line on the underside of the hind wing. The Black Hairstreak also normally has some orange-red spots near the margins on the upper side.

BLUE-SPOT HAIRSTREAK
Strymonidia spini
27-32 mm. Most often seen in hilly country up to 1,800 metres where there are patches of Buckthorn and Blackthorn. Appears in a single flight between June and early August in central and southern Europe (but not Britain). Overwinters as egg.

The caterpillar is green, striped with yellow and white. It feeds mainly on Blackthorn (*Prunus spinosa*), Buckthorn (*Rhamnus catharticus*), and hawthorns (*Crataegus*).

Identification The blue mark on the underside at the rear angle of the hind wing separates this species from all other European Hairstreaks.

GREEN HAIRSTREAK
Callophrys rubi
25-30 mm. A well camouflaged butterfly when the wings are closed and the green of the underside blends with a background of green leaves. The upper side is dull brown in both

sexes, but the male can be recognized by a small dark scent brand near the front edge of the front wing.

Appears between April and July in a single flight, and is generally common along overgrown hedgerows, thickets and the edges of woods from sea-level up to about 2,000 metres. Widely distributed in Europe (including Britain and the Arctic), North Africa, temperate Asia and North America.

The caterpillar is green and yellow, and feeds on the buds and shoots of gorse (*Ulex*), *Vaccinium* and other shrubs and low-growing plants.

SMALL COPPER
Lycaena phlaeas
25-30 mm. A common butterfly of dry fields and heaths, often visiting flowers or chasing away other butterflies in quick darting flights. The first European emergence is in April or May, the second in July and August, and there is sometimes a third flight, except in the north. Found in most of Europe, up to 2,000 metres, and in North and central Africa, the Canaries, Madeira, temperate Asia (including Japan), and North America.

The caterpillar is green, spotted with white and usually also with red. It feeds on sorrel (*Rumex*) and knotgrass (*Polygonum*), and overwinters either partly or full-grown.

SCARCE COPPER
Heodes virgaureae
32-35 mm. Locally distributed at low elevations in the north and up to 2,000

metres in the Alps in woodland meadows and more open, grassy places, especially near water. On the wing during June, July and August in a single flight. Probably bred in Britain over 200 years ago but now extinct. Absent also in western France and Holland, but found in much of central and northern Europe, including the Arctic. Overwinters in the egg stage.

The caterpillar is green, striped with yellow, and feeds on Sheep's Sorrel (*Rumex acetosella*) and other species of *Rumex*. It is often attended by ants.

PURPLE-SHOT COPPER
Heodes alciphron
30-36 mm. Found in both damp and dry, grassy places, often in hilly country. Locally common up to 1,800 metres in the Alps, and higher in the Atlas mountains of North Africa. On the wing, probably in a single flight, between May and August, often visiting Thyme (*Thymus*) and Bramble (*Rubus*) flowers. Found in North Africa, central and southern Europe (not Britain or Scandinavia), and across temperate Asia to Mongolia.

The caterpillar is green, striped with light green. It feeds on sorrels and docks (*Rumex*), often with ants in attendance, and hibernates from about September onwards.

Identification The violet tinge shown in the illustration is typical of males from central Europe. Males from southern Europe have much less purple. Females are brown or orange on the upper side, without any purple.

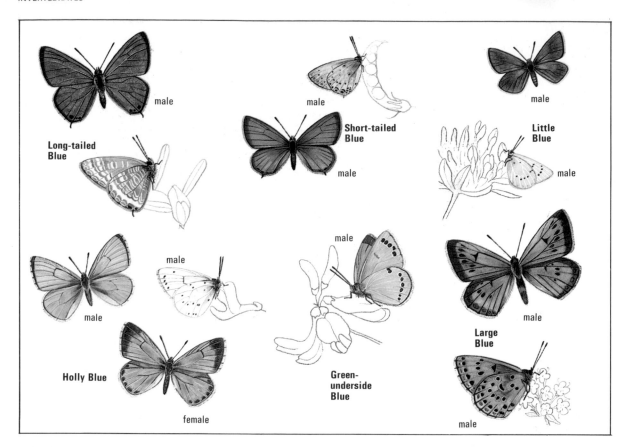

LONG-TAILED BLUE
Lampides boeticus
24-36 mm. A resident of southern Europe, but migrating regularly as far as northern Germany and occasionally even reaching Britain. Yet it never overwinters successfully north of the Alps or in cold climates probably because there is no hibernating phase in the life-history. Flies in Europe in open grassy country and fields of Lucerne (*Medicago sativa*) from June to October as two generations, but flies all year in warmer regions.
The caterpillar is green, striped with yellow and dark green, and feeds on the flowers and seed pods of Legumes, including Garden Pea (*Pisum*).
Identification The female is mostly brown above, but violet-blue towards the base of the wings.

SHORT-TAILED BLUE
Everes argiades
20-32 mm. On the wing in two or three flights from April to September in meadows, pastures and open, un-cultivated country up to about 2,000 metres. Resident in central and south-eastern Europe, across Asia to Japan, and in North America. Migrates northwards during the summer, and sometimes reaches Britain.
The caterpillar is at first green but becomes brown during hibernation. It feeds on the flowers and seeds of gorse, medick and other legumes.
Identification Female dark brown with a few blue scales at base.

LITTLE BLUE
Cupido minimus
18-28 mm. Usually restricted to chalk and limestone areas up to 2,400 metres, and found in small colonies, separated sometimes by only a 100 metres or so. Flies in June in the north and at high elevations, but has two flights elsewhere between April and August. Occurs in much of Europe, including Britain but excluding the Arctic, and across Asia to the Pacific.
The caterpillar is either green or yellow, striped with pink, and feeds on the flowers and seeds of Kidney Vetch (*Anthyllis vulneraria*) and other legumes. Autumn caterpillars overwinter amongst the dead flower-heads of the foodplant.
Identification Female is dark brown above, without any blue scales.

HOLLY BLUE
Celastrina argiolus
20-32 mm. Widely distributed and common in gardens, heaths and along hedgerows; usually in two flights in temperate climates, the first as early as April. Often rests on Ivy and holly leaves. Found up to 1,500 metres in most of Europe (including Britain), North Africa, North and Central America and much of temperate Asia.
The caterpillar is green, marked with darker and lighter green, and feeds on the shoots, flowers and berries of holly, ivy, gorse, dogwoods and other shrubs.

GREEN-UNDERSIDE BLUE
Glaucopsyche alexis
26-34 mm. Rare north of the Alps, but locally common in hilly and mountainous areas up to 1,200 metres, usually in flowery places near woods. Emerges during April, May and June in a single flight in the north and at high elevations, but has two flights elsewhere between April and August. Found in Europe, from the Mediterranean to southern Scandinavia (but absent from Britain except as a rare vagrant), and in North Africa and across temperate Asia to Siberia.
The caterpillar is green or brown, striped with darker brown or green, and feeds on various legumes. Autumn caterpillars overwinter.
Identification Female is dark brown above, with some blue at base of wings.

LARGE BLUE
Maculinea arion
35-40 mm. Occurs in dry, grassy places up to 2,000 metres, often on south-facing slopes, in much of Europe, but not Britain, where it apparently became extinct in 1979, or in northern Scandinavia. The single yearly flight is in June and July.
The caterpillar feeds at first on Thyme (*Thymus*) flowers, but is later taken by ants into their nest. Here the caterpillar feeds on ant grubs, overwinters in the nest and eventually crawls to freedom as an adult butterfly.

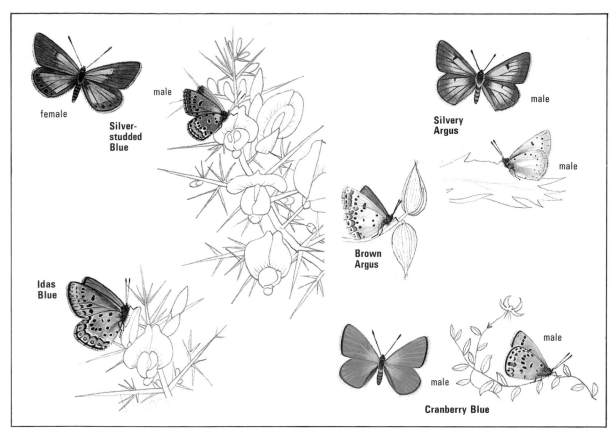

SILVER-STUDDED BLUE
Plebejus argus
28-34 mm. Sometimes common on sandy heaths and grassland up to 3,000 metres. Emerges as one flight during July or August in the north, but as two flights in the south from May to September. May fly until dusk if the weather is warm. Found in most of Europe, including Britain but excluding Ireland and northern Scandinavia. Overwinters in the egg stage.
The caterpillar is green or brown, striped with purple and white. It feeds on the shoots and flowers of gorse (*Ulex*), Birdsfoot (*Ornithopus perpusillus*) and other legumes.
Identification Male is deep violet-blue on upper side, with prominent black margins about 1 mm wide. Female may be almost completely brown, but usually with a good deal of blue at the base of the wings.

IDAS BLUE
Lycaeides idas
28-32 mm. Common in small colonies on heaths and pastures up to 2,000 metres during June and July in the north, and in two flights between May and August in the south. Found in Europe from the Mediterranean to the Arctic (but not in Britain), and eastwards to the Altai mountains of central Asia.
The caterpillar is green, striped with brown and white, and feeds on gorse

and other legumes, and on Sea Buckthorn. It is attended by ants and later taken to their nest, where it overwinters.
Identification This species is similar to the Silver Studded Blue, but normally a little larger. Male is a somewhat brighter blue and has narrower black margins to the wings.

CRANBERRY BLUE
Vacciniina optilete
22-25 mm. Mainly an alpine and Arctic species in Europe, but also found on moors in Germany. Emerges between June and August in a single flight; seldom common, and usually found near the foodplants. Occurs in the Alps and central Germany, across northern Asia to Japan, and in North America.
The caterpillar is green, striped with yellow, white and black, and feeds on the shoots and flowers of Cranberry (*Vaccinium oxycoccus*), other species of *Vaccinium* and on bell heathers (*Erica*). It overwinters partly grown.
Identification Females are brown above, with a scattering of violet scales at the base of the wings.

BROWN ARGUS
Aricia agestis
24-28 mm. Prefers chalk and limestone areas, and can be locally fairly common on downland and flowery, grassy slopes up to 1,000 metres. It also occurs on many areas of heathland. There is one flight each year in

the north during May and June, but two or more in the south from May to about September. Occurs in the Canary Islands, North Africa, western Asia and much of Europe, including southern England, but not in most of Scandinavia where it is replaced by the very similar Mountain Argus (*A. artaxerxes*).
The caterpillar is green, striped with dark green, brown, pink and white. It feeds on Storksbill (*Erodium*) and also on rockrose. It overwinters.
Identification The upper-side ground-colour in both sexes is brown.

SILVERY ARGUS
Pseudoaricia nicias
23-25mm. Found between 900 and 2,000 metres in dry, sunny places in the Alps and Pyrenees, and at lower elevations in much of eastern Scandinavia. On the wing during July and August in a single flight. Also present in Asia as far east as the Altai mountains of central Asia. Overwinters in the egg stage.
The caterpillar is green, striped with darker green, and feeds on species of Cranesbill (*Geranium*).
Identification Distinguished by the silvery-blue colour of the male upper side, and by the lack of orange spots on the underside of both sexes. Females are brown above.

Mazarine Blue

Damon Blue

Adonis Blue
male

male

female

male

Chalk-hill Blue
male

female

male

Common Blue
female

male

caterpillar

The male common blue — one of the commonest of the European butterflies.

MAZARINE BLUE
Cyaniris semiargus
26-34 mm. A generally common butterfly of open, flowery places, from sea-level to 1,800 metres in Europe, and up to 2,500 metres in the south of its range. Emerges during June and July at high elevations, but has two flights in the lowlands between May and August. Often drinks from wet mud. Resident in North Africa, most of Europe (but not Britain, except as a rare migrant) and Asia.
The caterpillar is yellow-green, striped with green, and feeds on trefoils (*Lotus*) and other legumes. Autumn caterpillars overwinter.
Identification The female is brown above.

DAMON BLUE
Agrodiaetus damon
30-35 mm. A rare mountain butterfly found in small colonies up to 3,000 metres in grassy places or light scrub on chalk or limestone soils. Flies during June, July and early August in a single generation. Occurs in the Pyrenees, Alps, Apennines and the mountains of the Balkans and western Asia. The female is brown.

The caterpillar, which overwinters, is yellowish-green, striped with dark green, yellow and red. It feeds on the flowers of Sainfoin (*Onobrychis*), and is attended by ants.

ADONIS BLUE
Lysandra bellargus
30-36 mm. Fairly common in colonies on grassy chalk and limestone regions up to 2,000 metres. The usual two flights are in May and June and August and September. Found in southern England, continental Europe, except for Scandinavia, and eastwards to Iran. Protected by law in France.
The caterpillar is green, striped with yellow, and feeds at night, chiefly on leaves of Horseshoe Vetch (*Hippocrepis comosa*). It overwinters, often soon after hatching.
Identification The males are brilliant blue above. Females may be confused with female Chalk-hill Blues (*L. coridon*), but have blue, not silvery-blue, scales on the upper side.

CHALK-HILL BLUE
Lysandra coridon
29-36 mm. A common species of chalk and limestone grassland up to

3,000 metres, emerging during July or August. Attracted to flowers and animal droppings. Found in most of Europe but absent from much of the south-west, Ireland, Scotland and Scandinavia.
The caterpillar overwinters on the foodplant as a caterpillar inside the unbroken egg-shell. When full grown it is green, striped with yellow, and feeds at night on the leaves and flowers of Wild Liquorice (*Astragalus glycyphyllos*), and other legumes, attended by ants.

COMMON BLUE
Polyommatus icarus
25-33 mm. The commonest European Blue in grassy, flowery places from the Arctic to the Mediterranean; found also in North Africa, the Canary Islands, and much of temperate Asia. Appears between May and July in the north, but in two or three flights in the south between April and October.
The caterpillar is green, striped with dark green and white, and feeds on trefoils (*Lotus*) and other legumes. Autumn-generation caterpillars overwinter at the base of the foodplant in a frail, silken shelter.

SKIPPERS
Family Hesperiidae

The skippers are mostly small species, with a broad head and body, and most make only short, swift, darting flights. The club of the antenna is usually rather pointed and curved; all six legs are well developed. Many are sombrely coloured above, and the underside provides the best guide to identity. Females differ little from the males in colour-pattern, but the males of several species have a dark scent brand on the front wing. They rest either with the wings folded together above the back or held in a tent-like fashion.

GRIZZLED SKIPPER
Pyrgus malvae
20-29 mm. Found in grassy places up to 1,700 metres, and usually fairly common. There is usually a single flight in the north during May and June, but two flights in the south from April to August. The range includes North America, western Europe (excluding northern Scotland, Ireland and northern Scandinavia).
The caterpillar is green, striped with pink and brown, and feeds on strawberry (*Fragaria*), mallow (*Malva*) and other plants.
Identification The row of white spots close to the outer margin on the upper side of the forewing separates this species from other European Skippers.

DINGY SKIPPER
Erynnis tages
24-30 mm. Prefers dry, open places and is generally common on heaths and in meadows up to 2,000 metres. Emerges during May and June in the north, or from April to late summer as two generations in the south. Often basks on bare ground, seldom on leaves. Breeds in most of Europe (including Britain, but excluding the Arctic), and in Asia eastwards to Siberia.
The caterpillar is green, and feeds on trefoils (*Lotus*), vetches (*Coronilla*) and other legumes. It overwinters in a silken shelter on the foodplant, changing to a chrysalis in the spring.

LARGE CHEQUERED SKIPPER
Heteropterus morpheus
33-36 mm. Mainly a lowland butterfly, locally distributed in grassy woodland clearings up to about 500 metres. Appears usually in a single flight during June, July and August, but may have two generations in the south. Rare in Scandinavia and absent from Britain, but found in much of Europe and across temperate Asia to the Pacific.
The caterpillar is green or yellow, striped with dark green and white, and feeds on grasses. Autumn caterpillars overwinter inside a tube of grass and silk.
Identification Bold spots on underside.

SMALL SKIPPER
Thymelicus flavus
25-30 mm. The yearly flight extends from June to September in open, grassy places up to 1,500 metres. Common locally in North Africa, Britain, southern and central Europe, and east to Iran.
The caterpillar is green and white, lives in a silk tube and feeds on grasses. It overwinters.
Identification Closely resembles the Essex Skipper (*T. lineola*, not illustrated), but the tip of the antenna is orange below, not black.

SILVER-SPOTTED SKIPPER
Hesperia comma
28-31 mm. Locally common in July and August in grassy places, mainly in chalk and limestone areas up to 2,500 metres. Found in North Africa, most of Europe and temperate Asia and in western North America. Overwinters as an egg.
The caterpillar is green and black, lives in a tube of silk and grass, and feeds on fescues (*Festuca*) and other grasses.
Identification The silvery spots on the underside separate this species from the other European skippers.

LARGE SKIPPER
Ochlodes venatus
27-35 mm. Inhabits meadows up to 1,800 metres, flying from May to August in one or more generations. Found in much of Europe, including Britain, and across Asia to Japan.
The caterpillar is mostly green, and lives in a silk tube on brome (*Bromus*) and other grasses. It overwinters at the grass base in a silk shelter.
Identification Similar to the Silver-spotted Skipper (*Hesperia comma*), but has yellow spots on the underside.

Grizzled Skipper

Dingy Skipper

Large Chequered Skipper

Small Skipper

Silver-spotted Skipper

male

male

male

Large Skipper

caterpillar

male

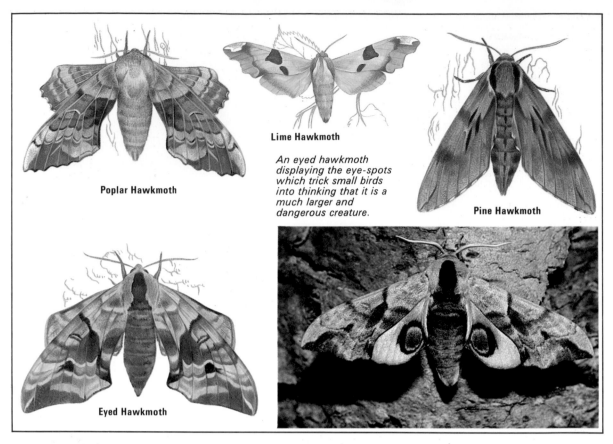

Poplar Hawkmoth

Lime Hawkmoth

An eyed hawkmoth displaying the eye-spots which trick small birds into thinking that it is a much larger and dangerous creature.

Pine Hawkmoth

Eyed Hawkmoth

Moths

Like the butterflies, the moths belong to the order Lepidoptera and their wings are clothed with minute scales. There are over 100,000 known species, in many different families. There is no single difference between all the moths on the one hand and all the butterflies on the other, but the antennae are a good guide. Moth antennae vary a great deal but, with the exception of the burnets and a few other groups, they are not clubbed, whereas all European butterflies have clubbed antennae. Moth antennae are often feathery, especially in the males. Most species are nocturnal and generally well camouflaged during the daytime when they are at rest. The caterpillars are with or without hairs and they normally pupate either in silken cocoons or in subterranean chambers.

The measurements given in the following pages indicate wingspan.

HAWKMOTHS
Family Sphingidae

These are fast-flying, stout-bodied moths with relatively narrow, pointed front wings. Some do not feed as adults, but others have enormously long tongues which they plunge deep into flowers while hovering in front of them. The family is found mainly in the tropics, but 23 species occur in Europe. Nine are resident in the British Isles and eight more occur as regular or irregular immigrants. The caterpillars are hairless, often with diagonal stripes, and most have a curved horn at the end.

POPLAR HAWKMOTH
Laothoe populi
70-90 mm. Wings distinctly scalloped, greyish-brown often with a pinkish tinge. Hind wing has a large brick-coloured spot, concealed at rest but exposed when the insect is disturbed and displayed like the eyed hawkmoth's 'eyes'. Flies May-June, with a partial 2nd brood in late summer. Found in most of Europe; common in gardens.
Caterpillar: up to 60 mm long, is bright green or bluish-green, speckled with yellow dots. The stripes are yellow and the horn yellowish-green. It eats poplar and sallow June-July.

LIME HAWKMOTH
Mimas tiliae
75 mm. Basically green and brown, often with a pinkish tinge; outer edge of front wing very 'ragged'. Flies May-June and does not feed. Most of Europe: southern Britain only.
Caterpillar: up to 60 mm long, is pale green with yellow stripes and a bluish horn. It feeds July-September on lime, elm and various other trees.

PINE HAWKMOTH
Hyloicus pinastri
70-80 mm. Dark grey with some black dashes near centre of front wing. Hard to see at rest on pine trunks. Flies May-August, feeding on various flowers. Most of Europe: but s. England only.
Caterpillar: up to 75 mm long, feeds on pine and spruce July-September. Green with white stripes at first, it becomes mottled with brown later.

EYED HAWKMOTH
Smerinthus ocellata
75-95 mm. Pinkish brown with darker markings; hind wing has a large eye-spot, concealed at rest but exposed when the moth is disturbed. The moth then sways menacingly and scares small birds. It flies May-July but does not feed. Most of Europe.
Caterpillar: up to 70 mm long, is green with yellow or lilac stripes and a

bluish tail. It feeds on apple, sallow and various other trees June-September, often resting upside-down and looking like a curled leaf.

PRIVET HAWKMOTH
Sphinx ligustri
100-120 mm. The largest resident British moth, this species flies June-July and regularly visits flowers at dusk. At rest, the wings are pulled tightly back along the sides of the body and the insect resembles a broken twig. Brownish front wings, pink bands on hind wings, and blackish thorax distinguish it from the Convolvulus Hawkmoth. Most of Europe, but mainly southern in Britain.
Caterpillar: reaches 75 mm and is bright green with purple and white stripes and a black horn. It feeds on privet, ash and lilac July-September and is very well camouflaged by its stripes. It often sits with the front end raised in a sphinx-like attitude. Several other hawkmoth larvae do this, and in America the insects are known as sphinx moths.

DEATH'S HEAD HAWKMOTH
Acherontia atropos
100-135 mm. Named for the skull-like pattern on the thorax, this handsome moth is one of Europe's largest insects. The species is essentially a native of Africa, but it flies to Europe each spring, often in large numbers, and produces a European generation during the summer. Specimens reach Britain mainly in August, but rarely more than a few each year, and larvae can be found in potato fields in September and October. The species cannot survive the winter in Europe. The moth does not visit flowers, but it is very fond of honey and is commonly found in bee hives. If picked up, it can produce a loud squeak by forcing air out through its proboscis.
Caterpillar: reaches 125 mm and is yellowish-green (sometimes yellow or brown) with purplish stripes and a yellow horn. It feeds in summer and autumn on potato plants and related wild species such as the nightshades.

CONVOLVULUS HAWKMOTH
Agrius convolvuli
90-120 mm. The abdomen is banded with pink like the Privet Hawkmoth, but the entirely grey wings distinguish this species. It is a strongly migratory moth, found in many parts of the Old World, and it arrives in Europe each spring from North Africa. Occasional specimens reach the British Isles in late summer and may produce larvae, but the species cannot survive the winter. It flies all summer and autumn in Europe and feeds at tubular flowers. Its tongue can be up to 130 mm long — much longer than the body — and needs a special case in the pupal stage, which looks like a jug handle sticking out from the body.
Caterpillar: reaches 100 mm and is bright green or deep purplish-brown with yellowish stripes. The horn is brownish-red with a black tip. It feeds on bindweeds and related plants in summer and autumn.

caterpillar

Privet Hawkmoth

Death's Head Hawkmoth

Convolvulus Hawkmoth

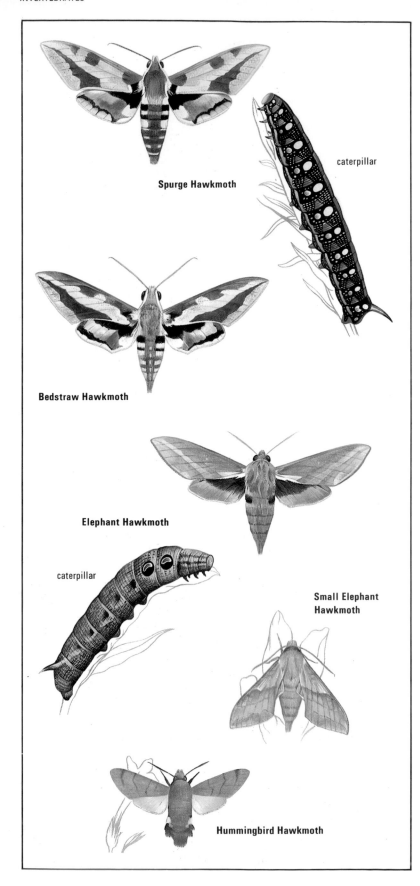

Spurge Hawkmoth

caterpillar

Bedstraw Hawkmoth

Elephant Hawkmoth

caterpillar

Small Elephant Hawkmoth

Hummingbird Hawkmoth

SPURGE HAWKMOTH
Hyles euphorbiae
75 mm. Resident in southern and central Europe, this moth is a sporadic summer visitor to Britain and other more northerly areas. It flies June-July. The pink tinge on the front wings may be replaced by yellowish-green. The broad pink band on the hind wing distinguishes the moth from the closely related Bedstraw Hawkmoth.
Caterpillar: up to 80 mm long, is one of the most colourful of all caterpillars; its red, black and cream pattern being a clear warning of its poisonous nature. It feeds on various kinds of spurge in late summer.

BEDSTRAW HAWKMOTH
Hyles gallii
75 mm. Widely distributed in Europe, this moth is a sporadic summer visitor to Britain, although more frequent than the Spurge Hawkmoth, from which it is easily distinguished by the unbroken brown stripe on the front margin of the front wing. It flies May-July and is most common in sandy areas.
Caterpillar: up to 80 mm long, is pale green at first, becoming darker and sometimes almost black with a row of large yellow spots on each side. It feeds on bedstraws in summer.

ELEPHANT HAWKMOTH
Deilephila elpenor
70 mm. Flying in June, this moth is very fond of Honeysuckle flowers. At rest, with its wings swept back like an arrowhead — a feature of many hawk-moths — it is very hard to see on the vegetation. Most of Europe.
Caterpillar: up to 85 mm, is brown (rarely green) with 2 pairs of pink eye-spots just behind the thorax. When disturbed, the head and thorax are pulled into the abdomen, causing the eye-spots to swell. The caterpillar then sways to and fro and frightens birds away. It feeds on willowherbs and bedstraws July-August.

SMALL ELEPHANT HAWKMOTH
Deilephila porcellus
50 mm. More brightly coloured than the previous species, this moth flies May-July in most of Europe.
Caterpillar: up to 50 mm long, is pale brown or green. It has the eye-spots and defensive behaviour of its larger relative, but lacks a tail horn. It feeds on bedstraws and occasionally willow-herbs July-August.

HUMMINGBIRD HAWKMOTH
Macroglossum stellatarum
50 mm. This day-flying moth is most often seen as a brown blur as it hovers to feed at flowers. It flies all year in southern Europe, where it has three or four generations, although the adults hibernate in the coldest months. Large numbers fly north in spring and breed all over Europe in summer.
Caterpillar: up to 60 mm long, is green or brown with white spots and a bluish horn. It feeds on bedstraws.

OAK HAWKMOTH
Marumba quercus

120 mm. This handsome insect resembles a large and yellowish Poplar Hawkmoth, although it rests in a very different position. The hind wings are largely orange-brown. The moth is confined to southern Europe and is found mainly in the hilly cork oak woods around the Mediterranean. It flies May-August.

Caterpillar: reaches 80 mm in length and is a variable green (often quite bluish) with yellow stripes and a bluish horn. It feeds July-August, mainly on cork oak leaves although it will eat other oaks.

PROSERPINUS PROSERPINA

35-60 mm. Unknown in Britain, this pretty little hawkmoth lives in southern and central Europe, with headquarters in southern Germany and Switzerland, although it is never common. As well as the typical green form, there is a grey form and a brown one with an orange band across the front wings. It flies around mid-summer.

Caterpillar: up to 60 mm long, is dull green when young, becoming greyish brown with darker diagonal bars on the sides. Each bar slopes forward and surrounds an eye-like spiracle. There is no horn on the tail in the later stages. It feeds on willowherbs and purple loosestrife in late summer.

BROAD-BORDERED BEE HAWKMOTH
Hemaris fuciformis

50 mm. This is a day-flying moth which revels in bright sunshine. It flies May-June in most parts of Europe, with a 2nd brood in August in the south. Woodland glades and margins are its favourite haunts and it is most often on the wing before noon. It is remarkably bee-like when at rest as well as when hovering at flowers, but it has a much quicker darting flight than a bumble bee. It is especially fond of rhododendron flowers. The wings are clothed with brownish-green scales when the moth first emerges, but most of the scales fall during the first flight, leaving just the brown margins and veins.

Caterpillar: up to 50 mm long, is green on top and reddish-brown below, with red spots around the spiracles. The horn is brown with a violet base. It feeds on honeysuckle and bedstraws July-August (and again in September in southern Europe).

NARROW-BORDERED BEE HAWKMOTH
Hemaris tityus

45 mm. Distinguished from the previous species by its narrower borders, this moth has very similar habits, but also occurs on wet heaths and moorland. It is especially fond of bugle flowers. All Europe, including the far north.

Caterpillar: reaches 40 mm in length and is green with reddish spots and stripes and a reddish-brown horn. It feeds on various kinds of scabious.

Oak Hawkmoth

Proserpinus proserpina

Broad-bordered Bee Hawkmoth

Narrow-bordered Bee Hawkmoth

A narrow-bordered bee hawkmoth at rest, showing its striking resemblance to a bumblebee.

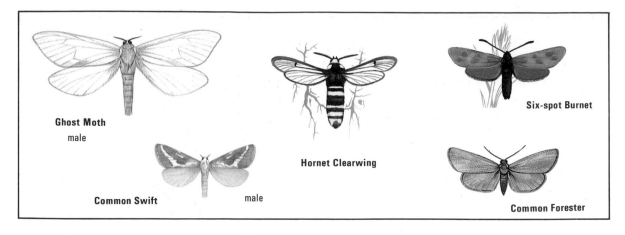

Ghost Moth
male

Common Swift

male

Hornet Clearwing

Six-spot Burnet

Common Forester

SWIFT MOTHS
Family Hepialidae

The swifts are rather primitive, fast-flying moths with all four wings of similar shape. The antennae are very short and the adults do not feed. The wings are folded along the sides of the body at rest. The caterpillars, usually white with brown heads, all feed on roots from summer to late spring.

GHOST MOTH
Hepialus humuli
46 mm. The male, silvery-white above and dull brown below, drifts ghost-like over grassy places at dusk June-July. The female is brownish-yellow. Northern and central Europe.

COMMON SWIFT
Hepialus lupulinus
25-40 mm. Female is larger than male and often has virtually no wing markings. It flies May-July in most of Europe.

CLEARWING MOTHS
Family Sesiidae

The clearwings are day-flying moths which, because the wings are largely devoid of scales, bear striking resemblances to various bees and wasps, especially when in flight. They like to sunbathe on leaves. The caterpillars are pale and maggot-like and most live inside the stems or roots of trees and shrubs, usually for two years. A few tunnel in the roots of herbaceous plants.

HORNET CLEARWING
Sesia apiformis
30-40 mm. One of the largest of the clearwings, this species resembles a wasp, except that it lacks the narrow waist. It flies May-July in most parts of Europe.
Caterpillar: about 25 mm long, tunnels in the roots and lower parts of the trunks of poplars.

BURNETS and FORESTERS
Family Zygaenidae

These are mostly brightly coloured, day-flying moths with rather sluggish flight. Many species live in Europe, especially in the south. The burnets have clubbed antennae, but the tip thickens more gradually than in the butterflies. The foresters have toothed antennae.

SIX-SPOT BURNET
Zygaena filipendulae
30 mm. The deep metallic green (often appearing black) and red colours are typical of the burnets and advertise their poisonous nature, although the red is replaced by yellow in some individuals. The two outer spots of each front wing may join up. It flies May-August in flowery grasslands.
Caterpillar: up to 25 mm long, is cream with black spots. It feeds on trefoils and related plants in autumn and spring. Like most burnets, it pupates in a papery cocoon.

COMMON FORESTER
Adscita statices
20 mm. Bluish or bronzy green front wings. It flies in damp, flowery meadows May-July. Most of Europe.
Caterpillar: about 25 mm long, is yellowish with darker spots. It feeds on sorrel in autumn and spring.

TIGERS and ERMINES
Family Arctiidae

Most of these moths are brightly coloured and very hairy, warning birds that they are distasteful. The adults often do not feed. The caterpillars are also very hairy in most species and pupate in cocoons made largely from the hairs.

Left: A garden tiger moth displays its striking warning coloration.

caterpillar

Jersey Tiger

Garden Tiger

caterpillar

Buff Ermine

male

Cymbalophora pudica

Cinnabar

White Ermine

GARDEN TIGER
Arctia caja
50-80 mm. Extremely variable in size and also in the wing pattern, with the dark markings sometimes linking up and sometimes almost absent. The hind wing may be yellow instead of orange. It flies July-August and is common all over Europe.
Caterpillar: reaches 60 mm in length and is commonly known as a 'woolly bear' because of its dense fur coat, made up of long black hairs with white tips, and shorter brown hairs. It feeds on a wide variety of low-growing plants, beginning in late summer but hibernating when small and feeding up in the spring.

JERSEY TIGER
Euplagia quadripunctaria
50-65 mm. Hind wings may be yellow. It flies by day June-September, but only in sunshine. It is common in southern and central Europe and in the Channel Islands, but in Britain it is established only in a small area of Devon. In some southern localities the moths roost in huge swarms on the trees, one of the most famous places being the 'Valley of Butterflies' on the island of Rhodes.
Caterpillar: up to 50 mm long, has greyish-brown hair and a yellow stripe along the back. It behaves just like the Garden Tiger caterpillar.

CYMBALOPHORA PUDICA
40-50 mm. The dark markings vary in extent and pattern in this little tiger moth, and the ground colour of the front wings ranges from white to rosy pink. It lives in southern Europe and is often extremely common in Mediterranean areas in late summer and autumn.
Caterpillar: up to 30 mm long, has short greyish-brown hairs and feeds on grasses from autumn to spring. Unlike the last two species, it does not hibernate, although it becomes inactive during cold spells.

CINNABAR
Tyria jacobaeae
35-45 mm. The red markings vary a little in size and sometimes join up. Very rarely they are replaced by yellow. The moth flies May-July in grassy places. Although nocturnal, it is easily disturbed by day and it flies weakly away to find another resting place. It occurs in most parts of Europe, but is mainly coastal in the north – often on sand dunes.
Caterpillar: up to 25 mm long, is easily identified by its black and yellow banding. It feeds on ragwort July-August, freely exposed but well protected by its efficient warning coloration. It has been used in some places in attempts to control ragwort in grazing land.

BUFF ERMINE
Spilosoma lutea
30-40 mm. The wings are often quite yellow in the male (seen here), but much paler in the female. The black markings also tend to be paler in the female, but they are very variable: the wings may be almost black, with yellow just on the veins, while at the other extreme there may be no black at all. The antennae are distinctly feathered in the male and thread-like in the female. It flies May-August in a wide variety of habitats nearly all over Europe.
Caterpillar: about 40 mm long, is brown with distinct tufts of rust-brown hair. It feeds on a wide variety of low-growing plants June-October and walks surprisingly quickly when alarmed.

WHITE ERMINE
Spilosoma lubricipeda
35-50 cm. The black dots vary in number and size and may be absent altogether. The wings may be yellowish in Irish specimens. The antennae are feathered in male and thread-like in female. It flies May-August in many habitats throughout Europe.
Caterpillar: up to 50 mm long, is clothed with tufts of dark brown hair and has a distinct reddish stripe along the middle of the back. It feeds and behaves like the Buff Ermine caterpillar.

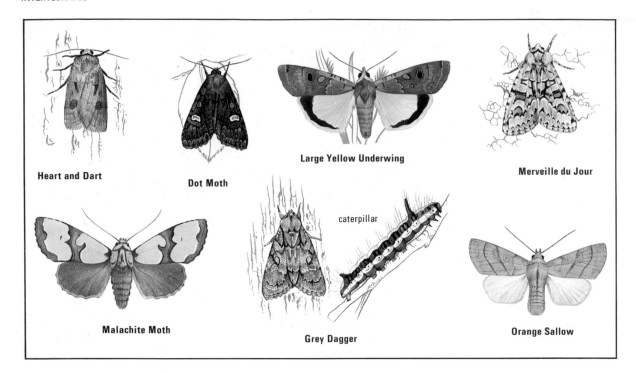

Heart and Dart

Dot Moth

Large Yellow Underwing

Merveille du Jour

Malachite Moth

caterpillar

Grey Dagger

Orange Sallow

NOCTUID MOTHS
Family Noctuidae

Sometimes known as owlet moths, or simply noctuids, the members of this large family are all nocturnal. They have fairly stout bodies and relatively sombre front wings which provide good camouflage when at rest by day. Most also have dull hind wings. The caterpillars are mostly without conspicuous hairs and nearly all pupate in the soil. The pupae are normally shiny and bullet-shaped.

HEART AND DART
Agrotis exclamationis
35-45 mm. Front wings vary from very pale to very dark brown but usually clearly show the dark dart near the middle and the heart-shaped mark just beyond it which give the moth its name. Hind wings are dirty white, sometimes with a dark border. At rest, the wings lie more or less flat over body, not roof-wise as in most other noctuids. It flies May-July, with a second brood in southern Europe. All Europe; especially common in cultivated regions.
Caterpillar: up to 40 mm, is brown above and greyish below and feeds on a wide range of herbaceous plants June-September.

DOT MOTH
Melanchra persicariae
35-50 mm. Named for the prominent white spot on the bluish-black front

wing; hind wings are greyish-brown. Very common June-September in many habitats, but especially common in cultivated regions. Most of Europe, but less frequent in the north.
Caterpillar: reaches 45 mm and varies from greyish-green to dark brown, but is most commonly pale green with darker arrow-like marks on the sides. There is a hump at the hind end. It feeds July-October on many trees and shrubs as well as on herbaceous plants. It is often a pest in gardens.

LARGE YELLOW UNDERWING
Noctua pronuba
50-60 mm. One of several species with yellow hind wings, this very common moth flies June-September. Front wings range from pale greyish-brown (female only) to deep chestnut or almost black (male only). At rest, they lie flat over the body. When disturbed, the moth flies rapidly away and the flashing yellow of hind wings confuses a pursuing bird: the moth drops quickly to the ground and covers hind wings, leaving the bird searching unsuccess-fully for something yellow. All Europe.
Caterpillar: 50 mm long and tapering towards the front, is usually brown with black dashes at the sides. It feeds July-April on a wide variety of her-baceous plants at about ground level and often under the ground.

MERVEILLE DU JOUR
Dichonia aprilina
40-50 mm. Beautifully camouflaged on lichen-covered tree trunks by day, this moth has dull grey hind wings. It flies August-October in all parts of Europe where oak trees grow.
Caterpillar: up to 40 mm long, is olive green or brownish with a white line and 2 zig-zag black lines along the

back. It feeds March-June on oak buds and leaves, often resting in bark crevices by day.

MALACHITE MOTH
Calotaenia celsia
50 mm. On the wing in autumn, this beautiful moth inhabits the open pine forests of northern and central Europe, especially in the eastern parts: not in Britain. Like the Merveille du Jour, it is well camouflaged on mossy and lichen-covered tree trunks by day.
Caterpillar: 40-50 mm long, is yel-lowish-green with black spots and a brown head. It feeds on grasses in summer.

GREY DAGGER
Apatele psi
35-45 mm. Named for the little dagger-like markings on the front wings, this common moth flies May-June in most parts of Europe. Hind wings are pale grey.
Caterpillar: (illustrated above) reaches 50 mm and feeds on a wide range of trees and shrubs July-September. (The Dark Dagger *A. tridens* is externally indistinguishable as an adult, but it has a quite distinct larva.)

ORANGE SALLOW
Xanthia citrago
3·5-4 cm. Front wings usually orange but sometimes distinctly reddish. It flies July-September and is common in southern and central Europe wherever lime trees flourish; less frequent in the north (rare in Scotland).
Caterpillar: reaches 3·5 cm and is red-brown with rows of black and white spots. It feeds April-June on lime and pupates in a chamber made by drawing leaves together with silk.

MULLEIN MOTH
Cucullia verbasci
50 mm. Streaky brown front wings and the tuft of hair on the thorax give the resting moth a striking resemblance to a broken twig or sliver of bark. Hind wings are greyish-brown. It flies April-June in many parts of Europe: uncommon in northern Britain.
Caterpillar: (illustrated below) reaches 50 mm and feeds openly on leaves and flower spikes of mulleins June-August. Its bold colours warn of its unpleasant taste.

ANGLE SHADES
Phlogophora meticulosa
40-50 mm. Front wings of fresh moths are a beautiful mixture of pink, green and brown, with a bold olive-green V across the middle, but colours soon fade. The curious way in which wings are folded at rest gives the moth a remarkable similarity to a dead leaf. It flies at all times of year, even in winter, but most commonly May-September. Most of Europe.
Caterpillar: up to 45 mm, is plump and soft and usually bright green with faint white dots and lines. It eats all kinds of herbaceous plants, mainly in autumn, and pupates in a flimsy cocoon on the ground.

DARK ARCHES
Apamea monoglypha
50 mm. This extremely common moth ranges from pale grey to almost black. It flies June-August and sometimes later in most parts of Europe.
Caterpillar: up to 60 mm, is grey, often with pinkish tinge, with black spots and a dark head. It feeds August-June on grass bases.

LIGHT ARCHES
Apamea lithoxylaea
50 mm. Closely related to the Dark Arches, this moth is pale fawn all over with just a few rust-coloured patches. It flies June-July in most parts of Europe.
Caterpillar: like that of the Dark Arches, but with a pale brown head.

HERALD MOTH
Scoliopteryx libatrix
40-50 mm. The attractive front wings conceal plain grey-brown hind wings. It flies August-October and then hibernates in hollow trees and outhouses before reappearing to fly again March-June. Most of Europe.
Caterpillar: 45 mm long, is slender and bright green. It feeds on willows and poplars June-August.

RED UNDERWING
Catocala nupta
70-90 mm. One of several very similar species, it flies July-October in most parts of Europe. When disturbed, it behaves like the yellow underwings.
Caterpillar: reaches 70 mm and feeds on poplar and willow April-July. Its greyish-brown body blends perfectly with the twigs on which it lies at rest.

SILVER Y
Autographa gamma
30-45 mm. Named for the silvery mark in middle of front wing, this common moth flies by day and night. Resident in southern Europe, it spreads north to nearly all parts in summer and breeds there.
Caterpillar: up to 40 mm, is green with black dots and faint white lines. It has only 2 pairs of prolegs in front of the claspers. It feeds in summer on various low-growing plants.

BURNISHED BRASS
Diachrysia chrysitis
30-45 mm. The brassy patches may be golden or green. Hind wings are dull brown. It flies May-September.
Caterpillar: (illustrated below) reaches 40 mm. It feeds on many low-growing plants. It hibernates.

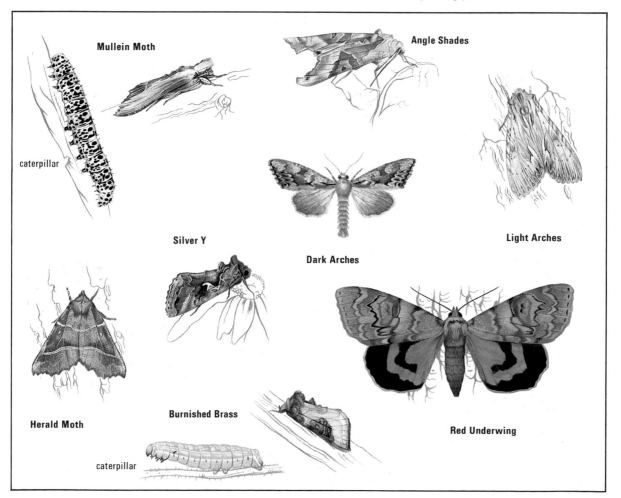

Mullein Moth

caterpillar

Angle Shades

Silver Y

Dark Arches

Light Arches

Herald Moth

Burnished Brass

caterpillar

Red Underwing

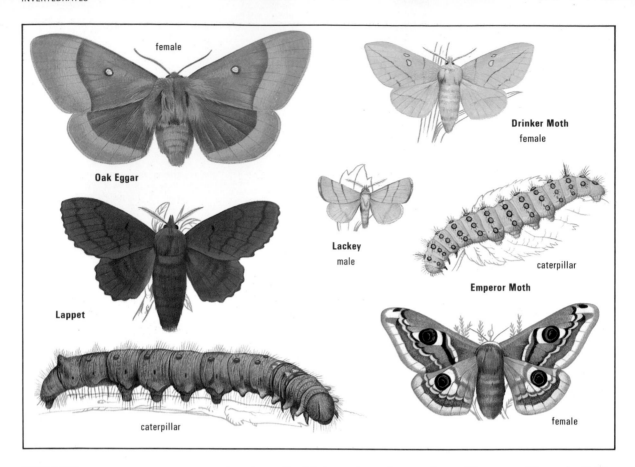

female

Oak Eggar

Drinker Moth
female

Lackey
male

Lappet

caterpillar

Emperor Moth

caterpillar

female

EGGARS
Family Lasiocampidae

The moths in this family are mostly rather stout and furry. Females are larger than males. Antennae are feathery in both sexes, but especially so in the males. Adults do not feed. The caterpillars are generally hairy and often brightly coloured.

OAK EGGAR
Lasiocampa quercus
60-90 mm. The female, illustrated above, flies by night to scatter her eggs. The male is much darker, with a yellowish band across the outer part of the wings, and he flies by day in search of resting females for mating. The moths fly May-August on heathlands and lightly-wooded places. Northern specimens may be darker.
Caterpillar: up to 90 mm, is brown and very furry and feeds on heather, bramble and many other plants, including hawthorn. It begins to feed in summer, but then hibernates and completes its growth in spring. It pupates in a silken cocoon, usually among dead leaves on the ground.

LAPPET
Gastropacha quercifolia
50–80 mm. Usually purplish-brown, but often yellowish-brown in southern Europe. At rest, hind wings are laid almost flat, while front wings are held roof-like over body, producing a good imitation of a dead leaf. It flies June-August in southern and central Europe (southern Britain only).
Caterpillar: (illustrated above) reaches 100 mm and feeds on blackthorn and various other trees, including apple. It hibernates while small, its furry coat blending well with the twigs on which it sleeps. Growth is completed April-May.

DRINKER MOTH
Philudoria potatoria
40-70 mm. Female, illustrated above, is yellowish; male is reddish-brown, with some yellowish clouding on front wing. It flies May-August in grassy places throughout Europe.
Caterpillar: up to 60 mm, is dark grey with yellowish markings and a mixture of black, brown, yellow and white hairs. There is a slender brown tuft just behind the head and another thicker one at the hind end. It feeds on grasses late summer and again in spring after hibernation. It pupates in a long, papery cocoon on a stem.

LACKEY
Malacosoma neustria
30-45 mm. Female has longer and more pointed wings than male shown above. Some specimens are much more orange. It flies July-August.

Caterpillar: up to 50 mm, is slightly hairy and decorated with blue, red and black stripes. Until nearly ready to pupate, it leads a communal life in a large silken web, feeding on a variety of trees and often damaging orchard and garden plants.

FAMILY SATURNIIDAE

This family contains some of the world's largest moths, including the giant silkmoths. Adults do not feed. Most are tropical; 4 species live in Europe, including the Giant Peacock Moth – Europe's largest moth, spanning about 15 cm. Only the Emperor Moth lives in Britain.

EMPEROR MOTH
Saturnia pavonia
50-80 mm. Male much brighter than female shown here, with orange hind wings. On the wing April-May in most parts of Europe, inhabiting heathland, scrub and hedgerow. Male flies by day, picking up female's scent with his large antennae. She flies by night.
Caterpillar: (illustrated above) is orange and black when young. It reaches 70 mm and feeds May-July on bramble, blackthorn, heather and many other plants. It pupates in a tough silken cocoon.

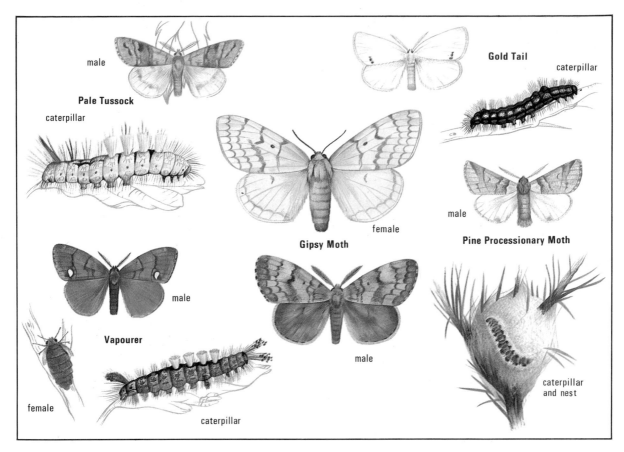

male

Pale Tussock

caterpillar

Gold Tail

caterpillar

female

Gipsy Moth

male

male

Pine Processionary Moth

Vapourer

male

female

caterpillar

caterpillar and nest

TUSSOCK MOTHS
Family Lymantriidae

A family of fairly stout and hairy moths, many of them known as tussocks. Female is usually larger than male and often has a dense tuft of hair at tip of abdomen. Antennae are strongly feathered in male. Adults do not feed. Caterpillars are very hairy, often with dense tufts or tussocks on various parts of the body. Hairs often cause irritation if handled. Pupation occurs in a silken cocoon incorporating many of the larval hairs.

PALE TUSSOCK
Dasychira pudibunda
50-70 mm. Front wings are larger and paler in female than in male shown above, and her hind wings are almost white. Melanic (black) males are quite common in some places (see page 193). It flies April-July in northern and central Europe (absent from northern Britain); rests on tree trunks with front legs stretched forwards.
Caterpillar: (illustrated above) reaches 45 mm. It feeds May-September on many deciduous trees; also on hops.

GOLD TAIL
Euproctis similis
35-45 mm. Also known as the Yellow Tail, this moth has a tuft of golden hairs at tip of abdomen in both sexes; tuft is larger in female, who uses hairs to cover her eggs. Pure white wings, often with black smudge near hind margin of front wing. It flies June-August. Rests with wings steeply roofwise over body.
Caterpillar: (illustrated above) reaches 35 mm. It feeds late summer, then hibernates and completes growth April-May. It feeds on hawthorn and many other trees.

VAPOURER
Orgyia antiqua
35-40 mm (male only). Female wingless. Adult June-October, with 2-3 broods in southern regions, the male flies by day and seeks out females, which never venture further than the surface of their cocoons. Eggs are laid on the cocoon.
Caterpillar: (illustrated above) reaches 40 mm. It feeds on a wide range of deciduous trees and shrubs April-September.

GIPSY MOTH
Lymantria dispar
40-65 mm. Sexes very different, as illustrated above. Males fly by day July-September; females do not fly and remain close to their cocoons after emergence. Eggs are laid in batches and covered with hairs from female abdomen. Most of Europe; extinct as a breeding species in Britain, but occasional males reach southern and eastern coasts from the continent.
Caterpillar: reaches 60 mm and is mottled grey with blue and red spots bearing loose tufts of hair. It feeds on a wide range of deciduous trees and shrubs and is a serious pest in many woodlands in spring.

FAMILY THAUMETOPOEIDAE

PINE PROCESSIONARY MOTH
Thaumetopoea pityocampa
30-50 mm. Female larger than male. It flies in early summer among pine trees in southern and central Europe; not in Britain.
Caterpillar: about 50 mm long, is dark brown with black markings and tufts of irritating brown and white hairs. It lives communally in a large silken nest among the pine twigs, resting by day and going out to chew pine needles by night. When on the move, the larvae walk in single file, each one just nudging the back of the one in front — hence the name processionary. They feed late summer and autumn and hibernate in the nest before completing growth in spring. Young trees may be completely stripped of needles, and the larvae may even move to other trees to feed.

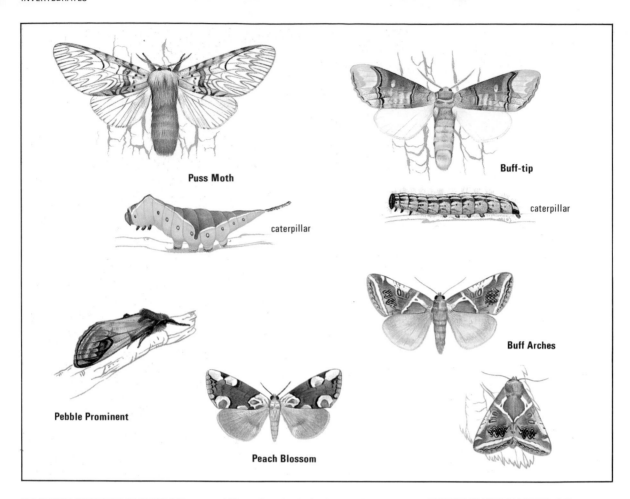

Puss Moth

caterpillar

Buff-tip

caterpillar

Buff Arches

Pebble Prominent

Peach Blossom

FAMILY NOTODONTIDAE

Mostly fairly large, stout–bodied moths with relatively long front wings and fast flight. They resemble noctuids in some ways, including their generally sombre colours, but differ in wing venation. Many are known as prominents because front wings bear tufts of scales which stand out above the body when at rest – best seen from the side. The caterpillars are generally hairless and many have fleshy outgrowths on the back. Many raise both ends of the body when at rest, gripping the twigs with just the 4 pairs of prolegs.

PUSS MOTH
Cerura vinula
60-80 mm. Body and legs very furry; hind wings often darker in female, especially in northern areas. It flies May-July all over Europe.
Caterpillar: (illustrated above) reaches 70 mm. The last pair of legs — the claspers — are modified as 'tails'.

When disturbed, the larva raises them and protrudes red whip-like filaments from them; at the same time, it pulls the head into the front part of the thorax, swelling it up to display a threatening 'face'. Eats willow and poplar June-September. Pupates in tough cocoon welded to bark.

BUFF-TIP
Phajera qucephala
50-70 mm. Named for the pale wing tips and the yellowish hairs on the thorax. At rest, with wings pulled tightly round body, the moth looks just like a broken twig. It flies May-July in most parts of Europe.
Caterpillar: (illustrated above) reaches 80 mm and feeds on many deciduous trees June-September; gregarious in early stages.

PEBBLE PROMINENT
Eligmodonta ziczac
40-50 mm. Named for the pebble-like wing]tip mark; hind wing is dirty white. Tuft of scales characteristic of prominents is clearly seen from the side. Flies May-October all over Europe.
Caterpillar: about 40 mm long, is pinkish-grey with a green head and a large rust-coloured patch near hind end; tapers strongly towards front, with 2 fleshy horns near middle. Eats willow and poplar June-November.

FAMILY THYATIRIDAE

PEACH BLOSSOM
Thyatira batis
30-40 mm. Female with slightly larger pink spots than male; pink sometimes replaced by yellowish-brown. It flies May-July and sometimes again in autumn. Essentially a woodland insect, it occurs in northern and central Europe.
Caterpillar: reaches 40 mm and is reddish-brown freckled with white. There are several prominent ridges across the back. It feeds on bramble June-September and rests with the hind region raised.

BUFF ARCHES
Habrosyne pyritoides
30-45 mm. Rests with wings held quite steeply over body in a distinctly triangular fashion; well camouflaged among dead leaves. It flies June-July and sometimes again in autumn in woods, gardens and hedgerows. Mainly central Europe; common in England and Wales.
Caterpillar: reaches 40 mm and is blackish-brown above and rusty brown below. It feeds mainly on bramble August-September.

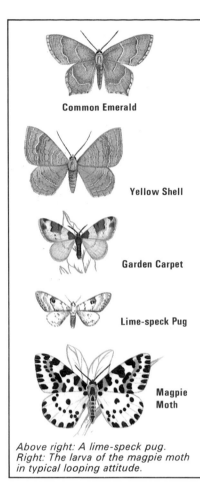

Common Emerald

Yellow Shell

Garden Carpet

Lime-speck Pug

Magpie
Moth

Above right: A lime-speck pug.
Right: The larva of the magpie moth
in typical looping attitude.

GEOMETER MOTHS
Family Geometridae

Collectively known as geometers, the moths in this very large family are mostly rather flimsy and slender-bodied. The majority rest with wings held flat, sometimes covering the abdomen and sometimes held well out to the sides. A few species rest with wings held vertically over the body like butterflies. The larvae, often known as loopers or inchworms, have only 2 pairs of prolegs at the hind end, including the claspers. They move by alternately stretching the front end forward and then bringing the hind end up to it, throwing the body into a high loop in the process. This habit is also responsible for the name geometer, which means 'ground measurer'. Many species pupate in cocoons in the vegetation, but others pupate under the ground.

COMMON EMERALD
Hemithea aestivaria
20-30 mm. One of several similarly coloured moths but easily recognized by the chequered fringes. The green is bright in freshly emerged moths, but soon takes on a greyish tint. It flies June-July in wooded areas and hedgerows. Southern and central Europe; absent from northern Britain.
Caterpillar: up to 30 mm is very slender; yellowish-green with chestnut markings. It feeds on various trees before and after hibernation.

YELLOW SHELL
Camptogramma bilineata
20-30 mm. Varies from bright yellow to brown, with the cross lines sometimes almost black. Abundant in woodland, gardens, hedgerows and other scrubby places throughout the summer. Most of Europe.
Caterpillar: up to 25 mm, is green or brown. It feeds on grasses and other low-growing plants August-May.

GARDEN CARPET
Xanthoroe fluctuata
20-30 mm. Black markings often less distinct than shown, and the whole insect often brownish-grey. It flies from spring to autumn in many habitats in most parts of Europe.

Caterpillar: about 25 mm long, is green, grey or brown; feeds June-October on plants in the cabbage family.

LIME-SPECK PUG
Eupithecia centaureata
20-25 mm. Like other pug moths, which are all very slender, it rests with wings widely spread: front edge of front wing almost at right angles to body and hind wing almost concealed under front wing. Well camouflaged on lichen-covered bark (above); resembling a bird-dropping on leaves. It flies all summer in most parts of Europe; common in gardens.
Caterpillar: about 20 mm long, is green, usually with a dark red network on it. It feeds on flowers of various composites summer and autumn.

MAGPIE MOTH
Abraxas grossulariata
35-40 mm. Pattern variable, but easily recognized; bold colours warn of its unpleasant taste. Very common in gardens and hedgerows June-August. Most parts of Europe.
Caterpillar: (see above) reaches 40 mm and also has an unpleasant taste. Feeds on various shrubs, especially blackthorn and gooseberry, August-June. Pupates in a flimsy cocoon.

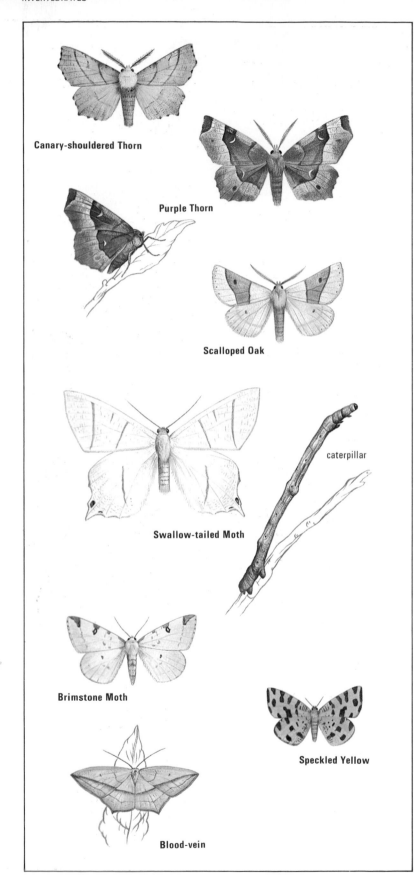

Canary-shouldered Thorn

Purple Thorn

Scalloped Oak

Swallow-tailed Moth

caterpillar

Brimstone Moth

Speckled Yellow

Blood-vein

CANARY-SHOULDERED THORN
Ennomos alhiaria
30-40 mm. Named for the very bright yellow hairs on thorax; flies August-October in damp woods and other moist habitats. Most of Europe.
Caterpillar: about 35 mm long, is purplish-brown, warty, and very twig-like. It feeds on birch, alder and other trees May-July.

PURPLE THORN
Selenia tetralunaria
30-45 mm. Underside resembles upper-side; rests with wings vertically over body. Flies April-May and July-August; summer moths much paler than spring one seen here. Southern and central Europe.
Caterpillar: up to 50 mm, is blotchy brown and twig-like; feeds on various trees June-July and in autumn.

SCALLOPED OAK
Crocallis elinguaria
40-50 mm. Ground colour ranges from cream to reddish-buff. It flies June-August in most parts of Europe.
Caterpillar: about 40 mm long, is twig-like; greyish-brown with a dark, broad zig-zag line along the back. Feeds on a wide range of trees in spring.

SWALLOW-TAILED MOTH
Ourapteryx sambucaria
50-60 mm. Named for the little 'tail' on hind wing, this moth flies June-July, drifting ghost-like over gardens and hedgerows and around woodland margins in most parts of Europe.
Caterpillar: (illustrated left) reaches 60 mm and is extremely twig-like. It feeds on ivy, hawthorn and many other shrubs August-June, hibernating during the coldest months.

BRIMSTONE MOTH
Opisthograptis luteolata
30-40 mm. Flies April-August in gardens and all kinds of scrubby and woody places; 2 generations.
Caterpillar: about 30 mm long, is brown and twig-like with a distinct hump in the middle. It feeds mainly on hawthorn June-July and again in autumn; late larvae hibernate and complete their growth in spring.

SPECKLED YELLOW
Pseudopanthera macularia
20-30 mm. A day-flying species of lightly wooded regions; active May-June in most parts of Europe. The amount of brown is variable.
Caterpillar: about 25 mm long, is relatively stout and green, with white lines along it. Feeds July-August on members of deadnettle family.

BLOOD-VEIN
Calothysanis amata
30-40 mm. Named for the bright pink line on the wings, this moth flies May-August in hedgerows and other scrubby places. Most of Europe.
Caterpillar: some 25 mm long, is greyish-brown with darker spots: eats many low-growing plants from late summer to spring.

PEPPERED MOTH
Biston betularia
45-65 mm. Exists in two main forms (right). Black (melanic) form, first recorded in northern England in 1859, spread to many industrial areas in late 19th century and became common because it was camouflaged against sooty trees and buildings. Original speckled form almost disappeared from these areas, but more common again now that pollution is being controlled. Speckled form remained common in rural areas, but black moths occur there too. Several intermediate forms are also known. The moth flies May-August all over Europe.
Caterpillar: (illustrated right) reaches 60 mm and is green or brown; twig-like with a distinct notch in the head. It feeds on many trees and shrubs June-September.

FAMILY DREPANIDAE

PEBBLE HOOK-TIP
Drepana falcataria
30-40 mm. The hooked wing-tips (found in most members of the family) and the pebble-like mark in middle of front wing give this moth its name. Wings range from dirty white to rich brown and 'pebble' is sometimes indistinct. It flies May-September in 2 broods. Northern and central Europe.
Caterpillar: up to 30 mm long, is brown above and green below; slightly hairy. Like other hook-tip larvae, it has no claspers and the body tapers to a point. Both ends are raised when at rest. It feeds June-October, mainly on birch.

FAMILY PYRALIDAE

SMALL MAGPIE MOTH
Eurrhypara hortulata
25-35 mm. Pattern somewhat variable. Unrelated to the Magpie Moth (page 191), this species flies June-July, usually at about dusk, in areas rich with nettles and other rank vegetation. Most of Europe, but less common in the north.
Caterpillar: about 25 mm long, is flesh-coloured. It feeds August-September, mainly on stinging nettle; usually gathers leaves together with silk to form a shelter.

FAMILY PTEROPHORIDAE

WHITE PLUME MOTH
Pterophorus pentadactylus
20-30 mm. Pure white wings form 5 feathery plumes on each side – 2 in the front wing and 3 in the hind wing. Flies June-July; most of Europe, but rare in the north.
Caterpillar: about 20 mm long, is green and hairy. Feeding on hedge bindweed, it hibernates while small and completes its growth in spring.

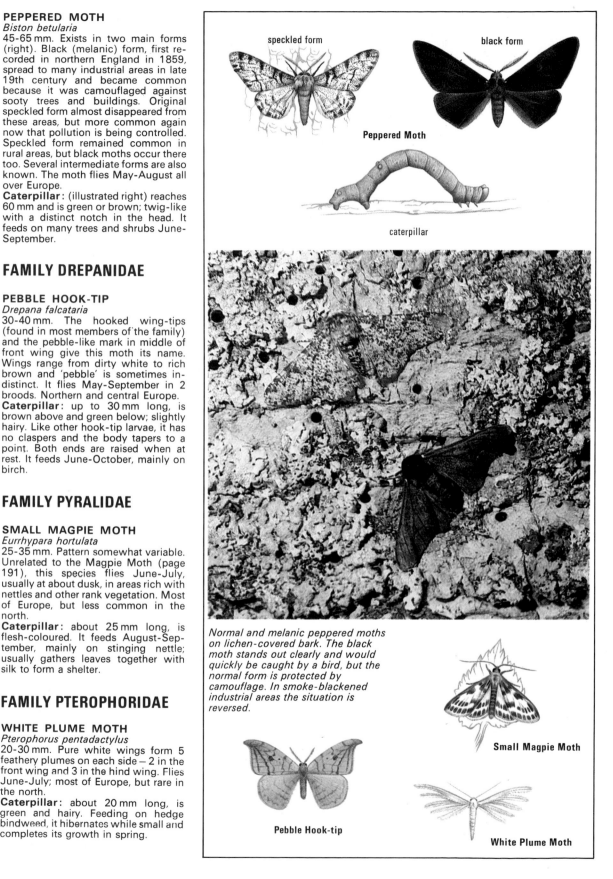

speckled form

black form

Peppered Moth

caterpillar

Normal and melanic peppered moths on lichen-covered bark. The black moth stands out clearly and would quickly be caught by a bird, but the normal form is protected by camouflage. In smoke-blackened industrial areas the situation is reversed.

Small Magpie Moth

Pebble Hook-tip

White Plume Moth

True Flies

The true flies belong to the order Diptera and have only one pair of functional wings. The hind wings are reduced to tiny pin-like bodies called halteres, which help to maintain balance in flight. A few parasitic species, such as the sheep ked, are completely wingless. All flies are liquid-feeders, either mopping up free fluids, such as nectar, or piercing other animals to suck blood. The larvae are all legless, but otherwise are extremely varied. Many of them live in water.

CRANE-FLY
Tipula maxima
Family Tipulidae
50-60 mm. Largest of many quite similar species which are also known as daddy-long-legs. Male abdomen not pointed. Summer, especially in woods. The larva lives in waterlogged soil. The larvae of some other species are the notorious leatherjackets which damage plant roots.

CRANE-FLY
Nephrotoma quadrifaria
30-40 mm. Abundant everywhere May-September. The larva attacks the roots of many garden crops.

WINTER GNAT
Trichocera annulata
Family Trichoceridae
15 mm. Like a small crane-fly, but distinguished by the sharply-bent vein near hind edge of wing. Swarms in large numbers, especially on winter afternoons. Rests with wings flat over body. The larvae live in decaying vegetation. Several very similar species.

MOSQUITO
Culex pipiens
Family Culicidae
12 mm. One of the commonest mosquitoes, especially in buildings. As in all mosquitoes, only male has feathery antennae and only female sucks blood (this species rarely attacks humans): male prefers nectar. One of many species holding abdomen parallel to surface on which they are resting. Larva lives in stagnant water. All year.

MIDGE
Chironomus annularis
Family Chironomidae
15 mm. Mosquito-like, but with no piercing beak: probably does not feed as adult. Males often dance in large swarms. Rests with wings roof-like over body, but wings much shorter than abdomen. Only male has feathery antennae. Larva is a 'blood-worm' living in stagnant water. All year.

ST MARK'S FLY
Bibio marci
Family Bibionidae
20 mm. Common in gardens and fields March-May. Flies lethargically, males often in swarms, and visits flowers. Female eyes much smaller than those of male. Larvae feed on roots and decaying matter in soil.

ROBBER-FLY
Asilus crabroniformis
Family Asilidae
35-45 mm. A fast-flying insect, catching other insects in mid-air and sucking them dry. Late summer. Larvae live in cow dung.

HORSE-FLY
Tabanus sudeticus
Family Tabanidae
30-50 mm. Female larger than male and usually seen around horses and other livestock from which she sucks blood. Male frequents flowers. Mainly on pastureland, especially near water, June-August. The larvae feed on other animals in damp soil.

HORSE-FLY
Chrysops relictus
15-20 mm. One of several similar flies with beautiful iridescent eyes. Females often attack people. June-August, usually near water and often in wooded country.

BEE-FLY
Bombylius major
Family Bombyliidae
25 mm. A very bee-like fly commonly seen hovering over low-growing flowers in spring. The larva lives as a parasite in nests of solitary bees.

HOVER-FLY
Syrphus ribesii
Family Syrphidae
20-25 mm. As in all hover-flies, some veins turn and run parallel to hind edge of wing, forming a false margin. Abundant on hogweed and other umbels in summer, protected by wasp-like coloration. Maggot-like larva eats aphids.

HOVER-FLY
Rhingia campestris
20 mm. Easily recognized by the snout. Very common on flowers in hedges and meadows. The larva feeds in cow dung. Spring and summer.

DRONE-FLY
Eristalis tenax
20-30 mm. Named for its bee-like appearance, this hover-fly is common on spring flowers. A super hoverer. The larva is the rat-tailed maggot, living in muddy ditches and breathing with a telescopic 'snorkel'.

HOUSE-FLY
Musca domestica
Family Muscidae
15 mm. Common in houses for much of the year, but not the commonest fly indoors. Abundant in stables. Mops up all kinds of liquid food. Larva is a white maggot living in decaying matter.

BLUEBOTTLE
Calliphora vomitoria
Family Calliphoridae
20-25 mm. Metallic blue. Buzzes noisily indoors. Maggot feeds on dead flesh. Most of the year.

GREENBOTTLE
Lucilia caesar
20 mm. One of several similar flies. Less common indoors than bluebottle. Maggot feeds on living and dead flesh.

FLESH-FLY
Sarcophaga carnaria
25 mm. Common near buildings, but rarely indoors. Adults visit flowers and carrion. Female gives birth to young maggots on carrion. Most of the year.

DUNG-FLY
Scathophaga stercoraria
Family Scathophagidae
20 mm. Abundant on cow-pats and other dung from early spring onwards. Female is greyer and less furry. Larvae feed in dung: adults prey on smaller flies.

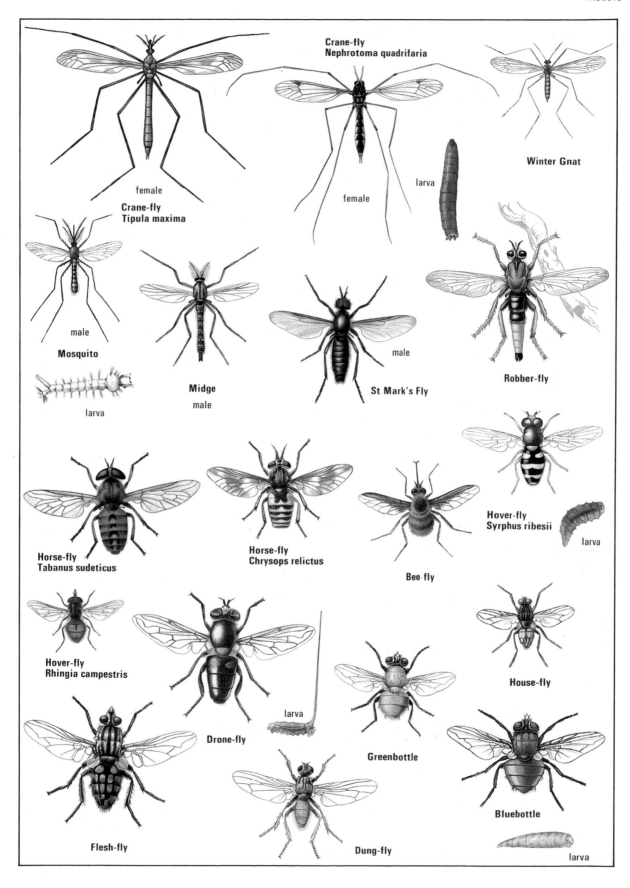

Crane-fly
Nephrotoma quadrifaria

Winter Gnat

female

larva

female

Crane-fly
Tipula maxima

male

Mosquito

Midge
male

male

St Mark's Fly

Robber-fly

larva

Horse-fly
Tabanus sudeticus

Horse-fly
Chrysops relictus

Bee-fly

Hover-fly
Syrphus ribesii

larva

Hover-fly
Rhingia campestris

House-fly

larva

Drone-fly

Greenbottle

Flesh-fly

Dung-fly

Bluebottle

larva

Bees, Wasps, Ants and their relatives

These insects all belong to the order Hymenoptera, an extremely variable group with well over 100,000 species. They have little in common except that most have two pairs of membranous wings, often with few veins and several large cells. The hind wings are often quite small and are linked to the front wings by a row of tiny hooks. All have biting jaws, although the bees have suctorial mouthparts as well for nectar-feeding.

There are two distinct sub-orders – the Symphyta and the Apocrita. The Symphyta contains the sawflies, in which the thorax and abdomen are broadly joined without any 'waist'. These insects get their name because most of the females have tiny saw-like ovipositors (egg-layers) with which they cut slits in plants before laying their eggs there. Most larvae feed on leaves and look like moth caterpillars except that they have more stumpy legs on the abdomen. Some live inside plants and have no abdominal legs. Adult sawflies feed mainly on pollen.

The Apocrita contains all the other hymenopterans, all with the typical 'wasp waist'. The ichneumons and many others are parasites, the females using needle-like ovipositors to lay eggs inside the young stages of other insects. The parasitic grubs gradually destroy their hosts, but not until the parasites themselves are fully grown and ready to pupate. Gall wasps lay their eggs in plants and the presence of the developing larvae causes the plant tissues to swell and form galls, with the grubs feeding on the nutritious tissues inside them.

Social behaviour is well developed in some bees and wasps and in all the ants. The insects live in large colonies which are always founded by females, or queens. All the other members of a colony are the queen's children. Most of them are sterile females called workers, and these do all the building and food-gathering chores as well as tending their younger sisters. The females of the bees and wasps and many of the ants have powerful stings, which are modified ovipositors. Many wasps use their stings to paralyze prey, but otherwise the stings are used for defence. Having laid the foundations of their nests, the queens do nothing but lay eggs. The queen honey bee does not even do any building: she always has a band of workers to help her right from birth. Males occur only at certain times of year among the social insects and do nothing but mate with the new queens.

Most bees and wasps are actually solitary insects, each female excavating or constructing a small nest – often in the ground – and laying a few eggs in it. The nests are always stocked with food – pollen and nectar for the bees, and paralyzed insects or spiders for the wasps (although adult wasps feed mainly on fruit and nectar). Because the larvae are always surrounded by food and do not need to move, they are all legless. This is true of the social and parasitic hymenopterans as well.

Below: Walking astride its victim's body, a digger wasp displays enormous strength as it drags a paralyzed bush cricket to its burrow. The wasp's jaws have a firm grip on one of the cricket's antennae.

SOLITARY BEES

TAWNY MINING BEE

Andrena fulva Family Andrenidae
20-25 mm. One of several species with flattened abdomens which dig nest burrows in lawns and similar places. Female is bright orange-brown: male is much duller. Very common in spring, especially on blackthorn blossom and also on garden currants and gooseberries, which it pollinates very efficiently. It has a short tongue and cannot reach the nectar in deep-throated flowers. After stocking the nest and laying her eggs, the female seals it up and abandons it, like most other solitary bees and wasps.

LEAF-CUTTER BEE

Megachile centuncularis
Family Megachilidae
15-20 mm. Resembles a small honey bee, but venation is different and the abdomen is fringed with golden hairs, especially on the lower surface. The female cuts neat semi-circular pieces from leaves, especially rose leaves, and uses them to construct neat sausage-shaped cells in a hollow stem or some other suitable crevice. The cells are then stocked with food and an egg is laid in each. May-August in northern and central Europe.

LONG-HORNED BEE

Eucera longicornis
Family Anthophoridae
20-25 mm. Named for the great length of the male's antennae. Female antennae are of normal length and she has pale, wedge-shaped marks on the sides of her abdomen. Female makes a nest in the ground. April-July.

CARPENTER BEE

Xylocopa violacea Family Xylocopidae
40-50 mm. This striking, fast-flying bee appears in late summer, feeding on a wide variety of flowers to stock up with nectar before going into hibernation. It reappears in spring and female excavates a nest burrow in a dead tree or other timber. Mainly southern Europe, but occasionally further north.

SOCIAL BEES
Family Apidae

These insects include the honey bee and the bumblebees, all of which make their nests with wax from their own bodies. Honey bee colonies are perennial, but bumblebee colonies last for just one season: young mated queens hibernate and begin new colonies in the spring. The social bees all have long tongues and can obtain nectar from deep-throated flowers. They carry pollen on their hind legs, held by stiff hairs which form the pollen baskets'.

HONEY BEE

Apis mellifera
20-25 mm (worker). Male (drone) and queen are larger, but queen is not normally seen outside the hive. There are many races, some with orange patches on the front of the abdomen. Originally a tropical insect, it is now almost world-wide. Most honey bees live in artificial hives, but wild colonies live in hollow trees and similar places. The nest consists of vertical sheets of 6-sided cells. The bees survive the winter on honey stored up during the previous summer.

WHITE-TAILED BUMBLEBEE

Bombus lucorum
20-40 mm. One of several similar bees, but the bright yellow bands distinguish it. Queens spend a lot of time at flowers in spring, being especially fond of sallow blossom. They usually nest just under the ground, often in old mouse holes. Small workers are soon reared and they take over the building and foraging work. Later workers get progressively larger until, by late summer, they are almost as large as the queen. New queens and males are reared in late summer.

RED-TAILED BUMBLEBEE

Bombus lapidarius
20-40 mm. Male, seen only in late summer, has a yellow collar just behind the head. Life cycle is just like that of the previous species. It often nests under stones.

CARDER BEE

Bombus pascuorum
20-32 mm. A very common bumble bee, particularly fond of white dead-nettle flowers. Its life cycle is like that of the previous species, but the nest is usually built in rough grass.

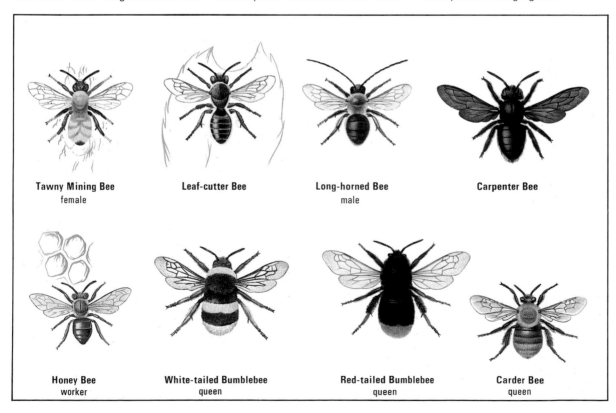

| Tawny Mining Bee | Leaf-cutter Bee | Long-horned Bee | Carpenter Bee |
| female | | male | |

| Honey Bee | White-tailed Bumblebee | Red-tailed Bumblebee | Carder Bee |
| worker | queen | queen | queen |

SOCIAL WASPS
Family Vespidae

These insects all form annual colonies like those of the bumble bees (page 197), but they build their nests with paper, which they make by chewing wood. The larvae are fed insects and other animal matter. Queen usually much larger than workers.

HORNET
Vespa crabro
30-50 mm. The largest European wasp. Nests in hollow trees, often reducing entrance holes with its brittle yellow paper. No more than a few hundred colony members. April-October.

COMMON WASP
Vespula vulgaris
25-45 mm. One of several very similar black and yellow species. Usually with an anchor-shaped mark on face. Nests under the ground or in roof cavities, building a football-sized nest of yellowish paper: cells are enclosed by delicate, overlapping 'shells'. Spring to autumn. Up to 6,000 wasps in a colony.

PAPER WASP
Polistes dominulus
20-25 mm. Lives in small colonies of just a few dozen insects. Nest is a small umbrella with a few dozen cells. Queens no larger than workers. Spring to autumn in southern and central Europe: not in Britain.

SOLITARY WASPS

ECTEMNIUS CEPHALOTES
Family Sphecidae
15-30 mm. One of several rather similar digger wasps. Makes nest in rotten tree stumps and stocks it with paralyzed flies. June-September.

BEMBEX ROSTRATA
25-35 mm. Another digger wasp, nesting in sandy soil and stocking up with flies. June-August, from southern Scandinavia southwards: not in Britain.

AMMOPHILA SABULOSA
25 mm. Often called a sand wasp, it nests in sandy soil and stocks the nest with caterpillars. June-September.

BEE-KILLER WASP
Philanthus triangulum
16-35 mm. Female much larger than male. Catches bees on flowers, paralyzes them and puts them in nest — usually in sandy ground. July-September. Southern and central Europe: rare in Britain.

ANOPLIUS VIATICUS
Family Pompilidae
20-30 mm. Female larger than male. Long legs are a feature of this wasp and its relatives, all of whom capture spiders to stock their subterranean burrows. All summer.

SPINY MASON WASP
Odynerus spinipes
Family Eumenidae
15-20 mm. Nests in vertical sandy banks and also in the mortar of old walls. Stocks nest with small caterpillars. May-August.

ANTS
Family Formicidae

Social insects in which the workers are usually much smaller than queens and always wingless. Queens and males are winged for mating flight, but queens lose wings before starting nest. The nests have no elaborate cells of wax or paper. Insects active in all but coldest months.

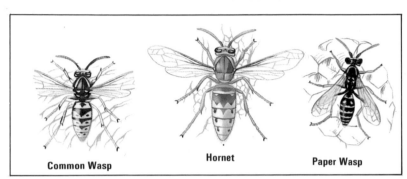

Common Wasp   Hornet   Paper Wasp

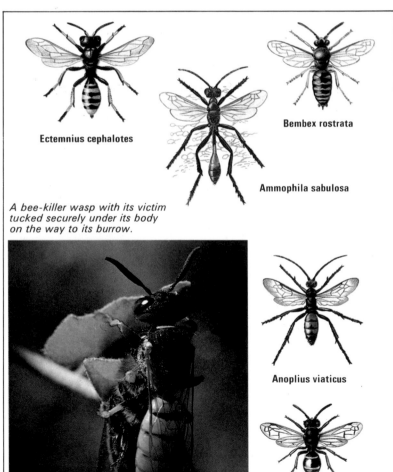

Ectemnius cephalotes

Bembex rostrata

Ammophila sabulosa

A bee-killer wasp with its victim tucked securely under its body on the way to its burrow.

Anoplius viaticus

Spiny Mason Wasp

WOOD ANT
Formica rufa
5-11 mm long. Nests in large mounds in woods, covering mounds with twigs and leaves. Omnivorous.

BLACK ANT
Lasius niger
3-5 mm long. Nests under stones and paths, and even under houses. Very common. Eats other insects and is very fond of honeydew from aphids.

RED ANT
Myrmica ruginodis
5-10 mm. 'Waist' of 2 distinct segments. Has a sting. Very common; nests in soil and in tree stumps. Mainly carnivorous, but enjoys honeydew.

SAWFLIES

HORNTAIL
Urocerus gigas
Family Siricidae
40-60 mm. Female has a drill-like ovipositor with which she lays eggs in pine trunks. Summer.

HAWTHORN SAWFLY
Trichiosoma tibiale
Family Cimbicidae
30-35 mm. Fast-flying: May-June. Larva is pale green with a brown head and eats hawthorn leaves in summer.

GOOSEBERRY SAWFLY
Nematus ribesii
Family Tenthredinidae
10-15 mm. Male is smaller than female and has much black on abdomen. All summer on gooseberries and currants. Larvae live in groups and strip leaves.

PARASITIC HYMENOPTERA

GALL WASP
Biorhiza pallida
Family Cynipidae
10 mm. Develops inside oak apples on oak twigs. June-July.

APANTELES GLOMERATUS
Family Braconidae
4 mm. Grows up in large white butterfly larvae and pupates in silken cocoons around empty skin. Spring and summer.

ICHNEUMON FLY
Ophion luteus
Family Ichneumonidae
30 mm. One of several species developing in moth caterpillars. Summer.

RUBY-TAILED WASP
Chrysis ignita
Family Chrysididae
14 mm. Found on walls and tree trunks spring and summer. A parasite of various solitary bee and wasp larvae.

SCOLIA HIRTA
Family Scoliidae
35 mm. Common on flowers in sandy places June-September. Larva parasitizes various beetles. Southern and central Europe: not in Britain.

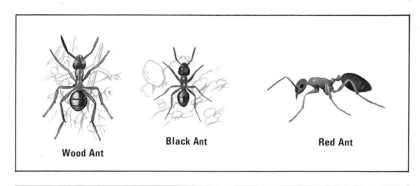

Wood Ant

Black Ant

Red Ant

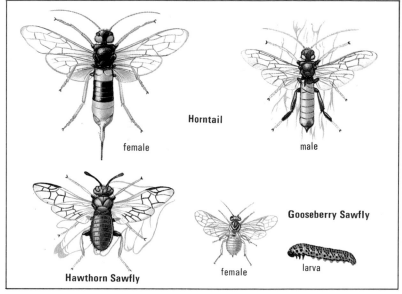

Horntail

female

male

Hawthorn Sawfly

female

Gooseberry Sawfly

larva

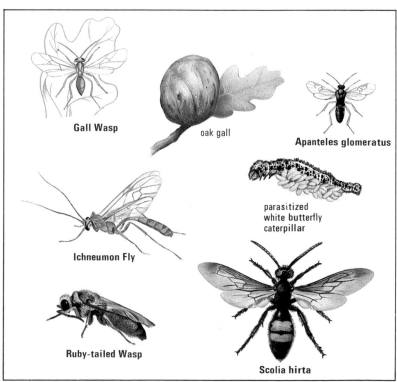

Gall Wasp

oak gall

Apanteles glomeratus

parasitized white butterfly caterpillar

Ichneumon Fly

Ruby-tailed Wasp

Scolia hirta

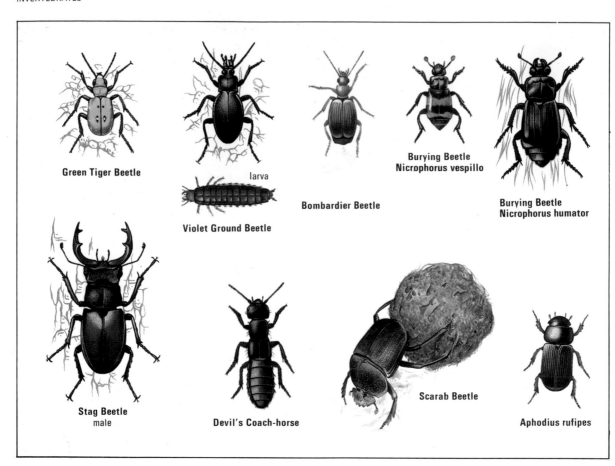

Green Tiger Beetle

larva

Violet Ground Beetle

Bombardier Beetle

Burying Beetle
Nicrophorus vespillo

Burying Beetle
Nicrophorus humator

Stag Beetle
male

Devil's Coach-horse

Scarab Beetle

Aphodius rufipes

Beetles

The beetles form the order
Coleoptera which, with about
250,000 known species, is the
largest of all the insect groups.
They exhibit a tremendous range
of size, shape and habits. The
front wings, known as elytra, are
tough and horny and they conceal
the membranous hind wings.
They also conceal the whole
abdomen as a rule, although some
beetles, such as the rove beetles,
have short elytra. Most beetles
can fly, but some have no hind
wings and in some ground-living
beetles the elytra are fused
together for extra protection.
Water beetles carry their air
supply under the elytra, renewing
it from time to time at the
surface. All beetles have biting
mouthparts, and between them
they feed on just about everything. The larvae are also
extremely varied, but they all
have powerful jaws and often
feed on the same kinds of foods
as the adults.

GREEN TIGER BEETLE
Cicindela campestris Family Carabidae
10-15 mm. A fast-flying and fast-
running predator of ants and other
insects. Active only in sunshine, it lives
mainly on heathland. Spring and summer. The larva lives in a burrow and
darts out to catch prey in its large jaws.

VIOLET GROUND BEETLE
Carabus violaceus
20-30 mm. A flightless, nocturnal predator of slugs and other small invertebrates. Often found under logs and
stones by day. The violet sheen is
especially marked on edges of thorax
and elytra. All year. The larva is also an
active hunter.

BOMBARDIER BEETLE
Brachinus crepitans
7-10 mm. A carnivorous beetle named
because, when alarmed, it fires a puff
of volatile, corrosive liquid from its
anus, accompanied by a slight bang.
Ground-living on well-drained soils:
mainly on chalk in Britain. Most common in early summer.

BURYING BEETLE
Nicrophorus vespillo
Family Silphidae
15-20 mm. One of several similarly-
coloured species, but distinguished by
the two uninterrupted orange bands
and the strongly curved hind legs. Also
known as sexton beetles, these insects

bury the corpses of small birds and
mammals by digging soil from under
them. The beetles usually work in pairs
and eggs are laid on the buried corpse.
The grubs feed on the decaying meat
and also on fly maggots and other
scavengers. Adults are active mainly in
the summer and often fly to lights at
night.

BURYING BEETLE
Nicrophorus humator
18-30 mm. Antennal club is reddish-
yellow. The beetle's habits are just like
those of *N. vespillo*.

DEVIL'S COACH-HORSE
Ocypus olens
Family Staphylinidae
20-30 mm. This ground-living predator
is one of the rove beetles, with very
short elytra. When disturbed, it opens
its huge jaws and bends the abdomen
forward over the rest of the body in a
threatening attitude – leading to its
alternative name of cocktail. Commonly
found under stones and in compost
heaps, it comes out to hunt at night.

STAG BEETLE
Lucanus cervus
Family Lucanidae
Male 50-70 mm. Female lacks the
'antlers', which are really enlarged
jaws, and is 20-40 mm long. Males use
antlers to fight over females, just like
male deer. Flies well on summer

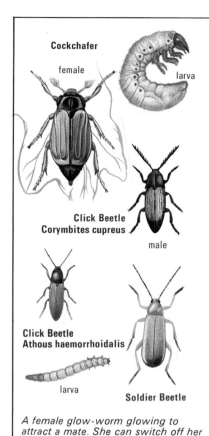

Cockchafer
female
larva

Click Beetle
Corymbites cupreus
male

Click Beetle
Athous haemorrhoidalis

larva

Soldier Beetle

A female glow-worm glowing to attract a mate. She can switch off her light at will.

evenings. Found mainly in and around old woodland and parks with old trees. Larva is like that of the cockchafer, but feeds for several years in old tree trunks and decaying stumps. Southern and central Europe.

SCARAB BEETLE
Scarabaeus sacer
Family Scarabaeidae
25 mm. One of a number of dung beetles famed for their habit of rolling balls of dung about until they find a suitable spot in which to bury them. Eggs are then laid in the dung and the larvae feed on it. Adults also eat dung and sometimes fight over possession of it. All year in Mediterranean region.

APHODIUS RUFIPES
10-12 mm. A very common dung beetle which tunnels in cow-pats and other dung in both adult and larval stages. All legs are quite broad for tunnelling and, as in all other dung beetles and chafers, the antennal club is composed of a number of very thin leaf-like flaps.

COCKCHAFER
Melolontha melolontha
20-25 mm. Female has much smaller flaps to antennal club, and only 6 flaps to the male's 7. Also known as the May-bug because it is often abundant on May evenings, crashing into cars and lighted windows as it flies. It usually flies around trees and feeds on

the leaves, often causing great damage when present in numbers. Larvae feed on roots and also do much damage to cereals and other crops.

CLICK BEETLE
Corymbites cupreus
Family Elateridae
11-16 mm. Female antennae are less feathery than those of male seen here. Lives in grassland, especially in upland regions, in summer. Northern and central Europe. It is one of numerous slender beetles known as click beetles because, when turned on their backs, they leap into the air and right themselves with a loud click.

CLICK BEETLE
Athous haemorrhoidalis
10-13 mm. One of the commonest click beetles, found almost everywhere in spring and early summer. Especially common on hedgerow flowers. The larva is one of the notorious wire-worms which live in the soil and feed on plant roots. This species prefers pasture to arable land, but does a lot of damage to potatoes and cereal roots. It is also fond of dock roots.

SOLDIER BEETLE
Rhagonycha fulva
Family Cantharidae
10-15 mm. Elytra rather soft. Abundant everywhere on flower-heads of hog-weed and other umbellifers where it

catches other small insects throughout the summer. The beetles are called bloodsuckers in many country areas because of their red colour, but they are harmless. There are several similar species, some known as sailor beetles.

GLOW-WORM
Lampyris noctiluca
Family Lampyridae
Only the male (10-13 mm long) looks like a beetle, with soft brown elytra that gape slightly at the hind end. A broad shield covers the head and thorax. Female (10-18 mm) is wingless and looks more like a flat brown wood-louse except that she has only three pairs of legs. Pale yellow patches on the underside of her abdomen give out a strong greenish light as she sits in the grass at night (above). The light attracts the flying males, and if you pick up a glowing female in the dark you will often find a male with her. The larva is very like the adult female and feeds on small snails, often going right inside their shells to devour them. Adults rarely feed. Mainly in chalk and limestone areas, especially in more more northerly parts, and absent from northern Britain. Appears to be getting rarer. May-August.

The related Firefly, *Luciola lusi-tanica,* lives in parts of southern Europe. The males flash their lights as they fly and are answered by flashes from the females on the ground.

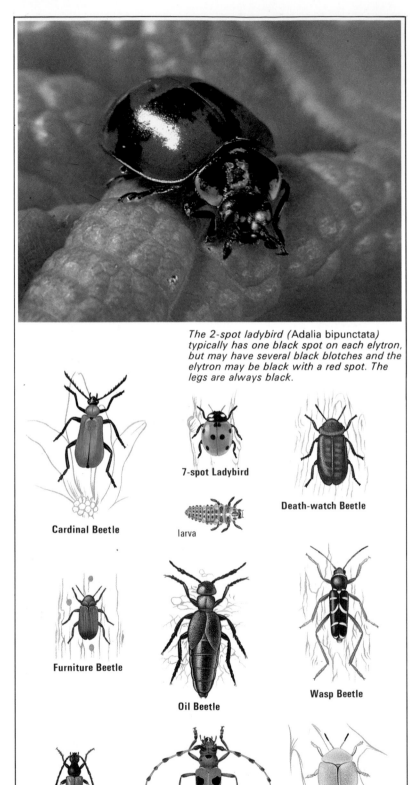

*The 2-spot ladybird (*Adalia bipunctata*) typically has one black spot on each elytron, but may have several black blotches and the elytron may be black with a red spot. The legs are always black.*

Cardinal Beetle

7-spot Ladybird

larva

Death-watch Beetle

Furniture Beetle

Oil Beetle

Wasp Beetle

Leptura rubra

Rosalia alpina

Tortoise Beetle

CARDINAL BEETLE
Pyrochroa coccinea
Family Pyrochroidae
13-18 mm. A flattened, predatory beetle commonly seen on flowers May-July. The larvae, very flat and shiny brown, feed on small animals under loose bark. Northern and central Europe.

7-SPOT LADYBIRD
Coccinella 7-punctata
Family Coccinellidae
5-8 mm. Named for its aphid-eating habits in both larval and adult stages, this is one of the commonest ladybirds, found on a wide variety of plants for much of the year. It goes into hibernation in autumn, often in huge colonies, in attics and outhouses. The larva is steely blue with a few yellow spots. There are several similar species, varying in spot pattern.

DEATH-WATCH BEETLE
Xestobium rufovillosum
Family Anobiidae
5-7 mm. Head almost covered by thoracic shield (pronotum). Larvae tunnel in dead trees in the wild and are very serious pests of timbers in old buildings, especially oak. Young adults knock their heads against the timber to attract mates and the loud ticking sound was once thought to herald a death in the house. April-June.

FURNITURE BEETLE
Anobium punctatum
3-5 mm. Head almost covered by pronotum. Larvae (woodworm) bore in dead trees and also in furniture and other household timbers. Small holes show where adults have emerged. May-July.

OIL BEETLE
Meloe proscarabaeus
Family Meloidae
13-32 mm. Female larger than male but with even shorter elytra and less of a bulge in antennae. Flightless. Discharges an oily fluid when alarmed. Larvae parasitize various bees in their nests. March-June; mainly southern.

WASP BEETLE
Clytus arietis Family Cerambycidae
9-18 mm. One of the longhorn beetles. Flies well in sunshine May-July, often visiting flowers for pollen and nectar. Harmless, but protected by wasp-like colours and movements. Larva lives in dead wood.

LEPTURA RUBRA
10-20 mm. Another longhorn beetle. Female larger than male, with redder elytra and reddish-brown thorax. Larvae live in fallen conifers. Summer.

ROSALIA ALPINA
15-38 mm. A beautiful longhorn from the mountain beechwoods of central Europe. Flies in summer. Rare.

TORTOISE BEETLE
Cassida viridis Family Chrysomelidae
7-10 mm. One of several similar leaf beetles. Very hard to see at rest on leaves. Summer.

COLORADO BEETLE
Leptinotarsa decemlineata
6-12 mm. 5 black stripes on each elytron. Native to North America, this leaf beetle is now a serious potato pest in many parts of Europe. Adult and fleshy pink larva both eat potato leaves (and also related plants). All year, but hibernates in winter. Not in Britain: report it at once if you do find one.

BLOODY-NOSED BEETLE
Timarcha tenebricosa
11-18 mm. This large flightless leaf beetle roams in grassy places in spring, eating bedstraws and other low-growing plants. When alarmed, it exudes bright red blood from its mouth. The blood has a burning taste and birds soon learn to leave the beetle alone. Southern and central Europe.

CHRYSOMELA POPULI
10-12 mm. May-August on sallow and related trees. Adults and larvae all nibble the leaves.

NUT WEEVIL
Curculio nucum
Family Curculionidae
6-9 mm. Snout is longer than in most weevils, especially in female, who uses it to drill into young hazel nuts where she lays her eggs. Larvae feed in the developing kernels. Adult visits various flowers in spring.

PHYLLOBIUS POMACEUS
7-9 mm. A very common weevil, showing the typical snout or rostrum of the group. Clothed with metallic green or golden scales, but these easily rub off and black elytra commonly show through. Abundant on nettles and many other plants in spring and summer. There are many similar species.

ELM BARK BEETLE
Scolytus scolytus
Family Scolytidae
3-6 mm. The infamous carrier of the Dutch elm disease fungus which has killed millions of elm trees. The larvae live under the bark, making the familiar galleries as they chew through the nutritious tissues. Adults emerge through small holes May-July.

GREAT DIVING BEETLE
Dytiscus marginalis
Family Dytiscidae
30 mm. Female has ridged elytra and no swelling on front leg. A fierce predator in ponds and streams. Flies well at night. Larva has huge curved jaws for piercing prey. All year.

WHIRLIGIG BEETLE
Gyrinus natator
Family Gyrinidae
5-7 mm. Whirls rapidly round and round on surface of ponds and slow streams, 'skating' with the aid of the short middle and hind legs. It catches small insects on the surface or below it. Dives when alarmed. Spring to autumn, and hibernates in the mud. The larva is long and slender, with numerous feathery outgrowths.

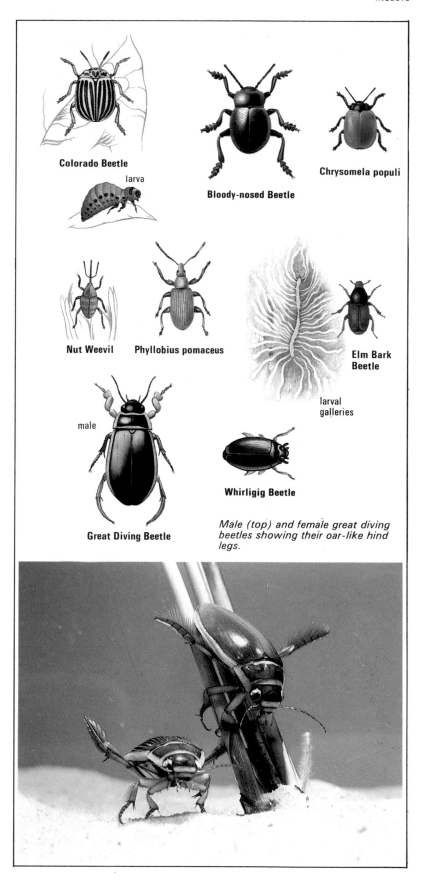

Colorado Beetle

larva

Bloody-nosed Beetle

Chrysomela populi

Nut Weevil   Phyllobius pomaceus

Elm Bark Beetle

larval galleries

male

Great Diving Beetle

Whirligig Beetle

Male (top) and female great diving beetles showing their oar-like hind legs.

The insects on these three pages belong to a number of smaller orders. Some orders are completely wingless, either because they are primitive groups which have never evolved wings (springtails and silverfish) or because they have lost their wings in association with their parasitic habits (lice and fleas).

Mayflies

The mayflies (order Ephemeroptera) fly weakly on flimsy wings: hindwings small and sometimes absent. 2 or 3 tails. Antennae very short. Adults short-lived and do not feed: always near water in which young grow up. There is no pupal stage.

ISONYCHIA IGNOTA
Family Isonychidae
30 mm. Female often with large egg mass protruding from her body, ready to be dropped into the water. Lakes and rivers in southern and central Europe: not in Britain. Summer.

Stoneflies

The stoneflies (order Plecoptera) are weak-flying insects which grow up in water – usually in fairly fast streams, but some species in still water. Adults feed little: may nibble algae and pollen. They rest with wings flat over body or wrapped tightly round it. There are 2 tails, sometimes very short.

PERLODES MICROCEPHALA
Family Perlodidae
30-40 mm (female). Male has short wings. Stony streams. March-July.

Earwigs

Easily recognized by the pincers at the hind end, which are quite strongly curved in males and straighter and thinner in females. Front wings short and horny: hind wings extremely thin and elaborately folded under front wings, protruding as little triangular flaps. Hind wings often lacking, however, and many species lack front wings as well. Mainly nocturnal, earwigs eat both plant and animal matter. They hide by day under stones and loose bark. Female looks after eggs and young. The earwigs belong to the order Dermaptera.

COMMON EARWIG
Forficula auricularia
Family Forficulidae
9-17 mm. Male sometimes has much longer pincers. All year in many habitats. The only earwig commonly seen in Britain.

Cockroaches and Mantids

These insects (order Dictyoptera) have long, spiky legs and the front wings (when present) are leathery. Cockroaches are nocturnal scavengers, while mantids are fierce predators, catching other insects in their strongly-spined front legs. Mantids lay their eggs in frothy masses which become tough and horny as they dry. Cockroach eggs are laid in horny 'purses'. There is no pupal stage.

GERMAN COCKROACH
Blatella germanica Family Blatellidae
9-14 mm. A native of North Africa, now a widely distributed pest in warehouses, bakeries and other buildings; also on rubbish dumps. All year.

PRAYING MANTIS
Mantis religiosa Family Mantidae
40-80 mm (female usually longer than male and stouter). Stalks prey or lies in wait in low vegetation. Flies well in warm weather. Southern and central Europe: not in Britain.

Thrips

These minute black, brown or yellow insects (order Thysanoptera) have four feathery wings. They suck juices from a wide variety of plants, including fungal threads. Many are found in flowers, and in thundery weather they often take to the air in millions. Many hibernate as adults in our houses. There is no pupal stage.

ONION THRIPS
Thrips tabaci Family Thripidae
Family Thripidae
1-2 mm. Yellow or brown. Attacks leaves and flowers of many plants, including various crops, and often causes stunting. All year.

Booklice and Barklice

The booklice and barklice (order Psocoptera) are very small, winged or wingless, with relatively large eyes and long antennae. Many live on tree trunks, chewing algae and pollen grains: others live in debris and some are household pests. There is no pupal stage.

COMMON BOOKLOUSE
Liposcelis divinatorius
Family Liposcelidae
1-2 mm. One of several very similar wingless species found in buildings, where they chew all kinds of starchy materials, including the glue of book-bindings and wallpaper. Can be a pest in stamp collections. All year.

Scorpion Flies

Named because the males of most species have a scorpion-like tail although the insects are quite harmless. Jaws at the tip of a stout beak. Omnivorous scavengers. Larvae are caterpillar-like and live in damp soil. The scorpion flies belong to the order Mecoptera.

PANORPA COMMUNIS
Family Panorpidae
30 mm. May-August in hedgerows and gardens and other shady places: especially fond of nettle beds. One of several very similar species.

Lacewings and their relatives

A variable order of carnivorous insects (Neuroptera), mostly with densely netted wings held roof-wise over the body at rest. They undergo a complete metamorphosis, the young stages being bristly, shuttle-shaped larvae.

ALDER FLY
Sialis lutaria Family Sialidae
30 mm. Weak-flying and rarely far from the still or slow-moving water in which larva lives. Rests on stones and plants: rarely feeds. May-July.

SNAKE FLY
Raphidia notata Family Raphidiidae
25 mm. Mainly on trees and shrubs, feeding on aphids. Rests with long, snake-like neck raised. Larva eats insects under bark and in dead wood. One of several similar species. May-August in woodland.

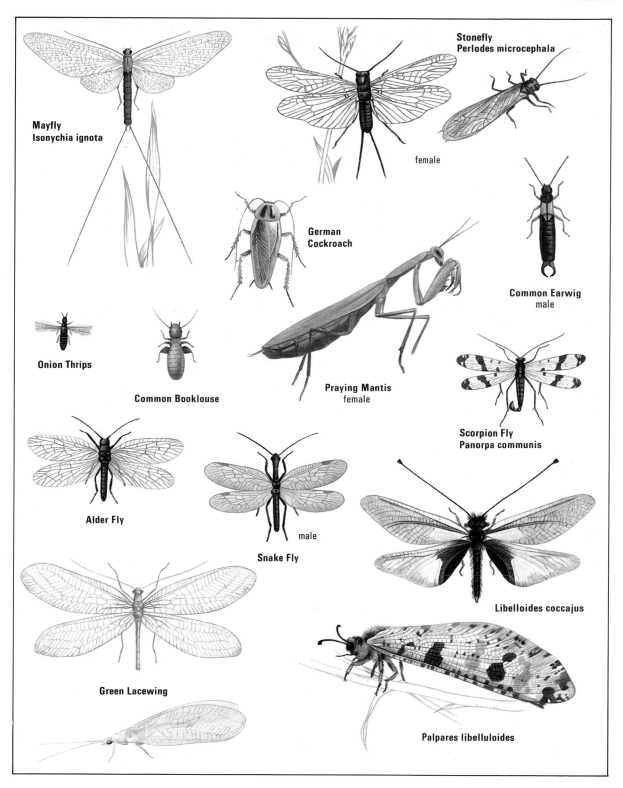

Mayfly
Isonychia ignota

Stonefly
Perlodes microcephala

female

German
Cockroach

Common Earwig
male

Onion Thrips

Common Booklouse

Praying Mantis
female

Scorpion Fly
Panorpa communis

Alder Fly

Snake Fly
male

Libelloides coccajus

Green Lacewing

Palpares libelluloides

GREEN LACEWING
Chrysopa septempunctata
Family Chrysopidae
30-40 mm. One of several similar species. Adult and larva eat aphids. Nocturnal. Woods, hedges and gardens. May-August. Not in north.

LIBELLOIDES COCCAJUS
Family Ascalaphidae
50 mm. Fast-flying, catching other small insects in mid-air. May-August in grassy places, mainly in hills. Southern and central Europe: not in Britain.

PALPARES LIBELLULOIDES
Family Myrmeleonidae
100 mm. Slow-flying, catching other insects in flight or on vegetation. It is one of the antlions, some of whose larvae dig pits to trap ants. May-August. Southern Europe.

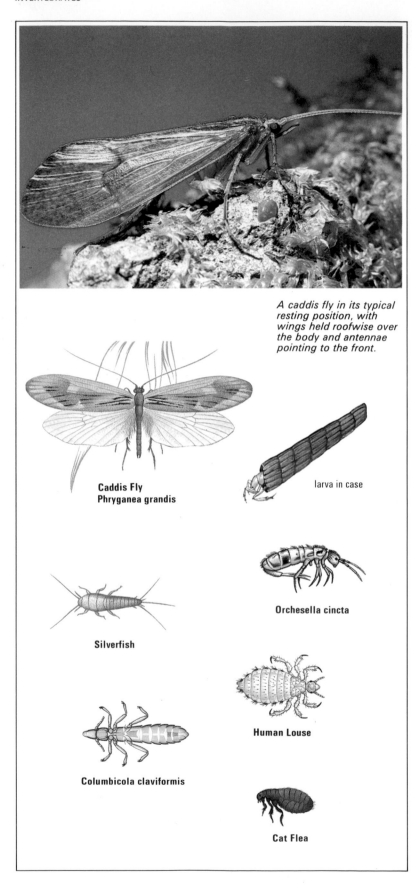

A caddis fly in its typical resting position, with wings held roofwise over the body and antennae pointing to the front.

**Caddis Fly
Phryganea grandis**

larva in case

Silverfish

Orchesella cincta

Human Louse

Columbicola claviformis

Cat Flea

Caddis Flies

Mostly brownish, rather moth-like insects, but wings are clothed with hairs instead of scales and there is no tongue or proboscis. They rarely feed and the mouth-parts are often vestigial. Most fly by night. The larvae nearly all live in water and many make portable shelters or cases with sand grains or plant fragments. Each species has its own case pattern. The caddis flies belong to the order Trichoptera.

PHRYGANEA GRANDIS
Family Phryganeidae
35-40 mm. Breeds in still water with plenty of vegetation, the case being made of leaf fragments. Summer.

Wingless Insects

SILVERFISH
Lepisma saccharina
7-10 mm. A member of the order Thysanura, a primitive group whose bodies are loosely clothed with scales and have three tails. Young are just like adults. The silverfish is found only in buildings and feeds on starchy foods. All year. Related species live under stones on seashore.

ORCHESELLA CINCTA
2-4 mm. One of the springtails, in the order Collembola. The forked springing organ on the hind end shoots the insect forward when it is disturbed. Lives in woodland, under stones and moss. All year. Young are just like adults.

COLUMBICOLA CLAVIFORMIS
3 mm. One of the biting lice (order Mallophaga) that are found chiefly on birds. It lives on wood pigeons, chewing the skin and feather bases at all times of the year. The body is flattened and strong claws help the louse to maintain its grip. Young are very like adults. Many similar species.

HUMAN LOUSE
Pediculus humanus
2-3 mm. One of the sucking lice (order Anoplura) that feed on the blood of mammals. It infests only man and chimpanzees and can carry several diseases. Like the biting lice, it is flattened and endowed with strong claws. Young are very like the adults.

CAT FLEA
Ctenocephalides felis
3 mm. Attacks many mammals, including man, but breeds only where there are cats. Like all fleas (order Siphonaptera), it sucks blood. Body is flattened from side to side, to slip through fur easily, and long hind legs are used for jumping. Young are slender maggots, living in cats' sleeping quarters and growing up via a pupal stage.

Centipedes and Millipedes

Centipedes

The centipedes form the class of arthropods known as the Chilopoda. They are elongate animals with one pair of legs on each body segment. They are mostly fast-moving and all are carnivores, catching and killing other animals with a pair of poison claws surrounding the head. Most are active at night.

LITHOBIUS FORFICATUS
Family Lithobiidae
18-30 mm. 15 pairs of legs when mature, including the hind legs which trail behind body and act rather like antennae. Hides under stones and loose bark by day.

HAPLOPHILUS SUBTERRANEUS
Family Himantariidae
50-70 mm. 77-83 pairs of legs (always an odd number), the last pair resembling the antennae. Lives in soil and leaf litter.

SCUTIGERA COLEOPTRATA
Family Scuterigidae
30 mm. 15 pairs of long legs, the hind pair extremely long and thin. The antennae are also extremely long. A very fast runner. Native in Mediterranean region, in caves and rocky places: found in buildings further north, rarely in Britain.

Millipedes

Millipedes (Class Diplopoda) are elongate arthropods with two pairs of legs on most body segments. They are relatively slow-moving herbivores.

TACHYPODIULUS NIGER
Family Iulidae
50 mm. One of several very similar cylindrical species which curl up like watch springs when disturbed. Very common in many habitats, especially on lime-rich soils. Often climbs trees.

POLYDESMUS ANGUSTUS
Family Polydesmidae
25 mm. One of the flat-backed millipedes, most common in leaf litter and other decaying matter.

PILL MILLIPEDE
Glomeris marginata
Family Glomeridae
20 mm. Much stouter than other millipedes and often confused with woodlice, but has 17-19 pairs of legs compared with the 7 pairs of the woodlouse. It is also much shinier than the woodlouse, which distinguishes it when rolled up. Turf and leaf litter.

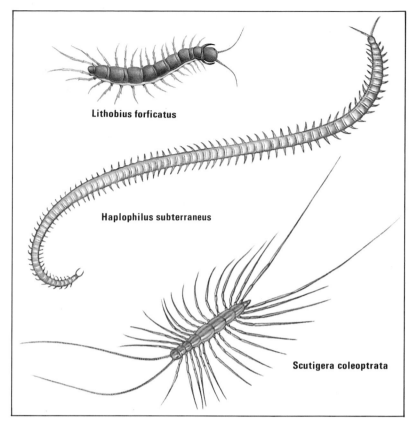

Lithobius forficatus

Haplophilus subterraneus

Scutigera coleoptrata

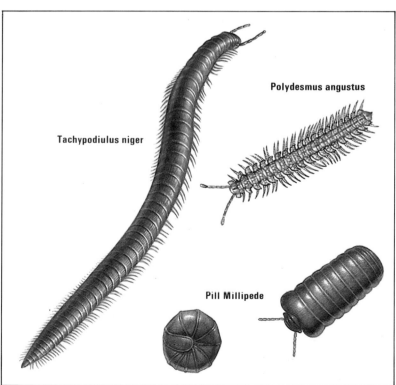

Tachypodiulus niger

Polydesmus angustus

Pill Millipede

Worms

The name worm is given to several quite distinct groups of animals with long, thin bodies, including the tapeworms (Phylum Platyhelminthes) and roundworms (Phylum Nematoda) that live parasitically in the bodies of other animals. The most familiar worms, however, are the segmented worms or annelids (Phylum Annelida), whose bodies are divided into many rings or segments. There are three classes. In the Oligochaeta, which includes the earthworms and various aquatic worms, each body segment has just a few bristles. The leeches belong to the Hirudinea and have suckers fore and aft, but no bristles. Most are aquatic and generally prey on other animals, but some are blood-suckers. The Polychaeta contains the bristleworms, in which there are many bristles on each segment. The sides of the segments are often expanded to form simple paddle-like limbs and it is possible that the arthropods evolved from worms of this kind. Bristleworms are all marine and include both free-swimming and sedentary forms. The latter filter food particles from the water or mud, but the free-swimming species are often predatory.

Bristleworms

RAGWORM
Nereis diversicolor Family Nereidae
10 cm. 90-120 segments. Green to red, but usually yellowish and always with a red line on the back. Lives in burrows in muddy and sandy shores, often in estuaries. Strong jaws may snatch passing animals, but the worm also feeds by straining particles from the mud and water. It can crawl on the mud and also swim weakly.

LUGWORM
Arenicola marina Family Arenicolidae
Up to 35 cm. Green to black, with feathery red gills. Lives in U-shaped burrow in muddy and sandy shores. Sucks in sediment, digests the edible content and voids the rest at surface.

SERPULA VERMICULARIS
Family Serpulidae
5 cm. Secretes a trumpet-shaped limestone tube around itself, attached to stones or shells in shallow water. Filters food particles from water. Closes tube with a stopper.

PEACOCK WORM
Sabella pavonina Family Sabellidae
Up to 25 cm. Lives in a slender tube built of sand grains and filters food. Usually below low-tide level. Tentacles withdrawn if uncovered, leaving tubes sticking up like pencils.

COMMON EARTHWORM
Lumbricus terrestris
Family Lumbricidae
9-30 cm. 110-160 segments. Reddish-brown above, yellowish below. Front end pointed, hind end flattened. The swollen region known as the clitellum or saddle covers segments 32-37 in adult worms. Like all earthworms, the species is hermaphrodite, with both male and female organs in each individual. Feeds by swallowing soil as it tunnels and digesting the organic matter in it. May come to the surface at night. All year, but goes very deep to avoid winter cold.

HORSE LEECH
Haemopis sanguisuga
Family Hirudidae
30 cm when extended, but can contract to an oval blob. Green, brown or black. Swims with beautiful sinuous movements, but actually spends much time hunting worms and other soft-bodied animals in damp soil near the water's edge. The prey is crushed with the leech's blunt teeth and usually swallowed whole. The leech cannot pierce even human skin to suck blood and has nothing to do with horses. It can be found all year in muddy ponds and ditches.

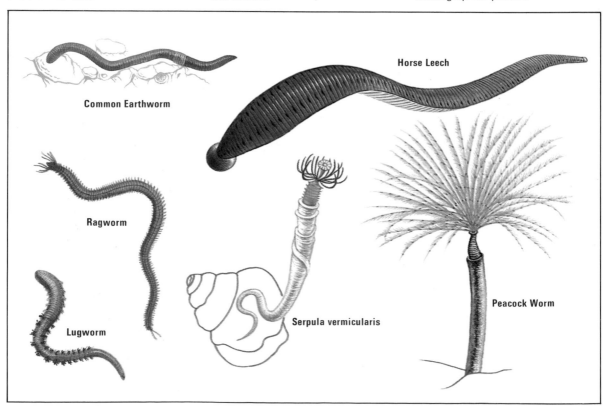

Common Earthworm

Horse Leech

Ragworm

Lugworm

Serpula vermicularis

Peacock Worm

Coelenterates

These animals belong to the Phylum Coelenterata. They have no skeleton, no head, and no real sense organs, although a simple network of nerves runs through the body. There is just one opening, through which food is taken in and waste is passed out. It is usually surrounded by food-catching tentacles. The animals are carnivorous and usually well-endowed with stinging cells which are fired into the prey like tiny harpoons. There are two main types of body – the polyp, which is fixed and roughly cup-shaped, and the free-swimming medusa or jellyfish type. The sea anemones and the corals form the Class Anthozoa, which is entirely marine. Jellyfishes (Class Scyphozoa) are also entirely marine, but the Class Hydrozoa contains several freshwater animals, such as *Hydra*, as well as marine ones.

DAHLIA ANEMONE
Tealia felina
Up to 15 cm long when stretched, but usually about 5 cm. Normally 80 short tentacles clothed with stinging cells. Attached to rocks and common in rock pools quite high on the shore, especially where shaded by seaweeds. When uncovered by the tide, the animal pulls its tentacles right inside the body and contracts to a blob of jelly. One of many colourful species, it often gathers small stones and shells and sticks them to its body.

COMMON JELLYFISH
Aurelia aurita
Up to 40 cm across. Easily recognized by the four circular violet reproductive organs. Often floats in large shoals. It feeds on small planktonic animals, which it catches by means of the stinging cells on the long lips surrounding the mouth. It is often washed up on the shore.

Hydrozoa

PORTUGUESE MAN O' WAR
Physalia physalis Family Physalidae
A colonial animal, consisting of numerous small polyps clustered under a gas-filled blue or pink float. The colony drifts with the wind and current, trailing long tentacles in the water. The tentacles, armed with stinging cells powerful enough to cause severe injury to people, capture small fishes and pull them up to the feeding polyps just under the float for digestion. The food is then shared by the whole colony. Usually seen off-shore in the Atlantic and Mediterranean.

BROWN HYDRA
Hydra oligactis Family Hydridae
Up to 10 mm long when extended, this slim animal lives in ponds and streams, attached to water plants; often hangs down from water lily leaves. The relatively few slender tentacles capture water fleas and other small animals and push them into the mouth, causing prominent bulges in the body until they are digested. Small buds often grow on the body and develop into new individuals which eventually drop off and become independent. Hydra can also reproduce sexually by producing sperm and egg cells in autumn. It then passes the winter in the embryonic stage, surrounded by a tough coat. There are several similar green or brown species.

Comb Jellies

Marine animals once grouped with the coelenterates, but they have no stinging cells and now form the Phylum Ctenophora.

SEA GOOSEBERRY
Pleurobrachia pileus
2-3 cm diameter. Drifts through the water by beating the iridescent cilia which form 8 rows along the body. Small animals are caught with sticky lasso-like threads on the retractile tentacles and then brought up to the mouth. Often washed up on beaches, like soft crystal-clear marbles.

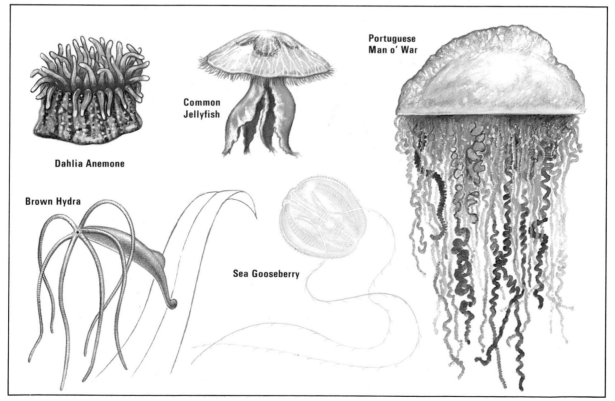

Dahlia Anemone

Common Jellyfish

Portuguese Man o' War

Brown Hydra

Sea Gooseberry

Chapter Six
Wild Flowers

Flowering plants belong to the most advanced group of plants, known as the Angiosperms, and they can be found in every kind of habitat. The flower is the reproductive part of the plant, where the seeds are formed. A typical flower consists of several greenish sepals forming the *calyx* on the outside, a number of colourful petals, several or many pollen-producing stamens, and one or more carpels which eventually form the fruits and carry the seeds.

Flowers

Flowers may be carried singly on their stems, but they are more often grouped into inflorescences. Some of the main types are shown in the diagrams. In a *cyme*, the main growing point ends in a flower and growth continues by one or more side branches: the oldest flower is thus in the centre. In the other types, the axis goes on growing until the inflorescence is complete: the oldest flowers are then at the bottom or the outside. A *corymb* is a type of raceme in which the lower flower stalks are longer than the upper ones, thus bringing all the flowers to about the same level. A *panicle* is a branched raceme.

Seeds do not develop until pollen of the right kind falls on to the stigma on top of the carpels. This is known as pollination and it may be brought about by the wind or by insects. Brightly coloured petals attract insects, but wind-pollinated flowers often have small and dull petals, or even none at all. Either carpels or stamens may be missing, giving rise to male or female flowers respectively.

Fruits

Fruits are of many different kinds. *Capsules* vary in shape and split open in various ways to scatter their seeds. A *follicle* is a slender fruit which splits down one side, while a *pod* splits down both sides. An *achene* is a small dry or leathery fruit with one seed. It does not split open and the germinating seed pushes its way out. A *berry* is a juicy fruit containing many seeds.

Leaves

Leaf shapes are also important in identifying plants, and several are shown in the diagrams. The leaf margin may be quite smooth (entire), but is usually toothed or lobed. *Compound leaves* are split into several distinct leaflets. *Bracts* are small leaves at the bases of flower stalks. *Stipules* are outgrowths from the bases of leaves.

The flowering plants are split into two major divisions – the Dicotyledons (page 212) and the Monocotyledons (page 279). Each group is then split into numerous families, whose names nearly all end in -aceae. Unless otherwise stated, all the plants described in the following pages are *perennials*, living from year to year. *Annuals* complete their lives in one year or less, while *biennials* take two years.

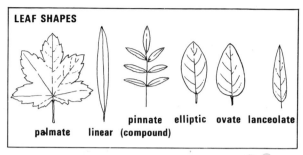

LEAF SHAPES

palmate · linear · pinnate (compound) · elliptic · ovate · lanceolate

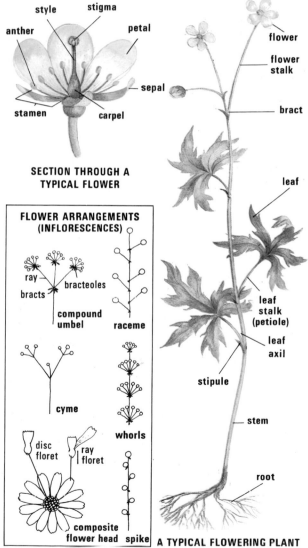

SECTION THROUGH A TYPICAL FLOWER

style · stigma · anther · petal · sepal · stamen · carpel

FLOWER ARRANGEMENTS (INFLORESCENCES)

ray · bracteoles · bracts · compound umbel · raceme · cyme · whorls · disc floret · ray floret · composite flower head · spike

A TYPICAL FLOWERING PLANT

flower · flower stalk · bract · leaf · leaf stalk (petiole) · leaf axil · stipule · stem · root

Left: Oxlip, a close relative of the primrose, grows in old woodlands on heavy soils. In Britain, it is confined to the chalky boulder clays of East Anglia and the East Midlands.

Dicotyledons

BUTTERCUP FAMILY
Ranunculaceae

Most of the 2,000 or so plants in this family are herbaceous species from the north temperate regions. The flowers are regarded as rather primitive, with few specializations. There are many stamens and usually many carpels. The sepals, normally 5 in number, are often petal-like and true petals are then absent. When present, there are five separate petals.

WOOD ANEMONE
Anemone nemorosa

A rather delicate, hairless plant of broad-leaved woodland, hedgebank and upland meadow, it grows 6-30 cm high. Like many woodland plants the Wood Anemone makes use of the sunlight of early spring for flowering before the trees come into leaf.

Flower: white or pink-tinged, 2-4 cm across, no petals but 6-7 petal-like sepals; stamens many.
Flower arrangement: solitary, terminal.
Flowering time: March-May.
Leaf: 1 or 2 long-stalked basal leaves of 3 segments, each segment deeply dissected, coarsely toothed, shortly stalked; upper leaves in whorl of 3, smaller with flattened stalks.
Fruit: many downy achenes.

MARSH MARIGOLD
Caltha palustris

Although this stout plant has flowers that look like large buttercups, its broad, shining, heart-shaped leaves and hollow flower stalks betray its true identity. It grows in marshy ground, often near streams, and may either be erect, to a height of 15-30 cm, or creeping.

Flower: bright golden yellow, 1·5-5 cm across; petal-like sepals, 5 or more; stamens many.
Flower arrangement: few-flowered cyme.
Flowering time: March-July.
Leaf: broadly heart-shaped, teeth blunt or pointed; basal leaves long-stalked, upper often kidney-shaped, stalkless.
Fruit: head of 5-15 follicles, erect or curved back.

MEADOW BUTTERCUP
Ranunculus acris

Commonly found in meadows and pasture, this buttercup grows up to 100 cm high. The stem is much branched and erect above.

Flower: glossy, bright yellow, 1·5-2·5 cm across; petals 5; sepals lying against petals; stamens many; flower stalk not furrowed.
Flower arrangement: irregular cyme.
Flowering time: April-October.
Leaf: more or less hairy; lower leaf with long stalk, palmate with 2-7 deeply toothed segments, middle segment not stalked; uppermost leaves stalkless, deeply cut.
Fruit: achenes many, hairless, each with short hook, in a round head.

BULBOUS BUTTERCUP
Ranunculus bulbosus

This plant, named for the bulb-like tuber at the base, resembles the last species but grows in drier grassland. The middle leaf-lobe has a long stalk, and the flower-stalk is furrowed. The stem is less branched, but when in flower the plant is best distinguished by the reflexed sepals. It grows to about 50 cm, flowering April-July.
The very similar Creeping Buttercup (*R. repens*), a common garden weed, has a creeping, rooting stem. Its middle leaf-lobe is stalked and the flower stalk is furrowed.

Bulbous Buttercup

Meadow
Buttercup

Marsh
Marigold

Wood
Anemone

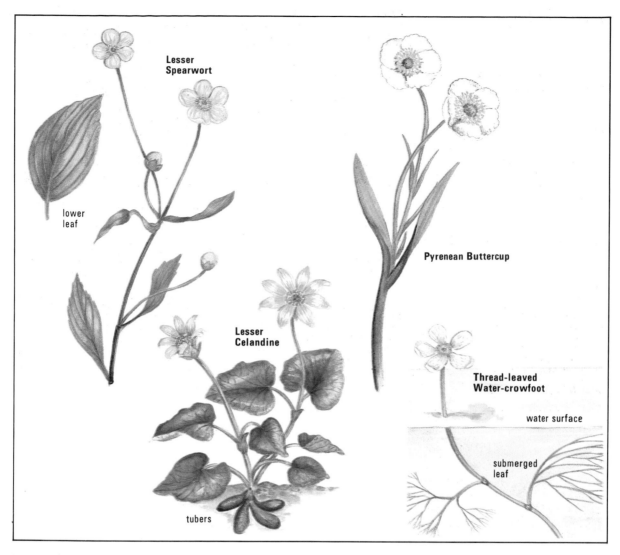

Lesser Spearwort

lower leaf

Pyrenean Buttercup

Lesser Celandine

Thread-leaved Water-crowfoot

water surface

submerged leaf

tubers

LESSER CELANDINE
Ranunculus ficaria
One of the early spring flowers, Lesser Celandine has more petals than a buttercup and glossy, heart-shaped leaves. It grows 5-30 cm high on hedgebanks, in woods and stream-sides. The roots form tubers.
Flower: bright golden yellow, whitening with age at petal-base, opening only on fine days, 1·5-5 cm across; petals 8-12, more or less pointed; sepals 3; stamens many.
Flower arrangement: solitary.
Flowering time: March-May.
Leaf: broadly heart-shaped, dark green, hairless; basal leaves long-stalked, in a rosette.
Fruit: achenes, many, downy.

LESSER SPEARWORT
Ranunculus flammula
This is a Buttercup of wet places easily distinguished by its undissected leaves and pale, rather than golden, yellow flowers. Erect or creeping, with a hollow stem, and usually hairless, it grows between 8 and 80

cm high. Irritant poisons are present in larger amounts than in other butter-cups.
Flower: pale yellow, glossy, 8-20 mm across, petals 5; sepals 5; stamens many; flower stalk grooved.
Flower arrangement: solitary or in a cyme.
Flowering time: May-September.
Leaf: lower leaves ovate, stalked; upper leaves stalkless, smaller, pointed, parallel-veined, with or without teeth.
Fruit: achenes, hairless, in a round head.

THREAD-LEAVED WATER-CROWFOOT
Ranunculus trichophyllus
This Water-crowfoot has small, white flowers and grows in ponds, slow streams and ditches. There are no floating leaves, and the needle-like segments of the submerged leaves do not lie flat. Several other species of Water-crowfoot grow in N. Europe, some of which have floating leaves in

addition to submerged.
Flower: white, petal-base yellow, 8-10 mm across; petals 5, not touching at edges; stamens 5-15.
Flower arrangement: solitary, opening above surface of water.
Flowering time: May-June.
Leaf: all submerged, finely dissected, bristle-like, not lying in one plane, 2-4 cm, shortly stalked.
Fruit: hairy achenes; stalk usually less than 4 cm.

PYRENEAN BUTTERCUP
Ranunculus pyrenaeus
A low-growing mountain species of damp limestone pastures in the Alps as well as in the Pyrenees, it occurs at altitudes from 1,700 to 2,800 m.
Flower: white, 10-20 mm across with 5 rounded petals and whitish sepals: many yellow stamens.
Flower arrangement: solitary or in twos and threes. May-July.
Leaf: bluish-green, hairless: strap-shaped, untoothed and unstalked (sometimes broader in Alps).
Fruit: a cluster of achenes.

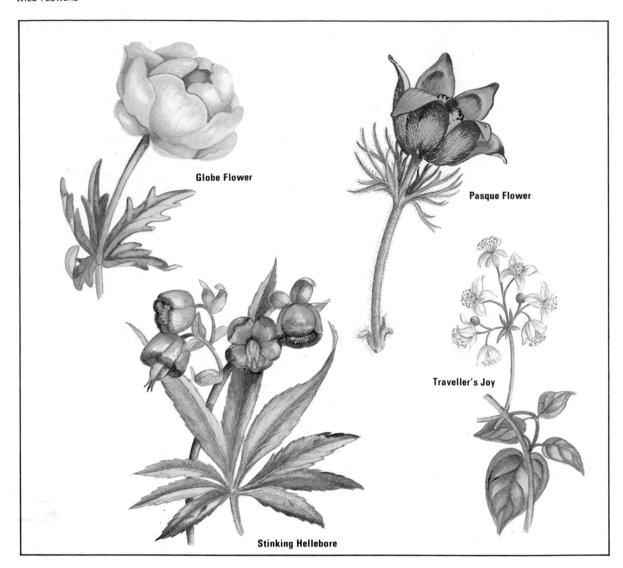

Globe Flower

Pasque Flower

Traveller's Joy

Stinking Hellebore

GLOBE FLOWER
Trollius europaeus
Named for the almost spherical shape of the flower, this plant grows in damp woods and meadows, mainly in upland regions but also lower down in the north. It reaches 60 cm.
Flower: golden yellow, 2·5-5 cm across: 5-15 petal-like sepals forming the globe and enclosing the strap-shaped nectar-secreting petals and numerous stamens and carpels.
Flower arrangement: usually solitary: May-August.
Leaf: shiny, deep green above and paler below: lower ones stalked and deeply 3-5 lobed, upper ones stalkless and 3-lobed.
Fruit: a cluster of beaked follicles.

STINKING HELLEBORE
Helleborus foetidus
This much-branched evergreen plant, named for its unpleasant smell, is widely distributed in the southern half of Europe, where it grows in open woods and scrub on limestone slopes. It reaches 80 cm.

Flower: shaped like an inverted cup, up to 3 cm across. Petals absent: 5 yellowish-green sepals, edged with purple: many stamens and usually 3 carpels.
Flower arrangement: a drooping cyme. January-April.
Leaf: all on stems (none radical): lower ones dark bluish-green, palmately divided with up to 11 narrow leaflets: upper ones paler and undivided.
Fruit: a cluster of beaked follicles surrounded by opened sepals.

PASQUE FLOWER
Pulsatilla vulgaris
This hairy plant, with feathery leaves, grows in chalk and limestone grassland, usually on south-facing slopes: widely distributed in northern and central Europe, but generally uncommon. It reaches 30 cm.
Flower: 6 sepals, deep purple above, paler and silky below: 5-8 cm across. Numerous stamens and carpels. Upright at first and then nodding. A whorl

of hairy bracts below flower.
Flower arrangement: Solitary. April-June.
Leaf: all from base: finely divided and coated with grey hairs.
Fruit: a cluster of achenes, each with a feathery plume.

TRAVELLER'S JOY
Clematis vitalba
Also known as Old Man's Beard, this climber — one of the few woody plants in the family — can reach 30 m, scrambling over shrubs and trees and clinging to them with its twining leaf stalks. Found from the Netherlands southwards, but only on chalk and limestone in northern parts of its range.
Flower: 2 cm across, with 4 greenish-white sepals and no petals: fragrant.
Flower arrangement: dense panicles. June-August.
Leaf: pale green: compound, with 3-5 well separated heart-shaped or oval leaflets, each up to 10 cm long.
Fruit: clusters of hairy achenes, each with a long plume — the 'beard'.

POPPY FAMILY
Papaveraceae

The flowers of this family have 2 sepals, which fall as the flowers open, and 4 petals – often very crinkly in the poppies themselves. The plants all contain a white or yellowish latex. Several kinds of poppy are weeds of cultivation, although less common today owing to the use of herbicides. The weed species are mostly annuals, with long-lived seeds that can germinate after being buried for many years.

GREATER CELANDINE
Chelidonium majus
There seems little resemblance between this plant, with its small, yellow flowers, and its flamboyant relatives, the Poppies. Despite the common name, it is not related to Lesser Celandine. It has surprising bright-orange sap and grows 30-90 cm high on hedgebanks and walls, usually near buildings.
Flower: bright yellow, 2-2·5 cm across; petals 4; stamens many.
Flower arrangement: umbel of 2-6 flowers.
Flowering time: May-August.
Leaf: pinnate, leaflets 5-7, glaucous, blunt-toothed.
Fruit: a capsule 3-5 cm, straight, opening from below by 2 valves.

LONG-HEADED POPPY
Papaver dubium
The flowers are smaller and more orange than those of the Common Poppy. The stem is stiffly hairy. The plant grows 20-60 cm high, in waste places and as a weed of cultivation.
Flower: orange-pink, sometimes with a dark spot at petal-base; 3-7 cm across; petals circular, overlapping at base; stamens many, purple; stigma disc flat with 7-9 radiating ridges.
Flower arrangement: solitary.
Flowering time: June-July.
Leaf: greyish green, shortly hairy; basal leaves deeply lobed, end lobe not enlarged.
Fruit: long, narrow capsule, 1·5-2 × 0·5-0·75 cm, tapered at base, hairless, often ribbed. Opening by pores under the cap.

COMMON POPPY
Papaver rhoeas
The Common Poppy, with its large, scarlet flowers and covering of stiff hairs, grows 25-90 cm high. If cut, it exudes milky-white latex. Like the previous species, it is an annual and a very common plant of roadsides and field margins.
Flower: scarlet, often with dark blotch at petal-base; 7-10 cm across; petals thin; stamens many; stigma disc more or less flat with 8-12 radiating ridges.
Flower arrangement: solitary.
Flowering time: June-August.
Leaf: stiffly hairy, 1- to 2-pinnate; segments coarsely toothed.
Fruit: capsule, rounded at base, top flat, length 1-2 cm, hairless, opening by pores under top.
Uses: Poppies were thought to cause headaches and thunderstorms, but were also used to treat headaches. Although slightly poisonous, the red poppy does not contain the opium of the Opium Poppy (*P. somniferum*).

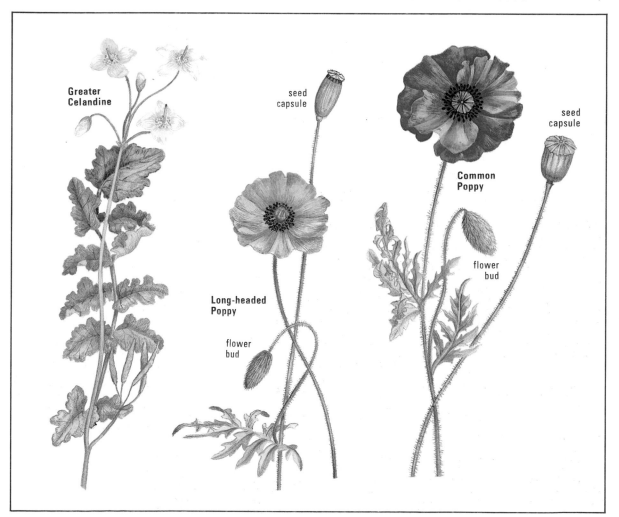

Greater Celandine

seed capsule

Long-headed Poppy

flower bud

Common Poppy

seed capsule

flower bud

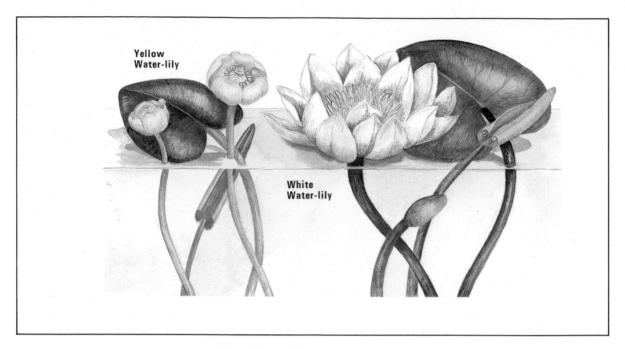

Yellow Water-lily

White Water-lily

WATER-LILY FAMILY
Nymphaeaceae

Water-lilies grow in still or slow-moving fresh water, with their roots and stout rhizomes in the mud. Leaves and flowers grow up on long stalks, most leaves floating on the surface and often covering large areas. The flowers may float or stand clear of the water. Like the buttercups, the water-lilies have flowers with many stamens and no specialized pollination mechanisms.

YELLOW WATER-LILY
Nuphar lutea

Growing in freshwater lakes, ponds and slow streams, the Yellow Water-lily is more widely distributed than the White. The floating leaves are oval compared with the almost circular White Water-lily leaves.
Flower: bright yellow, cup-shaped, smelling of alcohol, 4-6 cm across, rising clear of the water; sepals 4-6, large, petal-like, rounded; stamens many; 15-20 radiating stigmas on top of flask-shaped ovary.
Flower arrangement: solitary.
Flowering time: June-August.
Leaf: floating, oval, 12-40 × 9-30 cm, entire with a deep cleft where stalk joins; submerged leaves thin, lettuce-like.
Fruit: bottle-shaped, ripening above water.
Uses: Water-lilies, not surprisingly, were held to have cooling properties. Gerard's *Herbal* of 1597 states, 'the root of the Yellow cureth hot diseases of the kidnies and bladder.'

WHITE WATER-LILY
Nymphaea alba

The White Water-lily grows in standing or slow-flowing water up to a depth of 3 m. It is more tolerant of polluted water than many other water plants. The large, floating flowers are scented.
Flower: white, 10-20 cm across, floating; 20-25 pointed petals; sepals 4; stamens many; 15-20 radiating stigmas.
Flower arrangement: solitary, on long stalks.
Flowering time: June-September.
Leaf: floating, more or less circular, 10-30 cm, entire with deep cleft where stalk joins, veins joined around edge of leaf.
Fruit: flask-shaped, sometimes spherical, ripening underwater; seeds float, aiding dispersal.
Uses: the rhizomes were sometimes eaten in parts of N. Europe, and Elizabethans ate seed and root to promote chastity.

FUMITORY FAMILY
Fumariaceae

Fumitories are sprawling weeds of cultivated or disturbed ground. The leaves are finely cut, reminiscent of Maidenhair Fern. They are hairless, often greyish-green and waxy. The small flowers are tubular and 2-lipped.

COMMON FUMITORY
Fumaria officinalis

Common Fumitory is a slender, glaucous, long-stemmed annual, climbing or almost erect. It is a weed of arable land and prefers light soils.

Common Fumitory

Flower: purplish pink, tips blackish red; tube-like corolla 7-9 mm long, spurred behind, 2-lipped and consisting of 2 outer petals and 2 narrow inner ones; 2 very small sepals.
Flower arrangement: raceme, usually of more than 20 flowers, longer than its stalk.
Flowering time: May-October.
Leaf: all arising from stem, finely divided into flat segments.
Fruit: more or less spherical, 2-3 mm.

CABBAGE FAMILY
Cruciferae

The members of this large family, with some 3,500 species, typically have 4-petalled flowers resembling a cross – hence the Latin name – and 6 stamens. The flowers are very often yellow or white and carried in racemes, tightly packed at first but elongating after the first flowers open. The fruits are commonly long and narrow. The family contains many important vegetables, such as turnips and cabbages, as well as many weeds.

GARLIC MUSTARD
Alliaria petiolata
A rather tall, upright biennial, un-branched, up to 120 cm, Garlic Mustard smells faintly of garlic when crushed. The plant can be seen along hedgerows, walls and wood margins.

Flower: white, 6 mm across.
Flowering time: April-June.
Leaf: pale, rather bright green, heart-shaped, toothed; shape reminiscent of nettle leaf.
Fruit: long, very narrow capsule, 2-7 cm long, opening by 2 valves from below.

SHEPHERD'S PURSE
Capsella bursa-pastoris
Hardly a walk can be taken, whether in town or country, without seeing Shepherd's Purse, an annual 3-40 cm high, of wayside, cultivated land and waste places. Distributed through-out the world, having followed man as a weed of agriculture.

Flower: white, about 2.5 mm across. crowded at the top of a raceme, becoming less dense in fruit.
Flowering time: all the year.
Leaf: basal leaves in rosette, deeply lobed or not; base of upper leaves clasping stem.
Fruit: heart-shaped, 6-9 mm across, the 2 valves breaking apart to dis-perse pale brown seeds – the 'money' in the 'purse'.

CUCKOO FLOWER
Cardamine pratensis
A very pretty plant of damp places and stream sides, the Cuckoo Flower or Lady's Smock, reaches 60 cm.

Flower: lilac, pink or white, 12-18 mm across; petals may be notched.
Flowering time: April-June.
Leaf: pinnate, up to 7 oval or circular leaflets; end leaflet enlarged; basal leaves in rosette.
Fruit: 2.5-4 cm, thin, on long stalks opening from below by 2 valves.

COMMON SCURVY GRASS
Cochlearis officinalis
A common coastal plant the scurvy grass got its name because sailors used to eat it as a source of vitamin C to combat scurvy. With rather lax and often sprawling reddish stems, it reaches 50 cm.

Flower: white, rarely pale lilac, about 1 cm across. Fragrant. May-August.
Leaf: deep shiny green, hairless and rather fleshy: basal leaves in a rosette, more or less heart-shaped on long stalks. Stem leaves oblong or almost triangular, mostly clasping stem.
Fruit: globular, 3-7 mm across.

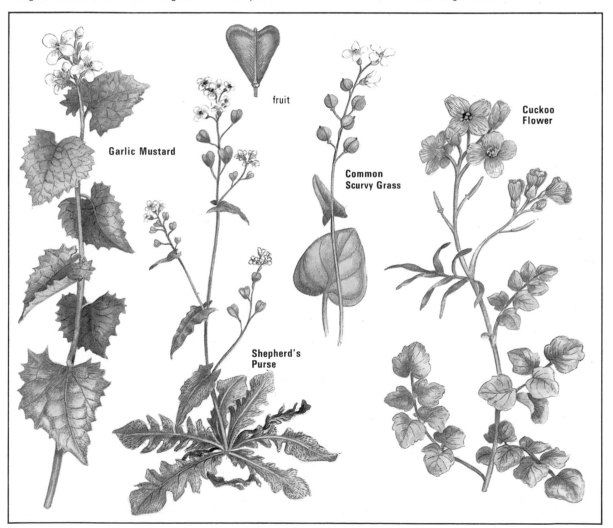

Garlic Mustard

fruit

Shepherd's Purse

Common Scurvy Grass

Cuckoo Flower

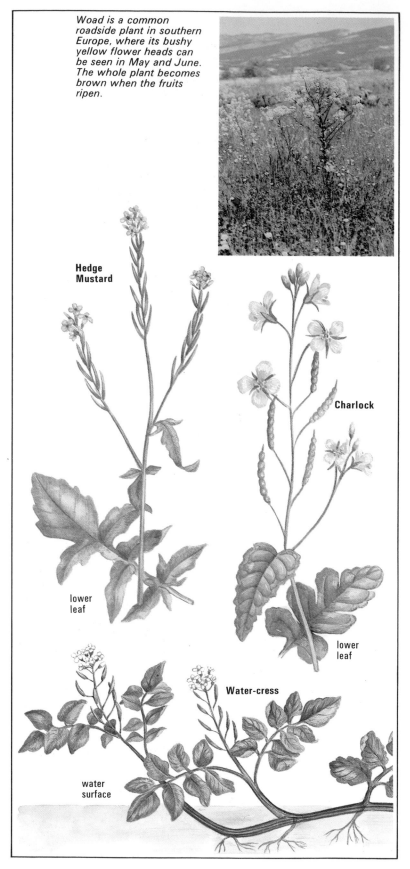

Woad is a common roadside plant in southern Europe, where its bushy yellow flower heads can be seen in May and June. The whole plant becomes brown when the fruits ripen.

Hedge Mustard

Charlock

lower leaf

lower leaf

Water-cress

water surface

WOAD
Isatis tinctoria
Famed as the source of the blue dye used by the ancient Britons, the woad is a native of southern and central Europe, where it grows abundantly on waste ground and roadsides. A much-branched biennial, it reaches 1·5 m.
Flower: yellow, up to 4 mm across, in large branched racemes (panicles). June-August.
Leaf: bright green in basal rosette, slightly hairy, with wavy edges; lanceolate, to 15 cm long. Upper leaves arrow-shaped, grey-green and hairless; clasping stem.
Fruit: dark brown and winged, with one seed like a small ash key: hanging in dense clusters.

HEDGE MUSTARD
Sisymbrium officinale
Hedge Mustard, familiar if not pleasing to the eye, grows in waste places in town and country to a height of 90 cm. An annual, it is stiffly erect and branched above, like candelabra.
Flower: pale yellow, small.
Flower arrangement: in dense racemes.
Flowering time: June-July.
Leaf: lower leaves in a rosette, deeply lobed; end lobe larger than rest.
Fruit: very thin, cylindrical, 10-20 mm, straight, pressed to the stem, which elongates in fruit.

CHARLOCK
Sinapis arvensis
Charlock grows up to 80 cm and often has stiff hairs on the base of the stem. It is a serious weed of arable land. An annual.
Flower: bright yellow, 1·5-2 cm; petals narrowed at base.
Flower arrangement: dense raceme, spreading as fruit ripens.
Flowering time: May-July.
Leaf: up to 20 cm, alternate, roughly hairy; lower leaf stalked, deeply lobed; end lobe large, coarsely toothed; upper leaves stalkless, without lobes.
Fruit: 2·5-4·5 cm long, narrow, abruptly narrowed at tip, indented between seeds, smooth or stiffly hairy.

WATER-CRESS
Rorippa nasturtium-aquaticum
Water-cress grows in masses in wet places where there is fresh, moving water. It is 10-60 cm high, hairless, creeping, often rooting: ascending at the tip.
Flower: white, 4-6 mm across, petals about twice as long as sepals.
Flower arrangement: clustered at the top of a raceme.
Flowering time: May-October.
Leaf: pinnate, lower leaves with 1-3 circular or broadly ovate leaflets; upper leaf with 5-9.
Fruit: 13-18 mm, curving slightly upward.
Uses: commercial cultivation as a salad crop started at the beginning of the 19th century.

VIOLET FAMILY
Violaceae

The flowers in this family are markedly irregular, with 5 petals of which the lowest has a long spur at the back. The sepals have small flaps. After producing normal flowers in spring, violets often produce flowers which do not open and which fertilize themselves. The fruits are rounded capsules which split open into three parts.

SWEET VIOLET
Viola odorata
Although cultivated in gardens and often escaping, the scented Sweet Violet is also a native of Europe. It grows in hedgebanks, scrub and woods, and is 5-15 cm high.
Flower: deep violet or white with lilac spur, about 1·5 cm, scented; petals 5, unequal, lower petal forming spur behind; spur longer than sepal appendages; sepals rounded at tip.
Flower arrangement: solitary, on long stalks.
Flowering time: February-April.
Leaf: heart-shaped, rounded or pointed at tip, blunt-toothed, sparsely hairy, long-stalked.

COMMON DOG-VIOLET
Viola riviniana
This violet can be very variable in size. It lacks creeping stems and grows in woods, on hedgebanks or in grassland.
Flower: usually blue-violet though varying; spur paler; lower petal with many long, dark veins; unscented, 1-2·5 cm; spur 2-5 mm, stout, often curved up, notched at tip; sepals with appendages about 2-3 mm.
Flower arrangement: solitary.
Flowering time: April-June.
Leaf: in loose rosette; stalked, heart-shaped, blunt-toothed, up to 8 cm; stipules toothed.

WILD PANSY
Viola tricolor
This ancestor of the garden pansy grows on cultivated and waste ground and in short grassland. It is normally 15-45 cm high, but a dwarf form 3-15 cm high grows on dunes and grassland by the sea. Grassland plants are normally perennial, but those growing on disturbed land are annuals.
Flower: blue-violet or yellow, or a mixture of the two: scentless; 1-3 cm vertically. Petals usually longer than sepals, the latter being pointed and rather shorter than spur.
Flower arrangement: solitary, several arising from each stem.
Flowering time: April-September.
Leaf: alternate; lower leaf ovate or heart-shaped, blunt-toothed; upper leaf narrower; stipules leaf-like deeply lobed.

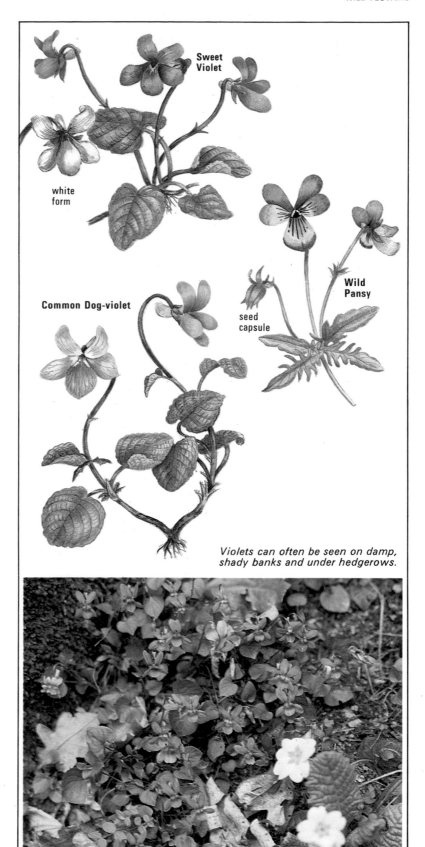

Violets can often be seen on damp, shady banks and under hedgerows.

MILKWORT FAMILY
Polygalaceae

This world-wide family includes shrubs and small trees but all the North European members are small plants growing in short grassland. The 3 true petals of the flowers are enclosed within the 5 petal-like sepals.

COMMON MILKWORT
Polygala vulgaris
This is a rather low, much branched plant, 10-30 cm high, to be found in short grassland, heaths and dunes. The tiny flowers are almost enclosed by 2 enlarged, coloured sepals.
Flower: blue, pink or white, 6-8 mm; sepals 5, the two inner enlarged, coloured, petal-like.
Flower arrangement: a raceme.
Flowering time: May-September.
Leaf: alternate, narrow, entire, more or less pointed; lower leaves 5-10 mm, upper leaves longer.
Fruit: flat, heart-shaped capsule.
Uses: herbalists formerly prescribed this little plant for nursing mothers, to increase the flow of milk.

ST JOHN'S WORT FAMILY
Hypericaceae

A family of approximately 1,000 species. Glands, appearing as black or translucent dots on the plants, are characteristic of this family. There are 5 petals, and the many stamens are joined at their bases into bundles.

PERFORATE ST JOHN'S WORT
Hypericum perforatum
There are tiny translucent dots (seen if the plant is held to the light) and black dots to look for on this plant. Running down the stem are 2 raised lines. The plant is hairless, erect and 10-100 cm high, growing in grassland and scrub.
Flower: yellow, about 2 cm across; petals 5, tiny black dots around margins; sepals 5, pointed, with or without black dots; stamens many.
Flower arrangement: branched cyme.
Flowering time: June-September.
Leaf: alternate, with many translucent dots; 1-3 cm, elliptic to linear.

ROCKROSE FAMILY
Cistaceae

This family of about 250 herbs and small shrubs is centred on the Mediterranean region, where the plants thrive on dry, sunny

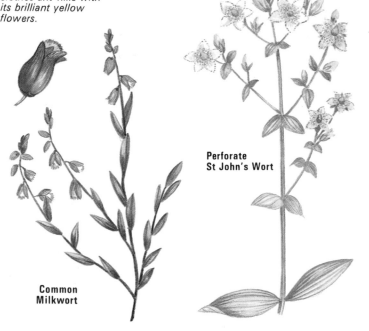

The common rockrose grows on chalk and limestone and often clothes ant-hills with its brilliant yellow flowers.

Perforate St John's Wort

Common Milkwort

slopes. There are generally 5 petals, numerous stamens, and 5 strongly-veined sepals of which three are much larger than the other two. Individual flowers are short-lived, with the petals falling after just one day.

COMMON ROCKROSE
Helianthemum chamaecistus
This creeping, mat-forming plant has a sturdy woody base from which spring many slender branches — soft at first but becoming wiry. It reaches 30 cm and is best described as an under-shrub. It grows on grassy and rocky slopes, especially on limestone, in many parts of Europe.
Flower: bright yellow, 2·5 cm across; petals creased at first. Up to 12 flowers in a loose cyme with downy stalks. May-September.
Leaf: oval, to 2 cm long: deep green above, pale and furry below.
Fruit: an egg-shaped capsule splitting into three lobes.

STITCHWORT FAMILY
Caryophyllaceae

This large family includes Carnations, Pinks and many other garden plants, as well as widespread weeds such as the Chickweeds. The flowers have 4 or 5 petals, which are notched, except in the Sandworts and Spurreys. Stamens are normally twice as numerous as petals. Some flowers open or emit scent only at night to attract moths for pollination.

CORN SPURREY
Spergula arvensis
Corn Spurrey is a pale green annual, 5-70 cm high, slightly to very sticky, with weak, branched stems and whorls of leaves. It is a weed of cultivated land, preferring sandy soils.

Flower: white, 4-7 mm across; petals 5, rounded, slightly longer than sepals.
Flowering time: June-August.
Leaf: 1-3 cm long, needle-shaped, in whorls, slightly fleshy, channelled beneath, sticky.
Fruit: capsule, 5 mm, opening by 5 teeth; seeds blackish, warty.
Uses: various forms of this weed are grown in Germany and the Netherlands as a nutritious fodder crop for sheep and cows. When cultivated it may grow 90 cm high.

SAND SPURREY
Spergularia rubra
Sand Spurrey, with its tiny, pink flowers, is a straggling plant, 5-25 cm high, found on sandy soils in open ground. The upper parts of the plant have slightly sticky hairs. An annual.

Flower: pink, paler at base of petals, 3-5 mm, petals 5; sepals longer than petals.
Flower arrangement: few-flowered cyme.

Flowering time: May-September.
Leaf: in clusters along stem, very narrow, tapering to stiff, sharp point, not fleshy; stipules silvery, conspicuous.
Fruit: capsule, 4-5 mm, opening by 3 teeth; seeds tiny, dark brown.

SEA SANDWORT
Honkenya peploides
The Sea Sandwort is a small, fleshy plant, 5-25 cm high, partly creeping on sand and shingle by the sea. It can withstand brief immersion in salt water.

Flower: greenish white, 6-10 mm; petals 5, rounded, as long as or shorter than the sepals.
Flower arrangement: solitary, in leaf axils and forks of branches.
Flowering time: May-August.
Leaf: opposite, ovate, fleshy, stalkless. Bright green.
Fruit: capsule, spherical, opening by 3 teeth; seeds large, pear-shaped, reddish-brown.

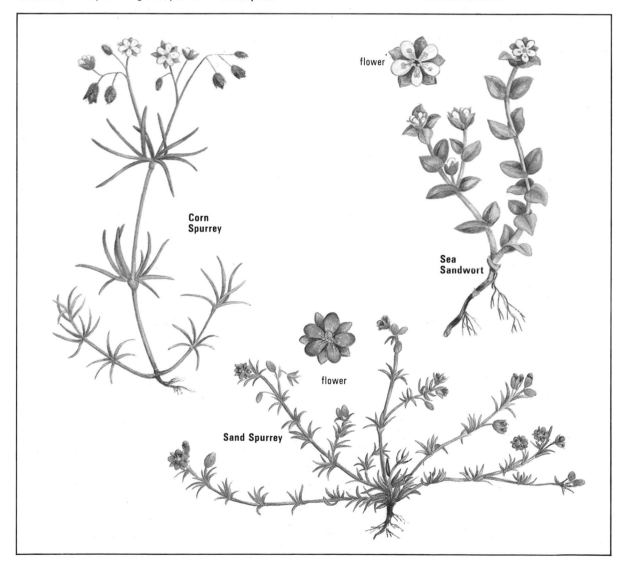

Corn Spurrey

Sea Sandwort

flower

Sand Spurrey

flower

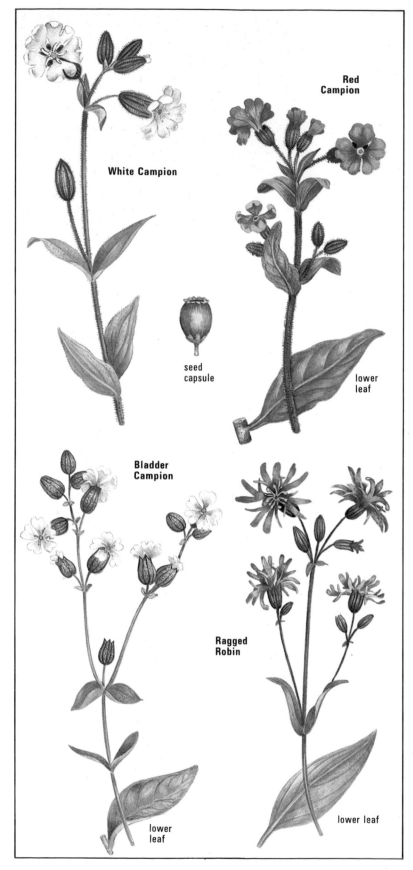

White Campion

Red Campion

seed capsule

lower leaf

Bladder Campion

Ragged Robin

lower leaf

lower leaf

WHITE CAMPION
Silene alba
The White Campion is a branched, softly hairy weed of cultivated land and grows to 80 cm. As with the Red Campion, the flowers are unisexual. They open in the evening when they are slightly scented to attract moths as pollinators.
Flower: white, 2·5-3 cm across; petals 5, deeply cleft, narrowed at base; calyx-tube hairy, sticky.
Flower arrangement: cyme.
Flowering time: May-September.
Leaf: opposite, ovate, stalked; stem leaves stalkless.
Fruit: capsule 1-1·5 cm, ovoid, opening by 10 teeth.

RED CAMPION
Silene dioica
The Red Campion grows in woods and hedgerows. The whole plant is softly hairy and grows up to 80 cm high. There are separate male and female flowers. Red Campion interbreeds readily with White Campion, the offspring having pale pink flowers.
Flower: bright rose, 18-25 mm across; petals 5, deeply cleft, narrowed at base; calyx-tube hairy, slightly sticky.
Flower arrangement: cyme.
Flowering time: May-June.
Leaf: opposite, broadly ovate; the basal leaf blade continuous as thin border down each side of stalk; upper leaves stalkless.
Fruit: capsule 1-1·5 cm, spherical or ovoid, opening by 10 teeth which curve back.
Uses: Campions were associated with snakes, the pounded seed being used to treat snake bite.

BLADDER CAMPION
Silene vulgaris
This erect, often grey-green, branching plant is usually without hairs and grows up to 90 cm high. The 'bladder' is the inflated calyx-tube. It is found in grassland and arable land, and along roadsides.
Flower: white, about 1·5 cm across; petals 5, deeply cleft, narrowed at base; calyx-tube inflated, net-veined; bracts papery.
Flower arrangement: loose cyme.
Flowering time: June-August.
Leaf: often greyish-green, opposite, ovate; lower leaves short-stalked, upper stalkless.
Fruit: capsule, with 6 erect teeth, enclosed by persistent calyx.
The Sea Campion (*S. maritima*), growing on cliffs and shingle, is similar but shorter. Its greyish leaves form dense mats. Petals are broader.

RAGGED ROBIN
Lychnis flos-cuculi
The rose-red, finely dissected flower petals of the Ragged Robin are striking. The stem and leaves are slightly rough to the touch. The height of the branched stem is 20-90 cm. The plant is a lover of damp places.

Flower: rose-red, 3-4 cm across; petals deeply cut into thin segments; calyx-tube 5-toothed; stamens 10.
Flower arrangement: cyme.
Flowering time: May-June.
Leaf: opposite; basal leaves ovate, stalked, slightly rough to touch; upper leaves stalkless.
Fruit: capsule 6-10 mm, opening by 5 teeth.

COMMON MOUSE-EAR
Cerastium holosteoides
The flowering stems of this very common little plant reach 45 cm. It is found in grassland and waste places almost everywhere, growing in loose, straggling tufts. The leaves and stem are hairy.
Flower: white; petals 5, deeply notched, equalling sepals; sepals with narrow, papery margins and showing between petals of open flower; stamens 10 or 5.
Flower arrangement: loose clusters.
Flowering time: April-September.
Leaf: 10-25 × 3-15 mm, stalkless, tip pointed or rounded.
Fruit: capsule, curved; seeds warty.

GREATER STITCHWORT
Stellaria holostea
The slender, flowering stems are 15-60 cm high and 4-angled, the angles being slightly rough to the touch. The plant is slightly greyish-green and grows in hedgerows and woods.
Flower: white, 2-3 cm, long-stalked; petals 5, notched to about half their length; sepals with narrow, papery margins; stamens 10.
Flower arrangement: loose forking cymes.
Flowering time: April-June.
Leaf: rather greyish-green, opposite, 4-8 cm long, lanceolate, tapering to sharp point, stalkless.
Fruit: capsule, spherical; seeds reddish-brown, warty.
Uses: seed of Stitchwort was powdered, added to wine and used against pains or 'stitches' in the side.

COMMON CHICKWEED
Stellaria media
The straggling stems of this world-wide annual weed are 5-40 cm long. The tiny flowers are inconspicuous and there is a single line of hairs running down the stem.
Flower: white, 8-10 mm; petals very deeply cleft; sepals same length as petals with narrow, papery margins, showing between petals of open flower.
Flower arrangement: loose clusters.
Flowering time: all year.
Leaf: opposite, ovate; lower leaves stalked, upper stalkless.
Fruit: capsule, stalk curved down.
Uses: young plants can be eaten in salads and sandwiches. Small birds love the seed.

The conspicuous white flowers of a member of the stitchwort family.

Greater Stitchwort

Common Mouse-ear

Common Chickweed

ROCK SOAPWORT
Saponaria ocymoides
This sprawling, hairy plant grows in the Alps and Pyrenees, where it clothes many rocky and stony slopes with beautiful pink cushions or carpets throughout the summer. It can be found at altitudes up to 2,400 m.
Flower: deep pink to purple 6-10 mm across. Calyx tube long and reddish-brown and clothed with glandular hairs. In dense clusters. March-October.
Leaf: greyish green and hairy; oval or spoon-shaped up to 1 cm long.

MESEMBRYANTHEMUM FAMILY Ficoidaceae

The 1,200 or so members of this family come from the warmer parts of the world, especially from South Africa. They are herbs and undershrubs and all are adapted for life in dry places. Many have fleshy leaves. The flowers often look like large daisies, but they are not related: each is a single flower with many petals, and not a composite head (see page 270). One of the best known members of the family is the Mesembryanthemum itself, whose brilliant flowers make it a favourite garden plant.

HOTTENTOT FIG
Carpobrotus edulis
Introduced from South Africa, this striking plant has become naturalized on many parts of the European coast-line. It is a sprawling plant, 25-30 cm high, forming dense carpets on cliffs and shingle banks.
Flower: deep pink (magenta) or yellow, up to 5 cm across, with many strap-shaped petals and many stamens; calyx tube with 5 leafy lobes. Borne singly on swollen stalks. April-July.
Leaf: bright green, fleshy and sausage-shaped; to 10 cm long and triangular in cross-section.
Fruit: a fleshy capsule: edible: Several closely related species have now been introduced to various parts of the European coastline.

Above left: Rock soapwort growing high in the Alps. The plant flourishes on stony ground and on roadside walls.

Left: Hottentot fig grows on many European coasts, on sand dunes and shingle as well as on cliffs.

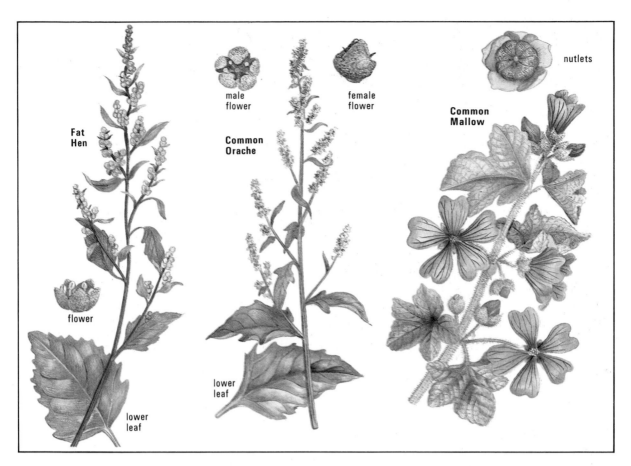

Fat Hen

flower

lower leaf

male flower

female flower

Common Orache

lower leaf

nutlets

Common Mallow

GOOSEFOOT FAMILY
Chenopodiaceae

This family contains some 1,500 species, including such economically important plants as beetroot and spinach. The flowers are inconspicuous, clustered into slender spikes and wind-pollinated. The leaves of many species have a pale mealy coating composed of minute bladder-like hairs. Many are salt-loving species, growing in both moist coastal habitats and desert regions. Common saltmarsh and seashore species include Glasswort, Sea Beet, and Sea Purslane. There are also many common agricultural weeds in the family, most of them annuals.

FAT HEN
Chenopodium album
Growing 10-150 cm high, Fat Hen often has a red tinge to the grooved stem. The plant is deep green with a mealy covering and grows on cultivated and waste land. It is very variable and there are several other similar species. An annual.

Flower: green, inconspicuous, bisexual.
Flower arrangement: spikes, arising from leaf-axils.
Flowering time: July-October.
Leaf: alternate, mealy, diamond-shaped to narrowly ovate, stalked, toothed, sometimes nearly 3-lobed or entire.
Fruit: black achene.

COMMON ORACHE
Atriplex patula
The plant is branched, up to 150 cm high and slightly mealy. The stems are ridged and striped white and green or red and green. This is a weed of waste places and cultivated ground. Although similar to Fat Hen, Common Orache can be distinguished by its separate male and female flowers. An annual.
Flower: green, inconspicuous, unisexual, males with 5 green 'petals' and 5 stamens, females with 2 stigmas and enclosed by 2 diamond-shaped bracts.
Flower arrangement: spikes arising from leaf-axils.
Flowering time: July-September.
Leaf: alternate, diamond-shaped, base tapering into leaf-stalk, toothed or entire; upper leaves narrow, entire, stalkless.
Fruit: black, enclosed by 2 bracts.

MALLOW FAMILY
Malvaceae

Mallows, Cotton and Hollyhock all belong to this family. The 5 petals are twisted in the pointed bud, and the many stamens are bunched on a central tubular stalk. There is an epicalyx, usually of three segments, below the 5 true sepals. The plants are downy and a lens reveals that the hairs of most species are branched and star-shaped.

COMMON MALLOW
Malva sylvestris
This very variable plant is erect or straggling up to 150 cm high, and the stem is woody at the base. The plant favours dry, open places on waste and cultivated land.
Flower: rose-purple, dark-striped, 2·5-4 cm across; petals 5, thin, narrowed at base, notched; several stalked flowers arising from each leaf-axil.
Flowering time: June-September.
Leaf: palmately lobed, blunt-toothed, often folded along main veins; basal leaves long-stalked.
Fruit: nutlets, arranged in circle, covered by network of ridges.

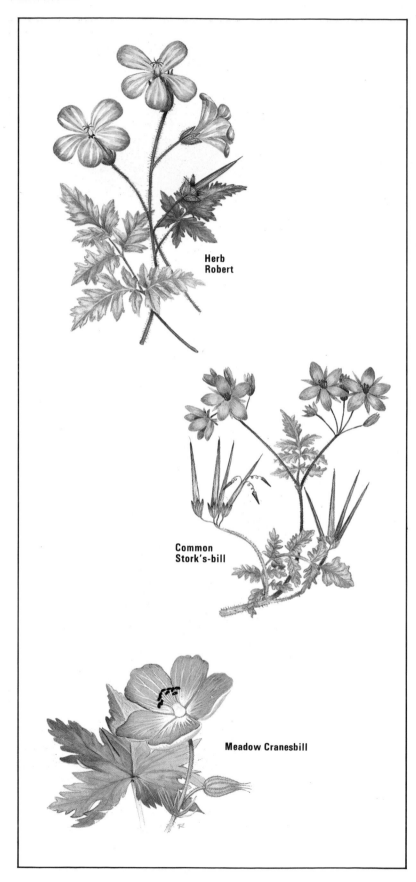

Herb
Robert

Common
Stork's-bill

Meadow Cranesbill

GERANIUM FAMILY
Geraniaceae

Many species in the Geranium family have long, soft hairs, and the flowers are usually brightly coloured, with 5 petals. The characteristic fruit is arranged around the base of the stiff, persistent style and splits into 5 one-seeded sections when ripe.

HERB ROBERT
Geranium robertianum
The stem and leaves of Herb Robert are hairy and often turn bright red. The plant grows 10-50 cm high, is branched and erect or straggling. If bruised, it smells unpleasant. It is most often found in hedgerows but also grows among rocks, on walls and in woodland.
Flower: bright pink-mauve, 2 cm across, long-stalked; petals 5, narrowed at base; sepals erect, with bristle-like tips.
Flowering time: May-September.
Leaf: in 3 main segments, each deeply and repeatedly dissected; long-stalked.
Fruit: arranged around base of stiff, persistent style to which segments are attached by thin strands.

COMMON STORK'S-BILL
Erodium cicutarium
This plant looks rather similar to Herb Robert but differs in the clustered flowers, the pinnate leaf-segments and the spiralling strands attached to the fruits. The stem and leaves are slightly to very hairy. The plant grows up to 60 cm high in dry, open places, particularly near the sea.
Flower: bright rose-purple; petals 5, 12-14 mm across, upper 2 sometimes with black spot at base, sepals spreading, with bristle-like tips. 5 of the 10 stamens lack anthers.
Flower arrangement: 3-12 flowers in umbel-like cluster.
Flowering time: June-September.
Leaf: doubly pinnate.
Fruit: arranged around base of stiff, persistent style to which segments attached by thin, spiralling strands.

MEADOW CRANESBILL
Geranium pratense
This handsome and rather hairy plant grows in grassy places and reaches 100 cm (sometimes more in damp places). It occurs in many parts of Europe, especially on limestone.
Flower: violet-blue, or occasionally sky-blue, with paler veins; saucer-shaped 25-35 mm across. Paired in loose cymes. June-September.
Leaf: lower ones up to 15 cm across, palmately lobed, each of the 5-7 lobes deeply toothed: upper leaves smaller and 3-lobed.
Fruit: hairy, drooping at first and becoming upright as it ripens.

WOOD SORREL FAMILY
Oxalidaceae

The flowers in this family have 5 petals and 10 stamens. The family is mainly distributed in the tropics. Some *Oxalis* species are grown as ornamentals in gardens, and a few have edible tubers.

WOOD SORREL
Oxalis acetosella
A small plant of woodland and shaded hedgebanks, Wood Sorrel has leaves composed of 3 leaflets, like clover leaves but a paler, more delicate green. In cold weather and at night the leaves fold down.
Flower: white, lilac-veined, bell-shaped, nodding; petals 5, 8-15 mm long; sepals 5.
Flower arrangement: solitary.
Flowering time: April-May.
Leaf: in 3 rounded, notched leaflets, pale yellow-green.
Fruit: capsule, rounded, 5-angled, 3-4 mm long; seeds light brown.

BALSAM FAMILY
Balsaminaceae

The Balsams are hairless plants with juicy, easily broken, translucent stems often with stalked, sticky glands. The flowers are irregular in shape, with 5 petals forming a broad lip, a hood and a curved spur behind. Typically the flower dangles from the flower stalk. The fruits explode on being touched.
The yellow flowered Touch-me-not Balsam (*Impatiens noli-tangere*) gets its name from this explosive habit.

INDIAN BALSAM
Impatiens glandulifera
Introduced as a garden plant from the Himalayas in 1839, and naturalized along waterways and in waste places, this tall, stout-stemmed species grows 100-200 cm high. It is hairless and the stems reddish. There is no mistaking the rather orchid-like dangling mauve flowers.
Flower: purplish pink, 2·5-4 cm, petals 5, forming a broad, lower lip and hood; sepals 3, lower forming a mauve, spurred bag. The plant is also known as the Policeman's Helmet because of the flower shape.
Flower arrangement: long-stalked racemes arising from leaf-axils.
Flowering time: July-October.
Leaf: opposite or in threes, 5-18 cm long, elliptic, toothed; reddish glands along basal margins.
Fruit: capsule, club-shaped, opening by 5 valves which spring into coils, shooting out seeds.

Wood Sorrel

Indian Balsam

PEA FAMILY
Leguminosae

The flowers in this very large family are easily recognizable, being composed of an upright 'standard' petal, 2 side 'wing' petals and a pair of fused, boat-shaped petals under the standard, as in the Sweet Pea. The 5 sepals are fused into a calyx tube, and stamens and style are usually enclosed by the petals. The flowers are loosely clustered or in small, dense heads. Leaves are usually trifoliate or pinnate, often with a tendril at the end. The fruit is typically a pod, and many important food crops like soybeans and peas belong to this family. Clover and Lucerne are very widely grown as fodder and green manure. The roots form nodules which contain nitrogen-fixing bacteria and act as a natural fertilizer.

COMMON REST-HARROW
Ononis repens
A shrubby, hairy plant of 40-70 cm, this species is prostrate, often with upturned tips bearing the pink flowers. The stems are hairy all round. The plant grows • in rough grassland and dunes.
Flowers: pink, 1·5-2 cm long, on shortly hairy stalks; wing petals as long as keel; calyx tube with 5 long teeth, densely hairy.
Flowering time: June-September.
Leaf: 1-3 leaflets, oval, finely toothed, hairy, short-stalked.
Fruit: pod, hidden by calyx.

COMMON BIRD'S-FOOT TREFOIL
Lotus corniculatus
This plant is usually almost hairless and grows in grassland. Plants growing on the coast may have small, fleshy leaves. The prostrate stems, 5-35 cm long, turn up at the tips.
Flowers: yellow, often tinged or streaked with red, 1-1·5 cm long.
Flower arrangement: 2-7 flowers. in outward-facing ring on erect stalk
Flowering time: June-September.
Leaf: of 5 elliptic or almost circular leaflets, each 3-10 mm long, rounded at tip or with a short point; short leaf-stalk often between lower and upper leaflets.
Fruit: pod, 1·5-3 cm long, cylindrical, straight; spreading out from stem like the toes of a bird – hence the common name.

Sainfoin is a native of eastern Europe, but widely cultivated for fodder and naturalized in many dry grasslands in western Europe.

Common Bird's-foot Trefoil

Common Rest-harrow

Sainfoin

Ribbed Melilot

RIBBED MELILOT
Melilotus officinalis
A native of southern Europe, but now widely distributed, this rather slender, hairless biennial is often abundant on roadsides and other bare or waste places: also on dunes and as a weed of cultivation. It reaches 120 cm.
Flower: bright yellow, 5 mm long: in slender, tapering racemes up to 50 mm long. May-September.
Leaf: trifoliate, each leaflet being oval, up to 20 mm long, and strongly toothed.
Fruit: a brown oval pod to 5 mm long.

SAINFOIN
Onobrychis viciifolia
A rather downy and generally upright herb, the Sainfoin resembles a small lupin when in flower. It reaches 50 cm and occurs widely in dry grassland and on roadsides in southern half of Europe: widely cultivated for fodder.
Flower: 10-12 mm across; deep pink with darker veins. In dense conical spikes. May-September.
Leaf: pinnate, with 6-12 pairs of leaflets each up to 3 cm long.
Fruit: a semi-circular, one-seeded pod that does not split open.

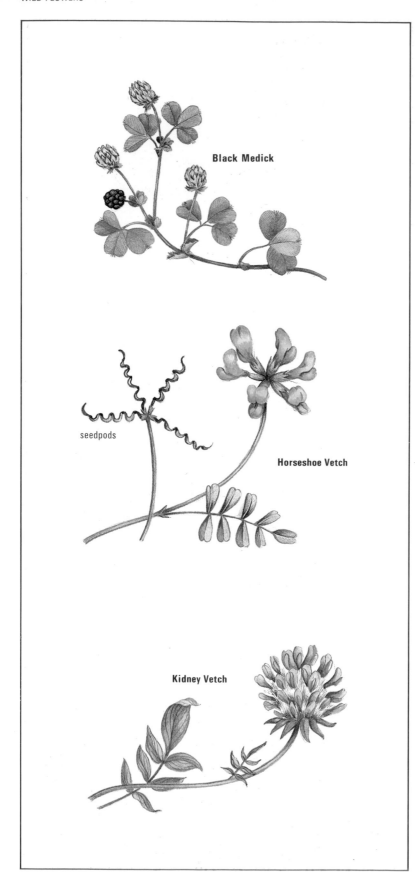

Black Medick

seedpods

Horseshoe Vetch

Kidney Vetch

BLACK MEDICK
Medicago lupulina
The leaves of Black Medick are clover-like and the flowers yellow.
The plant is sprawling, 5-50 cm high and downy, growing in open places such as roadsides, cultivated fields and at the coast. It is an annual or short-lived perennial.
Flower: bright yellow, 2-3 mm.
Flower arrangement: grouped into small, round heads 3-8 mm across, on stalks longer than the leaf-stalks.
Flowering time: April-August.
Leaf: of 3 leaflets, each narrowed towards base, finely toothed, often shallowly notched at tip in which is a minute bristle; stipules finely toothed.
Fruit: tightly curved disc, about 2 mm across, containing 1 seed, covered by a network of ridges. Black when ripe and clustered tightly at top of flower stalk.
Uses: this Medick is sometimes grown for fodder.
The Lesser Trefoil (*Trifolium dubium*) is very similar to Black Medick, but is an almost hairless annual. Its fruits are brown and straight and always covered with the dead petals.

HORSESHOE VETCH
Hippocrepis comosa
Spreading out from a woody rootstock, this plant forms beautiful carpets of yellow when in flower on chalk and limestone grasslands and on limestone rocks. It reaches heights of about 20 cm. It is much like the Bird's-foot Trefoil (p 229) but its leaves are longer and the characteristic seed pods easily distinguish it.
Flower: bright yellow, 6-10 mm long: up to 10 in a flat-topped whorl at top of stem up to 10 cm long. May-July.
Leaf: pinnate, to 8 cm long: 4 or 5 pairs of leaflets plus a terminal one, all oblong and blunt-ended (not pointed as in Bird's-foot Trefoil).
Fruit: a cluster of pods radiating from top of stem: each pod to 30 mm long and strongly waved; breaking up into several horseshoe-shaped, one-seeded sections.

KIDNEY VETCH
Anthyllis vulneraria
Clothed with silky hairs, this is a rather variable species – sometimes prostrate and creeping, at other times erect and reaching 30 cm. Normally a perennial, but occasionally behaving as an annual, it grows on calcareous grasslands, dunes, and cliffs.
Flower: normally yellow, sometimes orange; occasionally red, pink, or white by the sea. Tightly packed into rounded or kidney-shaped heads 2-4 cm across. June-September.
Leaf: pinnate, to 6 cm long, very silky below. 4 or 5 pairs of linear leaflets plus a terminal one, the latter large and lanceolate in lower leaves and linear in upper leaves.
Fruit: a flat pod about 3 mm long.

RED CLOVER
Trifolium pratense

Red Clover grows erectly 5-100 cm high in grassland, and is more or less hairy.

Flower: pink-purple; individual flowers 15-18 mm long.

Flower arrangement: in compact, rounded or ovoid heads of 2-4 cm.

Flowering time: May-September.

Leaf: of 3 elliptic leaflets, each 1-3 cm long, often with pale crescent, usually rounded at tips; leaf-stalk up to 20 cm; pair of short-stalked leaves immediately below flower head; stipules conspicuous, joined up the leaf-stalk, with 2 free points, each ending in bristle.

Fruit: pod, about 2 mm.

Uses: several varieties of red clover are grown for hay and silage, usually in mixed stands with various grasses. They are also sown with grasses to produce a good sward for new roadside verges, the nitrogen-fixing abilities of the clovers helping to nourish the grasses.

Several similar species of clover can be seen growing wild and in meadows. Zig-zag Clover (*T. medium*) has deeper red flowers and much brighter leaves than Red Clover, with at most a small white spot on each leaflet, and its stem is angled at each node to produce a zig-zag effect. Long-headed Clover (*T. incarnatum*) has very hairy, cylindrical flower heads up to 20 mm long, with the pale pink or cream flowers almost hidden among the hairs. It grows mainly on sea cliffs. A widely cultivated variety of this species, known as Crimson Clover, usually has bright crimson flowers on elongated heads up to 40 mm long.

WHITE CLOVER
Trifolium repens

A very familiar little plant of grassland, including lawns and verges. The stems of White Clover creep along the ground rooting at intervals. The plant is hairless and may grow as long as 50 cm.

Flower: white or pink-tinged, scented, individual-flowers 8-13 mm, turning down and becoming brown from base of head upwards; calyx-tube white, green-veined with narrow, pointed teeth.

Flower arrangement: round head on long, grooved stalk.

Flowering time: June-September.

Leaf: of 3 rounded leaflets, minutely toothed, each 1-3 cm long, each often with pale crescent; stipules joined, sheathing stem, with 2 free points.

Fruit: pod, hidden by dead flower.

Uses: bees use the nectar to produce clover honey, and several varieties are grown for fodder.

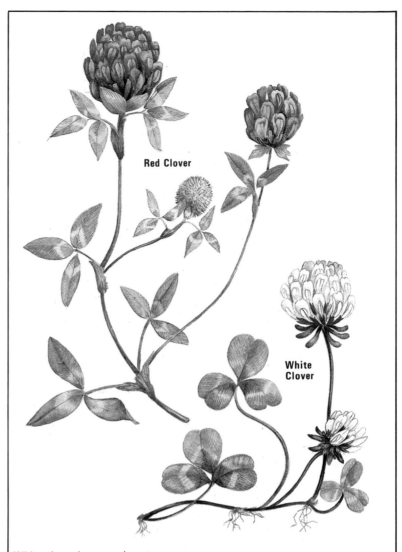

White clover has creeping stems which root at intervals and forms distinct patches among the grasses.

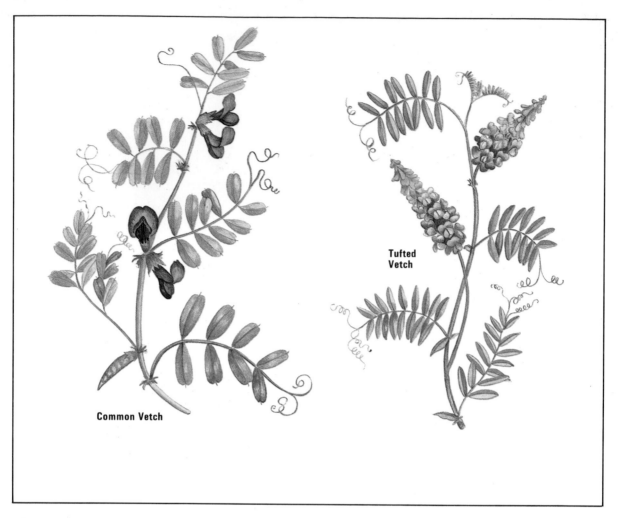

Tufted
Vetch

Common Vetch

COMMON VETCH
Vicia sativa
The Common Vetch is a slightly hairy plant, scrambling or climbing in hedges or grassy places. It can grow up to 120 cm.
Flower: purplish red, 1-3 cm long; calyx teeth about equal.
Flower arrangement: solitary or in pairs, on very short stalks or stalkless.
Flowering time: May-September.
Leaf: pinnate, with 3-8 pairs of narrow leaflets, each 1-2 cm long, often wider at tip than base, with minute bristle, notched or pointed; tendrils branched or not; stipules toothed or not, often with dark spot.
Fruit: pod, 2.5-8 cm long, yellow-brown to black, hairless or slightly hairy; seeds 4-12.
Uses: a form of this Vetch is often grown as a fodder crop.

TUFTED VETCH
Vicia cracca
Tufted Vetch is a weak-stemmed plant which gains support by clambering over other vegetation. It is 60-200 cm long, slightly hairy and grows in hedges and bushy places. The long, crowded racemes

of flowers are characteristic of this species.
Flower: blue-purple, 8-12 mm long, each drooping on short stalk; style equally hairy all round; upper teeth of calyx-tube minute; lower teeth about as long as calyx-tube.
Flower arrangement: dense raceme of 10-40 flowers on stalk 2-10 cm long.
Flowering time: June-August.
Leaf: pinnate, with 6-15 pairs of narrow leaflets, each 1-2.5 cm long, pointed or with minute bristle; leaf ends in branched tendril; stipules untoothed.
Fruit: pod, brown, hairless, 1-2.5 cm long; seeds 2-6.

BUSH VETCH
Vicia sepium
Climbing or scrambling in grassy or bushy places, the Bush Vetch grows 30-100 cm long. The leaves and stem have short hairs or are almost hairless.
Flower: pale purple, 1-1.5 cm; lower calyx teeth much shorter than calyx-tube, and tips curving toward each other.
Flower arrangement: raceme of 2-6 flowers, very shortly stalked.

Flowering time: May-August.
Leaf: pinnate, with 3-9 pairs of leaflets, each 1-3 cm long, variably shaped; tips rounded or pointed, with or without minute bristle at centre of slight notch at leaflet-tip; tendrils branched; stipules sometimes toothed, with black spot.
Fruit: pod, 2-3.5 cm long, black, hairless; seeds 3-10.

MEADOW VETCHLING
Lathyrus pratensis
This Vetchling, with or without short hairs, scrambles over vegetation in grassy or bushy places. It is 30-120 cm in length and has a sharply angled stem.
Flower: yellow, 10-18 mm long; teeth of calyx-tube narrowly triangular.
Flower arrangement: raceme of 5-12 flowers on long stalk.
Flowering time: May-August.
Leaf: 1-2 pairs of narrow, pointed leaflets, 1-3 cm long; tendril branched or not; stipules leaf-like, 1-2.5 cm, arrow-shaped.
Fruit: pod, 2-4 cm long, black; seeds 5-12.

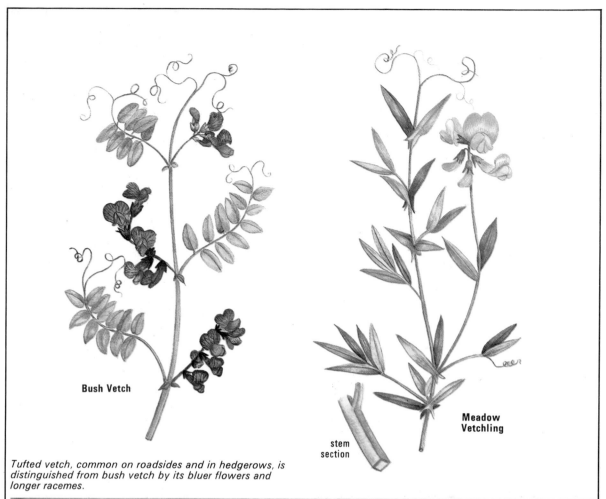

Bush Vetch

Meadow Vetchling

stem section

Tufted vetch, common on roadsides and in hedgerows, is distinguished from bush vetch by its bluer flowers and longer racemes.

Bramble

Dog
Rose

*The scarlet rose hips each contain
numerous small seeds.*

ROSE FAMILY
Rosaceae

This ancient family is among the
more primitive of the flowering
plant families. The flowers are
often conspicuously coloured, but
very rarely blue. The regular,
unspecialized flowers attract a
wide range of insects. There are
normally 5 petals and many
stamens. The fruits are varied
and include achenes, follicles,
drupes (stone–fruit), and the
apples and pears, which are false
fruits known as pomes.

The popular modern roses of
gardens are complicated hybrids,
far from their wild ancestors.

DOG ROSE
Rosa canina
The Dog Roses are extremely variable
shrubs, 1-3 m high, with stems that
arch and scramble in hedgerow
and scrub. The prickles are hooked.
Flower: pink or white, 4-5 cm
across; petals 5, notched; sepals 5,
lobed, falling before fruit ripens;
stamens many; stigmas in a head.
Flower arrangement: cluster of
1-4 flowers, stalks hairless.
Flowering time: June-July.
Leaf: pinnate, with 2-3 pairs of
elliptic, toothed, usually hairless
leaflets; stipules joined to leaf-stalk.
Fruit: rose hip, scarlet, about
1·5-2 cm long, spherical or ovoid.
Uses: jelly and syrup may be made
from the fruit, rich in vitamin C. More
than 500 tons of hips were collected
in Britain in 1943 to provide children
with rose-hip syrup.

BRAMBLE
Rubus fruticosus
The stems of these woody shrubs
often arch over, rooting at the tip
and bearing hooked prickles, some
of which may be straight. The
Brambles are extremely variable.
About 2,000 micro-species may be
recognized in the *Rubus fruticosus*
group. This huge number is thought
to have arisen by a combination of
hybridization and self-fertilization.
Flower: pink or white, 2-3 cm
across; petals 5; stamens many.
Flower arrangement: solitary or
clustered.
Flowering time: May-September.
Leaf: of 3-5 toothed leaflets.
Fruit: the 'blackberry'.
Uses: blackberries have been eaten
and enjoyed for thousands of years.
Healing powers were associated with
the leaves and stems, mainly for
relieving burns and swellings.

WATER AVENS
Geum rivale

A plant of shady, wet places and cleared woodland, the Water Avens is 20-60 cm high and shortly hairy. The flowers may easily be overlooked due to their nodding habit.

Flower: orange-pink, nodding; petals 5, 1-1·5 cm long, shallowly notched, abruptly narrowed at base; sepals purple, 5 as long as petals alternating with 5 shorter; stamens many; styles many, in central tuft.

Flower arrangement: few-flowered cyme.

Flowering time: May-September.

Leaf: pinnate, with 3-6 pairs of toothed leaflets; end leaflets enlarged, more or less rounded; leaf-stalk long; upper leaves smaller with fewer leaflets.

Fruit: head of achenes; styles persistent, becoming hooked; dispersed by clinging to fur of passing animals.

WOOD AVENS or HERB BENNETT
Geum urbanum

Growing erect in shady places, the Wood Avens is 20-60 cm tall and shortly hairy.

Flower: yellow, 10-18 mm across; petals 5, oval; sepals 10, 5 as long as petals, alternating with 5 shorter; stamens many; styles many, in central tuft.

Flowering time: June-August.

Leaf: basal leaves pinnate, stalked, with 2-3 pairs of toothed leaflets, 5-10 mm long; end leaflet enlarged; stipules leaf-like.

Fruit: like that of Water Avens.

TORMENTIL
Potentilla erecta

Erect or creeping but not rooting, Tormentil is 10-30 cm high. It grows in grassland and may be found on mountains to a height of about 1,000 m. Not on lime.

Flower: yellow, 7-11 mm across; petals 4, shallowly notched, longer than sepals; sepals 8; stamens many.

Flower arrangement: on long slender stalks in loose cymes.

Flowering time: June-September.

Leaf: of 3 toothed segments; stalked basal leaves in rosette, often withering before flowering; stem leaves stalkless with large, toothed, leaf-like stipules (leaf appearing 5-segmented).

Fruit: achenes, hairless, in a head.

WILD STRAWBERRY
Fragaria vesca

This plant grows 5-30 cm high, with long runners which root and form new plants. It grows in woods and on hedgebanks.

Flower: white, 12-18 mm across; petals 5, rounded, not notched, edges touching or overlapping; sepals 10, in 2 layers; stamens many.

Flower arrangement: long-stalked cyme; stalk hairs lie flat.

Flowering time: April-July.

Leaf: divided into 3 toothed segments, each 1-6 cm long, ovate, bright green, paler with silky hairs beneath; leaf-stalks long, hairy.

Fruit: strawberry; smaller than the cultivated strawberry but very good to eat.

BARREN STRAWBERRY
Potentilla sterilis

This plant is like the Wild Strawberry but has only short runners and duller, bluish-green leaves. It is easily distinguished in flower by its notched or heart-shaped petals. The fruit does not become fleshy.

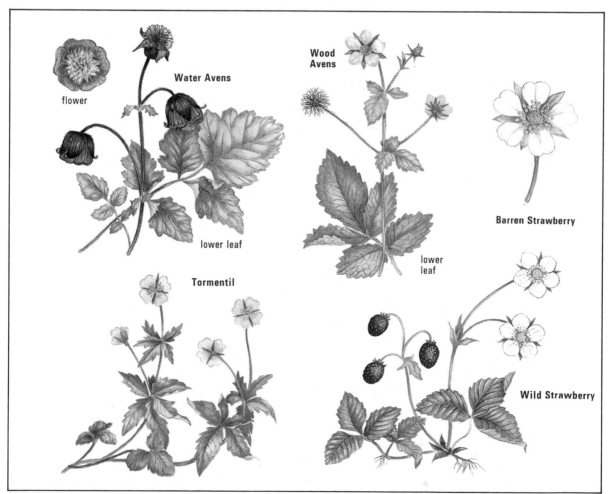

flower

Water Avens

lower leaf

Wood Avens

lower leaf

Tormentil

Barren Strawberry

Wild Strawberry

SALAD BURNET
Poterium sanguisorba

Abundant on dry grassland, especially on chalk and limestone, this plant has a strong smell of cucumber when crushed and makes a pleasant addition to salads. It reaches 50 cm.

Flower: minute and without petals: 4 greenish sepals. Tightly packed into globular heads about 10 mm across. Upper flowers are female, with purplish-red stigmas; lower ones are male with hanging yellow stamens. Wind-pollinated. May-August.

Leaf: almost hairless; bluish-green. Pinnate with 4-12 pairs of leaflets each up to 20 mm long and strongly toothed. Basal ones form rosette.

Fruit: a cluster of achenes, each with a corky covering.

The Greater Burnet (*Sanguisorba officinalis*) is larger, with elongated maroon flower heads. It grows in damp grassland.

MEADOWSWEET
Filipendula ulmaria

This is a rather tall, erect plant, 60-200 cm high, of wet places, including damp meadows. The small, cream-coloured flowers with long stamens are in frothy, irregular masses. The stems are often reddish.

Flower: cream, scented, 4-10 mm across; stamens many, twice length of petals.

Flower arrangement: in loose, irregular masses.

Flowering time: June-September.

Leaf: pinnate, with 2-5 pairs of large, ovate, toothed leaflets with small leaflets between; usually white and downy beneath.

Fruit: carpels becoming twisted together to form achenes about 2 mm.

Uses: Meadowsweet was formerly used against malaria when forms of that disease were common in undrained lowland areas. Strewn on floors, it also gave out a tangy odour like today's air fresheners.

COMMON AGRIMONY
Agrimonia eupatoria

This is an erect plant, 30-60 cm high, with a slender spike of yellow flowers above and densely leafy below. The reddish stems have long hairs, and the plant favours dry roadsides and field edges.

Flower: yellow, 5-8 mm across; petals 5; sepals 5, hairy; ring of hooked bristles immediately below; stamens many.

Flower arrangement: slender spike.

Flowering time: June-August.

Leaf: pinnate, with 3-6 pairs of toothed, elliptic leaflets, 2-6 cm long; hairy, greyish beneath, not glandular; smaller leaflets between; stipules leaf-like.

Fruit: grooved; top covered with hooked bristles which point forward; dispersed by catching onto clothing, or fur of passing animals.

SILVERWEED
Potentilla anserina

The name describes the silvery, silky hairs with which this plant is covered. The leaves form a rosette from which creep rooting runners up to 80 cm long. The plant grows in damp roadside places and meadows.

Flower: yellow, 1·5-2·0 cm across; petals 5, rounded; sepals 10, in 2 layers, outer layer toothed and half as long as petals; stamens many.

Flower arrangement: solitary, on long stalk.

Flowering time: June-August.

Leaf: pinnate, 5-25 cm, with 7-12 pairs of deeply toothed leaflets, alternating with much smaller leaflets; dense, silver, silky hairs beneath or silky both sides.

Fruit: hairless, achenes in a head.

Uses: the fleshy roots were eaten in the poorer parts of Britain as a vegetable or made into meal for bread and porridge.

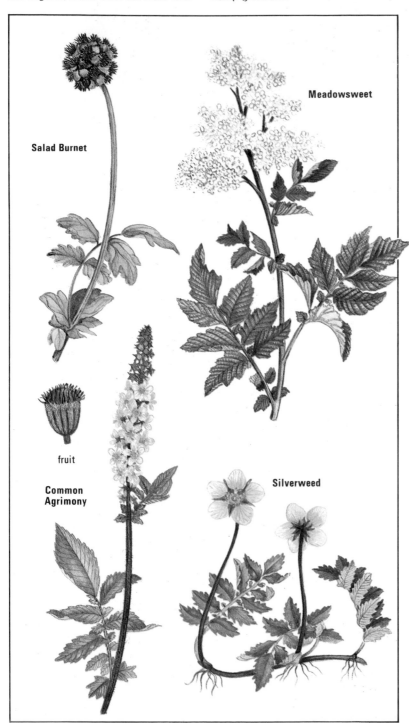

Salad Burnet

Meadowsweet

fruit

Common Agrimony

Silverweed

Cobweb houseleeks in flower: a rosette dies when it has flowered, but younger rosettes take its place.

Biting Stonecrop

Purple Loosestrife

the three style and stamen arrangements

STONECROP FAMILY
Crassulaceae

Members of this family are adapted to mountain slopes and other dry habitats such as walls and stony places. Many grow on rocky banks and some grow on sand dunes. They have fleshy (succulent) stems and leaves, all with waxy coatings, and the leaves are usually tightly packed, often forming dense rosettes – all features which help to conserve water. The flowers are usually star-shaped with pointed petals and they are often grouped into broad, domed heads. The fruits are dry and many-seeded.

The two main groups within the family are the stonecrops themselves (*Sedum* spp) and the houseleeks (*Sempervivum* spp). Stonecrops normally have 5 petals, while the houseleeks have 8–16 petals. Several species are grown in rock gardens, where the Ice-Plant (*Sedum spectabile*), with its greyish-green leaves and broad heads of nectar-rich pink flowers, is famed as a butterfly attractant. The Common Houseleek (*Sempervivum tectorum*) was once planted on cottage roofs, where its spreading root system and tightly-packed rosettes helped anchor the slates.

COBWEB HOUSELEEK
Sempervivum arachnoideum
One of the few hairy plants in this family, the Cobweb Houseleek grows on acidic rocks in the Alps and the Apennines, reaching altitudes of over 3,000 m. It is a favourite windowsill plant, for it thrives with little soil. Each rosette produces numerous short, radiating runners which quickly form new rosettes around the parent and soon cover large areas.
Flower: reddish-pink, star-like about 15 mm across; on short stems from the older rosettes. July-September.
Leaf: greyish green, in tight rosettes to 20 mm across: wispy hairs clothe the rosettes and help to conserve moisture. Several closely related, but hairless species of houseleek grow in the mountains of Europe. Most have pink flowers, but there are some yellow-flowered species.

BITING STONECROP
Sedum acre
Growing in mats on dry, stony or sandy ground or on walls, the Biting Stonecrop gets its name from the burning taste of its small, fleshy leaves.
Flower: bright yellow, star-shaped, about 12 mm across; petals 5, pointed; sepals 5; stamens 10.
Flower arrangement: in small clusters at the ends of the branches.
Flowering time: June-July.
Leaf: very fleshy, hairless, rounded, 3-6 mm long, overlapping on non-flowering shoots.

Fruit: group of spreading follicles, each with many tiny seeds.

LOOSESTRIFE FAMILY
Lythraceae

This is a small family of plants which favour damp places. The flowers have 4-6 petals which are crumpled in bud. Some species in this family produce dyes, one of the best known being henna.

PURPLE LOOSESTRIFE
Lythrum salicaria
This is an erect plant, 50-150 cm tall with a 4-angled stem and varying from almost hairless to densely hairy. It is found in damp places such as river banks. The flowers are insect-pollinated and are of 3 kinds, differing in the relative lengths of their styles and stamens. Each plant bears only one kind of flower. When bees visit the flowers they pick up pollen from long stamens in just the right position to transfer it to a long stigma of another flower. Similarly, pollen from short or medium length stamens can be transferred to short or medium length stigmas.
Flower: red-purple, 1-1·5 cm across; petals 6, flimsy; calyx tubular, ribbed, with 12 teeth; stamens 12.
Flower arrangement: in whorls on a tall spike.
Flowering time: June-August.
Leaf: opposite or in threes; narrow, pointed, 4-7 cm long, stalkless.
Fruit: capsule, ovoid, enclosed by calyx.

Livelong saxifrage flourishes in mountain crevices and often cascades like snow from vertical rock faces.

Rue-leaved Saxifrage

Round-leaved Sundew

SAXIFRAGE FAMILY
Saxifragaceae

Many species of Saxifrage are short, mountain plants and several are commonly grown in gardens. The flowers have 5 petals and sepals and 10 stamens. The leaves often form rosettes.

LIVELONG SAXIFRAGE
Saxifraga paniculata
One of several similar mountain-dwellers, this saxifrage occurs on rocks and screes to a height of 2,700 m. Not in Britain.
Flower: white or cream, occasionally pale pink: 8-11 mm across in loose upright or drooping panicles.
Leaf: oblong-oval and encrusted with lime: in open rosettes.

RUE-LEAVED SAXIFRAGE
Saxifraga tridactylites
This is a slender, often red-tinged plant ot 3-8 cm, though sometimes taller, often branched and covered in sticky hairs. In sunshine the ring-shaped nectaries at the flower centres exude glistening nectar. Mainly on dry walls in lowland areas.
Flower: white, 4-6 mm across.
Flower arrangement: loose cyme.
Flowering time: April-June.
Leaf: 3-5-lobed; basal leaves not forming rosette, often withered at flowering time.
Fruit: 2-lobed capsule; seeds brown.

SUNDEW FAMILY
Droseraceae

The members of this family are insectivorous plants, trapping and digesting insects with the aid of special leaves. They live in boggy or waterlogged places and the insects supplement the meagre supplies of minerals in such places. The Venus' Fly Trap of America is one of the best known species. Several species of sundew live in Europe.

ROUND-LEAVED SUNDEW
Drosera rotundifolia
Stalked, sticky red glands on the leaves of this little plant often lend a red tinge to the ground of bogs and wet moors where it grows. Insects stick to the glands which slowly bend toward the leaf centre, further enmeshing the insect. Eventually the prey is digested and the glands return to their former positions.
Flower: white, 5 mm across; petals 5 or 6. On a slender spike.
Flowering time: June-August.
Leaf: circular, long-stalked, in a rosette, upper surface covered in sticky, red, stalked glands.

WILLOWHERB FAMILY
Onagraceae

This widespread family includes some shrubs and water plants as well as the familiar willowherbs which spring up on roadsides and waste ground. There are also a number of garden plants in the family, including the Evening Primroses (*Oenothera* species). The flowers have 4 petals, which are formed into a tube in the fuchsias. There are commonly 8 stamens and the stigma is often 4-lobed. The fruit is usually a long, slender capsule, which opens by 4 longitudinal slits to release large numbers of plumed wind-scattered seeds.

GREAT WILLOWHERB
Epilobium hirsutum
This willowherb is tall, up to 150 cm, erect and densely covered in soft hairs. It often forms stands in marshes and on the banks of streams.
Flower: deep purplish pink, 1·5-2·5 cm across; petals 4, notched; sepals 4, erect, pointed; stamens 8; stigma cream-coloured.
Flower arrangement: raceme, flower stalks arising from leaf-axils.
Flowering time: July-August.
Leaf: rather narrow, opposite, pointed, teeth curved forward; stalkless, leaf base weakly clasping stem.
Fruit: 5-8 cm long.

ROSEBAY WILLOWHERB
Epilobium angustifolium
The tall, almost hairless plants are up to 120 cm high. In Britain a century ago this species was confined to certain localities but has since spread widely. It has a preference for burnt ground, and covered bombed sites in World War II.
Flower: rosy-purple, 2-3 cm across; petals 4, upper 2 slightly larger; sepals 4, narrow, purple; stamens 8.
Flower arrangement: raceme, long, many-flowered.
Flowering time: July-September.
Leaf: narrow, pointed, alternate, 5-20 cm long, entire or with small, widely spaced teeth.
Fruit: 2·5-8 cm long.

BROAD-LEAVED WILLOWHERB
Epilobium montanum
This is a small, sparsely hairy plant. The stems are erect, 20-60 cm high and reddish. It is found in gardens, woods, hedges and stony places.
Flower: pale mauve, 6-9 mm across; petals 4, notched; sepals 4, erect, pointed; stamens 8.
Flower arrangement: solitary or small racemes in leaf-axils.
Flowering time: June-August.
Leaf: ovate, opposite, toothed, shortly stalked.
Fruit: 4-8 cm long.

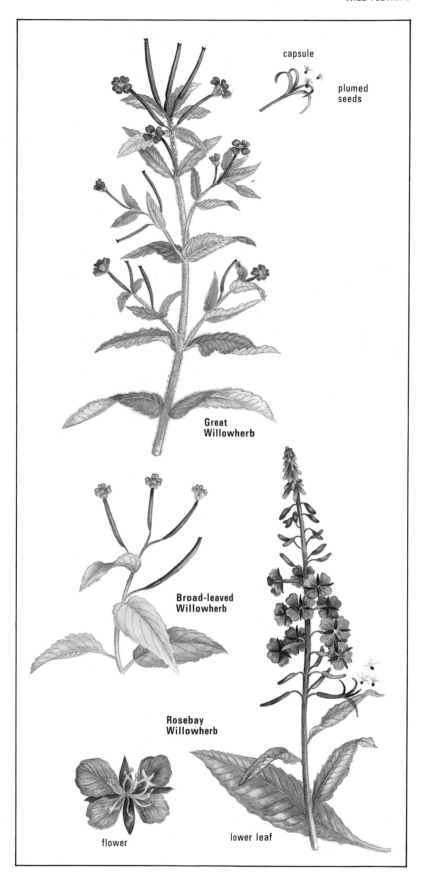

capsule

plumed seeds

Great Willowherb

Broad-leaved Willowherb

Rosebay Willowherb

flower

lower leaf

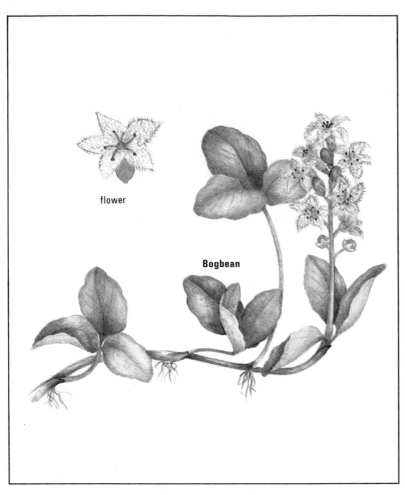

flower

Bogbean

BOGBEAN FAMILY
Menyanthaceae

This is a small family of water plants in which the 5 white, pink or yellow flower petals are often fringed with stout hairs. Apart from the Bogbean itself, the only European species is the Fringed Water-lily (*Nymphoides peltata*), which has floating, heart-shaped leaves and floating yellow flowers. Unlike the true water-lilies, the flowers are borne in clusters.

BOGBEAN
Menyanthes trifoliata
The leaves and beautiful fringed, pink and white flowers of this hairless water plant are borne above the surface of shallow water, the stems creeping through the mud. It is found in marshes, lake-edges and upland pools.
Flower: pink, paler within, about 1·5 cm across; petals 5, covered in long, white hairs, joined at base; anthers reddish.
Flower arrangement: clustered, on long stalk.
Flowering time: May-July.
Leaf: of 3 rounded leaflets, 3·5-7 cm, alternate, on stalk with sheathing base.
Fruit: capsule, spherical, with persistent style.
Uses: the underground stem contains a bitter substance called menyanthin, which was used as a tonic and to bring down fever.

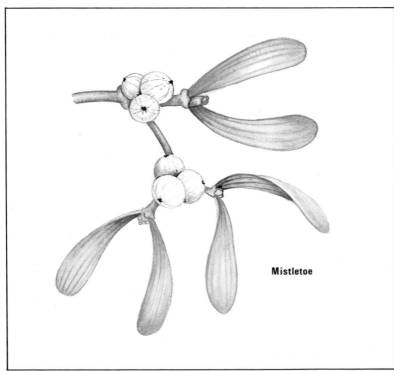

Mistletoe

MISTLETOE FAMILY
Loranthaceae

Most of the 1,500 or so species in this family are semi-parasitic shrubs – they contain chlorophyll but rely on various other plants for their water and some of their food, which they obtain by sending suckers into the host root or stem.

MISTLETOE
Viscum album
Well-known as a Christmas decoration, this much-forked shrubby plant grows on a wide variety of deciduous trees, especially apple and poplar: occasionally on conifers. Its tangle of green branches may form a ball as much as 1 m across.
Flower: small and green with 4 petals: male and female flowers on separate plants. February-April.
Leaf: yellowish-green, thick and leathery: elongated oval to 8 cm long. In pairs.
Fruit: a white berry with sticky flesh, ripening November-February. Birds eat the flesh and then wipe their beaks on the tree branches, leaving the seeds glued to the bark and ready to grow.

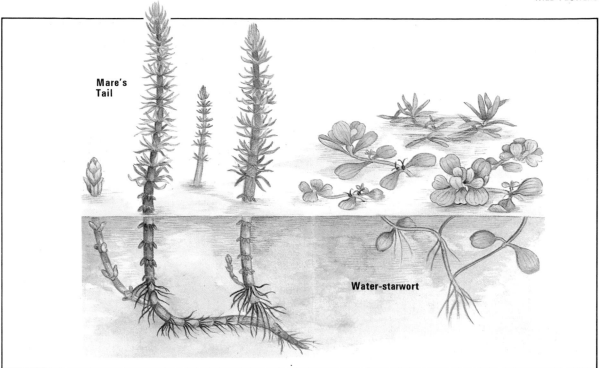

STARWORT FAMILY
Callitrichaceae

The Starwort family consists of one genus of 25 species. They are small, slender water plants. Some species grow and are pollinated underwater, some grow in or beside water and others only on wet mud. The flowers are minute and unisexual.

WATER-STARWORT
Callitriche stagnalis
These small, hairless water plants may be found creeping and rooting on wet mud, or floating or submerged in ponds, streams or lakes. The stems grow 1-25 cm long on land and to 100 cm in water. The species is extremely variable and difficult to separate from several of its close relatives. Leaf shape depends on whether the plants are submerged or not, and on water depth and movement.
Flower: inconspicuous, green, without petals, unisexual.
Flower arrangement: in leaf-axils.
Flowering time: April-October.
Leaf: oval or strap-shaped, opposite, often forming rosettes at tips of emerging shoots.
Fruit: 4-lobed.

MARE'S TAIL FAMILY
Hippuridaceae

There is only one species, *Hippuris vulgaris*, in this family.

MARE'S TAIL
Hippuris vulgaris
Growing 25-75 cm high in still or slow-moving fresh water, the un-branched shoots of Mare's Tail bear many whorls of narrow leaves. The leaves are flattened, not tubular as in the superficially similar Horse-tails, which are relatives of the ferns.
Flower: inconspicuous, without petals, greenish, wind-pollinated.
Flower arrangement: in the leaf-axils of aerial shoots.
Flowering time: June-July.
Leaf: very narrow, 1-7·5 cm long, in whorls, stalkless; submerged leaves very thin, pale, limp.
Fruit: nut, green, 2-3 mm.

IVY FAMILY
Araliaceae

This is a family of mainly tropical herbs, shrubs and trees. The small flowers are green or white, and the fruits are berry-like. Climbing species often have special aerial roots which cling to tree trunks and other surfaces.

IVY
Hedera helix
The familiar, evergreen Ivy climbs to 30 m on trees, cliffs and buildings. Short, thick roots up one side of the stem help it to cling to a support. It may also be found carpeting the ground in woods.
Flower: yellow-green; petals 5, 3-4 mm long, pointed; calyx with 5 tiny teeth; stamens 5; style surrounded by nectar-secreting disc.
Flower arrangement: in rounded, umbel-like clusters on unshaded, high parts of plant.
Flowering time: September-November. The nectar-rich flowers are eagerly sought by insects, especially young wasp queens stocking up their bodies for the winter.
Leaf: glossy, stalked, of 2 kinds: those on non-flowering branches 3-5-lobed, those on the flowering not lobed, ovate or more or less diamond-shaped.
Fruit: black, berry-like, 8-10 mm.

Ivy

climbing roots

fruit cluster

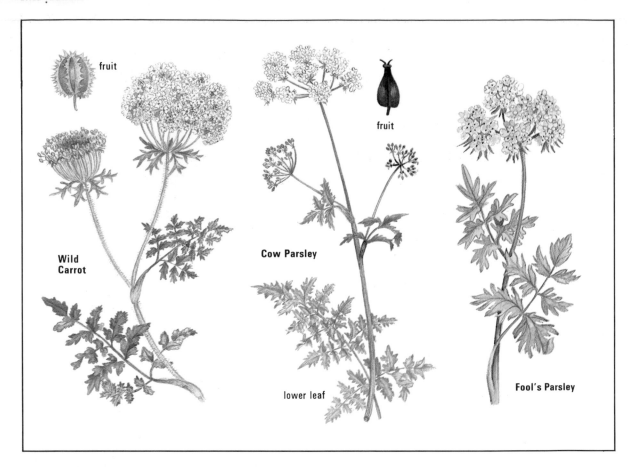

fruit

Wild
Carrot

Cow Parsley

fruit

lower leaf

Fool's Parsley

CARROT FAMILY
Umbelliferae

Among the most easily recognizable features of this large family is the arrangement of tiny flowers in umbels. These are flat-topped clusters of flowers, with the bases of the stalks (*rays*) all joining at one point. Most species have compound umbels. These are umbels formed, in turn, of smaller umbels. Bracts may be present at the base of a compound (*primary*) umbel and smaller bracts (*bracteoles*) at the bases of the individual (*secondary*) umbels. The fruits and bracts are important for identification. There are 5 separate petals in each flower, often of markedly different sizes. There may be 5 sepals, but they are often absent. The massed heads attract plenty of insects to the freely exposed nectar.

There are many herbs and spices in the family, including parsley, fennel and dill, as well as many poisonous plants.

WILD CARROT
Daucus carota

The Wild Carrot usually has stiffly hairy stems, ridged, not hollow and 30-100 cm high. It grows in grassy places, and at the coast. It is a biennial, flowering and fruiting in its second year. The widely cultivated carrot with a swollen edible tap root is a form of the Wild Carrot.

Flower: white, middle flower of umbel often red; petals 5, tips incurved; petals of outer flowers enlarged.
Flower arrangement: compound umbel, 3-7 cm across; rays many; bracts conspicuous, each of 3 or more long points; bracteoles similar.
Flowering time: June-August.
Leaf: finely dissected, often fleshy if growing by the sea.
Fruit: ovoid; ridges spiny; 2-4 mm; umbel becoming hollow in fruit.

COW PARSLEY
Anthriscus sylvestris

One of the commonest white-flowered umbels, Cow Parsley is also among the earliest to flower. A tall, slightly downy plant, it grows up to 150 cm high in hedges and wood borders. The stems are hollow, grooved and may be tinged red.
Flower: white, 3-4 mm across; petals 5, tip often slightly notched and curved inward.

Flower arrangement: in compound umbels, 2-6 cm across; no bracts; bracteoles 5 or 6.
Flowering time: April-June.
Leaf: 2- or 3-pinnate, up to 30 cm long, shortly hairy beneath, leaf-stalk sheathing stem at base.
Fruit: of 2 oblong, joined carpels, black, smooth, 5-10 mm, each bearing short, persistent style.

FOOL'S PARSLEY
Aethusa cynapium

This common weed of gardens, field margins, and waste places is a rather shiny, bright green annual. It is quite hairless and the stems are very smooth — pale green with prominent darker striations. Reaching 120 cm, it is a poisonous plant and its vague resemblance to cultivated parsley has given it its name.
Flower: white, 2 mm across with very unequal petals. Borne in compound umbels 2-6 cm across. Bracts are usually absent, but slender, strap-shaped bracteoles about 1 cm long hang from the secondary umbels like beards and make this plant easily identified when in flower. June-October.
Leaf: triangular in outline and 2-3 pinnate; with membranous flaps where leaf bases clasp the stems.
Fruit: egg-shaped and clearly ribbed: not spiny.

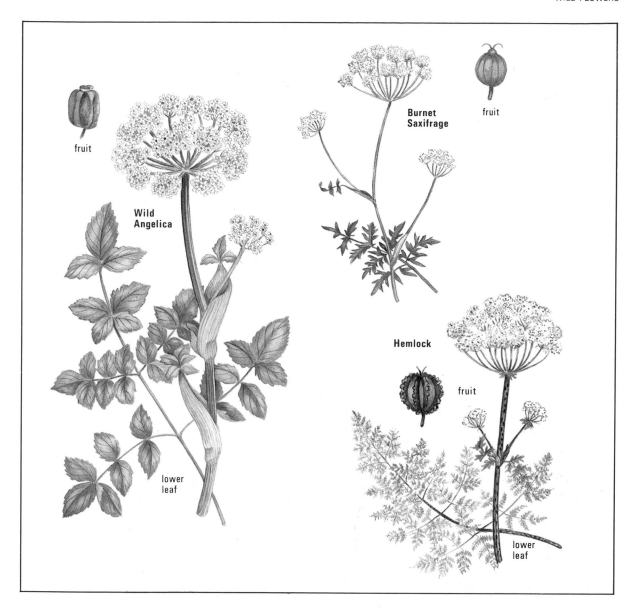

fruit

Wild
Angelica

Burnet
Saxifrage

fruit

Hemlock

fruit

lower
leaf

lower
leaf

WILD ANGELICA
Angelica sylvestris

Often stout and up to 200 cm or more high, this Umbellifer is almost hairless. It favours damp, shady places. The hollow, grooved stem is often purple with a whitish cast or bloom.

Flower: white or pink, 2 mm across; petals 5, incurved.

Flower arrangement: compound umbel, rounded, 3-15 cm across; rays many, slightly hairy; few or no bracts; bracteoles few, bristle-like.

Flowering time: July-September.

Leaf: doubly or trebly pinnate; leaflets 2-8 cm, ovate, toothed, leafstalks deeply grooved on upper side, widely sheathing stem at base. Upper leaves are little more than sheaths with a tuft of leaflets at the tip, often with small umbels in axils.

Fruit: ovoid, 4-5 mm, flattened, winged; persistent styles curved.

HEMLOCK
Conium maculatum

Hemlock is extremely poisonous in all parts. It can be recognized by the smooth, purple-spotted stem and a 'mousy' smell if the plant is crushed. The hairless plant grows up to 2·5 m in damp habitats, near water and on waste land. It is a biennial.

Flower: white, 2 mm across; petals 5, tips shortly incurved.

Flower arrangement: compound umbel, 2-5 cm across; rays 10-20; bracts 5-6; bracteoles on outer sides of secondary umbels.

Flowering time: June-July.

Leaf: finely dissected, up to 30 cm.

Fruit: spherical, 2·5-3·5 mm, ridges bumpy.

Uses: traditionally this was the drug used to poison Socrates. Medicinal use of Hemlock was revived in the late 18th century but discontinued due to the uncertain effects.

BURNET SAXIFRAGE
Pimpinella saxifraga

This species has a downy and tough but slender stem, weakly ridged. It grows 30-100 cm high in dry grassland, very often on chalk or limestone. The seed of a Mediterranean species of *Pimpinella* is the aniseed of seed cake and sweets.

Flower: white, 2 mm across; petals 5, tips incurved.

Flower arrangement: compound umbel, 2-5 cm across, flat-topped; rays 10-20; no bracts or bracteoles.

Flowering time: July-August.

Leaf: pinnate; leaflets ovate, coarsely toothed, stalkless; upper leaves doubly pinnate, leaflets narrow.

Fruit: ovoid, 2-3 mm.

The Greater Burnet Saxifrage (*P. major*) is a taller, hairless relative, often with pink flowers (especially in the north). All leaves are once pinnate. It grows on heavier and damper soils.

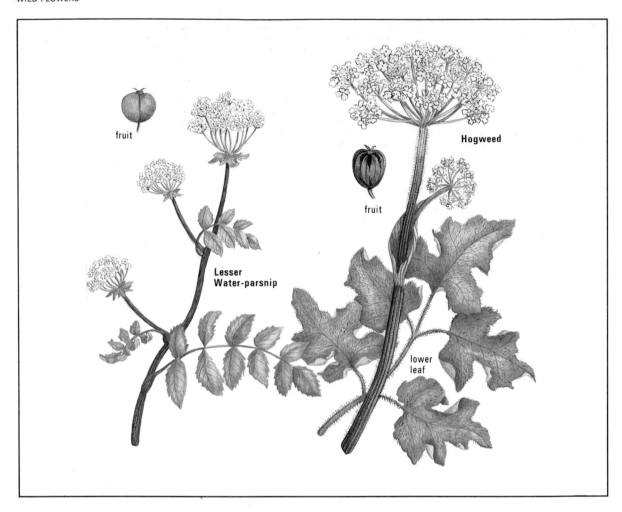

fruit

Hogweed

fruit

Lesser
Water-parsnip

lower
leaf

LESSER WATER-PARSNIP
Berula erecta
These hairless plants, 30-100 cm high, grow in shallow fresh water, often forming sprawling masses. The stems are hollow and ridged. Fool's Water-cress (*Apium nodiflorum*) is similar to this species. They cannot easily be told apart unless flowers or fruit are present.
Flower: white, 2 mm across; petals 5, tips incurved.
Flower arrangement: compound umbel, 3-6 cm across, on long stalk; rays 10-20; bracts and bracteoles many, often with a few teeth.
Flowering time: July-September.
Leaf: pinnate, up to 30 cm long; 7-14 pairs ovate, toothed leaflets; dull, blue-green.
Fruit: 2-lobed, 1·5-2 mm, a little wider than high; persistent styles curved. A poisonous species.

HOGWEED
Heracleum sphondylium
The stout stem of Hogweed is grooved, hollow and stiffly hairy, the hairs bent sharply down. The plant is found in grassland, hedges and woods, growing 50-200 cm high. The Giant Hogweed (*H. mante-*

gazzianum) is up to 5 m and has a red-blotched stem up to 10 cm thick.
Flower: white or pink, 5-10 mm across; petals 5, incurved, enlarged in outer flowers.
Flower arrangement: compound umbel, 5-15 cm across; rays 7-20, few or no bracts; bracteoles bristle-like.
Flowering time: June-September.
Leaf: pinnate, 15-60 cm; leaflets broad, toothed and lobed, stiffly hairy; bases of stalks widely sheathing stem.
Fruit: ovoid, flattened, whitish, 7-8 mm; persistent styles short, curved.
Uses: the leaves are fed to pigs.

GROUND ELDER
Aegopodium podagraria
The leaves of Ground Elder have broad, undissected leaflets, unlike the finely dissected leaves of many other Umbellifers. The plant is hairless, with hollow, grooved stems, and grows in shady places and gardens, where it can be a stubborn weed.
Flower: white, sometimes pink, 1 mm across; petals 5, tips incurved.
Flower arrangement: in com-

pound umbels, 2-6 cm across; rays 15-20; few or no bracts or bracteoles.
Flowering time: May-July.
Leaf: of 3 leaflets, each 4-8 cm, ovate, toothed, on long, 3-angled leaf-stalk sheathing stem at base.
Fruit: ovoid, 4 mm, ridged; persistent styles curved down.

ALEXANDERS
Smyrnium olusatrum
This tall and rather imposing biennial grows mainly in coastal regions. Its stout branched stems and shiny foliage form dense banks on roadsides, cliffs, and waste ground. It reaches 150 cm and has a distinct smell of celery. A native of the southern half of Europe, it is now well established in Britain. It was once cultivated as a pot herb.
Flower: yellow, 1-5 mm · across in domed or globular compound umbels with few bracts or bracteoles. April-June.
Leaf: bright green, often yellowish when young. Basal leaves 30 cm long or more and much divided (thrice trifoliate); leaflets — diamond-shaped. Upper leaves twice trifoliate.
Fruit: black and globular, about 8 mm long.

SANICLE
Sanicula europaea
This hairless plant grows 20-60 cm high and forms dense carpets in many woodlands, especially beechwoods.
Flower: greenish white, often with a pinkish tinge; very small and packed into small globular umbels, 3 or 4 of which are in turn grouped into loose compound umbels. Bracts 3-5 mm long and pinnately lobed: bracteoles slender and undivided. May-August.

Leaf: deep green and shiny with reddish stalks; palmately lobed.
Fruit: oval, 3 mm long and clothed with hooked bristles.

SEA HOLLY
Eryngium maritimum
An inhabitant of sand dunes and shingle banks by the sea, this beautiful plant forms a blue haze over the ground when in flower. It reaches 60 cm, but is often shorter.

Flower: bright blue and packed into a simple spiny umbel which is oval and up to 4 cm long. The umbel is surrounded by broad and spiny leaf-like bracts. July-September.
Leaf: grey-green with a waxy coating and sharply spined edges reminiscent of true holly. The basal leaves are often markedly fan-shaped.
Fruit: oblong, about 5 mm long and covered with hooked bristles.

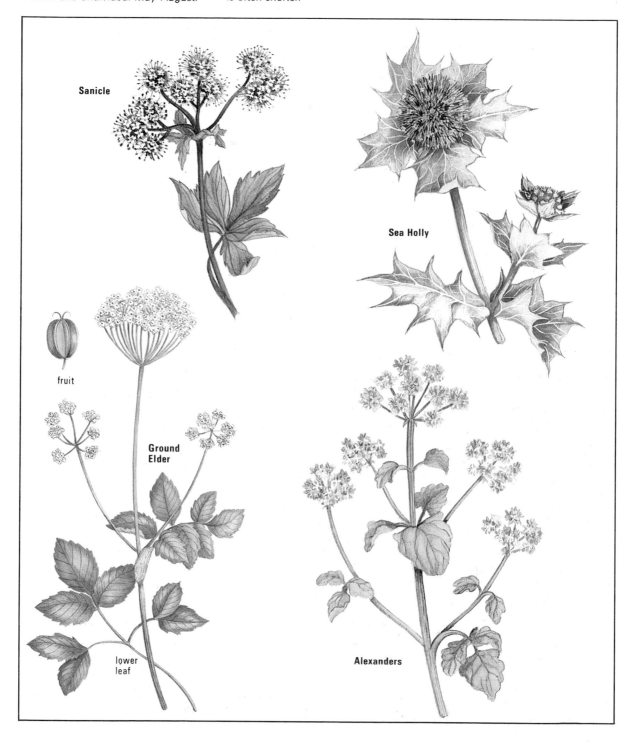

Sanicle

fruit

Sea Holly

Ground Elder

lower leaf

Alexanders

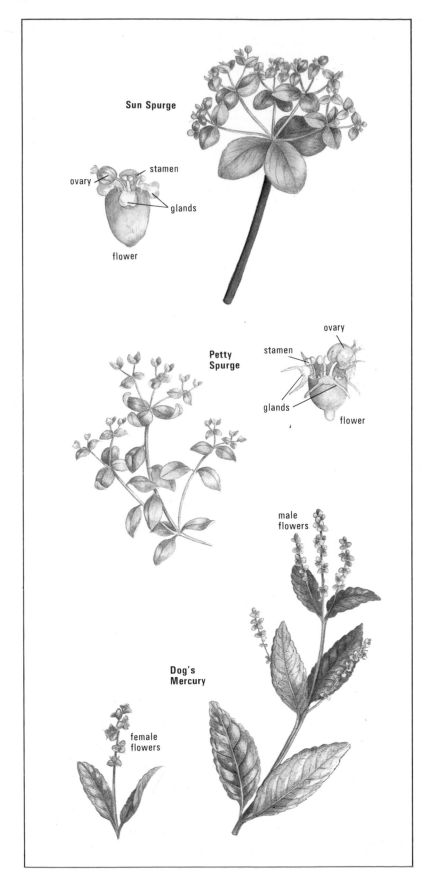

Sun Spurge

ovary — stamen
— glands
flower

Petty
Spurge

ovary
stamen
glands
flower

male
flowers

Dog's
Mercury

female
flowers

SPURGE FAMILY
Euphorbiaceae

This large, mainly tropical family includes plants which produce rubber and castor oil. Many are trees and shrubs, but all the European species are herbaceous. Spurges have very distinctive flowers without petals. A typical inflorescence consists of a little cup in which there are several minute, one-stamened male flowers and a single female flower with three stigmas. Nectar-secreting glands around the edge attract insects. All members of the family contain a poisonous and often milky sap.

SUN SPURGE
Euphorbia helioscopia
The whole plant is hairless, 10-50 cm high and erect. The characteristic yellowish bracts of the flowers lend a yellow-green look to the plant. The stem is often red. An annual living on disturbed ground.
Flower: minute; glands on rim green; kidney-shaped, surrounded by yellowish, leaf-like bracts.
Flower arrangement: in umbel-like, 5-stalked clusters.
Flowering time: May-October.
Leaf: rounded, lower leaf often tapering at base; minutely toothed.
Fruit: capsule, smooth, 3-5 mm, stalked, nodding over rim of flower.

PETTY SPURGE
Euphorbia peplus
Growing 10-30 cm high in cultivated ground, this annual is hairless and light green. The minute flowers are surrounded by leaf-like bracts.
Flower: minute; glands on rim crescent-shaped with long, pointed tips, surrounded by opposite, leaf-like bracts.
Flower arrangement: flower stalks repeatedly dividing in two.
Flowering time: April-November.
Leaf: oval, not toothed, alternate.
Fruit: capsule, ridged, 2 mm, stalked, nodding over rim of flower.

DOG'S MERCURY
Mercurialis perennis
Poisonous to humans and livestock, Dog's Mercury is erect, up to 40 cm, unbranched and shortly hairy. The plant smells unpleasant if crushed, and grows in woods and shady places.
Flower: inconspicuous, green; male and female on separate plants.
Flower arrangement: males in slender spikes, females in small, stalked clusters.
Flowering time: February-April.
Leaf: elliptic, blunt-toothed, opposite, 2-8 cm long, shortly stalked.
Fruit: spherical, hairy, 6-8 mm.

male flowers

fruit

Hop

female flower

HEMP FAMILY
Cannabiaceae

There are two main divisions in this family. One contains the Hops. The other contains species used for their plant fibre (hemp) and the drug cannabis. The flowers are either male or female, borne on separate plants.

HOP
Humulus lupulus
The Hop is found climbing with rough stems in hedges and, although native in N. Europe, is often an escape from cultivation. The 'cones' of pale bracts on the female plants are easy to recognize.
Flower: males and females on separate plants; females enclosed by yellow-green bracts; males tiny, green; petal-like lobes 5.
Flower arrangement: female bracts in hanging 'cone'; male flowers in branched clusters.
Flowering time: July-August.
Leaf: 3-5 lobed, coarsely toothed, roughly hairy, opposite, 10-15 cm, yellow glands dotting underside.
Fruit: enclosed by enlarged bracts dotted with yellow resin glands.
Uses: the female 'cones' are used to flavour beers. Cultivation of Hops began in Britain in about 1520, earlier in the rest of Europe.

GOURD FAMILY
Cucurbitaceae

Most members of this family are tropical climbing herbs. They grow rapidly and climb by means of spring-like tendrils. There are usually 5 sepals and 5 petals. Well-known members of the family include melons, marrows, and cucumbers – all with thick-skinned berries as fruit.

White Bryony

WHITE BRYONY
Bryonia dioica
This rather dull green climber is abundant in hedgerows and woodland margins, where its bristly angular stems readily reach heights of 4 m. Its tendrils coil in two different directions and their great elasticity allows the plant to sway in the wind without risk of breaking away from its support.
Flower: in small clusters, male and female on separate plants: pale green with hairy petals. Female flowers 10-12 mm across, male flowers 12-18 mm. May-September.
Leaf: hairy and palmately lobed with 3-5 toothed lobes. The unbranched tendrils arise close to the leaf stalks and may be modified stipules, although their exact nature is not clear.
Fruit: a red berry. Poisonous. The plant is in no way related to the Black Bryony (p 283) which often grows with it.

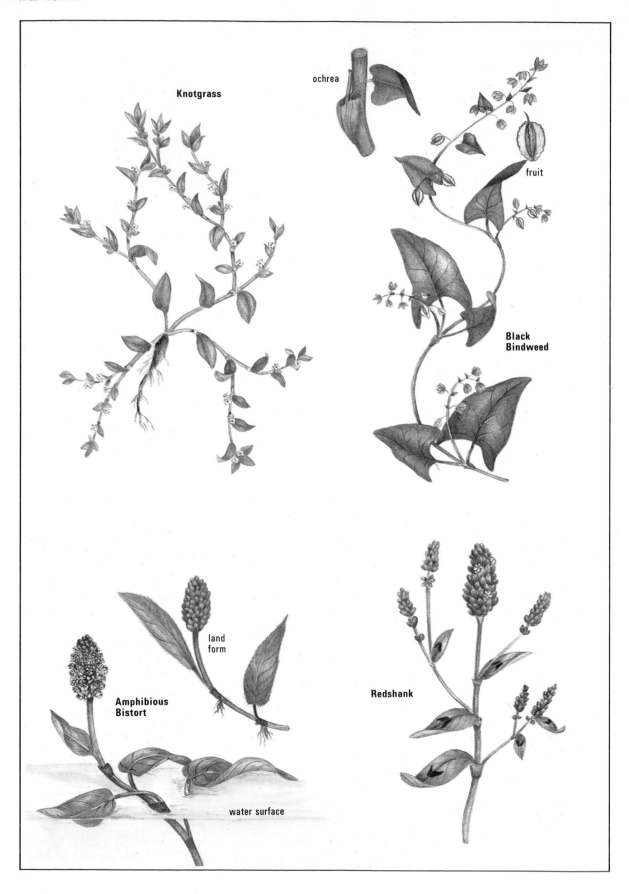

Knotgrass

ochrea

fruit

Black
Bindweed

land
form

Amphibious
Bistort

water surface

Redshank

DOCK FAMILY
Polygonaceae

Most members of this large family are from the northern temperate zone. Useful species include buckwheat and rhubarb. The leaves have a characteristic papery sheath called an ochrea encircling the stem at the leaf-base. The small flowers have no true petals, but the sepals are white, green, or pink and petal-like. The fruit, a small nut enclosed by the persistent flower, is important in identification.

KNOTGRASS
Polygonum aviculare
Knotgrass is a ragged-looking annual, erect (up to 2 m high) or straggling in mats on trampled ground and at the coast. The plant is hairless and branched, and the ochreae are ragged and silvery.
Flower: pink or white; petal-like lobes 5.
Flower arrangement: 1-6 flowers in the leaf-axils.
Flowering time: July-October.
Leaf: elliptic to very narrow, tips more or less pointed, almost stalkless; leaves on main stem larger than branch leaves; ochreae silvery, torn.
Fruit: nut, 3-angled, hidden by dead flower.

BLACK BINDWEED
Polygonum convolvulus
The grooved stem of the climbing Black Bindweed twines clockwise around its support to a height of 30-120 cm. It is an annual growing on waste and cultivated land.
Flower: greenish white; petal-like lobes 5, 3 outer with ridge; each flower stalk 1-2 mm.
Flower arrangement: loose spike or raceme in the leaf-axils.
Flowering time: July-October.
Leaf: spear-shaped, stalked, powdery white beneath, usually alternate; ochrea rim at an angle.
Fruit: nut, dull, black.

AMPHIBIOUS BISTORT
Polygonum amphibium
The stems and leaves of this water plant float on the surface of still or slow-moving water. The stems grow 30-75 cm long and root along their length. A slightly differing form, with short, stiff hairs on the leaves and ochreae, grows at the water's-edge and in damp grassland.
Flower: pink; petal-like lobes 5; stamens 5, red.
Flower arrangement: dense, short spike, 2-4 cm long, stalked.
Flowering time: July-September.
Leaf: long—ovate, hairless, shiny stalked, alternate.
Fruit: nut, shiny, brown.

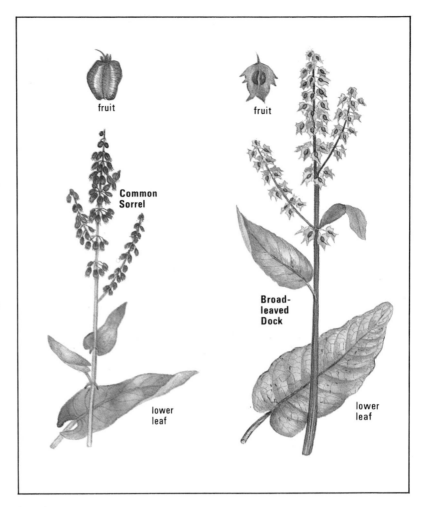

fruit

fruit

Common Sorrel

Broad-leaved Dock

lower leaf

lower leaf

REDSHANK
Polygonum persicaria
The stem, often reddish, is more or less erect, branched and 25-80 cm high. There are dense spikes of tiny pink flowers, and the leaves often bear a dark blotch. The whole plant is almost hairless and grows on waste and cultivated ground. It is an annual.
Flower: pink; petal-like lobes 5.
Flower arrangement: compact spike, up to 3·5 cm long.
Flowering time: June-October.
Leaf: narrow, tapering to point, often dark-blotched; ochreae brownish, fringed with hairs.
Fruit: nut, black, shiny.

COMMON SORREL
Rumex acetosa
Growing up to 100 cm but usually much smaller, this almost hairless plant grows in grassland, to which the flowers and fruits can give a reddish tinge.
Flower: green and red, tiny; male and female flowers on separate plants; wind-pollinated.
Flower arrangement: in whorls on branched raceme.
Flowering time: May-July.

Leaf: spear-shaped, basal lobes pointing down, acid-tasting, up to 10 cm long; upper leaves almost stalkless; ochreae fringed.
Fruit: 3-4 mm, with 3 papery wings, tinged red, enclosing 3-angled nut.
Uses: a sharp-tasting sauce, to be eaten with fish or pork, can be made from the leaves simmered in butter with salt and black pepper.

BROAD-LEAVED DOCK
Rumex obtusifolia
This is a very common dock, 50-120 cm high, of waste places and cultivated land. There are several similar species of dock which can be distinguished by their fruits.
Flower: green, tiny, wind-pollinated.
Flower arrangement: in whorls, on branched raceme.
Flowering time: June-October.
Leaf: oblong, broad, tip pointed or rounded, lobed at base, alternate, up to 25 cm long.
Fruit: 5-6 mm, with 3 green, deeply toothed wings alternating with 3 unequal red swellings enclosing 3-angled nut.
Uses: traditionally dock leaves are rubbed on nettle stings to reduce irritation.

249

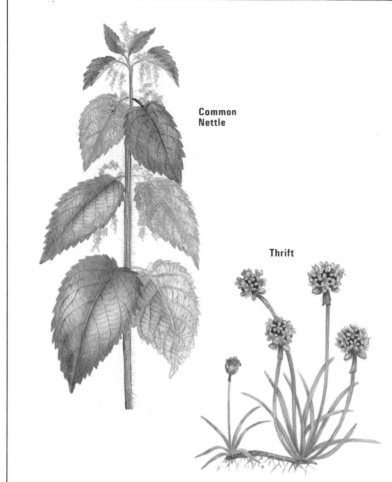

Common
Nettle

Thrift

*Sea lavender turns many salt marshes
lilac in July and August. The domed
heads are formed by hundreds of tiny
pale lilac flowers.*

NETTLE FAMILY
Urticaceae

Stinging hairs crop up in many
members of this family. The
flowers are inconspicuous and
without petals. The stamens are
flicked out as the flowers open,
expelling pollen in puffs.

COMMON NETTLE
Urtica dioica
Notoriously covered in stiff, stinging
hairs, the Common Nettle grows
30-150 cm high in all kinds of disturbed
places. When touched, the hair-tip
breaks off. The remaining hollow
hair injects the skin with fluid
containing an irritant poison.
Flower: green, tiny; male and
female flowers on separate plants
in loose-hanging spikes; wind-pollinated.
Flowering time: June-August.
Leaf: ovate, toothed, opposite, 4-
8 cm long
Uses: In World War II, the tough plant
fibres were made into textiles.

THRIFT FAMILY
Plumbaginaceae

Many members of this family
grow on the coast. The remainder
are alpine, Arctic or desert
species. The flowers have 5 petals
and papery sepals.

THRIFT
Armeria maritima
Thrift forms cushions of narrow
leaves and pink flowers mainly in
rocky places at the seaside, in
salt marshes, or inland on mountains
and sandy places.
Flower: pale to deep pink; petals 5.
Flower arrangement: in dense,
rounded head, 1·5-2·5 cm across;
bracts below, greenish; flower stalk
5-30 cm high, surrounded by brown,
papery sheath above.
Flowering time: April-October.
Leaf: grass-like, slightly fleshy, hairy
or not, 2-15 cm long, up to about
4 mm wide.
Fruit: surrounded by papery calyx.

COMMON SEA LAVENDER
Limonium vulgare
This is a saltmarsh plant growing to
about 40 cm, often turning the marshes
blue with flowers in summer.
Flower: up to 8 mm across, with a
papery pale lilac calyx and 5 purplish-
blue petals: densely clustered on arching spikes to form flat-topped heads.
July-August. Calyx persists after flowering.
Leaf: all from the base; elliptical to
12 cm long; hairless.

HEATHER FAMILY
Ericaceae

As well as heathers and heaths, this family also contains the rhododendrons. The members are small or large shrubs, mainly from temperate areas, with evergreen, often needle-like leaves. The flowers are normally bell-shaped. Most species prefer acid soils, and many have a fungus growing inside the roots.

HEATHER
Calluna vulgaris
This low-growing, wiry shrub grows 15-80 cm high, preferring acid soil and carpeting large tracts of heath, moor and open woods. Heather differs from the similar species of Heath in that the flower petals are not joined into a bell and the leaves are opposite, not whorled.
Flower: mauve, scented; petals 4, hidden by 4 petal-like sepals, about 4 mm long.
Flower arrangement: spikes, 3-15 cm.
Flowering time: July-September.
Leaf: needle-like, opposite, pressed to stem, 1-3·5 mm long, overlapping on short, side shoots.
Fruit: capsule.
Uses: hives of bees are kept on Heather moors in late summer, the resulting honey being particularly good. Heather also feeds sheep and shelters red grouse.

BELL HEATHER
Erica cinerea
Often confused with the previous species, this sprawling under-shrub is abundant on dry heathland in western Europe. The upright stems reach 60 cm and are clothed with short leafy shoots. Less branched and contorted than Heather.
Flower: bell or urn-shaped, 5-6 mm long; deep pink or purple with dark green sepals. In short racemes. July-September.
Leaf: bristle-like, dark green and hairless; 3-6 mm long. In whorls of 3 on the shoots.
Fruit: a many-seeded capsule.

CROSS-LEAVED HEATH
Erica tetralix
This small undershrub is closely related to Bell Heather, but is rarely more than 30 cm high and is less branched. It is a downy plant and favours wet heaths and bogs. It is absent from the drier heathlands.
Flower: pale pink, 6-7 mm long and flask-shaped with a narrow opening; sepals short, green and downy. Borne in small drooping clusters at tips of shoots.
Leaf: greyish and downy, tightly rolled; 2-5 mm long. In whorls of 4 in the shape of a cross.

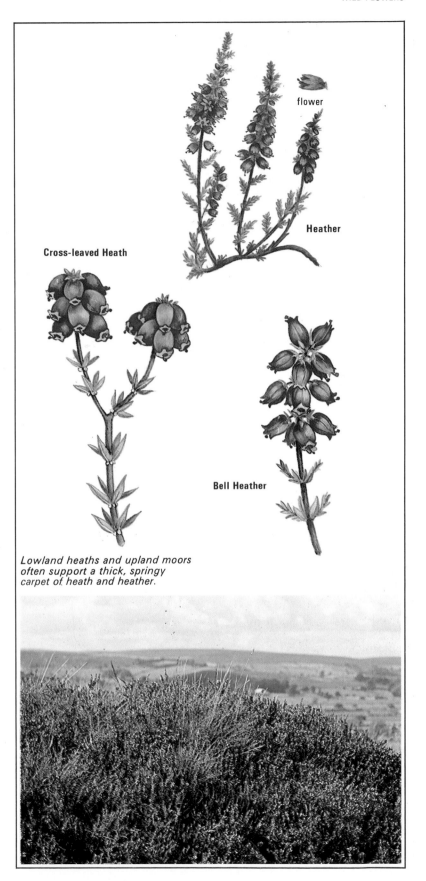

flower

Heather

Cross-leaved Heath

Bell Heather

Lowland heaths and upland moors often support a thick, springy carpet of heath and heather.

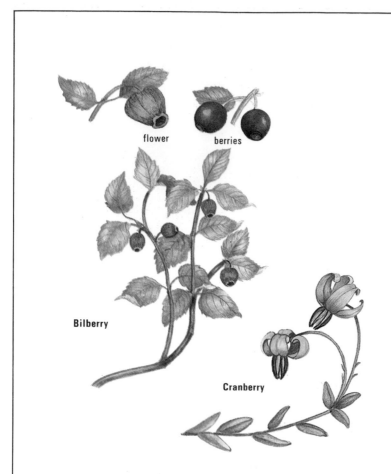

flower

berries

Bilberry

Cranberry

An alpenrose plant, hugging the ground on a windswept scree slope 2,000 metres up in the Alps.

BILBERRY
Vaccinium myrtillus
A low, hairless shrub 15-35 cm high, the Bilberry is known for its sweet, black berries. It grows in woods, and on moors and mountains to an altitude of over 1,200 m. The twigs are 3-angled and green.
Flower: pink, tinged green; petals joined into a globe shape, 4-6 mm.
Flower arrangement: solitary or paired.
Flowering time: April-June.
Leaf: ovate, tip pointed, minutely toothed, bright green, short-stalked, alternate, 1-3 cm long.
Fruit: berry, blue-black, edible.
Uses: the berries are worth the labour of gathering. If too bitter for eating raw then they make good tarts and jam.

CRANBERRY
Vaccinium oxycoccus
This prostrate, creeping evergreen undershrub, a relative of the previous species, grows in acidic bogs, where its thread-like stems creep over the peat and root at intervals.
Flower: drooping, with 4 deep pink petals about 5 mm long and strongly reflexed, leaving the cluster of dark stamens projecting downwards like a beak. Borne singly or in pairs on slender reddish stalks up to 3 cm. June-August.
Leaf: oval, 4-10 mm long, carried alternately on the creeping stems. Dark green above, waxy grey beneath, with margins rolled under.
Fruit: a spherical or pear-shaped berry, 6-8 mm across, red or brown and usually heavily speckled. It is unpalatable when raw but widely used in preserves.

ALPENROSE
Rhododendron ferrugineum
This is a low-growing evergreen shrub of mountain slopes, to an altitude of 3,200 m in the Alps and Pyrenees, mainly on acidic rocks. It grows to a height of 1 m and forms neat, rounded bushes on windswept scree slopes. The bushes may join up to form extensive thickets. The plant also carpets open woodland on the mountains.
Flower: pale pink to deep red, bell-shaped or funnel-shaped about 15 mm long; sepals very short. Borne in small clusters at tips of the branches.
Leaf: elliptic or oblong, 3-5 cm long: dark green above and clothed with reddish-brown scales beneath: margins rolled under.
Fruit: a dry capsule.
The Hairy Alpenrose (*R. hirsutum*), confined to the Alps, is similar but lacks the brown scales under the leaves.

PRIMROSE FAMILY
Primulaceae

This is a large family in which the petals are joined together and often form a tube, as in the primroses themselves. Many species have two kinds of flowers – *pin-eyed*, in which the stigma shows in the throat of the tube with the stamens far below it, and *thrum-eyed* with the stamens in the throat and the stigma below them. Such an arrangement encourages cross-pollination.

PRIMROSE
Primula vulgaris
This much-loved plant grows in grassy places, woods and hedges, flowering before the trees come into leaf and shade the ground.
Flower: pale yellow, deep yellow in throat, 2-3 cm across; petals joined at bases into tube with 5 spreading, notched lobes; calyx tubular, 5-toothed.
Flower arrangement: solitary on long, softly hairy stalks.
Flowering time: December-May.
Leaf: oblong, tip rounded, tapering gradually at base into stalk, wrinkled, shortly hairy beneath.
Fruit: capsule, ovoid, enclosed by calyx.

COWSLIP
Primula veris
Cowslip is only locally common and is decreasing owing to the ploughing of old pasture where it grows. The plants are 5-30 cm high.
Flower: pale or deep yellow, orange in throat, nodding; petals joined at bases into tube with 5 notched lobes; calyx tubular, pale green, 5-toothed.
Flower arrangement: 1-30 drooping flowers in umbel-like cluster on shortly hairy stalk.
Flowering time: April-May.
Leaf: oblong, rounded at tip, abruptly narrowed into stalk, wrinkled, shortly hairy all over.
Fruit: capsule, ovoid, hidden by calyx.

BIRD'S-EYE PRIMROSE
Primula farinosa
This beautiful little plant grows in moist meadows in upland regions of northern England and Scandinavia and on damp mountain slopes elsewhere in Europe. It grows to 20 cm.
Flower: pink or purple, occasionally white, with a yellow eye; about 1 cm across. Grouped into a loose umbel at the top of a mealy white stem (mealiness may disappear from older stems). May-July.
Leaf: spatula-shaped, 1-5 cm long, lightly toothed; light green above, densely mealy white below.
Fruit: a small capsule.

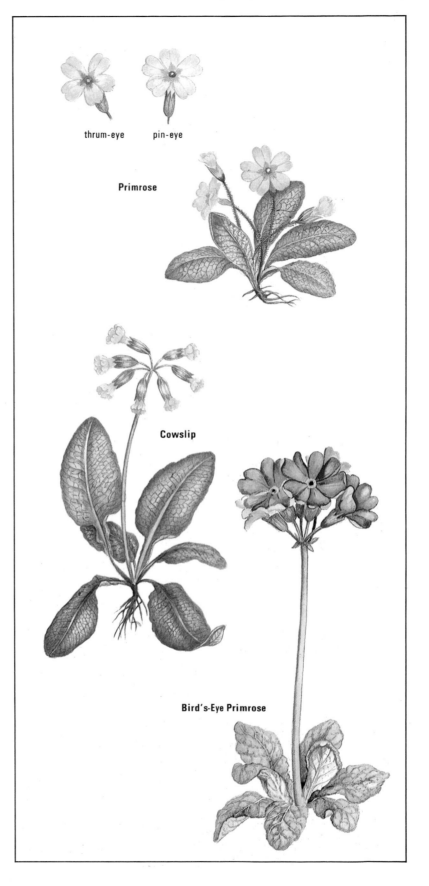

thrum-eye   pin-eye

Primrose

Cowslip

Bird's-Eye Primrose

253

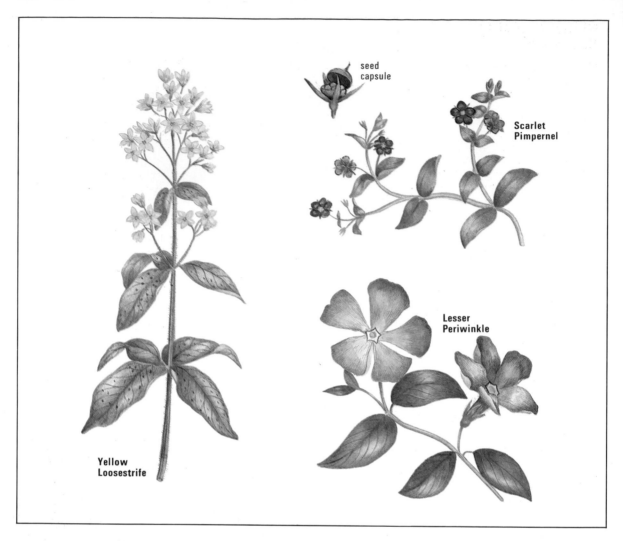

seed capsule

Scarlet Pimpernel

Lesser Periwinkle

Yellow Loosestrife

YELLOW LOOSESTRIFE
Lysimachia vulgaris
The tall, erect, shortly hairy plants of Yellow Loosestrife grow 60-150 cm high. They are found along riversides and other damp places. This species is absent from N. Scotland, Sweden and much of Norway.
Flower: yellow, about 1.5 cm across; petals 5; sepals 5, orange-margined.
Flower arrangement: in loose, branched heads.
Flowering time: July-August.
Leaf: long, narrow, pointed, in pairs or whorls of 3 or 4; stalkless, dotted with black glands.
Fruit: capsule, spherical, opening by 5 valves.

SCARLET PIMPERNEL
Anagallis arvensis
One of the very few scarlet-flowered plants native to N. Europe, the Scarlet Pimpernel reaches 30 cm on dry grassland and as an annual weed on cultivated ground.
Flower: scarlet or salmon pink, rarely blue, up to 14 mm across;

petals 5, more or less rounded; sepals 5, sharply pointed.
Flower arrangement: on thin stalks, longer than leaves, arising from each leaf-axil.
Flowering time: June-August.
Leaf: ovate, pointed, opposite, stalkless, black glands beneath.
Fruit: capsule, spherical, with persistent style, splitting around middle.
Uses: the flowers can be used to tell the time and approaching weather. They open from about 8 am to 3 pm and close in the damp, cool air of impending rain.

PERIWINKLE FAMILY
Apocynaceae

Members of this large family are mainly tall rain-forest trees of the tropics. The rest are shrubs and woody climbers, or herbs in northern Europe, with a milky, often poisonous latex, used in the tropics to tip arrows for hunting.

LESSER PERIWINKLE
Vinca minor
This species has long been grown in gardens. It has escaped and become naturalized in shady places but is truly native in many parts of Europe, where it is common on the floor of many woodlands. Probably native in Britain only in the south.
It is an evergreen plant with long, rooting stems of 30-60 cm covering the ground.
Flower: blue-purple or white, 2.5-3 cm across; petals 5, wide and blunt at tip, joined at base; calyx tube 5-toothed, hairless.
Flower arrangement: solitary, stalked, in leaf-axil.
Flowering time: March-May.
Leaf: elliptic, opposite, glossy, hairless, short-stalked.
Fruit: pair of follicles, rarely ripening in Britain, forked at tip.
The Greater Periwinkle (*V. major*) is very similar but its trailing stems root only at their tips. The flowers are 4-5 cm across with fringed sepals: up to 4 flowers at each node of the stem.

GENTIAN FAMILY
Gentianaceae

Many of the species in this family grow in arctic regions and on mountains. They are nearly all herbaceous plants and their leaves are quite hairless. The flowers, of 5 joined petals, are often blue, bell-shaped or trumpet-shaped, and erect. The Gentian family is one in which a fungus commonly lives within the roots, benefitting both plant and fungus. The bitter roots have been much used medicinally.

COMMON CENTAURY
Centaurium erythraea

Common Centaury varies between 2 and 50 cm high, with a branched stem bearing flat clusters of pink flowers. It is a hairless plant growing in dry grassland and dunes. It is an annual.
Flower: rose-pink, 1-1·5 cm across; petals joined into tube below; lobes 5, spreading flat; calyx with 5 long, narrow teeth.
Flower arrangement: in more or less flat-topped clusters.
Flowering time: June-October.
Leaf: opposite, basal leaves in rosette; elliptic, tip rounded or pointed, stalkless.
Fruit: capsule.
Uses: Common Centaury has been called Gall of the Earth due to its bitterness. A tonic can be made from an infusion of dried plants.

SPRING GENTIAN
Gentiana verna

This intensely blue gentian, one of several similar species, is found mainly on the mountains, although it occurs (rarely) at lower altitudes in Britain and Ireland. It prefers calcareous soils, where it displays sheets of blue flowers on the screes and grasslands as soon as the snows melt. Absent from northern Europe.
Flower: deep blue, with a tube up to 2·5 cm long and 5 oval lobes spreading star-like to 2 cm across. Borne singly on stems to 6 cm high. March-August.
Leaf: bright green and leathery: oval to 15 mm long. In a dense rosette, with a few smaller leaves on the flowering stems.

TRUMPET GENTIAN
Gentiana acaulis

This is one of the most striking gentians and a favourite species for the rock garden. It grows in the Alps, Pyrenees, and Apennines, reaching altitudes of 3,000 m. Preferring acidic rocks, it grows in turf and stony places, especially where there is plenty of moisture.

Spring Gentian

Common Centaury

The trumpet gentian grows in damp mountain pastures, especially close to rocks. The deep blue flowers often open before all the snow has gone from the higher slopes.

Flower: a deep, erect trumpet up to 7 cm tall, with 5 spreading, pointed lobes. Deep, bright blue with patches of green spots around the throat. Carried singly on leafy stalks up to 5 cm long. May-August.
Leaf: dark and slightly greyish green; elliptical to 15 cm long: in a loose rosette.

FORGET-ME-NOT FAMILY
Boraginaceae

Members of this family are almost always hairy, often stiffly so. The blue or mauve, sometimes white, flowers are very often pink in bud and arranged in one-sided cymes which uncoil as the flowers open.

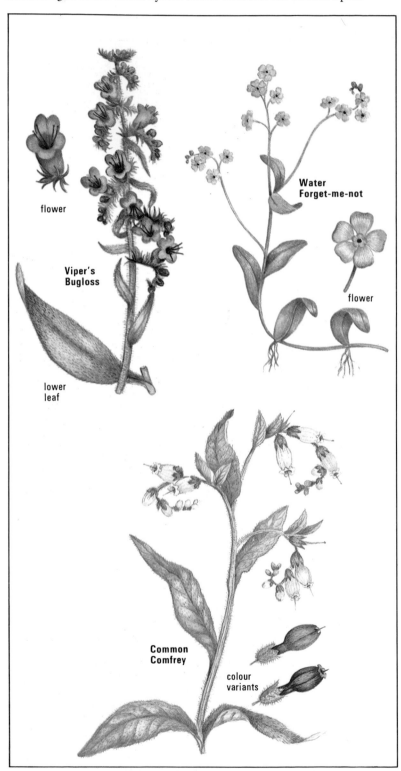

flower

Viper's Bugloss

lower leaf

Water Forget-me-not

flower

Common Comfrey

colour variants

WATER FORGET-ME-NOT
Myosotis scorpioides
Growing in damp or wet places, this forget-me-not has a slightly ridged, hairy stem, 15-45 cm high, the base of which often creeps and roots. The important characteristics of this species are the flower size and the notched petal-lobes. Several similar species, annual or perennial, grow on the drier soils of woods and fields.
Flower: sky-blue, yellow in throat, 4-10 mm across; petals joined into tube at base; lobes 5, shallowly notched; calyx 5-toothed with straight hairs; buds pink.
Flower arrangement: cyme, uncoiling as flowers open, without bracts.
Flowering time: May-September.
Leaf: oblong, usually rounded at tip, stalkless, shortly hairy or almost hairless.
Fruit: 4 nutlets, black, shiny, enclosed by calyx.

VIPER'S BUGLOSS
Echium vulgare
An erect, stout biennial, 20-90 cm tall and densely covered in stiff, whitish hairs with swollen bases, Viper's Bugloss has bright blue flowers, pink in bud, forming an exciting colour combination. It grows in dry places and is common on roadsides in many sandy areas.
Flower: bright blue, 1-2 cm; petals joined into tube at base; 5-lobed; calyx 5-toothed; stamens 5, 4 protruding.
Flower arrangement: a panicle of short, curved or coiled cymes.
Flowering time: June-September.
Leaf: lanceolate, tapering gradually to base, up to 15 cm long, stalkless, lowest shortly stalked.
Fruit: 4 nutlets, enclosed by calyx.
Uses: this plant was linked from ancient Greek times with snakes. The nutlet, supposed to resemble a snake's head, was consequently used to treat snake bite.

COMMON COMFREY
Symphytum officinale
Common Comfrey is a branched, stout, stiffly hairy plant of 30-120 cm. The stem has thin prominent ridges, and the plant grows in damp places.
Flower: cream, white, pink or purple, 15-17 mm long; petals joined into tube with 5 short lobes at rim; calyx 5-toothed; style protruding from petal-tube.
Flower arrangement: in nodding cymes, uncoiling as flowers open.
Flowering time: May-June.
Leaf: ovate to lanceolate, tip pointed, bases running down stem in thin, often wavy ridges.
Fruit: 4 nutlets, black, shiny, enclosed by calyx, style persistent.
Uses: in Bavaria the young leaves are fried in batter. Manure water to feed tomato or marrow crops can also be made by soaking Comfrey plants in water for a week. The resulting water is rich in potassium.

Hedge Bindweed

Field Bindweed

The common dodder smothering a gorse bush with a tangled mass of slender, food-stealing stems.

BINDWEED FAMILY
Convolvulaceae

The flowers in this family are bell- or trumpet-shaped on stems which often climb by twining. The sap is quite often milky

HEDGE BINDWEED
Calystegia sepium
This climbing bindweed covers such supports as railings and hedges with a blanket of arrow-shaped leaves and large, white trumpet-shaped flowers. These are visited at dusk by hawk moths. The stems grow 1-3 m long, twisting anti-clockwise.
Flower: white, trumpet-shaped, 3-4 cm across, scentless; sepals 5, enclosed by 2 slightly longer bracts.
Flower arrangement: solitary, on long stalks.

Flowering time: July-September.
Leaf: arrow-shaped, up to 15 cm long, stalked, shortly hairy or not.
Fruit: capsule, enclosed by bracts.
Great Bindweed (*C. sylvatica*) is similar but flowers to 7·5 cm across and swollen bracts hide sepals.

FIELD BINDWEED
Convolvulus arvensis
The invasive rhizomes make this little creeping or climbing plant a stubborn weed of farm and garden. The stem coils anti-clockwise.
Flower: pink or white, striped darker outside, trumpet-shaped, 1·5-3 cm across, scented; sepals 5.
Flower arrangement: 1-3 flowers on long stalk with 2 small bracts half-way up.
Flowering time: June-September.
Leaf: arrow-shaped, 2-5 cm long, stalked, shortly hairy or not.
Fruit: capsule, spherical.

COMMON DODDER
Cuscuta epithymum
This is a parasitic annual quite devoid of chlorophyll. A hair-like red stem 0·1 mm thick emerges from the minute seed and creeps over the ground. If it meets a suitable host plant – a wide variety of herbs and small shrubs will do – it begins to climb and soon sends tiny suckers into the host to absorb food. The dodder stem can then grow rapidly and branch repeatedly until it may completely smother the host, although the stems do not get much thicker. The plant is most common on heathland.
Flower: minute and bell-shaped; pale pink and scented. In dense clusters up to 1 cm across. July-September.
Leaf: reduced to minute red scales on the stem.
Greater Dodder (*C. europaea*) is a little larger (stems 1 mm thick) and usually found on stinging nettles.

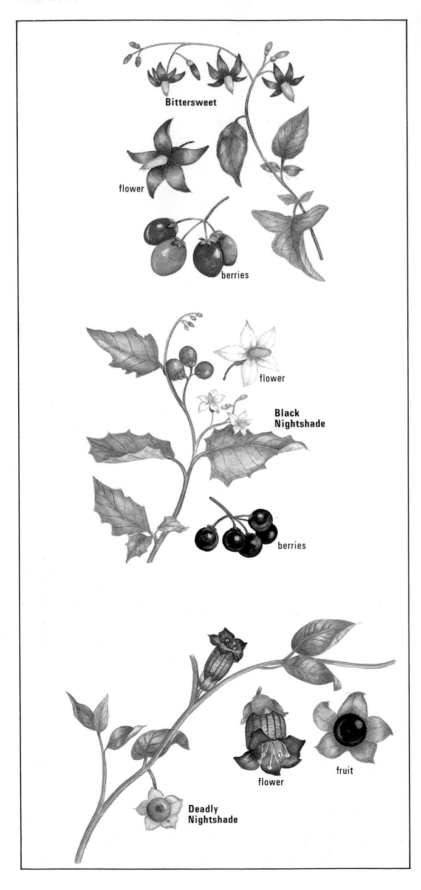

Bittersweet

flower

berries

flower

Black
Nightshade

berries

flower

fruit

Deadly
Nightshade

POTATO FAMILY
Solanaceae

Most of the 2,000 or so species in this family come from the tropics. They include many important food plants, such as the potato and tomato. Red peppers, chillis, and tobacco also belong to this family. Many species are poisonous, including Henbane, Thorn-apple and the night-shades. The flowers often have a central cone of yellow anthers. The fruits are usually berries.

BITTERSWEET
Solanum dulcamara
The small, purple flowers, each with a cone of yellow anthers, are unmistakeable. The plant is mildly poisonous and climbs 30-200 cm high in hedges, woods or waste places. It is also called Woody Night-shade.
Flower: purple, with central cone of yellow anthers, 1-1·5 cm across; petals 5, pointed.
Flower arrangement: cyme.
Flowering time: June-September.
Leaf: ovate, pointed, stalked, with or without 1-4 lobes at base.
Fruit: berry, poisonous, shiny, ovoid, green when unripe, becoming yellow, then red.

BLACK NIGHTSHADE
Solanum nigrum
This annual is poisonous. The plant is hairless or with short hairs and grows up to 60 cm high on waste and cultivated land.
Flower: white, with central cone of yellow anthers, about 5 mm across; petals 5, pointed.
Flower arrangement: cyme.
Flowering time: July-September.
Leaf: ovate or diamond-shaped, pointed, stalked, toothed or not.
Fruit: berry, poisonous, black.

DEADLY NIGHTSHADE
Atropa bella-donna
This uncommon, highly poisonous, narcotic plant grows in dry places on chalk or limestone. It is stout, branched and grows up to 150 cm high.
Flower: lurid violet or greenish, 2·5-3 cm, nodding, bell-shaped, lobes pointed; sepals pointed.
Flower arrangement: solitary.
Flowering time: June-August.
Leaf: alternate, ovate, up to 20 cm.
Fruit: berry, 1·5-2 cm across, shiny, black, surrounded by persistent calyx.
Uses: the poisonous and medicinal properties of this plant have long been known. An infusion of plant juice was formerly dropped in women's eyes causing dilation of the pupils to produce a 'wide-eyed' look, hence the name *bella-donna* (beautiful lady).

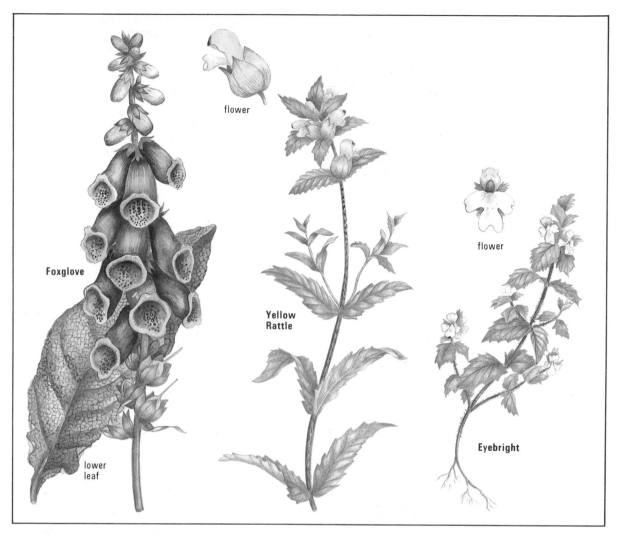

flower

Foxglove

lower leaf

Yellow Rattle

flower

Eyebright

FOXGLOVE FAMILY
Scrophulariaceae

This large family contains about 3,000 species, most of which are native to the northern temperate regions. All the European species are herbaceous plants. Some species are semi-parasites, mainly attacking grasses. The flowers are usually tubular and irregular, with two lips, and they often attract specialist insect pollinators. The fruits are many-seeded capsules and the seeds are often extremely small. The mint family (page 263) has some similar flowers, but the stems are square in section and the fruits are quite different. Many members of the foxglove family are cultivated in gardens. The snapdragons are good examples.

FOXGLOVE
Digitalis purpurea
The upright, softly hairy Foxglove plants with their spikes of purple bells are easy to recognize. They prefer acid soils and grow in open woodland, heaths and field borders. Children poke their fingers in the flowers to make a wish.
Flower: pinkish purple, sometimes white, 4-5 cm long, bell-shaped, shallowly 5-lobed, spotted and whiskery within; sepals 5.
Flower arrangement: long spike.
Flowering time: June-September.
Leaf: ovate, blunt-toothed, softly hairy above, woolly beneath; narrow border on each side of leaf-stalk.
Fruit: capsule, ovoid, with long, persistent style.
Uses: Foxgloves are still cultivated for the heart drug digitalin.

YELLOW RATTLE
Rhinanthus minor
This annual is semi-parasitic on grasses, amongst which it grows. The stem may be branched, 10-50 cm high and marked with black.
Flower: yellow, 1-1·5 cm long, tubular, 2-lipped, teeth of upper lip purple; calyx 4-toothed, inflated.
Flower arrangement: crowded with leaf-like bracts at top of stems.
Flowering time: May-August.
Leaf: oblong to lanceolate, toothed, opposite, stalkless, rough to touch.
Fruit: formed from enlarged calyx in which ripe seeds rattle.

EYEBRIGHT
Euphrasia officinalis
The eyebrights are extremely difficult to tell apart. The following description covers a group of species. All are semi-parasites on grasses and grow 1-40 cm high in grassy places. The stems are hairy and branched. The plants are annuals.
Flower: white or mauve, with yellow and purple marks; 2-lipped, lower lip of 3 notched lobes; calyx 4-toothed; bracts leaf-like.
Flower arrangement: in leaf-axils.
Flowering time: May-September.
Leaf: circular or oval, deeply toothed.
Fruit: capsule, fringed with hairs.
Uses: this little plant was used in the past to treat eye disorders.

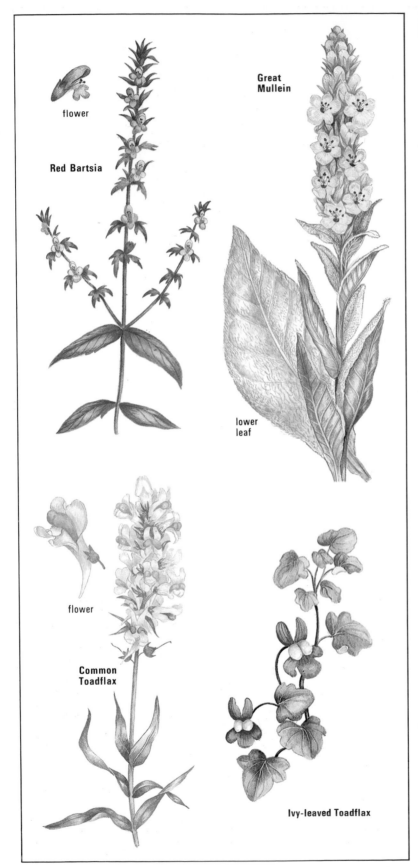

flower

Red Bartsia

Great Mullein

lower leaf

flower

Common Toadflax

Ivy-leaved Toadflax

RED BARTSIA
Odontites verna
This is a semi-parasitic annual, much branched and downy. It grows to 50 cm in grassland, on waste land, and on the margins of cultivated fields. It obtains water and minerals from the roots of grasses.
Flower: purple-pink, about 1 cm, tubular; 2-lipped, lower lip 3-lobed; calyx of 4 teeth; bracts leaf-like.
Flower arrangement: in spikes, flowers pointing one way.
Flowering time: June-August.
Leaf: lanceolate, toothed, opposite, stalkless. Often tinged with maroon.
Fruit: capsule, seeds ridged.

GREAT MULLEIN
Verbascum thapsus
The leaves and stem of this tall biennial are thickly covered in white wool. It grows in dry, waste places and chalk grassland.
Flower: yellow, 1·5-3 cm across; petals 5, rounded, joined at base; sepals 5, pointed; 3 stamens covered with pale hairs, 2 hairless.
Flower arrangement: tall, dense spike.
Flowering time: June-August.
Leaf: oblong, pointed or rounded at tip; base running down stem as narrow border; basal leaves in rosette.
Fruit: capsule, enclosed by sepals; seeds tiny.

COMMON TOADFLAX
Linaria vulgaris
The flowers look like miniature yellow garden Snapdragons, to which Toadflax is related. Nectar is stored in the long spur behind the flower, accessible only to long-tongued bees. The plant is almost hairless, 30-80 cm high and grows along hedges and in grassy places.
Flower: yellow, top part of lower lip orange; 1·5-2·5 cm long; 2-lipped; spur almost straight; sepals 5, pointed.
Flower arrangement: dense raceme.
Flowering time: June-October.
Leaf: narrow, strap-shaped, pointed, alternate, 3-8 cm long, grey-green beneath.
Fruit: capsule, ovoid; seeds winged.
Uses: the plant is said to make a good fly poison if boiled in milk, the milk serving as an attractant.

IVY-LEAVED TOADFLAX
Cymbalaria muralis
This attractive little plant is a native of the Mediterranean region, but now established throughout Europe. It is a hairless trailing plant that grows best on dry rocks and walls.
Flower: 8-10 mm across; lilac with a white swelling (the palate) on lower lip and a yellow spot at the mouth. Borne singly on slender curving stalks. May-September.
Leaf: shiny green above, often purplish below: shaped like a tiny ivy leaf, about 2·5 cm across.

flower

flower

Common Figwort

Brooklime

Germander Speedwell

flower

COMMON FIGWORT
Scrophularia nodosa
This is a rather tall, hairless plant growing in wet woods and ditches. The stem is 4-angled. The dull maroon flowers smelling of decay attract wasps by mimicking carrion. Normally 40-80 cm high, the plant may reach a height of about 1 m.
Flower: upper part maroon, lower green, 1 cm long; 5-lobed, upper 2 slightly longer; sepals 5, rounded.
Flower arrangement: branched clusters with sticky hairs on the flower stalks.
Flowering time: June-September.
Leaf: ovate, pointed, toothed, opposite, 6-13 cm long.
Fruit: capsule, ovoid, pointed.
Uses: the knobs on the rhizomes were taken as signs that this plant cured both piles and goitre.

BROOKLIME
Veronica beccabunga
Both stem and leaves of this water-loving plant are hairless and rather fleshy. The bases of the hollow stems creep and root in wet mud or shallow fresh water. The plant reaches a height of about 60 cm.
Flower: blue, 5-8 mm across; petals 4, upper petal larger than lower 3; sepals 4; stamens 2.
Flower arrangement: racemes in leaf-axils.
Flowering time: May-September.
Leaf: circular to oval, opposite, slightly fleshy, shiny, blunt-toothed, short-stalked.
Fruit: capsule, spherical, slightly notched.
Uses: the sharp-tasting leaves have been eaten as a substitute for Water-cress.

GERMANDER SPEEDWELL
Veronica chamaedrys
Common in grassy places, hedges and woods, this small speedwell grows 7-25 cm high. The stem, with its 2 lines of hairs, lies along the ground, rooting at intervals and turning up at the tip. Speedwell flowers characteristically drop from the calyx at the lightest touch.
Flower: bright blue, white circle at centre, 1 cm across; petals 4, upper largest; sepals 4; bracts shorter than or equalling individual flower stalks; stamens 2.
Flower arrangement: raceme springing from leaf-axil.
Flowering time: March-July.
Leaf: oval, blunt-toothed, hairy, shortly stalked or stalkless.
Fruit: capsule, heart-shaped, hairy, shorter than sepals.

BROOMRAPE FAMILY
Orobanchaceae

Members of this family are total parasites, without chlorophyll and drawing all their food supplies from the roots of various host plants. Stems and flowers are usually brown, yellow, or pinkish. Flowers are tubular and 2-lipped. Fruit is a capsule with numerous tiny seeds.

COMMON BROOMRAPE
Orobanche minor
One of several rather similar plants, which are best distinguished by their host plants and by the colour of their stigma lobes, this spiky annual is often abundant on roadside verges and other rough grassland. It parasitizes clovers and other legumes and also various composites. The upright pinkish-brown stem reaches 50 cm.
Flower: up to 18 mm long, yellowish brown with purple veins and spots: tube strongly and smoothly curved: stigma lobes purple. Clustered into a dense spike (sometimes just a few flowers). May-July, or even later.
Leaf: simple brown scales on stem.

BUTTERWORT FAMILY
Lentibulariaceae

The members of this small family are insectivorous plants of water and wet places. The flowers are 2-lipped, with a prominent spur. Apart from the butterworts, the family contains the bladderworts – rootless water plants which have suction traps to catch small animals.

COMMON BUTTERWORT
Pinguicula vulgaris
This is a plant of wet heaths and moors and damp rocky places in general. It grows mainly in upland regions.
Flower: up to 12 mm wide: violet coloured and often mistaken for a violet when seen without the leaves; a white patch in the throat, and lower lip split into 3 lobes. Borne singly on slender, leafless stems up to 15 cm. May-July.
Leaf: pale yellowish green; elongated oval to 8 cm long. Margins inrolled. Forming a neat, flat rosette. Leaf surface covered with minute glands exuding a sticky fluid which traps insects and digests them. Leaf rosette dies in autumn and plant passes winter as a rootless bud just under the ground.

Above left: Common broomrape flowers in June and July, but its papery dead stems stand until well into winter.
Left: Common butterwort growing on an upland moor. There may be several flower stalks.

MINT FAMILY
Labiatae

This large family contains about 3,500 species, concentrated in the Mediterranean region. Many members are aromatic and they include many popular kitchen herbs, such as Sage, Marjoram, and Thyme, as well as the mints. The stems are square in cross section and the leaves are in opposite pairs. The flowers are borne in whorls. The calyx is funnel-shaped and the petals are joined into an irregular, 2-lipped tube. The ovary is 4-lobed, each lobe producing a 1-seeded nutlet deep in the persistent calyx. Chemicals called terpenes are found in the family and they often suppress the growth of surrounding plants.

WATER MINT
Mentha aquatica
The often reddish stems of Water Mint are erect, rising from a creeping underground stem, and 15-90 cm tall. Water Mint grows in wet places.
Flower: mauve; petals 4; calyx 5-toothed, hairy; stamens long with red anthers.
Flower arrangement: shoots ending in dense, rounded heads of 1-3
Flowering time: July-October.
Leaf: ovate, teeth blunt or pointed, opposite, more or less hairy, stalked; if growing in water, the submerged leaves are rounded, toothless.
Fruit: 4 nutlets, smooth.
Uses: as with many other mints, Water Mint has been used as a stomach medicine and as a herb for strewing on floors of houses.

MARJORAM
Origanum vulgare
This is a plant of dry places on chalk or limestone, smelling aromatic when crushed, due to tiny translucent oil-filled glands on the leaves, seen if held to the light. The 4-angled stems, 30-80 cm long, are erect and branched in the upper parts.
Flower: mauve, 6-8 mm across; 4-lobed; calyx 5-toothed; stamens 4; bracts often purple.
Flower arrangement: in flat-topped or rounded clusters.
Flowering time: July-September.
Leaf: ovate, opposite, slightly toothed or not, short-stalked.
Fruit: 4 nutlets, each ovoid.
Uses: this native species is more pungent than the cultivated, frost-tender species from the Mediterranean used in cooking. Tea can be made from the dried leaves.

GROUND IVY
Glechoma hederacea
Many species in the mint family have purplish, 2-lipped flowers, all looking rather similar. Ground Ivy is distinguished by having only 2-5 flowers in each whorl and the top petal-lobe being flat, not hooded. Creeping and rooting, it grows in woods and waste places.
Flower: pale violet, 1·5-2 cm long; 2-lipped, upper lip flat, not hooded, lower purple-spotted; calyx 5-toothed.
Flower arrangement: in loose whorls, directed to one side.
Flowering time: March-May.
Leaf: kidney-shaped to almost circular, blunt-toothed, often tinged purple, opposite, long-stalked.
Fruit: 4 nutlets, smooth.

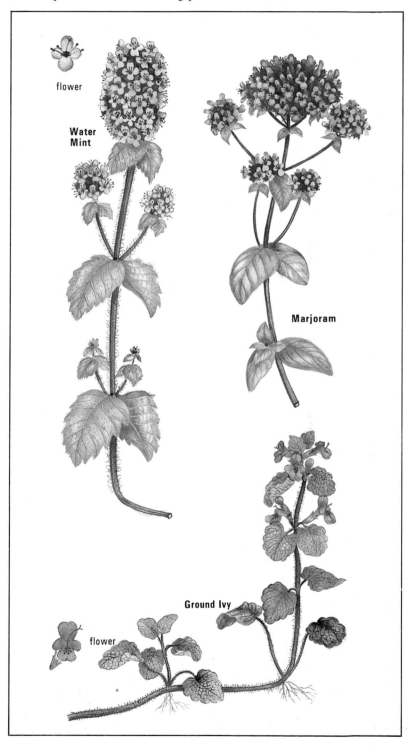

flower

Water Mint

Marjoram

Ground Ivy

flower

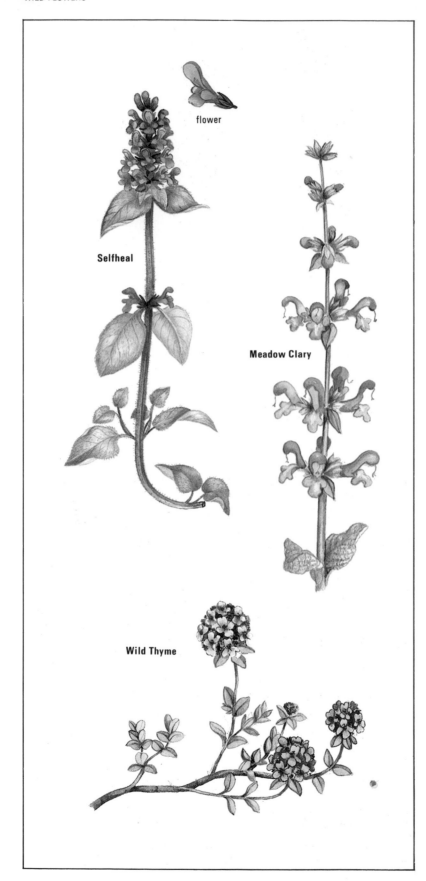

flower

Selfheal

Meadow Clary

Wild Thyme

SELFHEAL
Prunella vulgaris
Selfheal is a low-growing, slightly hairy plant of grassland, often tinged purple. The stem is 4-angled, creeping in the lower part and ending in an oblong head of flowers. The plant has no smell when crushed.
Flower: violet, 1-1·5 cm long; 2-lipped, upper lip hooded, lower 3-lobed; calyx of 5 teeth in 2 lips; bract beneath each flower almost circular, hairy and purplish.
Flower arrangement: in oblong or squat head at top of stem, pair of leaves immediately beneath.
Flowering time: June-September.
Leaf: ovate, tip pointed, 2-5 cm long, shallowly toothed or not, opposite, stalked.
Fruit: 4 nutlets, each oblong.

MEADOW CLARY
Salvia pratensis
This hairy and slightly aromatic plant, a relative of the cultivated Sage, grows in rough, calcareous grassland. Confined to the most westerly parts of Europe, from Denmark southwards, it is most abundant in France. It reaches a height of 1 m.
Flower: brilliant blue, up to 2·5 cm long, with a strongly curved upper lip forming a distinct hood: stamens and style project beyond petals. Borne in whorls on stiff, leafless stems. June-July. Some plants carry only female flowers.
Leaf: basal leaves up to 15 cm long, in a rosette: oval to lanceolate and very wrinkled. Stem leaves smaller, the upper ones stalkless.
Fruit: 4 smooth triangular nutlets. Wild Clary (*S. horminoides*) of France and southern Britain is similar, but flowers are more purplish-blue with shorter style: leaves are more jagged.

WILD THYME
Thymus drucei
A small relative of the true Thyme (*Thymus vulgaris*) which is used in cooking, this creeping plant has wiry stems and forms thick carpets in dry grassland — where it very commonly covers ant hills — and on dunes and rocks. It rarely exceeds 7 cm in height. The species may be separated from several other very similar plants by looking at the upright shoots: they are very hairy on 2 opposite sides and almost hairless on the other 2 sides. Large Thyme (*T. pulegioides*) is hairy only on the angles of the stem, while Breckland Thyme (*T. serpyllum*) is hairy all round the stem.
Flower: pink or purple; 3-5 mm across, with stamens protruding well beyond petal tube. In small whorls at the top of upright shoots. May-August.
Leaf: oval, 4-8 mm long: dark shining green and sometimes hairy.
Fruit: smooth ovoid nutlets.

LAVENDER
Lavandula angustifolia
This is a low-growing, much branched shrub famed for its aromatic oils which are widely used in perfumes. It is a native of southern Europe, where it grows on dry, rocky hillsides, usually on limestone. It reaches heights of about 75 cm. It is cultivated in large fields for the perfume industry, the strongly-scented flowers being gathered just as they begin to open. They are then distilled to yield lavender oil. The bushes are regularly trimmed into neat domes about 50 cm high to encourage fresh new shoots. Lavender is also a popular garden plant in many parts of Europe.
Flower: purplish-blue (lavender), 3-5 mm across: upper lip not hooded. Calyx tubular and grey-green. Borne in dense oblong spikes at the top of downy, grey-green stems. June-August.
Leaf: grey-green and downy, more or less linear: up to 4 cm long.

FRENCH LAVENDER
Lavandula stoechas
This much-branched, strongly-scented undershrub is a close relative of the Common Lavender, but often develops into larger and more straggly bushes. Another native of the Mediterranean region, it thrives on dry, stony hillsides. It is often a major associate of the cork oak trees on the acidic soils of southeast France. It reaches about 1 m. The flowers are sometimes gathered to provide oil for perfumes.
Flower: individual flowers are similar to those of the Common Lavender, grouped into dense oblong spikes, but the top of each spike carries a number of large purple bracts which help to attract insects to the spikes. Smaller bracts among the flowers are papery and purplish-green. April-July.
Leaf: greyish-green and velvety: more or less linear to about 4 cm.

YELLOW ARCHANGEL
Galeobdolon luteum
This rather stiff and hairy plant, a close relative of the White Deadnettle, is found in woodlands and shady hedgebanks on rich, damp soils, especially in calcareous regions. It reaches a height of about 60 cm. Long creeping runners spread out and take root in all directions, producing extensive patches of the plant, often with little else growing amongst it.
Flower: about 2 cm long, with upper lip forming a distinct hood: bright yellow with rust-coloured streaks on the 3-lobed lower lip. Borne in open whorls, well separated on upper parts of stem.
Leaf: 4-7 cm long, oval and coarsely toothed.
Fruit: 4 triangular nutlets, concealed, as in all labiates, deep in the persistent calyx.

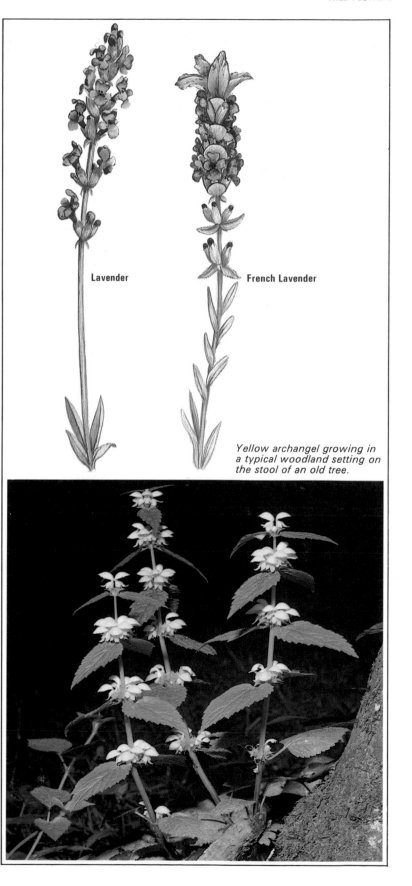

Lavender

French Lavender

Yellow archangel growing in a typical woodland setting on the stool of an old tree.

RED DEAD-NETTLE
Lamium purpureum

Red Dead-nettle is a softly hairy weed of cultivated ground. It has a 4-angled stem and grows 10-45 cm high. It is an annual, branching freely from the base. Dead-nettles, as the name implies, have no stinging hairs.

Flower: mauve-purple, 1-1·5 cm long; 2-lipped, upper hooded, lower spotted; ring of hairs near flower base; calyx 5-toothed.

Flower arrangement: in dense whorls with leaf-like bracts.

Flowering time: March-October.

Leaf: ovate to almost circular, blunt-toothed, often tinged purple, surface puckered, opposite, stalked.

Fruit: 4 nutlets, 3-angled.

WHITE DEAD-NETTLE
Lamium album

Although a very common plant of waste places and roadsides, the tight whorls of plump-looking, pure white flowers make this an attractive plant. The 4-angled stem is un-branched, hairy and 20-80 cm high. Unlike the Red Dead-nettle, this species is a perennial plant and has a mat of creeping rhizomes which spread through the soil and throw up new shoots to produce dense clumps.

This dead-nettle is not related to the Common Nettle and does not sting,

although the leaves are similar.

Flower: white, 2-2·5 cm long; 2-lipped, upper lip pronouncedly hooded, hairy, lower lip with 2 or 3 short teeth each side; calyx with 5 narrow, pointed teeth.

Flower arrangement: in compact whorls.

Flowering time: May-December.

Leaf: ovate, tapering to point, coarsely toothed, opposite, stalked.

Fruit: 4 nutlets, 3-angled.

Uses: country children have made whistles out of the hollow stems and they also enjoy sucking nectar from the flowers.

A closely related species (*L. maculatum*), whose leaf blades commonly bear a large white blotch, is often cultivated in gardens. It has pinkish flowers.

COMMON HEMP-NETTLE
Galeopsis tetrahit

The branched, roughly hairy stem has red or yellow glandular hairs and is swollen where the leaf stalks join. The swellings contain special cells to enable the plant to make slight movements. This plant is 10-100 cm tall and found on cultivated land, less often in damp places. It is an annual.

Flower: mauve with darker markings, occasionally white or pale yellow, 1·5-2 cm long; 2-lipped,

upper lip hooded, lower 3-lobed, middle lobe notched or not; calyx with 5 narrow teeth.

Flower arrangement: in whorls.

Flowering time: July-September.

Leaf: ovate, tapering to point, blunt-toothed, stalked, blue-green.

Fruit: 4 nutlets, 3-angled.

HEDGE WOUNDWORT
Stachys sylvatica

The tough stems of this rather tall plant are roughly hairy and 4-angled. The plant grows 30-120 cm high in the shadier parts of hedgerows. and also in woods and waste places. If crushed the whole plant, in particular the creeping, underground stem, gives off a foul smell.

Flower: light maroon with white marks, 1-1·5 cm; 2-lipped; calyx with 5 narrow teeth and glandular hairs.

Flower arrangement: spike of whorls usually with about 6 flowers in each whorl; upper whorls closely spaced.

Flowering time: July-August.

Leaf: ovate, tip pointed, toothed, stalked, opposite, sparsely hairy.

Fruit: 4 nutlets.

Uses: the common name refers to the old use of this plant in staunching bleeding wounds. The plant also contains antiseptic properties.

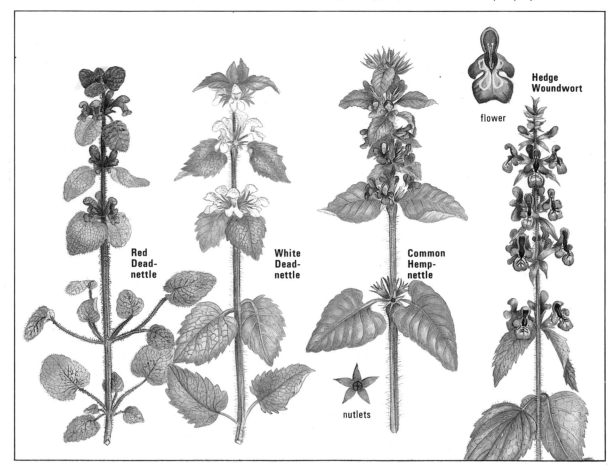

Hedge Woundwort
flower

Red Dead-nettle

White Dead-nettle

Common Hemp-nettle

nutlets

PLANTAIN FAMILY
Plantaginaceae

This is a small family with about 300 species, mainly from temperate areas or tropical mountains. The small flowers are clustered tightly into spikes and are mainly wind-pollinated. They produce large amounts of powdery pollen and, together with the grasses, the plantains are major causes of hay-fever. Among the plantains the lowest flowers on the spike open first and they die before the uppermost flowers have opened. A ring of pendulous stamens thus moves slowly up the spike. Several species of plantain are stubborn weeds, although Ribwort Plantain is quite nutritious and a useful component of pasture land.

GREATER PLANTAIN
Plantago major
The rosettes of tough, ribbed leaves, often flattened by, but very resistant to trampling, are seen at the sides of almost every path and piece of trodden ground.
Flower: greenish yellow, tiny; anthers mauve, becoming yellow, protruding, wind-pollinated.
Flower arrangement: in long, dense, stalked spike, 10-15 cm, encircled by whorl of anthers.
Flowering time: May-September.
Leaf: broadly elliptic, in rosette; 10-15 cm long, usually without teeth, strongly ribbed, abruptly narrowed into broad stalk.
Fruit: capsule, 2-5 mm.
Uses: when in seed the flower spikes may be hung up for cage-birds to feed on.

RIBWORT PLANTAIN
Plantago lanceolata
The ribbed leaves of this plantain are long and narrow, forming rosettes. The plant grows in grassy places.
Flower: browny-black, tiny; anthers cream, protruding, wind-pollinated.
Flower arrangement: in dense, short spike of 1-2 cm, on grooved, tough stalk, much longer than leaves.
Flowering time: April-August.
Leaf: lanceolate, in rosette; 10-15 cm long, usually without teeth, strongly ribbed. There is no obvious demarcation between blade and stalk.

Fruit: capsule, about 5 mm.
Uses: the seeds become slimy-coated when wet. In France the coating was used as a fabric stiffener, especially of muslin.

HOARY PLANTAIN
Plantago media
Growing in fairly dry grassy places, especially on chalk and limestone soils, this species resembles the Greater Plantain, but has markedly furry, greyish-green leaves.
Flower: white and scented, with lilac or white anthers, producing a distinctly pale spike. The latter is 2-8 cm long and borne on a smooth stalk to 30 cm. Pollinated partly by insects.
Flowering time: May-August.
Leaf: greyish-green and clothed with fine greyish hairs. Ovate to elliptical, usually 4-6 cm long, gradually narrowing into a short stalk. In a rosette and usually pressed close to the ground.
Fruit: a 4-seeded capsule.

Hoary plantain can be recognized from a distance by the hazy mass of pale lilac stamens.

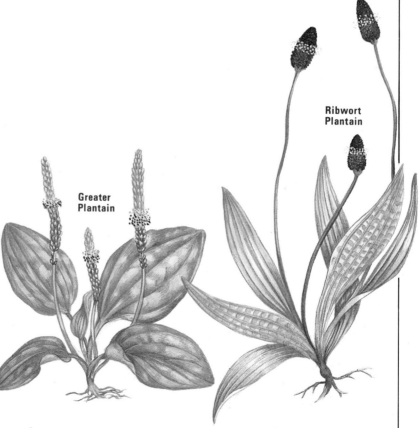

Greater Plantain

Ribwort Plantain

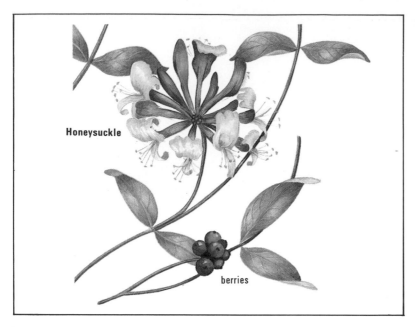

Honeysuckle

berries

HONEYSUCKLE FAMILY
Caprifoliaceae

Most of the species in this family are shrubs, some of them climbing. The flowers are often tubular, and the fruits are usually berries.

HONEYSUCKLE
Lonicera periclymenum
A climbing shrub of up to 6 m, Honeysuckle may also be found sprawling over the ground. It grows in hedges and woods and is planted in gardens for the scented flowers.
Flower: cream, tinged with pinky red; trumpet-shaped with 4 upper lobes, 1 lower; 4-5 cm long, stamens and style protruding.
Flower arrangement: in head, flowers directed outwards.
Flowering time: June-October.
Leaf: elliptic or oblong, tip usually pointed, stalkless, 3-9 cm long, dark green above, paler beneath.
Fruit: tight head of red berries.

BELLFLOWER FAMILY
Campanulaceae

Many of the flowers in this family are blue and bell-shaped and are grown as garden ornamentals. A sugar (*inulin*) occurs in the sap that is identical to that found in plants of the Daisy family. The two families are thought to be closely related.

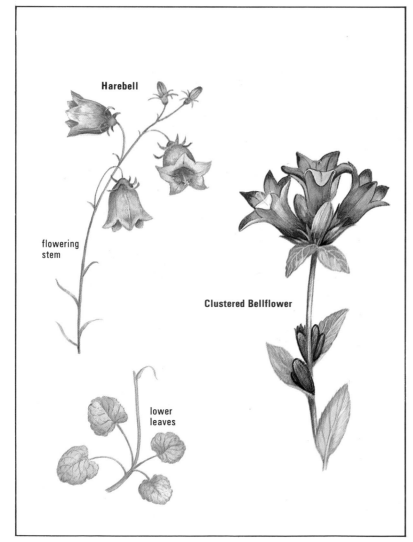

Harebell

flowering stem

Clustered Bellflower

lower leaves

HAREBELL
Campanula rotundifolia
Called Bluebell in Scotland, the Harebell is unrelated to the English Bluebell (p 280). It is a very slender, hairless plant of dry, grassy places and grows 15-40 cm.
Flower: pale blue, 1-2 cm, bell-shaped with 5 pointed lobes, nodding; calyx with 5 narrow, pointed teeth; stigmas 3.
Flower arrangement: solitary or in loose cluster, on thread-like stalk.
Flowering time: July-September.
Leaf: very narrow, pointed, un-stalked on stem; basal leaves ovate or circular, blunt-toothed, stalked.
Fruit: capsule, papery, 3-5 mm.

CLUSTERED BELLFLOWER
Campanula glomerata
This erect, downy plant grows on rough calcareous grasslands and reaches heights of about 30 cm.
Flower: bell-shaped, with mouth upwards: 15-20 mm long with 5 pointed lobes. Deep purplish-blue. Borne in dense clusters at top of normally un-branched stem.
Leaf: basal leaves oval to triangular; long stalked: blade to 8 cm long and lightly toothed. Stem leaves ovate to lanceolate, upper ones stalkless.

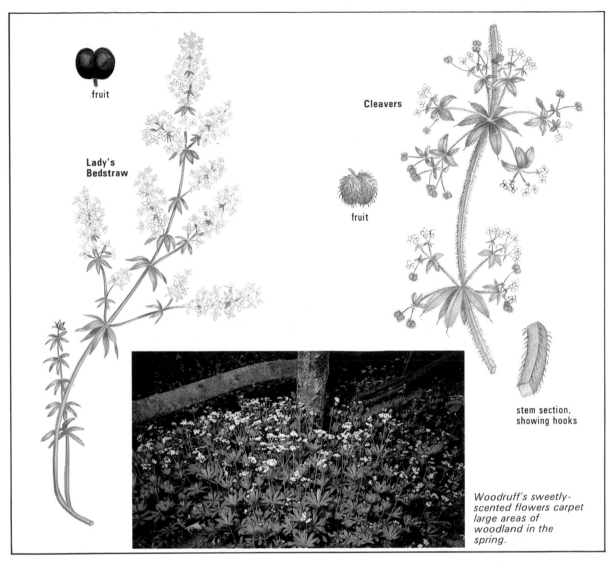

fruit

Cleavers

Lady's
Bedstraw

fruit

stem section,
showing hooks

*Woodruff's sweetly-
scented flowers carpet
large areas of
woodland in the
spring.*

BEDSTRAW FAMILY
Rubiaceae

This large family contains many
tropical trees and shrubs,
including the coffee plant.
European members are all herbs.
Leaves appear to be whorled, but
each 'whorl' has just two
opposite leaves and a number of
leaf-like stipules. The flowers are
always small, with 4 or 5 joined
petals.

LADY'S BEDSTRAW
Galium verum
The stems of this yellow-flowered
bedstraw are more or less erect,
15-100 cm high, and without the
minute, hooked bristles used by other
bedstraw species for climbing. The
plant grows in dry grassland.

Flower: golden yellow, 2-4 mm
across; petals 4.
Flower arrangement: in many-
flowered clusters at ends of branches.
Flowering time: July-August.
Leaf: in whorls of 8-12, grass-like,
6-25 mm long, bristle-tipped; margins rolled under; dark green and
shiny above, paler beneath.
Fruit: of 2 joined lobes, 1·5 mm,
hairless, black when ripe.
Uses: this bedstraw in particular
was used to turn and colour the
milk in cheese-making.

CLEAVERS
Galium aparine
This scrambling plant of 15-180 cm
clings to other vegetation, often
in dense masses, with minute hooked
bristles, rough and tacky to the
touch. Also called Goose-grass, it
grows in hedges and woods and is a
weed of cultivation.
Flower: white, 2 mm across; petals
4.

Flower arrangement: in clusters of
2-5, on long stalks, with whorl of
leaf-like bracts.
Flowering time: June-August.
Leaf: in whorls of 6-9, narrow, tip
ending in bristle, single-veined.
Fruit: of 2 joined lobes, 3-6 mm,
covered with tiny, white, hooked
bristles; purplish when ripe.

WOODRUFF
Galium odoratum
This fragrant woodland plant, smelling
strongly of vanilla or fresh hay, grows
on both calcareous soils and heavy
clays, but avoids sandy areas. Its erect,
unbranched stems spring from creeping rhizomes and reach 45 cm.
Flower: white and funnel-shaped,
deeply 4-lobed, to 6 mm across. Packed
into umbel-like heads. May-June.
Leaf: lanceolate and hairless but with
spiny edges, bright green: 6-8 in a
whorl.
Fruit: rounded, 2-3 mm: with hooks.

269

TEASEL FAMILY
Dipsacaceae

This small family includes the various kinds of scabious as well as the teasels. The tight heads of flowers resemble those of the daisy family, except for the stamens which stand out from each tubular flower. Each flower head has a cluster of bracts under it, and there may be small bracts among the flowers as well. In the Teasel itself, these small bracts are spiny.

FIELD SCABIOUS
Knautia arvensis
The beautiful mauve flower-heads, made up of many tiny flowers, are often larger than the other scabious species. The erect plants grow 25-100 cm high on dry banks and fields, and the stem has rough bristles, at least at the base.
Flower: mauve, 4-lobed; outer flowers larger than inner; stamens protruding.
Flower arrangement: in flattish head, 3-4 cm across, on long stalk; bracts directly below head ovate, in 2 overlapping layers, not reaching edge of head.
Flowering time: July-September.

Leaf: variable, deeply lobed, opposite, hairy; basal leaves often forming rosette, some unlobed.
Fruit: 5-6 mm, crowned by 8 bristles; dispersed by ants, which find them attractive.

DEVIL'S BIT SCABIOUS
Succisa pratensis
This scabious has undivided leaves and an erect, slightly hairy stem 15-100 cm high. It grows in damp places, including woods. The curious root gives the plant its name. After the first year's growth the tip of the thick root falls away leaving an abrupt end, as if bitten off.
Flower: mauve, 4-lobed; outer flowers not much larger than inner; stamens protruding.
Flower arrangement: in domed head, 1·5-2·5 cm across, on long stalk; sepal-like bracts lanceolate, in 2 overlapping layers, reaching edge of head. Leafy bracts among flowers.
Flowering time: June-October.
Leaf: elliptic, tip pointed or rounded, opposite, untoothed or with a few teeth; basal leaves form rosette.
Fruit: 5 mm, crowned by 5 bristles.

DAISY FAMILY
Compositae

This enormous family of about 25,000 species includes many common weeds as well as numerous cultivated plants. The family is characterized by tiny flowers (florets) which are packed into tight heads. The florets are of 2 kinds – a simple tube (disc floret) or a tube with a strap-like outgrowth on one side (ray floret). The heads may have only disc florets (thistle), only ray florets (dandelion), or a mixture (daisy). Florets may be male, female, or hermaphrodite. With sepal-like bracts underneath, each head may look like a single flower. The fruits (achenes) often have a parachute of hairs (pappus) for wind dispersal. Cultivated species include lettuces, asters, and sunflowers.

DAISY
Bellis perennis
Familiar in the short grass of meadow, lawn and verge, the Daisy flower stalks rise straight from a rosette of leaves. The flowers close at night and in wet weather.
Flower: ray florets white, tinged pink beneath, many; disc florets yellow; head 1·5-3 cm across.
Flower arrangement: head solitary, on long stalk.
Flowering time: March-October.
Leaf: spoon-shaped.
Fruit: achene, 1·5-2 mm, downy.

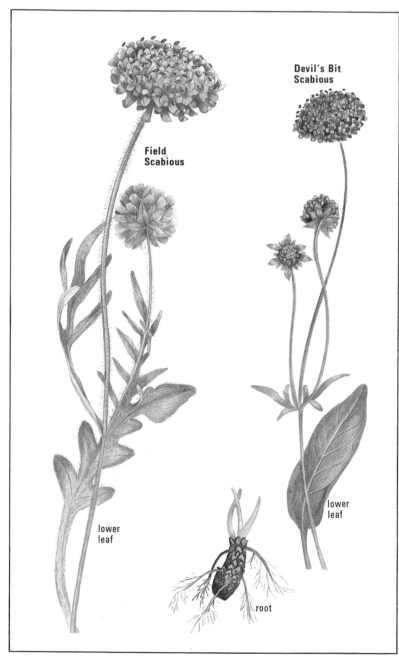

Field Scabious

Devil's Bit Scabious

lower leaf

lower leaf

root

Daisy

Ox-eye Daisy

flower bud

Scentless Mayweed

Pineappleweed

PINEAPPLEWEED
Matricaria matricarioides
Named for the strong aromatic smell, supposed to resemble pineapple scent, when crushed, this low-growing annual is a weed of cultivation and waste places, especially where trampling is heavy. Introduced to Europe, probably from north-east Asia, it has ferny leaves.
Flower: yellow-green; no ray florets: heads domed, 5-8 mm across and resembling a miniature pineapple: sepal-like bracts rounded and pale-bordered.
Flower arrangement: heads loosely clustered on branched stems.
Flowering time: June-July.
Leaf: finely dissected, fern-like.
Fruit: a small achene.

SCENTLESS MAYWEED
Tripleurospermum maritimum
This mayweed has daisy-like flower-heads and ferny leaves. It has no smell when crushed. The branched stem is 10-30 cm high, usually prostrate. The whole plant is hairless Grows on waste ground and as an arable weed.
Flower: ray florets white; disc florets yellow; heads 1·5-5 cm across; sepal-like bracts with narrow, papery margins.
Flower arrangement: heads loosely on branched stems.
Flowering time: July-September.
Leaf: ferny, very finely dissected .
Fruit: achene, with 2 dark dots near top.

OX-EYE DAISY
Leucanthemum vulgare
The Ox-eye Daisy has large, daisy-like flower-heads, smaller in exposed places. The almost hairless stems grow 20-70 cm tall in grassy places.
Flower: ray florets white; disc florets yellow; head 2·5-5 cm across; sepal-like bracts with purplish borders.
Flower arrangement: heads solitary, on long stalks.
Flowering time: June-August.
Leaf: Often forming non-flowering rosettes, dark green, toothed; lower stem leaves rounded or spoon-shaped, long-stalked; upper leaves oblong, stalkless.
Fruit: achene, pale grey, ribbed.

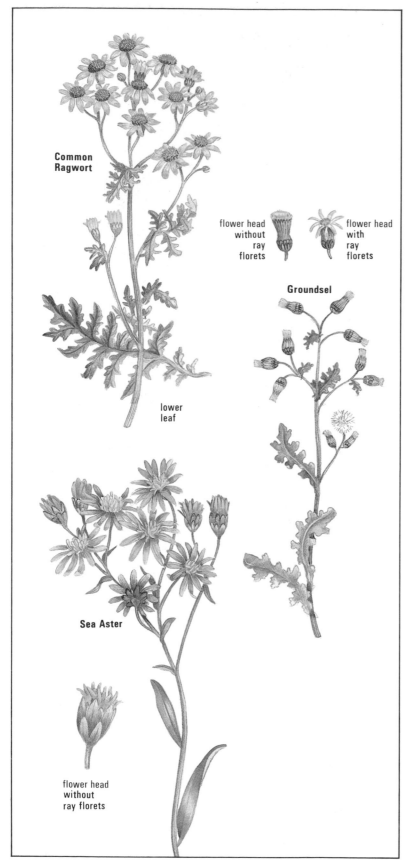

Common Ragwort

flower head without ray florets

flower head with ray florets

Groundsel

lower leaf

Sea Aster

flower head without ray florets

GROUNDSEL
Senecio vulgaris
Groundsel grows on waste and cultivated ground. The branched stem is 8-45 cm high. The common name is very old, coming from an Anglo-Saxon word meaning 'ground swallower', from the way this weed spreads. It is an annual.
Flower: yellow; disc florets only, occasionally rayed; heads about 4 mm across; sepal-like bracts dark-tipped, outer short.
Flower arrangement: heads in loose clusters.
Flowering time: all year.
Leaf: lobed, the lobes irregularly toothed; upper leaf bases clasping stem; hairless or slightly hairy.
Fruit: achene, with pappus forming clocks.

COMMON RAGWORT
Senecio jacobaea
Neglected fields are often overgrown with this biennial species. It is also found on waste ground and sand dunes. The grooved stem branches above the middle and grows 30-150 cm high.
Flower: ray florets yellow, 12-15; disc florets orange; heads 1·5-2·5 cm across; sepal-like bracts black-tipped.
Flower arrangement: heads in flat-topped corymbs.
Flowering time: June-October.
Leaf: deeply lobed, lobes blunt-toothed, end lobe rounded; dark green, hairless or with sparse hairs beneath.
Fruit: achene, ribbed, with pappus.
The Oxford Ragwort (*S. squalidus*) is a shorter and bushier annual, with more slender, pointed leaf lobes. Bracts with conspicuous black tips. A native of southern Italy, it is now well established on waste ground in many parts of Europe: particularly common on old walls and along railway lines. It flowers May-December.

SEA ASTER
Aster tripolium
Closely related to the Michaelmas Daisy of gardens and with similar flowers, Sea Aster has fleshy leaves and grows 15-100 cm high in salt marsh and on sea cliffs.
Flower: ray florets mauve or whitish, many or none; disc florets yellow; head 8-20 mm across; sepal-like bracts rounded at tip.
Flower arrangement: in loose corymbs.
Flowering time: July-October.
Leaf: fleshy, hairless; upper leaves narrow, pointed, stalkless; lower leaves rounded at tip, stalked.
Fruit: achene, with brownish pappus.
The cultivated Michaelmas Daisies originated in North America. They often escape from gardens and become established in waste places, especially along railway lines and around rubbish dumps.

WELTED THISTLE
Carduus acanthoides

The common name refers to the matted white hairs on the stem and undersides of the leaves, though the degree of hairiness varies. Thin, spiny ridges run up the stem, ending short of the flower head. The plant grows 30-150 cm tall in hedges, and on verges and stream-sides, mainly on calcareous soils. It is a biennial.

Flower: reddish purple; disc florets only; head 2-2·5 cm across; sepal-like bracts many, sharply pointed.

Flower arrangement: in loose clusters of 3-5.

Flowering time: June-August.

Leaf: margins spiny, wavy, white hairs beneath; upper leaves narrow, lower deeply lobed.

Fruit: achene, with long pappus.

SPEAR THISTLE
Cirsium vulgare

Thin, spiny ridges run down the stems of this common biennial. The stems have white, woolly hairs and grow 30-150 cm tall in fields and waste places, and by roadsides.

Flower: mauve; disc florets only; head 3-5 cm across; sepal-like bracts spiny, hairy.

Flower arrangement: solitary, or cluster of 2-3.

Flowering time: July-October.

Leaf: lanceolate, margins wavy, very spiny; end segment sword-shaped; white-hairy or rough beneath.

Fruit: achene, yellow with black streaks; pappus long, white.

CREEPING THISTLE
Cirsium arvense

Creeping Thistle is a stubborn weed on cultivated and waste land. The creeping roots send up new plants and produce dense clumps of upright stems. Ploughing does not destroy the weed, for cutting through the roots simply increases the number of pieces that can throw up new shoots.

The grooved stem is not continuously spiny-ridged, as in the common Spear Thistle, and grows 30-120 cm high.

Flower: mauve; disc florets only; head 1·5-2·5 cm across; sepal-like bracts sharply pointed but not spiny, purple-tinged. Fragrant. Male and female florets are sometimes borne on separate plants, the male plants then never producing the familiar thistledown.

Flower arrangement: solitary, or in clusters.

Flowering time: July-September.

Leaf: lanceolate, margin undulating, very spiny, hairless above, white-hairy or not beneath.

Fruit: achene; pappus long, fawn.

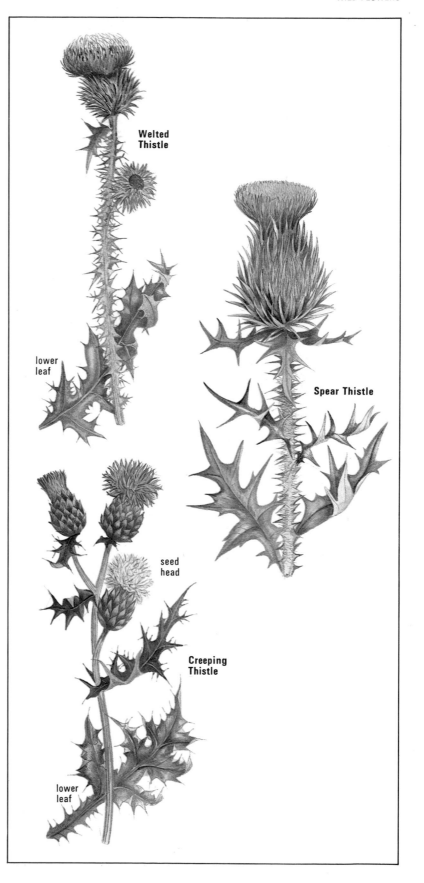

Welted Thistle

lower leaf

Spear Thistle

seed head

Creeping Thistle

lower leaf

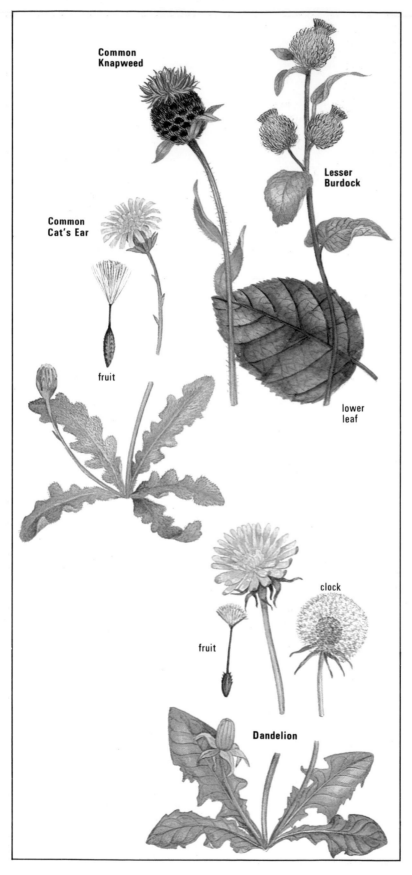

Common Knapweed

Lesser Burdock

Common Cat's Ear

fruit

lower leaf

clock

fruit

Dandelion

COMMON or BLACK KNAPWEED
Centaurea nigra
The thistle-like flower heads of this knapweed, shaped like a shaving brush, are very hard. The unspined plants grow 15-100 cm tall in grassland and along roadsides.
Flower: reddish purple; disc florets only; head 2-4 cm across; sepal-like bracts browny-black and fringed.
Flower arrangement: solitary.
Flowering time: June-September.
Leaf: lanceolate, with or without a few teeth, hairy; lower leaves stalked.
Fruit: achene, fawn; pappus short.

LESSER BURDOCK
Arctium minus
Stout, sometimes bushy, Lesser Burdock grows 50-150 cm high in waste places and on roadsides. After flowering the hooked bracts of the seed-heads attach themselves as burs to clothing and animal fur, so transporting the seeds. Biennial.
Flower: red-purple; disc florets only, in thistle-like, ovoid heads, 1·5-4 cm; bracts hooked.
Flower arrangement: in racemes; upper heads clustered.
Flowering time: July-September.
Leaf: ovate, tip pointed, toothed, up to 30 cm long; hairless above, sparse hairs beneath; stalk hollow.
Fruit: achene, with short pappus; whole seed-head forming bur.

COMMON CAT'S EAR
Hypochoeris radicata
Important features are the rosette of rough, lobed leaves and tiny bracts on the upper parts of the branched, hairless stem. The stem bears dandelion-like flower-heads and exudes milky sap if broken. The plant grows 20-60 cm high in grassy places.
Flower: yellow; ray florets only, outer green or grey beneath; heads 2·5-4 cm across.
Flower arrangement: heads on hairless, few-branched stalks with tiny bracts.
Flowering time: June-September.
Leaf: in basal rosette, roughly hairy, lobed, end lobe rounded.
Fruit: achene, pappus fawn, stalked.

DANDELION
Taraxacum officinale
There are many species of dandelion, all very variable and difficult to identify. This description covers a group of species. Dandelions grow in grassy and waste places. The pappus forms the familiar 'clocks' of children's games.
Flower: yellow; ray florets only, outer brown or mauve beneath; heads 3-7·5 cm across; outer sepal-like bracts turned down or spread out.
Flower arrangement: heads solitary, stalk unbranched, stout, hollow, exuding milky sap if broken.
Flowering time: March-October.
Leaf: in basal rosette, lobes deep, toothed, pointing down, hairless.
Fruit: achene, with stalked pappus.

WALL LETTUCE
Mycelis muralis
This slender, much-branched plant is hairless and grows 20-100 cm high on walls, and in rocky places and woods in calcareous regions.
Flower: pale yellow; 5 ray florets only; heads about 1 cm across; sepal-like bracts in cylinder shape.
Flower arrangement: heads on branched stalks.
Flowering time: July-September.
Leaf: alternate, deeply lobed, coarsely toothed; basal lobes of upper leaves clasping stem; often purple-tinged, red-veined.
Fruit: achene, with pappus.

GOAT'S-BEARD
Tragopogon pratensis
The solitary dandelion-like flower-head of this biennial is overtopped by long bracts and closes around noon. The stem bears grass-like leaves and grows 30-70 cm high in grass- and wasteland.
Flower: yellow; ray florets only; heads broad; sepal-like bracts longer than head, narrow.
Flowering time: June-July.
Leaf: grass-like, often clasping stem at base, white-veined, hairless.
Fruit: achene, with stalked pappus, forming large clock.

AUTUMNAL HAWKBIT
Leontodon autumnalis
The outer petals of the dandelion-like flower-heads are often striped red beneath. The stems are branched, usually hairless, with tiny bracts towards the top. If broken, the stem exudes milky sap. The plants grow 5-60 cm high in grassy places.
Flower: yellow; ray florets only, striped red beneath; heads 1-3.5 cm across; buds erect; sepal-like bracts hairless (with dark hairs on mountain plants).
Flower arrangement: heads on branched, usually hairless stalks.
Flowering time: June-October.
Leaf: in rosette, lobed or with widely spaced teeth, tip pointed, hairless or slightly hairy.
Fruit: ribbed achene, with pappus.

SMOOTH HAWK'S-BEARD
Crepis capillaris
The branched stems of this rather slender, dandelion-like plant are 20-100 cm high. It grows in grass-land and waste places.
Flower: bright yellow; ray florets only, outer often reddish beneath; heads 1-2.5 cm across; sepal-like bracts lanceolate, with black bristles or not, in 2 layers, outer bracts pressed close to inner.
Flower arrangement: loose clusters.
Flowering time: June-September.
Leaf: variable; lower leaves with many narrow lobes or toothed; upper leaves narrow, stalkless, with base having 2 pointed lobes clasping stem.
Fruit: achene, curved, 10-ribbed; pappus white.

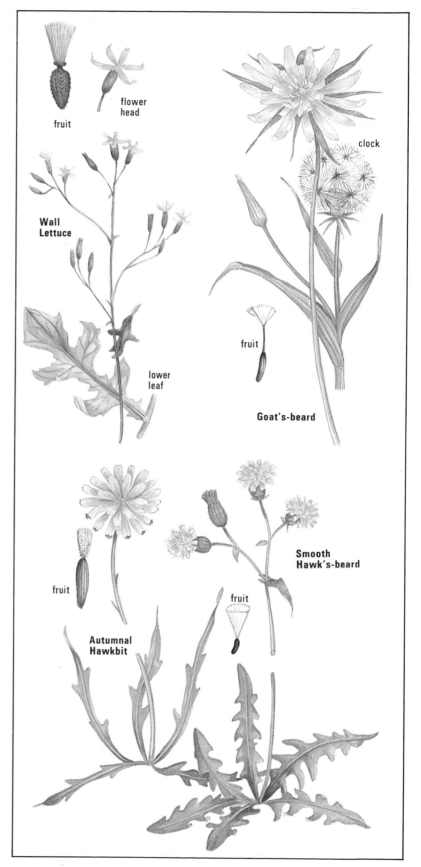

fruit

flower head

clock

Wall Lettuce

lower leaf

fruit

Goat's-beard

Smooth Hawk's-beard

fruit

Autumnal Hawkbit

fruit

275

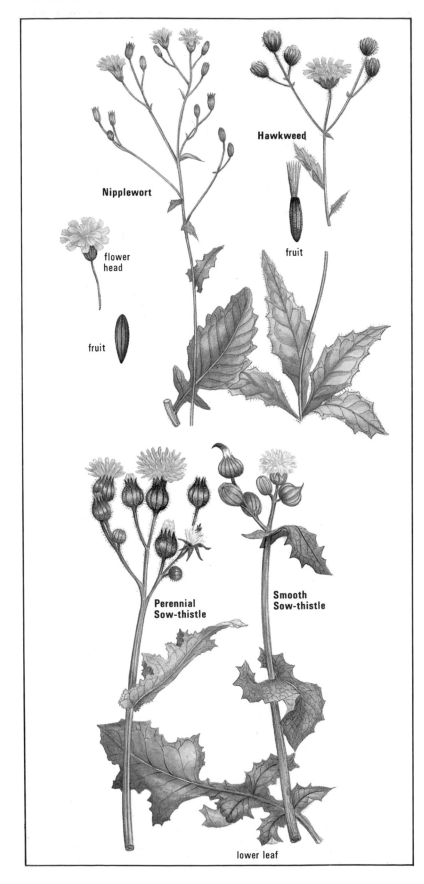

Nipplewort

flower
head

fruit

Hawkweed

fruit

Perennial
Sow-thistle

Smooth
Sow-thistle

lower leaf

NIPPLEWORT
Lapsana communis
The flower-heads are like small dandelions on branched stalks, and the leaves grow up the stem. The plant can grow up to 90 cm high in shady, waste places. The common name is said to come from the shape of the flower buds. An annual.
Flower: yellow; ray florets only; heads 1·5-2 cm across; sepal-like bracts narrow, tips rounded, dark-striped down centre.
Flower arrangement: heads on branched stalks.
Flowering time: July-September.
Leaf: alternate, toothed; lower leaves with toothed lobes; all often slightly hairy.
Fruit: achene, ribbed, no pappus.

HAWKWEED
Hieracium Sect. Vulgata
Hawkweed species are extremely numerous and difficult to identify. A section containing some of the most common species is described here. The branched, hairy stem grows 15-80 cm tall and exudes milky sap if broken: Hawkweeds are found in a wide variety of places.
Flower: yellow; ray florets only, Dandelion-like; sepal-like bracts dark green, glandular, hairy.
Flower arrangement: heads on branched, glandular hairy stalks.
Flowering time: June-September.
Leaf: elliptic to lanceolate, variably toothed, not lobed, both ends narrowed, hairy in parts; basal leaves in rosette.
Fruit: achene; pappus brownish.

PERENNIAL SOW-THISTLE
Sonchus arvensis
The plant has dandelion-like flower-heads, and leaves with rounded basal lobes. The hollow stem is 30-150 cm tall with sticky hairs on the upper parts. If cut, the stem oozes milky sap. The plant grows in waste places, by streams and on the coast.
Flower: golden yellow; ray florets only; heads 4-5 cm across; sepal-like bracts with yellow-tipped, sticky hairs.
Flower arrangement: heads in loose, flat-topped clusters.
Flowering time: July-October.
Leaf: oblong, lobed, margins weakly spiny; leaf bases clasping stem with 2 rounded lobes.
Fruit: achene, with white pappus.

SMOOTH SOW-THISTLE
Sonchus oleraceus
This annual has dandelion-like flower-heads and pointed basal lobes to the leaves. The stem is hollow, 20-150 cm high and usually lacks sticky hairs. If cut, it oozes milky sap. The plants grow in waste places and as a weed of cultivation.
Flower: pale yellow; ray florets only; heads 2-2·5 cm across; sepal-like bracts usually without sticky hairs.

Flower arrangement: heads clustered.
Flowering time: June-August.
Leaf: variable in shape, often deeply lobed, margins weakly spiny; leaf bases clasping stem with 2 pointed lobes; blue-green.
Fruit: achene, with white pappus.

COLTSFOOT
Tussilago farfara
Coltsfoot is found on waste and arable land, especially on clay soil. The flowering stems appear before the leaves in early spring, rising from a creeping, underground stem, as do the leaves later on.
Flower: yellow; disc florets surrounded by many narrow ray florets; head 1·5-3·5 cm across, drooping after flowering.
Flower arrangement: head solitary; stalk thick, scaled, 5-15 cm high.
Flowering time: February-April.
Leaf: appearing after flowers, 10-30 cm across, in clumps, heart-shaped, irregularly toothed, stalked, white-woolly beneath.
Fruit: achene, pappus forming clock.

BUTTERBUR
Petasites hybridus
The rather stout, large-leaved plants of Butterbur are found in damp places, often growing in masses. Flowering stems with broad bracts appear before the leaves.
Flower: pink or mauve; disc florets only; heads 3-12 mm; sepal-like bracts narrow, purplish.
Flower arrangement: heads in dense racemes. Male and female florets usually on separate plants.
Flowering time: March-May.
Leaf: 10-90 cm across, kidney-shaped, toothed, grey beneath, stalked, up to 1 m high.
Fruit: achene, with pappus.
Uses: the leaves were used to wrap butter, hence the common name.

CHICORY
Cichorium intybus
This much-branched plant, with tough, wiry stems, is most commonly seen on roadsides and waste places, mainly on calcareous soils. The stems are grooved and more or less hairy and reach about 120 cm.
Flower: clear sky-blue, 2·5-4 cm across: ray florets only. Carried in small clusters in leaf axils.
Leaf: basal leaves deeply lobed or toothed, rather like dandelion leaves: upper leaves less divided and clasping stem. Often hairy.
Fruit: a ribbed achene: no pappus, but toothed scales on the top.
Uses: Some varieties are cultivated for their stout tap roots, which are roasted and ground and blended with coffee. Other varieties are grown under cover for their succulent basal leaves which, under the right conditions, form compact heads like cos lettuces. Such heads are not found in wild plants.

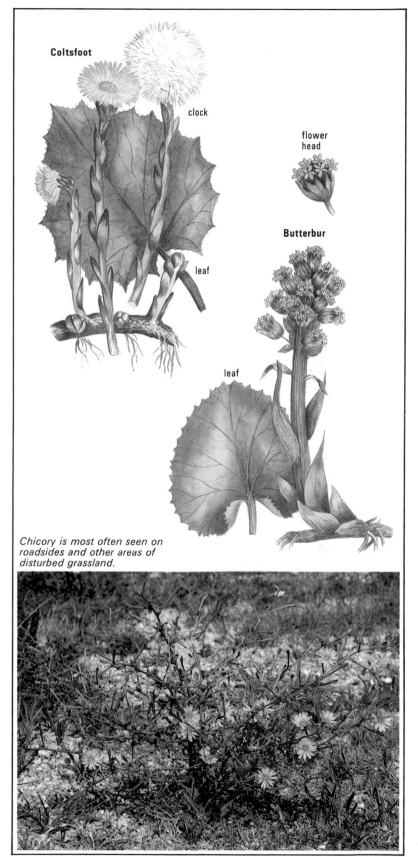

Chicory is most often seen on roadsides and other areas of disturbed grassland.

flower head

Mugwort

Yarrow

flower head

Hemp Agrimony

Tansy

YARROW
Achillea millefolium
The stem is erect and 8-60 cm high, with soft hairs. Yarrow grows in grass- and waste land and the narrow, ferny leaves may be found creeping through lawns. The plant looks Umbellifer-like, except that the flower stalks do not all join at one point. If crushed, the plant smells aromatic.
Flower: ray florets white or pink, 5; disc cream; head 4-6 mm across.
Flower arrangement: in flat-topped corymbs.
Flowering time: June-August.
Leaf: very finely dissected, fern-like, 5-15 cm long; lower leaves stalked.
Fruit: achene, 2 mm, greyish.

MUGWORT
Artemisia vulgaris
The backs of the finely cut leaves are strikingly white, and the plant is faintly aromatic. The stem is 60-120 cm tall, erect and often red. It grows on roadsides and in waste places.
Flower: brownish-yellow; disc florets only in bell-shaped heads, 3-4 mm long; sepal-like bracts hairy.
Flower arrangement: branched raceme.
Flowering time: July-September.
Leaf: deeply dissected, segments toothed, main vein translucent, almost hairless above, densely white-hairy beneath.

HEMP AGRIMONY
Eupatorium cannabinum
The tall plants grow 30-170 cm high in masses in damp places. The tiny pink flower-heads are gathered in fairly loose clusters.
Flower: pinkish; disc florets only; styles protruding; head of 5-6 florets, 2-5 mm across; sepal-like bracts purple-tipped.
Flower arrangement: heads in rather loose, domed clusters.
Flowering time: July-September.
Leaf: divided to base into 3-5 toothed segments, almost stalkless, opposite; upper leaves undivided.
Fruit: achene, black, with pappus.

TANSY
Tanacetum vulgare
The flower-heads are like little yellow buttons clustered at the ends of stems 30-100 cm high. The plant is highly aromatic and grows in hedgerows and waste places. It is often found as an escape from gardens, where it has been grown for ornament and medicine.
Flower: orange-yellow; disc florets only; heads 7-12 mm across.
Flower arrangement: heads in flat-topped clusters.
Flowering time: July-September.
Leaf: ferny, divided into narrow, toothed segments, alternate, dark green, hairless, gland-dotted, 15-25 cm long.
Fruit: achene, 5-ribbed.

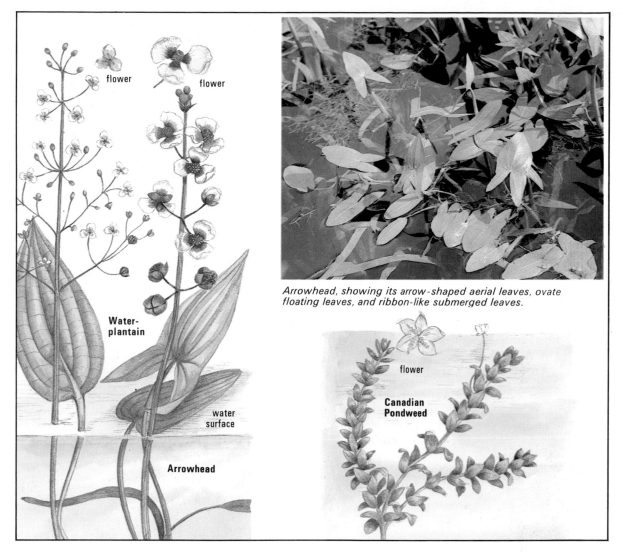

Arrowhead, showing its arrow-shaped aerial leaves, ovate floating leaves, and ribbon-like submerged leaves.

Monocotyledons

WATER-PLANTAIN FAMILY
Alismataceae

All the plants in this small family grow near or standing in fresh water. The flowers have 3 white or pink petals rarely lasting more than a day.

COMMON WATER-PLANTAIN
Alisma plantago-aquatica
This is a pretty plant which grows in the wet mud or shallow water of ditches, ponds and slow rivers. The whole plant is hairless and 20-100 cm high. This water-plantain differs from other, more narrow-leaved species in its ovate leaves with abrupt, not tapering bases.
Flower: very pale pink to white, up to 1 cm across; petals 3, rounded; sepals 3; open 1-7 pm.

Flower arrangement: in branched whorls.
Flowering time: June-August.
Leaf: broadly ovate, tip pointed; base joining long stalk abruptly, not tapering.
Fruit: flat seeds in a ring.

ARROWHEAD
Sagittaria sagittifolia
The arrow-shaped leaves and 3-petalled flowers on stout, 3-sided stems poke up out of shallow water. From root to tip the plant is 30-90 cm tall and hairless.
Flower: white, purple blotch at centre, 2 cm across; petals 3, rounded; sepals 3.
Flower arrangement: in short-stalked whorls of 3-5 on long stems. Upper flowers male, lower ones female.
Flowering time: July-August.
Leaf: arrow-shaped, long-stalked, held above water; floating leaves ovate with smaller basal lobes; submerged leaves ribbon-like.
Fruit: in tight, rounded head.

FROG-BIT FAMILY
Hydrocharitaceae

Members of this family grow partly or wholly submerged in water. Some are rooted, while others float free.

CANADIAN PONDWEED
Elodea canadensis
This waterweed has many little dark green leaves closely spaced up the long stems. It grows submerged in slow-moving fresh water and rarely flowers.
Flower: white, tinged pink, 5 mm across; petals 5.
Flower arrangement: solitary, floating, on long stalk.
Leaf: dark green, translucent, lanceolate, tip pointed or rounded, in overlapping whorls of 3.
Uses: this plant is widely grown in aquaria for the large amounts of oxygen it produces and for the shelter it provides.

LILY FAMILY
Liliaceae

This is one of the largest of the flowering plant families. Many members have bulbs as storage organs. Included in the family are onions, leeks and many garden flowers such as tulips and lilies. The flowers appear 6-petalled, having 3 true petals and 3 petal-like sepals, which may or may not be joined into a tube. The ovary is superior (above or inside the petal bases).

LILY-OF-THE-VALLEY
Convallaria majalis

This little plant may sometimes be found escaped from gardens, where it is commonly grown. It is also native to Europe in woods, mostly on chalk or limestone. There is a pair of broad leaves at the base of the flowering stem.
Flower: white, sweet-scented, bell-shaped, nodding, 8 mm.
Flower arrangement: in raceme of 6-12 flowers, all directed one way.
Flowering time: May-June.
Leaf: broad, elliptic, stalked, hairless, in a pair; scales sheathing base of leaf-stalks and flowering stem.
Fruit: red berries.

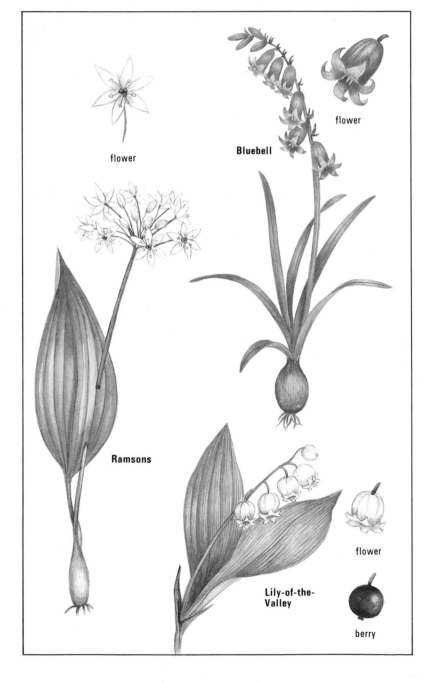

flower

Bluebell

flower

Ramsons

Lily-of-the-Valley

flower

berry

Uses: the plant contains a heart drug close to that found in Foxgloves. It was used to revive gassed soldiers in World War I.

BLUEBELL
Endymion non-scriptus

This species of bluebell is native to the western, Atlantic part of Europe. It was not known to the ancient Greek recorders of plants, hence the species name of *non-scripta*, meaning 'not written upon'. The plant grows 20-50 cm high, often carpeting woods.
Flower: purplish blue, 1·5-2 cm long, bell-shaped; rim with 6 curled-back teeth; anthers cream; bracts paired, bluish.
Flower arrangement: raceme, drooping at tip; buds erect; open flowers nodding, all directed to one side of long stem.
Flowering time: April-June.
Leaf: long, narrow, all rising directly from bulb, keeled, shiny.
Fruit: a capsule about 15 mm.
Uses: a slimy glue can be obtained by scraping the bulbs.

RAMSONS
Allium ursinum

Walkers through woods may notice the strong garlic smell before the plants themselves. Ramsons also grows in hedges. There is a small narrow bulb at the base of the 3-angled stem. The leaves are broad and spring from the bulb.
Flower: white; petals 6, pointed; stamens 6.
Flower arrangement: 6-20 flowers in rounded umbel on unbranched, 3-angled stem 10-45 cm high.
Flowering time: April-June.
Leaf: broad-elliptic, tip pointed, stalked, hairless.
Fruit: 3-lobed, with black seeds.

ASPHODEL
Asphodelus albus

This beautiful and imposing plant is a native of southern Europe, where it flourishes on dry and stony ground, especially on the over-grazed lands around the Mediterranean. It also ascends the southern slopes of the Alps and other mountains to a height of 1600 m, growing in the meadows as well as on the dry scree slopes. Often forming dense clumps, its stout flowering stems reach 1·5 m. There are several similar species.
Flower: white, often with a pink tinge, each petal having a brownish mid-rib. Star-shaped, 3-6 cm across. Borne in dense racemes on leafless branched or unbranched stems. April-July.
Leaf: long and blade-like, V-shaped in cross section: up to 50 cm long and 4 cm broad.
Fruit: a brown capsule with brown seeds.

Right: Asphodels thrive on stony hillsides and dry pastures in southern Europe.

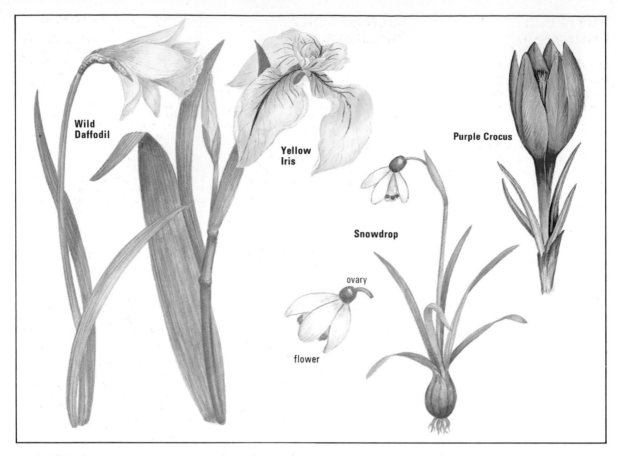

Wild
Daffodil

Yellow
Iris

Purple Crocus

Snowdrop

ovary

flower

DAFFODIL FAMILY
Amaryllidaceae

This family, centred in tropical and sub-tropical regions, contains many popular cultivated plants. Many are bulbous plants from dry areas. There are 3 petals and 3 petal-like sepals, which may or may not be joined. The ovary is always inferior (below, or outside the petals). The flowers are enclosed in a sheath at first.

SNOWDROP
Galanthus nivalis
Snowdrops are native to Central and S. Europe. In N. Europe they are commonly planted in gardens and widely naturalized in damp woods and hedges. There is a small bulb at the base of the plant, from which spring the leaves and flower stem.
Flower: white and green, bell-shaped, 14-17 mm long; outer petals 3, white; inner petals 3, shorter than outer, deeply notched, green-tipped and striped, forming tube; flower-sheath green.
Flower arrangement: solitary, nodding, on long stem.
Flowering time: January-March.
Leaf: linear, grey-green, keeled.
Fruit: capsule.

IRIS FAMILY
Iridaceae

Many members of this family, including crocuses, gladioli, and the various kinds of irises, are grown in gardens. A large proportion of the thousand or so species live in hot and dry areas. Many have underground storage organs in the form of corms or rhizomes. The 3 petals and 3 petal-like sepals, which may or may not be of similar shape, are joined into a tube at the base.

WILD DAFFODIL
Narcissus pseudonarcissus
The Wild Daffodil is native in woods and grassland. The flower stem and leaves end in a bulb of 2-3 cm.
Flower: trumpet golden yellow, as long as or slightly shorter than surrounding 6 paler yellow petals, 3·5-6 cm long; flower-sheath brown, papery.
Flower arrangement: solitary, drooping, on flattened stalk 20-35 cm high.
Flowering time: February-April.
Leaf: linear, 12-35 cm long, grey-green.
Fruit: capsule.

YELLOW IRIS
Iris pseudacorus
The leaves and flower-stem are tall and stiff, growing 40-150 cm high in river or ditch margins, marshes or marshy woods. The thick rhizomes often arch up above the soil surface.
Flower: yellow, 8-10 cm across; outer petals 3, broad, drooping, often dark-veined; inner petals 3, erect; stigmas 3, petal-like, forked at tip.
Flower arrangement: 2-3 on long, flattened stem.
Flowering time: May-July.
Leaf: very long, narrow, blue-green, 1·5-2·5 cm across, midrib raised; together, leaves form a flattened fan-shape at base.
Fruit: capsule; seeds brown.

PURPLE CROCUS
Crocus vernus
One of several rather similar species, this plant is a native of the mountains of southern and central Europe, often pushing up its delicate flowers before the snows have melted from the meadows. Introduced and naturalized in grasslands elsewhere in Europe.
Flower: purple or violet, to 6 cm high. 6 petals, opening widely in sunshine. 3 stamens and a feathery orange stigma. The 'stalk' is the base of the petal tube. February-June.
Leaf: bristle-like, 4-5 cm long.
Fruit: a capsule at ground level.

YAM FAMILY
Dioscoreaceae

Most members of this family are tropical climbers with tuberous rhizomes. Most are herbaceous, but a few are woody. Several species, known as yams, are cultivated in the tropics for their starch-filled tubers. About 6 species occur in Europe. Unlike most monocotyledons, the leaves are net-veined.

BLACK BRYONY
Tamus communis
The only widespread European species in the family, this clockwise-twining herbaceous climber is common in hedgerows and woodland margins. Its slender, hairless stems reach heights of 4 m. New stems spring from the rhizome each year. Absent from the north.
Flower: greenish-yellow, funnel or star-shaped, 4-5 mm across. 3 sepals and 3 petals alike and joined into a tube at the base. Borne in slender, loose racemes in leaf axils. Male and female flowers on separate plants. May-August.
Leaf: heart-shaped, to 10 cm long on long curving stalks: deep glossy green.
Fruit: clusters of shiny red berries. Poisonous.
(See also White Bryony – page 247.)

ORCHID FAMILY
Orchidaceae

This very large family, with over 20,000 species, is famed for the beauty and intricacy of its flowers and many tropical species are cultivated commercially. There are 3 sepals, usually more or less alike and often brightly coloured, and 3 petals. The lowest petal, known as the lip or labellum, is very different from the others – often of bizarre shape and pattern, and remarkably like an insect in the bee orchid and its relatives. It is often prolonged as a nectar-filled spur. The elaborate shapes and colours, combined with scent and nectar, are designed to attract pollinating insects, but they are often so specialized that only one kind of insect can pollinate them. The pollen is normally in sticky clumps. The seeds are minute. Several species, such as the Bird's Nest Orchid, are saprophytes – devoid of chlorophyll and obtaining food from dead leaves. Most orchids flower sporadically and should never be picked.

COMMON SPOTTED ORCHID
Dactylorhiza fuchsii
This conspicuous orchid is also one of the more common, and grows 15-50 cm high in damp or dry grassy places and open woods. Like many other orchids, this one hybridizes readily with other species.
Flower: pale pink or whitish with dark red marks; segments each side of hood pointing up; lip broad, 3-lobed; middle lobe pointed, slightly longer than broader side lobes; spur 5·5-8·5 mm long; bracts equalling or longer than flowers.
Flower arrangement: dense spike.
Flowering time: June-August.
Leaf: usually dark-blotched; lower leaves broad-elliptic, tip rounded.
Fruit: capsule.

FRAGRANT ORCHID
Gymnadenia conopsea
The scent of this orchid is strongest in the evening, when it attracts pollinating moths. The spurs on the flowers are very narrow and long.
15-40 cm high in grassland and marshy ground, particularly on chalk or limestone.
Flower: pink-lilac; lip of 3 rounded lobes; spur 11-13 mm long, slender; bracts equalling flowers.
Flower arrangement: dense spike.
Flowering time: June-August.
Leaf: long, narrow, folded down midrib, tip more or less rounded, slightly fleshy; bases sheathing stem.
Fruit: capsule.

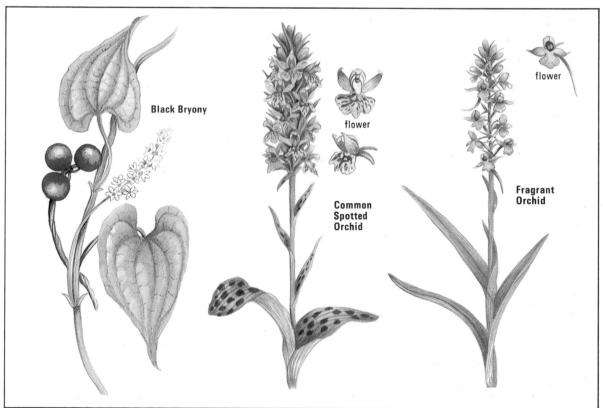

Black Bryony

flower

Common Spotted Orchid

flower

Fragrant Orchid

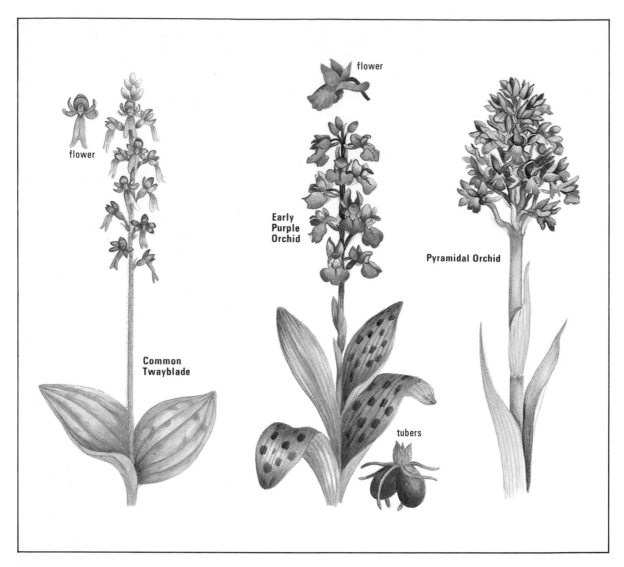

flower

flower

Early
Purple
Orchid

Pyramidal Orchid

Common
Twayblade

tubers

COMMON TWAYBLADE
Listera ovata
The common name refers to the 2 broad leaf-blades just below the middle of the stem. The stem is 20-60 cm high and hairy above the leaves. The plant grows in damp woods and grassland, particularly on limestone or chalk, and seems equally happy in shade or bright sunlight. The plant has slender roots without tubers. Lesser Twayblade (*L. cordata*) is a much smaller plant with reddish flowers. It grows in pine woods and on peat bogs and moorland, where it flowers June-September.
Flower: yellow-green; lip oblong, furrowed down centre, forked at tip; no spur; bracts tiny.
Flower arrangement: long spike. with few to many flowers: up to 25 cm long.
Flowering time: May-July.
Leaf: pair of very broad, ovate leaves, slightly fleshy; bases sheathing stem.
Fruit: capsule.

EARLY PURPLE ORCHID
Orchis mascula
These spring-flowering orchids grow 15-60 cm high in moist woods and grassland. They often grow among bluebells and Dog's Mercury. The lovely purple or mauve flowers have the unlovely smell of tom cats.
Flower: purple or mauve; lip pale with dark spots at top-centre, broad, 3-lobed; spur thick, blunt; bracts purple.
Flower arrangement: spike.
Flowering time: April-June.
Leaf: usually dark-spotted, alternate, slightly fleshy, oblong, tip shortly pointed or rounded; bases sheathing stem.
Fruit: capsule.
Uses: because of the twin tubers, looking like testicles, this orchid was used as an aphrodisiac. The name orchid comes from the Greek for testicle. Most European orchids grow from tubers.

PYRAMIDAL ORCHID
Anacamptis pyramidalis
Named for the markedly pyramidal shape of the young flower spike, this beautiful plant grows on dry, grassy slopes, especially on calcareous soils, and on shelly sand dunes by the sea. Rising from 2 oval tubers, it reaches a height of about 50 cm.
Flower: pale to deep pink and usually unspotted; lip about 5 mm long and deeply 3-lobed with a long curved spur. 2 parallel ridges at base of lip guide insect tongue past the pollen masses as it probes the spur for nectar. Flowers borne in dense pyramidal clusters at first, becoming oblong with age. May–August.
Leaf: narrow; greyish green and unspotted: 5-8 in a rosette.
Fruit: a capsule with many seeds.

Right: A cluster of bee orchids showing the pale pink sepals and the furry, bee-like lips.

Below Right: A single flower of the lady orchid, showing the 'skirt' and 'bonnet' which give the plant its name.

flower

Broad-leaved Helleborine

Lizard Orchid

rhizome

BROAD-LEAVED HELLEBORINE
Epipactis helleborine
This helleborine has up to 3 stems, often tall, short-hairy at the top. They rise from a short length of underground stem and grow up to 80 cm high in hedgerows and woods. The cup-shaped lip of the flower holds nectar for bees and wasps.
Flower: green to dull purplish, scentless; lip cup-shaped with narrow, turned-back tip; no spur; bracts almost equalling flowers.
Flower arrangement: loose spike of drooping flowers turned to one side.
Flowering time: July-October.
Leaf: alternate, broadly ovate, tip pointed, middle leaves longest, margins rough.
Fruit: capsule.

LIZARD ORCHID
Himantoglossum hircinum
Named for the long, ribbon-like lip, this is one of Europe's largest orchids, occasionally reaching 1 m. It grows mainly on dry, calcareous grassland: very rare in Britain, but locally common in southern and central Europe.
Flower: sepals and 2 upper petals greenish, forming a hood; lip cream, fawn, or pinkish with darker spots, divided into 3 ribbon-like lobes of which the central one reaches 5 cm. Smells of goats. Carried in long spikes. May-July.
Leaf: pale greyish-green, lanceolate, up to 20 cm: 6-8 root leaves in a rosette, withering as flower stem grows. Upper leaves sheathe stem.
Fruit: a many-seeded capsule.

BEE ORCHID
Ophrys apifera
The lip of this fascinating orchid looks like a bee. It even smells like a female bee and in some parts of Europe it is pollinated by male bees which try to mate with it. Elsewhere it is normally self-pollinated. Reaching 40 cm, it is not uncommon in grassland and on rough ground on calcareous soils.
Flower: sepals pink (occasionally white), oval to 1·5 cm long: 2 upper petals greenish or pink, usually narrow and blunt-ended: lip rounded, rich brown and furry with pale U or W mark, to 1·5 cm long. Up to 10 well-spaced flowers on a spike. May-July.
Leaf: pale green, ovate to lanceolate: basal leaves form rosette which withers as flowers appear.
Fruit: a ribbed capsule.

LADY ORCHID
Orchis purpurea
Each flower of this beautiful plant resembles a lady in a poke bonnet and broad skirt. Although very rare in Britain, it is not uncommon elsewhere in open woods and scrub on calcareous soils. It reaches 50 cm.
Flower: 3 sepals form a purplish-brown hood or bonnet enclosing 2 upper petals. Lip, about 1·5 cm long, is white or pale pink with tufts of tiny crimson hairs; 3-lobed, the middle one broad and skirt-like, sometimes split up the middle. In dense spike. April-July.
Leaf: bright green, to 15 cm long: mostly in a basal rosette.
Fruit: a capsule with many seeds.

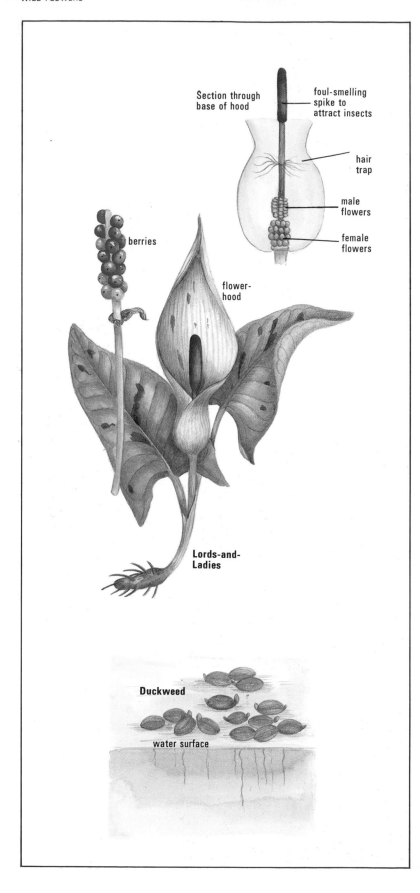

Section through base of hood

foul-smelling spike to attract insects

hair trap

male flowers

female flowers

berries

flower-hood

Lords-and-Ladies

Duckweed

water surface

ARUM FAMILY
Araceae

Members of this large, mainly tropical family include Arum Lilies of florists' shops (not lilies at all) and the Swiss Cheese Plant (*Monstera deliciosa*), a common house-plant. The poker-like flower-spike is surrounded by a large sheath; many exude unpleasant smells to attract pollinating flies.

LORDS-AND-LADIES
Arum maculatum
The tiny flowers are hidden at the base of a purple, poker-shaped stalk, half-enclosed by a yellow-green hood. Midges are trapped in the base of the hood and pollinate the flowers. They later escape and effect cross-pollination by becoming trapped in other flower-hoods. The plants grow in shady hedges and woods. 15-50 cm high.
Flower: unisexual, without petals or sepals.
Flower arrangement: clustered at base of spike: female flowers at bottom, then male flowers, and then a ring of sterile flowers forming a ring of hairs. Insects can push down past the hairs, but cannot get out again. Female flowers open first; male flowers then open and dust insects with pollen; hairs then wither and insects escape to carry pollen to other spikes.
Flowering time: April-May.
Leaf: arrow-shaped, usually dark-blotched, shiny; stalks rising directly from roots.
Fruit: spike of orange berries.

DUCKWEED FAMILY
Lemnaceae

The plants in this family are very small and made up of simple, leaf-like lobes which float on fresh water. Included in the family are species of *Wolffia* – the smallest known flowering plants.

DUCKWEED
Lemna minor
The tiny, round, leaf-like lobes of this plant spread on the surface of still water, often covering large areas. A single thread-like root hangs in the water from each plant. The plants normally reproduce by the budding of new lobes, and over-winter in the mud of pond- or ditch-bottoms. Each lobe is 1·5-4 mm across.
Flower: minute; unisexual with just 1-2 stamens or 1 carpel. Carried in a pouch on lobe margin, but rare.
Flowering time: June-July.

BUR-REED FAMILY
Sparganiaceae

Some plants in this small family float in fresh water, while others grow erect at the water-side. The tiny flowers are gathered into spherical heads, with male and female flowers in separate clusters on the same stem. Most species are found in temperate regions.

BRANCHED BUR-REED
Sparganium erectum
This is a stout, erect, hairless plant of 50-150 cm, growing at the edge of still or slow-moving fresh water. The long, stiff leaves look like iris leaves except for the 3-angled bases. The less common Unbranched Bur-reed (*S. emersum*) has a single stem of flower-heads.
Flower: tiny, with 6 greenish, black-edged papery scales.
Flower arrangement: males and females in separate, round heads on branched, leafy stem (male above female).
Flowering time: June-August.
Leaf: long, narrow, 3-angled and sheathing stem at base.
Fruit: in bur-like head, each bearing spike.
Uses: stands of Bur-reed shelter wild-fowl, and the fruits provide food for them in winter.

REEDMACE FAMILY
Typhaceae

Most species in this small family are very tall and grow in shallow, fresh water. The tiny flowers form a long, dense club-shape. The plants are commonly known as 'Bulrushes'.

GREAT REEDMACE ('BULRUSH')
Typha latifolia
Great Reedmace is very tall (1·5-2·5 m), and grows in large stands in the shallows of still or slow-moving fresh water. It is often found growing with Reed (*Phragmites communis*), a tall water-side grass.
Flower: tiny and unisexual. No petals but surrounded by hairs — brown in female, yellow in male.
Flower arrangement: females in large, dense club-shape, continuous with thinner, paler male spike above (Lesser Reedmace, *T. angustifolia*, has a gap between).
Flowering time: June-July.
Leaf: very long, narrow, 10-18 mm wide, grey-green, rather leathery.
Fruit: wind-borne achene.
Uses: the leaves can be used for weaving and basketry.

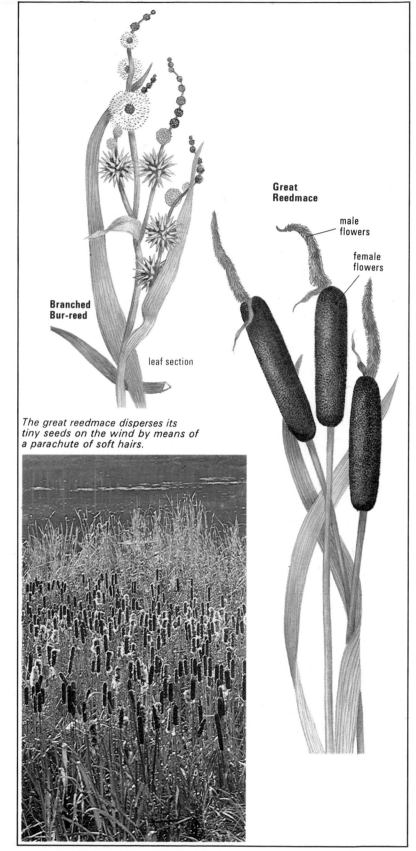

Branched Bur-reed

leaf section

Great Reedmace

male flowers

female flowers

The great reedmace disperses its tiny seeds on the wind by means of a parachute of soft hairs.

Soft Rush

Jointed Rush

Field Woodrush

RUSH FAMILY
Juncaceae

The rushes are often confused with grasses, but they are not closely related. Rushes are slender herbs, usually with creeping rhizomes, and they bear small and inconspicuous flowers, although these may be gathered into large bunches. There are 6 perianth segments (3 sepals and 3 petals), all alike and usually greenish white or brown, with a chaffy texture. There are usually six stamens and three stigmas, and the flowers are wind-pollinated. True rushes (*Juncus* species) usually have hairless and rather spiky cylindrical leaves, while woodrushes (*Luzula* species) have flat and hairy leaves. Most true rushes flourish in damp places and many of the 300 or so species grow in cold climates.

SOFT RUSH
Juncus effusus
This very common rush grows in tufts in wet places almost everywhere. The glossy green stems are quite smooth, up to 3 mm thick and reaching 1·5 m in height.
Flower: brown with narrow segments. Sprouting in a cluster in upper part of stem. The cluster may be tightly packed or loosely branched. June-August.
Leaf: reduced to reddish brown scales at base of stem.
Fruit: a many-seeded capsule.

JOINTED RUSH
Juncus articulatus
This rather weak-stemmed rush is named because the leaves contain transverse partitions, which can be felt by pulling a leaf between the fingers. (Several other rushes also have these partitions.) The stem is dark green and smooth and reaches 80 cm. It grows on wet ground almost everywhere.
Flower: dark brown with pointed segments. In loose, much-branched heads at top of stems. June-October.
Leaf: deep green, usually curved and slightly compressed: 2-7 on a stem.
Fruit: a many-seeded capsule.

FIELD WOODRUSH
Luzula campestris
Abundant in grassy places almost everywhere, this grass-like little plant grows in loose tufts and reaches about 15 cm.
Flower: chestnut brown with conspicuous yellow stamens: star-like, 3-4 mm across. Carried in a loose panicle. March-June.
Leaf: bright green, to 4 mm wide: thinly clothed with long hairs.
Fruit: a 3-seeded capsule.

SEDGE FAMILY
Cyperaceae

Members of this family are grass-like herbs, but they differ from grasses in having solid, unjointed stems, often triangular in cross-section. The slender leaves are also arranged in a triangular fashion around the shoots. The flowers are very small, without petals, and grouped into brown spikes. In the true sedges (*Carex* species) the flowers are unisexual and the male and female flowers often form separate spikes. They are wind pollinated. The fruits are like little grains – globular or distinctly 3-cornered – and often important for identifying the species. Most of the 4,000 or so sedges flourish in wet places, but several small species, such as the bluish-leaved Glaucous Sedge (*Carex flacca*), also grow in dry grassland.

COMMON COTTONGRASS
Eriophorum angustifolium
Despite its name, this wiry plant is a sedge. Reaching 60 cm, it is abundant on wet heaths and bogs, forming extensive patches with the aid of its creeping rhizomes and forming white drifts as the fruits ripen.
Flower: very small, hermaphrodite: no petals, but each flower has a ring of hairs which become long and cottony after flowering – hence the common name. Flowers grouped into several nodding spikes. June-August.
Leaf: deep green, up to 20 mm long and 6 mm wide; deeply channelled. Becoming brown and dying by flowering time, to be replaced by fresh green leaves in late summer.
Fruit: a 3-cornered nutlet, surrounded by the long white hairs.
Harestail Cottongrass (*E. vaginatum*) has its flowers grouped into a single oval spike. It is common on moorland.

GREAT POND SEDGE
Carex riparia
This is a typical waterside sedge, growing in dense clumps around ponds and slow-moving streams. The robust stems are stiff and hairless and distinctly 3-cornered. They reach 1·5 m.
Flower: unisexual, with male and female flowers in separate spikes. Up to 7 male spikes closely grouped at top of stem; dark brown, becoming yellow as stamens open and shed pollen. Up to 5 female spikes lower down, greenish and up to 9 cm long; lower ones often nodding. Long tapering bracts below each spike. May-June.
Leaf: bluish-green, up to 1·5 cm wide, sharply keeled and with sharp edges: often taller than stems.
Fruit: an ovoid or 3-cornered nutlet.

Great Pond Sedge

Common cottongrass – a sedge and not a true grass at all – grows in boggy places. It has narrow, channelled leaves and several cottony heads to each stem.

289

GRASS FAMILY
Gramineae

With over 10,000 species, this is one of the most important plant families – providing the staple diet of many wild and domestic animals and also giving us all our cereals. Grasses grow in all parts of the world and in all kinds of habitats. Most are small herbaceous plants with hollow, jointed stems, although the woody bamboos are also grasses. The flowers have no petals and consist of a single carpel and 3 stamens. They are wind-pollinated. They are enclosed in spikelets, which consist of two outer scales called glumes and a number of smaller inner scales. There may be one or more flowers in a spikelet, and the spikelets may be borne in dense spikes (ears) or in spreading panicles. Most species flower May–July. The lower parts of the leaves ensheathe the stem, and where they join it there is a little membranous collar called a ligule. The shape of this ligule, seen by pulling back the leaf blade, is important in identifying grasses. The fruit is normally a 1-seeded grain.

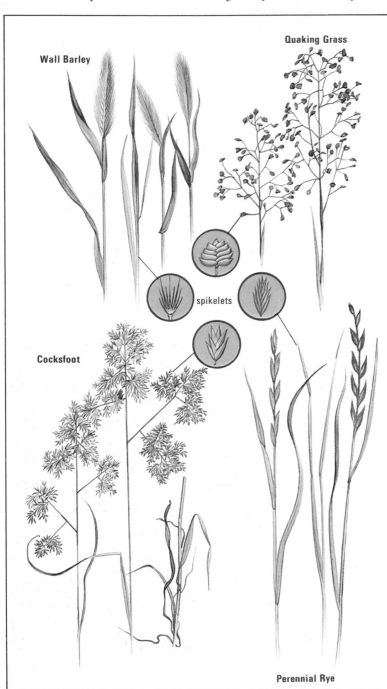

Quaking Grass

Wall Barley

spikelets

Cocksfoot

Perennial Rye

WALL BARLEY
Hordeum murinum
This common annual of waste places and disturbed ground reaches 60 cm in loose tufts.
Leaf: light green, to 20 cm long: finely pointed. Ligule very short and ring-like.
Spikelet: with fine, stiff bristles (awns): borne in 3's on a somewhat flattened bristly spike which children like to throw like darts. Only the middle one of each trio has a flower.

QUAKING GRASS
Briza media
This delicate grass occurs in all kinds of grassland, including roadside verges. It grows in loose tufts and reaches 75 cm. It gets its name for its drooping and freely-swaying spikelets.
Leaf: bright green, hairless, to 15 cm. Ligule up to 1·5 mm: blunt-ended.
Spikelet: flattened, oval or triangular to 7 mm long. Shining brown, often purplish, with up to 12 flowers. In a loosely branched, pyramidal panicle.

COCKSFOOT GRASS
Dactylis glomerata
Named for the resemblance of the panicle to a chicken's foot, this grass forms dense clumps in all kinds of rough grassland. It is nutritious and regularly sown for hay. It reaches 1·5 m.
Leaf: pale or greyish green to 45 cm: folded down centre when young. Ligule to 12 mm long: more or less triangular.
Spikelet: to 9 mm long with 2-5 flowers: in dense clusters, all facing one way on a few-branched panicle.

PERENNIAL RYE GRASS
Lolium perenne
This very nutritious, but rather tough grass is extensively sown for pasture and for lawns, where its wiry flower stems often defeat the mower. It reaches about 1 m when not cut or grazed. There are many varieties.
Leaf: bright green and hairless, to 20 cm long; folded along mid-rib when young. Basal sheaths often pink. Ligule ring-like, to 2 mm high.
Spikelet: stalkless, oval and flat, with only 1 glume and up to 14 flowers. Placed alternately on opposite sides of a slender spike, with narrow edge facing the stem.

COMMON REED
Phragmites communis
Forming dense stands in fens and marshes and around the edges of lakes and rivers, this grass reaches heights of 3 m. Its tough stems are in great demand for thatching.
Leaf: greyish green, to 60 cm or more long and 3 cm wide, with a fine tapering point. Ligule is a fringe of tiny hairs.
Spikelet: up to 15 mm long, with 2-6 flowers; very hairy. Grouped into dense purplish or brownish feathery panicles.

FALSE OAT GRASS
Arrhenatherum elatius
Abundant on roadsides and other rough grassland, this loosely-tufted grass is very attractive as its shiny heads sway in the breeze. It reaches 1·5 m.
Leaf: bright green, rough textured and usually lightly haired; to 40 cm long. Ligule to 3 mm long, smoothly rounded at end.
Spikelet: up to 11 mm long, usually 2-flowered and with 1 or 2 long bristles (awns). Shiny, green at first becoming brown or purplish. Panicle slender at first, but branches — in well-spaced clusters — later spreading and nodding.

MEADOW FOXTAIL
Alopecurus pratensis
This grass is especially common on rich, moist soils, particularly in riverside meadows. It reaches 1·2 m and is highly nutritious. It is one of the earliest-flowering grasses.
Leaf: mid-green, tending to bluish; hairless but often slightly rough. Ligule more or less square, to 2·5 mm long.
Spikelet: flattened, oval, 4-6 mm long; 1-flowered and hairy, with a straight bristle. Packed into dense cylindrical spikes to 13 cm long, greyish-green or purplish and very soft to the touch.

WAVY HAIR GRASS
Deschampsia flexuosa
This slender grass forms neat cushion-like tufts on heaths and moorlands. Its reddish stems reach 1 m.
Leaf: bright green and hairless; tightly in-rolled and bristle-like to 20 cm or more long. Ligule conical, to 3 mm long and bluntly pointed.
Spikelet: up to 6 mm long, usually 2-flowered. Shiny brown or purple. Borne on wavy, hair-like stalks in loose panicles.

YORKSHIRE FOG
Holcus lanatus
This is a very furry grass of roadsides, waste ground, and run-down pastures. It reaches 1 m.
Leaf: greyish-green and clothed with soft hair; to 20 cm long and finely-pointed. Ligule flat-topped, to 4 mm.
Spikelet: to 6 mm long, 2-flowered; white, green, pink, or purple. Borne in rather dense hairy panicles, lanceolate at first but opening to a pyramidal shape.

Wavy Hair grass growing in its typical heathland habitat.

Panicles of Yorkshire fog in various stages of opening.

291

Roadside verges support many kinds of grasses, most of which flower in June. This verge is dominated by cocksfoot grass.

TIMOTHY GRASS
Phleum pratense
Reaching 1·5 m, this loosely tufted and very nutritious grass is characteristic of low-lying meadows, but is sown extensively for hay and pasture. It also grows on many roadsides.
Leaf: green or grey-green, up to 45 cm long; hairless, but rough to touch, at least on upper surface. Ligule up to 6 mm long, oval with blunt tip.
Spikelet: oblong, flat, 3-4 mm long; 1-flowered, with 2 short bristles. Packed into a dense cylindrical spike 6-30 cm long; greyish-green or purple and rough to the touch.

COMMON BENT GRASS
Agrostis tenuis
One of several very similar grasses, this species is abundant almost everywhere, but especially on the drier acidic soils of heathlands and on the rough grazings of the uplands. It reaches about 70 cm and its delicate flower heads form a brown mist over the ground.
Leaf: bright green and hairless, to 15 cm long, finely pointed and often in-rolled. Ligule ring-like to 2 mm.
Spikelet: 2-4 mm long, 1-flowered, green at first becoming purplish-brown. Borne on spreading branches on a rather pyramidal panicle.

FEATHER GRASS
Stipa pennata
This beautiful grass grows on dry, stony slopes in the Alps, reaching altitudes of 2,500 m. Up to 1 m in height, it is quite unmistakable because of its long plumed awns.
Leaf: blue-green, to 50 cm or more; bristle-like and in-rolled, especially in dry weather.
Spikelet: to 2 cm long, pale brown when ripe; 1-flowered with a feather-like awn to 35 cm long. A small cluster of spikelets at top of stem. The awn carries the fruit away, and twisting movements in response to humidity changes drive the pointed grain into the ground.

MARRAM GRASS
Ammophila arenaria
This grass grows on coastal sand dunes, where its extensive creeping rhizomes help to bind and stabilize the sand.
Leaf: greyish-green to 60 cm long; tightly in-rolled. Ligule to 3 cm long, very narrow and pointed.
Spikelet: to 16 mm long, 1-flowered. Packed into dense, pale spike-like panicles, to 22 cm long.

ROUGH-STALKED MEADOW GRASS
Poa trivialis
Abundant in meadows and pastures, especially on the moister soils, this grass also occurs on waste land and as a weed of cultivation. Loosely tufted and up to 1 m high, it is one of several similar species, but distinguished by its rough stems.
Leaf: deep green, often with a purplish tinge, to 20 cm long and abruptly pointed. Ligule 4-10 mm long, parallel-sided with a triangular tip.
Spikelet: ovate to 4 mm long; 2-4 flowers; dull green, often with a purplish tinge. Borne on a distinctly pyramidal panicle.

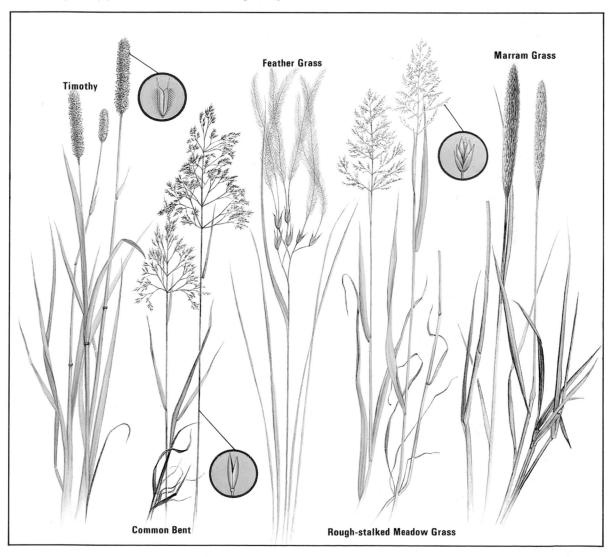

Timothy

Feather Grass

Marram Grass

Common Bent

Rough-stalked Meadow Grass

Chapter Seven
Trees and Shrubs

Trees and shrubs are plants with perennial woody stems. A tree normally has just one main stem, known as the trunk, while a shrub is a species that normally has several main stems arising at or near ground level. Shrubs are rarely more than about 5 metres high. A tree which is cut to ground level may send up several new trunks and appear shrub-like for a few years. It does not become a true shrub, but it may be called a bush. This term is commonly used for any fairly low woody plant with several stems, whether it normally grows as a tree or a shrub. The shrubs included in the following pages all reach at least a metre in height. Lower-growing species, many of which creep prostrate over the ground, are included with the wild flowers (pages 210–293).

Flowers and Cones
Most of the trees and shrubs are flowering plants (Angiosperms) and, except that they are usually longer-lived, their life cycles are identical to those of the smaller, herbaceous plants. Their flower structures are exactly the same. There are, however, a number of cone-bearing species among the trees and shrubs. These belong to the group of plants called Gymnosperms and they are slightly less advanced than the flowering plants.

Gymnosperm pollen is carried in small male cones and blown to the female cones by the wind. Seeds later develop in the female cones, but they are never completely enclosed in fruits as they are in the flowering plants. Male and female cones may be borne on the same tree or on different trees. The flowering trees often carry male and female parts in one flower, but there are many species with single-sexed flowers. Like the cones, these male and female flowers may grow on the same tree or on different trees.

Evergreen and Deciduous
Species that retain their leaves in winter are called evergreens, while those that drop their leaves in autumn are known as deciduous trees. Most conifers are evergreens, while most European flowering trees are deciduous. Flowering trees are also called broad-leaved, because their leaves are quite broad in comparison with the needle-like leaves of the conifers. Evergreen trees and shrubs grow mainly in the colder regions, and also in the Mediterranean region where the summers are very hot and dry. The tough leaves have waxy coats which cut down water loss.

Identification
The general shape of a tree, especially its crown of branches, is often characteristic for each species when

Left: Deciduous trees, such as this fine sycamore, dominate the landscape in many parts of Europe, where the relatively warm and moist climate is ideal for tree growth.

the trees are growing alone, but shape cannot be used in woodland, where neighbouring trees interfere with growth and alter the shape. The bark is also distinctive in many trees, and winter buds can be used to identify many deciduous trees. The colour of the shoots – the youngest parts of the branches – is a useful guide when identifying certain shrubs. Flowers afford the surest way of identifying most of the flowering trees, although they are present only at certain times of the year. Many trees carry their flowers in catkins – elongated clusters of unisexual flowers which may hang down or stand erect on the branches. Cones may be used to identify the coniferous species.

Leaf shape is a very useful guide, and some of the main shapes are shown in the diagrams below. The margin may be quite smooth (entire), but is normally toothed to some extent and often deeply lobed. Compound leaves are divided into several distinct leaflets.

Fruits may be dry or fleshy. The *nut* is a common dry fruit, with a woody coat and a single seed. *Berries* are juicy fruits with several seeds. The skin is often thin, but may be quite thick as in oranges. *Drupes*, or stone fruits, have a woody inner layer (the stone) surrounding a single seed. The outer part of the fruit is usually fleshy. Cherries, plums, and peaches are examples. The walnut is also a drupe, but its outer region is leathery. Apples and pears are known as *pomes*. The fleshy, edible part here is the swollen top of the flower stalk in which the seeds are embedded.

A variety of tree leaves

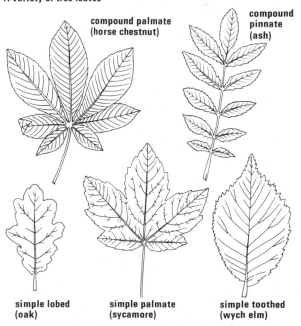

compound palmate
(horse chestnut)

compound pinnate
(ash)

simple lobed
(oak)

simple palmate
(sycamore)

simple toothed
(wych elm)

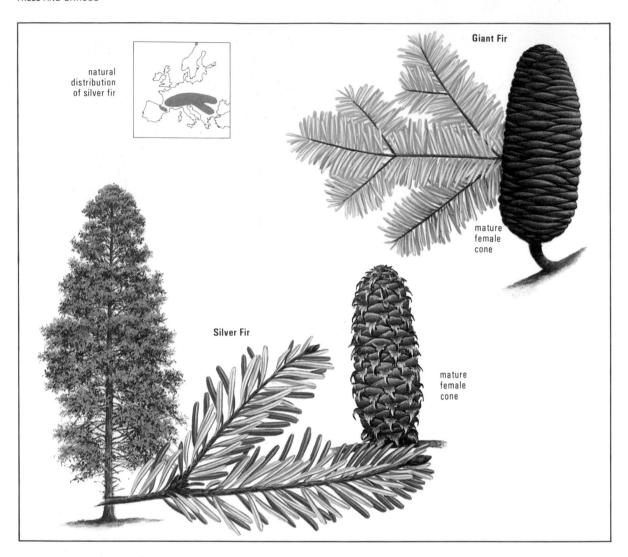

natural
distribution
of silver fir

Giant Fir

mature
female
cone

Silver Fir

mature
female
cone

Cone-bearing Trees

PINE FAMILY
Pinaceae

This important family of over 300 species occurs in the Northern hemisphere, forming forests in the cooler northern regions and restricted to mountains in the south. The trees belonging to it – firs, cedars, larches, spruces, pines, and hemlocks – all have needle-like leaves and woody cones made up of spirally arranged scales. Nearly all are evergreens.

SILVER FIR
Abies alba
This European conifer forms pure forests in mountainous regions of central Europe, from the Pyrenees across the Alps to the Balkan mountains. It is widely cultivated for its timber and other useful products and it grows to 57m.
Crown: narrow and conical, with level branches that have upturned tips.

Bark: smooth, dark grey, and blistered in young trees, becoming cracked into small square plates with age.
Shoots: grey-buff, with dark hairs.
Buds: red-brown and egg-shaped.
Leaves: thick needles with notched tips, dark green above with two narrow white bands beneath; 2–2·5cm long. They are arranged in two rows along the twigs.
Cones: erect and cylindrical, 10–15cm long, ripening from green to orange-

brown. The large scales have bracts turned towards the base of the cone; they fall off when ripe leaving a central axis on the tree.
Uses: soft yellow-white timber best for planks, joinery, boxes, carving, paper pulp, etc. Oil of turpentine, distilled from the leaves and wood, is used in medicine and veterinary work for sprains and bruises; Strasbourg turpentine, obtained from the bark blisters, is used in paints and varnishes.

GRAND or GIANT FIR
Abies grandis
A native of the west coast of North America, this fast-growing tree is planted for its timber in northern and central Europe, where it grows to 56m.
Crown: narrow and conical, with the branches in regular whorls.
Bark: brown-grey, with resin blisters, becoming darker and cracked into small square plates with age.
Shoots: smooth and olive green.
Buds: purple, becoming coated with resin; 2mm long.

Leaves: soft needles with notched tips, shiny green above with two silver bands beneath; 2—5cm long. They are arranged in two rows along the twigs.
Cones: erect and cylindrical, 7—10cm long, maturing from light green to red-brown.
Uses: pale cream or white timber for boxes, paper pulp, etc.

ATLAS CEDAR
Cedrus atlantica
Outside its native Atlas Mountains in North Africa, this cedar is commonly planted as an ornamental tree in parks and gardens and is sometimes grown for timber in southern Europe; it reaches a height of 40m.
Crown: broad and conical; the branches grow up from the trunk and their tips turn upwards.
Bark: smooth and dark grey, becoming cracked and scaly with age.
Buds: light red-brown and egg-shaped with black-tipped scales; 2—3mm long.
Leaves: stiff green or bluish-green needles, 1—3cm long, growing in tufts of up to 45 on short spurs; they form flat plates of foliage on the branches.
Male cones: conical, 3—5cm long.
Female cones: erect and barrel-shaped, with a hollow at the tip, maturing in 2 years to a pale purple-brown colour; 5—8cm long. The fan-shaped scales fall off to release winged seeds, leaving a central axis on the tree.

CEDAR OF LEBANON
Cedrus libani
A native of the Lebanon Mountains, Syria and south-east Turkey, the cedar of Lebanon is widely planted as an ornamental tree in parks, gardens, and churchyards; grows to 40m. It is distinguished from the Atlas cedar by the following features:
Crown: conical, becoming flat-topped with wide-spreading level branches.
Leaves: dark grass-green needles, 2—3cm long, growing in tufts of 10 to 20 on short spurs.
Female cones: like the Atlas cedar but larger — 7—12cm long.

EUROPEAN LARCH
Larix decidua
Native to central Europe — from the Alps to the West Carpathians — this graceful deciduous conifer is planted in northern and western Europe as an ornamental tree and for its strong, highly-prized timber; it grows to 40m.
Crown: narrow and conical, becoming flat-topped with age. The branches tend to droop down, then turn up at the tips.
Bark: grey-brown and smooth, splitting into vertical cracks with age.
Shoots: pale yellow or pale pink, long, and hanging down from the branches.
Buds: brown, scaly, and resinous.

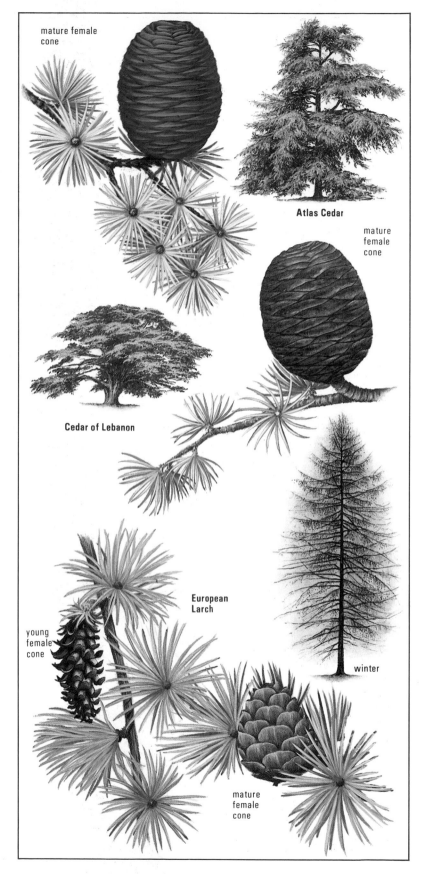

mature female cone

Atlas Cedar

mature female cone

Cedar of Lebanon

European Larch

winter

young female cone

mature female cone

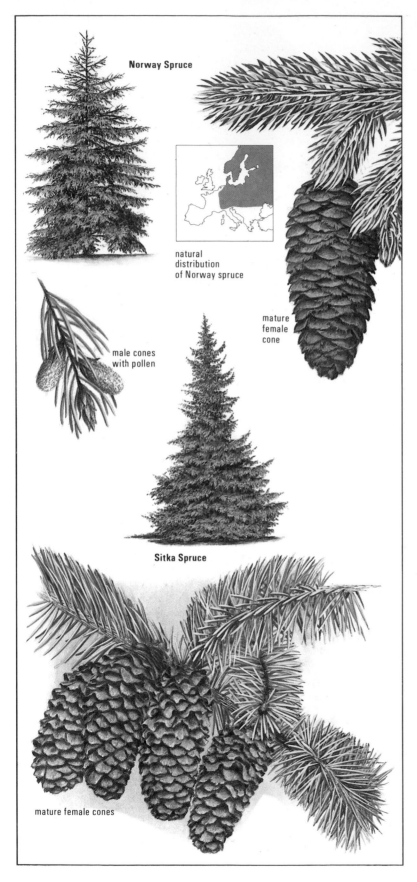

Norway Spruce

natural
distribution
of Norway spruce

male cones
with pollen

mature
female
cone

Sitka Spruce

mature female cones

Leaves: soft needles, 2–3cm long, growing in clusters of 20 to 30 from short spurs on the twigs. Emerald green in March, they become darker, and finally golden in autumn.
Male cones: small, round, and golden, 0·5–1cm long.
Female cones: pale to rose-red, and flower-like, 1cm long, maturing to brown, egg-shaped cones, 2–4cm by 2–3cm, with rounded scales.
Uses: strong durable resinous timber, with yellowish sapwood and red-brown heartwood, used for fencing, gates, planking for fishing boats, staircases, wall panelling, light furniture, telegraph poles, railway sleepers, pit-props, etc.
The Japanese larch (*L. kaempferi*) is now widely planted for its quicker growth and greater disease resistance. Its mature cones have wavy edges and its needles are slightly wider than those of the common larch.

NORWAY SPRUCE
Picea abies
A conifer of central and northern Europe, the Norway spruce is widely grown in forests, plantations, shelter belts, gardens, etc., for Christmas trees and timber; it grows to 40m.
Crown: narrow and conical; the branches are level except at the top, where they grow up from the trunk.
Bark: smooth and reddish-brown, becoming dark purple with age and flaking into small rounded scales.
Shoots: reddish or orange-brown.
Buds: smooth, brown, and pointed.
Leaves: dark-green sharp-pointed four-sided needles, 1–2cm long, growing from pegs all round the twigs.
Male cones: globular and yellow, 1cm long, hanging down from the tips of the shoots.
Female cones: erect, oval, green or dark red; when fertilized they become dark brown and cylindrical, 12–18cm long, and hang down.
Uses: strong light elastic pale-yellow timber for boxes, interior joinery, barrels, paper pulp, chipboard, violin and cello bellies, etc. The wood fibres are woven into mats and screens. Turpentine is extracted from blisters on the trunk and branches.

SITKA or SILVER SPRUCE
Picea sitchensis
Native to the coastal regions of western North America, from Alaska to North California, this fast-growing spruce is now widely planted in certain coastal areas of northern and western Europe for its useful timber; grows to 80m in North America, 50m in Europe. It can be recognized by the following features:
Crown: narrow and conical, with a long spire-like tip; in older trees the branches droop and the crown broadens.
Bark: dark grey or grey-brown and speckled; it flakes off in purplish scales in older trees.

Leaves: slender flat sharp-pointed needles, 1–3cm long, bluish-green above with two blue-white bands beneath.

Ripe female cones: light brown to whitish, blunt, and cylindrical, 5–10cm long; the scales are thin and papery with crinkled edges.

Uses: strong light fine-grained timber for interior joinery, boxes, carpentry, paper pulp, chipboard, pit-props, etc.

AROLLA or SWISS STONE PINE
Pinus cembra

This pine occurs at an altitude of just under 3000m in the Alps and Carpathians (which is close to the limit for tree growth). It is planted in other parts of Europe for ornament and timber and grows to a height of 25m.

Crown: columnar; stout level branches with upturned tips grow right from the base of the trunk.

Bark: dark grey or orange-brown, becoming scaly and rugged with broad cracks.

Shoots: greenish-brown, densely covered with orange-brown down.

Leaves: needles, 7–9cm long, growing in dense bunches of five; their outer surface is shiny dark green, the inner surface green-white.

Cones: egg-shaped, 8 by 6cm, ripening from purple to shiny red-brown. The edible seeds are released after the cone has fallen and rotted.

Uses: the pale resinous timber, which is easily worked, is used for furniture, turned articles, and toys.

MONTEREY PINE
Pinus radiata

This wind-resistant tree, native to Monterey Bay in South California, is grown in mild coastal regions of western Europe for shelter and ornament; fast-growing, it is planted commercially in Spain, South Africa, Australia, and New Zealand. It grows to 30m.

Crown: conical, becoming broader and round-topped with age; branches grow low down on the trunk.

Bark: dark brown or dull grey, with deep cracks.

Buds: brownish, pointed, and covered with resin; 1–2cm long.

Leaves: slender bright-green needles, growing in threes; 10–15cm long.

Cones: large and irregular – 7–14cm by 5–8cm and flattened on the side nearest to the stem – with glossy brown scales. These cones grow in clusters of 3 to 5 and remain on the tree for many years.

Uses: timber for boxes and paper pulp.

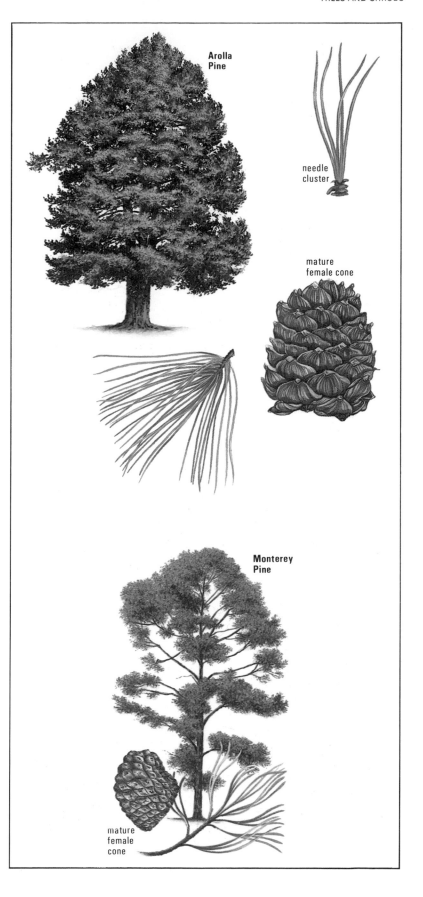

Arolla Pine

needle cluster

mature female cone

Monterey Pine

mature female cone

SCOTS PINE
Pinus sylvestris

Native over much of Europe and northern and western Asia, the Scots pine is very widely planted for its valuable timber; it also makes an attractive hardy ornamental tree, thriving in light acid soils. Grows to 35—40m.

Crown: pyramid-shaped or conical when young, becoming flat-topped or rounded with age, with the branches sparsely arranged high up on the trunk.

Bark: at the base of the trunk reddish or grey-brown and cracked; on the upper trunk and branches orange-red to pink, and scaly.

Shoots: hairless and pale green, becoming brown.

Buds: cylindrical, dark brown or red.

Leaves: blue-grey or blue-green needles, often twisted, growing in pairs; 3—7cm long.

Male cones: small, yellow, and rounded, clustered near the tips of the shoots in early summer.

Female cones: pink and globular when fertilized, becoming green and turning down on the stem during the next year. Mature third-year cones, 3-8cm long, are grey-brown, ovoid, and pointed.

Uses: yields a good multi-purpose resinous timber with reddish heart-wood and pale-brown sapwood: one of the best softwoods for general construction, telegraph poles, railway sleepers, fencing, pit-props, paper pulp, chipboard, etc. Other products are pitch and tar; oil of turpentine and rosin (from the resin); and a reddish-yellow dye (from the cones).

STONE or UMBRELLA PINE
Pinus pinea

Native to the western Mediterranean, this wind-resistant pine has been planted in coastal regions all over the Mediterranean region since Roman times; it grows to 30m.

Crown: umbrella-shaped, with large spreading branches supported on a short trunk: an unmistakable feature of the Mediterranean landscape.

Bark: red-brown or orange, deeply cracked and scaly.

Shoots: pale greyish-green and curved.

Buds: red-brown, with deeply fringed white scales that turn out.

Leaves: dark greyish-green sharp-pointed needles, growing in pairs; 12-20cm long.

Cones: shining brown, globular, and flat-based, 10—15cm by 8—10cm; the scales are rounded and each has a central boss. The seeds are edible.

Uses: the rich oily seeds are eaten raw or roasted and used as a flavouring; the timber is used locally for furniture.

WEYMOUTH PINE
Pinus strobus

A native of eastern North America, the Weymouth pine is widely cultivated in central and western Europe for its timber; it grows to 30—40m.

Crown: narrow and conical, becoming irregular and flat-topped with age.

Bark: smooth and greenish-brown in young trees, becoming grey-black and cracked with age.

Shoots: slender and bright green, becoming greenish-brown with fine hairs at the bases of the needle bundles.

Leaves: slender bluish-green needles, 8—12cm long, growing in bundles of five, form horizontal masses on the branches.

Cones: brown and banana-shaped, 10—15cm long, hanging down from the stem; scales curve outwards. Young cones are green and straighter.

Uses: pale-brown, light, fine-textured timber for pianos, stringed instruments, doors, window frames and general purposes.

AUSTRIAN PINE
Pinus nigra var. *nigra*

Native to Austria, central Italy, and the Balkans, this hardy wind-resistant pine is commonly planted on coasts as a wind-break and screen and to stabilize dunes; it grows to 33m.

Crown: irregular and spreading, with dark black-brown upper branches.

Several stems normally rise from a short bole, making this a poor timber tree.

Bark: black-brown to dark grey, very scaly and coarsely ridged.

Shoots: shining yellow-brown, stout and ridged.

Buds: pale-brown and broad-based, 1cm long, tapering to a sharp point.

Leaves: stiff dark-green to black needles, curved and sharp-pointed, growing in pairs; 10—15cm long.

Cones: yellow- to grey-brown, egg-shaped and pointed; 5—8cm long.

CORSICAN PINE
Pinus nigra var. *maritima*

This fast-growing pine, native to Corsica, southern Italy, and Sicily, is planted for shelter and yields a useful timber; grows to 35m. It can be distinguished from the Austrian pine by the following features:

Crown: narrow and conical, with level branches. One main trunk.

Bark: pink-grey to dark brown, with shallow cracks.

Buds: 2cm long, with a long point.

Leaves: flexible grey-green or sage-green needles, often twisted, growing in pairs; 12—18cm long.

Uses: hard strong timber, with reddish heartwood surrounded by pale-brown sapwood, used for general construction work in the Mediterranean (see Scots pine for details); it also yields a useful resin.

mature
female
cone

Weymouth
Pine

Corsican
Pine

Austrian Pine

mature
female cone

Scots Pine

mature
female
cone

Stone Pine

mature
female cone

natural
distribution
of Scots pine

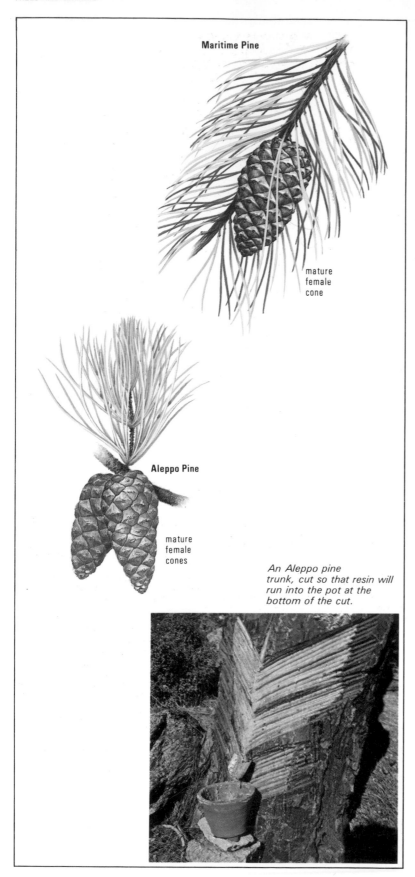

Maritime Pine

mature
female
cone

Aleppo Pine

mature
female
cones

*An Aleppo pine
trunk, cut so that resin will
run into the pot at the
bottom of the cut.*

MARITIME PINE
Pinus pinaster
The maritime pine is native to the coasts of central and western Mediterranean regions: it grows best in light well-drained soils and is often planted for shelter and to reclaim sand dunes, as well as for its timber; grows to 30m.

Crown: pyramid-shaped, with spreading branches growing high up on the trunk.

Bark: pale grey or reddish-brown with deep cracks, becoming darker with age.

Shoots: pinkish- or reddish-brown and hairless.

Buds: bright red-brown and non-resinous, with fringed scales.

Leaves: stout leathery sharp-pointed needles, growing in pairs; 15—25cm long.

Cones: bright glossy brown and pointed, up to 22cm long; the scales each have an upturned prickle. Cones remain on the branches for several years before opening.

Uses: tapped for resin, which yields turpentine oil (used in solvents for paints and varnishes) and rosin (used in paints, varnishes, soaps, and linoleum); timber used for general construction work, telegraph poles, pit-props, and paper pulp.

ALEPPO PINE
Pinus halepensis
A Mediterranean species, the Aleppo pine is a familiar sight in hot dry coastal regions. It thrives on exposed limestone hills and rocky ground, checking soil erosion and acting as a wind-break, and has many important uses in the Mediterranean region; it grows to 20m.

Crown: narrow when young, becoming domed with age with twisting branches supported on a stout trunk.

Bark: purple- or reddish-brown, with deep cracks.

Shoots: pale and slender, greenish-brown or yellowish.

Buds: red-brown, cylindrical, 1cm long.

Leaves: long slender flexible bright-green needles, usually in pairs; 9—15cm long.

Cones: bright reddish-brown, pointed or egg-shaped, 5—12cm long; borne on short down-turned stalks, they remain on the tree for several years.

Uses: coarse-grained resinous timber for furniture, ships, houses, pitch, and fuel. The tree is also tapped for resin, which yields turpentine oil and is used for preserving wine; its bark is used for tanning skins.

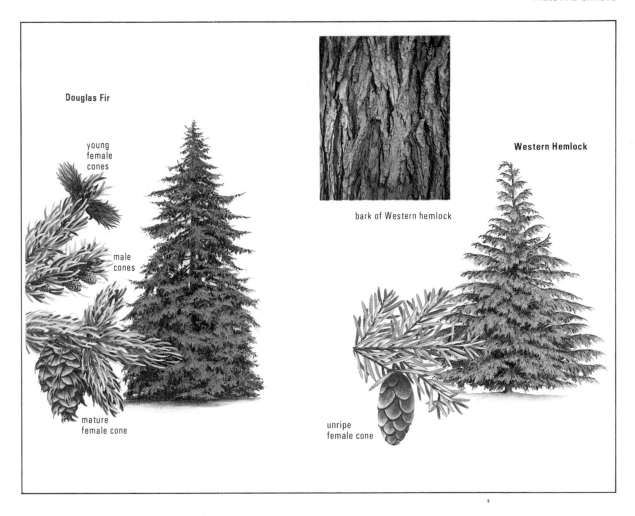

Douglas Fir

young female cones

male cones

mature female cone

bark of Western hemlock

Western Hemlock

unripe female cone

DOUGLAS FIR
Pseudotsuga menziesii

Native to western North America, this tall fast-growing tree is very widely planted in Europe for its timber. Growing to 100m in North America, it attains a height of 50m or more in Europe. It is not closely related to the true firs and can be distinguished from them by its cones.

Crown: pyramid-shaped, becoming flat-shaped with age.

Bark: dark grey and resin-blistered in young trees, becoming red-brown or purplish and corky, with deep cracks and ridges, with age.

Shoots: pale- or yellowish-green, covered with fine hairs.

Buds: pale brown and spindle-shaped, up to 7mm long; non-resinous.

Leaves: flexible aromatic needles, 2–3cm long, with two white bands underneath each side of the midrib; they grow singly on the stems and leave smooth oval scars when they fall.

Cones: dull brown and cylindrical, 5–8cm by 2·5cm, hanging down from the stem; the scales each have a three-lobed bract, which points towards the tip of the cone.

Uses: strong durable timber, with pinkish-brown heartwood and pale brown sapwood, for construction, flooring, joinery, fencing, pit-props, paper pulp, telegraph poles, and masts.

WESTERN HEMLOCK
Tsuga heterophylla

This graceful fast-growing conifer is native to the west coast of North America, where it may reach a height of 70m. A producer of good-quality timber, it is widely grown in north-west Europe; it prefers shade and is frequently planted under hardwood trees. It grows to 50m.

Crown: pyramid-shaped or conical, with a spire-like tip that arches over; the tips of the branches droop down.

Bark: brown, smooth, and flaky in young trees; becomes darker, with deep furrows and scaly ridges, with age.

Shoots: ribbed, pale yellow-brown, and covered with long hairs.

Buds: small, brown, and globular.

Leaves: flattened aromatic needles of different sizes 5–15mm long, with rounded tips; shining dark green above, they have two white bands along each side of the midrib on the lower surface. The needles have short stalks, and leave round orange scars on the twigs when they fall.

Cones: pale brown and egg-shaped, 2–3cm long, with smooth rounded scales; they hang down from the ends of the twigs. Unripe cones are green.

Uses: produces strong fine-textured pale-yellow timber with a darker heartwood, used for construction, joinery, boxes, paper pulp, etc.

EASTERN HEMLOCK
Tsuga canadensis

A native of eastern North America, this hemlock is similar to the western species but its timber is of inferior quality. It is often planted in Europe for ornament and occasionally for timber; it grows to 32m. It can be distinguished from the other species by the following features:

Crown: broad and conical.

Buds: egg-shaped; green with a brown tip.

Cones: small — 1·5–2cm.

mature female cone

Giant Sequoia or Wellingtonia or Big Tree

The enormous trunks of the giant sequoia or 'big tree'. The bark is very soft and can be punched without hurting one's fist.

Coast Redwood

mature female cone

REDWOOD FAMILY   Taxodiaceae

Most of the trees in this primitive family, which was once large and widely distributed, are now extinct. Those that remain – about 14 species – can be regarded as living fossils. They have awl-like or flattened needles and usually rounded, woody or leathery, cones. There are both evergreen and deciduous species.

COAST REDWOOD
Sequoia sempervirens
This majestic tree is native to western North America, its natural range being restricted to a narrow strip of coast from south-west Oregon to California. An important timber tree in North America, it is planted in Europe mainly for ornament in parks and gardens but occasionally for its timber. The redwood is considered to be the tallest tree in the world: a specimen of over 112m has been recorded in California; it grows to about 40m in Europe. It is also one of the longest lived: some Californian trees are over 2000 years old. It is an evergreen.
Crown: columnar, with level or drooping branches.
Bark: rusty red, soft, and fibrous, becoming darker, thicker, and deeply cracked with age.
Shoots: green and hairless, surrounded by green scale leaves.
Buds: short and scaly.
Leaves: hard, flattened, and blade-like, 1·5—2cm long, dark green above with a white band along each side of the midrib beneath; arranged in two rows along the side-branches. The leaves on the main stems of the branches are smaller and awl-shaped.
Male cones: small, rounded, and yellowish, in clusters at the tips of the main shoots.
Female cones: woody and globular, 2—2·5cm long, with wrinkled red-brown scales attached to the centre of the cone. They produce winged seeds.

Uses: soft strong durable timber, with pale-yellow sapwood and red-brown heartwood, suitable for garden furniture, fencing, etc., as well as for cabinet work.

GIANT SEQUOIA
Sequoiadendron giganteum
The most massive — but not the tallest — tree in the world, the giant sequoia forms natural forests in California's Sierra Nevada, where it grows to over 80m, with a girth of 24m, and lives for over 3000 years. In Europe it is planted for ornament, reaching a height of 50m and a girth of 7m.
Crown: narrow and conical; the ends of the branches curve upwards; the trunk is often buttressed at its base.
Bark: reddish-brown, thick, soft, and fibrous; becomes darker, fluted, and deeply cracked with age.
Leaves: blue-green or dark-green pointed scales, 4—7mm long, densely covering the branchlets. Evergreen.
Cones: brown and egg-shaped, 5—8cm long, drooping down from stalks at the ends of the branches; the scales are attached at the centre.

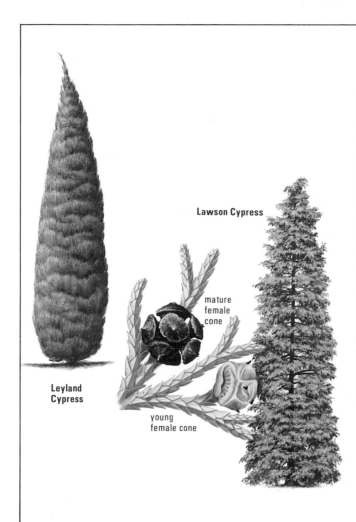

Lawson Cypress

mature
female
cone

Leyland
Cypress

young
female cone

Several varieties of Lawson cypress growing in a landscaped garden.

CYPRESS FAMILY Cupressaceae

The hundred or more species of evergreens in this family are found in the cooler regions of both hemispheres and on mountain tops in the tropics and subtropics. They often have two kinds of leaves – needle-like juvenile leaves and scalelike adult leaves – and small woody cones (except the junipers, which have fleshy cones).

LAWSON CYPRESS
Chamaecyparis lawsoniana
A tree of western North America – from north-west California and south-west Oregon — Lawson cypress is very widely planted in northern and central Europe for shelter and ornament. Many cultivated varieties are seen in parks, gardens, and church-yards; the tree is also planted commercially for timber on a small scale. Growing to 60m in America, it reaches a height of 38m in Europe.
Crown: narrow and conical; the tips of the branches droop down.
Bark: smooth, grey-brown, and shiny, becoming purplish-brown, cracked, and flaking off in older trees.

Leaves: bright green, triangular, and scale-like, borne on flattened branched twigs in horizontal sprays, like fern fronds. There are also cultivated varieties with golden and blue-green foliage.
Male cones: crimson and club-shaped, 5mm long, at the tips of the branches.
Female cones: green and globular, borne at the tips of the shorter branches, ripening to woody purple-brown cones, 7–8mm in diameter, producing winged seeds.
Uses: produces strong light durable timber, with yellow-white sapwood and dark-brown heartwood, for joinery, fencing, and underwater construction.

LEYLAND CYPRESS
x *Cupressocyparis leylandii*
This hybrid occurred in 1888 in the garden of C J Leyland as some chance seedlings, although their hybrid nature was not realized until the 1920s. The parents were the Nootka cypress (*Chamaecyparis nootkatensis*) and the Monterey cypress (*Cupressus macrocarpa*). Since then several hardy, fast-growing varieties have been raised and the tree is now widely planted in parks and gardens in north-west Europe. Growing to 30m, it is usually propagated by cuttings.
Crown: columnar, tapering to a pointed tip.
Bark: dark red-brown, with shallow cracks.
Leaves: scale-like, of various colours (dark grey-green to blue-green, depending on the variety), clothing branched sprayed twigs.
Male cones: brown and club-shaped, yellow at the tips of the shoots.
Female cones: globular and greenish, ripening to grey or chocolate-brown cones, up to 1·5cm in diameter.

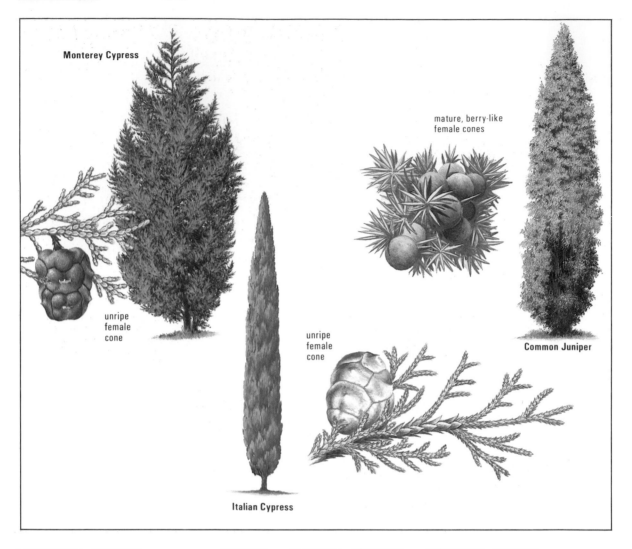

Monterey Cypress

unripe female cone

mature, berry-like female cones

Common Juniper

unripe female cone

Italian Cypress

MONTEREY CYPRESS
Cupressus macrocarpa

Native to California, the Monterey cypress — quick-growing and salt-resistant — is planted in western and southern Europe for both shelter and ornament in parks, gardens, church-yards and by the sea, and also for its timber. It reaches a height of 37m.

Crown: columnar, with a pointed top, becoming spreading and flat-topped with age.

Bark: brown with shallow ridges, becoming grey with thick peeling ridges in very old trees.

Leaves: scale-like and blunt-tipped, bright- or dark-green with paler margins; 1–2mm long. They completely cover the twigs and smell of lemon when crushed.

Male cones: yellow and egg-shaped, 3mm long, borne on small side-shoots.

Female cones: egg-shaped, green and purple, 6mm long, on central shoots; they ripen to rounded lumpy cones, 3–4cm long, with shining purple-brown scales each with a central boss.

ITALIAN or FUNERAL CYPRESS
Cupressus sempervirens

This handsome Mediterranean cypress is commonly planted in gardens and cemeteries, especially in the Mediter-ranean region; it also yields a highly valued timber. The tree grows to 23m.

Crown: usually narrow and columnar, tapering to a pointed tip, but may be pyramid-shaped, with spreading level branches.

Bark: brown-grey, with shallow spiralled ridges.

Leaves: dark green, scale-like, and triangular, 1mm long, arranged in overlapping rows that completely cover the twigs.

Male cones: greenish and egg-shaped, 3mm long, at the tips of the twigs.

Female cones: greenish and globular, becoming dark red-brown and finally dull grey, 4 by 3cm; the scales each have a central spine.

Uses: strong durable fragrant timber, resistant to decay, used for carving, furniture, stakes, and vine props. The crushed leaves and seeds have medicinal properties.

COMMON JUNIPER
Juniperus communis

Very widely distributed in the northern hemisphere — from North America to south-west Asia and from Siberia to the Mediterranean — this adaptable small tree or shrub grows well on poor soils in a variety of habitats; it reaches a height of 6m.

Crown: variable — usually pointed but may be wide-spreading and broad.

Bark: reddish-brown.

Leaves: sharp-pointed needles, 1cm long, spreading out from the stems in whorls of three; there is a whitish band on the upper surface and the lower surface is grey-green.

Male cones: solitary, yellow, and cylindrical; 4mm long.

Female cones: greenish and glob-ular, ripening in 2 to 3 years to blue-black berry-like fruits, 6–9mm in diameter.

Male and female cones grow on separate trees, in the axils of the needles.

Uses: the ripe berries are used for flavouring gin and seasoning food; oil of juniper is distilled from the unripe fruits.

Prickly Juniper

mature female cones

mature female cone

Western Red Cedar

The fan-shaped leaves and young male cones of the Maidenhair tree — the only living member of a very ancient group of plants.

CADE or PRICKLY JUNIPER
Juniperus oxycedrus

The prickly juniper is widespread in its native Mediterranean region, growing in coastal parts, dry hills, rocky ground, and woods; it reaches a height of 8m.

Crown: basically conical and densely branched. On windswept slopes it may be no more than a large 'cushion' hugging the ground.

Leaves: sharp-pointed or blunt needles, 16mm long, with two white bands along either side of the mid-rib on the upper surface.

Female cones: (on separate trees from the males): rounded and berry-like, ripening from green to reddish or yellowish; 6–10mm in diameter.

Uses: oil of cade, used in medicine and veterinary work, is distilled from the wood; the wood is very resistant to decay and is used for making charcoal.

WESTERN RED CEDAR
Thuja plicata

An important timber tree of western North America, the western red cedar is cultivated in parks, gardens, and plantations in Europe for shelter and timber. Noted for its quick growth, it reaches a height of 40m.

Crown: narrow and conical, with a spire-like tip and upswept branches; it broadens with age.

Bark: reddish-brown and fibrous, becoming grey-brown and peeling off in strips.

Leaves: blunt and scale-like, growing in sprays on flattened twigs; the upper surface is bright glossy green, the undersurface paler with white streaks.

Male cones: yellow and very small, at the tips of the smallest shoots.

Female cones: leathery and egg-shaped, ripening from green to brown, 1·5cm long; they are each made up of 10 to 12 thin overlapping spreading spine-tipped scales and are borne at the tips of the branches.

Uses: soft light durable timber, used for joinery, fencing and other outdoor construction.

MAIDENHAIR FAMILY
Ginkgoaceae

MAIDENHAIR TREE
Ginkgo biloba

The sole living member of a very ancient group, the maidenhair is a native of China. It is widely planted for ornament in parks and gardens. Although a gymnosperm, it has no cones and looks more like a flowering tree. It is deciduous and reaches heights of 30m. There are separate male and female trees.

Crown: variable, but normally tall and slender with short and elegant branches.

Bark: greyish brown, with a network of ridges and furrows when older.

Leaves: leathery, pale green, and fan-shaped — quite unlike those of any other tree. Up to 12cm across. Turn yellow before falling.

Male flowers: in thick yellow catkins 6–8cm long.

Female flowers: like small yellowish acorns: one or two on a slender stalk. Globular fruit 2·5cm across, green at first, ripening to brown.

YEW FAMILY
Taxaceae

YEW
Taxus baccata

Widely distributed in Europe, North Africa, and south-west Asia, the yew is commonly planted in many cultivated varieties in parks, gardens, and churchyards. Yews can live to a great age — it is estimated that some are over a thousand years old — and reach a height of 25m; their bark, shoots, leaves, and seeds are all poisonous.

Crown: rounded or pyramid-shaped and densely branched; the branches are level or upturned.

Bark: reddish-brown and flaking; becomes deeply furrowed with age.

Leaves: leathery, sharp-pointed needles, 1–4cm by 3 mm, very dark green above and yellowish-green underneath. They are arranged in two rows along the side branches.

Male cones: small, rounded, and yellow, with overlapping scales.

Female cones: bright red and berry-like, enclosing a single seed; 1cm long.

Male and female cones grow on separate trees in the axils of the leaves.

Uses: the wood is hard, heavy, durable, strong, and elastic; in the Middle Ages it was used for bows, and more recently for cabinetwork, wood sculpture, etc.

Yew

mature berry-like female cones

bark of yew

MONKEY-PUZZLE FAMILY
Araucariaceae

MONKEY PUZZLE
Araucaria araucana

The monkey puzzle — a native of Chile and Argentina — is quite widely planted in Europe as an ornamental tree for its curious branching system. It can grow to 30m but cultivated trees are smaller.

Crown: broad and rounded; the stout branches grow in regular tiers, drooping down at the base of the tree, and all have up-turned ends.

Bark: smooth and grey.

Leaves: leathery, green, and triangular, 3–4cm long, each with a spiny tip; they overlap each other and completely cover the twigs and branches.

Male cones: dark-brown and cylindrical, 10–12cm long.

Female cones: nearly spherical, 15cm across, green with golden spines; they break up into scales on the tree. The large brown seeds are edible and usually eaten roasted.

Male and female cones usually grow on separate trees.

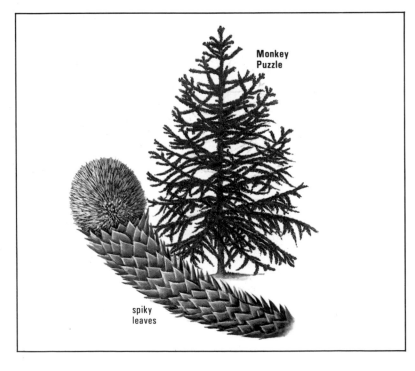

Monkey Puzzle

spiky leaves

Flowering Trees

PALM FAMILY
Palmae

This family of flowering plants is widespread in the tropics, and some palms are cultivated in subtropical and warm regions. Unlike the other trees, palms do not produce true wood, and their stems – which are unbranched – are covered with layers of strong tough fibres, rather than bark. The trunks do not get much thicker as they get older. Palm stems are crowned by a tuft of leaves. In the feather palms each leaf consists of a row of leaflets along each side of the midrib; in fan palms the leaflets arise from the same point at the top of the leaf stalk. The palms are all evergreens.

CHUSAN PALM
Trachycarpus excelsus
Native to south China and Japan, this tall fan palm is often grown as an ornamental both in the Mediterranean and also in warm regions elsewhere. The stout shaggy stem is covered with a mass of hard brown fibres and the woody bases of shed leaves; the tree reaches a height of 11m.
Leaves: rounded, each made up of 50–60 long narrow pointed leaflets. Borne on spiny leaf stalks, the leaves are a rich dark green, turning bright yellow and then dull brown before falling.
Flowers: yellow and very small, growing in drooping clusters, 60cm long; male and female flowers are usually in separate clusters.
Fruit: blue-black and globular; 1–1·5cm across.

DWARF FAN PALM
Chamaerops humilis
The only native European palm, the dwarf fan palm is found in dry regions along the Mediterranean coast – from Italy westwards but excluding France. It is widely cultivated; most forms are stemless but some have stout, fibre-covered trunks and may reach a height of 6–7m.
Leaves: rounded, each made up of 12 to 15 stiff pointed leaflets and borne on a slender spiny leaf stalk.
Flowers: small and yellow, in dense clusters that are at first sheathed in red spathes.
Fruit: brownish-yellow and globular; 2cm across.

Chusan Palm

The dwarf fan palm, with the trunk covered by fibrous old leaf bases.

Dwarf Fan Palm
with flower clusters

underside of leaf

White Poplar

ripe male catkins

ripe female catkins

winter

bark of black poplar

WILLOW FAMILY
Salicaceae

The willows and poplars constitute nearly all the 300 or more species of deciduous trees and shrubs that make up this family. They all have flowers grouped into single-sexed catkins. Willow catkins produce nectar and are pollinated partly by insects. Poplar catkins are always pollinated by the wind. The dry fruit – a capsule – splits to release seeds, which are covered in silky hairs.

WHITE POPLAR
Populus alba
Native to central and southern Europe and central and western Asia, the white poplar is widely planted as an ornamental in parks and gardens; it grows to 30m.
Crown: broadest at the top, with twisted spreading branches.
Bark: smooth and grey-white in young trees, becoming black and rough at the base and patchy above.
Shoots and buds: densely covered with white woolly down.
Leaves: either large (9 by 8cm) and 5-lobed or small (5 by 5cm) and usually oval, with toothed or lobed margins; all have stalks 3–4cm long. The undersurface and stalks are white and downy.
Male catkins: crimson and grey.
Female catkins: pale green or greenish yellow, producing fluffy seeds. Male and female flowers (catkins), 4–8cm long, grow on separate trees.

BLACK POPLAR
Populus nigra
Widely distributed over much of Europe, this poplar is often planted as an ornamental tree; it grows to 35m and there are many varieties and hybrids.
Crown: broad, with upturned branches; the trunk is short and thick and often carries large burrs.
Bark: grey-brown to black, deeply furrowed into broad ridges.
Leaves: triangular to diamond-shaped, 5–8cm by 6–8cm, with translucent toothed margins; borne on 3–4cm-stalks, they are deep green above and paler beneath, turning a soft yellow.
Male catkins: grey, becoming crimson; 5cm long.
Female catkins: greenish-white, 6–7cm long, producing white woolly seeds.
Male and female flowers grow on separate trees.
Uses: soft light nearly white wood used for packing cases and general purposes.

Right: A beechwood displaying the autumn coloration typical of many deciduous trees.

Lombardy Poplar

ripe female catkins

Aspen

underside of leaf

summer and autumn leaves

ripe female catkin

White Willow

natural distribution of white willow

LOMBARDY POPLAR
Populus nigra var. *italica*
This variety of the black poplar, produced in Italy, is now very widely grown for ornament and for shelterbelts, where its quick growth is much appreciated: it grows to 36m.
Crown: narrow and columnar, with a pointed tip and upswept branches.
Leaves: triangular, with a rounded base and small curved teeth; 6 by 4·5cm. Bright green, they are borne on flattened stalks, 2·5cm long.

ASPEN
Populus tremula
Very widely distributed over the whole of Europe – and extending into the Arctic Circle – the aspen is most commonly found on hillsides and in damp places; it grows to 25m.
Crown: conical and sparsely branched, becoming broader with age.
Bark: greenish-grey and smooth, becoming brown and ridged at the base.
Buds: red-brown, sticky, and pointed.
Leaves: rounded, with curved irregular teeth; 4–6cm by 5–7cm. Borne on slender flattened stalks, 4–6cm long, they are dull rich green above and pale grey-green beneath. The leaves flutter in the slightest breeze, giving rise to the tree's alternative name of trembling poplar.
Male catkins: purplish-grey and downy, becoming yellow with pollen.
Female catkins: green, 4cm long, becoming woolly and white when they shed their seeds.
Male and female catkins grow on separate trees.
Uses: soft light white wood excellent for matches and paper pulp.

WHITE WILLOW
Salix alba
This willow is widely distributed in Europe, central Asia, and North Africa, often found growing by streams and rivers; it reaches a height of 25m.
Crown: conical, becoming rather shapeless with spreading branches.
Bark: dark grey with thick ridges.
Shoots: greyish-pink to olive-brown, slender, and hairy.
Buds: dark pinkish, covered with grey hairs.
Leaves: narrow and pointed, 7–8cm long, with toothed margins; blue-grey and covered with silky hairs.
Male catkins: yellow, with 2 stamens to each flower.
Female catkins: green and slender, becoming white and fluffy with seed.
Male and female flowers grow on separate tree.
Uses: light tough timber for flooring, cart bottoms, etc.; the pliant young twigs are used for basketry. Cricket bats are made from a quick-growing variety of this species known as the cricket-bat willow. It has purple shoots and bluer leaves than the normal white willow.

GOAT WILLOW or SALLOW
Salix caprea
Native from Europe to north-east Asia, the sallow is common in damp wooded regions and coppices; it grows to 16m.
Crown: open, with upswept branches.
Bark: smooth and grey in young trees, becoming brown with wide cracks.
Shoots: deep red-brown and initially covered with long hairs.
Buds: red, oval, and pointed; 3—4mm.
Leaves: usually oval with a pointed tip and wavy margins; 10 by 6cm. Dark grey-green above and grey and woolly beneath, they have dark red hairy stalks with 2 small leaves at the base.
Male catkins: egg-shaped, 3cm long, and covered with silvery hairs; later they sprout golden-tipped stamens.
Female catkins: arched, slender (5—6cm long), and pale green with whitish styles, producing fluffy seeds. Male and female flowers grow on separate trees and appear long before the leaves.

CRACK WILLOW
Salix fragilis
Found all over Europe and as far east as western Siberia and Iran, the crack willow is common in damp places, e.g. by rivers; it grows to 25m.
Crown: broad and conical with up-swept branches, becoming domed with twisted branches.
Bark: grey and scaly, developing thick brownish ridges with age.
Shoots: greenish-brown, snapping off cleanly and readily at the base.
Buds: brown, slender, and pointed.
Leaves: narrow and pointed, 12cm long, bright green and glossy above, grey-green and waxy beneath.
Male catkins: yellow; 2—5cm long.
Female catkins: green, 10cm long, becoming white and fluffy with seed. Male and female flowers grow on separate trees and appear with the leaves; they are slender, cylindrical, and pointed.

WEEPING WILLOW
Salix vitellina var. *pendula*
One of several types of weeping willow, this hybrid is widely planted as an ornamental tree in parks, gardens, and by rivers; it grows to 22m.
Crown: broad and domed; the curved branches bear long slender yellow shoots that hang straight down.
Bark: pale grey-brown, with a network of shallow ridges.
Leaves: narrow and pointed, 10cm long; pale green above, bluish-white beneath, and covered with fine hairs.

Goat Willow

female catkins

male catkins with pollen

Crack Willow

female catkins

Weeping willows are popular ornamental trees for parks and watersides. They come into leaf earlier than many other trees.

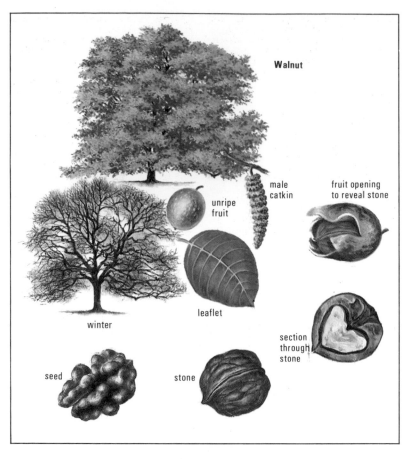

Walnut

male catkin

unripe fruit

fruit opening to reveal stone

leaflet

section through stone

winter

seed

stone

WALNUT FAMILY
Juglandaceae

WALNUT
Juglans regia

Thought to be native to south-east Europe and south-west Asia, the walnut is now naturalized in many parts of Europe; it grows to 30m.

Crown: rounded or spreading.

Bark: very pale grey, becoming deeply furrowed with age.

Buds: broad and squat; deep purple-brown to black.

Leaves: compound, with 3 to 4 leaflets down each side of the stalk and one (the largest) at the tip. Each leaflet is leathery and oval with a pointed tip, 8–20 by 4–10cm, and aromatic when crushed. Orange-brown when they first open, they become dull green above and paler beneath.

Male flowers: greenish-purple catkins, 5–10cm long, in the leaf axils.

Female flowers: greenish-yellow, 1cm long, in erect clusters of 2 to 5 at the tips of the shoots. They develop into globular dark-green fruits (drupes), the outer layer decaying to reveal the stone within.

Uses: the seeds are edible and yield a useful oil; the unripe fruits are pickled. A fast brown dye is obtained from the fruits and other parts. Walnut timber is hard, heavy, and fine-grained, with a pale grey-brown sapwood and chocolate-brown heartwood, and is attractively figured; it is highly valued for furniture, gunstocks, etc.

BIRCH FAMILY
Betulaceae

The deciduous trees and shrubs of this family – about 120 species – grow in northern temperate regions. Their flowers are grouped into separate male and female inflorescences on the same tree: the males are in long drooping catkins; the females in shorter catkins or erect clusters.

HORNBEAM
Carpinus betulus

The natural range of this slow-growing wind-resistant tree is from the Pyrenees to southern Sweden and east as far as south-west Asia. It makes excellent hedges and produces hard timber; it grows to 30m.

Crown: rounded, with upswept branches and a deeply fluted trunk.

Bark: smooth and pale grey, sometimes with fine pale-brown stripes.

Buds: pale brown, slender, pointed, and turned in towards the stem.

Leaves: oval and pointed, with reddish stalks, double-toothed margins, and about 15 pairs of prominent parallel veins; 8–10 by 5–6·5cm. Very dark green above and yellowish beneath, they turn old gold in autumn.

Male flowers: bright yellow-green

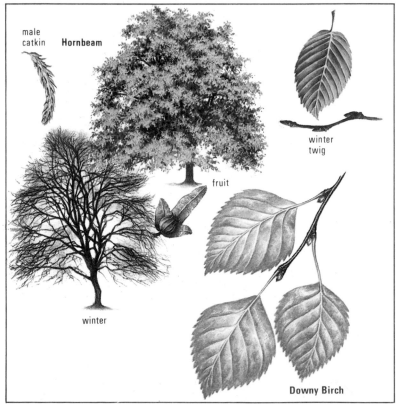

male catkin

Hornbeam

winter twig

fruit

winter

Downy Birch

drooping catkins, 2·5–5cm long.

Female flowers: shorter catkins, made up of green leafy bracts each carrying two crimson-styled flowers. They develop into clusters of 3-lobed bracts, each 3·5cm long and bearing a pair of small nutlets.

Uses: tough heavy nearly white wood used for chopping blocks, mallets, skittles, wooden rollers, etc.

DOWNY BIRCH
Betula pubescens

This slender and elegant tree resembles the silver birch but prefers damper soils. It is common in fens and on wet heaths and it forms extensive stands in the Scottish Highlands. It completely replaces the silver birch in some northern areas. Its bark never has the black diamonds of the silver birch. The branchlets do not droop and are clothed with soft hairs. The petiole is also densely hairy, while the leaf is more rounded than that of the silver birch and its margins are uniformly toothed.

SILVER BIRCH
Betula pendula

This graceful slender tree, native to most of Europe and south-west Asia, grows well on light peaty sandy soils; it reaches a height of 30m.

Crown: narrow and conical with upswept branches, becoming rounded, with long hanging branchlets and a deeply fluted trunk.

Bark: shiny purplish-brown in young trees, becoming pinkish-white and finally white with black diamond-shaped markings, smooth and peeling above, black and knobbly at the base.

Shoots: dark purple-brown, with raised white warts.

Leaves: emerald green and triangular, with rounded bases and double-toothed margins; 3–7cm long.

Male flowers: clusters of 2 to 4 drooping yellow catkins, 3cm long, at the tips of the shoots; young catkins are pale purple-brown and visible all winter.

Female flowers: clusters of about 6 catkins on branched stalks below the males; at first erect, green, and club-shaped, 1–1·5cm long, they become brown and hang down, 2–3cm long, and release small winged fruits.

Uses: the hard strong pale-brown wood is used for small turned articles and, in Scandinavia, for plywood, flooring, and skis; the twigs are used for brooms and brushes and the bark for roofing, tanning, etc.

The leaves of the silver birch become brilliant yellow in the autumn.

winter

young female catkin

male catkin

Silver Birch

developing female catkins

winged fruit

ripe female catkin

autumn leaf

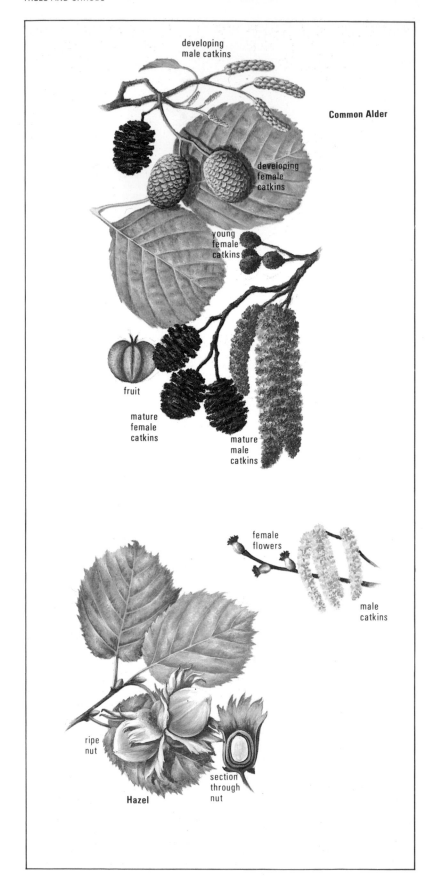

developing
male catkins

Common Alder

developing
female
catkins

young
female
catkins

fruit

mature
female
catkins

mature
male
catkins

female
flowers

male
catkins

ripe
nut

section
through
nut

Hazel

COMMON ALDER
Alnus glutinosa

Found all over Europe and also in Siberia and North Africa, the common alder grows by open water — from mountain streams to lowland fens; it reaches a height of 25m.

Crown: broad and conical or pyramid-shaped; the spreading branches are at first upswept and later level.

Bark: purplish-brown, becoming dark grey-brown and cracked into small square plates.

Shoots: green and sticky, becoming purple with orange markings.

Buds: green to purple, 7mm long, borne on short stalks, 3mm long.

Leaves: oval, with a pointed base, a rounded tip, and wavy or toothed margins; 10 by 7cm. Pale orange-brown when they first open, they become very dark green.

Male and female flowers (catkins) appear before the leaves.

Male catkins: in clusters of 3 to 5, maturing from dull purple to dark yellow; 5cm long.

Female catkins: present all the year round in short erect clusters; dark red catkins, 5–6mm long, mature into green egg-shaped cones, 8–15mm long, which become dark brown and woody when ripe.

Uses: the wood is strong, easily worked, and durable under water; it is used for piles, barrels, toys, broom-heads, hat blocks, etc., and paper pulp. This alder is often planted to conserve river and lake banks; it also improves the fertility of the soil.

The grey alder (*A. incana*) is similar, but can be distinguished by its duller leaves which are sharply pointed and strongly toothed. It flourishes in dry soils and is often planted when rubbish tips and similar places are being reclaimed.

HAZEL
Corylus avellana

Widely distributed in Europe and south-west Asia, the hazel is found in woods, thickets, and hedgerows; it can grow to 12m but is usually shorter (6m).

Crown: usually a broad bush, sometimes with a short trunk.

Bark: smooth and shiny grey-brown, with horizontal rows of pores.

Shoots: pale-brown, covered with long swollen-tipped (glandular) hairs.

Buds: smooth, blunt, and egg-shaped, changing from brown to green.

Leaves: rounded with a pointed tip and double-toothed margins, up to 10 by 10cm, borne on hairy stalks. Hairy and deep green above, they turn brown and finally yellow.

Male flowers: brownish-yellow catkins that appear in autumn, becoming yellow and longer (5cm) by spring.

Female flowers and fruit: small brown buds with protruding crimson stigmas develop into clusters of 1 to 4 nuts, each partly enclosed in a toothed green husk; the nuts change from whitish-green to pale pink-brown and finally brown by autumn.

Cork Oak

underside
of leaf

ripening
acorn

bark of
cork oak

unripe acorn
in spiny cup

Holly Oak

A recently-stripped cork oak. Bark-stripping must be done very carefully to avoid damaging the living tissues beneath.

BEECH FAMILY
Fagaceae

This large and commercially important family – containing about 1,000 species of deciduous or evergreen trees and shrubs – is widely distributed in all temperate regions of the world. The male flowers are borne in catkins, while the female ones are borne singly or in small clusters. The fruit is a nut, partly or completely enclosed in a cup–like husk.

CORK OAK
Quercus suber
Native to south Europe and North Africa, the evergreen cork oak is planted for ornament in parks and gardens as well as commercially (mainly in Portugal and south-west Spain) for its corky bark; grows to 20m.
Crown: domed and spreading, with low heavy twisting branches.
Bark: very rugged, with thick spongy ridges of pale brown or pale grey cork between wide dark cracks. Stripped trunks are pinkish-red.
Leaves: oval and pointed, with 5–6 shallow spine-tipped lobes on each side; 4–7 by 2–3cm. Blackish-green above and densely hairy beneath, they have hairy stalks, 1cm long.
Fruit: acorns, 1·5–3cm long, in deep cups with spreading upper scales.
Uses: cork, removed from the trunk every 8–10 years, is used for bungs,

shoe soles, flooring, floats, life buoys, etc. The heavy wood is used for joinery and fuel.

HOLLY OAK
Quercus coccifera
Also known as the kermes oak, this evergreen species is abundant on the hot, dry hillsides of the Mediterranean basin. It can reach 6m in height, but more commonly grows as a dense holly-like bush just a metre or so high. On some hillsides these oaks form impenetrable thickets.
Leaves: bronze and slightly hairy when young, becoming dark green and very prickly. 2–4cm long and hairless below when mature.
Flowers and Fruit: male catkins yellow, 2–4cm long, appearing with young leaves in spring. Acorns, hidden among foliage, ripen in second summer: cup clothed with sharp spines.

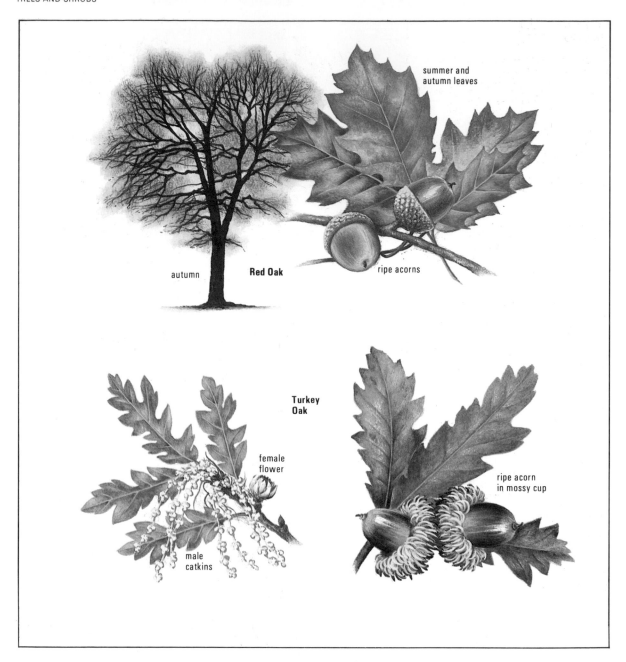

summer and autumn leaves

autumn **Red Oak** ripe acorns

Turkey Oak

female flower

ripe acorn in mossy cup

male catkins

TURKEY OAK
Quercus cerris

The Turkey oak, native to south-west Asia and south and central Europe, is now widely naturalized in Europe. One of the fastest-growing oaks, it is widely planted for shade and ornament; it grows to 38m.
Crown: wide and broadly domed with straight up-growing branches.
Bark: dull dark-grey and roughly cracked.
Buds: pale brown and downy, surrounded by long twisted whiskers.
Leaves: variable, but usually with 7 to 14 deep triangular lobes down each side; 9–12 by 3–5cm. Borne on hairy stalks, 2cm long, the leaves are rough and dull green, becoming shiny, above; paler and woolly beneath.
Male flowers: in catkins, 5–6cm long, maturing from red to yellow.
Female flowers: oval, 5mm long, with dark-red stigmas surrounded by yellowish scales.
Fruit: narrow egg-shaped acorns, 2·5 by 1·4cm, either stalkless or on very short stalks and surrounded by a mossy cup, 1cm deep, with long pointed pale-green scales.

RED OAK
Quercus borealis

This oak from eastern North America is commonly planted in Europe as an ornamental tree, for its attractive autumn foliage; for shelter; and, particularly in central Europe, for timber. It grows to 35m.
Crown: broad and domed, with straight radiating branches and a short straight trunk.
Bark: smooth and silvery-grey.
Leaves: oblong, 12–22cm long, with a pointed base and tip and 4 to 5 sharply angled lobes on each side, the tip of each lobe extending into a bristle. Borne on yellow stalks, 2–5cm long, the leaves turn from pale yellow to dark green above, pale grey beneath, and become dull red or red-brown in autumn before they fall.
Fruit: flat-based dark red-brown acorns, 2 by 2cm, in shallow scaly cups with incurved rims and stout 1-cm stalks.

PENDUNCULATE or COMMON OAK
Quercus robur

The most widespread European oak: a long-lived slow-growing tree occurring in forests, woods, parks, and gardens all over Europe, from Spain to North Africa, north-east Russia, and south-west Asia; it grows to 45m. It can be distinguished from the sessile oak by the following features.

Crown: wide and domed, with wide-spreading branches (the lower ones are massive and twisted).

Leaves: oblong, with an ear-like lobe at the base on each side of the stalk and 4–5 pairs of rounded lobes with wavy or toothed margins; 10–12 by 7–8cm. Borne on short stalks (4–10mm), they are dull dark green above and paler beneath, turning rich orange-brown in autumn.

Fruit: acorns, 1·5–4cm long, with shallow cups, usually growing in pairs on stalks 4–8cm long. They mature from whitish-green to dark brown.

Uses: strong heavy timber, with white sapwood and golden-brown heartwood, is durable and resistant; used for furniture, fencing, gates, railway carriages, panelling, chests, etc., and, in the past, for shipbuilding. The bark is used in tanning leather and the acorns provide mast for pigs.

HOLM OAK
Quercus ilex

This evergreen south European oak is widely planted for shelter and ornament, especially by the sea, being resistant to salty winds and pollution in towns; it grows to 30m.

Crown: dense and rounded, usually with a short trunk and straight up-growing branches.

Bark: brownish-black to black, cracked into small square plates.

Shoots: slender, dull greyish-brown, and woolly.

Buds: fawn and downy, 1–2mm long.

Leaves: vary from long and narrow to oval, with spiny-toothed, wavy, or smooth margins; 5–10 by 3–8cm. The upper surface is rough and shiny blackish-green, the lower surface greyish-green and densely hairy; the leaf-stalks are woolly and 1–2cm long.

Male flowers: in pale-gold catkins, 4–7cm long.

Female flowers: grey-green and hairy with pink tips, 2mm long, growing on woolly stalks in clusters of 2 to 3.

Fruit: light-green acorns, 1·5–2cm long, with deep cups covered with rows of grey-haired fawn scales.

Uses: the hard, heavy, tough highly figured wood is used for wheels, joinery, vine-props, fuel, and charcoal; the bark is used for tanning leather and dyeing.

winter

Pendunculate Oak

stalked acorns

Holm Oak

ripening acorns

319

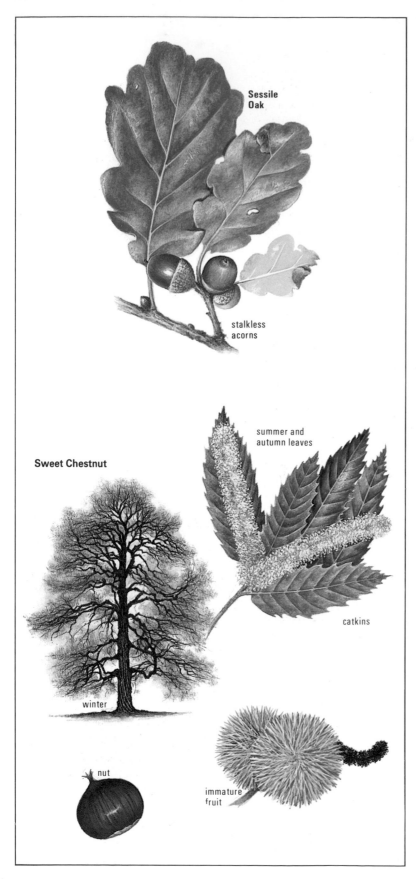

Sessile Oak

stalkless acorns

Sweet Chestnut

summer and autumn leaves

catkins

winter

nut

immature fruit

SESSILE or DURMAST OAK
Quercus petraea

The sessile oak — native to Europe (including Britain) and west Asia — forms forests over much of its natural range. It grows best on light acid soils and reaches a height of 30–40m.
Crown: open and domed, with straight branches radiating from a straight trunk.
Bark: grey, with fine, usually vertical, cracks and ridges.
Leaves: oblong, with a wedge-shaped base and 5 to 9 pairs of rounded lobes; 8–12 by 4–5cm. Dark green and leathery, they are borne on long yellow stalks (1–2cm).
Male flowers: in slender pale-green catkins.
Female flowers: tiny and greenish-white, with red-purple stigmas.
Fruit: rounded acorns, either stalk-less or on very short stalks (5–10mm), ripening from green to brown.
Uses: (timber) see Pedunculate oak.

SWEET or SPANISH CHESTNUT
Castanea sativa

This Mediterranean tree is widely grown for its edible nuts — it should not be confused with the horse chestnut whose seeds (conkers) are inedible. Long-lived and fast-growing, it does best on dry sandy soils; it reaches a height of over 30m.
Crown: conical and open when young, becoming columnar, and finally rounded and spreading.
Bark: silvery-grey, but becoming dark with deep, spirally arranged, cracks.
Shoots: stout and shiny purple-brown; smooth or downy.
Buds: rounded, yellow-green to red-brown.
Leaves: oblong, with a pointed tip and prominent parallel veins each extending into a bristly tooth on the margin; 10–25 by 9–10cm. Borne on red or yellowish stalks, 2·5cm long, they turn from bronze to glossy dark green, and finally pale yellow or rich brown in autumn.
Male flowers: minute with long stamens, growing in clusters on yellow catkins 10–12cm long. Catkins appear in summer.
Female flowers: in groups of 1–3 at the base of late catkins of male flowers. Each is surrounded by a green spiny cup from which the styles protrude.
Fruit: shiny red-brown nuts grouped in pairs or threes in a yellow-green husk, 3 by 4cm, covered with radiating spines. The nuts are released when the husk splits.
Uses: the nuts are eaten roasted and used to make flour, bread, etc., and for fattening livestock. The timber, grown as a coppice crop, is much used for fencing.

ripe fruit in husk

winter bud

female flowers

male flowers

Beech

autumn

BEECH
Fagus sylvatica
Native to most of Europe (except northern Scandinavia), the beech is a dominant forest tree; it is also widely planted for ornament, shelter, hedges, and timber. It grows to 30m.
Crown: slender and conical, becoming rounded with spreading branches.
Bark: smooth and silvery-grey.
Buds: slender and pointed, 2cm long, covered with brown papery scales.
Leaves: oval with a pointed tip, wavy margins, and 5 to 7 parallel veins on each side; 10 by 7cm. Clear green and silky at first, they become dark shiny green above and paler beneath with hairs on the larger veins, turning pale yellow and finally rich orange-brown before falling.
Male flowers: rounded greenish-yellow clusters, each of about 15 tiny flowers, on long drooping stalks.
Female flowers: in a rounded green head on a short stiff hairy stalk.
Male and female flowers grow in separate clusters on the same tree and open with the leaves.
Fruit: a pointed green husk, 2·5cm long, covered with soft green hairs; turns brown and splits into 4 to release 1 to 2 shiny brown nuts, triangular in section.
Uses: the strong, hard, fine-grained

wood, bright buff with brown flecks, is used for furniture and turnery (e.g. tool handles, bowls, spoons, chair legs); the nuts provide mast for pigs, cattle, and poultry.

ELM FAMILY
Ulmaceae

SMOOTH-LEAVED ELM
Ulmus carpinifolia
Native to Europe, North Africa, and south-west Asia, this species is the common elm of continental Europe; it grows to 30m.
Crown: tall, narrow, and domed, with the branches growing up nearly vertically from the trunk and arching over into long hanging branchlets.
Bark: grey-brown, with long deep vertical cracks and long thick ridges; bark on the branches has fine black vertical cracks.
Shoots: pale brown, slender, and hairless.
Buds: egg-shaped, dark red, and hairy.
Leaves: oval, 6–8cm long, with a pointed tip, an oblique base, and toothed margins. Borne on hairy stalks

5mm long, the leaves are bright shiny green above and turn yellow in autumn.
Flowers and fruit: small red flowers with white stigmas appear before the leaves and develop into transparent winged fruits with the seed towards the tip of the membrane.

Smooth-leaved Elm

English Elm

summer and autumn leaves

fruit

flowers

winter

Wych Elm

flowers

winter

fruit

winter twig

WYCH ELM
Ulmus glabra

Native to northern and central Europe and west Asia, the wych elm grows naturally in woods and hedgerows and is often planted in exposed situations and polluted atmospheres; it grows to 40m.

Crown: broadly domed, with branches spreading and arching out from low down the trunk, which is often forked.

Bark: smooth and silvery-grey in young trees, becoming brown with a network of broad grey-brown ridges.

Shoots: stout and dark red-brown, covered with hairs when young.

Buds: pointed and dull red-brown with a covering of reddish hairs.

Leaves: oval, with a pointed tip, double-toothed margins and a very unequal base (the base on one side forms a rounded lobe that covers the stalk); 10–18 by 6–9cm. Borne on thick hairy stalks, 2–5mm long, the leaves are dark green and very rough above, paler with soft hairs beneath.

Flowers and fruit: dark purplish-red flowers grow in dense clusters that appear before the leaves. They develop into round winged fruits, 2–5cm wide with the seed at the centre of the membrane, which ripen from light green to brown.

Uses: the pliable strong wood is used for boat- and carriage-building, tool handles, shafts, and furniture.

ENGLISH ELM
Ulmus procera

This elm is native to Britain and occurs in many varieties and local forms in southern and central Europe; it grows to 35m.

Crown: tall, narrow, and domed, with massive twisting branches growing upwards from high up on the trunk.

Bark: dark brown or grey, deeply cracked into small square plates.

Shoots: long, slender, reddish-brown, and densely hairy.

Buds: pointed, dark brown, and downy; 2–3mm.

Leaves: rounded, or oval and pointed, with double-toothed margins, an oblique base (one side may be lobed), and 10 to 12 pairs of veins; 4–10 by 3·5–7cm. Borne on 5mm downy stalks, they are dark green and rough with hairs on the upper surface and turn yellow or bright golden in autumn.

Flowers and fruit: dark purplish-red flowers with tufts of stamens appear before the leaves. They develop into sterile winged fruits, with the seed close to the notched tip of the rounded membrane, which mature from pale green to brown. The tree is propagated by root suckers.

Uses: the reddish-brown timber is strong, firm, heavy, and does not split easily; used for coffins, indoor and outdoor furniture, and – since it is durable under water – for bridges, piles, and groynes. The inner bark has medicinal properties.

NETTLE TREE
Celtis australis
A graceful deciduous tree from the Mediterranean region, often planted for ornament and shade in the south. It reaches heights of 25m.
Crown: an irregular dome with flexible, drooping shoots.
Bark: greyish brown, smooth with just a few gentle wrinkles.
Leaves: elongated heart-shaped with prominent teeth and wavy margins and often with a long, twisted point. Rough above and softly hairy below. 10-15cm long.
Flowers: small and green, hanging on long stalks among the leaves.
Fruit: cherry-like, 9-12mm in diameter: green at first, becoming dark brown or black when ripe. The flesh is edible, with a sweet taste. The fruits of related American trees are known as hackberries.

Nettle Tree

MULBERRY FAMILY
Moraceae

FIG
Ficus carica
Native to west Asia, the fig is widely cultivated — both as an important fruit crop (mainly in south Europe) and for shelter and ornament (it is often trained against walls); it grows to about 10m.
Crown: spreading, with stout knobbly upswept branches.
Bark: smooth and metallic grey, finely patterned in darker grey.
Leaves: thick and leathery, up to 30 by 25cm, with a heart-shaped base and 3 to 5 coarsely toothed lobes, the middle lobe being the largest. Borne on stalks 5–10cm long, they are dark green and rough with hairs above and beneath.
Flowers: tiny, enclosed in a fleshy pear-shaped structure with a small hole at the top through which pollinating insects enter.
Fruit: dark green and pear-shaped, becoming larger and either violet or blackish when ripe.
Uses: the fruit is eaten either fresh or dried; it also has laxative properties.

BLACK or COMMON MULBERRY
Morus nigra
The black mulberry, native to central and west Asia, is widely cultivated in south Europe for its fruit and is grown elsewhere mainly for ornament; it reaches a height of 12m.
Crown: low and broadly domed, with rough stout twisting branches arising from a short trunk.
Bark: dark orange, with wide cracks and many bosses and burrs.
Shoots: stout and downy, turning from pale green to brown.
Buds: stout and pointed, shiny dark purplish-brown.

Fig

Black Mulberry

ripe fruit

unripe fruit

ripe fruit

Leaves: heart-shaped, with toothed or lobed margins; 8–12 by 6–8cm. Growing on stout hairy stalks, 1·5–2·5cm long, they are rough, hairy, and deep green above, paler and finely hairy beneath.
Flowers: male and female flowers grow in separate pale-coloured catkins, the males being short and stout and the females rounded.
Fruit: rounded and raspberry-like, made up of a cluster of fleshy blobs each surrounding a central seed. Green at first, they become orange-scarlet and finally deep blackish-red and sweet enough to eat.

323

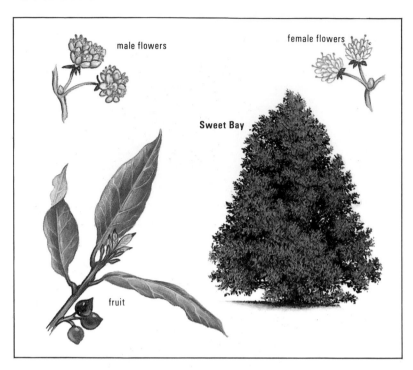

male flowers

female flowers

Sweet Bay

fruit

LAUREL FAMILY
Lauraceae

SWEET BAY or BAY LAUREL
Laurus nobilis

In its native Mediterranean region this attractive evergreen tree reaches a height of 20m; it is widely grown elsewhere as an ornamental pot plant or shrub. Laurel leaves — worn in wreathes as a sign of ·victory or honour in classical times — are today used in cooking to season food.

Crown: dense and conical, with spreading up-growing branches.

Bark: smooth and blackish, with paler cracks in older trees.

Leaves: lance-shaped with wavy margins and dark-red basal veins; 5–10 by 2·5–3cm. Borne on dark-red stalks, 6mm long, they are leathery and very dark green above, yellow-green beneath, and aromatic when crushed.

Flowers and fruit: pale yellow inconspicuous flowers, 1cm across, develop into shiny berries, 8–10mm across, ripening from green to black.

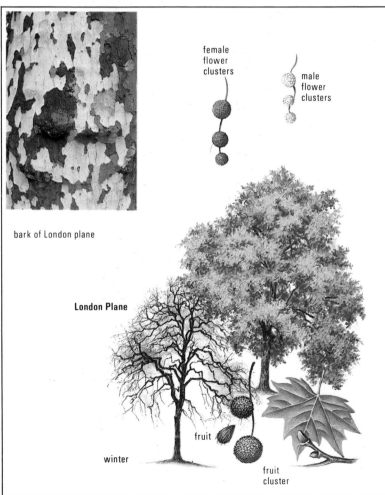

bark of London plane

female flower clusters

male flower clusters

London Plane

winter

fruit

fruit cluster

PLANE FAMILY
Platanaceae

LONDON PLANE
Platanus x *hispanica*

A fast-growing hybrid between the Oriental plane and the American plane (*Platanus occidentalis*), this tree is widely planted for shade and ornament in city streets and squares; it is resistant to pollution, thrives in restricted rooting space, and withstands heavy pruning. Grows to 35m.

Crown: domed, with large spreading branches supported on a long trunk.

Bark: smooth, thin, and grey-brown, flaking off to reveal greenish or yellow patches.

Shoots: pale green, becoming stout and brown.

Buds: conical and red-brown, with a large protruding base and covered with a single scale.

Leaves: 5-lobed, each lobe being triangular with coarsely toothed margins. Borne on red-brown tube-like stalks, the leaves are bright shiny green above and paler beneath.

Flowers: male and female flowers grow in separate rounded clusters hanging on long stalks on the same tree. The males are yellow; the females crimson.

Fruit: in brown globular clusters, 3cm across, that remain on the tree all winter and break up the following spring. Each fruit is 1cm long with a style projecting from the top and a parachute of yellow hairs at the bottom.

ORIENTAL PLANE
Platanus orientalis
Native to south-eastern and eastern Europe, Asia Minor, and India, the Oriental plane is often planted for shade and ornament in southern and eastern Europe; grows to 30m. Slower growing than the London plane and less tolerant of pollution, it can be distinguished from this tree by its leaves.
Leaves: 5- to 7-lobed, 18 by 8cm; the lobes are longer and narrower than those of the London plane. Borne on yellowish stalks, 5cm long, each with a thick red base, the leaves turn from pale orange-brown to yellow-green and finally to pale bronze-purple.

ROSE FAMILY
Rosaceae

Distributed all over the world, this vast family contains over 2,000 species of trees, shrubs and herbaceous plants, including many important fruit trees. The members are distinguished by their flowers, which have 4-5 petals and an equal number of sepals.

HAWTHORN or MAY
Crataegus monogyna
This small spiny tree is very widely distributed in Europe, growing in thickets, hedgerows, and at the edges of woods; it is also planted as a windbreak and boundary hedge. It reaches a height of 10m.
Crown: spreading or rounded, with intertwining branches.
Bark: smooth and brown at first, becoming darker and rugged.
Shoots: dark purple-red or reddish-brown with straight thorns, 1–2·5cm long.
Buds: very small, reddish-black, and scaly.
Leaves: divided into 3 to 7 deep lobes with smooth or sparsely toothed margins; up to 8 by 7cm (usually 3·5 by 4cm). Shiny green above: tufts of hairs at the bases of the veins beneath.
Flowers: 8–15mm across, with 5 white overlapping petals, purple-tipped stamens, and one style; they grow in dense fragrant clusters of 16 or more.
Fruit: round, 8–10mm across, with a persistent style at the tip and containing (usually) one nutlet; ripens from green to dark red.
Uses: the heavy dense wood has been used for tool handles, mallet heads, and other small articles; makes good charcoal.

MIDLAND HAWTHORN
Crataegus laevigata
Similar to the previous species, but much less common and found mainly on heavy soils — especially in damp woodlands. It can be distinguished

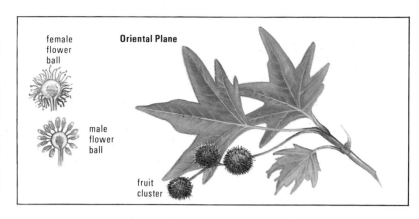

Oriental Plane

female flower ball

male flower ball

fruit cluster

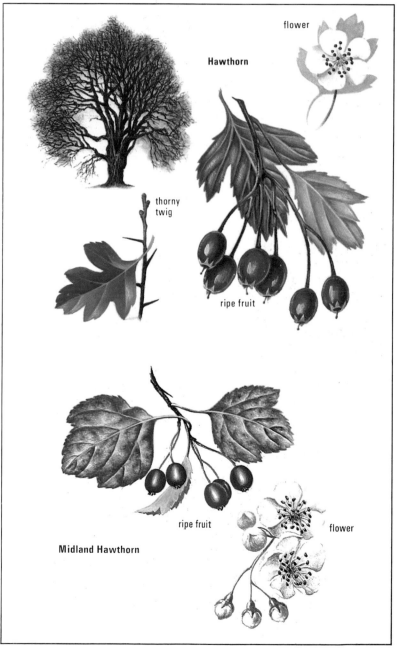

flower

Hawthorn

thorny twig

ripe fruit

Midland Hawthorn

ripe fruit

flower

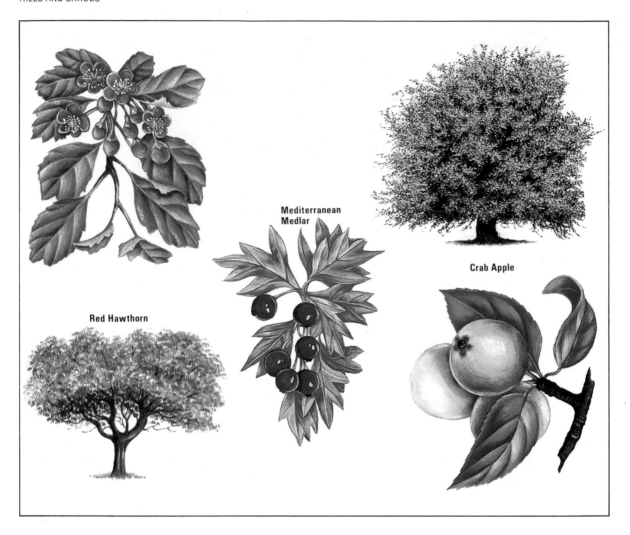

Mediterranean Medlar

Crab Apple

Red Hawthorn

from the common hawthorn by the following features:

Leaves: have shorter and blunter lobes, with the incisions rarely reaching half way to the mid-rib; lobes always toothed; no hair tufts on lower surface.
Flowers: usually with 2 styles.
Fruit: normally with two persistent styles at tip and two nutlets.

Hybrids between the two species are very common. Both species have cultivated varieties with pink or red flowers — the red hawthorns. Some of these have double flowers.

MEDITERRANEAN MEDLAR
Crataegus azarolus
Widely distributed in the Mediterranean region, this shrub or small tree is cultivated for its fruit in southern Europe; grows to 4-12m.
Shoots: downy.
Leaves: pale green in colour, 3—7cm long, divided into lobes usually without teeth and with hairs on the lower surface.
Flowers: small and white, with purple-tipped stamens, growing in downy clusters 5—7·5cm across.
Fruit: large (2—2·5cm across) and round, orange-red or yellow, and

containing 1 to 3 nutlets.
Uses: the fruit, which has a pleasant slightly acid taste, is made into jams and jellies.

CRAB APPLE
Malus sylvestris
The crab apple commonly grows in woods, thickets, and hedgerows of Europe and south-west Asia; it reaches a height of 10m. One of the species from which the orchard apple was derived, it is often grown as a rootstock on which garden varieties are grafted; some forms of crab apple are grown as flowering ornamentals.
Crown: dense, low, and domed, with many twisting spiny branches.
Bark: greyish-brown or dark brown, splitting into small thin square plates.
Shoots: ribbed and often thorny; dark purple above, pale brown beneath.
Buds: small (4—5mm) and pointed, dark purple and covered with grey hairs.
Leaves: oval, with a rounded or wedge-shaped base, pointed tip, and toothed margins; 5—6 by 3—4cm. Borne on downy grooved stalks, 2·5cm long, they are bright green above, paler and downy beneath.

Flowers: small, with 5 white petals, usually tinged with pink, and many yellow stamens; they grow in clusters from short spurs.
Fruit: globular, 2·5 by 2·8cm, with a hollow at each end and a central 'core' containing brown seeds (pips). The apples are glossy yellow-green with white spots and become speckled or flushed with red in autumn.
Uses: the fruit, though too sour to be eaten, is made into crab-apple jelly; the red-brown wood — hard, tough, and fine-grained — is used for ornamental carving, mallet handles.

MEDLAR
Mespilus germanica
Native to south-eastern Europe and western and central Asia, the medlar has long been cultivated, especially in western and central Europe, for its fruit; it reaches a height of 6m.
Crown: low and spreading, with tangled branches.
Bark: grey-brown and deeply cracked into oblong plates that flake off.
Shoots: downy; they sometimes develop spines.
Leaves: oblong, with a pointed tip and smooth or toothed margins; 15 by

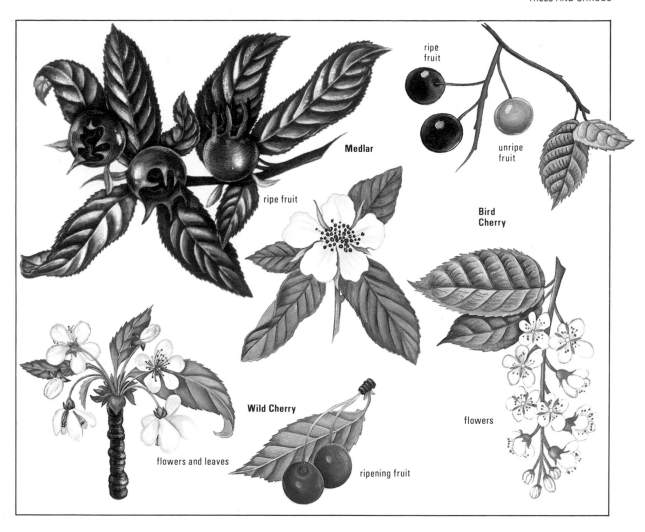

Medlar

ripe fruit

ripe fruit

unripe fruit

Bird Cherry

flowers

Wild Cherry

flowers and leaves

ripening fruit

5cm. The upper surface is dull green, with indented veins, and is sometimes hairy; the lower surface is paler and densely hairy. The leaves are borne on very short (5mm) hairy stalks.

Flowers: stalkless, 3—6cm across, with 5 broad white petals, 5 long (4cm) green sepals, and many brown-tipped stamens.

Fruit: globular, 5—6cm across, ripening from green to brown. Persistent sepals surround an open pit at the tip through which the brown 'seeds' (actually individual fruits) can be seen.

Uses: the fruit is edible only when soft and over-ripe; it can also be made into a jelly. The wood is hard and fine-grained.

WILD CHERRY or GEAN
Prunus avium

In its wild state this tree grows in woodlands in most parts of Europe; it reaches a height of 20m. It is the ancestor of all cultivated forms of sweet cherry and is widely grown in many varieties both for its fruit and for its blossom and attractive autumn foliage.

Crown: spreading, with branches growing up from a tall straight trunk.
Bark: purplish-grey, marked with horizontal orange-brown corky ridges and peeling off in thin horizontal strips.
Shoots: greyish-brown.
Buds: shiny red-brown and pointed.
Leaves: oval, with a pointed tip, finely-toothed margins, and 2 glands near the base; 10 by 4·5—7cm. Drooping from stalks 2—3·5cm long, which are red above and yellow beneath, the leaves are pale green (downy beneath) and turn crimson or yellow in autumn.
Flowers: white and sweetly scented, growing on slender stalks in clusters at the tips of the branches.
Fruit: rounded and shiny, 2·5cm across, growing on a red-brown stalk 3—5cm long and ripening from green to bright red and finally purple. Sweet-tasting when ripe, they are dispersed by birds.
Uses: the fruit of cultivated varieties is eaten fresh, made into jams, liqueurs, etc.; the golden-brown wood is heavy, hard, and tough and prized for furniture and turned articles (such as bowls, pipes and similar musical instruments). Large trunks yield valuable veneers,

with a gleaming surface and interesting grain patterns.

BIRD CHERRY
Prunus padus

Native to northern and central Europe and Asia Minor, the bird cherry grows in woods, especially by streams, as a low shrub or a tree up to 15m tall.

Crown: rounded, with sharply ascending upper branches and spreading or drooping lower ones.
Bark: smooth and dark brown, with a strong unpleasant smell of bitter almonds.
Shoots: olive green, turning dark brown.
Buds: slender and sharply pointed; shiny brown.
Leaves: oval, with a pointed base and tip and finely-toothed margins; 10 by 7cm. Borne on dark red stalks, 2cm long, they are dull green above and pale green beneath, turning pale yellow or red in autumn.
Flowers: small, white, and fragrant, grouped in long (8—15cm) spreading or drooping clusters.
Fruit: globular and shiny, 8mm across, ripening from green to black. Bitter-tasting, they are dispersed by birds.

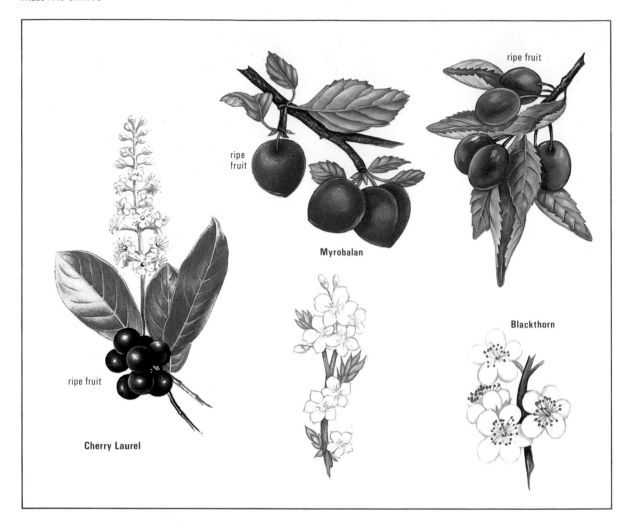

Myrobalan

Blackthorn

ripe fruit

ripe fruit

ripe fruit

ripe fruit

Cherry Laurel

CHERRY LAUREL
Prunus laurocerasus
A native of S. E. Europe and western Asia, this large evergreen is commonly grown for ornament and hedging, and also as cover for pheasant rearing. It is naturalised in many woodlands. Reaching 14m in some western areas, it is more often a spreading bush, casting such deep shade that nothing grows beneath it. The plant is often simply called laurel, but this causes confusion with the bay laurel or true laurel (page 324). The leaves contain prussic acid (cyanide): entomologists sometimes crush them and use them for killing insects.
Crown: usually broad and spreading.
Bark: brownish grey with prominent lenticels (breathing pores), often a squared pattern.
Leaves: thick and leathery, oval, up to 20cm long: bright and shiny on upper surface, pale green at first and becoming darker with age.
Flowers: creamy white and fragrant, carried in erect spikes in spring. Plant flowers only when growing freely in good light: clipped bushes rarely flower.
Fruit: purplish black berries up to 2cm in diameter.

MYROBALAN or CHERRY PLUM
Prunus cerasifera
Native to the Balkans and central Asia, the myrobalan is planted in central Europe for its edible fruit (the cultivated plum is probably a hybrid between this tree and the blackthorn); it grows to about 8m. There are also several early-flowering cultivated varieties, which are widely grown as ornamentals.
Crown: open and spreading.
Bark: brownish-black.
Shoots: smooth and glossy green.
Leaves: oval with blunt-toothed margins; 4–7cm long. Borne on purple-green stalks, 1cm long, the leaves are glossy green above, paler and matte beneath (some ornamental varieties have reddish leaves).
Flowers: white, 2cm across, with 5 petals; cultivated ornamental varieties have white or pink flowers.
Fruit: globular and grooved down one side, ripening from pale glossy green to yellow or red, and containing a flattish stone.

BLACKTHORN or SLOE
Prunus spinosa
The blackthorn is widely distributed in Europe and parts of Asia, growing in hedgerows, on waste ground, scrub, hillsides, etc.; it produces suckers and grows to a height of 4m.
Crown: dense and upright, with a tangled mass of thorny branches.
Bark: black; in old trees it is deeply cracked into small square plates.
Buds: small, oval, and pointed; reddish-purple to black in colour.
Leaves: small (4cm long), dull green, and oval, with a bluntly pointed tip and shallow-toothed margins.
Flowers: white, 1–1·5cm across, with 5 petals and long orange-tipped stamens; they usually open well before the leaves.
Fruit: globular, 1·5–2cm across, ripening from green to purple-black with a waxy bloom; the green flesh has a very bitter taste.
Uses: the fruit is used for jams and jellies, flavouring gin, and is fermented into sloe wine.

ALMOND
Prunus dulcis
A native of west Asia and North Africa, this small tree is widely cultivated – in warm regions for its seeds, and elsewhere for ornament in gardens. It reaches a height of about 6m.

Crown: open and rounded, with up-growing branches.

Bark: purplish-black, deeply cracked into small square plates.

Leaves: oval, 7–12cm long, with a pointed tip and finely toothed margins. Dark green or yellowish-green in colour, they are often folded along the midrib into a V shape.

Flowers: pink, 3–5cm across, with 5 petals and many stamens; they open well before the leaves. Some cultivated varieties have white or double flowers.

Fruit: oval and pale green, 4cm long, splitting when ripe to reveal a pale brown stone within which is the edible kernel or seed.

Uses: seeds from the sweet almond are eaten raw and used for cooking, flavouring etc. The hard reddish wood is used for veneers.

The peach (*P. persica*) is very similar but has a large juicy fruit.

APRICOT
Prunus armeniaca

A native of Asia, the apricot is widely grown in S. Europe for its fruit. Susceptible to frost, it is grown further north only in sheltered places.

Crown: sturdy and rounded, to 10m.

Bark: brownish grey, often ridged.

Leaves: oval, to 10cm long, with long reddish stalks: reddish when young, becoming bright green.

Flowers: white or pale pink in early spring, before leaves appear.

Fruit: yellow to orange, with furry coat: stone smooth.

ROWAN or MOUNTAIN ASH
Sorbus aucuparia

This attractive tree grows wild in woodlands and rocky mountainous regions of Europe, south-west Asia, and North Africa; it is also widely planted as an ornamental tree in streets, parks, and gardens. It reaches a height of 20m.

Crown: oval and open, with up-growing branches.

Bark: smooth and shiny silver-grey, becoming light grey-brown and marked with a network of thin scaly ridges.

Shoots: purplish- or brownish-grey, hairy at first, becoming smooth.

Buds: dark purple-brown, 1·7cm long, covered with grey hairs.

Leaves: compound, 22cm long, consisting of 5 to 7 pairs of leaflets and one terminal leaflet (each is oval, with toothed margins; 6 by 2cm). Hairy at first, they become smooth and deep green above, grey-green beneath; the leaves of some cultivated varieties turn bright red in autumn.

Flowers: creamy white and 5-petalled, 1cm across, growing on woolly stems in flat-topped sweetly scented clusters, 10–15cm across.

Fruit: round berries, 1cm across, maturing from yellow to orange and finally scarlet.

Uses: the fruit, rich in vitamin C, is made into jelly; the smooth hard purple-brown wood is used for carved and turned articles.

Almond

unripe fruit

ripe fruit

Apricot

Rowan

ripe fruit

winter

ripe
fruit

Whitebeam

downy underside
of leaf

summer and
autumn leaves

Wild
Service
Tree
winter

ripe fruit

WHITEBEAM
Sorbus aria

The whitebeam, native to southern and central Europe and parts of Britain, is found in woodlands, rocky regions, and on southern mountains; reaches a height of 25m. It grows well on chalk and limestone, and, because it withstands pollution, it is often planted in city streets.

Crown: domed, with up-swept radiating branches.

Bark: smooth and grey, developing shallow cracks and ridges with age.

Shoots: brown and hairy at first, becoming smooth and grey.

Buds: green, with brown-tipped scales and a white hairy tip; 2cm long.

Leaves: oval, with shallow-toothed or lobed margins; 8 by 5cm. The upper surface is dull green, the lower surface is densely covered with white hairs, giving the whole tree a glistening white appearance when the leaves first appear. The leaves turn yellow or pale brown in autumn and finally pale grey before falling.

Flowers: white, 1·5cm across, growing on white woolly stalks in clusters 5—8cm across.

Fruit: rounded, 8—15cm across, ripening from green to orange-red and finally deep scarlet; they are dispersed by birds.

Uses: the hard, heavy, tough wood — yellowish-white and fine-grained — is sometimes used for handles, spoons, etc.; the fruit is made into a jelly.

WILD SERVICE TREE
Sorbus torminalis

This tree is widely distributed in Europe (except the north), North Africa, and parts of Asia; it grows to a height of 25m.

Crown: conical when young, becoming domed and spreading, with up-growing branches.

Bark: pale grey to black-brown; it cracks into thin plates that flake off.

Shoots: brown and shiny.

Buds: glossy green and globular; 4—5mm long.

Leaves: divided into 3 to 5 pairs of triangular toothed lobes that decrease in size towards the tip of the leaf; 10 by 8cm. Borne on yellowish-green stalks, 2—5cm long, the leaves are shiny deep green above and yellow-green beneath, turning yellow, deep red, and purple in autumn.

Flowers: 1·2cm across, with 5 white petals and yellow stamens; they are grouped into loose domed clusters, 10—12cm across.

Fruit: oval, 1cm or more long, ripening from green to brown with rust-coloured specks. Acid-tasting, they are said to have medicinal properties and have been used in the past as a cure for colic.

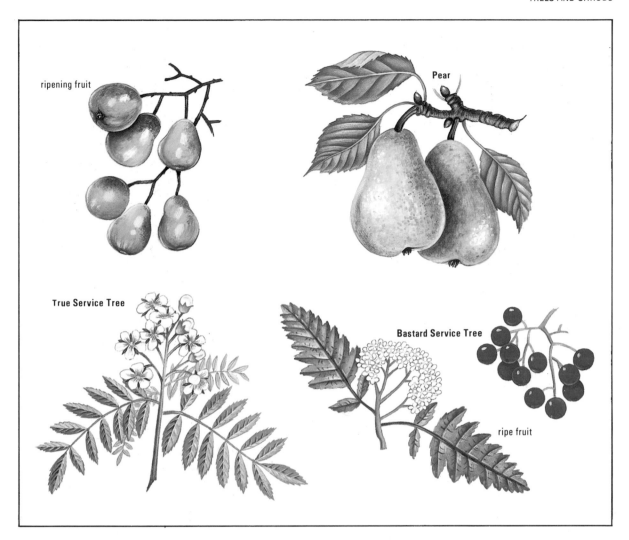

ripening fruit

Pear

True Service Tree

Bastard Service Tree

ripe fruit

TRUE SERVICE TREE
Sorbus domestica

The service tree — native to southern Europe, North Africa, and west Asia — is widely planted for ornament and (particularly in central Europe) for its fruit; it grows to a height of 20m. When not bearing fruit, it can be distinguished from the rowan — a similar species — by its bark and buds.

Crown: domed, with spreading level branches.

Bark: orange- to dark-brown, cracked (often deeply) into rectangular plates.

Buds: egg-shaped, glossy bright green, and resinous; 1cm long.

Leaves: compound, 15–22cm long, with 6 to 10 pairs of leaflets and one terminal leaflet, each oblong and sharply toothed, 3–6cm long, dark yellow-green above, downy beneath.

Flowers: 1·5–2cm across, with 5 cream-coloured petals, triangular sepals, and 5 styles; they grow in domed erect clusters, 10 by 14cm.

Fruit: globular or pear-shaped, 2–3cm long, ripening from green to brown. They are edible when over-ripe and are used in continental Europe for making alcoholic beverages.

BASTARD SERVICE TREE
Sorbus x thuringiaca

A hybrid between the rowan (mountain ash) and the whitebeam, the bastard service tree is grown for ornament, mostly in town streets; it reaches a height of 15m.

Crown: oval and upright, becoming dense and leaning to one side.

Bark: dull grey with shallow cracks.

Shoots: pink-grey with a purple tip.

Buds: dark red-brown; 8mm long and with few scales.

Leaves: oblong, 11 by 7cm, with lobes that decrease in size towards the tip of the leaf; 1–4 pairs of toothed leaflets grow at the base of each leaf. Borne on stout red stalks, 2cm long, the leaves are dark grey-green above and white with down beneath.

Flowers: white, 1cm across, grouped in downy clusters, 6–10cm across.

Fruit: bright red, 1·2cm across, growing in clusters of 10 to 15.

The Swedish whitebeam (*S. intermedia*) is a very similar tree, but its leaves lack free leaflets at the base. A native of the Baltic region, it is widely planted for ornament in towns. It is tolerant of smoke pollution.

PEAR
Pyrus communis

The parent species from which the numerous orchard and garden varieties of pear are derived, this tree grows wild in woods, hedgerows, etc., of Europe and west Asia; it reaches a height of 20m.

Crown: slender, with a rounded top and up-growing branches.

Bark: grey-brown or black, breaking into small deep squares.

Shoots: brown, often downy, and sometimes thorny.

Leaves: oval to heart-shaped, 5–8cm long, with a pointed tip and smooth or toothed margins. Borne on long (2–5cm) stalks, they are glossy dark- or yellow-green.

Flowers: 2–4cm across, with 5 white petals and dark-red stamens; they grow in dense clusters, 5–8cm across, that open before the leaves.

Fruit: varies from globular to oblong, 2–4cm long, ripening from green to brown; the flesh is sweet when ripe.

Uses: the hard compact pinkish-brown wood is used for furniture, turned articles, wood blocks, etc.; it also makes good fuel and charcoal.

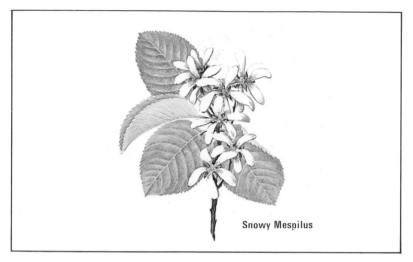

Snowy Mespilus

SNOWY MESPILUS
Amelanchier ovalis

This small, much branched shrub grows on rocky hillsides in southern and central Europe, especially on limestones. The young leaves and twigs are clothed with white fur, and when the flowers open in spring the bush appears completely white — hence its common name. It reaches 4m in height.

Bark: dark grey to black on mature branches, but pale grey and furry when young.

Leaves: oval and coarsely toothed, 1·5cm long: clothed with white hairs below when young, soon becoming hairless and bright green.

Flowers: 2cm across, white with narrow, widely separated petals: in small clusters.

Fruit: small and round, blue-black with sweet, edible flesh.

PEA FAMILY
Leguminosae

The 7000 or more species of this family – which includes peas, beans, and other herbaceous plants as well as trees and shrubs – are found all over the world. They are distinguished by their fruit – a pod. Because their roots bear nodules containing nitrogen-fixing bacteria, leguminous plants improve the fertility of the soil in which they grow.

LABURNUM
Laburnum anagyroides

The common laburnum grows wild in woods and thickets in mountainous regions of southern and central Europe; it reaches a height of 7m. It is very widely planted as an ornamental tree in parks, gardens and streets, the hybrid *L. × vossii* being particularly popular. All parts of the tree, especially the seeds, are poisonous.

Crown: narrow, open, and irregular, with up-growing branches.

Bark: smooth; green at first, becoming greenish-brown.

Shoots: grey-green and covered with long grey hairs.

Buds: egg-shaped, pale grey-brown, and hairy.

Leaves: compound, with 3 oval pointed leaflets, 3–8cm long. Borne on stalks 2–6cm long, the leaves are greyish-green above, blue-grey and covered with silky hairs beneath.

Flowers: bright yellow and shaped like those of the pea, 2cm long, growing in hanging clusters, 10–30cm long.

Fruit: slender pods, 4–8cm long, containing black seeds. Hanging in bunches, they are hairy when young, becoming dark brown and hairless.

unripe pods

Laburnum

ripe pod

Right: The long, hanging flower clusters of the laburnum give the tree its other name of 'golden rain'. Like the other parts of the tree the flowers are poisonous.

Locust Tree

winter

winter

Judas Tree

ripe pods

ripe
pods

FALSE ACACIA or LOCUST TREE
Robinia pseudoacacia
Native to eastern North America, the false acacia has long been planted in Europe as an ornamental tree in parks, gardens, etc. It grows well on sandy soils and is often planted to stabilize the soil; it reaches a height of 30m.
Crown: irregular and open, with twisted branches and a fluted and burred trunk.
Bark: smooth and brown in young trees, becoming dull grey and rugged, with a network of deep ridges and cracks, with age.
Shoots: dark red and ribbed, each with a pair of short spines at its base.
Buds: small and hidden by the leafstalks until autumn.
Leaves: compound, 15–20cm long, made up of 3 to 7 pairs of oval leaflets and one terminal leaflet (each 2·5–4·5cm long). The leaves vary from yellow-green to light green and spines are often present at the base of the leafstalks.
Flowers: white and resembling those of the pea, growing in dense hanging fragrant clusters, 10–20cm long.
Fruit: dark brown pods, 5–10cm long, each containing 4 to 16 seeds; they hang from the branches in bunches well into winter.

JUDAS TREE
Cercis siliquastrum
Said to be the tree on which Judas Iscariot hanged himself, the beautiful Judas tree grows wild in rocky regions of southern Europe and western Asia. It is often planted — especially in warmer regions — for ornament in parks and gardens; it reaches a height of 10–12m.
Crown: low and irregularly domed.
Bark: purplish, becoming pinkish-grey with fine brown cracks.
Shoots: dark red-brown.
Buds: dark red, narrow, and conical, 3–5mm long.
Leaves: nearly circular, with a heart-shaped base and smooth margins; 8–12 by 10–12cm. Borne on stalks 5cm long, they are yellow- or dark-green above and paler beneath.
Flowers: rosy pink and resembling those of the pea, 2cm long, growing in clusters (often directly from the trunk) that open before the leaves have appeared.
Fruit: flat red-purple pods, becoming brown and remaining on the tree throughout winter.

Gorse

flower

flower

Broom

seed pod

Spanish broom growing on a dry Mediterranean hillside. It is often accompanied by several kinds of spiny broom.

GORSE
Ulex europaeus
A spiny evergreen shrub which covers large areas of heath and rough grassland. Its golden, scented flowers are favoured by bees. On being touched, the flowers explode pollen on to the visiting insect. Can reach 3m when growing erect, but in exposed places or when subject to heavy grazing it forms low cushions.

Leaves: trifoliate and clover-like in seedlings and young plants, but in the form of stiff, branched spines 1·5-2·5cm long in mature plants: slightly greyish green. The spines are soft on young shoots and readily grazed by animals.

Flowers: golden yellow, about 1·5cm long on short velvety stalks: calyx of sepals yellowish, 2-lipped and hairy. Appear mainly in spring, but often in mid-winter in mild seasons.

Fruit: pod, black, 11-20mm long, hairy, barely longer than the calyx, bursting when ripe to expel seeds.

Uses: an old use for gorse was as a fuel and, after crushing, as fodder.

BROOM
Sarothamnus scoparius
A shrub similar to gorse but without spines, the broom grows up to a height of 2m. The twigs are 5-ridged and hairless. The flowers respond to the landing of visiting insects by expelling pollen onto their undersides. The shrub is found on heaths and dunes and in woods.

Leaves: composed of three elliptic leaflets, short-stalked or stalkless and slightly hairy. Although the leaves are deciduous, the green stems give the broom an evergreen appearance.

Flowers: golden yellow, about 2cm long on stalks up to 1cm: style forming a loop. Calyx of sepals 2-lipped and hairless. Flowering May-June.

Fruit: pod, black, 2·5-4cm long; hairs on margins only.

Uses: the shoots are still used to stimulate urine production, and the long, supple branches were made into brooms for sweeping.

SPANISH BROOM
Spartina junceum
This much-branched upright shrub is a native of the dry, sun-drenched slopes of southern Europe and is much planted elsewhere for its brilliant yellow flowers. The slender, whippy twigs are green and rush-like throughout the year and the plant looks much like the previous species except that it has very few leaves or even none at all. When they are present they are very small and either oval or strap-like.

Flowers: brilliant yellow and pea-like, 2-2·5cm long and sweetly scented: in clusters near tips of branches. Much of the summer.

Fruit: a pod: green and hairy at first, becoming black and hairless: 5-8cm long with several brown seeds.

Sweet Orange

fruit

Seville
Orange

Lemon

CITRUS FAMILY
Rutaceae

This family includes over 1000 species, mostly of tropical and subtropical regions. The citrus trees – none of which is native to Europe – were originally from South East Asia but have been widely cultivated in warm regions (particularly the Mediterranean) since ancient times. They all have glossy evergreen leaves, whose glands secrete aromatic oils, and 5-petalled flowers.

LEMON
Citrus limon
Probably native to India, this small spiny tree is the least hardy of the citrus trees; grows to a height of 6–7m.
Crown: irregular and spreading.
Shoots: reddish and bearing stout spines.

Leaves: dark green and oval, with a pointed tip and crinkly or toothed margins. The leafstalks are jointed and narrowly winged.
Flowers: fragrant, growing singly or in pairs, and developing from reddish buds. The petals are white, tinged with purple on the outside, and there are 20 to 40 stamens. In some flowers both stamens and ovaries are functional; in others only the stamens are fertile.
Fruit: egg-shaped, with a nipple-like projection at the tip; the rind is pale yellow and the flesh acid-tasting. Lemons are used principally for beverages and flavouring.

SWEET ORANGE
Citrus sinensis
Native to China, the sweet orange is the most adaptable of all the citrus trees to growing at lower temperatures, although it is prone to attack by pests and disease; it reaches a height of 9–13m. As well as being grown for its fruit, it is a popular ornamental pot plant.
Crown: rounded or pyramid-shaped.
Leaves: oval, 7·5–10cm long, with a pointed tip, smooth margins, and narrowly winged leafstalks. The leaves

are dark green above, paler beneath.
Flowers: white and fragrant, growing singly or in small clusters.
Fruit: rounded with tough yellow, orange, or orange-red rind and sweet-tasting flesh. It is eaten fresh, made into orange juice, or used for flavouring.

SEVILLE ORANGE
Citrus aurantium
Similar to the sweet orange, this small tree can be distinguished chiefly by its fruit.
Crown: rounded or spreading.
Leaves: like those of the sweet orange, but the leafstalks are more broadly winged.
Flowers: white and fragrant, growing singly or in small clusters in the axils of the leaves.
Fruit: rounded, about 7·5cm across, but flattened slightly at both ends; the aromatic rind is orange or reddish-orange and rough, and the flesh is bitter-tasting.
Uses: the fruit is used for marmalade, beverages (including the liqueur curaçao), and confectionery (as candied peel); oil of Neroli, used in perfumery, is distilled from the flowers.

Tangerines are dark green before they ripen and acquire their orange colour.

The heavy, ripe fruit of the grapefruit, ready for picking.

The citron is slightly more pointed than the grapefruit.

TANGERINE
Citrus deliciosa

The tangerine is a small spiny tree with distinctive fruits.
Leaves: narrow and oval, with a pointed tip and narrowly winged leaf-stalks.
Flowers: white, growing singly or in small clusters.
Fruit: rounded, 5—7·5cm across, and flattened or depressed at both ends. The rind — thin and bright orange — separates readily from the sweet-tasting flesh when the fruit is ripe.
It is also known as the mandarin.

GRAPEFRUIT
Citrus paradisi

The grapefruit is thought to be native to south-east China; it reaches a height of 10—15m.
Crown: rounded or pyramid-shaped.
Leaves: oval, with a pointed tip, smooth margins, and very broadly winged leafstalks (up to 1·5cm wide).

The leaves, which often have spines in their axils, are light green when they first open, becoming darker on the upper surface.
Flowers: white, growing either singly or in clusters.
Fruit: globular, 10—15cm across, with thick smooth pale-yellow or yellow-orange rind and sweet or slightly acid-tasting flesh.

CITRON
Citrus medica

This small tree was the first citrus species to be brought from the Far East for cultivation in Europe.
Crown: irregular and spreading.
Leaves: oval, with toothed margins and rounded or narrowly winged leaf-stalks. Short spines grow in the axils of the leaves.
Flowers: large and fragrant, developing from purple buds, with pinkish-white outer petals and many stamens.

Fruit: oblong or oval and very large (15—25cm long), with very thick rough yellow rind and pale green or yellow flesh with a sweetish or acid taste.

BOX FAMILY
Buxaceae

BOX
Buxus sempervirens

The evergreen box, a native of southern and central Europe, parts of Britain, and North Africa, grows as a shrub or small tree on hillsides; it reaches a height of 10m. It is widely planted in parks, gardens, and churchyards, particularly as a screening and decorative hedge; it clips well and is commonly used for topiary work.
Crown: (tree form) dense and rather narrow, on a slender trunk.
Bark: thin and pale brown, patterned with small squares, becoming pale grey in old trees.
Shoots: green, covered with orange down; they are square in section.
Buds: domed, pale orange-brown, and hairy.
Leaves: hard, leathery, and oval, with a tendency to be inrolled; 1·5—3cm long. Borne on very short (1mm) stalks, they are glossy and dark green above, paler beneath.
Flowers: male and female flowers grow in loose clusters at the base of the leaves. They lack petals, consisting only of stamens (4 per flower) or styles (3 per flower).
Fruit: rounded 3-part capsules bearing the remains of the styles; they split when ripe to release small glossy black seeds.
Uses: the hard heavy close-grained wood is used for carving (e.g. chess pieces), engraving, tool handles, drawing instruments, etc.

Box

fruit

Purple grapes ready for harvest.

Buckthorn

fruit

Alder Buckthorn

fruit

VINE FAMILY
Vitidaceae

GRAPE VINE
Vitis vinifera
A native of S. E. Europe and S. W. Asia, the grape vine is grown throughout the warmer parts of Europe for the wine which is made from the fruit juice. It is essentially a climbing plant, with branching tendrils, but is normally cultivated as a small bush trained on wires. Many varieties are grown, most of them hybrids between American and European vines.
Leaves: palmately lobed.
Flowers: small and green, in dense clusters.
Fruit: juicy berries, green or purple according to variety.
Uses: apart from wine, the fruits of certain varieties are eaten fresh or dried (as raisins and sultanas).

BUCKTHORN FAMILY
Rhamnaceae

BUCKTHORN
Rhamnus cathartica
Also called purging buckthorn, this rather thorny species thrives in woodland margins and hedgerows and commonly springs up on chalk and limestone hillsides when grazing is stopped. It occurs in most parts of Europe apart from the far north and the Mediterranean area. It grows as a bush or a small tree, reaching 6m in height. Many of the short twigs end in spines.
Bark: dark grey, becoming black with age.
Leaves: bright green; oval and finely toothed, often with a notch at the tip; 2-4 pairs of lateral veins. 5cm long.
Flowers: 4mm across; sweetly scented with four green petals; sexes separate. In clusters in May.

Fruit: berries 6-10mm; green and then black: poisonous, with powerful purgative action.

ALDER BUCKTHORN
Frangula alnus
Growing as a shrub or small tree and reaching 5m in height, this plant resembles the buckthorn in general appearance but differs in several details. It grows in most parts of Europe, mainly in damp woods and fens. It has no thorns.
Bark: black with clear brown pores.
Leaves: like those of buckthorn but with smooth margins and 7-9 pairs of veins.
Flowers: bisexual; 3mm across with 5 pale green petals; solitary or in small small clusters in May
Fruit: small berries, ripening from green, through red, to black.

HOLLY FAMILY
Aquifoliaceae

HOLLY
Ilex aquifolium
This evergreen grows as a shrub or small tree in woods, thickets, and hedgerows in western, central, and southern Europe; it reaches a height of 20m. Since it withstands clipping, the holly is grown as a hedge in gardens; there are also many ornamental varieties with attractive foliage and berries.
Crown: conical and spired, with up-turned branches, in young trees; becomes dense and irregular with age.
Bark: smooth and silvery-grey, becoming rough and gnarled with age.
Shoots: bright green or purple; stout and grooved.
Buds: green, very small, and sharply pointed.
Leaves: very variable, but usually leathery and oval, 6-8cm long, with a pointed tip; glossy dark green above, bright green and matt beneath. Leaves on the lower branches have spiny margins, those higher up have wavy or smooth margins. Some cultivated ornamental varieties have variegated foliage.
Flowers: male and female flowers grow on separate trees in crowded fragrant clusters at the base of the leaves. Each flower is small (6–8mm across) and white, opening from a purple bud.
Fruit: poisonous berries, 7–10mm across, ripening from green to scarlet. Borne on a stalk 4–8mm long, each contains 3 to 4 black seeds. Some ornamental varieties have yellow berries. Fruit, of course, is borne only on female trees.
Uses: the ivory-white wood — hard, heavy, and fine-grained — is valued for turned articles, inlay work, and carving.

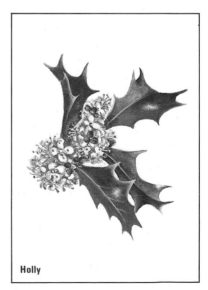

Holly

ripe fruit

Tree of Heaven

winter

autumn leaves

ripe fruit

autumn

Spindle Tree

QUASSIA FAMILY
Simaroubaceae

TREE OF HEAVEN
Ailanthus altissima
This fast-growing Chinese tree is widely grown for shade and ornament in streets, parks, and gardens (it is naturalized in parts of southern and central Europe); it withstands pollution and is often planted for soil conservation. It reaches a height of 25m.
Crown: a tall loose irregular dome, with stout wavy up-growing branches supported on a straight trunk.
Bark: smooth, grey-brown to black, with white vertical streaks; it becomes dark grey and roughened with age.
Shoots: stout and orange-brown.
Buds: small and egg-shaped, maturing from red-brown to scarlet.
Leaves: compound, 30–60cm long, consisting of 5 to 22 pairs of leaflets. Each leaflet is narrow, oval, and pointed, 7–15cm long, with 1 to 3 large teeth on each side at the base with a large gland underneath each tooth. Borne on red stalks, 7–15cm long, the leaves are deep red when they first open, becoming deep green above and paler beneath.
Flowers: small and greenish, growing in large clusters; male and female flowers often grow on separate trees.
Fruit: twisted wings, each with a seed in the centre; 4cm long. They grow in large hanging clusters, 30 by 30cm, ripening from yellow-green to bright orange-red.

SPINDLE TREE FAMILY
Celastraceae

SPINDLE TREE
Euonymus europaeus
The attractive spindle tree is found throughout Europe (except in the extreme north), growing as a shrub or small tree in woods, thickets, and hedgerows, especially on chalk or limestone; reaches a height of 6m.
Bark: smooth and green, becoming grey or pale brown with age.
Buds: green and egg-shaped.
Leaves: oval to lance-shaped, 3–10cm long, with a pointed tip and finely toothed margins. Borne on stalks 6–12mm long, they are shiny blue-green above and paler beneath, turning yellow, russet, and crimson in autumn.
Flowers: small (1cm across), with 4 greenish-white petals and 4 stamens; they grow in loose long-stalked clusters of 3 to 8 at the base of the leaves.
Fruit: 4-lobed seed-pods, 10–15mm across, ripening from green to bright pink. When ripe they split to reveal the seeds, each covered by a fleshy orange-red coat (aril); the seeds themselves, which are poisonous, are white and surrounded by a pink seed coat.
Uses: the whitish wood is hard, smooth, and tough; it has been used for spindles, knitting needles, pegs, toothpicks, etc., and makes excellent artists' charcoal.

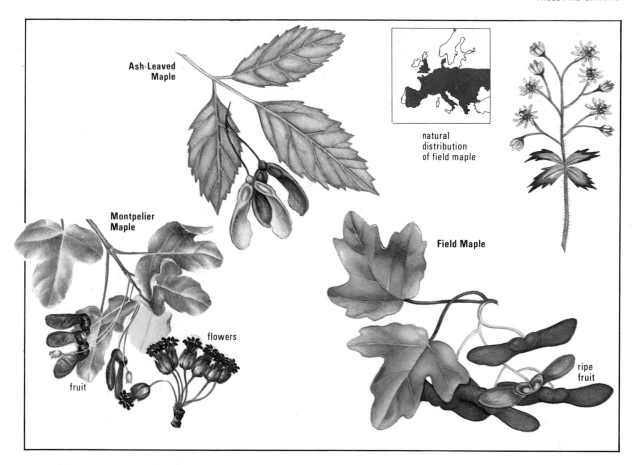

Ash-Leaved Maple

natural distribution of field maple

Montpelier Maple

Field Maple

flowers

fruit

ripe fruit

MAPLE FAMILY
Aceraceae

Most of the trees in this family (which contains about 150 species) are maples (genus *Acer*). Their flowers – small and greenish-yellow – grow in clusters and their fruits consist of 2 wings joined by the seeds at their bases. Most are deciduous.

MONTPELIER MAPLE
Acer monspessulanum
This small maple, growing in dry hilly and rocky districts of southern Europe and western Asia, is sometimes planted for ornament in parks and gardens; it reaches a height of 15m.
Crown: dense and broadly domed.
Bark: dark grey to black, with vertical cracks.
Shoots: smooth, slender, and pale brown.
Buds: small (3mm), egg-shaped, and dark orange-brown.
Leaves: hard and leathery, 4 by 8cm, with 3 rounded untoothed lobes. Borne on orange-pink stalks, 4cm long, the leaves are bright green on opening, becoming dark green above and grey-blue beneath.
Flowers: grouped in flat-topped erect (later drooping) clusters.
Fruit: paired brown nutlets attached to parallel or overlapping wings— green or pinkish, each 1·2cm long and borne on a 4cm stalk.

BOX ELDER or ASH-LEAVED MAPLE
Acer negundo
This North American maple is widely cultivated in Europe for shelter and ornament, being planted in town streets, parks, and gardens; short-lived and fast-growing, it reaches a height of 20m.
Crown: irregularly domed, leaning to one side with age.
Bark: smooth and grey-brown at first, becoming darker and cracked.
Shoots: green and straight, becoming covered with purple bloom in the second year.
Buds: small, white, and silky.
Leaves: compound, up to 20 by 15cm, with 3 to 7 irregularly toothed leaflets. Borne on pale-yellow or pink stalks, 6–8cm long, the leaves are pale green, but the colour varies in ornamental varieties (var. *variegatum* has white-margined leaves).
Flowers: male and female flowers grow on separate trees in hanging clusters before the leaves open.

Fruit: the wings, 2cm across, are set at an acute angle; pale brown when ripe, they remain on the tree after the leaves have fallen.

FIELD MAPLE
Acer campestre
Often growing as a small tree or shrub in hedgerows, especially on chalk or limestone soils, the hardy field maple is found throughout Europe, extending to southern Sweden, North Africa and northern Iran; reaches a height of 25m. It is grown for ornament and hedges.
Crown: domed and usually low.
Bark: pale brown with wide cracks or split into squares; becomes darker with age.
Shoots: brown, covered with fine hairs and, later, corky ridges.
Buds: brown and hairy; 3mm long.
Leaves: up to 8 by 12cm, with rounded lobes each with a shallow notch near the tip (the middle, largest, lobe has parallel sides or is wedge-shaped). Borne on slender green or pink stalks, 5–9cm long, the leaves open pinkish, becoming dark green above (paler beneath) and bright gold or reddish in autumn.
Flowers: grow in erect widely spaced clusters of about 10 and open with the leaves.
Fruit: horizontal wings, 5–6cm across, yellow-green tinged with crimson, ripening to brown.

339

Norway Maple

ripe fruit

winter

Sycamore

fruit

winter

NORWAY MAPLE
Acer platanoides

The Norway maple is found all over Europe (except the extreme north); grows to a height of 30m. It is often planted as a shelter belt and for shade and ornament, particularly in city streets (since it tolerates smoke).

Crown: tall, domed or spreading, and dense, often on a very short trunk.

Bark: smooth and grey-brown, with a network of shallow ridges.

Shoots: pinkish-brown.

Buds: egg-shaped, dark red or brown (at the tips of the branches).

Leaves: 5-lobed, with the tip and teeth of each lobe ending in long slender points; 12 by 15cm. Borne on long (15cm) slender stalks containing milky sap, the leaves open rusty red, becoming bright green above and paler beneath, and turning yellow then orange-brown before falling.

Flowers: greenish-yellow and quite showy; grow in erect clusters of 30–40 that open before the leaves.

Fruit: the wings, 6–10cm across, are very widely spread; they ripen from yellow-green to brown.

Uses: the hard heavy fine-grained wood — white or greyish — is used for furniture and turned articles.

SYCAMORE
Acer pseudoplatanus

Growing wild in mountainous regions of southern and central Europe, the sycamore is widely planted for shelter, ornament, and timber (it has become naturalized in many parts); since it tolerates pollution, it is often grown in towns and cities. It reaches a height of 35m.

Crown: dense and broadly domed, with spreading branches.

Bark: smooth and grey, becoming pinkish-brown and flaking off in irregular plates.

Buds: green and egg-shaped; 8–12mm long.

Leaves: up to 18 by 26cm, divided into 5 pointed coarsely toothed lobes. Borne on reddish stalks, up to 15cm long, the leaves are orange or reddish when they first open, becoming deep green and matt above and pale blue-green beneath.

Flowers: grow in dense narrow hanging clusters of 50 to 100, 6–12cm long.

Fruit: the wings, about 3cm long and set more or less at right angles, are green tinged with red, turning brown when the fruit is ripe.

Uses: the hard yellowish-white fine-grained timber is used for furniture, turned articles (bowls, spoons, etc.), carving, textile rollers, violins and other musical instruments, and veneers.

CASHEW FAMILY
Anacardiaceae

A largely tropical family of about 600 species, but with seven species in Europe. All have small flowers, usually with 5 petals, grouped into branching clusters. Most are resinous and several are used as sources of resin and gums. They are also used for tanning leather. The European species all form thickets on the dry, stony hillsides of the Mediterranean region.

SMOKE TREE
Cotinus coggygria
Named for its smoky appearance when in fruit, this dense shrub grows to 2-5m.
Leaves: smooth and rounded, bluish-green and becoming brilliant red in autumn: 3-8cm long with clear veins.
Flowers: yellow, in loose conical clusters.
Fruit: small and rounded, brownish when ripe: in loose clusters whose stalks carry plume-like hairs, giving the tree its smoky look in late summer. Hairs vary from yellow to greyish brown.

SUMACH
Rhus coriaria
Recognized by its hairy shoots, this shrub is almost evergreen, retaining at least a few leaves for most of the winter. Reaches 3m; common by many Mediterranean roadsides.
Leaves: thick and velvety, deep green with numerous coarsely toothed oval leaflets. 20cm or more long.
Flowers: greenish, packed into dense, erect spikes.
Fruit: purplish brown and hairy; currant-sized in dense clusters.

TURPENTINE TREE
Pistacia terebinthus
Also known as the terebinth, this grey-stemmed, strongly aromatic shrub or small tree reaches 5m.
Leaves: bright green, 10cm or more long; leathery, with 3-9 oblong leaflets.
Flowers: green to purple in large clusters.
Fruit: pea-sized, bright red becoming brown.

MASTIC TREE
Pistacia lentiscus
Also known as the lentisc, this evergreen and strongly aromatic species is usually a low, spreading bush: occasionally reaches 8m.
Leaves: dark green and leathery; up to 5cm, with 6-12 narrow leaflets.
Flowers: dull red in small tight bunches: unisexual.
Fruit: pea-sized, red becoming black.
Uses: the resinous gum from stems is used as chewing gum.

PISTACHIO
Pistacia vera
This Asiatic tree is grown in S. Europe for its edible green seeds. It reaches 10m.
Leaves: to 10cm with up to five oval greyish-green leaflets.
Fruit: egg-shaped; 2·5cm long, hard-shelled in loose bunches.

leaves

Smoke Tree

The smoke tree in full fruiting glory, the smoky haze being created by the hairy fruit clusters.

Turpentine Tree

fruit

Sumach

fruit

Pistachio

fruit

Mastic Tree

fruit

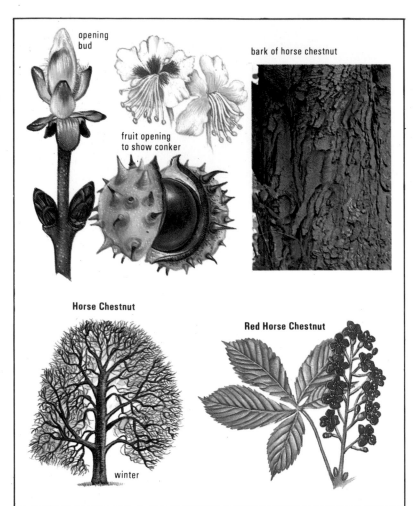

opening bud

bark of horse chestnut

fruit opening to show conker

Horse Chestnut

winter

Red Horse Chestnut

HORSE CHESTNUT FAMILY
Hippocastaneae

This small family, with about 30 species, has its headquarters in North and Central America, where the trees are commonly called buckeyes. Almost all are large and showy trees and all have the familiar digitate leaves and erect flower spikes.

HORSE CHESTNUT
Aesculus hippocastanum
Native to the Balkans, this fast-growing impressive tree is very widely planted for ornament and shade; it withstands pollution and is naturalized in some parts of Europe. It reaches a height of 30m.
Crown: tall and domed, on a short thick trunk.
Bark: dark grey-brown or reddish-brown, flaking off in scales.
Shoots: stout; grey or pink-brown.
Buds: large and pointed (2·5 by 1·5cm), shiny dark red-brown, and sticky with resin.
Leaves: compound, with 5 to 7 toothed leaflets (up to 25 by 10cm), which are pointed and broadest near the tip, arising from the same point on the stout yellow-green stalk (up to 20cm long). Bright green at first, they become darker above, yellow-green beneath, and turn gold, orange, or scarlet in autumn; they leave horseshoe-shaped scars when they fall.
Flowers: 2cm across, with fringed white petals tinged with crimson or yellow at the base; they grow in erect clusters, 15-30cm long. The flowers at the top of each cluster have only male organs (stamens) and therefore produce no fruit.
Fruit: green, globular, and spiny, splitting when ripe (brown) to reveal 1 to 3 shiny brown seeds (conkers).
Uses: the soft white wood has been used for joinery, cabinetwork, turnery, etc.; the seeds provide fodder for cattle in eastern Europe.

RED HORSE CHESTNUT
Aesculus x carnea
This hybrid between the horse chestnut and the American red buckeye (*A. pavia*) is widely planted as an ornamental; reaches a height of 20m.
Buds: egg-shaped, 1·5—2·5cm, but not sticky.
Leaves: similar to those of the horse chestnut but the leaflets are darker, crinkled, sometimes shiny above, and have broader, more jagged, teeth.
Flowers: red, in erect clusters 12—20cm long.
Fruit: usually not spiny; each contains 2 to 3 small dull-brown seeds.

Left: The full beauty of horse chestnut flowers is seen in April and May.

LIME FAMILY
Tiliaceae

Most of the 300 to 400 species of this family are native to tropical and warm regions. The limes, widely distributed in northern temperate regions, all have small fragrant flowers (with 5 sepals, 5 petals, and many stamens) hanging in clusters from leafy strap-like bracts; they develop into nut-like fruits, each with 1 to 3 seeds. The soft white wood is used for carving, turnery, hat blocks, piano keys, and wood pulp. The soft fibres of the inner bark are known as bast and are very strong and flexible. They were once used for making ropes and matting and even fishing nets and coarse clothing.

Lime trees are also known as lindens, and in North America they are called basswoods. They must not be confused with the limes which yield lime juice: these are citrus fruits related to the lemon and orange.

SMALL-LEAVED LIME
Tilia cordata
Growing wild throughout Europe, the small-leaved lime is also widely planted for shade and ornament, especially in avenues; it grows to 30m.
Crown: tall, dense, and domed.
Bark: smooth and grey, becoming dark grey and cracked into plates.
Shoots: red above, olive beneath.
Buds: smooth, shiny dark red, and egg-shaped.
Leaves: heart-shaped, 4–7 by 3–5cm, with finely toothed margins. Borne on yellow-green or pinkish stalks 3·5cm long, they are dark shiny green above, and paler — with tufts of reddish hairs at the bases of the veins — beneath.
Flowers: greenish-white, growing in nearly erect or spreading clusters of 4 to 15 from pale green bracts, 6cm long.
Fruit: small (6mm across), rounded, and smooth or indistinctly ribbed.

LARGE-LEAVED LIME
Tilia platyphyllos
Another widespread European lime (although not extending as far north as the small-leaved species), this tree is planted for ornament. It grows to a height of 40m.
Crown: tall and domed, with up-growing branches.
Shoots: reddish-green and hairy.
Leaves: rounded, with a pointed tip and sharply toothed margins; 6–15 by 6–15cm. Borne on hairy stalks, 2–5cm long, they are dark green and

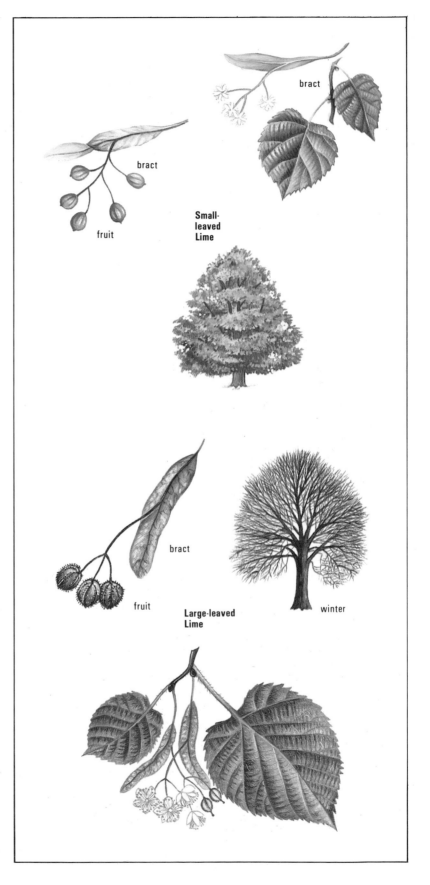

bract

bract

fruit

Small-leaved Lime

Large-leaved Lime

bract

fruit

winter

underside
of leaf

Silver Lime

fruit

bract

**Common
Lime**

fruit

winter

*Dense clusters of shoots springing
from the base of the trunk are
characteristic of lime trees.*

hairy above, and paler — with white
hairs on the veins — beneath.
Flowers: yellowish-white, hanging in
clusters of 3 to 4 from whitish-green
bracts, 5—12cm long.
Fruit: rounded, 8—10mm across, each
with 3 to 5 prominent ribs and densely
covered with hairs.

SILVER LIME
Tilia tomentosa
Native to south-east Europe (the
Balkans) and south-west Asia, the
silver lime is quite often planted for
ornament; it grows to 30m.
Crown: broadly conical or domed,
with steeply up-turned branches.
Bark: dark greenish with vertical
markings, becoming grey with a network of flat ridges.
Shoots: whitish and densely downy,
becoming dark grey-green above and
bright green beneath.
Buds: egg-shaped and hairy, 6—
8mm long; green and brown.
Leaves: rounded, with a pointed tip,
toothed margins, and an unequal base;
12 by 10cm. Borne on downy 5-cm
stalks, the leaves are dark green and
crinkled above, pale grey and downy
beneath.
Flowers: yellow-white, growing in
clusters of 6 to 10 from yellow-green
bracts, 9 by 2cm.
Fruit: egg-shaped and warty, 6—
10mm long.

COMMON LIME
Tilia x *europaea*
This tree — a hybrid between the
small-leaved and large-leaved limes —
is often planted for shade and ornament, especially in streets and avenues
in north-west Europe; it produces
numerous suckers from the base and
from the trunk itself, the region from
which the suckers arise often swelling
up to form a prominent bulge or boss.
Sucker shoots also spring in quantity
from the cut ends of the branches, and
large bosses develop here as well.
Many limes in parks and avenues are
clipped back to these bosses each
year, causing them to swell even more
and give the trees a strangely attractive
tufted appearance.
Crown: tall and domed, with up-
turned branches (the lower branches
are arched).
Bark: dull grey and smooth, becoming
rough with a network of shallow ridges
and (usually) bosses.
Shoots: green tinged with red.
Buds: reddish-brown and egg-shaped.
Leaves: heart-shaped, 6—10cm long,
with toothed margins and an unequal
base. Borne on green hairless stalks,
2—5cm long, they are dull green
above, pale green and rather shiny
beneath with tufts of buff or white
hairs at the bases of the veins; the
leaves turn yellow in autumn.
Flowers: yellowish-white, hanging
in clusters of 4 to 10 from yellow-
green bracts.
Fruit: egg-shaped, downy, and slightly
ribbed; 8mm across.

POMEGRANATE FAMILY
Punicaceae

POMEGRANATE
Punica granatum

Originally from south-west Asia, this small, much-branched tree is now widely grown in southern Europe for its fruit (it is naturalized in some parts); the pomegranate is occasionally grown for its ornamental flowers in temperate regions. It reaches a height of 6m.

Shoots: angled and hairless.

Leaves: slender and shining bright green, 2–8cm long, growing on short stalks.

Flowers: orange-red and showy, 3–4cm across; the sepals are united in a tube from which 4 crumpled petals and many stamens emerge. Some ornamental varieties have double flowers.

Fruit: a large berry, 5–8cm across, with a brownish-red leathery skin enclosing a sweet or acid-tasting purple to white pulp divided into compartments containing many seeds.

Uses: the fruit is eaten raw and its juice can be drunk fresh or made into wine; the seeds are used in jams and syrups. The bark, rind, and roots of the tree were formerly used medicinally (especially as a worm powder).

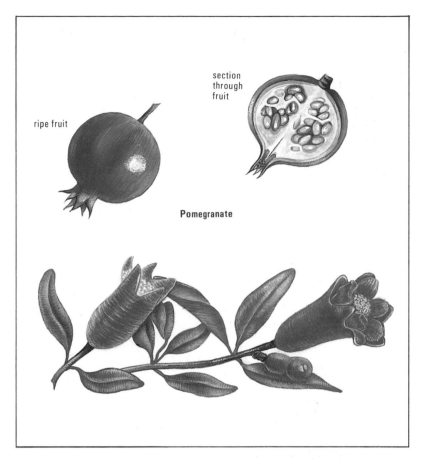

ripe fruit

section through fruit

Pomegranate

MYRTLE FAMILY
Myrtaceae

CIDER GUM
Eucalyptus gunnii

Native to Tasmania, the cider gum is the most commonly planted eucalyptus in north-west Europe, where it reaches a height of 20–30m.

Crown: conical at first, with upswept branches, becoming tall, domed, and heavily branched.

Bark: smooth and grey beneath pinkish-orange peeling strips.

Shoots: yellowish-white, covered with a pinkish-grey bloom.

Leaves: (mature) evergreen and oblong, 8–10 by 3–4cm, tapering to a point at the tip; borne on pale-yellow stalks 2·5cm long, these leaves are dark blue-grey above, yellow-green beneath, and smell of cider when crushed. Young leaves are rounded, 3–6cm across, and pale blue-grey.

Flowers: white and fluffy, in clusters of 3, opening from blue-white egg-shaped rimmed buds.

Fruit: white top-shaped flat-ended capsules, 5mm long.

flowers

Cider Gum

fruit

old fruit

Blue Gum

Myrtle

flower

flower bud

young flower

flower bud

MYRTLE
Myrtus communis
A dense much-branched evergreen shrub, the myrtle grows wild in dry sunny positions, woods, and thickets in the Mediterranean region; reaches a height of 5m. It is quite widely planted for ornament.
Shoots: downy.
Leaves: oval, 2–3 by 1·5cm, with a pointed base and tip. Dark green and leathery, the leaves are dotted with glands and are very aromatic when crushed.
Flowers: sweet-scented, 2cm across, with 5 white petals and numerous stamens. Opening from globular buds enclosed in 5 shiny brown sepals, the flowers grow on long stalks from the axils of the upper leaves.
Fruit: rounded purple-black berries, 6·5mm long.
Uses: the hard mottled wood is used for turned articles and charcoal; the leaves, flowers, and fruit yield an oil used in perfumery.

BLUE GUM
Eucalyptus globulus
This tall fast-growing evergreen from Australia is widely planted in frost-free parts of Europe for ornament and timber; reaches a height of 55m or more.
Crown: conical or domed, high, and dense, on a straight cylindrical trunk.
Bark: a pale-brown outer bark flakes off to reveal patches of grey, brown, and white smooth inner bark.
Leaves: (mature) lance- or sickle-shaped, 10–30 by 3–8cm, glossy dark blue-green and dotted with glands; (young) oblong, 10–15cm long, and pointed at base and tip; pale greyish-blue to white.
Flowers: whitish, about 4cm across, and borne singly; the petals and sepals are united to form a beaked cap and fall away to reveal numerous yellow stamens.
Fruit: large blackish top-shaped capsules, 1–1·5 by 1·5–3cm, with greyish-blue lids that open to release the seeds.
Uses: medicinal eucalyptus oil is obtained from the leaves.

ROCKROSE FAMILY
Cistaceae

GUM CISTUS
Cistus ladanifer
The tallest European member of the family, this much-branched evergreen shrub may reach 3m. Its foliage smells strongly of balsam. Like the other cistuses, it revels in dry, rocky places. It forms thickets in the western Mediterranean region.
Leaves: 4-10cm long, narrow; bright and sticky above, pale and furry below.
Flowers: 5-10cm across; five white petals, each with a brown or purple patch. Each flower lasts just one day in May and June.

SAGE-LEAVED CISTUS
Cistus salvifolius
A sprawling evergreen shrub up to 1m high, flowering March-May throughout the Mediterranean region.
Leaves: oval, up to 2cm long: bright green, soft like those of sage.
Flowers: 2-4cm across; white, with prominent tuft of yellow stamens.

GREY-LEAVED CISTUS
Cistus albidus
This much-branched, upright evergreen shrub from the western Mediterranean region reaches about 1m.
Leaves: velvety grey-green; oval, 2-3cm long.
Flowers: a beautiful pink, up to 6cm across: petals often creased and lasting just one day. April-July.

TAMARISK FAMILY
Tamaricaceae

TAMARISK
Tamarix anglica
A feathery shrub with slender, whip-like brown or purple branches, this plant is most frequently found on the coast or on shingly river banks. A native of S.W. Europe, it is now established in many other places.
Leaves: very small and scale-like, completely clothing the smaller twigs.
Flowers: 3mm across, pink or white; packed into dense spikes near tips of young shoots. July-September.

SEA BUCKTHORN FAMILY
Eleaginaceae

SEA BUCKTHORN
Hippophae rhamnoides
Unrelated to the true buckthorn (page 337), this densely branched, spiny shrub grows mainly by the sea, often being planted to stabilize dunes; also by mountain streams. Up to 10m.
Shoot: spine-tipped and clothed with golden brown scales.
Leaves: slender, 1-6cm long; greyish green at first, owing to coat of silvery hairs, becoming brighter and hairless.
Flowers: very small and green but clothed with brown scales; densely clustered; unisexual.
Fruit: clustered orange berries 6-8mm.

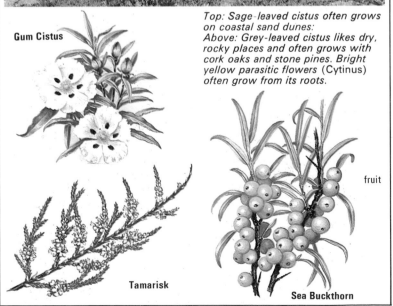

Top: Sage-leaved cistus often grows on coastal sand dunes:
Above: Grey-leaved cistus likes dry, rocky places and often grows with cork oaks and stone pines. Bright yellow parasitic flowers (Cytinus) often grow from its roots.

Gum Cistus

Tamarisk

Sea Buckthorn

fruit

flowers

Dogwood

winter
twig

Strawberry
Tree

flowers
and fruit

bark of strawberry tree

DOGWOOD FAMILY
Cornaceae

DOGWOOD
Cornus sanguinea
Found throughout Europe (except the far north), the dogwood grows as a shrub or small tree in hedgerows, thickets, woods, and scrub. It prefers chalky soils and produces suckers freely; it reaches a height of 4m.
Bark: greenish-grey.
Shoots: dark red and very conspicuous in winter.
Buds: slender and scaleless.
Leaves: oval, 4–10cm long, with a pointed tip and prominent curved veins. The leaves turn from pale green to dark red in autumn.
Flowers: small and white, with 4 wide-spreading petals, 4 sepals, and 4 stamens. The flowers grow in flat-topped clusters, 4–5cm across, at the tips of the branches.
Fruit: globular, 6–8mm across, ripening from green to shiny black. The bitter-tasting flesh encloses a hard stone containing 2 seeds.
Uses: the wood — tough, white, and smooth — was originally used to make skewers.

HEATHER FAMILY
Ericaceae

This is a family of 2,000 or so shrubs, together with a few small trees, spread through most of the cooler parts of the world, including the tropical mountains. Most, including the heather itself, are low-growing. Just a few of the taller species are described here.

STRAWBERRY TREE
Arbutus unedo
The small evergreen strawberry tree grows naturally in thickets, woods, and dry rocky places of south and south-west Europe as far north as south-west Ireland; it is sometimes planted for shelter and ornament. It reaches a height of 12m.
Crown: low, dense, and rounded, with up-growing branches supported on a very short trunk.
Bark: dark reddish, later peeling off and forming grey-brown ridges.
Shoots: hairy; pinkish above, pale green beneath.
Leaves: lance-shaped, with sharply toothed margins; 5–10 by 2–3cm. Borne on hairy pinkish stalks, 5–7mm long, the leaves are shiny dark green above, paler green beneath.
Flowers: white (tinged with green or pink) and flask-shaped, 8 by 8mm, growing in hanging clusters 5cm long. The flowers appear in autumn, at the same time as the ripe fruit from the previous year.
Fruit: rounded, 2cm across, with a rough warty skin, ripening from yellow to scarlet. Though edible, the fruit does not have a pleasant flavour.

Rhododendron

Lusitanian Heath

The rhododendron has become naturalized in many European woodlands, where it makes a fine sight in spring.

RHODODENDRON
Rhododendron ponticum

A native of southern Europe, this huge spreading evergreen shrub is widely planted for its beautiful flowers and has become naturalized in many parts of the continent, especially on sandy soils. It reaches 4m or more and forms impenetrable thickets in many woods.

Bark: Brownish grey, usually with numerous shallow fissures breaking it into small rectangular blocks.

Leaves: elongate-oval to 25cm long; leathery, dark green and shiny above, paler and duller below. Large green buds among leaves at branch tips.

Flowers: pale pink to mauve, bell-shaped up to 7cm across: 10 long curved stamens and a single style project from the bell. In dense rounded clusters in June.

Fruit: a dry, brown capsule.

Several other species are cultivated in parks and gardens, but they do not usually become naturalized. One exception is the yellow rhododendron (*R. luteum*), a deciduous species from S. E. Europe. It bears deep yellow flowers on leafless shoots in spring, before the rather pale green and sticky leaves appear. The flowers have only five stamens. The plant seeds readily and also spreads by means of suckers from the roots.

LUSITANIAN HEATH
Erica lusitanica

A native of the western Mediterranean region and the Iberian Peninsula, this densely branched evergreen shrub reaches 3-4m. It grows thickly in open woods and on exposed hillsides, and when in flower stands out like a hazy white cloud against the other shrubs.

Leaves: light green and needle-like, 3-5mm long in whorls on the hairy stems.

Flowers: white with a delicate tinge of pink (especially noticeable when in bud) and a red stigma; almost cylindrical, 4-5mm long, in dense elongated clusters towards the ends of the branches. Mid-winter to mid-summer. Fragrant.

The very similar tree heath (*E. arborea*) grows throughout the Mediterranean area. It is usually taller and has darker leaves, but it is best distinguished by its white bell-shaped flowers and yellow stigmas.

349

HONEYSUCKLE FAMILY
Caprifoliaceae

WAYFARING TREE
Viburnum lantana
The wayfaring tree is found over most of Europe (except the extreme north), growing at the edges of woods, in thickets, and in hedges, especially on chalk or limestone soils; reaches a height of 6m.
Shoots: covered with greyish down.
Buds: lack scales.
Leaves: heart-shaped and wrinkled, 5–12cm long, with toothed margins and densely covered with down on the lower surface: they are borne on short downy stalks.
Flowers: all are white, small (6mm across), and fertile, grouped in flat-topped clusters, 6–10cm across.
Fruit: small, oval, and flattened, in flat-topped or domed clusters, ripening unevenly from green to red and finally black.

GUELDER ROSE
Viburnum opulus
Native in most parts of Europe, the guelder rose grows in woodlands, scrub, hedgerows and thickets; especially on damp soils. It reaches a height of 4-5m. Cultivated forms, planted for their flowers, are sterile.
Crown: spreading.
Shoots: smooth and angled.
Buds: greenish-yellow and scaly.
Leaves: 3- to 5-lobed, 5–8cm long, with deeply toothed margins and 2 glands at the base. Borne on greenish-red stalks, 3–4cm long, each with pointed stipules at its base, the leaves are downy at first, becoming smooth above and turning scarlet in autumn.
Flowers: white, in dense flat-topped clusters 5–10cm across. The outer flowers are large (2cm across) and sterile (without stamens or ovaries) and serve to attract insects to the flower head; the inner flowers are smaller (6-8mm across) and fertile.
Fruit: red, translucent, and berry-like, 8mm across.

ELDER
Sambucus nigra
The elder grows throughout Europe as a shrub or small tree of woods, hedges, scrub, and waste ground; it reaches a height of 10m.
Crown: irregular and much-branched.
Bark: greyish-brown, with thick corky ridges and deep cracks.
Shoots: stout and grey, with corky pores and thick white pith.
Buds: scaly; brownish-red or purple.
Leaves: compound, with 2 to 3 pairs of leaflets and one terminal leaflet. Each leaflet is oval to lance-shaped, 3–9cm long, with sharply toothed margins and a pointed tip. Aromatic.
Flowers: small (5mm across) and creamy white, grouped into flat-topped clusters 10–20cm across.
Fruit: berry-like and juicy, in large clusters, ripening from green to black.
Uses: the fruit, rich in vitamin C, is made into wine, jam, and jelly; the flowers can also be brewed to make a beverage. The hard, whitish wood is used for small articles.

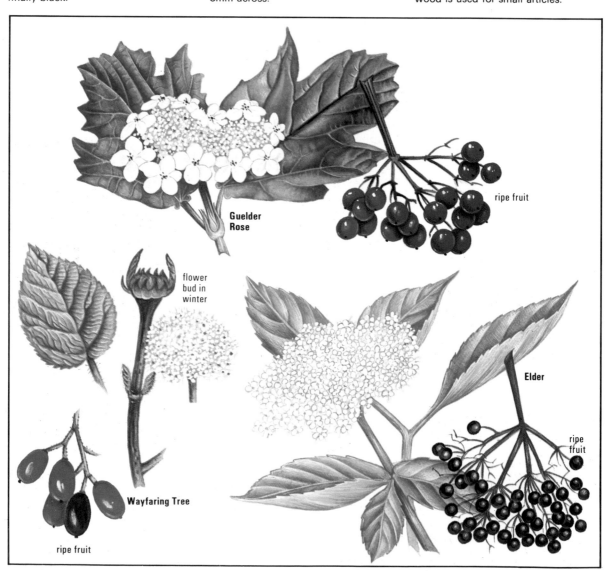

Guelder Rose

ripe fruit

flower bud in winter

Wayfaring Tree

ripe fruit

Elder

ripe fruit

Olive trees in a grove in southern Europe. The fruit is picked in autumn.

flowers

Olive

unripe fruit

ripe fruit

bark of olive

OLIVE FAMILY
Oleaceae

This widely distributed family of trees and shrubs (400 to 500 species) includes many ornamental trees (such as the lilac and jasmine) as well as the economically important olive and ash. Their flowers usually contain only 2 stamens.

OLIVE
Olea europaea

A slow-growing long-lived evergreen, the olive has been widely cultivated for fruit since ancient times in its native Mediterranean region; reaches a height of 15m. It grows wild in dry rocky places and is also planted in gardens for shade.

Crown: spreading (bushy in wild forms), supported on a twisted gnarled trunk.

Bark: smooth and grey at first, becoming darker and deeply pitted with age.

Shoots: covered with silvery scales.

Leaves: leathery and lance-shaped, 2–8cm long, dark green above and silvery-grey beneath. Wild trees often have small oval leaves.

Flowers: small and white, each with 2 yellow-tipped stamens, growing in dense clusters in the axils of the leaves. Some flowers have no pistils.

Fruit: egg-shaped, 1–3·5cm long, containing a single large seed; olives ripen from green to black or brownish-green.

Uses: the fruit is used as food and yields a high-quality oil (olive oil) used in cooking, medicine (as a lubricant, in ointments, and as a mild laxative), and in soap-making; the residue of the fruit (after the oil has been extracted) is used as cattle food. The wood, which is very hard, is used for carving, cabinetwork, fuel, and charcoal.

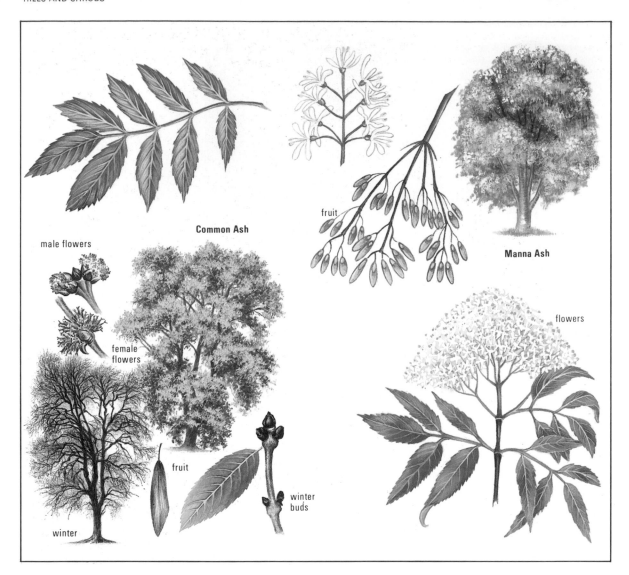

male flowers

female flowers

Common Ash

fruit

Manna Ash

flowers

fruit

winter buds

winter

COMMON ASH
Fraxinus excelsior
Widely distributed in Europe and south-west Asia, the common ash is found in woods and scrub (it grows particularly well on moist alkaline soils); reaches a height of 40m. It is valued for its timber and also grown for ornament in parks, churchyards, etc.
Crown: tall and rounded, with steeply up-growing branches.
Bark: pale grey; smooth at first, it later develops a network of ridges.
Shoots: stout; greenish-grey with white markings.
Buds: conspicuously black, squat, and angled.
Leaves: compound, 20–35cm long, with 4 to 6 pairs of leaflets and one terminal leaflet. The leaflets, up to 12cm long, are stalkless (or nearly so) and pointed, with sharply toothed margins; dull green above and pale and downy beneath, they turn yellow in autumn.
Flowers: usually, male and female

flowers grow on separate trees, but some trees bear both male and female flowers and others have hermaphrodite flowers. The flowers of both sexes are small and purplish, growing in small dense clusters that appear well before the leaves.
Fruit: strap-shaped keys, 2·5–5cm long, each with a notched tip. They ripen from shiny deep green to brown and remain on the tree after the leaves have fallen.
Uses: the pale tough elastic timber is used for sports equipment (oars, hockey sticks, etc.), tool handles, furniture, walking sticks, pegs, etc.; it also makes good fuel and charcoal.

MANNA or FLOWERING ASH
Fraxinus ornus
The manna ash is native to south, south-east, and central Europe, where it grows in dry rocky regions, woods, and thickets; reaches a height of 20m. It is widely planted as an ornamental

in parks, and is cultivated for commercial purposes in Italy.
Crown: rounded, with curving branches.
Bark: grey and very smooth.
Shoots: olive-green.
Buds: domed and densely covered with grey down; enclosed in 2 dark outer scales.
Leaves: compound, 25–30cm long, with 2 to 4 pairs of leaflets and one terminal leaflet. The leaflets (10 by 3·5cm) are stalked, lance-shaped, irregularly toothed, and covered with brownish or white down on the lower surface.
Flowers: white and fragrant, with very narrow 6-mm long petals, growing in dense conical clusters, 15 by 20cm, at the tips of the branches.
Fruit: slender wings ('keys'), 1·5–2·5cm long, each with a seed at its base. The keys hang in bunches and ripen from green to brown.
Uses: the branches yield a sap (manna), which hardens to form a gum used in pharmacy.

Lilac blossom opens in April or early May. The wild shrub has pale mauve flowers but cultivated varieties may be white or deep purple.

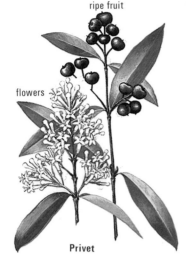

ripe fruit

flowers

Privet

Several varieties of buddleia are grown in gardens. Most have deep mauve or purple flowers. Some have globular flower heads instead of the tapering heads seen here on the variety Royal Red.

PRIVET
Ligustrum vulgare
The privet is a rather loosely branched, spreading shrub growing wild in most parts of Europe, especially on chalk and limestone soils. It is particularly common on wooded slopes and woodland margins. Reaching 4m, it is essentially deciduous, but some of the leaves, especially at the top, are reluctant to fall and may remain on the plant all winter.
Bark: smooth and grey, often reddish on young stems.
Leaves: elongate-oval, 3-6cm long; leathery with smooth margins; deep green, often becoming bronze in autumn.
Flowers: creamy white, 3-4mm across, funnel-shaped with four spreading lobes: in dense terminal spikes May-June. Strongly scented.
Fruit: a shiny black berry 6-8mm in diameter, with oily flesh. Poisonous. The garden privet used for hedging is *L. ovalifolium* from China and Japan. It has broader leaves and tends to be more evergreen. A yellow-leaved variety is often planted.

LILAC
Syringa vulgaris
Famed for its attractive and sweetly scented flowers, the lilac is a deciduous shrub or small tree, normally 3-4m high but occasionally reaching 7m. It is a native of rocky hillsides in the Balkans, but has been introduced to many places and has often become naturalized. Cultivated varieties, with flowers ranging from white to deep purple, are grown almost everywhere.
Leaves: pale green, smooth, and hairless; heart-shaped and untoothed: 4-10cm long.
Flowers: tubular or funnel-shaped, about 5mm across: normally pale mauve (lilac) in the wild but occasionally white. Very fragrant. In dense pyramidal heads up to 20cm long.
Fruit: a pointed leathery capsule with two compartments and two winged seeds in each.

BUDDLEIA FAMILY
Buddlejaceae

COMMON BUDDLEIA
Buddleja davidii
Known as the butterfly bush because of its great attraction for butterflies, the buddleia is a native of China, but widely grown in gardens and naturalized in many waste places, including railway yards and gravel pits and many urban areas. It was abundant on bombed sites after the war. A quick-growing and rather straggly shrub, it reaches 5m or more: new shoots can grow 2m in a season.
Leaves: lanceolate, to 25cm; dark green above, pale and woolly below; lightly toothed.
Flowers: tubular, pale mauve to deep purple with an orange throat; about 1cm long with four lobes and abundant nectar. In long, tapering spikes to 30cm in summer.
Fruit: a slender capsule with many tiny seeds.

353

Chapter Eight
Ferns and Mosses

The ferns and mosses are flowerless plants which reproduce by scattering minute spores instead of seeds. The ferns and the related horsetails and clubmosses form the group known as the Pteridophytes, while the mosses and liverworts are known as Bryophytes.

The Ferns

Fern stems are normally underground, and all that we usually see are the leaves, or fronds. The plants are mostly perennials and new fronds spring from the top of the stem each year. They are tightly coiled at first and uncoil in a very characteristic way. They are usually greatly divided. The spores develop in little capsules borne on the fronds – often on ordinary fronds, but sometimes on special fertile fronds, or on special parts of the fronds. The capsules are carried in clusters known as *sori* and they appear as rusty patches when the spores are ripe.

Clouds of spores are scattered in dry weather, but they do not grow directly into new fern plants. Given suitably moist conditions, each grows into a little green, heart-shaped plate called a *prothallus*. The sex organs are borne on this and, in damp conditions, males cells are released to swim to the female cells which remain embedded in the plate. After fertilization, the female cell grows into a new fern plant, drawing food from the prothallus at first and then putting down its own roots. Because moisture is essential for the reproductive process, ferns are abundant only in damp habitats, although individual plants may be able to survive in very dry places.

Horsetails and Clubmosses

The horsetails and clubmosses are built quite differently from the ferns and carry their spores in different ways, but their life cycles are similar, with two alternating generations. Clubmoss prothalli grow underground in association with soil-dwelling fungi.

Mosses and Liverworts

These are all low-growing plants with no true roots. Mosses all have slender upright or trailing stems with small leaves, but there are no water-carrying tubes such as are found in ferns and flowering plants. Most liverworts have stems and leaves like those of the mosses, but some look more like seaweeds, with just a flat green thallus undivided into stem and leaf. The moss or liverwort plant is really the equivalent of the fern prothallus, for this is where the sex organs are borne. Fertilization occurs in damp conditions, as among the ferns, and the fertilized cell grows into a stalked spore capsule. Although attached to the original plant, the capsule is really a separate organism and is equivalent to the whole fern plant.

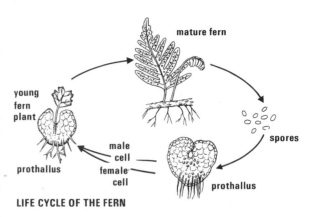

LIFE CYCLE OF THE FERN

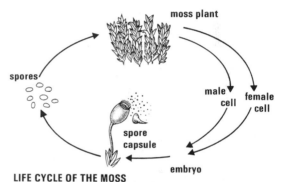

LIFE CYCLE OF THE MOSS

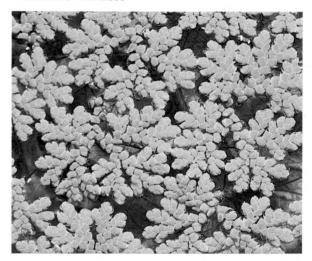

Above: Water fern floating on the surface. The plants break up very easily and each small branch grows into a complete plant, thus covering large areas of water very rapidly.

Left: Young fronds of male fern uncoiling in typical fashion in spring. Most of the previous year's fronds have died by this time.

355

sori

Male Fern

Hard Shield Fern

sori

Bracken

Ferns

European ferns are all herbaceous plants with leaves springing from underground stems. Most species have a short and stocky stem with a crown of fronds at the top, but some have creeping rhizomes which spread through the soil and send up fronds at intervals. The leaves of some species die down each autumn, but many survive until the next year's leaves are well developed and sometimes even longer.

The ferns are essentially plants of damp habitats and are much more abundant in western Britain than in the east. This is especially true of those species that grow on rocks and walls and as epiphytes on trees, for they are very dependent on a moist atmosphere.

The shape of the fronds and the position of the sori are important in the identification of the species. The following species belong to several different families in the order Filicales.

MALE FERN
Dryopteris filix-mas
One of the commonest woodland ferns, growing throughout Europe; often in hedgerows. The fronds grow in a ring, leaning out from the base and looking like a giant shuttlecock. One of several similar species.
Frond: up to 1·5 m long; stalk clothed with pale brown scales. Divided into 20-35 tapering lobes (pinnae); longest pinnae near the centre. Each pinna is again divided into a number of smaller lobes (pinnules), although these are not completely separated in the narrower part of the pinna. Pinnules are toothed and bluntly-rounded at the tips.
Sori: in 2 rows under each well-formed pinnule; up to 6 in a row. Each sorus covered by a heart-shaped flap which shrivels as spores ripen July-August.

HARD SHIELD FERN
Polystichum aculeatum
A fern of the woodland and hedgerow, found in most parts of Europe. Resembles Male Fern in growth form, but tougher and with several detailed differences.
Frond: up to 1 m long; stalk clothed with brown scales. As many as 50 pinnae on each side, each pinna with up to 15 pinnules on each side. Pinnules are toothed and bristly and the lowest one on each pinna is much larger than the others.
Sori: in 2 rows under each well-formed pinnule, but covered with a round flap (not heart-shaped as in the Male Fern). Spores ripe July-August.

BRACKEN
Pteridium aquilinum

The commonest of all ferns, found all over the world. Basically a woodland plant, it also grows on heathland and on many hillsides, but not in the most exposed areas because young fronds are damaged by frost and cold winds. Absent from the wettest soils and from limestones. It spreads rapidly by means of an extensive rhizome system and is a troublesome weed in many hill pastures. Because it spreads as much or more by the rhizomes as by spores, it is less confined to moist places than most other ferns.

Frond: grows singly from the rhizome, to a height of 4 m (usually much less). Blade is triangular and finely divided on a long stalk; early stage shaped like a shepherd's crook and clothed with soft brown hair.

Sori: in continuous lines around the edges of the leaf segments, protected by in-curved margin. Spores ripe July-August.

MAIDENHAIR SPLEENWORT
Asplenium trichomanes

A common fern of rock crevices and old walls in damp climates and shady places. Almost world-wide.

Frond: usually up to 20 cm long (may be as much as 40 cm in really moist places); hugs wall or rock quite closely. Stalk and mid-rib (rhachis) black, with up to 40 pairs of deep-green, oval leaflets. The latter fall in their second year, starting from the bottom and eventually leaving just the bare, wiry rhachis which is shed later.

Sori: oblong or linear, 1-2 mm long, on underside of leaflet and covered by pale flaps. Spores ripe May-October.

WALL RUE
Asplenium ruta-muraria

Grows in the same kinds of places as the previous species. Both prefer limestone rocks and are therefore quite happy with their roots in the mortar of old walls.

Frond: 3-15 cm long; stalk longer than blade. Latter is roughly triangular and divided into leaflets which may be round, triangular, or diamond-shaped.

Sori: linear, about 2 mm long, on underside of basal part of leaflet: merging into a single mass when mature. Spores ripe June-October.

HART'S TONGUE FERN
Phyllitis scolopendrium

An easily recognized fern of woodland and hedgerow, and also of rocks and walls in damp and shady places. Most of Europe, but rare in the north.

Fronds: up to 60 cm long, in dense tufts. Stalk purplish-black with brown scales at first. Blade tongue-shaped and undivided; very pale green at first, becoming bright and very glossy and then gradually darker. Fronds persist until well into their second year.

Sori: linear, forming long strips along the veins on the underside of the fronds; covered by a flap on each side at first, but pushing these aside as the capsules mature. Spores ripe July-October.

Maidenhair Spleenwort

Wall Rue

spore capsules

Hart's Tongue Fern

Hard Fern

Royal Fern

Common
Polypody

Adder's
Tongue

HARD FERN
Blechnum spicant
Named for its tough fronds, this is a fern of woods and heaths, especially in upland regions; most of Europe, but not on limestone.
Frond: 2 kinds. Sterile fronds, up to 50 cm long, spread more or less horizontally and are vaguely comb-like with up to 30 linear pinnae on each side. They persist for 2 years or more. The fertile fronds have more slender pinnae and stand ladderlike in the centre of the plant. They die away when they have shed their spores.
Sori: linear, under the pinnae of the fertile fronds. Spores ripe June-August.

ROYAL FERN
Osmunda regalis
A large and striking fern of fens, damp woodlands and other wet places. Widely distributed in Europe and elsewhere, but not common.
Frond: up to 3 m tall and 1 m wide, with numerous oblong leaflets (pinnules) up to 6 cm long. Outer fronds all sterile; inner ones with normal pinnules on lower part and small brown fertile pinnules higher up.
Sori: densely clustered around fertile pinnules, which have no green blade. Spores ripe June-August.

COMMON POLYPODY
Polypodium vulgare
One of 3 very similar species, this is a woodland fern, often growing epiphytically on tree trunks and branches; also on rocks and walls in wetter areas. It has a scaly, creeping rhizome, often on the surface, from which fronds arise singly.
Frond: up to 45 cm long, with up to 25 lobes (pinnae) on each side; pinnae often not completely separated.
Sori: rounded, 1-3 mm across, in 2 rows under pinnae. Spores ripe June-September.

ADDER'S TONGUE
Ophioglossum vulgatum
A small and very unfern-like fern, easily overlooked in damp grassland and woodland. All Europe, but less common in the north.
Frond: each plant produces just one stalked, oval frond each year, normally 5-20 cm long and undivided; easily mistaken for a plantain leaf, but lacks the prominent veins. In older plants a slender spike arises from the base of the blade; clusters of large spore capsules develop on this spike. Spores ripe May-August.

WATER FERN
Azolla filiculoides
Illustrated on page 355, this little plant floats on ponds, canals and slow-moving backwaters. The short stems bear lots of small, overlapping leaves which often turn red in autumn. Spores are borne on the undersides. A native of North America, but now widely distributed in southern and central Europe, including southern Britain. It belongs to the Order Salviniales.

Horsetails

Once major components of the great coal forests, these plants (Order Equisetales) are now reduced to about 25 small species. All are perennials with underground rhizomes and erect stems, often with whorls of slender branches. Leaves usually reduced to small scales on the stems. Spores are borne in cones – either at the tips of the ordinary stems or on special brown shoots.

GREAT HORSETAIL
Equisetum telmateia
Up to 2 m high in damp, shady places in most parts of Europe. Sterile stems white with collars of black-tipped scale leaves and dense whorls of bright green branches; die down in autumn. Fertile shoots pale brown, up to 40 cm high in spring; cone 4-8 cm long. Spores scattered April, after which fertile shoot dies. Field Horsetail (*E. arvense*) is smaller and with green sterile stems.

WATER HORSETAIL
Equisetum fluviatile
Up to 1·5 mm in swampy ground and at the edges of lakes and ponds all over Europe. Stem green, sometimes unbranched, but often with a few short branches in upper region; collars of black-tipped scale leaves. Cones, 1-2 cm long, at tips of normal stems; spores ripe June-July.

Clubmosses

Although they resemble mosses in their slender stems and small leaves, these plants (Order Lycopodiales) are more closely related to the ferns. Spores are borne in capsules at the bases of certain leaves, which are often grouped into club-shaped cones. Most of the 200 or so species are tropical.

FIR CLUBMOSS
Lycopodium selago
A plant of upland moors and rocky slopes. Its tufted upright stems reach 25 cm and are clothed with stiff, sharply-pointed leaves. Pale spore capsules grow in the axils of many of the leaves without cone formation. Spores ripe June-August.

STAG'S-HORN CLUBMOSS
Lycopodium clavatum
A widely distributed plant of upland moors, grasslands, and open woods; prefers acid soils. Its much-branched, wiry stems creep over the ground, rooting at intervals and reaching lengths of 1 m or more. Fertile branches bear 2 slender yellow cones. Spores ripe June-September.·

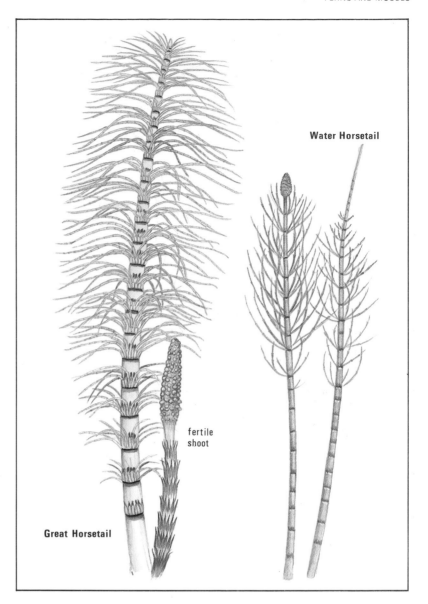

Water Horsetail

fertile shoot

Great Horsetail

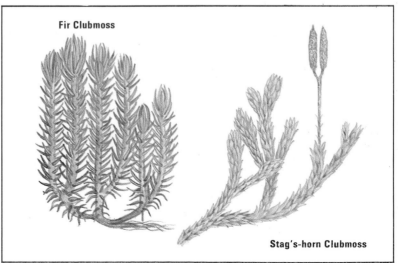

Fir Clubmoss

Stag's-horn Clubmoss

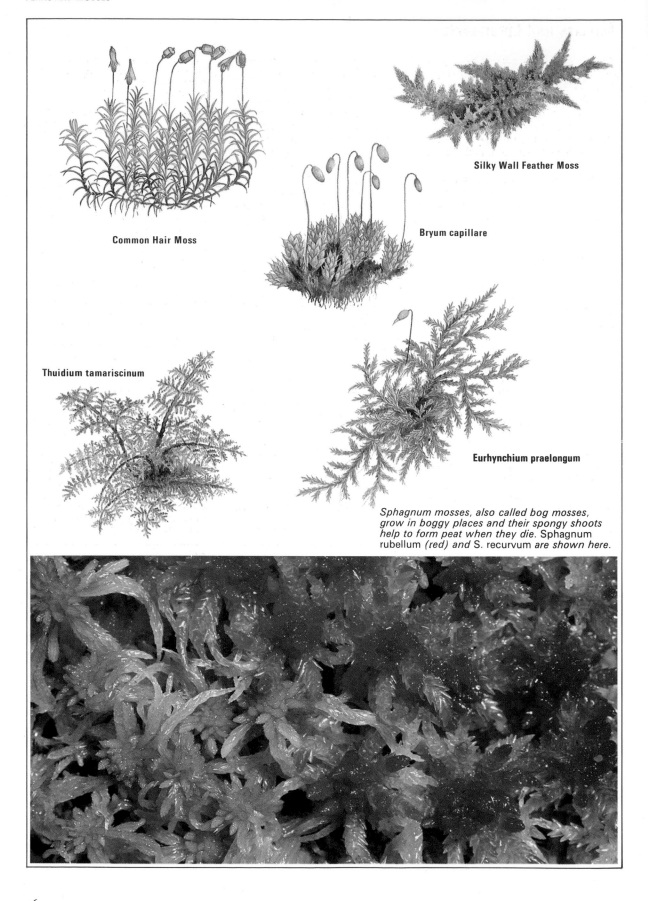

Common Hair Moss

Silky Wall Feather Moss

Bryum capillare

Thuidium tamariscinum

Eurhynchium praelongum

Sphagnum mosses, also called bog mosses, grow in boggy places and their spongy shoots help to form peat when they die. Sphagnum rubellum (red) and S. recurvum *are shown here.*

Mosses and Liverworts

Mosses (Class Musci) all have upright or creeping stems clothed with small leaves. Most liverworts (Class Hepaticae) have a similar build, but some (illustrated below) are flat and seaweed-like. Leafy liverworts usually grow in turf or among mosses and are easily overlooked, but may be distinguished from mosses by their lobed leaves without mid-ribs: moss leaves are unlobed and usually have mid-ribs. The main difference between the groups lies in the spore capsule. That of a moss is urn-shaped, with a detachable lid and a system of teeth which allow the spores to escape only in dry weather. Liverwort capsules are simple spheres that split open at maturity and look like little four-rayed stars. Some mosses and most liverworts also reproduce by scattering tiny flakes of tissue, called gemmae, which grow directly into new plants. Gemmae may be borne in little cups and splashed out by rain drops.

COMMON HAIR MOSS
Polytrichum commune
One of several similar species, forming extensive dark green mats on moors and bogs. Stems upright, reaching 20 cm or more. Leaves spear-like, 8-12 mm long with toothed edges. Separate male and female stems, the tips of male shoots being flower-like when male organs are ripe.
Spore capsule: 4-sided and box-like; horizontal when ripe; covered with a furry golden hood in early stages.

SILKY WALL FEATHER MOSS
Camptothecium sericeum
Forms extensive mats on walls and tree stumps; easily recognized by the shiny yellow tips of main shoots. Secondary shoots greener, forming a deep 'pile' in centre of mat. Leaf is a narrow triangle. Separate male and female plants.
Spore capsule: an erect yellowish-green cylinder 2-3 mm long.

BRYUM CAPILLARE
A very common moss forming neat cushions on tree stumps and rocks and especially on old walls. Stems up to 5 cm high. Leaves oblong, ending in a hair-like tip and strongly twisted when dry. Separate male and female plants.
Spore capsule: pear-shaped and drooping; bright green, becoming brown.

THUIDIUM TAMARISCINUM
This beautiful woodland moss is easily recognized by its regular, Christmas-tree-like branching. Leaf is heart-shaped or triangular, densely clothing the upper parts of the black stems. Separate male and female plants. It prefers shady places on heavy soils.
Spore capsule: sausage-shaped, borne horizontally on a red stalk, but rarely developed.

EURHYNCHIUM PRAELONGUM
Abundant in shady places on heavy soils; also clothes stones and piles of rubble. It is a trailing moss with fairly thick, but weak stems. Leaves on main stems are heart-shaped; those on side branches much narrower. Separate male and female plants.
Spore-capsule: egg-shaped, 1-3 mm long with a long beak when young; reddish-brown when ripe. Uncommon.

MARCHANTIA POLYMORPHA
A common thalloid liverwort of wet paths, river banks, greenhouses and other damp places: easily identified by the goblet-shaped gemma cups and the hexagonal pattern on the upper surface. Separate male and female plants, bearing sex organs on raised parasol-like structures. Simple spore capsules develop on underside of female parasols.

CRESCENT-CUP LIVERWORT
Lunularia cruciata
Easily recognized by the crescent-shaped gemma cups on the bright green thallus, this very common species occurs on river banks but is most frequent around human habitation – on damp paths and walls and in green-houses, where it is often a weed in flower pots. Separate male and female plants. Spore capsules rarely formed.

PELLIA EPIPHYLLA
A large thalloid liverwort carpeting sizeable areas of stream banks and other moist, shady places, especially on acid soils. Its irregularly-branched, shiny thallus is up to 1 cm wide and may be several centimetres long. No gemma cups. Male and female organs on the same plant, female organs under small flaps. Greenish-black spore capsules emerge from the flaps in early spring and rise on pale stalks to 5 cm.

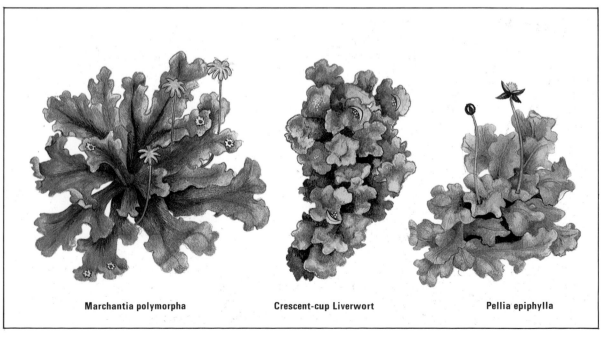

Marchantia polymorpha   Crescent-cup Liverwort   Pellia epiphylla

Chapter Nine
Fungi

The fungi are a large group of plants, with some 50,000 species all of which are completely without chlorophyll. They cannot, therefore, make their own food by photosynthesis in the way that normal plants do. Most fungi live as saprophytes, obtaining their food from dead and decaying matter – especially dead leaves on the forest floor – but there are also quite a number of parasitic species which attack living plants and animals. The fungus body consists essentially of a mass of slender threads called *hyphae*, which penetrate the food material and absorb nutrients from it.

Lower Fungi

All fungi reproduce by *spores* – minute, dust-like bodies that are normally scattered by the wind. The classification of the fungi depends mainly on the way in which the spores are produced. The more primitive fungi, known as the Lower Fungi or, more scientifically, the Phycomycetes, bear their spores in small capsules on fairly simple threads. They include many familiar moulds, such as the Pin Mould (*Mucor*) that often grows on stale bread.

Higher Fungi

With the exception of numerous mildews and yeasts and the *Penicillium* mould from which we get penicillin, the Higher Fungi produce their spores in relatively complex fruitbodies. These are formed of densely entwined threads and normally appear only at certain seasons of the year. Two main groups of Higher Fungi are recognized – the Ascomycetes and the Basidiomycetes. The spores of the Ascomycetes develop inside small club-shaped or cylindrical cells called *asci*. These cells are normally carried at the surface of the fruitbody, but the form of the latter is extremely varied. The spores of the Basidiomycete fungi develop, usually in fours, on the outside of club-shaped cells called *basidia*.

The Basidiomycetes include nearly all the familiar large fungi, and the following pages are devoted almost entirely to this important group. There are several divisions, of which the agarics are the best known. These are the typical mushrooms and toadstools, with a distinct cap on the underside of which there are numerous radiating gills. The term 'mushroom' was once restricted to the edible Field Mushroom (*Agaricus*

campestris) and Horse Mushroom (*A. arvensis*) and their cultivated relatives. All other gill-bearing agarics were known as toadstools. Under American influence, however, the word mushroom is now commonly used for all the agarics and also for many other large fungi.

The basidia of the agarics clothe the gill surfaces and fire off the spores when they are ripe. The spores then fall and are carried away by the wind. By carefully separating a ripe cap from its stem and placing it on a sheet of paper, one can obtain a spore-print faithfully reproducing the pattern of the gills. The colour of the spores is a useful guide to identification, and the connection between gills and stem is also important (see diagram). Some agarics exude a milky fluid when the gills are broken, and the nature of this 'milk' is a good guide to the identity of the species.

Other major divisions of the Basidiomycetes include the boletes and the polypores, in which the underside of the cap is sponge-like with numerous tiny pores. The basidia form the inner lining of the pores. The Gasteromycetes, represented by the puff-balls and stinkhorns, are yet another division, in which the basidia are completely enclosed within the fruitbody. In other groups, such as the jelly fungi, the basidia clothe much of the general surface.

Edible or Poisonous?

Many fungi, including the Field Mushroom and Horse Mushroom and most of the boletes, are very good to eat, but there are also some extremely poisonous species, such as the Death Cap (*Amanita phalloides*). There is no simple rule for distinguishing between edible and poisonous species, but in general you should always avoid white-spored species with both a cup at the base and a ring on the stem. The true mushrooms have a ring on the stem and purplish-black spores, but avoid any which turn bright yellow when scratched.

Lichens

Lichens (page 388) are composite plants consisting of a fungus – usually an Ascomycete – and an alga living in symbiosis. Each derives benefit from the partnership, but the fungus partner cannot survive alone and lichens are often regarded just as special fungi which require the help of an alga to survive.

Left: The colourful fly agaric toadstool grows under pines and birches in autumn. It is poisonous.

Right: Fruitbody shape and gill attachment. A. shallow convex cap with free gills (not attached to stem). B. funnel-shaped cap with decurrent gills (running down stem). C. conical cap with adnexed gills (attached to stem by only part of the width). D. broadly campanulate cap with adnate gills (attached to stem by their complete width). Sinuate gills have a distinct notch close to the junction with the stem.

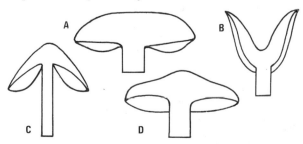

Amanita
phalloides

Amanita
citrina

Amanita
muscaria

Amanita
pantherina

Amanita
rubescens

Amanita
fulva

Basidiomycetes

GILL FUNGI (Agarics)

The agarics are those fleshy fungi
which bear gills. They grow on
the ground in pasture or
woodland, on dung, trees or on
woody debris. The stem may or
may not bear a ring and may or
may not show a sheathing, sac–like
structure (the volva) at its base.

AMANITA PHALLOIDES
Death Cap

Cap: 6-9 cm diam., convex then
shallowly convex; varying in colour
from olive-green at the centre to
yellowish-green nearer the smooth
margin. The cap surface appears indistinctly radially streaky; usually
naked, without trace of warts or
scales.
Stem: 7-9 cm high; 1-1·5 cm wide;
white, cylindrical or narrowed above
and sheathed below in a conspicuous
free-standing, white, sac-like volva.
Ring: near apex of stem; white.
Gills: white; virtually free.
Smell: when old unpleasant, cheesy.
Spore-print: white.
Habitat: deciduous woodland, especially with beech and oak. Autumnal. Fairly common.
POISONOUS, often fatal.

AMANITA CITRINA
False Death Cap

Cap: 6-8 cm diam.; convex then flat;

pale cream to pale lemon-yellow
ornamented with a few large, or
several smaller, thick, flat, whitish to
brownish patches of velar tissue.
Stem: 8-11 cm high, 1-2 cm wide,
tall in proportion to cap; white,
cylindrical with a conspicuous basal
bulb, up to 3 cm wide, with margin
indicated by a prominent rim representing the volva.
Ring: near apex; white.
Gills: white to very pale cream.
Smell: of raw potato.
Spore-print: white.
Habitat: deciduous and coniferous
woodland. Autumnal. Very common.

AMANITA MUSCARIA
Fly Agaric

Cap: up to 15 cm diam., convex,
flattened to saucer-shaped, scarlet

ornamented with white warts which gradually disappear and may be completely lacking. The cap colour often fades to reddish-orange. In the button stage the cap is covered by thick white velar tissue which eventually cracks to form the scales and expose more and more of the red surface as expansion occurs.

Stem: up to 20 cm high, 3 cm wide, white to pale-yellowish above, cylindrical and brittle with a slightly broader base surmounted by a series of concentric zones of white scales representing the volva.

Ring: near apex of stem, white to very pale-yellowish.

Gills: white, almost free.

Habitat: Under birch, occasionally with pine and other trees. Autumnal. Common. POISONOUS.

AMANITA PANTHERINA

Cap: 6-8 cm diam., convex, then flat, dark greyish-brown to olive-brown, sometimes paler and more yellowish-brown, ornamented with numerous, uniformly distributed small white pyramidal warts; margin somewhat striate.

Stem: 7-10 cm high, 1-1·5 cm wide, white, rather tall, cylindrical, slightly enlarged below where the volva disrupts into concentric rings, the uppermost forming a narrow, close-fitting but free collar or ridge.

Ring: near middle of stem, white.

Gills: white, free.

Flesh: white.

Spore-print: white.

Habitat: deciduous woodland. Autumnal. Rare. POISONOUS.

AMANITA RUBESCENS
The Blusher

Cap: 8-12 cm diam., at first strongly bell-shaped, then convex, finally flat to shallowly saucer-shaped, varying in colour from pale pinkish-brown with a darker red-brown centre to entirely red-brown, ornamented with thin mealy or hoary patches of whitish, greyish or pale volval tissue which tend to disappear with age.

Stem: 8-11 cm high, 2·5-3·5 cm wide, stout and stocky, cylindrical with somewhat enlarged base, whitish becoming pale pinkish-brown below, especially when handled. Volva reduced to inconspicuous rows of concentric scales.

Ring: near apex of stem; white.

Gills: white, often spotted red with age.

Flesh: white becoming pinkish when cut and in insect holes.

Spore-print: white.

Habitat: deciduous and coniferous woodland. Late summer and autumn. One of the first mushrooms to fruit. Very common. Edible, but best avoided owing to possible confusion with poisonous species.

AMANITA FULVA
Tawny Grisette

Cap: 3·5-5 cm diam., long remaining acorn-shaped, then bell-shaped,

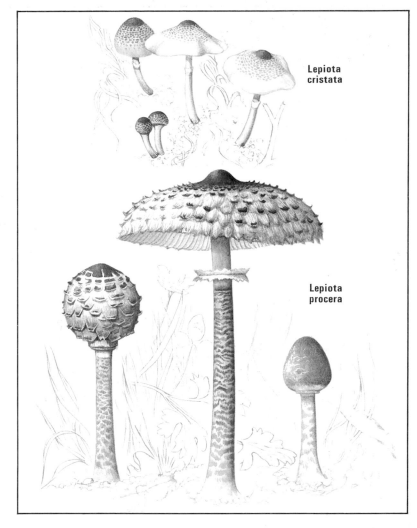

Lepiota cristata

Lepiota procera

finally flat but often with central boss, bright tawny-brown, often darker at centre, naked. Margin striate, fluted or grooved.

Stem: up to 11 cm high, 1 cm wide, tall, fragile, hollow, cylindrical, pale-tawny with well-developed, sac-shaped volva.

Ring: absent.

Gills: white, free.

Spore-print: white.

Habitat: coniferous and deciduous woodland. From late summer to autumn; one of the earliest mushrooms to appear. Very common. Edible.

LEPIOTA CRISTATA

Cap: 2-4 cm diam., broadly campanulate, surface disrupting into tiny red-brown scales on a white background; the scales rapidly disappear except around a small, central, similarly coloured disc.

Stem: 2-5 cm high, 4-6 mm wide, white, cylindrical to slightly enlarged below.

Ring: near apex of stem, white, membranous, deciduous.

Gills: white, free.

Smell: unpleasant, sour.

Spore-print: white.

Habitat: deciduous woodland, often in grass along rides. Autumnal. Common. POISONOUS.

LEPIOTA PROCERA
Parasol Mushroom

Cap: 12-22 cm diam., umbrella-shaped with nipple-like boss at centre, surface disrupting into large, often upturned, dark-brown scales on a dirty white, coarsely fibrillose background; scales larger and widely dispersed towards margin, smaller, more densely arranged at centre with nipple uniformly dark-brown.

Stem: 20-26 cm high, 1·5-2·0 cm wide, tall, narrow, cylindrical with bulbous base up to 4 cm wide, pale, ornamented with dark-brown, zig-zag markings.

Ring: large, spreading with double edge, whitish, movable.

Gills: soft to touch, free, attached to collar-like rim surrounding the stem apex.

Flesh: white.

Spore-print: white.

Habitat: pastures, edge of woods grassy rides. Autumnal. Occasional. Edible.

ARMILLARIELLA MELLEA
Honey Fungus
Cap: 6-12 cm diam., convex, then flat to saucer-shaped, tan, tawny or cinnamon-brown, paler towards the indistinctly striate margin; ornamented with delicate, dark-brown, hair-like scales, prominent and crowded in young specimens, eventually disappearing except at centre in old fruitbodies.
Stem: 9-14 cm high, 1-2 cm wide, tough, cylindrical, pale-tawny, whitish at apex.
Ring: near apex of stem, thick, cottony, whitish, often with yellow flocci at margin.
Gills: dirty-whitish to flesh-coloured; adnate.
Flesh: white, soft. Taste acrid.
Spore-print: cream.
Habitat: at base of living and dead trunks or stumps. Autumnal. Very common. Edible when young.

HYGROPHOROPSIS AURANTIACA
False Chanterelle
Cap: 3-6 cm diam., funnel-shaped with enrolled margin, surface suede-like, orange or yellowish-orange.
Stem: 2-4 cm high, 5-7 mm wide, same colour as cap, often brownish below when old.
Gills: decurrent, crowded, repeatedly forked, deep orange.
Smell: not distinctive.
Spore-print: white.
Habitat: coniferous woodland and heaths. Autumnal. Common. Edible but worthless.

CANTHARELLUS CIBARIUS
Chanterelle
Cap: 2·5-6 cm diam., top-shaped, often slightly depressed at centre, gradually narrowed below into the short stalk; smooth, moist, entire fungus bright egg-yellow.
Stem: 2-6 cm high, 6-16 mm wide, short and squat.
Gills: decurrent, blunt, irregularly branched, fold-like and interconnected.
Smell: pleasant (of apricots).
Spore-print: white.
Habitat: deciduous woodland, especially on sandy or clay banks amongst moss. Autumnal. Occasional. Edible. Much sought after and collected for sale in markets. Easily dried for use in cooking. It may be confused with the False Chanterelle, but is much paler and altogether more fleshy.

LACTARIUS TURPIS
The Ugly One
Cap: 8-20 cm diam., shallowly funnel-shaped or convex with depressed centre, surface sticky, smooth except for the enrolled felty margin, dark, dull olive-brown to almost black, brighter yellowish-olive towards edge.
Stem: 4·5-7 cm high, 2-2·5 cm wide; short, squat, sticky, same colour as, but paler than cap, often pitted.
Gills: more or less decurrent, dirty creamy-white becoming brown and discoloured when bruised.
Milk: white, plentiful, very peppery.
Spore-print: pale pinkish-buff.
Habitat: strictly associated with birch on heaths and commonland, often overgrown with grass. Autumn. Very common.

LACTARIUS RUFUS
Cap: 4-6 cm diam., shallowly funnel-shaped with prominent central nipple, rich red-brown, surface smooth, dry, minutely grained, appearing falsely granular.
Stem: 4·5-5·5 cm high, 5-7 mm wide, same colour as cap but paler, base whitish.
Gills: decurrent, yellowish.
Milk: white, plentiful, very peppery, but only after a minute or so.
Spore-print: pale pinkish-buff.
Habitat: coniferous woodland, very rarely with birch. Autumnal. Common.

LACTARIUS TABIDUS
Cap: 2·5-4 cm diam., flat or slightly depressed, irregularly radially wrinkled about a small central nipple,

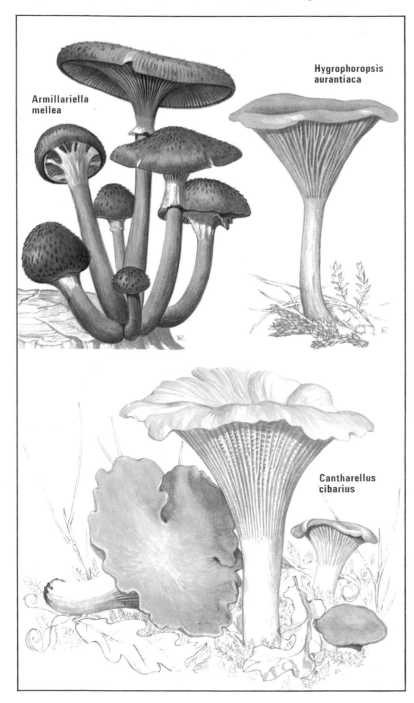

Armillariella mellea

Hygrophoropsis aurantiaca

Cantharellus cibarius

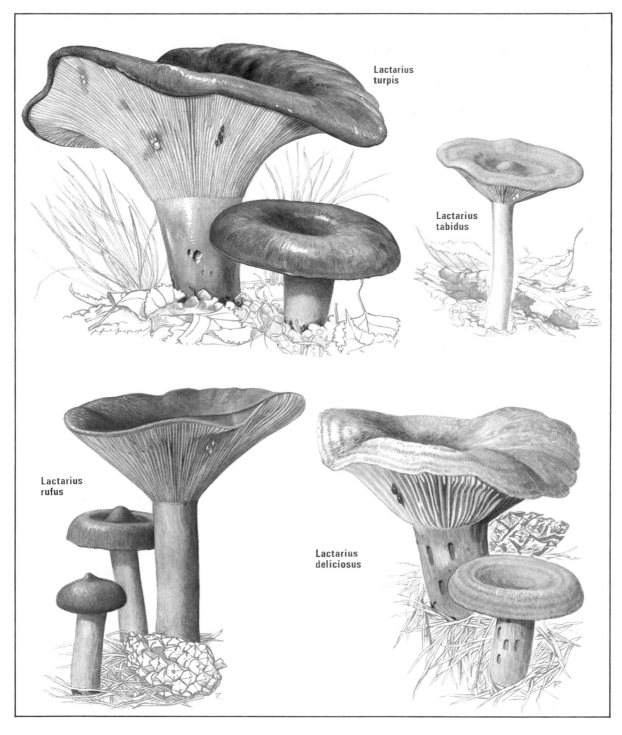

Lactarius
turpis

Lactarius
tabidus

Lactarius
rufus

Lactarius
deliciosus

orange-brown paling to yellowish-buff when dry, margin somewhat striate when moist.
Stem: 2-4 cm high, 4-6 mm wide, same colour as cap.
Gills: decurrent, buff.
Milk: mild, white, changing to yellow if allowed to dry on a handkerchief.
Spore-print: pale buff.
Habitat: deciduous woodland. Autumnal. Common.

LACTARIUS DELICIOSUS

Cap: 6-10 cm diam., convex with depressed centre or shallowly funnel-shaped, moist, reddish orange with darker greenish zones and variable development of green staining, surface appearing almost as if granular-stippled.
Stem: 6-8 cm high, 1·5-2·0 cm wide, orange, often pitted.
Gills: orange-yellow, staining greenish.

Milk: brilliant carrot-colour eventually becoming wine-red in 30 minutes.
Spore-print: pale pinkish-buff.
Habitat: coniferous woodland, especially pine. Autumnal. Common. Edible.

An unmistakable species due to its orange colour and green staining of all parts, and the presence of vivid carrot-coloured milk.

OUDEMANSIELLA MUCIDA
Poached Egg Fungus
Cap: 3-7 cm diam., soft, flabby, convex, very glutinous, white becoming flushed with grey, margin striate, almost translucent.
Stem: 5-7 cm high, 4-6 mm wide, often curved, tough, cartilaginous, cylindrical; often expanded disc-like at point of attachment; white to greyish.
Ring: spreading, white above, greyish below especially toward edge.
Gills: distant; deep, soft, white.
Spore-print: white.
Habitat: confined to beech, occurring in small clusters on trunks, branches, or on stumps. Autumnal. Common.

CLITOCYBE NEBULARIS
The Clouded Clitocybe
Cap: 7-16 cm diam., robust, fleshy, convex with a low central hump to more or less flat, cloudy-grey sometimes with a brown tinge, surface dry appearing to have a faint hoary bloom.
Stem: 7-10 cm high, 1·5-2·5 cm wide, cylindrical, same colour as cap but paler, often striate.
Gills: decurrent, crowded, dirty creamy-white.
Smell: characteristic, unpleasant.
Spore-print: creamy-white.
Habitat: deciduous woodland, especially in areas rich in humus, near piles of rotting leaves or grass, usually gregarious and sometimes forming fairy-rings. Autumnal. Common. POISONOUS.

RUSSULA EMETICA
The Sickener
Cap: 4-7 cm diam., convex then depressed, brilliant scarlet with a moist shiny surface, margin eventually coarsely striate.
Stem: 5-8 cm high, 1·5-2 cm wide, rather tall, fragile, pure white, the lower portion usually somewhat club-shaped.
Gills: adnexed, white.
Flesh: very hot.
Spore-print: pure white.
Habitat: coniferous woodland. Autumnal. Common. May cause sickness if eaten raw.

RUSSULA SARDONIA
Cap: 6-10 cm diam., convex to broadly bell-shaped, varying from dark reddish- or violet-purple to purplish-black.
Stem: 7-12 cm high, 1·5-2 cm wide, rather tall, beautifully purple.
Gills: adnexed, primrose, often with watery droplets along the edge.
Flesh: white, very hot.
Spore-print: cream.
Habitat: coniferous woodland. Autumnal. Common.

RUSSULA ATROPURPUREA
Cap: 4-10 cm diam., convex sometimes with slight hump, moist, dark reddish-purple to almost black, old specimens often mottled yellow at centre.
Stem: 5-7 cm high, 1·5-2 cm wide, short, squat, white, with rust-coloured base.
Gills: adnexed, whitish to pale cream, often discoloured with rusty spots.
Flesh: mild to slightly peppery.
Spore-print: white to off-white.
Habitat: deciduous woodland. Autumnal. Common.

RUSSULA OCHROLEUCA
Cap: 5-8 cm diam., shallowly funnel-shaped, moist, bright ochre-yellow to greenish-yellow.
Stem: 6-8 cm high, 1·5-2 cm wide, rather soft with firmer rind, white, eventually greyish, surface ornamented with faint, densely-crowded short, raised longitudinal lines.
Gills: whitish.
Flesh: mild to moderately hot.
Spore-print: pale-cream.
Habitat: coniferous and deciduous woodland. Autumnal but persisting late in the season. Very common.

RUSSULA CYANOXANTHA
Cap: 7-10 cm diam., convex, slightly depressed at centre, moist, dark greyish-purple with olive tones.
Stem: 8-11 cm high, 1·5-2 cm wide, white, hard.
Gills: white, softly pliable.
Flesh: mild.
Spore-print: white.
Habitat: deciduous woodland. Autumnal. Common.

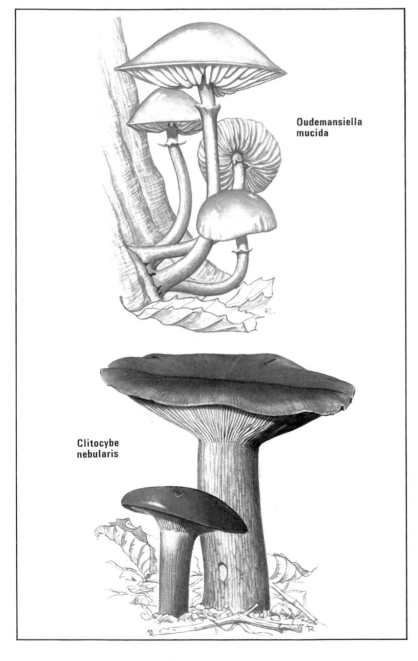

Oudemansiella mucida

Clitocybe nebularis

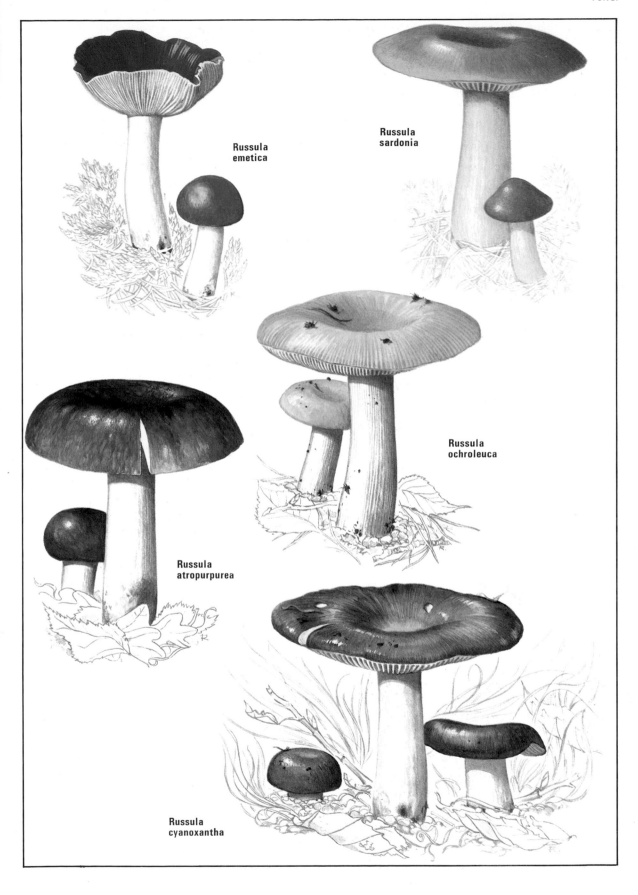

Russula
emetica

Russula
sardonia

Russula
ochroleuca

Russula
atropurpurea

Russula
cyanoxantha

369

FLAMMULINA VELUTIPES
The Velvet Shank

Cap: 2·5-5 cm diam., shallowly convex becoming flat, bright-yellowish or orangey-tan, often darker and more brownish at the centre, moist becoming sticky when wet, shiny when dry.
Stem: 2·5-5 cm high, 4-6 mm wide, very dark-brown and conspicuously velvety, paling to yellow nearer the cap.
Gills: adnexed, rather distant, pale creamy-yellow.

Habitat: on trunks and branches, especially of dead elm, often forming small tiered clusters.

TRICHOLOMOPSIS RUTILANS
Plums and Custard

Cap: 6-12 cm diam., convex to broadly bell-shaped, yellow, densely covered with tiny fleck-like purple scales which are continuous at centre but nearer the margin become pulled further apart to show more and more of the yellow background.
Stem: 6-9 cm high, 1-1·5 cm wide, similar in colour to cap, likewise densely flecked below with purple scales which disappear towards the yellow apex.
Gills: yellow.
Flesh: yellowish.
Spore-print: white.
Habitat: on conifer stumps. Autumnal. Fairly common.

LEPISTA SAEVA
Blewit

Cap: 6-8 cm diam., convex then flat, moist, varying from buff to greyish-buff.
Stem: 5-6 cm high, 1·5-2 cm wide, often enlarged at base, bright violet with streaky fibrillose surface.
Gills: whitish to pale flesh-coloured.
Spore-print: pale pinkish.
Habitat: in grassland, often forming fairy-rings. Autumnal. Uncommon. Edible and good, sometimes sold in shops.

LEPISTA NUDA
Wood Blewit

Cap: 6-10 cm diam., shallowly convex, becoming flat, often with greasy or water-soaked appearance, varying in colour from entirely violet to reddish-brown with violet tint localized to margin.
Stem: 6-8 cm high, 1·5-2 cm wide, bright bluish-lilac.
Gills: at first vivid violet becoming pinkish with age.
Spore-print: pale pinkish.
Habitat: deciduous woodland, compost heaps. Late autumn persisting into winter. Common. Edible and good, sometimes sold in shops.

LACCARIA AMETHYSTEA
Amethyst Deceiver

Cap: 2·5-4 cm diam., convex then shallowly convex, often depressed at centre, surface scurfy-felty, when moist entire fungus bright violet, but when dry this fades to pale buff with faint lilac tint.
Stem: 4-6 cm high, 6 mm wide, deep violet, but paler when dry.
Gills: deep, thick, distant, adnate or adnexed, bright violet fading to lilaceous-flesh-colour when dry.
Spore-print: white.
Habitat: deciduous woodland. Autumnal. Common.

LACCARIA LACCATA
The Deceiver

Cap: 2-4 cm, shallowly convex to broadly bell-shaped, sometimes slightly depressed at centre; surface felty or scurfy; when moist bright red-brown with striate margin, drying out to pale buff and opaque and not striate.
Stem: 4-5 cm high, 5 mm wide, tough, streaky fibrillose, reddish-brown, often twisted.
Gills: deep, thick, distant, pinkish flesh-colour with waxy appearance.
Spore-print: white.
Habitat: deciduous woodland and coniferous woodland, heaths. Often gregarious. Autumnal. Very common.

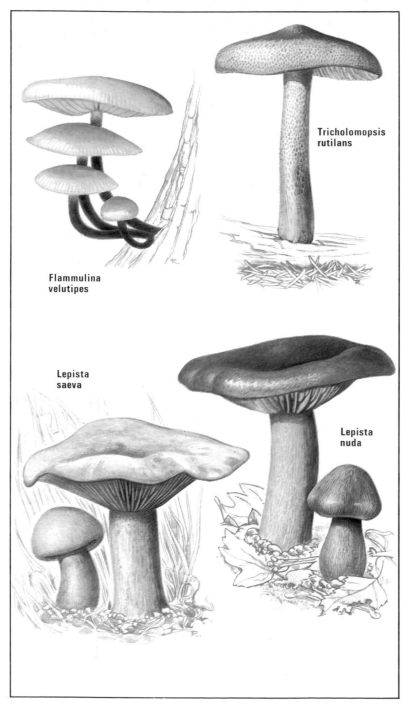

Flammulina velutipes

Tricholomopsis rutilans

Lepista saeva

Lepista nuda

Because of its variability in appearance due to the degree of moistness of the cap, it can be very difficult to recognize in all its guises, hence the common name. The thick, distant, waxy, flesh-coloured adnate or adnexed gills are a good guide to recognition.

COLLYBIA MACULATA
Foxy Spot
Cap: 5-9 cm diam., convex, white with pinhead-sized or larger red-brown spots, often becoming entirely pale red-brown with age.
Stem: 8-10 cm high, 1-1·6 cm wide, firm, white, often longitudinally striate, tapering below into a short rooting base.
Gills: densely crowded, shallow, pale-cream spotted with red-brown.
Habitat: coniferous woodland or amongst bracken in heathy situations where it sometimes forms fairy-rings. Autumnal. Common.

COLLYBIA FUSIPES
Spindle Shank
Cap: 3-7 cm diam., broadly bell-shaped with central boss, smooth, dark red-brown drying pinkish buff or pale tan.
Stem: 8-10 cm high, 1-1·5 cm wide, tough, similarly coloured to cap, gradually enlarged below then conspicuously narrowed into a rooting portion, surface distinctly grooved.
Gills: adnexed, broad, distant, whitish then flushed with red-brown, also often spotted with brown.
Spore-print: white.
Habitat: tufted at base of tree trunks, especially oak. Late summer to early autumn. Occasional.

COLLYBIA PERONATA
Wood Woolly Foot
Cap: 4-6 cm diam., very broadly bell-shaped to flat, sometimes with central boss, smooth, very tough and leathery, ochre-coloured to reddish-brown, drying paler.
Stem: 7-9 cm high, 5 mm wide, tall, narrow, but very tough, pale yellowish-buff, thickly covered toward base with pale yellowish woolliness.
Gills: tough, leathery, distant, adnexed, separating from around the top of the stem in a false collar; same colour as cap.
Flesh: thin, leathery, yellowish, taste peppery.
Spore-print: white.
Habitat: especially deciduous woodland amongst leaf litter. Autumnal. Common.

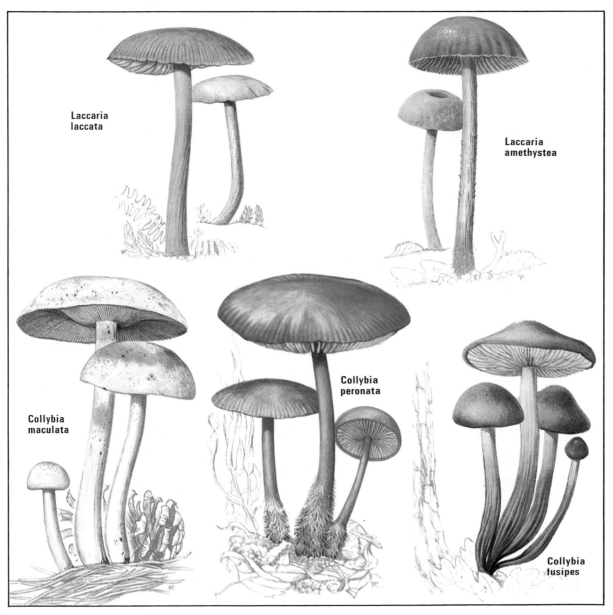

Laccaria laccata

Laccaria amethystea

Collybia maculata

Collybia peronata

Collybia fusipes

Marasmius oreades

Tricholoma gambosum

MARASMIUS OREADES
Fairy-Ring Champignon
Cap: 3-5 cm diam., convex with broad central boss, tough, smooth, pinkish-tan drying to pale buff, margin often grooved.
Stem: 4·5-5·5 cm high, 2·5-3 mm wide, firm, tough, pale buff.
Gills: adnexed, deep, distant, whitish.
Spore-print: white.
Habitat: pastures, lawns, roadside verges and the commonest cause of 'fairy-rings' in turf. Late summer to autumn. Common. Edible.

Recognized when forming fairy-rings by the tough, broadly bell-shaped, buff-coloured cap with distant gills. However it does not always grow in rings.

TRICHOLOMA GAMBOSUM
St George's Mushroom
Cap: 5-10 cm diam., shallowly convex, often with undulating margin, smooth, white to very pale buff at centre.
Stem: 4-7 cm high, 1·5-2 cm wide, short, squat, white.
Gills: sinuate, crowded, white.
Flesh: thick, smelling strongly of meal.
Spore-print: white.
Habitat: in pastures, roadside verges, hedge-bottoms. This whitish mushroom is readily recognized by its squat, fleshy fruitbodies which occur in spring, usually around St. George's Day (April 23rd), hence the common name. Edible.

ENTOLOMA CLYPEATUM
Cap: 3-6 cm diam., bell-shaped, then shallowly bell-shaped with central boss, grey-brown with darker radial streaks, drying paler.
Stem: 4-6 cm high, 6-15 mm wide, dirty-white to greyish with fibrillose surface.
Gills: sinuate, deep, distant, greyish becoming pink, edge irregularly wavy.
Flesh: greyish when water-soaked, white when dry, smelling of meal when crushed.
Spore-print: pink.
Habitat: often associated with rosaceous trees and shrubs, such as hawthorn. and common in hedgerows. Also in rich garden soil. Vernal.

HYGROPHORUS CONICUS
Cap: up to 3 cm high, acutely conical with fibrillose surface, yellow or orange becoming black on handling or with age.
Stem: up to 6 cm high, 5 mm wide, fibrillose, yellow, then blackening.
Gills: ascending, almost free, pale yellow.
Spore-print: white.
Habitat: in grassland. Autumnal. Fairly common.

The acutely conical fibrillose orange cap which, like the rest of the fruitbody blackens when handled, is very distinctive.

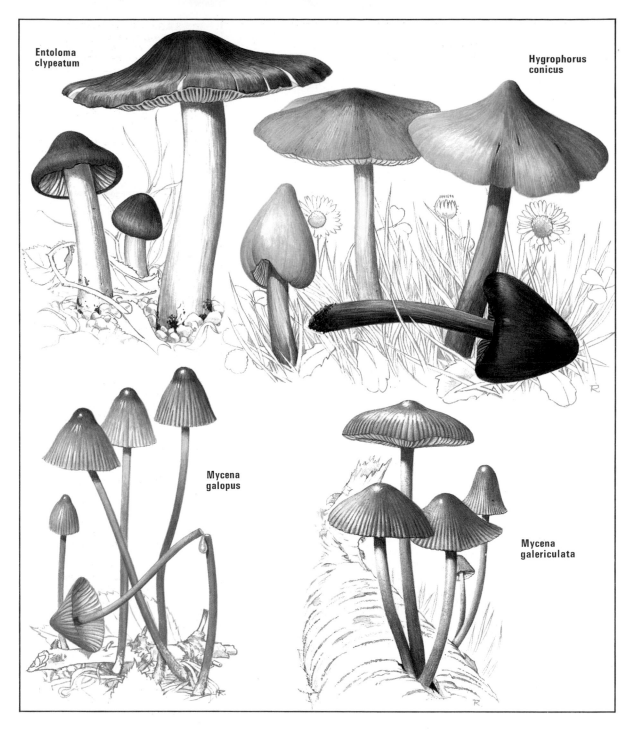

Entoloma clypeatum

Hygrophorus conicus

Mycena galopus

Mycena galericulata

MYCENA GALOPUS
Milking Mycena
Cap: 1 cm diam., broadly bell-shaped, pale with brown centre and radiating striae.
Stem: up to 5 cm high, 2 mm wide, greyish below, almost white above, when broken exuding a white milk.
Gills: adnexed, white.
Spore-print: white.
Habitat: woodland, hedge-bottoms, heaths etc. Autumnal. Very common.

The pale cap with brown radiating striae and presence of a white milk in the stem are distinctive characters, although it may not be possible to obtain milk from the stems of old fruiting bodies.

MYCENA GALERICULATA
The Leathery Mycena
Cap: 2-4·5 cm diam., broadly bell-shaped, flat with a central boss, tough, leathery, varying from grey-brown to buff, margin striate to somewhat grooved.
Stem: 7-10 cm high, 3-5 mm wide, tough, cartilaginous, smooth, polished, grey-brown.
Gills: adnate with decurrent tooth, deep, distant, interveined, whitish then flesh-coloured.
Smell: mealy when crushed.
Spore-print: white.
Habitat: clustered on stumps, or from buried wood. Typically autumnal, but occurring sporadically throughout the year. Very common.

373

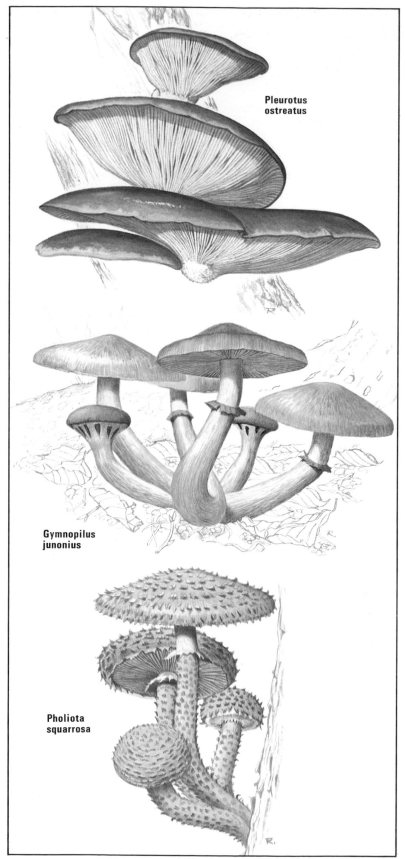

**Pleurotus
ostreatus**

**Gymnopilus
junonius**

**Pholiota
squarrosa**

PLEUROTUS OSTREATUS
Oyster Fungus
Cap: 5-12 cm wide, tiered, convex, bracket-shaped, smooth; variable in colour from blue-grey to buff when young, becoming dark brown with age.
Stem: 2-3 cm long, 1·5-2 cm wide, short, thick, lateral, hairy, white.
Gills: decurrent, distant, whitish.
Spore-print: lilac.
Habitat: in tiered clusters on standing or fallen trunks especially beech. Autumnal but found occasionally at other times of year. Common. Edible.

GYMNOPILUS JUNONIUS
Cap: 6-12 cm diam., convex, fleshy, bright tawny or golden yellow; surface fibrillose or disrupting into indistinct fibrillose scales.
Stem: 7-15 cm high, 1·2-3 cm wide, swollen near middle and then tapering towards base, fibrillose, same colour as cap, but paler, and with membranous ring near apex.
Ring: yellowish, soon collapsing back onto stem.
Gills: adnate, crowded, sometimes with decurrent tooth, yellow becoming rust-coloured.
Flesh: pale yellowish.
Spore-print: rusty-brown.
Habitat: forming dense tufts at the base of trunks (sometimes living) or on stumps of deciduous trees. Autumnal. Common.

PHOLIOTA SQUARROSA
The Shaggy Pholiota
Cap: 6-8 cm diam., convex, dry, pale ochre, entirely covered with prominent densely crowded up-turned bristly scales giving a coarse shaggy appearance.
Stem: 6-10 cm high, 1-1·5 cm wide, same colour as cap and covered with similar recurved scales below the fibrillose ring.
Gills: adnate with decurrent tooth, crowded, at first yellowish then pale rust-coloured.
Flesh: pale.
Spore-print: rusty-brown.
Habitat: parasitic on many species of deciduous trees, forming dense shaggy tufts at the base of living trunks. Autumnal. Fairly common.

GALERINA MUTABILIS
Cap: 2-3·5 cm diam., convex to broadly bell-shaped, watery date brown with striate margin when moist but drying out conspicuously from centre to tan colour. Fruitbodies when semi-dry are sharply two-coloured with tan centre and an abrupt, broad, watery-brown marginal zone.
Stem: 3-5·5 cm high, 3·5-5 mm wide, pale yellowish above becoming dark-brown and covered with recurved scales below the ring.
Gills: adnate with decurrent tooth, pale then cinnamon-brown.
Spore-print: cinnamon-brown.
Habitat: tufted on stumps of broadleaved trees. Autumnal. Fairly common. Edible.

PAXILLUS INVOLUTUS
The Roll Rim
Cap: 5-11 cm diam., convex with strongly enrolled margin, becoming shallowly depressed at centre, surface glutinous in wet weather, yellowish-brown, smooth except toward the edge which is often ribbed and downy.
Stem: 6-7 cm high, 1-1·2 cm wide, central, same colour as cap but paler, often streaky.
Gills: decurrent, yellowish-brown becoming dark red-brown when bruised.
Spore-print: ochre-brown.
Habitat: heathy places, associated with birch. Autumnal. Very common. POISONOUS.

AGROCYBE PRAECOX
Cap: 3-5 cm diam., convex, smooth, cream-coloured with ochre-coloured flush at centre.
Stem: 5-7 cm high, 5-7 mm wide, tall, slender, white, with ring.
Ring: membranous, whitish.
Gills: adnate, clay-brown, crowded.
Flesh: white in cap, brown in stem, smelling of meal when crushed.
Spore-print: clay brown.
Habitat: in grassy places, roadside verges. Vernal. Common.

PSATHYRELLA CANDOLLEANA
Cap: 2·5-5 cm diam., shallowly bell-shaped to flat, pale creamy-ochre to whitish especially when dry, with tiny tooth-like remnants of veil hanging from margin when young.
Stem: 4-6 cm high, 4-5 mm wide, white, hollow, very brittle.
Gills: adnate, for a long time whitish then lilac-grey and finally brownish-black.
Spore-print: almost black.
Habitat: tufted on wood, stumps, roots, fence-posts. Spring to Autumn. Common.

PSATHYRELLA GRACILIS
Cap: 1·5-2·5 cm diam., bell-shaped, dark brown or reddish-brown with striate margin when moist, opaque and pale biscuit colour when dry.
Stem: 8-10 cm high, 2 mm wide, very tall, fragile, pure white with white hairy fibrils at base.
Gills: adnate, blackish, with pink edge.
Habitat: solitary or gregarious, amongst grass or leaves, in deciduous woodland, hedge-bottoms, roadside verges. Autumn. Very common.

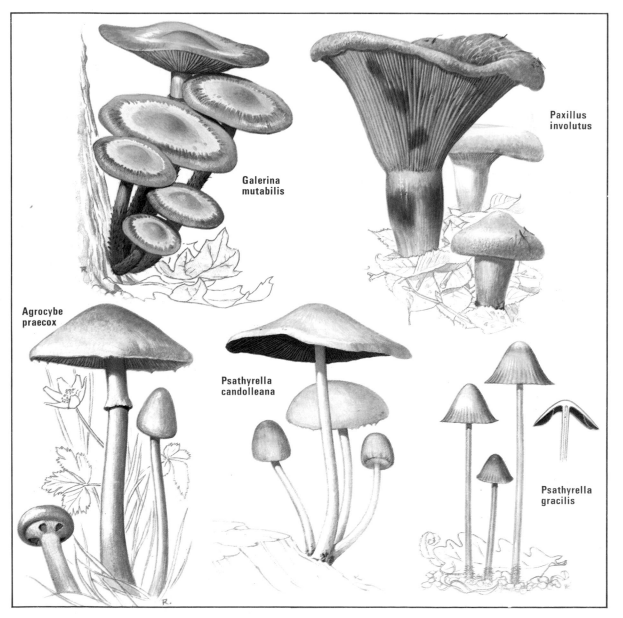

Galerina mutabilis

Paxillus involutus

Agrocybe praecox

Psathyrella candolleana

Psathyrella gracilis

COPRINUS PLICATILIS
The Little Japanese Umbrella
Cap: 2-3 cm diam., acorn-shaped, yellowish-brown and closely striate at first, then flat, coarsely grooved or fluted, grey with small depressed tan-coloured disc, very thin, short-lived, almost translucent.
Stem: 6-8 cm high, 3 mm wide, whitish, very delicate.
Gills: free, attached to a collar around stem apex, scarcely liquefying.
Spore-print: black.
Habitat: damp grass, lawns, roadside verges. Autumnal. Common.

COPRINUS COMATUS
Shaggy Ink Cap; Lawyers Wig
Cap: 6-14 cm high, cylindrical, opening slightly at base, eventually bell-shaped, white, with buff-coloured central disc, surface broken up into shaggy scales, margin closely striate becoming greyish, finally black on maturity. Entire cap gradually dripping away from margin as an inky fluid. This fluid contains the spores and has been used as ink.
Stem: up to 30 cm high, 1-1·5 cm wide, white with movable membranous ring toward base.
Gills: free, crowded, white near stem apex, then pink and finally black at margin.
Spore-print: black.
Habitat: gregarious on rubbish tips, roadside verges, fields and gardens. Autumnal. Fairly common. Edible, provided the gills have not started to liquefy.

COPRINUS ATRAMENTARIUS
Antabuse Ink Cap
Cap: 5-7 cm high, bell-shaped, irregularly ribbed and wrinkled almost to disc, grey, often with few inconspicuous brownish scales at centre.
Stem: 7-9 cm high, about 1 cm wide at base, where there is a conspicuous oblique ring-zone, white.
Gills: free, whitish, becoming grey, finally black, liquefying.
Spore-print: black.
Habitat: tufted in vicinity of stumps of deciduous trees or from roots, often in gardens, fields etc. Autumnal but sporadically throughout the year from early spring. Common. Edible, but causing sickness if eaten with alcohol.

COPRINUS DISSEMINATUS
The Trooping Crumble Cap
Cap: 5-10 mm high, acorn-shaped to hemispherical, pale yellowish-clay becoming greyish at the margin, closely grooved almost to the centre, minutely hairy under a very strong lens.
Stem: 1-3·5 cm high, 1-1·5 mm wide, white, very delicate and brittle.
Gills: adnate, dark grey to blackish, scarcely liquefying.
Spore-print: black.
Habitat: densely gregarious, covering entire stumps in myriads of tiny, brittle, bell-shaped, biscuit-coloured fruitbodies. Autumnal, but also sporadically throughout the year. Common.

AGARICUS CAMPESTRIS
Field Mushroom
Cap: 4·5-8 cm diam., convex then flat, white, surface often disrupting into indistinct fibrillose scales especially around centre.
Stem: 4-6 cm high, 1-1·5 cm wide, short, squat, with pointed base and ring.
Ring: poorly developed, simple, often little more than a torn fringe.
Gills: free, at first pink then purplish-brown.
Flesh: white, sometimes reddish in stem when cut.
Spore-print: purplish-brown.
Habitat: grassy places, pastures, often in fairy-rings. Autumnal. Occasional. Edible.

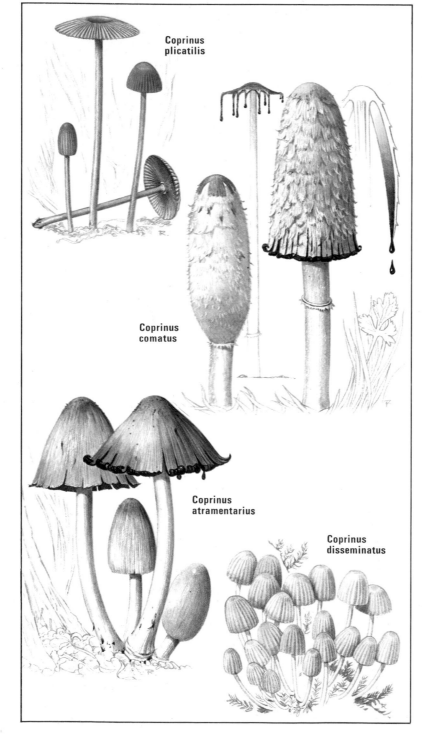

Coprinus plicatilis

Coprinus comatus

Coprinus atramentarius

Coprinus disseminatus

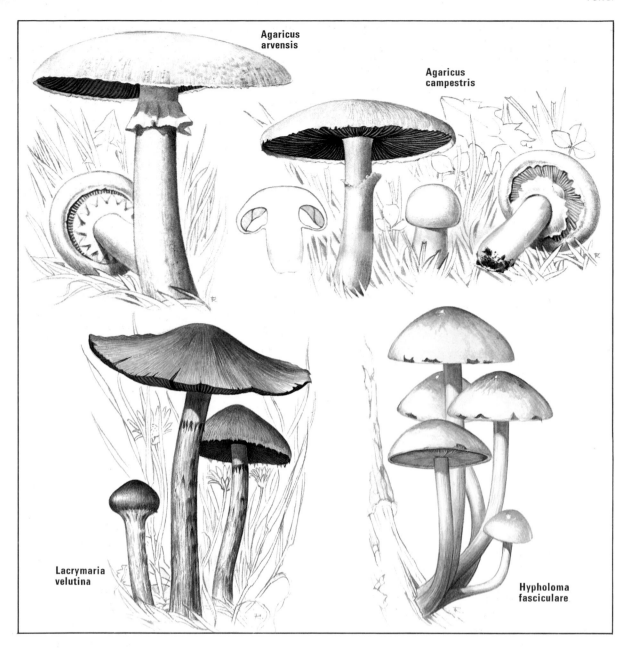

Agaricus
arvensis

Agaricus
campestris

Lacrymaria
velutina

Hypholoma
fasciculare

AGARICUS ARVENSIS
Horse Mushroom
Cap: 6-11 cm diam., hemispherical, becoming shallowly convex, white, often creamy with age, sometimes faintly yellow when handled, but never vividly so.
Stem: 8-12 cm high, 1·5-2 cm wide, tall, cylindrical, with bulbous base, white with membranous ring.
Ring: large, pendulous, high on stem, underside like radiating spokes of a wheel (cog-wheel-like).
Gills: white, then brownish, finally purplish-brown, never pink.
Flesh: white, unchanging.
Spore-print: purplish-brown.
Habitat: open grassland, hillsides, orchards etc, often in fairy-rings. Autumnal. Occasional. Edible.

LACRYMARIA VELUTINA
Weeping Widow
Cap: 4-6 cm diam., bell-shaped or convex, yellowish-brown to clay-brown, densely radially fibrillose, with enrolled woolly fringed margin.
Stem: 6-7 cm high, 5-8 mm wide, same colour as, but paler than cap, fibrillose or scaly, with prominent ring-zone of whitish cottony fibrils often becoming black due to trapped spores.
Gills: adnexed or adnate, almost black, mottled, with white edge bearing watery droplets in damp weather.
Spore-print: almost black.
Habitat: tufted from roots or buried wood, in deciduous woodland. Spring to autumn. Common.

HYPHOLOMA FASCICULARE
Sulphur Tuft
Cap: 2-4 cm diam., shallowly bell-shaped to shallowly convex, sulphur-yellow often with tawny flush at centre, margin with dark fibrillose remnants of veil.
Stem: 4-7 cm high, 4-8 mm wide, same colour as cap, sometimes flushed brown below, with poorly developed purplish-brown fibrillose ring-zone near apex.
Gills: sinuate, sulphur-yellow becoming olive.
Flesh: yellow with bitter taste.
Spore-print: purplish-brown.
Habitat: tufted at base of deciduous and coniferous tree-stumps. Autumnal, but sporadically throughout the year. Very common.

377

BOLETES

Fruitbodies are fleshy, with a cap and central stalk which may or may not bear a ring. The underside of the cap is sponge-like with tiny pores. These are the openings of densely crowded tubes lined with basidia which produce the spores.

SUILLUS BOVINUS
Jersey Cow Bolete
Cap: 4-7 cm diam., convex at first then flattened, glutinous when moist, buff to pinkish-buff with pale margin.
Stem: 4·5-7 cm high, 6-9 mm wide, tapering downward, same colour as cap.
Ring: lacking.
Pores: decurrent, large, irregular, compound (each pore subdivided into smaller pores), dirty-yellow to rusty.
Flesh: yellowish or pinkish, reddish in stem.
Habitat: coniferous woodland. Autumnal. Common. Edible.
   Recognized by its colour (resembling that of a Jersey cow) and large compound pores.

SUILLUS LUTEUS
Cap: 7-12 cm diam., bell-shaped, then flattened, often with slight central boss, glutinous when moist, dark chocolate or purplish-brown, sometimes becoming rusty-tan with age.

Stem: 6-8 cm high, 1·7-2 cm wide, yellow with darker glandular dots above the well developed ring, whitish or pale brownish below.
Ring: spreading, membranous, white or greyish, often dark with age.
Pores: adnate to decurrent, dull yellow to deep ochre-yellow.
Flesh: whitish to pale lemon-yellow especially in stem.
Habitat: coniferous woodland. Autumnal. Fairly common. Edible.

LECCINUM SCABRUM
Cap: 5-10 cm diam., convex to shallowly convex, grey-brown with an almost granular-mottled effect under a lens.
Stem: 8-12 cm high, 2-3 cm wide, tall, cylindrical, often enlarged below, white but rough with conspicuous black flocci.
Pores: almost free, minute, dingy buff, bruising yellowish-brown.
Flesh: white, unchanging or faintly pink.
Habitat: with birch, especially on

heaths. Autumnal. Very common. Edible.

BOLETUS BADIUS
Cap: 6-10 cm diam., shallowly convex, dark bay to chocolate-brown, slightly sticky in wet weather, shiny when dry but softly downy at margin.
Stem: 7-8 cm high, 1·5-2 cm wide, pale brown with darker streaks.
Pores: adnate or adnexed, small, cream to lemon-yellowish, turning blue-green when bruised.
Habitat: deciduous and coniferous woodland. Autumnal. Common. Edible.

BOLETUS CHRYSENTERON
Cap: 5-7 cm diam., convex, madder-brown sometimes with olive tint, cracking in a chequered manner showing pale pinkish flesh in between; surface minutely felty.
Stem: 6-8 cm high, 1 cm wide, yellowish streaked red below.
Pores: adnate to adnexed, large angular, at first pale dull yellow then olive-yellow.
Flesh: pink under cuticle, yellowish elsewhere often reddish in stem, turning slightly blue when cut.
Habitat: deciduous woodland. Autumnal. Very common.
B. subtomentosus, a common species of heathy areas, differs from *B. chrysenteron* in its velvety olive-tan

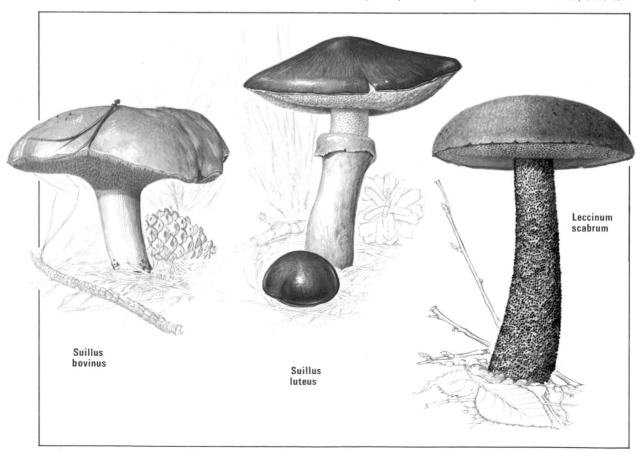

Suillus
bovinus

Suillus
luteus

Leccinum
scabrum

Boletus
badius

Boletus
erythropus

Boletus
chrysenteron

Boletus
edulis

Boletus
satanas

coloured cap which bruises dark brown on handling. Its cuticle also seldom cracks and it lacks the pink colour beneath it.

BOLETUS ERYTHROPUS

Cap: 7-11 cm diam., convex, dry, minutely downy, dark bay-brown to red-brown.
Stem: 8-11 cm high, 1·5-2·5 cm wide, yellow densely covered with very minute red granular-dots.
Pores: free, minute, blood-red.
Flesh: yellow, instantly indigo-blue when cut or bruised.
Habitat: deciduous woodland. Autumnal. Fairly common. Edible despite startling colour change of flesh.

BOLETUS EDULIS
Penny Bun Bolete
Cap: 10-16 cm diam., strongly convex, usually chestnut brown.
Stem: 6-12 cm high, 2·5-4 cm wide, cylindrical but sometimes conspicuously swollen at base to 10 cm wide; pale with whitish network at least at apex.
Pores: adnexed, whitish becoming greenish-yellow.
Flesh: whitish unchanging, sometimes faintly pink in cap.
Habitat: deciduous and coniferous woodland. Late summer to autumn. Fairly common. Edible and excellent. (The 'Cep' or 'Steinpilz' of continental gourmets and a major constituent of many 'mushroom' soups).

BOLETUS SATANAS
The Devil's Boletus
Cap: 10-18 cm diam., convex with enrolled margin, pale-greyish.
Stem: 7-12 cm high, enormously swollen below up to 12 cm wide, yellow above, red below with conspicuous red network.
Pores: free, minute, blood-red.
Flesh: pale yellow, turns faintly blue in stem apex and over tubes.
Habitat: beechwoods on chalk. Autumnal. Rare. POISONOUS.

The large size, pale grey cap, enormously swollen stem with red net and the red pores are the salient features.

379

POLYPORES

These are the bracket fungi and are recognized by the poroid undersurface. The spores are produced by the basidia which line the tubes, the openings of which form the pores. The fungi are mostly lignicolous (growing on wood). Most fruitbodies are laterally stalked or in the form of solitary or tiered bracket-like structures, commonly with a woody or leathery texture. Some form rosette-like clusters.

COLTRICIA PERENNIS

Cap: 2-10 cm diam., thin, leathery, funnel-shaped, adjacent fruitbodies often fused together, surface velvety, zoned in shades of tawny or rusty-brown but sometimes paling out to greyish-buff toward centre.
Stem: 3-5·5 cm high, 3-6 mm wide, velvety, rusty-brown.
Pores: small; lighter, brighter and more yellowish than stem, except when old, often with silky sheen.
Flesh: thin, fibrous, brown.

Spore-print: pale ochre.
Habitat: sandy heaths, sometimes on burnt ground. Autumnal but persisting for many months as discoloured blackened specimens.

GANODERMA APPLANATUM

Fruitbody: up to 30 cm diam. or more; flat, sessile, bracket-like, perennial, with thick, horny, dull crust, surface irregularly undulating, ornamented with conspicuous concentric grooves and varying in colour from buff to fawn or cocoa-brown; margin thin and rather acute.
Pores: very small, whitish, bruising brown.
Tubes: brown.
Flesh: fibrous, cinnamon-brown, thinner than tube layers.
Texture: very hard and woody.
Spore-print: cocoa-brown.
Habitat: parasitic on trunks and stumps, especially beech. Perennial. Very common.

POLYPORUS SQUAMOSUS
Dryad's Saddle

Cap: 13-50 cm diam., fan-shaped, pale fawn with concentric rings of brown scales.
Stem: 3-8 cm high, 3-8 cm wide, relatively short, pale above with

network due to rudimentary decurrent pores, black and swollen below.
Pores: white to cream, very large, 1-3 mm diam.
Flesh: white, rubbery, up to 4 cm thick behind, smell mealy.
Spore-print: white.
Habitat: parasitic on trunks of deciduous trees fruiting on the living or dead host, particularly common on elm, beech and sycamore, often at considerable height above ground. Spring to summer. Frequent. Edible but worthless.

GRIFOLA FRONDOSA

Fruitbody: up to 30 cm diam., consisting of a mass of small, thin, smoky-brown, often zoned, fan-shaped lobes, 3-7 cm across, each narrowed behind into a white stem-like portion attached to a common base.
Pores: decurrent, irregular, white.
Flesh: thin, white.
Spore-print: white.
Habitat: at base of living or dead stumps and trunks of deciduous trees, especially oaks. Summer to autumn. Occasional. Edible, but tough and with a mouse-like smell.

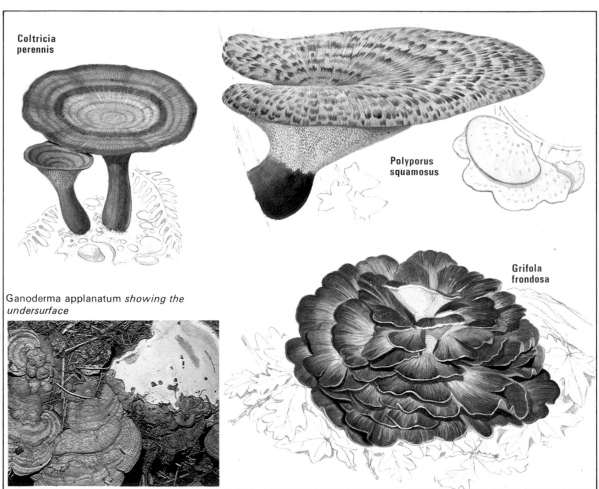

Coltricia perennis

Polyporus squamosus

Grifola frondosa

Ganoderma applanatum *showing the undersurface*

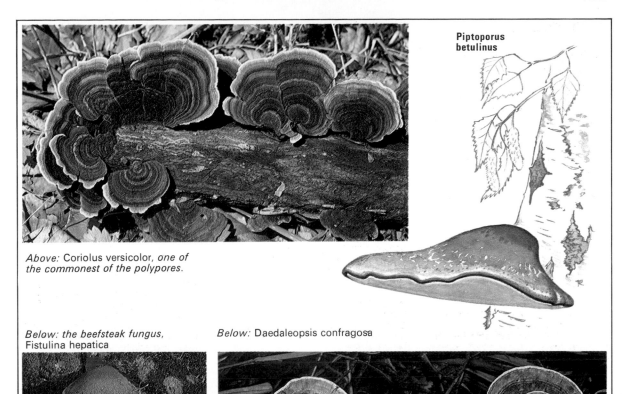

Piptoporus betulinus

Above: Coriolus versicolor, *one of the commonest of the polypores.*

Below: the beefsteak fungus, Fistulina hepatica

Below: Daedaleopsis confragosa

CORIOLUS VERSICOLOR

Fruitbodies: 3-8 cm diam., sometimes more when adjacent specimens merge together; thin, flexible sessile bracket-like, with felty surface ornamented with numerous colour zones varying from almost black or blue-black through smoky brown to tan or fawn especially at the margin. In addition to these colour zones there are often dark shining bands devoid of felt where the underlying surface shows through.
Pores: small, pale cream.
Flesh: white, about 2-3 mm thick.
Habitat: often conspicuously tiered, sometimes solitary, on stumps, trunks, fallen branches, bean poles or timber of both deciduous and coniferous trees throughout the year. Very common.

PIPTOPORUS BETULINUS
Birch Bracket

Fruitbody: up to 20 cm diam., hoof-shaped, occasionally with a basal boss forming a short pseudo-stem, surface covered by a greyish to pale-brown or brown separable smooth skin; margin rounded.

Pores: very small, late-forming, white.
Flesh: white, rubbery, up to 7 cm thick behind.
Habitat: parasitic on birch, fruiting on the living and dead trunks as individual brackets although several may be present at intervals up the same tree. All the year round. Very common.

FISTULINA HEPATICA
Beefsteak Fungus

Fruitbodies: up to 15 cm diam., solitary, fan-shaped with a narrow point of attachment, sometimes with a short stalk-like base, liver-coloured, the surface roughened toward the margin with minute warts which are rudimentary tubes, otherwise smooth.
Tubes: individually separate.
Pores: yellowish-flesh-coloured.
Flesh: up to 5 cm thick behind with colour, graining and texture of raw beef-steak, also exuding a red juice; strong acidic taste.
Habitat: on oak stumps or trunks, usually near the ground. Autumnal. Occasional. Edible but of poor quality.

DAEDALEOPSIS CONFRAGOSA

Fruitbodies: up to 15 cm diam., flattened, shell-shaped, sometimes with a thickened basal hump at point of attachment, surface concentrically grooved and often irregularly radially wrinkled, zoned in lighter or darker shades of red-brown; margin acute, often white.
Pores: radially elongated, slot-like, white to faintly grey, bruising red when rubbed if fruitbody is in active growth, and becoming lilac with a drop of ammonia; on old fruitbodies the pores become uniformly reddish-brown. Spore-print white.
Flesh: rubbery, zoned, whitish then reddish- or pale-brown.
Habitat: solitary or gregarious, several brackets often produced at intervals up a trunk or along branches of deciduous trees, especially willow. Throughout the year. Common.

The brackets usually occur on small trunks or branches and frequently appear to grasp them or encompass them.

STEREOID AND THELEPHOROID FUNGI

Fruitbodies either terrestrial or lignicolous. Variable in shape: bracket-like, rosette-like, or coral-like with flattened branches. Fertile surface either smooth or wrinkled, but devoid of gills, pores or spines.

THELEPHORA TERRESTRIS
Fruitbodies: 2-6 cm diam., forming small irregular rosettes, either ascending or closely pressed to the ground, dark chocolate-brown, with soft, spongy, felt-like surface marked with radiating fibrils. Undersurface somewhat wrinkled and ornamented with minute warts, cocoa-brown.
Habitat: on the ground in coniferous woodland or on open sandy heaths. Autumnal. Common.

The small brown rosettes with soft felty surface are characteristic.

CHONDROSTEREUM PURPUREUM
Silver Leaf Fungus
Fruitbodies: 2-4 cm diam., thin, flexible leathery brackets, often arising from a flat area, sometimes forming entirely flat patches. Upper surface felty with one or more concentric grooves, pale greyish-buff, often with dark line at or just in from the wavy margin. Undersurface bright lilac to purplish when in active growth, fading to brownish with age.
Habitat: saprophytic on a wide range of deciduous trees (stumps, branches etc) or parasitic especially on rosaceous trees and shrubs. When parasitic it sometimes causes silvering of the foliage as in Silver Leaf Disease of plum. All the year round. Common.

STEREUM RUGOSUM
Fruitbodies: forming extensive creamy flat patches on undersides of branches, only occasionally developing a very narrow, rigid, shelf-like portion, with dark-brown surface which may be slightly felty or naked. When scratched the cream-coloured surface reddens, and if broken the fruitbody is seen to have a stratified appearance under a lens.
Habitat: on small trunks, undersides of dead fallen or still attached branches of deciduous trees, especially hazel. All the year round. Common.

The creamy patches which redden when scratched are distinctive but if the fruitbody is dry when collected it may be necessary to moisten it before the red colour will develop.

HYMENOCHAETE RUBIGINOSA
Fruitbodies: 4-7 cm diam., densely-tiered, bracket-like, concentrically ridged and grooved, dark-brown to almost black and smooth, but when young with a minute rusty, velvety bloom. Lower surface chocolate-brown appearing as if waxed, with the extreme margin rust-brown or sometimes creamy-yellow. Flesh brown.
Habitat: old oak stumps. All the year round. Common.

The densely crowded dark brown to blackish brackets on oak stumps are easily identified, especially as they are rigid and brittle.

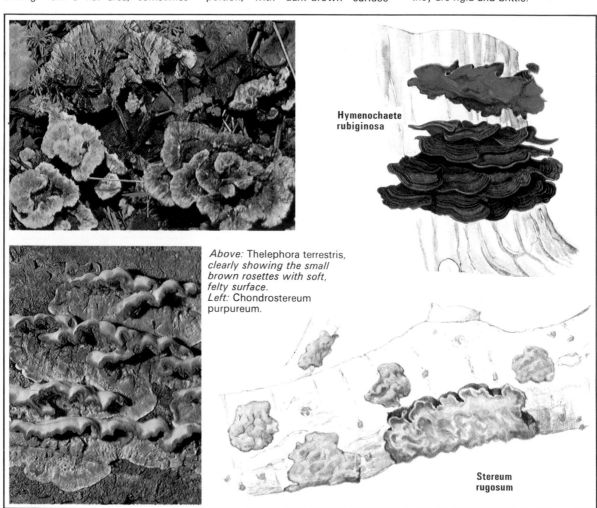

Hymenochaete rubiginosa

Above: Thelephora terrestris, *clearly showing the small brown rosettes with soft, felty surface.*
Left: Chondrostereum purpureum.

Stereum rugosum

Right: Tremella mesenterica

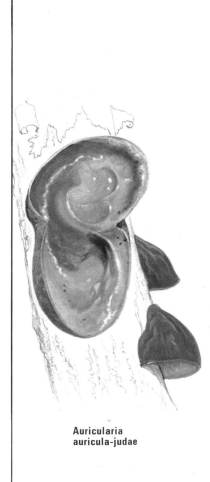

**Auricularia
auricula-judae**

Right: Calocera viscosa

JELLY FUNGI

Fruit bodies mostly lignicolous, growing on either living or dead wood: very variable in shape, but nearly always distinctly gelatinous and often brightly coloured when wet. They shrink a good deal if they become dry, assuming a rigid and horny texture and often becoming rather inconspicuous. Some dry right up to a varnish-like patch, but all regain their normal gelatinous and colourful state when they become wet again. Most of the 500 or so known species live in the tropics, where they run little risk of drying out.

AURICULARIA AURICULA-JUDAE
Jew's Ear
Fruitbodies: 3-6 cm diam., helmet-shaped, date-brown, firm-gelatinous or distinctly rubbery. Outer surface velvety. Undersurface, which bears the spores, has folds and ridges resembling the inside of an ear, pale purplish-brown; shiny.
Habitat: on branches of deciduous trees, especially elder. All the year round. Very common. Edible.

Distinctive because of its shape, colour and gelatinous texture. A white form also occurs and should be reported if found.

TREMELLA MESENTERICA
Fruitbodies: 1·5-5 cm diam., comprising pendant yellow gelatinous brain-like masses.
Habitat: on dead fallen or still attached branches of deciduous trees and shrubs. All the year. Common.

CALOCERA VISCOSA
Fruitbodies: 4-8 cm high, branched, club-shaped, bright egg-yellow, but of tough gelatinous texture; branches united below into a white rooting portion.
Habitat: on rotting conifer stumps. Autumnal. Common.

The bright yellow, branched, club-shaped fruitbodies on conifer stumps are distinctive. They are distinguished from the clavarias by their tough gelatinous texture, gliding easily between the fingers without breaking. The clavarias, commonly known as fairy clubs, are simple club-like or spiky fungi with very brittle flesh. Most are white, greyish, or yellow.

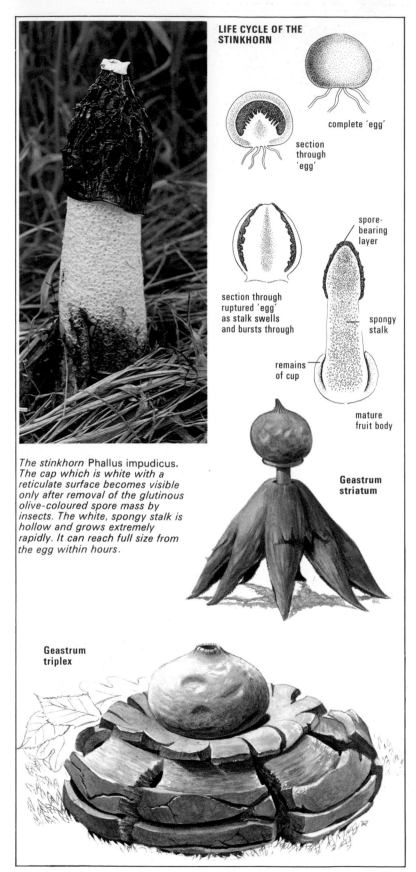

LIFE CYCLE OF THE STINKHORN

complete 'egg'

section through 'egg'

section through ruptured 'egg' as stalk swells and bursts through

spore-bearing layer

spongy stalk

remains of cup

mature fruit body

The stinkhorn Phallus impudicus. *The cap which is white with a reticulate surface becomes visible only after removal of the glutinous olive-coloured spore mass by insects. The white, spongy stalk is hollow and grows extremely rapidly. It can reach full size from the egg within hours.*

Geastrum striatum

Geastrum triplex

GASTEROMYCETES

The fungi in this group include puff-balls, earth stars (*Geastrum* species), stinkhorns, and bird's nest fungi. All produce their spores *inside* the fruiting body, which does not open until the spores are ripe. The Stinkhorn starts out as an egg-shaped body with a thick gelatinous wall, through which emerges the stout stalk and bell-shaped cap covered by the evil-smelling spore mass. Puff-balls and earth stars split open in various ways and the spores are puffed out when the fungus is disturbed. A single raindrop is enough to send out a cloud of spores, which are further dispersed by the breeze.

PHALLUS IMPUDICUS
Stinkhorn
Fruitbodies: 10-14 cm high, exceptionally up to 30 cm, comprising a fragile, white, spongy, hollow stalk with sac-like gelatinous remains of the egg forming a volva at its base, and supporting a pendulous bell-shaped cap at its apex.
Cap: white with reticulate surface which is only visible after removal of the glutinous, olive-coloured spore mass by insects.
Smell: extremely putrid, of rotting meat, so much so that the fungus is often smelled before it is seen.
Habitat: solitary or gregarious in deciduous woodland or gardens, attached by means of white strands to roots or buried wood. Summer to autumn. Very common. Edible in the egg stage.

GEASTRUM STRIATUM
Fruitbodies: 3-6 cm diam., when expanded.
Spore-sac: about 1 cm diam., shortly stalked, flattened or subglobose and flattened below, with a distinct rim or collar at base; bursts open through well-defined pore at top of a fluted cone, colour becoming almost blackish when old.
Rays: up to 8, becoming curled under fruitbody and lifting it clear off the ground.
Habitat: deciduous woodland. Autumnal. Occasional.

GEASTRUM TRIPLEX
Fruitbodies: 6-10 cm diam., when expanded.
Spore-sac: up to 3 cm diam., smooth, sessile, globular, pale-brown, seated in a shallow cup.
Rays: 4-8, thick, fleshy, yellowish to pale brown and curling under the spore sac and its cup.
Habitat: deciduous woodland. Autumnal. Occasional.

SCLERODERMA CITRINUM
Earth Ball

Fruitbodies: 5-10 cm diam., hemispherical, often slightly flattened above, with a basal chord-like attachment or sometimes with a mass of cottony threads, yellowish or ochre-coloured with a conspicuously rough, coarsely-scaly surface. When cut through the fruitbody is seen to have a thick whitish rind which often flushes pink, surrounding a firm, purplish-black spore mass which at maturity becomes powdery.
Habitat: sandy heaths or woodland. Summer to autumn. Very common.

CALVATIA EXCIPULIFORMIS

Fruitbodies: up to 12 cm high, pestle-shaped with fertile head and well-developed sterile stalk. The surface is pale greyish-buff, densely covered over the upper portion with fine, scurfy whitish hair-like spines, interspersed with minute granular warts. In section the fertile head is seen to contain the powdery olive-brown spores held in a mass of cottony threads, while the sterile base has a whitish sponge-like appearance.
Habitat: pastures, heaths or deciduous woodland. Autumnal. Occasional.

This puff-ball is easily recognized by its tall pestle-like fruit body.

VASCELLUM PRATENSE

Fruitbodies: 2-4 cm diam., pear-shaped with fertile head and sterile stalk, white to cream, ornamented with scurfy white granules and small spines which may be united at the tips. At maturity the spines and granules disappear leaving a more or less smooth, pale brown shiny surface. In this stage a section through the fruitbody shows the fertile head with its dark olive-brown powdery spores held in a cottony mass of threads, separated by a distinct diaphragm from the sterile stalk with its sponge-like texture.
Habitat: in open situations amongst short turf and lawns, often forming fairy-rings. Summer to autumn. Very common.

LANGERMANNIA GIGANTEA
Giant Puff-ball

Fruitbodies: up to 30 cm diam., occasionally even larger, resembling a smooth white ball with kid-like texture to the surface. The interior is initially white and fleshy becoming yellowish, but as the spores mature the colour changes to olive-brown and the texture becomes cottony. Attachment to the soil is by means of a tiny chord, such that mature fruitbodies often become free and get blown by wind scattering spores in the process.
Habitat: on the ground, in fields, gardens and woodland. Autumnal. Occasional. Edible if eaten while the flesh is still white.

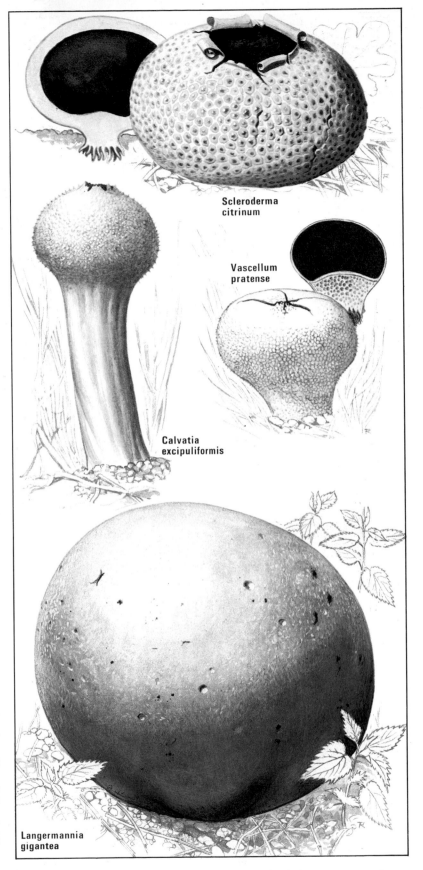

Scleroderma
citrinum

Vascellum
pratense

Calvatia
excipuliformis

Langermannia
gigantea

Above: Lycoperdon pyriforme *growing on an old stump.*

Lycoperdon perlatum

Above: Lycoperdon perlatum.

Bovista nigrescens

Cyathus olla

LYCOPERDON PYRIFORME
Fruitbodies: up to 6 cm high, 3 cm wide, club-shaped or pear-shaped, often narrowly so, pale greyish or pale brownish, densely covered by fine scurfy granules.
Stalk: arising from conspicuous, white, chord-like strands; internal structure sponge-like.
Spore-mass: greenish-yellow then olive-brown.
Habitat: gregarious, often in very large numbers on and around stumps of deciduous trees. Autumnal, but old weathered specimens can be found throughout the year. Very common. Although several other puff-balls grow on decaying leaves in the forests, this is the only one that actually grows on wood.

LYCOPERDON PERLATUM
Fruitbodies: up to 8 cm high, and 5 cm diam., club-shaped with a distinct head and long cylindrical stem, white to pale-brown, densely covered above with prominent, but deciduous, crowded, white pyramidal warts each surrounded by a ring of minute granules. In old specimens from which the warts have dis-appeared the surface has a reticulate pattern formed by the minute rings of granules.
Stalk: sponge-like.
Spore-mass: olive-brown.
Habitat: solitary, gregarious or even in small tufts in woodland. Autumnal. Very common.

BOVISTA NIGRESCENS
Fruitbodies: 3-6 cm diam., globular, at first white, but outer surface flaking away completely at maturity to expose the somewhat shiny blackish tissue beneath.
Stalk: lacking; fruitbodies with very tenuous attachment to the soil and usually becoming free. Old papery specimens persist for many months and may be blown for considerable distances scattering spores in the process.
Spore-mass: purplish-black.
Habitat: open grassland, dunes. Autumnal, but old weathered speci-mens may be found at any time.

CYATHUS OLLA
This is one of the bird's nest fungi, in which the spores are borne inside little egg-like bodies, which in turn are borne in nest-like cups. The eggs are attached at first, but become detached later and are splashed out by raindrops.
Fruitbodies: 9-15 mm high, 7-13 mm wide, funnel-shaped with broad flaring mouth and narrow base, outer surface felty varying from pale greyish-buff to yellowish-grey-brown or brown; inner surface smooth, shiny, ranging from pale to dark-grey.
Eggs: about 2·5 mm, disc-shaped, either dark-grey or blackish.
Habitat: gregarious, often in large numbers on bare soil in woods and gardens, sometimes in flower pots. Spring to autumn. Occasional.

Ascomycetes

The fungi in this group are extremely varied in shape, but all are characterized by bearing their spores in little sacs called asci. The asci may be borne inside the fruitbody or on the surface. The group includes the much sought-after edible truffles and morels, together with many colourful cup fungi and an assortment of smaller species.

MORCHELLA ESCULENTA
Common Morel
Cap: 6-8 cm high, yellowish-brown, with sharply angled pits.
Stem: 6-10 cm high, creamy white in colour, almost smooth, but slightly wrinkled at base.
Flesh: fairly thick, whitish, with a delicate flavour. This excellent edible mushroom should never be eaten raw.
Habitat: fields, woods and hedgerows.

TUBER AESTIVUM
Truffle
Fruitbody: 2-6 cm diam. Covered in coarse pyramidal warts. Grey-black. Interior pale greyish-lilac, marbled with darker veins. Asci inside fruitbody.
Habitat: a rare species on chalky soil, growing entirely underground. The related *T. melanosporum* is the famous truffle of France.

PEZIZA AURANTIA
Orange Peel Fungus
Looking like discarded pieces of orange peel, this rather brittle fungus forms a ragged cup 1-12 cm across. Bright orange inside, where the asci are embedded in the surface, it is downy white on the outside.
Habitat: bare ground or grassy places in woods and many other situations. Late autumn and winter.

NECTRIA CINNABARINA
Coral Spot Fungus
This very common lignicolous fungus has 2 visible stages. One consists of many pale pink spots on the wood, each producing numerous non-sexual spores called conidia. The other stage consists of darker red pustules which carry the asci.
Habitat: mainly dead twigs, including garden pea sticks; also on some living twigs, especially after wounding. All year, but asci normally autumnal.

XYLARIA HYPOXYLON
Candle-Snuff Fungus
This tough, leathery fungus forms strap-like fruitbodies which generally branch like tiny antlers. It gets its name from the powdery tips of the young branches, which resemble snuffed-out candle-wicks. The white powder consists of special spores called conidia. Asci develop later, embedded in small pits nearer the base of the fruit body.
Habitat: tree stumps and other dead wood almost anywhere. All the year.

DALDINIA CONCENTRICA
Cramp Balls
First appearing as rounded, dark brown 'buns' on dead trees, the fruitbodies eventually become jet black and very hard. Up to 9 cm across, they are also known as King Alfred's Cakes. Black spores develop just under the surface, which becomes very sooty when they are released.
Habitat: dead trunks and branches, especially ash trees. All the year.

Morchella esculenta

Tuber aestivum

Above: Orange peel fungus.
Right: Coral spot fungus growing on a twig.

Xylaria hypoxylon

Daldinia concentrica

Lichens

Lichens are very hardy plants which can survive in some of the hottest and coldest places on earth. Their bodies consist of fungal threads and minute algae in an intricate partnership. They are tough and dry and quite unlike ordinary fungi, although the fungus partner makes up the bulk of the body. Growth is usually very slow.

There are three main types of lichen. *Crustose* lichens form crusty coats on rocks and other surfaces. They may be broken into hexagonal plates, but they have no obvious lobes. *Foliose* lichens consist of numerous scales or leaf-like lobes, often forming circular patches. *Fruticose* lichens are like miniature bushes, standing erect or hanging in tufts from branches. Many lichens scatter powdery granules, called soredia, which grow directly into new plants. They also reproduce by spores, which are formed in certain regions. The spores are purely fungal and can grow into lichens only if they are quickly joined by the right kind of alga.

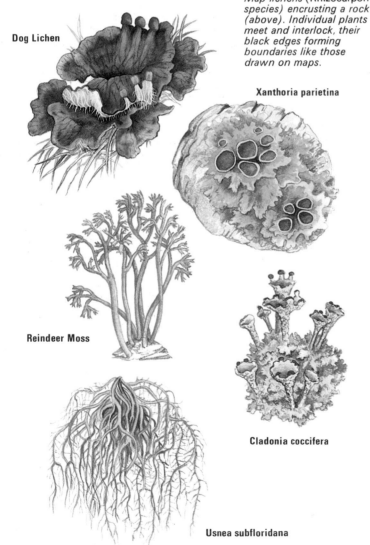

Map lichens (Rhizocarpon species) encrusting a rock (above). Individual plants meet and interlock, their black edges forming boundaries like those drawn on maps.

Dog Lichen

Xanthoria parietina

Reindeer Moss

Cladonia coccifera

Usnea subfloridana

DOG LICHEN
Peltigera canina
A large foliose lichen common on sand dunes and in grassy places. Underside is white and felt-like. Lobes are pale grey when dry. Spores are borne in chestnut-brown patches on the edges.

XANTHORIA PARIETINA
One of several similar species, this foliose lichen is abundant on rocks and old walls, on tree trunks and on asbestos roofs. It is especially common by the sea. Spores are formed in darker patches near the centre.

REINDEER MOSS
Cladonia rangiferina
A plant of the Arctic and high moors, this fruticose lichen is the staple diet of the reindeer.

CLADONIA COCCIFERA
One of the 'pixie-cup' lichens, this fruticose species is common on moorland and other areas of peaty soil. The cups grow up from clusters of scales and bear bright red spore-producing patches on their rims.

USNEA SUBFLORIDANA
One of the 'beard lichens', this fruticose species forms tangled clumps on tree trunks and branches. Young lichens are usually upright. Soredia are produced in white patches on the stems. The lichen is most abundant in the west, where the climate is damper.

Chapter Ten
Seaweeds and other Algae

The algae are simple flowerless plants, most of which live in water. There are no roots, and the body is never clearly divided into leaf and stem. Many forms, such as *Chlamydomonas* (page 390), consist of just a single free-swimming cell. These unicellular algae can multiply very rapidly by splitting into two or more new cells every few hours, and they are responsible for turning pond and aquarium water green in summer. They also play a vital role in the economy of the sea, for they form the *phytoplankton* – the 'soup' of minute drifting plants on which the marine animals depend for their food. A few unicellular algae live in damp soil, and also on tree trunks which they turn green in very wet conditions.

Seaweed Groups
There are several different groups of algae, not all closely related, and they are usually classified according to their colour. Seaweeds are the largest and most familiar of the algae and they belong to three main groups – green, brown and red algae. Some are several metres long and they have a much more complex structure than other algae. They are often attached to rocks by sucker-like discs called *holdfasts*, and there may be a stalk-like region between this and the flat blade, but there are never any special cells for carrying water and food such as are found in higher plants.

Although many seaweeds are brown or red, they all contain green chlorophyll and they all make their own food by photosynthesis in just the same way as other plants. The brown and red pigments that mask the chlorophyll improve the absorption of light under the water. Red is the best light-absorber under such conditions, and red seaweeds can grow in deeper water than brown and green ones. But no seaweed can survive in very deep water where there is no light.

Reproduction takes place in several ways and is often very complex, especially among the red algae. Many seaweeds resemble ferns (page 355) in having two distinct generations – one scattering spores into the water and the other bearing male and female organs. Both male and female cells are released into the water for fertilization, the mobile male cells being chemically attracted to the non-mobile female cells. Non-sexual reproduction is also common among the algae, the most frequent method being the release of flagellated cells called *zoospores*. These swim about and eventually grow directly into new plants exactly like the parents.

Below: A colourful array of green, brown and red seaweeds on Lundy Island. It is unusual for so many different kinds of seaweed to grow so close to each other.

Green Algae

Green algae (Chlorophyceae) live in fresh and salt water and a few live on land. Many are single-celled organisms, while many more exist as fine threads. Green seaweeds live in the shallowest waters around the shore and also cover the mud of many estuaries. They can withstand considerable exposure to the air. A coating of mucus ensures that they do not dry up too quickly, and also makes them slippery to walk on.

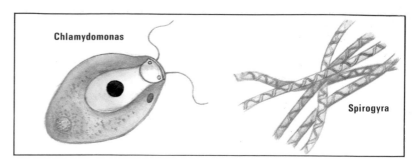

CHLAMYDOMONAS
A genus of microscopic unicellular algae, abundant in fresh water. The plant swims by waving its flagella. The red spot detects light and helps the alga to orientate itself in the best position for absorbing light into the cup-shaped chloroplast where food is made.

SPIROGYRA
A genus of filamentous green algae with several common species in ponds and streams — either floating or fixed to stones; commonly known as blanket weeds. Green chloroplasts run spirally round in each cell. Division of the cells leads to increased length of the filaments. Asexual reproduction takes place by fragmentation, each broken piece growing as a separate plant.

SEA LETTUCE
Ulva lactuca
A world-wide plant with fronds like very thin lettuce leaves, up to 45 cm long. Found on all shore zones, but mainly in the upper parts; especially common in muddy estuaries and bays and wherever fresh water runs over the shore. Edible.

ENTEROMORPHA INTESTINALIS
Sometimes known as grass kelp, this very common seaweed grows on rocks and mud in estuaries and on the upper shore zones, especially where streams trickle over the shore. The thallus, up to 60 cm long, is tubular, rather like a sausage skin inflated with gas.

Brown Algae

Nearly all the brown algae (Phaeophyceae) are marine and they include the largest seaweeds. None is unicellular. They are the commonest seaweeds of cool regions, occupying zones from the middle shore down to below low-tide level. They often form dense carpets on the rocks. This is especially true of the tough-fronded wracks, which can withstand a good deal of battering by the waves.

PEACOCK'S TAIL
Padina pavonia
The curved, fan-shaped frond is up to 15 cm high. It grows on rocks and stones in rock pools and around low-water mark. Common on Mediterranean and south-western coasts of Europe: reaches Britain, but uncommon and found only in summer and autumn — mainly on sunny sides of rock pools.

BLADDER WRACK
Fucus vesiculosus
Also known as popweed because of the air-filled bladders which buoy up the fronds in the water, this very tough seaweed occupies large areas of the middle shore. Fronds reach 90 cm. It often has no bladders where pounded by very strong waves. The pale swollen tips of the fronds house the reproductive organs.

SERRATED WRACK
Fucus serratus
Easily recognized by its serrated margins, this seaweed grows abundantly on the middle and lower shore — usually just below the bladder wrack zone; it avoids the most exposed areas where wave action is strongest. The fronds reach 1 m or more and are quite flat; swollen tips are much less obvious than in other wracks.

CHANNELLED WRACK
Pelvetia canaliculata
Named for the distinct channels along the branches, this seaweed is abundant on the upper zones of rocky shores and also on estuarine mud-flats and salt-marshes. It can survive out of water for several days at a time, relying on water trapped in its narrow channels. The fronds reach 15 cm.

THONGWEED
Himanthalia elongata
Grows on rocks on the middle and lower shore, usually just below the serrated wrack. The strap-like fronds may reach 3 m. Young plants resemble buttons until the thongs begin to grow.

OARWEED
Laminaria digitata
Also known as tangle, this seaweed forms dense beds from about low-water mark down to 30 m. A branched holdfast grips the rocks and the stalked, rubbery frond is up to 3 m long. It is split into numerous ribbon-like strips. When uncovered by the tide it lies flat: the stalks of the very similar species (*L. hyperborea*) remain upright.

Red Algae

The red algae (Rhodophyceae) are almost all marine and they are most common in the warmer seas. Some live in rock pools, but the majority inhabit deeper waters. They cannot survive much exposure to the air. The colour ranges from pale pink to violet or brownish-red and the range of form is tremendous. There are a few unicellular species; some encrust the rocks like lichens; many are filamentous; and others have leaf-like blades. The fronds are often elaborately branched. Many secrete coatings of calcium carbonate around themselves and are sometimes mistaken for corals.

CORAL WEED
Corallina officinalis
A stiff, bushy seaweed coated with lime and reaching 15 cm. Pink to purple in life; white when dead. It grows in shady pools and on stones from the middle shore down to fairly deep water. It can survive some exposure to the air in shady places.

RED LAVER
Porphyra umbilicalis
Has very thin, leaf-like lobes up to 25 cm across; often split into ribbon-like strips. Ranges from purplish-red to olive-green; usually green when young. Grows on rocks and stones on all parts of the shore, especially where there is sand as well. It is eaten in many places.

IRISH MOSS
Chondrus crispus
Also known as carrageen, this common seaweed grows in rock pools and on other rocks on the middle and lower shore. The fronds reach 15 cm and range from pink to deep reddish-brown; sometimes green in sunlit pools. Frond divisions may be much narrower in wave-battered areas. The plant is eaten in many places.

POLYSIPHONIA NIGRESCENS
The finely branched, feathery fronds reach 15 cm. It grows on rocks on the lower shore and below low-water mark, and may also be found growing on the larger brown seaweeds.

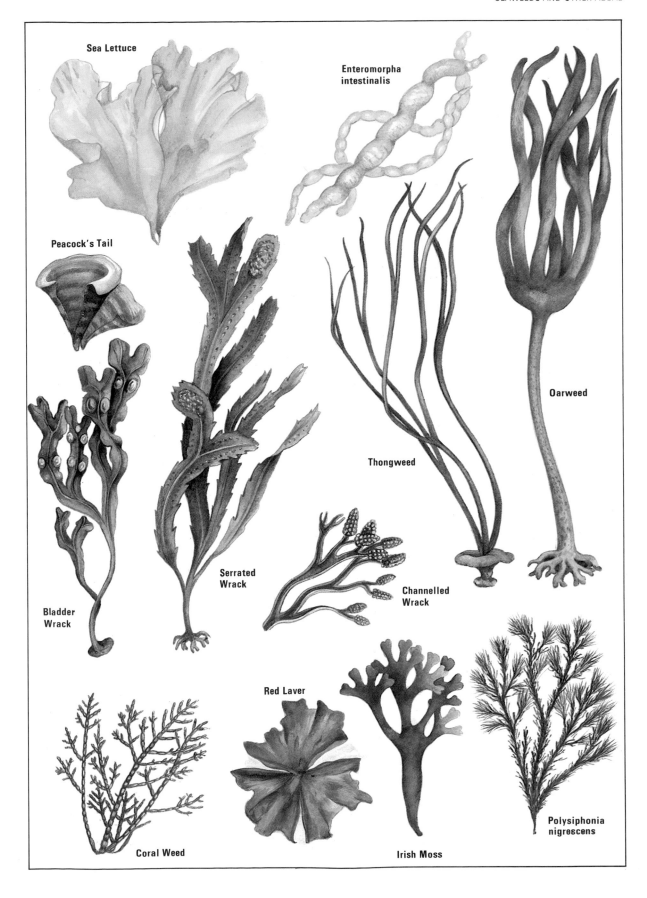

Sea Lettuce

Enteromorpha intestinalis

Peacock's Tail

Thongweed

Oarweed

Bladder Wrack

Serrated Wrack

Channelled Wrack

Red Laver

Coral Weed

Irish Moss

Polysiphonia nigrescens

Merveille du Jour 186
Mespilus, Snowy 332
Metalmarks 174
Midge 194, 195
Milkwort, Common 220
Millipede, Pill 207
Mink, European 28
Minnow 122, 123
Mint, Water 263
Mistletoe 240
Moderlieschen 122, 123
Mole, Northern 10
Mole-rat, Greater 18
Molluscs 134–141
Mongoose, Egyptian 30
Monkey Puzzle 308
Moorhen 61
Morel, Common 387
Mosquito 194, 195
Moss, Common Hair 360, 361
    Irish 390
    Reindeer 388
    Silky Wall Feather 360, 361
Moth, Brimstone 192
    Dot 186
    Drinker 188
    Emperor 188
    Ghost 184
    Gipsy 189
    Herald 187
    Magpie 191
    Malachite 186
    Mullein 187
    Peppered 193
    Pine Processionary 189
    Puss 190
    Small Magpie 193
    Swallow-tailed 192
    White Plume 193
Mouflon 32, 33
Mountain Ash see Rowan
Mouse-ear, Common 223
Mouse, Harvest 22, 23
    House 22
    Rock 21
    Striped Field 21
    Wood 21
    Yellow-necked field 21
Mugwort 278
Mulberry, Black or Common 323
Mullein, Great 260
Mullet, Red 127
    Thick-lipped Grey 128
Muntjac 35
Muskrat 19
Mussel, Common 140, 141
    Painter's 140
Mycena, Leathery 373
    Milking 373
Myrobalan see Plum, Cherry 328
Myrtle 346

Nase 122, 123
Natterjack 115
Nettle, Common 250
Nettle Tree 323
Newt, Alpine 116, 117
    Marbled 116
    Palmate 116
    Smooth 116, 117
    Warty 116
Nightingale 89
Nightjar 75
Nightshade, Deadly 258
    Black 258
Nipplewort 276
Noctuid Moths 186
Nutcracker 82, 83
Nuthatch 85

Oak, Cork 317
    Holly 317
    Holm 318, 319

Pendunculate or Common Red 318, 319
    Sessile or Durmast 320
    Turkey 318
Oak (moth), Scalloped 192
Oarweed 390, 391
Octopus, Common 136
Olive 351
Orache, Common 225
Orange Peel Fungus 387
Orange Sallow 186
Orange, Seville 335
    Sweet 335
Orange-tip 158
    Moroccan 158
Orchid, Bee 285
    Common Spotted 283
    Early Purple 284
    Fragrant 283
    Lady 285
    Lizard 285
    Pyramidal 284
Oriole, Golden 81
Ormer, Common 138, 139
Osprey 55
Otter 29
Ouzel, Ring 88
Owl, Barn 73, 74
    Eagle 74
    Little 74
    Long-eared 74
    Pygmy 74
    Scops 73, 74
    Short-eared 74, 75
    Snowy 74
    Tawny 74
Oxlip 210, 211
Oyster 140, 141
    Portuguese 140, 141
Oystercatcher 62
Oyster Fungus 374

Painted Lady 164
Palm, Chusan 309
    Dwarf Fan 309
Pansy, Wild 219
Parasol Mushroom 365
Parsley, Cow 242
    Fool's 242
Partridge 59
    Red-legged 59
    Rock 59
Pasque Flower 214
Peach Blossom (moth) 190
Peacock 163
Peacock's Tail 390, 391
Pear 331
Peewit see Lapwing
Pelican, Dalmation 43
    White 43
Pelican's foot 138, 139
Perch 118, 119, 125
Perching Birds 79–105
Peregrine 56
Periwinkle, Common 138, 139
    Flat 138, 139
Periwinkle, Lesser (flower) 254
Petrel, Leach's 42
    Storm 42
Phalarope, Red-necked 66, 67
Pheasant 59
Pholiota, Shaggy 374
Piddock, Common 140
Pike 121
Pimpernel, Scarlet 254
Pine, Aleppo 302
    Arolla or Swiss Stone 299
    Austrian 300, 301
    Corsican 300, 301
    Maritime 302
    Monterey 299
    Scots 300, 301

Stone or Umbrella 300, 301
Pineappleweed 271
    Weymouth 300, 301
Pintail 46, 47
Pipefish, Nilsson's 127
Pipistrelle, Common 13
Pipit, Meadow 97
    Rock 97
    Tawny 97
    Tree 97
    Water 97
Pistachio 341
Plaice 129
Plane, London 324
    Oriental 325
Plantain, Greater 267
    Hoary 267
    Ribwort 267
Plover, Green see Lapwing
    Golden 63
    Grey 62, 63
    Kentish 62
    Little Ringed 62
    Ringed 62
Plum, Cherry 328
Plums and Custard 370
Poached Egg Fungus 365
Pochard 48
    Red-crested 48
Polecat, Marbled 26, 27
    Steppe 26, 27
    Western 26, 27
Pollack 127
Polypody, Common 358
Pomegranate 345
Pond Skater, Common 154
Pondweed, Canadian 279
Poplar, Black 310
    Lombardy 312
    White 310
Poppy, Common 215
    Long-headed 215
Porcupine, North African Crested 16
Porpoise, Common 37
Portuguese Man o'War 209
Powan 121
Pratincole 67
Prawn, Common 142, 143
Praying Mantis 204, 205
Primrose 253
    Bird's eye 253
Privet 353
Prominent, Pebble 190
Psammodromus, Large 108
Ptarmigan 58
Puff-ball, Giant 385
Puffin 71
Pug, Lime-speck 181

Quail 59

Rabbit 14
Raccoon 30
Raccoon-dog 25
Ragworm 208
Ragged Robin 222
Ragwort, Common 272
Rail, Land see Corncrake
    Water 60
Ram's Horn, Great 137
Ramsons 280
Rat, Black or Ship 20
    Common or Norway 20
Rattle, Yellow 259
Raven 82
Ray, Sting 126
    Thornback 126
Razorbill 71
Redpoll 102
    Arctic 102
Redshank (bird) 65
    Spotted 65

Redshank (flower) 248, 249
Redstart 89
    Black 89
Red Wing 87
Redwood, Coast 304
Reed, Common 291
Reedling see Tit, Bearded
Reedmace, Great 287
Reindeer 34
Reptiles 106–112
Rest-harrow, Common 229
Rhododendron 349
Ringlet 171
    Almond-eyed 171
    Dewy 171
    Mountain 171
Roach, 122, 123
Robber-fly 194, 195
Robin 89
Rockling, Five-bearded 127
Rockrose, Common 220
Rodents 15–23
Roller 76
Roll Rim, The 375
Rook 82
Rose, Guelder 350
Rowan 329
Rudd 122
Rue, Wall 357
Ruff 66
Ruffe 125
Rush, Jointed 288
    Soft 288

Sainfoin 228, 229
St George's Mushroom 372
St John's Wort, Perforate 220
Salamander, Alpine 117
    Fire 117
    Spectacled 117
Sallow see Willow, Goat
Sallow, Orange 186
Salmon 120, 121
Sandeel, Greater 128
Sanderling 66
Sandpiper, Common 65
    Green 64
    Wood 65
Sand-smelt 128
Sandwort, Sea 221
Sanicle 245
Satyr, Black 170
Sawfly, Gooseberry 199
    Hawthorn 199
Saxifrage, Livelong 238
    Rue-leaved 238
Scabious, Devil's Bit 270
    Field 270
Scallop, Queen 140, 141
Scaup 48
Scorpion 147
Scorpion-fly 204, 205
Scorpion, Sea 129
    Water 154
Scurvy Grass, Common 217
Sea Buckthorn 347
Sea Cucumber, Common 133
Sea Gherkin 133
Sea Hare 138, 139
Sea Horse 127
Sea Lavender, Common 250
Seal, Common 36
    Grey 36
    Monk 36, 37
Sea Lettuce 390, 391
Sea Slug 138, 139
    Grey 138, 139
Sea Urchin, Edible 132
Seaweeds 389–391
Sedge, Great Pond 289
Selfheal 264

Sequoia, Giant 304
Serin 102
Serpent Star 133
Service Tree, Bastard 331
    True 331
    Wild 330
Shag 43
Shanny 128
Shearwater, Cory's 42
    Great 42
    Manx 42
    Sooty 42
Shelduck 49
Shell, Banded Carpet 140, 141
    Banded Wedge 140, 141
    Common Otter 140, 141
    Large Razor 140, 141
    Needle 138, 139
    Painted Top 138, 139
    Rayed Trough 140, 141
    Top 130, 131
    Tower 138, 139
    Yellow 191
Shepherd's Purse 217
Shoveler 46, 47
Shrew, Bicoloured White-toothed 11
    Common 11
    Greater White-toothed 11
    Pygmy 11
    Pygmy White-toothed (Etruscan) 11
    Water 11
Shrike, Great Grey 99
    Lesser 99
    Red-backed 99
    Woodchat 99
Shrimp, Common 142, 143
    Freshwater 142
Sickener, The 368
Silverfish 206
Silver Leaf Fungus 382
Silverweed 236
Silver Y 187
Siskin 100, 101
Skink, Three-toed 108
Skipper, Dingy 179
    Grizzled 179
    Large 179
    Large chequered 179
    Silver-spotted 179
    Small 179
Skua, Arctic 67
    Great 67
Skylark 79
Slater, Sea 142
Sloe see Blackthorn
Slow Worm 108
Slug, Budapest 136, 137
    Great Black 136, 137
    Great Grey 135, 136, 137
    Netted 136, 137
Smelt 121
Smew 49
Smoke Tree 341
Snail, Brown Lipped 137
    Garden 137
    Garlic Glass 137
    Great Pond 137
    Kentish 137
    Roman 137
    Round-mouthed 137
    Strawberry 137
    Two-toothed Door 137
Snake, Cat 111
    Grass 111
    Horseshoe Whip 110
    Ladder 110, 111
    Leopard 110, 111
    Montpellier 110
    Smooth 111
    Viperine 111
    Western Whip, 110, 111

Snake-fly 204, 205
Snipe 63
  Jack 63
Snout Butterflies 161
Snowdrop 282
Soapwort, Rock 224
Sorrel, Common 249
Sow-thistle, Perennial 276
  Smooth 276
Spadefoot, Common 114
Sparrowhawk 54
Sparrow, Hedge see Dunnock
  House 105
  Rock 105
  Spanish 105
  Tree 105
Spearwort, Lesser 213
Speedwell, Germander 261
Spider, Daddy-long-legs 144
  Garden 146
  House 144, 145
  Orb-web 130, 131, 146
  Water 144, 145
  Zebra 145
Spiders 144–147
Spindle Shank 371
Spindle Tree 338
Spirogyra 390
Spleenwort, Maidenhair 357
Spruce, Norway 298
  Sitka or Silver 298
Spurdog 126
Spurge, Petty 246
  Sun 246
Spurrey, Corn 221
  Sand 221
Squid, Common 136
Squirrel, Flying 15
  Grey 8, 9, 15
  Red 15
Starfish, Common 133
Starling 100
Stereoid Fungi 382
Stickleback, Nine-spined 125
  Three-spined 125
Stilt, Black-winged 66
Stinkhorn 384
Stitchwort, Greater 223
Stoat 26, 27
Stonechat 88
Stonecrop, Biting 237
Stonefly 204, 205
Stork, Black 45
  White 45
Stork's-bill, Common 226
Strawberry, Barren 235
  Wild 235
Strawberry Tree 348
Sturgeon 120
Sulphur Tuft 377
Sumach 341
Sundew, Round-leaved 238
Sunstar 130, 131, 133
Swallow 80
  Red-rumped 80
Swallowtail 156
  Scarce 156
Swan, Bewick's 51
  Mute 51
  Whooper 51
Sweet Bay 324
Swift (bird) 75
  Alpine 75, 76
Swift (moth), Common 184
Sycamore 294, 295, 340
Sympetrum, Ruddy 150, 151

Tamarisk 347
Tangerine 336

Tansy 278
Tarantula 145
Tawny Grisette 365
Teal 46
Tellin, Blunt 140, 141
  Thin 140, 141
Tench 122, 123
Tern, Arctic 70
  Black 70
  Common 70
  Little 70
  Roseate 70
  Sandwich 70
  Whiskered 70
Terrapin, European Pond 112
  Stripe-necked 112
Thelephoroid Fungi 382
Thistle, Creeping 273
  Spear 273
  Welted 273
Thongweed 390, 391
Thorn, Canary-shouldered 192
  Purple 192
Thrift 250
Thrips, Onion 204, 205
Thrush, Blue-rock 87
  Mistle 87
  Rock 87
  Song 87
Thyme, Wild 264
Tiger (moth), Garden 184, 185
  Jersey 185
  Wood 185
Tit, Bearded 86
  Blue 84
  Coal 84
  Crested 84
  Great 84
  Long-tailed 85
  Marsh 84
  Willow 84
Toad, Common 114, 115
  Green 114, 115
  Midwife 114
  Yellow-bellied 114
Toadflax, Common 260
  Ivy-leaved 260
Toothcarp, Spanish 124
Tormentil 235
Tortoise, Hermann's 112
Tortoiseshell, Large 163
  Small 130, 131, 163
Traveller's Joy 214
Treecreeper 86
  Short-toed 86
Tree of Heaven 338
Trooping Crumble Cap 376
Trout, Brown 120, 121
  Rainbow 121
Truffle 387
Turnstone 63
Turpentine Tree 341
Tussock, Pale 189
Twayblade, Common 284
Twite 100, 101

Ugly One, The 366, 367
Underwing, Large Yellow 186
  Red 187
Urchin, Rock 132
  Violet Heart 132

Vapourer 189
Velvet Shank, The 370
Vendace 121
Vetch, Bush 232, 233
  Common 232
  Horseshoe 231
  Kidney 231
  Tufted 232, 233
Vetchling, Meadow 232, 233
Vine, Grape 337
Violet, Common Dog, 219
  Sweet 219

Viper, Lataste's 111
Vole, Bank 18, 19
  Field 18, 19
  Northern Water 19
Vulture, Bearded see Lammergeyer
  Black 52
  Egyptian 52
  Griffon 52

Waders 62–67
Wagtail, Grey 98
  Pied 98
  White 98
  Yellow 98
Wallcreeper 85
Walnut 314
Warbler, Barred 92, 93
  Bonelli's 94
  Cetti's 94
  Dartford 94
  Garden 92, 93
  Grasshopper 90
  Great Reed 90
  Icterine 92, 93
  Marsh 92
  Melodious 92, 93
  Moustached 90
  Olivaceous 92, 93
  Orphean 92, 93
  Reed 90, 91, 92
  Savi's 90
  Sedge 92
  Willow 94
  Wood 94
Wasp, Bee-killer 198
  Common 198
  Gall 199
  Paper 198
  Ruby-tailed 199
  Spiny Mason 198
Water-cress 218
Water-crowfoot, Thread-leaved 213
Waterfowl 46–51
Water Lily, White 216
  Yellow 216
Water-parsnip, Lesser 244
Water-plantain, Common 279
Water-starwort 241
Waxwing 99
Wayfaring Tree 350
Weasel 26, 27
Weaver, Lesser 128
Weeping Willow 377
Wels 124
Wentletrap, Common 138, 139
Whale, Long-finned Pilot 37
Wheatear 88
  Black 88
  Black-eared 88
Whelk, Common 138
Whimbrel 64
Whinchat 88
White, Bath 158
  Black-veined 158
  Green-veined 157
  Large 157
  Marbled 168
  Small 157
  Western Marbled 168
Whitebeam 330
Whitefly, Cabbage 155
Whitethroat 94
  Lesser 94
Whiting 127
Wigeon 46, 47
Wild Boar 32, 33
Wild Cat 31
Willow, Crack 313
  Goat 313
  Weeping 313
  White 312
Willowherb, Broad-leaved 239
  Great 239
  Rosebay 239

Winkle, Sting 138, 139
Woad 218
Wolf 25
Wolverine 29
Wood (butterfly), Speckled 172, 173
Woodcock 64
Woodlark 79
Woodlice 142
Woodpecker, Black 77
  Great Spotted 78
  Green 77
  Grey-headed 77
  Lesser spotted 78
  Middle spotted 78
  Three-toed 77
  White-backed 78
Woodpigeon 72
Woodruff 269
Woodrush, Field 288
Wood Sorrel 227
Wood Woolly Foot 371
Worm, Peacock 208
Woundwort, Hedge 266
Wrack, Bladder 390, 391
  Channelled 390, 391
  Serrated 390, 391
Wrasse, Cuckoo 127
Wren 86
Wryneck 78

Yarrow 278
Yellowhammer 104
Yellow, Speckled 192
Yew 308
Yorkshire Fog 291

Zander 125

Scientific Names

Abies alba 296
  grandis 296
Abramis brama 122
Abraxas grossulariata 191
Acanthis cannabina 100
  flammea 102
  flavirostris 100
  hornemanni 102
Acanthosoma haemorrhoidale 154
Accipiter, gentilis 54
  nisus 54
Acer campestre 339
  monspessulanum 339
  negundo 339
  platanoides 340
  pseudoplatanus 340
Acherontia atropos 181
Acheta domesticus 152
Achillea millefolium 278
Acipenser sturio 120
Acrida ungarica 153
Acrocephalus arundinaceus 90
  melanopogon 90
  palustris 92
  schoenobaenus 92
  scirpaceus 92
Adscita statices 184
Aegithalos caudatus 85
Aegopodium podagraria 244
Aegypius monachus 52
Aeolidia papillosa 138
Aesculus hippocastanum 342
  x *carnea* 342
Aeshna grandis 150, 151
Aethusa cynapium 242
Agama stellio 108
Agaricus arvensis 377
  campestris 376, 377
Aglais urticae 163
Agrimonia eupatoria 236
Agrion splendens 150
Agrius convolvuli 181
Agrocybe praecox 375
Agrodiaetus damon 178
Agrostis tenuis 293
Agrotis exclamationis 186
Ailanthus altissima 338
Aix galericulata 46
Alauda arvensis 79
Alburnus alburnus 122
Alca torda 71
Alcedo atthis 76
Alces alces 34
Alectoris graeca 59
  rufa 59
Aleyrudes proletella 155
Alle alle 71
Alliaria petiolata 217
Alisma plantago-aquatica 279
Allium ursinum 280
Alnus glutinosa 316
Alopecurus pratensis 291
Alopex lagopus 25
Alytes obstetricus 114
Amanita citrina 364
  fulva 364
  muscaria 364
  pantherina 365
  phalloides 364
  rubescens 365
Amaurobius similis 144
Amelanchier ovalis 332
Ammophila arenaria 293
  sabulosa 198
Anacamptis pyramidalis 284
Anagallis arvensis 254
Anas acuta 46
  clypeata 46
  crecca 46

penelope 46
platyrhynchos 46
querquedula 46
strepera 46
Anax imperator 150
Andrena fulva 197
Anemone nemoròsa 212
Angelica sylvestris 243
Anguilla anguilla 124
Anguis fragilis 108
Anobium punctatum 202
Anoplius viaticus 198
Anser albifrons 50
anser 50
brachyrhynchus 50
erythropus 50
fabalis 50
Anthocharis belia 158
cardamines 158
Anthocoris nemorum 154
Anthriscus sylvestris 242
Anthus campestris 97
pratensis 97
spinoletta petrosus 97
spinoletta spinoletta 97
trivialis 97
Anthyllis vulneraria 230
Apamea lithoxylaea 187
monoglypha 187
Apanteles glomeratus 199
Apatele psi 186
Apatura ilia 162
iris 161
Aphanius iverus 124
Aphantopus hyperantus 171
Aphis fabae 155
Aphodius rufipes 201
Apis mellifera 197
Aplysia depilans 138
Apodermus agrarius 21
flavicollis 21
mystacinus 21
sylvaticus 21
Aporia crataegi 158
Aporrhais pespelecani 138
Apus apus 75
melba 76
Aquila chrysaetos 53
heliaca 53
Araneus diadematus 146
quadratus 146
Araschnia levana 164
Araucaria araucaria 308
Arbutus unedo 348
Arctia caja 185
Arctium minus 274
Arcyptera fusca 153
Ardea cinerea 44
purpurea 44
Ardeola ralloides 44
Arenaria interpres 63
Arenicola marina 208
Argiope bruennichi 146
lobata 146
Argynnis paphia 165
Argyroneta aquatica 145
Aricia agestis 177
Arion ater 137
Armeria maritima 250
Armillariella mellea 366
Arrhenatherum elatius 291
Arvicola terrestris 19
Artogeia napi 157
rapae 157
Arum maculatum 286
Asellus aquaticus 142
Asilus crabroniformis 194
Asio flammeus 75
otus 74
Asphodelus albus 280
Aspitrigla cuculus 129
Aspius aspius 122
Asplenium ruta-muraria
trichomanes 357
brichomanes 357
Asterias rubens 133
Asterina gibbosa 133

Aster tripolium 272
Astropecten irregularis 133
Athene noctua 74
Atherina presbyter 128
Athous haemorrhoidalis 201
Atriplex patula 225
Atropa bella-donna 258
Aurelia aurita 209
Auricularia auricula judae 383
Autographa gamma 187
Aythya ferina 48
fuligula 48
marila 48
nyroca 48
Azolla filiculoides 358

Balanus balanoides 143
Barbus barbus 122
Bellis perennis 270, 271
Belone belone 126
Bembex rostrata 198
Berula erecta 244
Betula pendula 315
pubescens 315
Bibio marci 194
Biorrhiza pallida 199
Biston betularia 193
Bitium reticulatum 138
Blatella germanica 204
Blechnum spicant 358
Blicca bjoerkna 122
Boletus badius 378, 379
chrysenteron 378, 379
edulis 379
erythropus 379
satanas 379
Boloria aquilonarius 166
Bombina variegata 114
Bombus lapidarius 197
lucorum 197
pascuorum 197
Bombycilla garrulus 99
Bombylius major 194, 195
Botaurus stellaris 45
Bovista nigrescens 386
Brachinus crepitans 200
Branta bernicla 50
canadensis 50
leucopsis 50
Brenthis daphne 165
Brintesia circe 170
Briza media 290
Bryonia dioica 247
Bryum capillare 361
Bubo bubo 74
Buccinum undatum 138
Bucephala clangula 49
Buddleja davidii 353
Bufo bufo 115
calamita 115
viridis 115
Buteo buteo 54
lagopus 54
Buxus sempervirens 336

Calidris alba 66
alpina 65
canuta 65
Callionymus lyra 128
Calliostoma zizyphinum 138
Calliphora vomitoria 194, 195
Callitriche stagnalis 241
Callophrys rubi 175
Calluna vulgaris 251
Calocera viscosa 383
Calonectris diomedea 42
Calotaenia celsia 186
Calothysanis amata 192
Caltha palustris 212
Calvatia excipuliformis 385
Calystegia sepium 257
Campanula glomerata 268

rotundifolia 268
Camptogramma bilineata 191
Camptothecium sericeum 361
Cancer pagums 143
Cantharellus cibarius 366
Canus aureus 24
lupus 25
Capra hircus 32
ibex 32
Capreolus capreolus 35
Caprimulgus europaeus 75
Capsella bursa-pastoris 217
Carabus violaceus 200
Carassius carassius 122
Carcinus maenas 143
Cardamine pratensis 217
Cardium echinatum 140
edule 140
Carduelis carduelis 100
chloris 100
spinus 100
Carduus acanthoides 273
Carex riparia 289
Carpinus betulus 315
Carpobrotus edulis 224
Cassida viridis 202
Castanea sativa 320
Castor fiber 16
Catocala nupta 187
Cedrus atlantica 297
libani
Celastrina argiolus 176
Celtis australis 323
Centaurea nigra 274
Centaurium erythraea 255
Cepaea nemoralis 137
Cepphus grylle 71
Cerastium holosteoides 223
Cercis siliquastrum 333
Cercopis vulnerata 155
Certhia brachydactyla 86
familiaris 86
Cerura vinula 190
Cervus dama 35
elaphus 34
nippon 35
Cettia cetti 90
Chalcides chalcides 108
Chamaecyparis
lawsoniana 305
Chamaerops humilis 309
Charadrius alexandrinus 62
dubius 62
hiaticula 62
Chazara briseis 169
Chelidonium majus 215
Chelon labrosus 128
Chenopodium album 225
Chichorium intybus 277
Chironomus annularis 194
Chlamydomonas 390
Chlamys opercularis 140
Chlidonias hybridus 70
niger 70
Chondrostoma nasus 122
Chondrus crispus 390
Chorthippus parallelus 153
Chrondrostereum
purpureum 382
Chrysis ignita 199
Chrysomela populi 203
Chrysopa septempunctata 205
Chrysops relictus 194
Cicadetta montana 155
Cicindela campestris 200
Ciconia ciconia 45
nigra 45
Ciliata mustela 127
Cinclus cinclus 86
Circaetus gallicus 53
Circus aeruginosus 55

cyaneus 55
pygargus 54
Cirsium arvense 273
vulgare 273
Citrus aurantium 355
deliciosa 336
limon 335
medica 336
paradisi 336
sinensis 335
Cladonia coccifera 388
Clamator glandarius 73
Clathrus clathrus 138
Clausilia bidentata 137
Clematis vitalba 214
Clethrionomys glareolus 19
Clitocybe nebularis 368
Clossiana chariclea 166
dia 166
euphrosyne 166
selene 166
Clupea harengus 126
Clytus arietis 202
Cobitis taenia 124
Coccinella 7-punctata 202
Coccothraustes
coccothraustes 100
Cochlearis officinalis 217
Coenonympha arcania 172
dorus 172
pamphilus 172
tullia 172
Colias crocea 159
hyale 159
palaeno 160
phicomone 159
Coltricia perennis 380
Collybia fusipes 371
maculata 371
peronata 371
Coluber hippocrepis 110
viridiflavus 111
Columba livia 72
oenas 72
palumbus 72
Columbicola claviformis 206
Conger conger 126
Conium maculatum 243
Convallaria majalis 280
Convolvus arvensis 257
Coprinus atramentarius 376
comatus 376
disseminatus 376
plicatilis 376
Coracias garrulus 76
Corallina officinalis 390
Cordulegaster boltonii 150, 151
Cordulia linaenea 150
Coregonus albula 121
lavaretus 121
Coriolus versicolor 381
Corixa punctata 154
Coronella austriaca 111
Cornus sanguinea 348
Corvus corax 81
corone cornix 81
corone corone 81
frugilegus 82
monedula 82
Corylus avellana 316
Corymbites cupreus 201
Coryphoblennius galerita 128
Cotinus coggygria 341
Cottus gobio 125
Coturnix coturnix 59
Crangon crangon 142
Crassostrea angulata 140
Crataegus azarolus 326
laevigata 325
monogyna 325
Crategus azarolus 326
Crepidula fornicata 138
Crepis capillaris 275

Crex crex 60
Cricetus cricetus 18
Crocallis elinguana 192
Crocidura leucodon 11
russula 11
Crocus vernus 282
Ctenocephalides felis 206
Cucullia verbasci 187
Cuculus canorus 73
Cucumaria planci 133
Culex pipiens 194
Cupido minimus 176
Cupressocyparis leylandii 305
Cupressus macrocarpa 306
sempervirens 306
Curculio nucum 203
Cuscuta epithymum 257
Cyaniris semiargus 178
Cyathus olla 386
Cygnus columbianus 51
cygnus 51
olor 51
Cymbalaria muralis 260
Cymbalophora pudica 185
Cynthia cardui 164
Cyprinus carpio 122

Dactylis glomerata 290
Dactylorhiza fuchsii 283
Daedaleopsis confragosa 381
Daldinia concentrica 387
Dasyatis pastinaca 126
Dasychira pudibunda 189
Daucus carota 242
Deilephila elpenor 182
porcellus 182
Delichon urbica 80
Delphinus delphis 37
Dendrocopos leucotos 78
major 78
medius 78
minor 78
Dendronotus frondosus 138
Deroceras reticulatum 137
Deschampsia flexuosa 291
Diachrysia chrysitis 187
Dicentrarchus labrax 127
Dichonia aprilina 186
Digitalis purpurea 259
Discoglossus pictus 114
Dolomedes fimbriatus 145
Donax vittatus 140
Dosina exoleta 140
Drepana falcataria 193
Drosera rotundifolia 238
Dryocopus martius 77
Dryopteris filix-mas 356
Dysdera crocata 145
Dytiscus marginalis 203

Echiichthys vipera 128
Echinus esculentus 132
Echium vulgare 256
Ectemnius cephalotes 198
Egretta alba 44
garzetta 44
Elaphe scalaris 111
situla 111
Eligmodonta ziczac 190
Eliomys quercinus 16
Elodea canadensis 279
Emberiza cirlus 104
citrinella 104
hortulana 104
schoeniclus 104
Emys orbicularis 112
Enallagma cyathigerum 150
Endymion non-scriptus 280
Engraulis encrasicolus 126
Ennomos alniaria 192

Enoplognatha ovata 145
Ensis siliqua 140
Enteromorpha intestinalis 390
Entoloma clypeatum 372
Epilobium angustifolium 239
  hirsutum 239
  montanum 239
Epipactis helleborine 285
Equisetum fluviatile 359
  telmateia 359
Equus caballus 32
Erebia aethiops 171
  alberganus 171
  epiphron 171
  pandrose 171
Eremophila alpestris 79
Erica cinerea 251
  lustianica 349
  tetralix 251
Erinaceus europaeus 10
Eriophorum angustifolium 289
Eristalis tenax 194
Erithacus rubecula 89
Erodium cicutarium 226
Eryngium maritimum 245
Erynnis tages 179
Eryx jaculus 110
Esox lucius 121
Eucalyptus globulus 346
  gunni 346
Eucera longicornis 197
Eudromias morinellus 63
Eupagurus bernhardus 143
Eupithecia centaureata 191
Euplagia quadripunctaria 185
Euproctis similis 189
Eurhynchium praelongum 361
Eurodryas aurinia 166
Eurrhypara hortulata 193
Euonymus europaeus 338
Eupatorium cannabinum 278
Euphorbia helioscopia 246
  peplus 246
Euphrasia officinalis 259
Everes argiades 176

Fabriciana adippe 165
  niobe 165
Fagus sylvatica 321
Falco columbarius 56
  naumanni 56
  peregrinus 56
  rusticolus 56
  subbuteo 56
  tinnunculus 56
Felis lynx 31
  sylvestris 31
Ficedula albicollis 95
  hypoleuca 95
  parva 95
Ficus carica 323
Filipendula ulmaria 236
Fistulina hepatica 381
Flammulina velutipes 370
Forficula auricularia 204
Formica rufa 199
Fragaria vesca 235
Frangula alnus 337
Fratercula artica 71
Fraxinus excelsior 352
  ornus 352
Fringilla coelebs 103
  montifringilla 103
Fucus serratus 390
  vesiculosus 390
Fulica atra 61
Fulmarus glacialis 42
Fumaria officinalis 216

Galanthus nivalis 282
Galemys pyrenaicus 10

Galeobdolan luteum 265
Galerida cristata 79
Galerina mutabilis 374
Galium aparine 269
  odoratum 269
  verum 269
Gallinago gallinago 63
Gallinula chlorepus 61
Gammarus pulex 142
Gandoderma applanatum 380
Garrulus glandarius 82
Gasterosteus aculeatus 125
Gastropacha querifolia 188
Gavia arctica 40
  immer 40
  stellata 40
Geastrum striatum 384
  triplex 384
Genetta genetta 30
Geranium pratense 226
  robertianum 226
Gerris lacustris 154
Geum rivale 235
  urbanum 235
Ginkgo biloba 307
Glaucidium passerinum 74
Glaucopsyche alexis 176
Glechoma hederacea 263
Glis glis 17
Globicephala melaena 37
Glomeris marginata 207
Glycimeris glycimeris 140
Gobio gobio 122
Gonepteryx cleopatra 160
  rhamni 160
Graphosoma italicum 154
Grifola frondosa 380
Grus grus 60
Gryllotalpa gryllotalpa 152
Gryllus campestris 152
Gulo gulo 29
Gymnadenia conopsea 283
Gymnocephalus cernuus 125
Gymnopilus junonius 374
Gypaetus barbatus 52
Gyps fulvus 52
Gyrinus natator 203

Habrosyne pyritioides 190
Haematopus ostralegus 62
Haemopis sanguisuga 55
Hallaeetus albicilla 55
Halichoerus grypus 36
Haliotis tuberculata 138
Hamearis lucina 174
Haplophilus subterraneus 207
Hedera helix 241
Helianthemum chamaecistus 220
Helix aspersa 137
  pomatia 137
Helleborus fuetidus 214
Hemaris fuciformis 183
  tityus 183
Hemithea aestivaria 191
Heocles alciphron 175
  virgaureae 175
Hepialus humuli 184
  lupulinus 184
Heradeum sphondylium 244
Herpestes ichneumon 30
Hesperia comma 179
Heteropterus morpheus 179
Hieraaetus fasciatus 53
  pennatus 53
Hieracium sect. Vulgata 276
Himanthalia elongata 390

Himantoglossum hircinum 285
Hipparchia fagi 168
  semele 169
Hippocampus ramulosus 127
Hippocrepis comosa 230
Hippolais icterina 92
  pallida 92
  polyglotta 92
Hippophae rhamnoides 347
Hippuris vulgaris 241
Hirundo daurica 80
  rupestris 80
  rustica 80
Holcus lanatus 291
Holothuria forskali 133
Homarus vulgaris 142
Honkenya peploides 221
Horcleum murinum 290
Humulus lupulus 247
Hydra oligactis 209
Hydrobates pelagicus 42
Hygrophoropsis aurantiaca 366
Hygrophorus conicus 372
Hyla arborea 115
Hyles euphorbiae 182
  gallii 182
Hyloicus pinastri 180
Hymenochaete rubiginosa 382
Hypericum perforatum 220
Hyperoplus lanceolatus 128
Hypholoma fasciculare 377
Hypochaeris radicata 274
Hystrix cristata 16

Iarus argentalus 68
  canus 68
  fuscus 68
  hyperboreus 68
  marinus 68
  minutus 68
  ridibundus 68
Iassus lanio 155
Ilex aquifolium 337
Impatiens glandulifera 227
Inachis io 163
Iphiclides podalirius 156
Iris pseudacorus 282
Isatis tinctoria 218
Isonychia ignota 204
Issoria lathonia 166
Ixobrychus minutus 45

Juglans regia 314
Juncus articulatus 288
  effusus 288
Juniperus communis 306
  oxycedrus 307
Jynx torquilla 78

Knautia arvensis 270

Labrus mixtus 127
Laburnum anagyroides 332
Laccaria amethystea 370
  laccata 370
Lacerta agilis 109
  lepida 109
  viridis 109
  vivipara 109
Lacrymaria velutina 377
Lactarius deliciosus 367
  rufus 366, 367
  tabidus 366, 367
  turpis 366, 367
Lagopus lagopus 58
  mutus 58
  scoticus 58
Laminaria digitata 390
Lamium album 266
  purpureum 266

Lampetra fluviatilis 120
Lampides boeticus 176
Lamprochernes nodosus 147
Lampyris noctiluca 201
Langermannia gigantea 385
Lanius collurio 99
  excubitor 99
  minor 99
  senator 99
Laothoe populi 180
Lapsana communis 276
Larix decidua 297
Lasiocampa quercus 188
Lasiommata maera 172
  megera 172
Lasius niger 199
Lathyrus pratensis 232
Laurus nobilis 324
Lavandula angustifolia 265
  stoechas 265
Leccinum scabrum 378
Leiobunum rotundum 147
Lemmus lemmus 19
Lemna minor 286
Leontodon autumnalis 275
Lepidochitona cinerea 138
Lepiota cristata 365
  procera 365
Lepisma saccharina 206
Lepista nuda 370
  saeva 370
Leptidea sinapis 160
Leptinotarsa decemlineata 203
Leptophyes punctatissima 152
Leptura rubra 202
Lepus capensis 14
  timidus 14
Leucanthemum vulgare 271
Leucaspius delineatus 122
Leuciscus cephalus 122
  idus 122
  leuciscus 122
Libelloides coccajus 205
Libellula depressa 150, 151
Libythea celtis 161
Ligia oceanica 142
Ligustrum vulgare 353
Limanda limanda 129
Limax maximus 137
Limenitis camilla 162
  populi 162
  reducta 162
Limnaea stagnalis 137
Limonium vulgare 250
Limosa lapponica 64
  limosa 64
Linaria vulgaris 260
Linyphia triangularis 145
Lipophyrys pholis 128
Liposcelis divinatorius 204
Listera ovata 284
Lithobius forficatus 207
Littorina littoralis 138
  littorea 138
Locusta migratoria 153
Locustella luscinioides 90
  naevia 90
Loligo vulgaris 136
Lolium perenne 290
Lonicera periclymenum 268
Lopinga achine 172
Lota lota 124
Lotus corniculatus 229
Loxia curvirostra 103
  pytyopsittacus 103
Lucanus cervus 200
Lucilia caesar 194
Lullala arborea 79

Lumbricus terrestris 208
Lunularia cruciata 361
Luscinia megarhynchos 89
  svecica 89
Lutra lutra 29
Lutraria lutraria 140
Luzula campestris 288
Lycaeides idas 177
Lycaena phlaeas 175
Lychnis flos-cuculi 222
Lycoperdon perlatum 386
  pyriforme 386
Lycopodium clavatum 359
  selago 359
Lycosa narbonensis 145
Lygocoris pabulinus 154
Lymantria dispar 189
Lymnocryptes minimus 63
Lyrurus tetrix 58
Lysandra bellargus 178
  coridon 178
Lysimachia vulgaris 254
Lythrum salicaria 237

Macroglossum stellatarum 182
Macrosiphum rosae 155
Mactra corallina 140
Maculinea arion 176
Malacosoma neustria 188
Malpolon monspelulanus 110
Malus sylvestris 326
Malva sylvestris 225
Maniola jurtina 171
Mantis religiosa 204
Marasmius oreades 372
Marchantia polymorpha 361
Marmota marmota 15
Martes foina 28
  martes 28
Marumba quercus 183
Matricaria matricariodes 271
Mauremys caspica 112
Medicago lupulina 230
Megachile centuncularis 197
Melanargia galathea 168
  occitanica 168
Meles meles 19
Melilotus officinalis 229
Meliteae cinxia 166
  didyma 166
  phoebe 166
Mellicta atha!ia 166
Meloe proscarabaeus 202
Melolontha melolontha 201
Mentha aquatica 263
Menyanthes trifoliata 240
Mercurialis perennis 246
Mergus albellus 49
  merganser 49
  serrator 49
Merlanguis merlangus 127
Merops apiaster 76
Mesoacidalia aglaja 165
Mespilus germanica 326
Micromys minutus 22
Microtus agrestis 19
Milax budapestensis 137
Miliaria calendra 104
Milvus migrans 55
  milvus 55
Mimas tiliae 180
Minois dryas 170
Misgurnus fossilis 124
Misumena vatia 147
Monacha cantiana 137
Monachus monachus 37
Monticola saxatilis 87
  solitarius 87
Montifringilla nivalis 105
Morchella esculenta 387

Morus nigra 323
Motacilla alba alba 98
　　alba yarrellii 98
　　cinerea 98
　　flava 98
Mullus surmuletus 127
Muntiacus reevesi 35
Murex brandaris 138
Musca domestica 194
Muscardinus avellanarius
　　17
Muscicapa striata 95
Mus musculus 22
Mustela erminea 26
　　eversmanni 26
　　lutreola 28
　　nivalis 26
　　putorius 26
Mya arenaria 140
Mycelis muralis 275
Mycena galericulata 373
　　galopus 373
Myocastor coypus 16
Myopus schisticolor 19
Myosotis scorpioides 256
Myotis daubentoni 13
　　myotis 13
　　mystacinus 13
　　nattereri 13
Myrmica ruginodis 199
Myrtus communis 346
Mytilus edulis 140

Narcissus
　　pseudonarcissus 282
Natrix maura 111
　　natrix 111
Nectria cinnabarina 387
Nematus ribesii 199
Neohipparchia stalinus
　　169
Neomys fodiens 11
Neophron percnopterus
　　52
Nepa cinerea 154
Nephrops norvegicus 142
Nephrotoma quadrifaria
　　194
Nereis diversicolor 208
Netta rufina 48
Nicrophorus humator 200
　　vespillo 200
Noctua pronuba 186
Noemacheilus barbatulus
　　124
Nordmannia illicis 174
Nucella lapillus 138
Nucifraga caryocatactes
　　82
Numenius arquata 64
　　phaeopus 64
Nuphar lutea 216
Nyctalus noctula 13
Nyctea scandiaca 74
Nyctereutes procyonoides
　　25
Nycticorax nyticorax 44
Nymphaea alba 216
Nymphalis antiopa 163
　　polychloros 163

Oceanodroma leucorhoa
　　42
Ochlodes venatus 179
Ocinebra erinacea 138
Octopus vulgaris 136
Ocypus olens 200
Odontites verna 260
Odynerus spinipes 198
Oecanthus pellucens 152
Oedipocla germanica 153
Oenanthe hispanica 88
　　leucura 88
　　oenanthe 88
Oeneis jutta 170
Olea europaea 351
Ondatra zibethicus 19
Oniscus asellus 142
Onobrychis viciifolia 229

Ononis repens 229
Ophioglossum vulgatum
　　358
Ophion luteus 199
Ophiothrix fragilis 133
Ophiura texturata 133
Ophrys apifera 285
Opisthograptis luteolata
　　192
Orchesella cincta 206
Orchestia gammarella 142
Orchis mascula 284
　　purpurea 285
Orgyia antiqua 189
Origanum vulgare 263
Oriolus oriolus 81
Orobanche minor 262
Oryctolagus cuniculus 14
Osmerus eperlanus 121
Osmunda regalis 358
Ostrea edulis 140
Otis tetrax 61
Otus scops 74
Oudemansiella mucida
　　368
Ourapteryx sambucaria
　　192
Ovis musimon 32
Oxalis acetosella 227
Oxychilus alliarius 137
Oxyura leucocephala 49

Padina pavonia 390
Palaemon serratus 142
Palinurus vulgaris 142
Palpares libelluloides 205
Panarus biarmicus 86
Panorpa communis 204
Papaver dubium 215
　　rhoeas 215
Papilio machaon 156
Paracentrotus lividus 132
Pararge aegeria 172
Pardosa amentata 145
Parnassius apollo 156
Parus ater 84
　　caeruleus 84
　　cristatus 84
　　major 84
　　montanus 84
　　palustris 84
Passer domesticus 105
　　hispaniolensis 105
　　montanus 105
Patella vulgaris 138
Patina pellucida 138
Paxillus involutus 375
Pediculus humanus 206
Pelecanus crispus 43
　　onocrotalus 43
Pellia epiphylla 361
Pelobates fuscus 114
Pelodytes punctatus 115
Peltigera canina 388
Pelvetia canaliculata 390
Perca fluviatilis 125
Perdix perdix 59
Perlodes microcephala
　　204
Pernis apivorus 53
Petasites hybridus 277
Petromyzon marinus 120
Petronia petronia 105
Peziza aurantia 387
Phalacrocorax aristotelis
　　43
　　carbo 43
　　pygmaeus 43
Phalangium opilio 147
Phalera bucephala 190
Phallus impudicus 384
Phasianus colchicus 59
Philaenus spumarius 155
Philanthus triangulum
　　198
Philudoria potatoria 188
Phleum pratense 293
Phlogophora meticulosa
　　187

Phoca vitulina 36
Phocoena phocoena 37
Phoenicopterus ruber 45
Phoenicurus ochruros 89
　　phoenicurus 89
Pholas dactylus 140
Pholcus phalangioides
　　144
Pholidoptera griseoaptera
　　153
Pholiota squarrosa 374
Pholis gunnellus 129
Phoxinus phoxinus 122
Phragmites communis
　　291
Phryganea grandis 206
Phyllitis scolopendrium
　　357
Phyllobius pomaceus 203
Phylloscopus bonelli 94
　　collybita 94
　　sibilatrix 94
　　trochilus 94
Physalia physalis 209
Pica pica 82
Picea abies 298
Picea abies 298
　　sitchensis 298
Picoides tridactylus 77
Picus canus 77
　　viridis 77
Pieris brassicae 157
Pimpinella saxifraga 243
Pinguicula vulgaris 262
Pinicola enucleator 102
Pinus cembra 299
　　halepensis 302
　　nigra 300
　　　var. maritima
　　　var. nigra
　　pinaster 302
　　pinea 300
　　radiata 300
　　strobus 300
　　sylvestris 300
Pipistrellus pipistrellus 13
Piptoporus betulinus 381
Pisaura mirabilis 145
Pistacia lentiscus 341
　　terebinthus 341
　　vera 341
Planorbis corneus 137
Plantago lanceolata 267
　　major 267
　　media 267
Platanus x hispanica 324
　　orientalis 325
Platichthys flesus 129
Plebejus argus 177
Plecotus auritus 13
Plectrophenax nivalis 104
Pleurobrachia pileus 209
Pleuronectes platessa 129
Pleurotus ostreatus 374
Pluvialis apricaria 63
　　squatarola 63
Poa trivalis 293
Podarcis muralis 109
Podiceps auritus 41
　　cristatus 41
　　grisegena 41
　　nigricollis 41
　　ruficollis 41
Podisma pedestris 153
Polistes dominulus 198
Pollachius pollachius 127
Polydesmus angustus 207
Polygala vulgaris 220
Polygonia c-album 164
Polygonum amphibium
　　249
　　aviculare 249
　　convolvus 249
　　persicaria 249
Polyommatus icarus 177
Polypodium vulgare 358
Polyporus squamosus
　　380
Polysiphonia nigrescens
　　390

Polystichum aculeatum
　　356
Polytrichum commune
　　361
Pomatias elegans 137
Pontia daplidice 158
Populus alba 310
　　nigra 310
　　　var. italica 312
　　tremula 312
Porphyra umbilicalis 390
Portunus puber 143
Porzana parva 60
　　porzana 60
　　pusilla 60
Potamobius pallipes 143
Potentilla anserina 236
　　erecta 235
　　sterilis 235
Poterium sanguisorba 236
Primula farinosa 253
　　veris 253
　　vulgaris 253
Procyon lotor 30
Promatoschistus microps
　　129
Proserpinus proserpina
　　183
Prunella collaris 96
　　modularis 96
　　vulgaris 264
Prunus armeniaca 329
　　avium 327
　　cerasifera 328
　　lavrocerasus 328
　　padus 327
　　spinosa 328
Psammodromus algirus
　　108
Psathyrella candolleana
　　375
　　gracilis 375
Pseudoaricia nicias 177
Pseudopanthera
　　macularia 192
Pseudotergumia fidia 169
Pseudotsuga menziesii
　　303
Pteridium aquilinum 357
Pteromys volans 15
Pterophorus
　　pentadactylus 193
Puffinus gravis 42
　　griseus 42
　　puffinus 42
Pulsatilla vulgaris 214
Pungitius pungitius 125
Punica granatum 345
Pyrgus malvae 179
Pyrochroa coccinea 202
Pyrrhocorax graculus 82
　　pyrrhocorax 82
Pyrrhosoma nymphula
　　150
Pyrrhula pyrrhula 102
Pyrus communis 331

Quercus borealis 318
　　cerris 318
　　coccifera 317
　　ilex 319
　　petraea 320
　　robur 319
　　sativa 320
　　suber 317
Quercusia quercus 174

Raja clavata 126
Rallus aquaticus 60
Rana esculenta 115
　　ridibunda 115
　　temporaria 115
Rangifer tarandus 34
Ranunculus acris 212
　　bulbosus 213
　　ficaria 213
　　flammula 213
　　pyrenaeus 213
　　trichophyllus 213
Raphidia notata 204

Rattus norvegicus 20
　　rattus 20
Reduvius personatus 154
Regulus ignicapillus 96
　　regulus 96
Rhagonycha fulva 205
Rhamnus cathartica 337
Rhinanthus minor 259
Rhingia campestris 194
Rhinocoris iracundus 154
Rhinolophus
　　ferrumequinum 12
Rhodeus sericeus 122
Rhododendron
　　ferrugineum 252
　　ponticum 349
Rhus coriaria 341
Riparia riparia 80
Rissa tridactyla 68
Robina pseudoacacia
　　333
Rorippa nasturtium-
　　aquaticum 218
Rosa canina 234
Rosalia alpina 202
Rubus fruticosus 234
Rumex acetosa 249
　　obtusifolia 249
Rupricapra rupicapra 32
Russula atropurpurea 368
　　cyanoxantha 368
　　emetica 368
　　ochroleuca 368
　　sardonia 368
Rutilus rutilus 122

Sabella pavonina 208
Sagittaria sagittifolia 278
Salamandra atra 117
　　salamandra 117
　　terdigitata 117
Salix alba 312
　　capraea 313
　　fragilis 313
　　vitellina var. pendula
　　313
Salmo gairdneri 121
　　salar 120
　　trutta 120
Salticus scenicus 145
Salvelinus alpinus 121
Salvia pratensis 264
Sambucus nigra 350
Sanicula europaea 245
Saponaria ocymoides 224
Sarcophaga carnaria 194
Sarothamnus scoparius
　　334
Saturnia pavonia 188
Satyns actaea 170
Saxicola rubetra 88
　　torquata 88
Saxifraga paniculata 238
　　tridactylites 238
Scarabaeus sacer 201
Scardinius
　　erythrophthalmus 122
Sciurus carolinensis 15
　　vulgaris 15
Scleroderma citrinum 385
Scolia hirta 199
Scoliopteryx libatrix 187
Scolopax rusticola 64
Scomber scombrus 128
Scolytus scolytus 203
Scophthalmus rhombus
　　129
Scrophularia nodosa 261
Scutigera coleoptrata 207
Scyliorhinus canicula 126
Sedum acre 237
Sehirus bicolor 154
Selenia tetralunaria 192
Sempervivum
　　arachnoideum 237
Senecio jacobaea 272
　　vulgaris 272
Sepia officinalis 136
Sequoia sempervirens
　　304